MW00779678

Château de Berneré. Pastel by Jean Reboux. Property of the author. Courtesy of the artist.

Facing the Revocation

Huguenot Families, Faith, and the King's Will

CAROLYN CHAPPELL LOUGEE

Oxford University Press is a department of the University of Oxford. It furthers the University's objective of excellence in research, scholarship, and education by publishing worldwide. Oxford is a registered trade mark of Oxford University Press in the UK and certain other countries.

Published in the United States of America by Oxford University Press
198 Madison Avenue, New York, NY 10016, United States of America.

Library of Congress Cataloging-in-Publication Data
Names: Lougee, Carolyn Chappell, author.
Title: Facing the revocation : Huguenot families, faith, and the king's will /
Carolyn Chappell Lougee.
Description: New York City : Oxford University Press, 2016. |
Includes bibliographical references and index.
Identifiers: LCCN 2016001873 (print) | LCCN 2016022267 (ebook) |
ISBN 9780190241315 (hardcover : alk. paper) | ISBN 9780190241322 (Updf) |
ISBN 9780190241339 (Epub)
Subjects: LCSH: Huguenots—France—History. | France—History—Louis XIV,
1643–1715. | Protestantism—France—History. | France—Emigration and immigration.
Classification: LCC BX9454.3 .C43 2016 (print) | LCC BX9454.3 (ebook) |
DDC 284/.509031—dc23
LC record available at https://lccn.loc.gov/2016001873

1 3 5 7 9 8 6 4 2

Printed by Sheridan Books, Inc., United States of America

"Why study one noble family? What can the social historian learn from a single case? Abandoning all claims to the typicality of the family in any statistical sense does not mean retreating to antiquarianism and the quaintness of the particular."

—Robert Forster, *The House of Saulx-Tavanes* (1971)

"Often it is the small things, rather than the big picture, that the mind can comfortably grasp . . . for instance, it is naturally more appealing to readers to absorb the meaning of a vast historical event through the story of a single family."

—Daniel Mendelsohn, *The Lost* (2006)

CONTENTS

PRINCIPAL PERSONAGES

Marie de La Rochefoucauld, Dame de Champagné

Josias de Robillard, Seigneur de Champagné. Husband of Marie de La Rochefoucauld

Susanne Isle. Grandmother of Marie de La Rochefoucauld, widow of Jean de Solière

Marie de Solière. Eldest daughter of Susanne Isle, wife of Casimir de La Rochefoucauld, mother of Marie de La Rochefoucauld and her five sisters

Madelene de Solière. Second daughter of Susanne Isle, wife of Louis de Salbert, aunt of Marie de La Rochefoucauld

Isaac Isle, Marquis de Loire. Cousin and advisor of Susanne Isle, Commissioner for the Edict of Nantes in Saintonge and Aunis

Casimir Prévost de Touchimbert. Brother-in-law of Josias de Robillard, guardian of Thérèse de Robillard

Charles de La Motte Fouqué, Baron de **Saint-Surin** and Seigneur de Tonnay-Boutonne. Friend of Josias de Champagné and future husband (in Holland) of Josias' and Marie's daughter **Susanne de Robillard**

Louis XIV, King of France, 1643–1715

Françoise d'Aubigné, Marquise de **Maintenon**. Morganatic second wife of Louis XIV

Additional Persons

Salbert family: **Louis de Salbert**, Seigneur de Soulignonne. Husband of Madelene de Solière; **Léa de Bessay**. Mother of Louis de Salbert, wife in her second marriage to Jean Isle de Beauchesne

Josias' cousins: **Philippe-Benjamin de Mazières, Gédéon Nicolas de Voutron, Marie-Marguerite Nicolas de Voutron** (wife of the admiral Duquesne-Guiton)

Other advisors to Susanne Isle: **Charles de Villedon**, Seigneur de Magezy; **François de La Rochefoucauld**, Seigneur de La Rigaudière; **Benjamin Green de Saint-Marsault**, Seigneur de Salignac; **François d'Ocoy**, Seigneur de Couvrelles; **Alphée Goulard**, Seigneur d'Anville

Jean Duvigier, Baron de Saint-Martin de La Monzie-Saint-Laurent. The magistrate in the Bordeaux Parlement charged with eliminating Protestantism in Saintonge

Intendants: **Charles Colbert de Terron, Honoré Lucas de Demuin, Pierre Arnoul, Michel Bégon, Armand-Jacques de Gourgue, Nicolas-Joseph Foucault**

Other officials: **Comte d'Avaux** (French ambassador in The Hague), **Louis François de Boufflers** (commander of troops in southwest France in 1685), **Marquis de Châteauneuf** (secretary of state for the R.P.R.), **Jean-Baptiste Colbert** (controller-general of finances and chief minister of Louis XIV), **Charles Colbert de Croissy** (intendant in Poitou, then secretary of state for foreign affairs), **Marquis de Louvois** (secretary of state for war), **Comte de Pontchartrain** (secretary of state for the king's household and controller-general of finances), **Marquis de Seignelay** (secretary of state for the navy and for the king's household)

Pierre Louis Pons de Tillieres, Sieur des Forges. A mole inside the refugee community in Holland who reported to the Comte d'Avaux

Eléonore d'Olbreuse, Duchess of Zell. Her brother Alexandre Desmier d'Olbreuse married **Madeleine-Sylvie de Sainte-Hermine de La Laigne**, later Madame von Bülow, who was a first cousin of Madame de Maintenon and the patron in Celle of Susanne de Robillard

NOTE: The appendix offers family trees for the Isle, La Rochefoucauld, Robillard de Champagné, Prévost de Touchimbert, Mazières-Voutron, and D'Aubigné-Olbreuse families.

GLOSSARY

Arrêt. A nonappealable decision from a sovereign authority (law court or royal council) on a question of fact or right.

Charente. The name given to both the river and the territory through which it flows. Since the Revolution split the territory into two *départements*—Charente around Angoulême and Charente-Maritime around La Rochelle—the region has been referred to in the plural as the Charentes. The old provinces of **Aunis** (around La Rochelle), **Saintonge** (around Saintes and Saint-Jean-d'Angély), and **Angoumois** (around Angoulême) fall within the Charentes. The neighboring provinces were **Poitou, Limousin, Périgord, and Guyenne.**

Chevalier de Saint-Michel, Chevalier de Saint-Louis. Knights honored with appointment by the king to two royal chivalric orders.

Coutumes. Customary laws that emerged over time from common practice and prevailed in many parts of France alongside or instead of Roman law.

Curé. Priest of a Catholic parish, who performed the rites of the church and kept the register of baptisms, marriages, and burials.

Distaff. A tool used in spinning onto which unspun fibers are wound. Since spinning was traditionally women's work, the distaff came to symbolize the woman's domain or the female side of a family.

Dowry and Dower. The assets a bride carried into a marriage and the property to which she was entitled when widowed.

Dragonnade. Lodging of mounted infantry soldiers (**dragoons**) in Protestant households from 1681 onward as a means of pressuring them to convert to Catholicism.

Factum. A legal brief written by a litigant's lawyer to lay out the facts of a case as the client saw them.

Gabare. A small river boat, wide and flat, typically used for transporting cargo or for fishing.

Généralité. The geographical area administered by an intendant. Most *généralités* contained several fiscal districts called ***élections***.

Governor. A royal appointee charged with oversight chiefly of military affairs in a province, city, or fortified place. His deputy was the **king's lieutenant** (*lieutenant du roi*) or **lieutenant-general de province**.

Hôpital général. Asylum for beggars, vagabonds, and the poor.

Intendant. Chief crown official administering a *generalité* or intendancy, overseeing all aspects of royal authority, seconded by his **subdelegate**.

League. The distance a person could walk in one hour, reckoned (in various localities) as 2–3 miles.

Légitime. In Roman law, the share of a parent's estate to which every child had a legal entitlement and from which the parent could not disinherit a child without sufficient legal cause.

Lettre de cachet. A letter issued over the king's signature, secured with his wax seal (*cachet*), and giving notice of his express personal will on any matter of urgent concern, sometimes an order for a subject's exile or imprisonment.

The Ligue. An ultra-Catholic party in the sixteenth-century Wars of Religion that fought to eradicate Protestantism, weaken the Huguenot nobility, and merge royal authority with religious orthodoxy.

Livre. The principal money of account in France, divisible into 20 *sols* (12 ***deniers*** per sol). The ***franc*** had the same monetary value as the *livre*, but the two terms were used differently in common parlance. An ***écu*** was generally reckoned the equivalent of three *livres*. Other common and legally valid currencies included ***Louis*** or Louis d'or (originally equivalent to 10 *livres*), ***pistoles*** (equivalent to *Louis*), and ***liards*** (3 *deniers*).

Nobles of the Sword, Robe, Cloche. Individuals recognized as having social and fiscal privileges originating in service to the military (Sword), administrative or judicial corps (Robe), and municipal offices (Cloche).

Parlements. Sovereign courts (from which there was no judicial appeal) with broad powers of police in Paris and across the kingdom.

Préciput. A preference legacy, usually favoring the eldest son, that was mandated by law regimes in some parts of France.

Presidial, sénéchaussée, siège royal. Ordinary royal law courts handling civil and criminal cases as tribunals of first instance or upon appeal from the lesser seigneurial courts. Officials who oversaw law cases included the **seneschal, counselors, lieutenant-criminal, lieutenant-general** (*de sénéchaussée*), lieutenant-particular, king's prosecutor (*procureur du roi*), **king's attorney** (*avocat du roi*), **clerk** (*greffier*). Also designates the geographical area subject to such a court's jurisdiction.

Recherches de noblesse. Royal investigations into the legitimacy of individuals' and families' claims to noble status.

Reconnaissance. An act by which refugees who had abjured under pressure in France confessed their fault, re-embraced Protestantism, and were reintegrated into the church community.

Religion prétendue réformée (R.P.R.). The official title for Protestantism in France, translatable as "supposedly reformed religion." Protestantism was also sometimes referred to as "**The Religion**" ("*la Religion*") and its adherents as "***Religionnaires***" or, more commonly, as "**Huguenots.**"

Rente. A loan at interest camouflaged as a sale, which was a common form of borrowing and lending at a time when lending at interest was suspect or prohibited by law. Government *rentes* were bonds secured on municipal revenues.

Seigneury. A landed estate in which were embedded certain economic, social, judicial, and honorific privileges and obligations. The holder of the estate was known as the **seigneur.**

Témoignage. A certificate from a former temple warranting that the bearer adhered to the Protestant faith and was worthy of admission as a member in another congregation.

Facing the Revocation

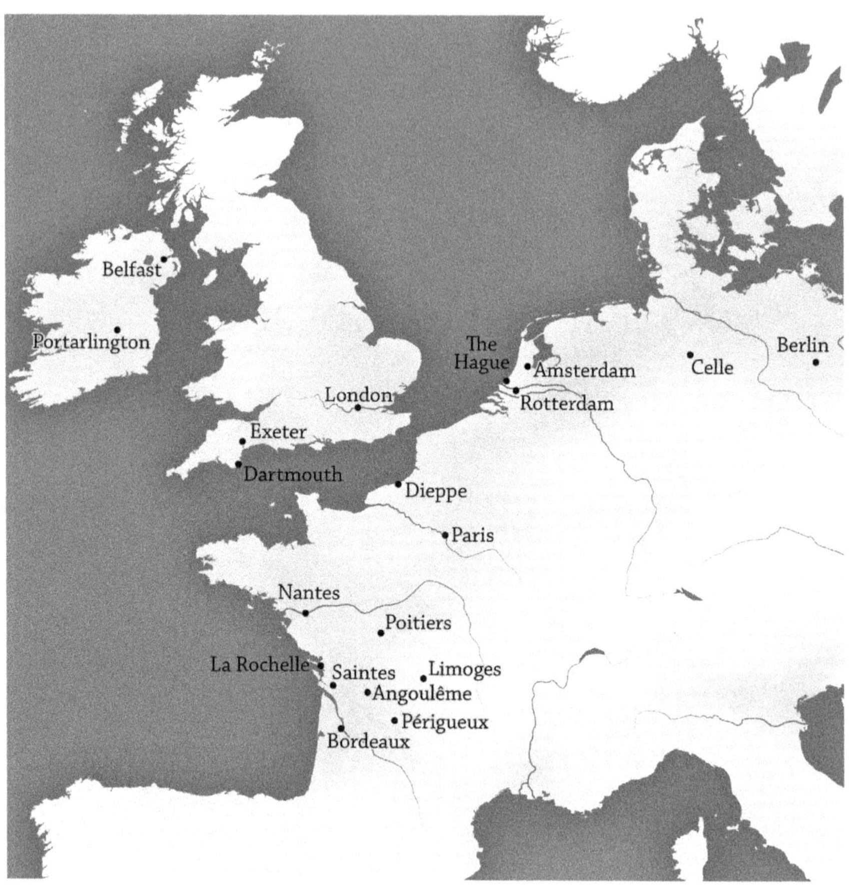

Itineraries of the Champagné. Created by Zephyr Frank and Erik Steiner at the Spatial History Project, Stanford University.

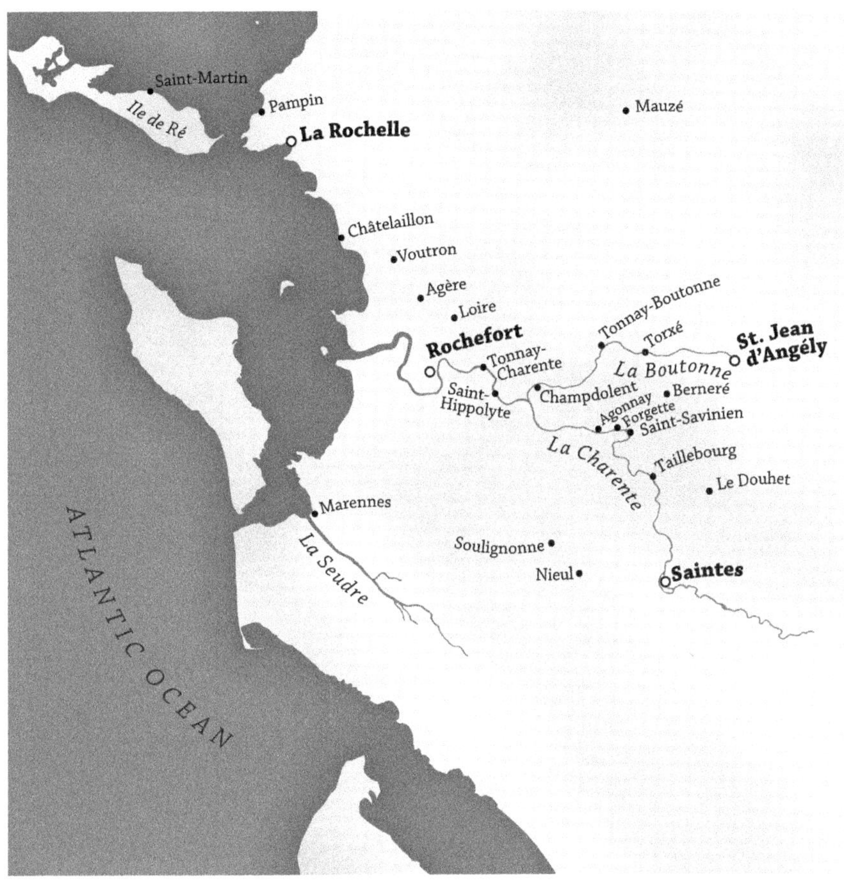

The Champagné's Charentes. Created by Zephyr Frank and Erik Steiner at the Spatial History Project, Stanford University.

Introduction

Before dawn on an April day in 1687, six children of the Protestant noble family Robillard de Champagné slipped among the wine casks belowdecks of an English eighteen-tonner and made their escape from La Rochelle to Devon. Their mother and eldest brother traced the same route to exile in June. Eleven months later, the father fled overland to Holland. A baby sister was left behind. Who were the Champagné, and why did they leave France? How did they manage to escape? And what became of these emigrants abroad, by contrast with those who stayed?

In her brief memoir of the emigration, the mother of the family, Marie de La Rochefoucauld,[1] offered an answer to each of these questions. She and her husband Josias de Robillard were French nobles, proprietors respectively of the noble estates of Berneré and Champagné in the southwestern province of Saintonge. They left France out of a desire for "liberty to worship God openly," which the policies of Louis XIV denied to Protestants like them. They succeeded in escaping by outwitting the authorities who closed possible emigration routes when the 1685 Revocation of the Edict of Nantes criminalized what was officially called the *Religion prétendue réformée* (R.P.R.) and forbade departures from the kingdom. In exile abroad they lost—for the sake of true religion—the economic advantages and social standing they could have continued to enjoy at home.

It is a storyline of many truths. Josias carried into exile—and his descendants preserved down into the twenty-first century—the genealogies, deeds, leases, contracts, and inventories of property that established the Champagné's identity as a noble landholding family and demonstrated Marie's inheritance of Berneré. Religion certainly did stand at the heart of the decision-making that led to the emigration. Both Josias and Marie inherited a familial Protestant identity from forebears who fought for the Reformed religion in the terrible wars of the Reformation and from those who coexisted with Catholicism after Henri IV's 1598 Edict of Nantes made France a kingdom with two lawful religions. It was Josias' and Marie's misfortune to found their own family and live as Protestants during the reign of Henri IV's grandson, Louis XIV, who gradually circumscribed their religious freedoms and civil privileges until, in October 1685, he revoked his grandfather's Edict of Nantes. While all the family members who escaped—the two parents and the seven children—remained faithful to Protestantism to the end of their days, neither the parents nor the children could enjoy, in exile, anything resembling the life they had expected at Berneré. Facing the Revocation changed everything.

Marie's telling of the Champagné story is, however, partial, for it masks much in order to establish a certain picture of their lives and of the decisions they made when facing the Revocation. Restoring the portions of experience she withheld is a key to restoring much more than one family's history. Her telling has seemed convincing for more than three centuries because it matched so closely the consensus narrative composed by numerous French Protestant exiles: the stability of life in France but for the Revocation, the religious motive for emigrating, the heroic clandestine escape against heavy odds, and the sacrifice of fortune for religious constancy. This framework, created by Huguenots themselves at the Revocation, has continued to encrust the Huguenot story. Because it emphasized how exceptional the Huguenot experience was vis-à-vis the evolution of state and society that is seen as the heart of the national story, it contributed to narrowing the place their story could claim in French memory.[2] Enlarging that claim is the broad objective of a recent quickening in revisionist histories that eschew the misleading tidiness of the standard Huguenot narrative, excavating stories "messier and more ambiguous . . . messier and more truthful . . . learning to remember with complexity."[3]

"Learning to remember with complexity" has transformed a number of historical fields from which this recollection of the Champagné experience takes inspiration. Family history and women's history have established strong reciprocal connections, over time, between private experience—the texture of family life, the strategies families adopt to promote their own prosperity and survival, the beliefs and attitudes generated in family contexts—and public processes. Autobiographical studies have pushed beyond literal reading of eyewitness testimonies, probing firsthand accounts for the selective inclusions and exclusions that reshape lives into the plausible rather than the true. "In every story is a story not told."[4] Migration studies, too, have generated new layers of meaning by reconceptualizing population movements. Rather than emphasizing, or limiting discussion to, migrants' adaptation to the receiving culture—"pick[ing] up the story only after the arrivals step off the vessel"—they seek to trace continuity and rupture across the full succession of stages from origin and exit to transit and resettlement. Rather than portraying given migrations as economic or political or religious, they aspire to embed individual agency within the full range of pertinent contexts. And they have developed comparative approaches, for example pairing migrants with non-migrants in order to illuminate both incentives to leave and options to stay.[5]

This history of the Champagné rests upon such strategic shifts. Here, the story of a single family as it faced the harshest domestic decision of Louis XIV's reign illuminates how the success of public policy, even under French absolutism, turned on private decision-making among those who were expected to comply. A bifocal reading of the firsthand accounts among its sources—one eye on the storyline and one on the way the story is fashioned—teases out the "story not told." Juxtaposing the stories told with information recoverable in other sources reveals, in several instances, the writer's unspoken, and perhaps unspeakable, intentions. Two further dimensions extend comparatively—across time (from well before departure to well after resettlement) and vis-à-vis other persons of their social set in Saintonge (who variously left, stayed as New Converts, or stayed as defiant Protestants).

In so doing, *Facing the Revocation* questions four widely assumed features of the Huguenot story. The first is the assumption that because those who left in the era of the Revocation were specifically Protestant, their motivations were patently religious. The complexity of considerations—familial, intellectual, legal, and financial as well as religious—that bore upon the Champagné as they decided whether to leave suggests, rather, that a cocktail of considerations—likely mixing differently with the desire "to worship God openly" in each individual case—tipped equally committed Protestants to, variously, leaving or staying. Likewise, the assumption that the state countered escapes with determination and punished those caught escaping to the letter of the law—"Men who were caught were sent to the galleys, women to prison"[6]—should seem implausible, given the sheer numbers who reached safety in the lands the Huguenots christened "The Refuge"—primarily England, Holland, Prussia, and Switzerland—and the inconsistent actions, even intimations of contrary intentions, from state officials, right up to and including the king. A third assumption—that the spectacular conversions of high nobles such as Turenne, La Trémoïlle, Rohan, and Soubise betokened a broad abandonment of the Reformed cause by French nobles well before the Revocation, often out of shallow religious commitment and for material advantage—is belied by the numbers of middling provincial nobles who remained Protestant down to the Revocation and then struggled to make their inherited religion viable under transformed circumstances. Alignment with the king's religion often did make material advancement possible, but conversion also allowed some kin and friends of the Champagné to enjoy once again the sort of familial solidarity they had prized before religious division deprived them of it, and some found in their new religion deep satisfactions that shaped the rest of their lives. Finally, characterizations of the culture of the Refuge as a modernizing force discontinuous with refugees' prior experiences must be strongly nuanced by the importance of relationships and values brought from France to the social patterns re-established abroad by the refugees. The Champagné were among the new refugees who traveled along old migration paths and, resettling in them, created communities that were more traditional in ideology and action than the characterization of Huguenot refugees as forerunners of modernity has implied.

The history of the Champagné, then, makes the Huguenot story less certain than before: more puzzling, more interesting, more inviting of close and systematic study, indeed more essential to an overall understanding of the grand lines of political and social developments in the France of Louis XIV.

This study has four Parts. Part One: The Champagné in Saintonge—the longest of the four—opens up the question of why Huguenots left at the Revocation by tracing the transformation of the Champagné's social and material circumstances as they made their decision to take the family out of France. When in 1677 Marie de La Rochefoucauld inherited Berneré from her grandmother, Susanne Isle, her family's future in the home of her ancestors seemed secure. Yet as persecution intensified and adherence to their religion came to be punished as disobedience to the king, pressures originating closer to home destroyed the social net that family solidarities had traditionally provided. For Susanne Isle's generation and for the six La Rochefoucauld granddaughters she raised, Protestantism was more than a set of beliefs; it was a shared religion that served to hold together both extended family and community. For some reasons directly linked to the Revocation and others only remotely connected to it, the solidarities of religion, family, and community enjoyed by the Isle and La Rochefoucauld dissolved in tandem. Their marriage alliances, inheritance strategies, financial practices, and interpersonal relations reveal that disputes among kin, a bitter contest over inheritance, and uncollectible debts upended the Champagné's lives and set them on ships to the Huguenot Refuge while fellow Protestants with different familial and community experiences chose to face the Revocation inside France.

Part Two: Escaping from France examines how Marie and Josias managed to escape and whether the successful escapes of some 150,000–200,000 fellow Protestants ought to force rethinking about the nature of the state they forsook and the intentions of the crown that failed to stop them. Details of how the Champagné planned their departures and crafted a continuity of both material means and memory confirm that escapees found ways to leave home without "leaving everything behind . . . departing with light baggage."[7] As for the authorities, their surveillance was intermittent enough and their practices ambivalent enough to allow considerable latitude to would-be escapees, despite the rigorous letter of the Revocation law.

Part Three: Those Who Stayed pursues the post-Revocation experience of members of the Champagné's kin and social set who stayed in France. Their stories mirror the experiences of those who left, allowing readers to imagine the lives the Champagné might have lived had they reached a different decision about departing. Some who stayed converted and settled comfortably into a transformed relationship between crown and nobility; others struggled to do, within changed circumstances, what consciences formed before the Revocation told them was right, in the end converting or, in at least one remarkable case, parrying for decades the crown's every effort to secure an abjuration. Family solidarity functioned in various cases to encourage or allay change, as a benefit recaptured when Protestant and Catholic lineages reconnected in a shared religion or as a protective shield enabling tepid adherence and continuing resistance. These histories demonstrate the important role played in conversions by the crown's practice of removing children from their Huguenot or New Convert parents for reeducation as Catholics. As an enforcer of this practice, Madame de Maintenon, one of the most famous and controversial daughters of the Charentes and morganatic second wife of Louis XIV, wove her way through the lives of Champagné kin. Bringing to the fore her actions toward Protestant children offers an alternate window on the perennial question of her influence on religious reunification in the era of the Revocation.

Part Four: Resettling Abroad illuminates the experience of exile and the way Marie de La Rochefoucauld refounded the family in changed circumstances. By the time of her death in Portarlington, Ireland, in 1730, Marie had lived in four countries and seen her children dispersed definitively in three. Wherever they went, Marie and her children carried with them, consciously or not, their native Saintonge and the ways of their class. Their craving for cultural persistence showed in the autobiographical memoirs they wrote as well as in the way they resettled, the occupations they adopted, and the social ties they wove and exploited in their new locations. Yet within this traditional expatriate society, Marie de La Rochefoucauld, once widowed, came into her own, taking independent charge of the patrimony and laying the foundation upon which this obscure French provincial noble family—"leaving everything behind" in order to stay Protestant—attained rank and renown in new homelands that far surpassed anything they could have dreamed of in the France from which they escaped in 1687.

PART ONE

THE CHAMPAGNÉ IN SAINTONGE

1

A Family of the Charentes in Distaff

Events of the early spring 1677 would have lasting consequences for public life in France as well as for private families, even for families as distanced from public functions and as obscure in historical memory as the Robillard de Champagné. Taking personal command in late February of the French armies in Flanders, Louis XIV touched off a cascade of springtime victories—Valenciennes, Cambrai, Mont-Cassel, Saint-Omer—that impressed French subjects with the qualities of their king and strengthened his hand at the peace negotiations begun in Nijmegen the previous year. Louis' decision to make Versailles his residence and capital set off an intensive phase of building orchestrated by Hardouin Mansart and the innovative, largely anti-Dutch decorative program devised by Charles Le Brun to showcase the personal glory of the Sun King.

Word of these developments could not have reached the Champagné by the morning of March 8, when Susanne Isle, widowed grandmother of the Dame de Champagné, divided the patrimony among her six granddaughters and retired. The family would surely have heard that their fellow Protestant Abraham Duquesne, in the company of some of their kin, had given France control of its southern sea through a succession of victories in the Mediterranean.[1] And they might even have caught whispers, from friends and relations who went occasionally to Paris, that a child of the region, Françoise d'Aubigné, Marquise de Maintenon, was beginning to be spoken of as the favorite of the king, displacing Madame de Montespan, whose ancestral château was just downriver at Tonnay-Charente. But on that day their attention had to be on their own intricate private affairs, and they could not have suspected how the events in Flanders and Versailles would undo their kin and their best, most careful stewardship of family lives.

The property division alone would be a complicated task. Susanne Isle's holdings would have to be enumerated and appraised. Nothing—neither assets nor liabilities—could be left out, and yet her properties were diverse and dispersed. Her family, the Isle, loomed as large in local landholding as their châteaux did in and around the Charente-side town of Saint-Savinien. In Saintonge since 1340 and in Saint-Savinien since 1435, the Isle were able, during the *recherches de noblesse* in the 1660s, to assemble and present to the king's commissioners proofs of nobility stretching back to 1336. Their Château de La Cave stood guard atop a cliff that the Charente had carved eons before from the calcareous bedrock for which Saint-Savinien would be famous. La Matassière, Beauchesne, and numerous other local properties were also in Isle hands. The Château de Forgette, on the downstream leg of the oxbow that turned along Saint-Savinien's quais, came to the Isle family as dowry in François Isle's marriage in 1556.[2] A venerable fortress, with its moat, quadrilateral main enclosure, triple towers, and large slate-roofed dovecote in the lower courtyard, it must have appeared in 1677 much as it would in 1718, when it was sketched by the king's engineer-geographer Claude Masse.[3]

Susanne's own estate, Berneré, had been carved out expressly for her from the seigneury of Forgette in 1632, with "full rights of high, medium, and low justice." Susanne's husband, Jean de Solière, Sieur de Lescure, first paid homage for Berneré in May 1632 to Henri de La Trémoïlle, Comte de Taillebourg, offering up the customary spearhead valued at twenty sols.[4] Their château, set on a gentle rise outside the town, bore a style of architecture and ornament

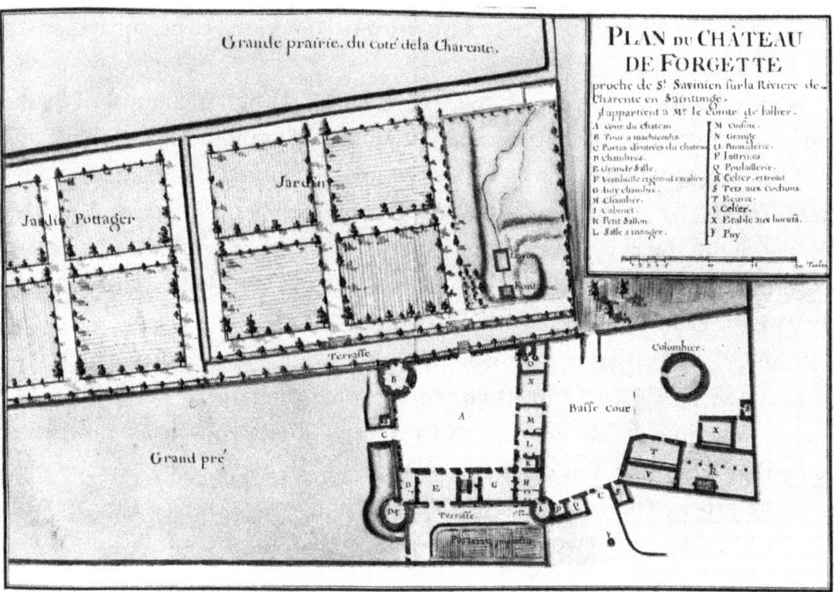

Figure 1.1 Plan of the Château de Forgette, near Saint-Savinien, from Claude Masse, "Recueil des Plans de Saintonge," 94[97] (pen & ink and w/c on paper) (b/w photo). Service historique de la Défense. Armée de Terre, Vincennes. By permission of Bridgeman Images.

typical for its time and place. A strong square central tower joining two roughly symmetrical wings exemplified a provincial interpretation of Louis XIII style that was much in vogue in contemporary Saintonge and neighboring Aunis. A single round tower with a pointed "pepper pot" roof gave it the strong corner typical of Saintongeais noble homes of the early seventeenth century. A decorative doorway, framed by fluted pilasters and garlanded with laurel leaves, raised high the helmeted coat of arms signifying the family of the seigneury and the date—1633—of the château's creation.[5]

Besides her own holdings, Susanne Isle had to identify and transfer title to the lands left by her late son-in-law Casimir de La Rochefoucauld, Seigneur

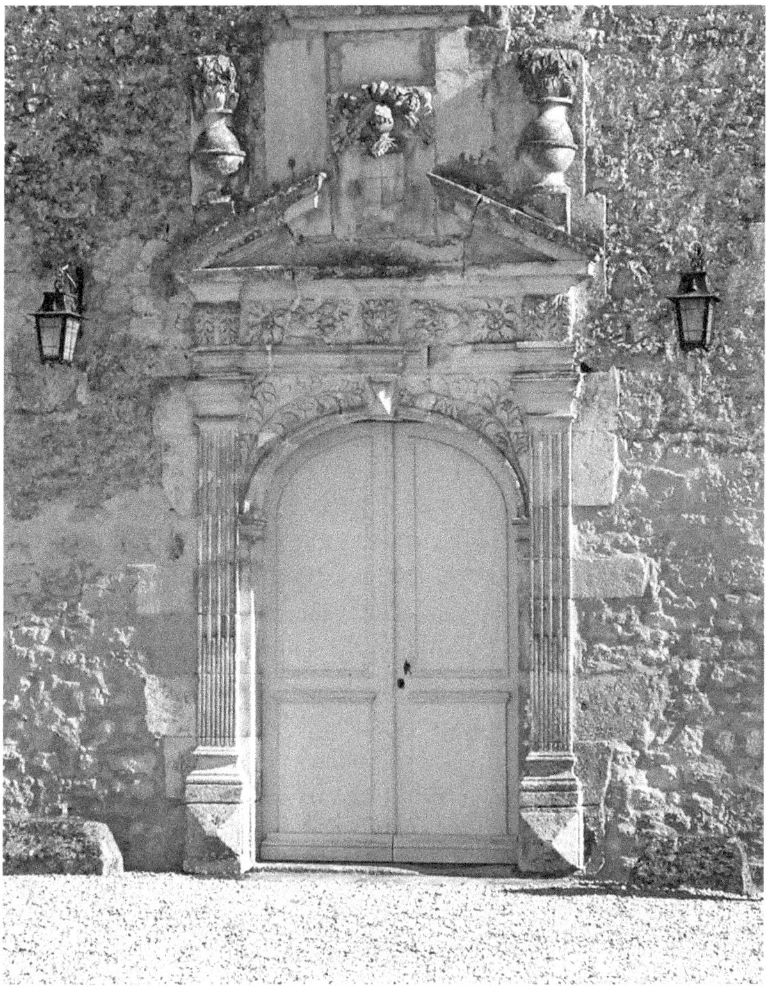

Figure 1.2 Portal of the Château de Berneré. Photo by Nicole and Jean Bardol, 2016. Courtesy of the proprietors of the Château.

des Touches, which she had been responsible for administering since his death in March 1660, following the death of his wife, her daughter Marie de Solière, in 1658 at the age of twenty-seven.[6] Those La Rochefoucauld holdings consisted of no fewer than thirty-two separate parcels of fields, vines, and pastures. Susanne had had to ask the laborers who farmed them for descriptions of their various boundaries and estimates of their overall size. Later, when her granddaughters decided to divide what she left them in common, they would engage a lawyer and a notary to visit the lands and formally appraise them. But not this time.

At least there did not seem to be other complications in identifying the holdings to be divided. Susanne had not remarried: French widows after the age of thirty usually did not, especially if their financial standing allowed them not to.[7] So there was neither a second set of children nor in-laws of a second husband to consider. No separate property from her late husband's side of the family remained to be passed along; what Jean de Solière brought to the marriage had been expended on Berneré itself or paid out long before as dowry. And her two younger daughters, Madelene and Susanne de Solière, had been provided for already. In 1646, when the eldest of the three daughters, Marie, married at the age of fifteen, Susanne Isle stipulated that Madelene and Susanne would receive 10,000 *livres* each upon her death. In 1654, when Susanne Isle named daughter Marie her universal heir, she raised the amount she promised each younger daughter from 10,000 to 12,000 *livres*. At the moment of her retirement, Susanne Isle simply referred back to these payments as "certain sums to the demoiselles Madelene and Susanne de Solière, her younger daughters, for their hereditary rights both paternal and maternal, which said sums have been paid and acquitted."[8]

Madelene de Solière was living nearby, at Soulignonne on the outskirts of Saintes, where her late husband, Louis de Salbert, had been seigneur. Susanne de Solière was living near Aubeterre on the estate of Louis de Lestang, Seigneur de Nabinaud, whom she had married in May 1663. Lestang created a stir a mere three months after the marriage, murdering another nobleman while out hunting. But Lestang was granted remission by the king in April 1668, and neither he nor his wife would figure in the troubles plaguing her mother's inheritance.[9] The absence of the daughters Madelene and Susanne from the March 1677 family gathering at Berneré reflected their mother's conviction that they had no further claim on the property being conveyed.

To finalize the division, Susanne Isle assembled at Berneré her six chosen heiresses, the husband of the only married heiress, and three representatives of the kin groups from whom the properties to be transmitted had derived. The occasion might have looked rather as Abraham Bosse, the great Protestant artist-engraver of the modest nobility and upper bourgeoisie, depicted the negotiation of a marriage contract: Susanne at the table before the great windows of Berneré with her advisors and the notary, Marie de La Rochefoucauld and her husband Josias nearby as interested parties but not principals in the main discussion, their young children at play in the midst of serious decision-making whose flaws would change the course of their lives. The heiresses were the six daughters of Susanne Isle's deceased daughter and universal heir Marie de Solière. Susanne had raised those six and served as their guardian since they were orphaned, at ages ranging from one to eleven.[10] A widow for over forty years, having long managed her own lands and theirs, she was old and prepared to withdraw, and they were ready to take over.

The three kin Susanne brought to the gathering were elders of the lineages whose properties she would be passing along. François de La Rochefoucauld, Seigneur de La Rigaudière, was the largest landowner in the parish of Saint-Hippolyte-de-Biard,[11] from the Parc d'Archiac branch of this distinguished family and a cousin of the orphaned heiresses. A second advisor, Charles de Villedon, Seigneur de Magezy in Saint-Vivien, had married a sister of the late Casimir and spoke for her on this occasion. The third family advisor, Isaac Isle, Marquis de Loire and a first cousin of the retiring grandmother, was the most

Figure 1.3 The Marriage Contract. Etching by Abraham Bosse, 1633. Metropolitan Museum of Art. By permission of Art Resource, NY.

distinguished member of the clan from which the bulk of Susanne's estate had issued. Educated at the Protestant Academy in Saumur, he subsequently served as a cavalry officer during the years of the Fronde and the war with Spain. He resided near Saint-Savinien at La Matassière, but his title derived from a tiny parish near the Atlantic coast. There, his seigneurial residence, perched on a rise above the village, enjoyed a wide view of the abundant grain fields and pastures of the surrounding countryside; a contiguous and immense dovecote bespoke the wealth and status of its proprietors. By 1715, when Claude Masse passed through Loire, the "rather lovely château adjoining the village that belonged to the marquis de Loirre" had gone to ruin. The passage of Loire from prosperity to ruin—left unexplained by Masse—resulted from the same complex interweaving of family politics and religious policy that, in parallel, would cost Susanne Isle's heirs their precious Berneré. When Susanne assembled her heirs and advisors in March 1677, that outcome was still in the future, if not entirely unforeseen.[12]

Susanne Isle brought together these kin even though legally she did not need to do so for her actions to be valid. In both customary and written (Roman) law, the widowed mother was assumed to administer the estate and serve as guardian of the children in default of an alternate designation in her husband's will, which seems to have been uncommon. Both legal regimes gave parents broad, but not total, discretion for determining how the estate would be passed down. The inheritance was to be divided among the children, but both the customary practice of *préciput* and the Roman law declaration of a "universal heir" could transfer the bulk of an estate to a single child, shrinking the interests of other sons and daughters in order to keep the patrimony largely intact.[13]

The menacing situation facing Susanne as she made her final will in March 1677 fell squarely in this area of parental power to favor one heir and was complicated by the issue of gender because her family had "fallen into distaff." Quite remarkably, for three generations the family had had only daughters—fourteen girls, no sons. Susanne herself was one of five girls, her three children were all girls, the heir among them (Marie de Solière) had six daughters. The pattern of female births would continue with the three daughters of Marie de La Rochefoucauld's sister Elisabeth de La Rochefoucauld, as well as the one daughter and three granddaughters of Susanne de Solière, the only lines of Susanne Isle's descendants who would remain in France.[14]

Having only female heirs was not so infrequent; it occurred in perhaps 20 percent of families in early modern France.[15] But fewer than 1 percent of cases would have had three successive all-girl generations in a line. Susanne Isle's side of the Isle clan was like an all-women pocket within the larger mixed network. The La Rochefoucauld sisters had one male first cousin (Zacharie de

Salbert, son of their aunt Madelene de Solière); otherwise, the nearest male relative was several degrees away.

"Falling into distaff"—as the very phrase implies—was menacing to families. For French monarchs, it meant the end of dynasties, as it had in 1589, for the French crown could never pass to or through a woman: "The lilies do not spin because France cannot fall to the distaff side."[16] This "male right" did not pertain to nonroyal families in distaff: their female heirs could inherit titles as well as fortunes. Still, "falling into distaff" presented all families with problems both of identity and of finances. In a society that transmitted family identity through the surname of the father, the lack of sons threatened symbolic loss. In this respect, the naming pattern of Susanne Isle's line is significant. Each generation of girls was given the first names of the Isle rather than of their father's family. Susanne Isle and Jean de Solière did not use the first names in his family—Catherine, Anne, Rachel—but the Marie, Madelene, and Susanne that had been traditional among Isle daughters for generations. Marie de Solière and Casimir de La Rochefoucauld dipped into the same naming pool— Marie, Elisabeth, Susanne, Madeleine—before turning to the La Rochefoucauld names of Henriette and Lidie. Marie de La Rochefoucauld and Josias de Robillard named their first daughters Susanne, Uranie, and Elisabeth. Elisabeth de La Rochefoucauld's three daughters were all given Isle first names: Marguerite, Marie, and Susanne. Susanne de Solière's daughter was Susanne de Lestang. This continuity in naming, which makes matters so confusing for the historian and the genealogist, was an instrument of solidarity in the kinship group. It created a bond not only between living and dead, but also between the male-descending lines that still bore the family surname and the female-descending lines that bore it no more. These girls carried the Isle first names as a token of lineal solidarity, of continuing identification with the Isle family, on the part of the lines "in distaff."

Identity aside, management of fortunes became difficult for families "in distaff." They would have the advantage of incurring no capital costs of offices or military commissions in order to provide employment and appropriate status for sons. But the capital costs of dowries for daughters compromised family fortunes if they were not compensated by dowries received in sons' marriages. For individual marriages, a family's objective would be relative equality of rank and resources. But for the totality of marriages in each generation, equality was not the goal: the optimal result would bring in as dowries from the marriages of sons more than was given out in dowries of daughters. Bringing a wife into the family increased its wealth; giving one to another family depleted it.[17] The lack of sons, then, meant that families "in distaff" had no opportunities for bringing in money as dowries, only for sending property out. Protestants may have had even more difficulty with distaff families than Catholics, for the respectable alternative of sending some daughters to convents with a pension more meager than a *légitime* or marriage dowry was unavailable to them. Of the fourteen Isle women named above, two died before marriage age and one never married. So eleven dowries left the lineage without any being received. The Isle did not comply with the dictum "Marry few daughters, for that is the ruin of a noble house."[18]

One expedient that could be used in such situations was intralineal marriage: matches between an heiress and her cousin or uncle that cycled dowries of lineage property back into the male line. The Isle arranged three intralineal marriages in the later seventeenth century, two of which paired daughters of Isle daughters with men from the lineage. In 1656, Susanne Isle's sister Léa Isle, having inherited Forgette, passed the estate in turn to her daughter (née Jacquette de Marbeuf), who married her second cousin Claude Isle des Groies, thus reintegrating Forgette into the Isle patrimony.[19] In 1685, Marguerite Isle, a sister of Jean Isle de Beauchesne, would marry her daughter Louise de Boisseau to Jean's son Henri, her first cousin.[20] The third intralineal marriage was Susanne Isle's doing, and it consolidated the Isle patrimony through a two-step process that advantaged the Isle line at the expense of the bride. In 1659, Madelene de Solière, second daughter of Susanne Isle, married the stepson of her mother's first cousin Jean Isle de Beauchesne (his wife's son by her first marriage). The marriage contract earmarked Madelene's cash dowry for paying the debts of the groom's family. In doing so, it freed Léa de Bessay, the cousin's wife and mother of the groom, to redirect her fortune from her first husband's family to the Isle line of her second husband.[21] Madelene de Solière's eventual protest that this arrangement violated her entitlements would have momentous consequences for Marie de La Rochefoucauld.

Although intralineal marriage was a familial strategy already in use by the Isle, Susanne did not arrange, either for her daughter-heir or for her La Rochefoucauld granddaughters, an intralineal marriage that would once again place the name of Isle on Berneré. As a consequence, in 1677, Berneré had had, in the forty-five years since its creation, only women "lords." In each generation, a male outsider moved into Berneré as consort to its heiress.[22] The conjugal unit in possession of the property changed in patronymic but, residing in the wife's estate, remained strongly identified with her kin group.

Susanne Isle's husband Jean de Solière, Sieur de Lescure in Nanteuil, hailed from Périgord, a younger son of a family that was on the move socially and religiously as well as geographically. Jean's father, Pierre de Sauliere, was the son of a mayor of Périgueux, himself a counselor at the Presidial of Périgueux.[23] Like many other minor noble families of Périgord, the Sauliere turned Protestant sometime in the 1560s. A number of these nobles would go to Paris for the wedding of Henry of Navarre in the summer of 1572 and die in the Massacre of

Saint Bartholomew, but the Sauliere survived and even prospered during the Wars of Religion. After the wars ended and Henry of Navarre became Henri IV, the king named Pierre de Sauliere Chevalier de Saint-Michel, no doubt as reward for his wartime services. Pierre reinvented his family of robe nobility in the image of the sword, as many other families were doing—such was the process whereby the French nobility was continuously renewed. The country seat Pierre acquired in southeastern Angoumois was the starkly imposing, heavy, fourteenth-century Château de Nanteuil, which dominated the valley of the Echelle. As if to write their newfound identity in stone, the family decorated Nanteuil in the seventeenth century with a crenelated parapet. And then they lived the life of military officers. Gabriel-Isaac de Sauliere would be known as Chevalier de Nanteuil in November 1763 when he was found murdered by a sword-cut in a Paris street, perhaps as a consequence of a duel. His brother and half-brother served in the king's military household.[24]

The scorn that could descend upon such newly minted nobility fell upon Pierre de Sauliere, Jean's father, from a particularly powerful pen. The famed courtly writer and soldier Pierre de Bourdeille, Abbé de Brantôme, like Pierre de Sauliere a man of Périgord, singled out Sauliere as an upstart whose knighthood in the Order of Saint-Michel illustrated "how this fair Order, so well instituted and sustained for men of honor, was vilified, debased, and ignobly abused. . . . I know two venerable and honorable gentlemen who, chagrined by such irreverence shown to this Order by letting it fall to this man of little worth, had agreed to take it from around his neck right in good company, if he were to appear there and threaten him that if he ever wore it again he would be

Figure 1.4 Château de Nanteuil. Photo property of the author.

beaten a hundred blows." Brantôme's savage verbal attack expressed the sentiments of the proud but hard-pressed old nobility who saw the honor meant for military heroes going to men of too low birth. But Brantôme's spleen may persuade posterity the less for the fact that the other upstart he cited was the justly celebrated Michel de Montaigne, "whose profession," Brantôme wrote, "was more truly to keep his pen writing his *Essays* than to exchange it for a sword that did not befit him so well."[25] A pairing with the great writer and statesman could, contrary to Brantôme's intent, shed only luster on the father of Jean de Solière, father-in-law of Susanne Isle.

The alliance through marriage of the Isle and the upwardly mobile family from Périgord was probably not exceptional; it was, for example, a common pattern in La Rochelle for the urban elite to marry with small nobles of the Charentes countryside. With his marriage, Jean de Solière transferred his life from Périgord to Saintonge. He refashioned his surname from the Occitan-style Sauliere of the South to the French-style Solière. He relocated his fortune to Saintonge. By the terms of his father's will, dated April 1, 1593, Jean inherited Lescure, in the parish of Nanteuil, which he would hold "nobly" as a fief in the seigneury of his brother Isaac, who was the universal heir. Jean also was to receive scattered villages and lands in the vicinity of Nanteuil. Later, Jean received a substantial cash gift from his mother, and in November 1608, his brother Isaac bought out all his rights to the inheritances, paternal and maternal.[26]

Casimir de La Rochefoucauld, Marie de Solière's groom in the second "son-in-law" marriage, was a younger son from Saint-Hippolyte, on the outskirts of Tonnay-Charente.[27] He moved into Berneré, his wife's home, at the time of their marriage in 1646. By the terms of their marriage contract, Susanne "willingly promised and would be bound to receiving in her House and providing for the said spouses with their entourage." By 1655 at the latest, he was in charge at Berneré, for in that year he sold fifteen cartloads of hay from the meadow of Forgette at a rate of twelve *livres* per cartload.[28]

Josias de Robillard, the third consecutive immigrating consort, came from Champagné, a seigneury west of Saint-Jean-d'Angély. The Robillard had been settled in the Charentes since long before the young Jean Calvin, taking refuge in Angoulême in 1533–1534, brought Reformed religion to the region.[29] André de Robillard was already established as a seigneur in the countryside near Saint-Jean-d'Angély in 1543 when he faced off against his brother Elie at the Parlement of Bordeaux. Since then, the marriages of the Champagné heirs had embedded each successive generation ever more deeply in local obligation and alliance. When Josias de Robillard (father of Marie de La Rochefoucauld's Josias) married Marie de Mazières in 1639, she enhanced the Robillard inheritance with the noble residence of Lisleau in the marsh of Agère as well as with three marshland cabins in Voutron, all in Aunis.[30]

Figure 1.5 Robillard Coat of Arms on the Proofs of Nobility presented for the *recherche de noblesse* in 1666. Champagné Papers A45. Courtesy of the Department of Special Collections, Stanford University Libraries.

The seigneury of Champagné, foundation of the Robillard family fortune, could not have been large. In its parish of Torxé alone, which boasted only eighty-seven households (*feux*) and 295 inhabitants in 1685, there were no fewer than nine seigneurs authorized to dispense justice, so small were the estates of that area's nobility.[31] Champagné itself and the village of Torxé sat on the marshy banks of the Boutonne, whose numerous locks and weirs created fishing ponds, diverted water flows to mills, and made the river navigable. Small *gabares* carried grain up to Saint-Jean-d'Angély for milling and downstream again to the markets at Rochefort, and also exported the famous wine of Saint-Jean. Torxé, with half its lands planted in grain and half in vines, had its role in both types of commerce.[32]

In 1662, Josias and his only sibling, an older sister named Marie de Robillard, who was already married to a nobleman named Casimir Prévost de Touchimbert, received their portions of the family inheritance from their widowed mother, Marie de Mazières. The occasion was an earlier parallel to what Susanne Isle would do in March 1677, with salient differences. Both women reserved a bit for their own lifetimes while settling the main properties on their descendants. Both included Charles de Villedon, Seigneur de Magezy, as an advisor. But consequential differences made Marie de Mazières' property division less vexed than Susanne Isle's. The Champagné had a male inheriting, and there was no deceased generation between the bestower and the receivers, as there was in Susanne Isle's case. Josias was given the entire undivided seigneury of Champagné plus assorted plots of land in the marshlands of Voutron, as well as five loans to be repaid by family and friends. Josias' sister received her own cluster of marshlands in Voutron for her maternal inheritance and three cash payments in lieu of her share in her parents' movables and her interest in Champagné and other paternal lands that fell undivided to her brother. Josias was obligated to pay her the three sums, totaling 7,690 *livres*, eventually, but she was not to ask for payment before their mother died and he attained his majority, settling in the meantime for only the payment of 5 percent interest from brother to sister.[33]

A further contrast between this 1662 Champagné property division and Susanne Isle's fifteen years later was how smoothly this earlier transfer was carried out. When more lands fell to brother and sister from another Mazières death after their mother's passing, the siblings split them with a document that could not have been more amicable and routine. The results bore out the hope expressed in Marie de Mazières' earlier document, which she had crafted from a desire "to anticipate and forestall the lawsuits and differences that could arise after her death between the said Sieur and the dame de Lilos, her children, with reference to the sharing and division of her properties and those of the said late Sieur de Robillard, her husband, and to preserve the peace and union between persons so close, since truly it is this very peace that renders families happy and flourishing."[34] How Susanne Isle might have envied that outcome! A final contrast was that there were no debts to be transmitted in the Champagné division—only lands and notes of credit. True, Josias assumed an obligation to his sister and would have to find a way to pay her every year until he could amass the principal to put in her hands. But neither he nor she was burdened by previous generations' outstanding obligations, as Marie de La Rochefoucauld would be.

The Champagné family fortune, then, was solvent. Marie de Mazières passed along all the lands she and her husband had inherited, and Josias enhanced the patrimony as a hands-on, engrossing landlord. From early in his years as seigneur, he steadily acquired parcels of land in the seigneury from resident peasants. From 1677 to 1680, he purchased, piece by piece, for "silver *louis* and other good moneys" the lands of the Simon family that had been morselized by the *coutume* of partible inheritance. Like other seigneurs, he took advantage of peasant indebtedness. In March 1686, Josias reunited to his domain the lands, all contiguous to his own, that the heirs of Jeanne Beauroy found they could not support. The Beauroy heirs were behind on their payments of seigneurial dues, and so after subtracting the arrears plus the procedure's cost, Josias needed to give them only sixteen *livres* for their entire small holding of meadow, cultivable land, and vines. As late as June 1688, the seigneurial judge-seneschal was pulling together an inventory of all the dues-paying farms in the seigneury, in an evident attempt to clarify the entitlements of the lord.[35] But by then, Josias would be gone.

Susanne Isle, then, knew "son-in-law" marriages from every angle. Her own had been one, she arranged one for the daughter who was her heir, and she arranged another for the granddaughter whose husband would take over management of Berneré. Those son-in-law marriages were crucial to her prosperity and that of the line. Long widowhoods like Susanne's were not unusual: women who married young often found themselves long-term widows. The widowhoods in the house of Lorraine, for example, stretched as long as sixty years.[36] But long widowhoods did pose specific challenges for the family. Maintaining the family wealth—keeping it from being consumed by the widow's maintenance or by poor management over many decades until the widow's death would distribute it to the descendants—was never easy. Susanne seems to have met this challenge well, to judge by the size of the estate she was able to pass along in 1677, more than four decades into her widowhood. In this she must have been, to some unavoidable degree, dependent upon the sons-in-law in each generation (Casimir and Josias) and on the solidarity of her kinship group.

Yet for most of her long widowhood Susanne had managed her own estate. She purchased land, negotiated leases, lent and borrowed money in her own name, sued and was sued. In doing so, she was not transgressive. About 10 percent of estates in areas of Roman law like Saintonge were held by women—slightly less than in the customary law provinces of the North, but substantial nonetheless. The number of female-headed households was on the rise in the seventeenth century, and women's activities in agricultural, as well as commercial, enterprises were expanding.[37] Changes in the law and social norms that increasingly limited women's capacity for independent action did not perceptibly affect Susanne's activity; her deferring to a son-in-law after 1646 and a grandson-in-law in 1677 more likely arose from a desire, as she aged, for relief from management that was no doubt onerous. The ceding of control to the next generation may well have been the best arrangement a Protestant widow could make for her old age.[38] Catholic women often turned to convents at this stage in their lives, "loaning" their money to an institution in return for cash annuities or room and board during their remaining years, and even for the privilege of burial and prayers for their soul. Protestant women like Susanne

Isle had to rely on their families, sometimes parlaying their control of property into old-age security—as Susanne did—through early transfer of inheritance. Such arrangements were not particularly common, perhaps because of the increased likelihood of conflicts between the generations if the widow did not withdraw completely from management of her (former) property. But it is precisely this to which Susanne Isle had recourse after 1646 and again in 1677, and, just as she no doubt feared, the combination of the two distaff-line transitions would before long upend the family's future.

Susanne Isle took counsel from her three kin advisors on March 8, 1677, in "a long and serious examination of the properties, rights, and obligations of the said inheritances" and then, "in the presence of all the parties, with their consent, and without any inducement, suggestion or constraint," Susanne Isle "divested and dispossessed herself from this day forward of all her properties, houses, domains, and inheritances in favor of the said dame de Champagné and the said demoiselles her sisters, her granddaughters, as her true heiresses."[39]

When the holdings of both the deceased La Rochefoucauld parents and the retiring Isle grandmother were divided among the six granddaughters, Marie de La Rochefoucauld, Dame de Champagné was the advantaged party. Her siblings received in common several substantial legacies: thirty-five parcels of land valued at 20,000 *livres* to be theirs at once and two additional sums to accrue to them after their grandmother's death—Susanne's 1655 loan to Catherine de La Valade, widow of the Seigneur de Chambon, in the amount of 3,187 *livres* 10 *sols* and an annual payment of 177 *livres,* in lieu of a *rente* capitalized at 3,538 *livres,* from their sister Marie.

Marie's capital inheritance included lands centering on Berneré as it had been carved out from Forgette nearly half a century before, supplemented by contiguous farms and meadows that Susanne Isle had inherited or purchased on her own or with her late husband.[40] In addition to the lands as immovable property, Marie received the lord's oven (*four banal*) in Saint-Savinien, in which most inhabitants were obliged to bake their bread. She would have half of Susanne Isle's personal effects after her grandmother's death and immediately enjoy a tapestry that hung in the upper chamber at Berneré, valued at 150 *livres,* as well as several beds.

Three features of this division set the stage for the turmoil it would impose on Marie and Josias in the very years when their religion was under assault and they would need to make the most fateful decision of their lives. The first was how traditional the components of Susanne's estate were. Her fortune was entirely invested locally and in standard rural assets. She held none of the government *rentes* that were so important in cities for the accumulation of capital and in which women were disproportionally heavily invested. Instead of bonds, her interest-accruing loans were to neighbors and kin, and they carried modest interest rates, with neither the upside opportunity for high rates one enjoyed in lending to the king nor the downside risk of default one endured thereby. Instead of commerce, her source of ready cash was the feudal lord's oven that had come into the Isle family along with the seigneury of Forgette in 1556, then was given to Susanne Isle and Jean de Solière on their marriage. The oven fetched a low return of less than 3 percent—well under what the same capital sum could earn in either loans or bonds. But it daily betokened the standing in the community of its owner, and so its social value surpassed the monetary.[41]

Along with the traditional character of her assets, Susanne's 1677 property division involved a certain reversal of standard usage that came from the distaff character of the family. Usually, younger siblings got their inheritance in money (as did Madelene and Susanne de Solière) or got the mother's property while the advantaged heir got the father's. In this case, when the remnants of two son-in-law marriages were passed to a third generation of girls, the advantaged Marie got the maternal holdings (Berneré) and the younger the paternal. At the time, this would have appeared as a strength: the father's lands sufficed to provide for the younger children without dividing the principal landed domain to be held by the universal heir (Berneré) and without borrowing, as Susanne herself had been forced to do for her own younger daughters. But Berneré was kept intact by making it and its appurtenances the core legacy to Marie. In the long run this would be the young woman's undoing.

The most consequential feature of this division of the estate was the absence of liquid assets. Marie would need liquidity in order to satisfy the obligations that came attached to the assets she inherited: a total of 7,250 *livres* in one-time debt taken over from Susanne and a life annuity of 500 *livres* to Susanne for the remainder of her life, to be replaced at her death by an annual payment of 177 *livres* to her five sisters. But in the absence of cash inheritance, liquidity would have to come from her landed properties themselves. The lord's oven proved a dependable source of cash income. The last time she let it out, in October 1686, Marie contracted the farming to a merchant living in Saint-Savinien, who would collect the fees that the locals paid for the obligatory baking of bread in the seigneurial oven, in return for a set payment to Marie of thirty *livres* per month.[42] And the land itself could be made to yield cash. Josias, as Marie's agent, in January 1687 sold some timber from the old-growth forest at Berneré to two merchants who were buying wood for construction of the king's vessels in the new naval port of Rochefort. The vines of Berneré also produced brandy that may have traveled far even before Marie de La Rochefoucauld in her exile marketed it in Holland.[43] Wine-production was one example of the precursors to modern industry that centered, in the Charentes, on seigneurial estates, under seigneurial regulation, and brought the Charentais seigneuries, by the seventeenth century, into a market-oriented economy.

Indeed, what the kin advisors did in the afternoon on March 8, 1677 explains this absence of liquid assets. Reassembling after the midday meal, the same group that signed the will in the morning drew up a second document, to assign Susanne Isle's accounts receivable—her liquid assets—to Marie de La Rochefoucauld. By this second agreement, whose language ties it to "the said contract of general property division made this day," Marie took possession of twelve *rentes* and promissory notes from kin and villagers totaling 3,000 *livres*. This transfer necessitated a separate document because the property was not to be Marie's own. Rather, her sisters and the other signatories "recognize that the 3,000 *livres* the said dame de Champagné is charged with . . . is to replace and pay the equivalent sum to dame Madelene de Solière, the said Susanne Ille's own daughter."[44] The debt had been mentioned in the vaguest of terms in the morning document: "the said dame de Champagné shall be bound to pay and acquit on behalf of the said inheritance up to the one-time sum of three thousand *livres* that all the parties assume to be due by the said dame Isle besides the above debts, the said parties declaring that they did not wish to reveal more on the present article for reasons known to them." Separating the two documents would seem to have been designed to distance the obligation toward Madelene de Solière from the heritages being passed down by Susanne Isle, both by declining to mention the purpose of the 3,000 *livres* in the document that distributed the bulk of Susanne's estate to the six heiresses of her choice and by specifying in the second document a separate funding source for the unexplained indemnification of Madelene de Solière.

The afternoon document, then, made Marie de La Rochefoucauld a creditor, a potential benefit to her, as the inheritance of receivables transferred power across generations in a way that mere cash did not. A particularly clear illustration of the way credit created a hierarchy of power that could extend across generations involved the sum of 32 *livres* 15 *sols* that a local cooper, Paul Boisaud, had owed Susanne Isle since 1665. Marie tried to call in the debt in September 1682, without success. So the week before Christmas 1683 she summoned the cooper to Berneré. He brought along his son and concluded an agreement with Marie, in the presence of a notary and witnesses, that would pay off the debt in kind. The cooper's son Abraham—thirteen or fourteen years old at the time; no one seemed quite sure of his age, but at any rate he was born well after his father incurred the debt—was indentured to work for Marie without salary or time off for five years, beginning immediately, as "cowherd, lackey, or other usage set by the said Dame in proportion to the age and strength of the said Boisaud." Abraham promised to serve Marie faithfully, she to feed him and maintain him with clothing, linens, and shoes as she judged necessary.[45] Here, transmuted into flesh and blood, was the hierarchy of power created by lending.

Dependencies created by lending and borrowing, however, ran both ways: lender and borrower became mutually dependent. Marie's new position as simultaneously a creditor and a debtor carried risks. Her ability to pay what might be due to Madelene de Solière would be contingent upon her own ability to collect sums from a dozen different debtors, some of whom had owed the money to Susanne Isle since the 1640s. Even as the borrowers were beholden to her, Marie became dependent for her own solvency upon their repaying the loans.

This, then, is what they signed: Susanne Isle, all six granddaughters, Josias de Robillard, Isaac Isle de Loire, François de La Rochefoucauld, Charles de Villedon, and a domestic servant from Champagné, Jean Poitevin. Marie inherited the family domain, armed with little cash other than what the estate itself could generate and responsible for making her grandmother's final payment to her daughter Madelene. Gradually, Marie gained more property, through the early deaths of two unmarried sisters: Henriette before May 1680 at age twenty-two and Lidie by December 1682, when she would have been twenty-five. Marie netted some 830 *livres* in lands and livestock as her 1/5 share of Henriette's property and a comparable gain from the passing of Lidie.[46] The jewel was still Berneré, however, and Berneré was to be Marie's, "for her and hers in perpetuity and forever." In this case, forever proved to be quite brief.

The Charentes

In time, Susanne Isle's distribution of property through a daughter to a granddaughter—involving, as it did, lesser shares for the other daughters and granddaughters—would have unforeseen and unwelcome effects. But for the moment, it provided Marie, Josias, and the survivors among their six children born at Champagné with a noble residence, a profitable estate, a familial social matrix, and—not insignificantly—a healthy environment. Before moving to Berneré, the family had spent a decade at Champagné and had lost half of the six children born there. Champagné was on low-lying land alongside the Boutonne, just at the limit of the sea tide in the river, and so it may well have shared the exceeding insalubrity of the nearby coastal marshes, which were endemically infected with malaria, scurvy, and fevers.[47] Along this coast, infant mortality was unusually high. Coastal families sent their newborns to wet nurses upstream, to Saint-Savinien and surrounding villages, to protect them from the "bad air" of the lowlands.[48] By moving to Saint-Savinien themselves, Marie and Josias improved the life chances of their children.[49]

As seigneuries went, Berneré was of middling size, but its seigneur had both judicial and economic power over a considerable number of persons. Because

Berneré had been carved out of Forgette, which had enjoyed rights of high justice since 1497, Josias and his predecessors at Berneré also had rights of high justice, meaning that their seigneurial court could mete out the death penalty. As for economic power, an estate survey drawn up around 1685 listed sixty-three tenants on the Berneré lands. Splendidly set among prairies of wheat and maize, paddocks and pastures, woods and vines, the estate probably had its part in all facets of the mixed agriculture for which Saint-Savinien was known: wheat, wine, hay, and livestock. The sharecropper Jean Michau, who worked the Berneré farm called "L'Hersant," delivered to the seigneur not only grains, half the milk produced by the cows and ewes Marie gave him, half the nuts he gathered from her trees, and half the flax and hemp he gathered in her fields, but also each year a hog worth ten *livres*, six capons, twelve hens, and a few ducklings if there were any. Jean Gabareau, who leased her farm at Vaufraiche in 1685, had to deliver to her door six pounds of butter yearly and a dozen-count of cheese, in addition to the customary hog, capons, and hens. Yet another lease, dated May 1683 at Berneré, stipulated that the salt-worker Jean Campain's farm, which included excellent marshes and vineyards, would cost him an annual rent of seventy-five *livres* plus the hay for a horse that Marie de La Rochefoucauld could send four times a year to fetch oysters and fish. This in-kind obligation probably supported a trip twenty miles to the seaside, to procure Oléron or Marennes oysters more savory than the fresh-water mollusks that could be found in the tidal sections of the river just below Saint-Savinien.[50]

The deep-water Charente, navigable as far upstream as Angoulême, was the focal point of communities like Saint-Savinien that lay on its banks. Flat-bottomed, single-masted *gabares* home-ported in Saint-Savinien, Taillebourg, Saintes, Cognac, and Jarnac carried salt upstream from the salt marshes along the coast as well as luxuries and staples from longer distances: linens and laces from Flanders, silks and spices and furs brought by Hanseatic ships, herrings and cod brought by the Dutch. Downstream they took the grain, timber, woad, tiles, and paper produced in inland reaches as well as cannons and muskets fabricated in the forges of Angoumois for the naval arsenal at Rochefort. A few regional specialties moved downstream in *gabares* and then were transferred to oceangoing ships toward international clienteles. From riverside Cognac and Jarnac flowed the premium champagne brandy prized notably by the aristocrats of London and Paris. And decorated earthenware from the centuries-old rural household workshops around La Chapelle-des-Pots, five miles east of Saintes, began on the Charente their transport to markets in the British Isles, Flanders, Scandinavia, and the French colonies across the Atlantic.[51]

Saint-Savinien was a linchpin of this fluvial and maritime commerce. Before its docks the Atlantic tides mixed with fresh water, and ocean ships

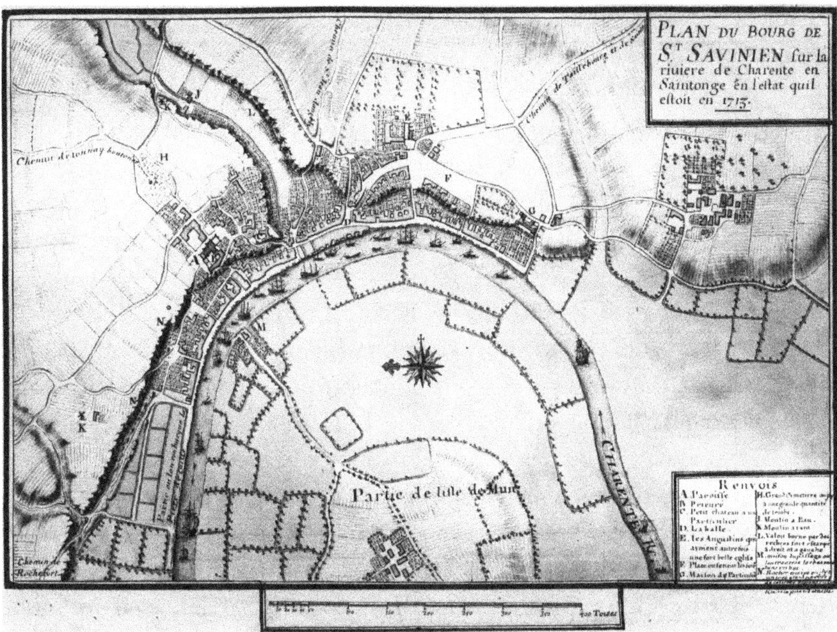

Figure 1.6 Map of Saint-Savinien on the Charente River in 1713, from Claude Masse, "Recueil des Plans de Saintonge," 96[99] (pen & ink and w/c on paper) (b/w photo). Service historique de la Défense. Armée de Terre, Vincennes. By permission of Bridgeman Images.

exchanged their cargos for the river's exports. Claude Masse noted at Saint-Savinien "always a good number of sea-going ships and other flat-bottoms," both of which were turned out in a shipbuilding facility at Forgette. From the Quai de La Grue, brandy distilled from local grapes was loaded directly into boats for shipment to northern Europe and to the colonies in America. Blocks of Saint-Savinien's white stone were dragged by oxen or horses from subterranean quarries to the wharf for export. Just miles downstream, the new naval city and arsenal of Rochefort was being built from this Saint-Savinien stone; so important was Saint-Savinien stone for the building of Rochefort that the intendant Bégon in 1693 provided price supports to keep the Saint-Savinien quarriers working. The inscription on Bégon's tombstone pegged his achievements—rather than to the New World flower that would ever bear his name—to this: "He found a city in wood scarcely begun, and he left it built in stone."[52]

Between Rochefort and the Atlantic shore lay the salt marshes whose exports made the "Charentais seaboard one of the nerve centers of the European economy."[53] Just to Rochefort's north was the great international commercial port of La Rochelle. Because it flowed out upon such a coast, the Charente opened the whole of Saintonge to the shaping force of distant demand. In the decades following the close of the Wars of Religion, the river's commerce transformed the land itself. A spectacular expansion of viticulture imprinted upon the landscape the particularities of Dutch taste. Precisely because the Dutch clamored for brandy of modest quality in large quantities, vines of mediocre stock grew everywhere in the Charentes region. Its grapes could not compete in flavor with those around Bordeaux, but they produced more beverage and greater profit. As Claude Masse would report in 1712, "a quarter of land that will produce five or six barrels of wine in Aunis will not produce one around Bordeaux." The Dutch brought this "brandywine" from France, for their own consumption and to transship around the globe, through Dutch merchant houses that controlled brandy trading in La Rochelle and Tonnay-Charente. But the Dutch traders did not work upstream. Rather, local wine-trading networks in the hinterlands were in French hands, specifically in Huguenot hands before the Revocation. Local Huguenots bought the wine from Charentais producers and sold it to Dutch factors in the port cities. In Saint-Savinien, Protestant merchants and distillers on the Quai de La Grue loaded onto *gabares* the brandy demanded by distant Dutch imbibers and re-exporters.[54]

This trade had far-reaching effects on the Charentes. It magnified the Dutch presence in the region, where Dutch investors and entrepreneurs had already modernized the paper mills of Angoulême and built the polders reclaiming dry land in the Marais Poitevin and Petite-Flandre. The river's commerce accustomed the region to the movement of money as well as men. The brandy trade familiarized locals with foreign bills of exchange and put Dutch money in many Charentais pockets. It gave the young men of the Charentes a special reason to go abroad. Like other Frenchmen, they were lured to venture far from home as soldiers (especially to Germany and the Low Countries), as theology students (especially to Geneva), as aspiring merchants (especially to Britain), and as artists (especially to Italy). But Charentais youth also went abroad (especially to Holland) to learn the brandy business. The fate of the Huguenots in the Charentes was strongly shaped by the fact that their religion was outlawed at this particular moment in the history of Charentais commercial relations with northwest Europe, during the heyday of Franco-Dutch and Franco-English commerce. It eventually facilitated their departure and their transfer abroad of funds to support them in the Refuge.

At the same time, the hybrid commercial-agricultural economy of Saint-Savinien and Saintonge lent the region a particular instability in the face of both natural and political impositions. Observers often waxed lyrical on its evident prosperity. Claude Masse would note that "the peasants are well-off relative to [those in] other areas. They are usually well housed, their houses are rather clean, rather well furnished, and ordinarily they are well dressed." It was probably already true, as François, future Duc de La Rochefoucauld, would write upon traveling in the region in 1783, that "Saintonge is the most beautiful province I crossed on my trip. It is filled with lovely meadows and good land. Cultivation there is quite perfected. This province abounds in all that is needed for good food, and there the peasant is less miserable than elsewhere."[55]

Yet Saintonge was only prosperous relative to the generally precarious economic conditions throughout the kingdom, and the region had never been as pacific as these idyllic descriptions suggest. The Charente had been "a sort of medieval Rhine," because it formed the border between the Plantagenet heirs of the Dukes of Aquitaine and the French crown, then served as a battleground in the Hundred Years' War, in the Wars of Religion, and in the Fronde. In the early seventeenth century, peasant uprisings emerged there. From April to August 1636, an "insurrectional epidemic" radiated out from Angoulême, responding to new taxes imposed to support the war against the Habsburgs. When it reached Saint-Savinien, rebels perpetrated a particularly vicious act of insurrectionary justice against a tax collector from Paris: "he was torn alive into small pieces, and each of them took a piece to fasten to the door of his house, where these pieces can still be seen."[56] Concern over the wine tax brought Saint-Savinien to the center of the uprising, since taxes on cargos of wine floating down the river were assessed and collected there.[57]

By the 1660s, when Josias de Robillard inherited Champagné, and the 1670s, when Susanne Isle's will installed him and Marie de La Rochefoucauld at Berneré, the peasant uprisings had disappeared from Saintonge, as they had across France generally. But the structural situation persisted and shaped economic life for both peasant and noble in the Saint-Savinien region. It was peasant indebtedness that allowed a noble like Josias de Robillard to engross his domain, but the excessive taxation that created peasant indebtedness also lay behind the endemic, widespread indebtedness of the nobles themselves, which runs as a leitmotif through the Champagné story. A common antitax interest, then, was shared by noble and peasant, for if taxes were so high that peasants could not pay from the proceeds of their labor, then landowning nobles could not collect seigneurial dues and rents. The uprisings of 1636 did not act out a conflict between peasant and seigneur—there were no attacks on châteaux, no protests against payment of the tithe to the church or dues to seigneurs, no proposals for changing power relations, no revolutionary vision. Complicity of the nobility may have been only passive, or the intendant may have been correct in observing that the nobility stirred the peasants up: "the clergy and gentry connived at their political gatherings." Passive or active, however, the Saintonge nobility—for the greater part still Protestant—did not align itself with the crown when the central government invaded the region. In 1636, there were no overt signs that religion played a role in the uprisings, but religious tensions were salient enough to be suspected. Some feared that, given how widespread Protestantism was among peasants and nobles alike, the revolts might take on a religious cast, and the revolts' principal historian has called them "a sort of continuation of the wars of religion."[58] When religion did come to the fore in 1685, with the imposition from Paris of the Revocation, the Saintonge nobility would have to rethink once again its interests and its obligation to obey.

Protestant Charentes

The watershed of the Charente was distinguished by its religious profile as well as by its economic activities. "This province has famously been infected with heresy more than any other in the realm. . . . the people have suckled the pernicious doctrine of Calvin with their milk." The Protestant presence in Aunis and Saintonge around 1660–1670 has been estimated at 79,000–84,000 faithful: 20,000–25,000 in the Saintes region, 13,000 in that of Saint-Jean-d'Angély, 14,000 in Aunis (including La Rochelle), and 32,000 along the Saintonge coast and on its islands.[59] Nobles were disproportionally attracted to, and instrumental in implanting, what Saintongeais would describe as "the religion we profess by the grace of God, that the edicts of the king oblige us to call supposedly reformed."[60] During the Wars of Religion, an estimated 20 percent of the nobility kingdom-wide turned Protestant. Noble conversions were especially numerous throughout the Southwest; in Saintonge and the diocese of La Rochelle as much as 70 percent of the nobility may have been won to the cause.[61] As late as 1664, the intendant Colbert de Croissy noted the continuing overrepresentation of nobles in Charentais Protestantism: "Perhaps around a tenth of the people of Poitou are of the R.P.R., and nearly half of the nobility, while for certain, in the bishopric of La Rochelle more than three-quarters of the gentlemen are of this religion." The minor landed nobility would sponsor the religion's rise and persistence in the Charentes, and when they ceased doing so in the era of the Revocation, the confession could not defend itself. "The defeat of the Protestant party was first and foremost the defeat of the nobility."[62] That is what makes the story of the Isle and Champagné families critical to an understanding of Huguenot history.

Typically, the first Protestant temple in a locality was built on a plot of land donated by a local noble family. On the coast, conversions to the Reformed religion occurred in less hierarchical, more populist fashion, incubated by a maritime openness to novel ideas. But in the Charentes hinterland, at least, Protestantism spread and took root by patronage of local noble powers. The La Trémoïlle family, regional magnates sometimes called "the little kings of Poitou" for their eminence and wealth, turned Protestant during the Wars of

Religion and fostered the implantation of Reformed religion in their lands.[63] The temple in Saint-Savinien was made possible by a concession from the La Trémoïlle. In 1604 the local pastor, sensing already the unusual numbers of Protestants in the town, petitioned the still-Protestant Duc de La Trémoïlle for help with "the preservation of this church that subsists under your authority . . . that we may have a temple for serving God as we see all our neighbors have, though they be less numerous and less well endowed than we are." Then in November 1612, the Comtesse de Taillebourg answered their plea, granting to the Protestants of the town "a place where the temple of Saint-Savinien was built, familiarly referred to as La Chaulme."[64]

Saint-Savinien had admitted the Reform from its earliest days. In May of 1547, the Parlement of Bordeaux ordered the arrest of four Savinois shoemakers for heresy. Seven years later, it ordered the arrest within a fortnight of a heretic locksmith who had fled to Saint-Savinien with the keys to Saint-Jean-d'Angély's Catholic church of Saint-Révérend. That same summer, another heretic Savinois was fined 200 *livres* by the Parlement of Bordeaux for creating a scandal in Saint-Savinien's (Catholic) parish church on Good Friday.[65] By 1564, the town's first temple had been founded; the Syndic of the Clergy of Saintes reported in that year that no Catholic services were held in Saint-Savinien and that Protestantism was so strong in the town's population that holders of Catholic benefices dared not reside there.[66] Saint-Savinien would become the most thickly Protestant locality in inland Saintonge. When the intendant of Limoges did a census of Protestants in 1682, he found that 1,145 individuals from 324 Saint-Savinien families were "*religionnaires*"—by far the most numerous Protestant community among the eighty-two communities in or near his *généralité* that he surveyed. The second largest concentration (1,027 individuals from 287 families) was in the much larger town of Saint-Jean-d'Angély.[67]

The families of Josias de Robillard de Champagné and Marie de La Rochefoucauld had long professed the *Religion prétendue réformée* and woven family solidarities with the threads of Protestant affiliation. Robillard, Sieur de La Grange was among the 579 Protestants condemned to death in absentia as rebels and heretics by the Parlement of Bordeaux in 1569.[68] Jean and André de Robillard had three sons and three daughters baptized by local pastors in neighbors' châteaux during the Wars of Religion. The end of the wars found the Champagné worshipping in the Protestant temple at Saint-Jean-d'Angély. This city would become one of the safe places established by the Edict of Nantes, where Protestants could worship free of harassment, because, as intendant Bégon reported, in the earliest days of the new religion its "inhabitants nearly all subscribed to the errors of Calvin."[69] Before their move to Berneré, Josias and Marie, like the many nobles in the Charentes who exploited the provision in the Edict of Nantes permitting gentlemen to hold Protestant services in their châteaux,[70] baptized four of their first five children (born 1669–1673) in their château at Champagné. From 1677 to 1680, they baptized three infants in the temple at Saint-Savinien. Throughout, Josias and Marie wrapped their babies in the protection of Protestant kin. Godparents included Charles de Villedon de Magezy, Marie's uncle and one of the kin advisors at the 1677 property division (Uranie, 1669); Marie de Robillard, sister of Josias (Uranie, 1669), and her husband Casimir Prévost de Touchimbert (Josias, 1673); Philippe Nicolas de Voutron, maternal cousin of Josias (Elisabeth Sylvie, 1671); Elisabeth de La Rochefoucauld, sister of Marie (Elisabeth Sylvie, 1671 and François Casimir, 1672); François de La Rochefoucauld, cousin of Marie (Josias, 1673); and Olympe de Cailhault, Josias' maternal aunt (Josias, 1673).[71]

The La Rochefoucauld, among the richest and most powerful families in the region, boasted some of the most devoted Protestants from the earliest days of the Wars of Religion. The senior branch of the family turned Protestant when François III, Comte de La Rochefoucauld, married a niece of the Admiral Coligny and became legendary for its leadership of the Reformed cause. The Parc d'Archiac branch of the family, to which Marie's father belonged, was one of the province's most steadfastly Protestant lineages, having given "striking proofs of its attachment to the Reformed Church." In September 1562, this line inherited the seigneury of La Rigaudière from Catherine Vigier, whose father Jean was beheaded by order of the Parlement of Bordeaux for attacking Catholic forces in the Gironde. Gédéon de La Rochefoucauld du Parc d'Archiac was a deputy to the church assembly in La Rochelle in 1612 and fought against the king's assault on La Rochelle in the 1620s.[72] François, Seigneur du Parc d'Archiac et de La Rigaudière, a brother of Marie's grandfather, was lieutenant of the governor Rohan in Saint-Jean-d'Angély in the years before Louis XIII wrested the city from Protestant hands. He commanded the fort of Saint-Martin-de-Ré for Soubise in September 1625, when Montmorency was attacking it for the king. His son, a family advisor at Susanne Isle's 1677 property division, would still be serving in Reformed synods as late as 1682.[73]

The Sauliere were Protestants in Périgord from at least one generation before Susanne Isle's husband Jean. In the late 1570s, Périgueux was at the center of hostilities between the royal forces and the Protestant armies fighting in the Southwest under the leadership of Henry of Navarre, then governor of Guyenne. André de Bourdeille, seneschal of Périgord for Charles IX and older brother of the writer who ridiculed Pierre de Sauliere, commanded the royal troops in the region. Pierre de Sauliere was among the town officials working to organize and mobilize the defense of the town against Bourdeille, up until the time it fell to his Catholic-crown forces in July 1581. Sauliere escaped the massacre of Protestants when the town changed hands but was captured and imprisoned. Henry of Navarre wrote to Bourdeille in August 1581 denouncing the attack as a violation of the king's peace and demanding redress: "once again, have everything returned and free all the said prisoners, principally Sauliere, so that nothing greater can be complained of." In the event, the Sauliere stayed Protestant longer than Henry of Navarre himself. Pierre's great-grandson Isaac was so militant in his Protestantism that he was fined 1,000 *livres* in 1681 and threatened with prison and confiscation of his seigneury if he continued to allow Protestant worship in his noble residence at Nanteuil. As late as May 1682, he was still defiantly holding such services in his capacity as seigneur with rights of justice, and as late as August 1699 his fifteen-year-old son was proclaiming publicly his "disdain for the [Catholic] religion . . . that he would ever be of the religion of his father and mother . . . that it was some wonderful religion in which one kneels before a bit of bread and idols."[74]

The Isle had long been among the leaders of Protestantism in the Charentes. As with the Champagné, their conversion dated as far back as the 1560s, when Jean Isle, Seigneur de La Matassière, was among those condemned to death by the Parlement of Bordeaux. The Wars of Religion found the Isle in Condé's forces. Isaac Isle's maternal grandfather, Jean Pallet, was physician to the Prince de Condé and one of the signatories of the report on the prince's March 1588 autopsy in Saint-Jean-d'Angély that concluded—erroneously—that he had been poisoned.[75] After the Edict of Nantes made peace between the confessions, the Isle perpetuated their Protestant commitments. Daniel Isle, Sieur de La Cave married the daughter, Madeleine, of the pastor Claude Heraud in 1634.

Then in 1663–1666, when the controller-general Jean-Baptiste Colbert subjected each Calvinist consistory in Saintonge and Aunis to an examination of its strict compliance with the provisions of the Edict of Nantes, Charles Colbert de Terron, first cousin of the Grand Colbert, served as the Catholic commissioner, and the lead negotiator on behalf of all the temples was Isaac Isle, Marquis de Loire, Marie's second cousin and one of the kin advisors at Susanne Isle's 1677 property division. These royal commissioners had been provided for in the Edict of Nantes and began their work immediately on its adoption, with one commissioner from each confession: the Catholic member usually an upper administrator or jurist, the Protestant a person of standing and reputation in the region, usually an important nobleman. The commissioners' original task was to oversee execution of the Edict's provisions and monitor its observance. But when the commissions were revived in the 1660s, they had a different intent: "not to find common ground for the advance of peace, but to limit the Edict of Nantes and impose greater restriction on the Huguenots."[76] Appointment of these later commissioners was part of Louis XIV's effort to roll back Protestantism by questioning each temple's right of public worship. So procedures in this phase of their work were weighted to favor the Catholic side. Temples were required to present their documentation, the clergy were invited to provide contrary testimony, and then the two commissioners would deliberate and draw their separate (often conflicting) conclusions.[77]

Even selection of the commissioners was skewed to the Catholic side. "The Reformed commissioners were chosen everywhere at the wish of the Catholic commissioner. The King's letters patent left the name of the Reformed blank, and the Catholic was ordered to fill it in. This is why one at first saw only persons on the commissions whose weakness Protestants feared, either because they were timid and indecisive or because they had business before the intendants that obliged them to be dangerously compliant or because they were suspected of seeking their own advancement and doing so even at the expense of their conscience." The authorities may have thought Isaac's dependence on royal favor as a military officer would force him to cooperate with their aims: "He was a gentleman who had spent part of his life in the army, he was not married, and (so it was said) he spent a great deal." But he was both knowledgeable and unbending in his defense of his family's religion. "Soon after, it was seen that those who had chosen him were mistaken in the opinion they had of his character. As he had a conscience and honor, he did nothing that violated them. He even made himself knowledgeable about the edicts and declarations pertaining to the Religion, with the result that he was not, as it had been alleged, easily controlled." The Rochelais scholar—later refugee—Abraham Tessereau considered Isaac a hero of the survival of Protestantism in the region after the accession of Louis XIV, placing him among "the most zealous for the Religion and the most capable whether in strengthening their fellows' attachment to it or in advising them on issues they faced." His fellow Protestants classed him among those commissioners who "nonetheless did their duty and for whom the Religion was stronger than all human considerations. . .whose tenacity made more difficulties for the clergy than they for him."[78] Because of Isaac's independence, because he construed his task as stemming the effects of the official anti-Protestant policy that would eventually culminate in the Revocation, his commission was withdrawn in 1677,[79] mere weeks after he advised his cousin Susanne Isle on the division of her estate.

Just as the Isle marriages with Protestant families—Robillard, La Rochefoucauld, Solière, and Heraud among them—merged religion with family ties, so did their practices of godparentage.[80] Their choices for the religious roles of godmother and godfather reveal the extent to which family cohesion derived from, and depended upon, their sharing of a common religion. Among the Isle, sibling solidarity was reinforced when a sister or brother of the new parent was asked to serve. Sara Isle de Loire asked Elisabeth Isle for her daughter in 1640 and their brother Isaac for her daughter in 1643. Marguerite Isle de Loire asked her brother Isaac to be godfather to her son in 1655. Isaac chose his sister Elisabeth in 1668 for his son Abimelec. Claude Isle des Groies asked his sister Esther for his son Daniel in 1658 and his son Isaac in 1660.

The cohesion of the extended family, too, was strengthened by godparent choices. The Isle made a special practice of crossing branches of the family for godparentage. So, for example, Susanne Isle and Jean de Solière asked her cousin Daniel Isle de La Cave to stand as godfather for their first daughter, who would be the mother of Marie de La Rochefoucauld. Daniel Isle de La Cave from the Des Groies line chose Isaac Isle de Loire from the La Matassière branch and Marie de Solière from the Forgette line for his son in 1645. Claude Isle des Groies turned to each of the three branches of the family, choosing his brother Paul and sister Esther for his son Daniel, his cousin Elisabeth Isle de Loire for his son Trajan, and his cousin Susanne Isle along with Daniel Isle de La Cave for his daughter Léa Susanne. Susanne Isle served as godmother in both of the main branches outside her own: for the son of Elisabeth Isle de Loire in 1640 and for the daughter of Claude Isle des Groies in 1657.

Susanne's three daughters were pulled into close Isle kin bonds in these ways. Sara Isle de Loire asked Marie de Solière to be godmother for her daughter in 1643, as did Daniel Isle de La Cave for his son in 1645. Each of Susanne Isle's other two daughters bonded as godmothers with one of Marie de Solière's babies: Madelene de Solière for Madeleine de La Rochefoucauld in 1651 and Susanne de Solière for Marie's youngest daughter, Henriette, on the last day of 1657 at the Château de Forgette. Godparenting did not merely cement the child to the church but also bonded the aunts and uncles to the child through the church. Godparenting further served as a rite of passage into adulthood. Marie de Solière served as godmother no fewer than four times in the four years preceding her marriage and Madelene de Solière no fewer than three times between 1649 and 1651. The "Mademoiselle des Touches" who served as godmother in September 1666 was probably Marie de La Rochefoucauld embarking on the same initiation before her marriage in 1667.

These Isle practices illustrate the codependence of religion and family within Protestantism before the intensified coercion leading up to the Revocation. Protestants tapped kin as godparents more frequently than Catholics did, perhaps from an understanding that their minority religion depended for its survival on family cohesion and bonds of mutual protection among its faithful. The Champagné case would soon illustrate the fate of Protestantism and Protestants in France when family cohesion eroded, in part from changes in religious commitments.

Meanwhile, in an increasingly Catholic country, Protestant interactions with Catholics were a fact of everyday life. Solidarities knit by religion were not incompatible with neighbor ties transcending confessions. As in Poitou, so in Saint-Savinien, "neighbors of different religions found ways to build bridges and place daily concerns ahead of confessional competition."[81] Susanne Isle's credit network included neighbors of both faiths. The husband of her debtor Elisabeth Gandouin was an officer in the consistory of Saint-Savinien's temple, but the family of her debtor La Valade were old Catholics. Josias and Marie made a joint will on April 26, 1683 before the notary Bouyer in Saint-Savinien in which they stipulated that "our burials . . . [be made] according to the usage observed in the *Religion prétendue réformée*, which we have always professed." One of the witnesses to this testament was the curé of Saint-Savinien, Jacques Bongirault, who also served as a witness when Marie leased one of Berneré's farms to a tenant of unknown religion in August 1683. Josias' and Marie's marriage contract, executed on February 22, 1667, was signed not only by a passel of Protestant Prévost de Touchimbert, Villedon, Robillard, Solière, and La Rochefoucauld but also by Charles Colbert de Terron, the crown commissioner representing Catholic interests in the negotiations for which Isaac Isle held up the Protestant side.[82] Terron was known, as was his cousin the controller-general, to care little about Huguenots' religious sentiments so long as they conformed politically and stayed within the strict provisions of the Edict of Nantes. Indeed, he took pride in his friendship with Protestant notables such as the Isle, and under Terron's leadership French naval forces mixed Protestant and Catholic with little distinction.[83]

Moreover, like most places, Saint-Savinien, though it had developed a concentration of Protestants, had its Catholic institutions, notably the Abbaye des Augustins that had been founded there in the thirteenth century. Among that community's few sources of income was their entitlement to half the profits from the lord's oven owned by Susanne Isle and then Marie de La Rochefoucauld.[84] It was the Augustinians who asked the judge of Taillebourg in June 1675 to prohibit the inhabitants of Saint-Savinien from having their dough baked elsewhere than in the lord's oven and to send officers to Saint-Savinien to enforce the order on the price of bread and against the local millers.[85] Just months after inheriting the oven from her grandmother, Marie joined with the Augustinians in requesting, successfully, a parlementary order against "Catherine Audebert and other sellers of bread in Saint-Savinien that forbids the bringing and selling of bread in the said Saint-Savinien that was not baked in the lord's oven of the said locality." But there were conflicts as well as cooperation. In 1679, Marie paid down a part of a debt Susanne Isle had owed the Augustinians since 1655. It took an order from the Parlement to get her to pay the remainder, which she did at last in June 1685.[86] So for the ten years preceding her flight into the Huguenot Refuge, Marie de La Rochefoucauld was business partner with the Catholic Church. As for the Champagné, in their *sénéchaussée* of Saint-Jean-d'Angély in 1686, 23 percent of the seigneurs of seigneuries were ecclesiastics. The largest landowner in Josias' own parish of Torxé was the bishop of Angoulême, by virtue of his benefice as prior of the priory of Saint-Pierre de Torxé.[87]

Within this increasingly Catholic country, minority Protestants had, perhaps most importantly, a family memory of involvement with their faith. The fathers and grandfathers of the actors in this story had been comrades in arms at the pivotal moments of Protestant crisis. When the Parlement of Bordeaux in 1569 sentenced 579 Protestants to death in absentia as "rebels, conspirators, traitors to the King, and public enemies of God," the nobles condemned to be drawn on a hurdle with their coats of arms dragging from the tail of a horse, then broken on the wheel, burned, decapitated, and their heads displayed on the ends of lances at the gates of the city, included François de La Rochefoucauld, Baron de Montendre; Nicolas de Valée, Sieur du Douhet; the Sieur de La Matassière (the last was an Isle: La Matassière and Le Douhet were identified as "both go-betweens in England for the rebels"); Gabriel de La Mothe, Sieur de Saint-Surin; Saint-Mesme; François Vigier, Sieur de Treillebois; Jean Goumard, Sieur d'Agonnay; and Robillard, Sieur de La Grange (Josias' ancestor). When the Protestant armies were defeated at Saint-Jean-d'Angély in 1621, those who signed the capitulation or were spoken for in the oath of obedience included an Isaac Isle (father of the future defender of Protestant temples) and two other Isle designated as Loire and Matassière, two Champagné brothers (including Josias' grandfather), the Baron de Saint-Surin (whose son would marry Josias' daughter Susanne in exile), and two La Rochefoucauld du Parc d'Archiac.[88] Both the men and the women in these families must have heard their fathers and mothers, their grandmothers and grandfathers talk about how they had defended the faith in the face of defeat.

Between the time Susanne Isle signed her will on March 8, 1677 and her death on December 8, 1679, the situation for Protestants in France shifted dramatically. Immediately upon assuming personal rule in 1661, Louis XIV had initiated efforts to reduce Protestant privileges to the literal minimum guaranteed in the Edict of Nantes. The regional commissions such as the one on which Isaac Isle served were part of this offensive of the young king, as were new laws excluding Protestants from various offices and privileges. Louis' first decade of personal rule was, then, the "prehistory of the persecution." Then the 1670s saw both a lessening of force due to the exigencies of the Dutch Wars and a turn to accommodations—"the golden age of attempts at resolution"[89]—perhaps an effect of optimism after the voluntary conversion of the Maréchal de Turenne in 1668.

But the end of hostilities to the north in 1678 allowed a reprise of persecution. The closure of temples resumed, and the large-scale dragonnades began in Poitou as the Peace of Nijmegen made soldiers available. A new rash of legislation outlawed mixed marriages and conversions to Protestantism, lowered the age of conversion to seven, granted a moratorium on debt payments for converts, and proliferated prohibitions on entry into professions. Louis XIV acknowledged the link between foreign affairs and religious policy in the preamble to the Edict of Revocation: "that peace having allowed [the king] to apply himself to reuniting to the Catholic church those who had separated from it, as his two predecessors had always hoped and sought to do but had unfortunately been prevented from doing by foreign wars and agitations in the realm." Peace abroad, then, ended the relative peace for Huguenots in France. How, indeed, would men and women who had heard their parents and grandparents talk about defending the faith respond to this next moment of crisis?

2

Faith of the Fathers and Will of the King

After the Revocation criminalized their religion, the Champagné joined countless small groups of escapees who added up to a torrent of emigrants from France. At the end of the seventeenth century, the intendant Michel Bégon would estimate that the population of the *généralité* of La Rochelle had fallen by more than a third. Some of that toll must have been wreaked by the general demographic catastrophe of the early 1690s: brutal mortalities brought on by overtaxation, food shortage, and germ cycles unrelated to religious division. But Protestant emigration was also a significant factor in the depopulation. One estimate suggests that perhaps 20,000 Protestants fled from Saintonge and Aunis in the years surrounding the Revocation. Another concludes that "the most reasonable estimate for the entire Charentes is around 25,000 departures." Perhaps 18,000 more fled from Poitou, an area of similar population size.[1]

Why did so many Protestants leave the kingdom? The escapees themselves testified that they left because ruthless persecution by the state, culminating in the Revocation, prohibited them from following religious truth. In October 1685, the Revocation of the Edict of Nantes did withdraw the privileges that had afforded them civil status and religious protection since 1598. The twelve articles of the Revocation obliged every subject of the French king to profess the Catholic religion, ordered the Protestants' temples demolished, closed Protestant schools, and prohibited their assemblies. They granted pastors a period of fifteen days in which to quit France without taking along any property or any children over the age of seven, but forbade others leaving the realm. In this last respect the Revocation was an act unique in seventeenth-century law: by constraining dissidents to convert to the religion of the prince without allowing them the option of leaving his territory, it violated the *jus emigrandi* or *beneficium emigrandi* that, since the Peace of Augsburg in 1555, had become a European norm.[2] Fugitives' property would be confiscated, and those caught in flight would be remanded to the galleys or prison for men, to prison or convent for women and children.

As if to balance the unprecedented rigor of the ban on departure and the radical erasure of all visible signs of the Protestant heresy, the final article of the Revocation granted toleration for private worship on the part of "the said persons of the R.P.R. until it should please God to enlighten them like the others," providing they eschewed assemblies and entrusted their children's education to Catholic personnel. For many, this concession of private worship might have seemed sufficient, since Protestants could worship without consecrated spaces, indeed mistrusted as superstitious the materializing of symbolic meanings in buildings and in the objects they contained. Calvin himself had rejected the notion that temples had a particular holiness: "as Paul says, we ourselves are the true temples of God . . . without any consideration of place, we worship God in spirit and in truth."[3] Aside from the Calvinist injunction to show forth the glory of God, their confession rested upon inner convictions that they could exercise in reading Scriptures and in praying as families or alone. But the crown never honored in practice the freedom of private worship that the Edict's final article granted. Private worship, like public, was to be Catholic.

Faced with repression of their religion, Huguenot emigrants framed their decisions to leave in terms of individual faith and personal character. They must bear witness. They must save their children from the path of idolatry. The Calvinist imperative of honest transparency would not permit them to dissemble their faith, even if they could devise a strategy for doing so in order to remain at home. Individually in their memoirs and collectively in the defenses of their faith published in the Refuge by leaders of their communities, especially the ministers, they formulated, and largely established, a heroic view of their own sacrifice for the faith.

The heroic view prevailed in historical memory, often in tandem with an exaggerated size of the exodus and a focus on the virtues of the refugees. "More than five hundred thousand Protestants (some historians raise this number to eight hundred thousand), braving rigorous penalties and preferring exile to apostasy, employed ingenious stratagems to quit the kingdom and go seek under other skies a hospitable soil where they would be permitted to worship God according to their conscience." Jules Michelet, in the mid-nineteenth century, lent the heroic view its most eloquent expression. In 1859, having been pushed to the sidelines by the Second Empire, he passed the summer in self-imposed internal exile in Saintonge. There, in "this land martyred by its bigotry," Michelet's discovery of "poor little Protestant France" put Louis XIV and his policies in a new light. The volume of Michelet's *Histoire de France* published the following year reshaped "the memory of the nation . . . the legend of

France," making the Revocation the culminating event of the seventeenth century, just as the Revolution was the apotheosis toward which all of the eighteenth century gravitated. The "martyrs of Calvinism," not Louis XIV, were the heroes of the Revocation, the victims of relentless persecution to whom history must at last render justice:

> The Protestant could stay; one tried to get them to stay. If he would but say one word, he would keep his properties and his homeland, be spared terrible dangers. The *émigré* of [17]93 wished to save his life; that of 1685 wished to keep his conscience. The flight of the Protestants was voluntary. It was an act of loyalty and sincerity, of horror for lying and respect for one's word. It is glorious for human nature that such a great number of men sacrificed everything in order not to lie, passed from wealth to poverty, risked their life, their family, in venturing such a difficult flight."[4]

Down to the present day, historians have repeated the heroic view and left fugitives' motivations unexamined. The numbers who fled, their geographical origins, their social rank and occupations, the dates of their departure, their routes and destinations: all these are staples of Huguenot histories. But for the emigrants' motives, it has seemed sufficient to list the laws and incidents of violence against Protestants after 1680 and allow the reader to infer that there was no question to be asked: Huguenots fled simply "to live their faith abroad," "to practice the faith to which they were attached," to find "a land with liberty of conscience where they could be free to worship God in their manner . . . to escape from the daily violation of their conscience."[5]

A variety of considerations have discouraged fuller examination of fugitives' motives. Histories of the emigrants have been largely a phenomenon of the countries of the Refuge. English, Dutch, German, and American writers, especially those descended from refugees, have been moved by familial piety, sectarian conviction, and national pride to celebrate the Huguenots' arrival. To the fugitives' courage and willingness to forsake their Catholic homeland, the descendants owed their own freedom to live as Protestants. To their advanced skills and their ability to integrate smoothly into the host cultures, the receiving nations owed a measure of their wealth and social peace. Such a focus on the aftermath of the emigration and orientation toward celebration have given descendants and their compatriots little incentive to question whether the reasons for the emigration were more complicated than what the refugees themselves described as their "exit from Babylon."

Within France, quite different polemical needs and scholarly interests kept attention focused on components of the Protestant story other than the emigrants.[6] French Protestant memory has been more invested in the pre-Revocation experience of persecution and the post-Revocation resistance by those who stayed.[7] Still feeling the sting of majority Catholics' calumnies, even after their religion was legalized and they were admitted fully to public life, the modest numbers of Protestants in post-Revolutionary France found solace in understanding their religious community as "our church of martyrs." Martyrologies and hagiographies by nineteenth-century Protestant historians recounted their confessional heritage as an unbroken line of persecution in which the heroes were those who did not flee. Their courageous persistence inside Babylon made possible a future for Protestantism in France and turned the Revocation into an event not merely tragic but sublime: "the beginning of terrible ordeals but also the occasion to strengthen a vitality and a resistance no one believed possible."[8]

A broader reorientation of French history during the Third Republic deflected interest in yet another way from the Protestant fugitives and the question of their motivations for fleeing. Secular histories directed attention to the state as decision-maker, aiming, among other objectives, to formulate a nonsectarian national history to which the religious allegiance of the citizen was irrelevant. They shied away from questions of religious experience and from "angry disputes" between zealots in the two confessional camps, to focus on the royal policymaking that had guided the destiny of the nation. "The Lavisse," the monumental textbook series from which generations of French youth would learn their national history, asked, with respect to the Revocation, not why Protestants could not bear to stay in France but why the monarchy could not countenance Protestants in the kingdom. Its answers played down religious motives in favor of political explanations and evocations of national character: fear that Huguenot republicanism "deformed" the monarchy, a typically French passion for order and unity, and a certain stylistic repugnance for Protestants' modesty, severity, and "foreign air"—these last so at odds with French classicist strivings for grandeur and glory.[9] Neither the Protestants who left nor those who stayed played a significant role in this story of state decisions.

Such state-centered histories cast a longer shadow over Huguenot history than over most other facets of French memory. Even down to the tercentenary of the Revocation in 1985, the Refuge remained "the least understood issue in France of all those raised by the Protestant policy of Louis XIV," and scholars—especially those who happened to be Protestant—felt constrained, even delicately apologetic, whenever they appraised Louis XIV's Protestant policy negatively. Daniel Robert, for example, at a 1967 session sponsored by the Société d'Etude du XVIIe Siècle prefaced his presentation—in which he attributed the Revocation to Louis XIV's aspiration to become Europe's new

Charlemagne—with a disclaimer: "I would hope, in offering this overview, not to offend anyone: but one ought in history to call a cat a cat, a persecution a persecution, and while not wallowing in the horror, not gloss over what was either sad or outrageous."[10] Others, though, feeding upon the springs of social history that had refashioned historical writing from the 1930s onward through the work of the Annales, reconnected with Michelet's interest in the rank and file rather than leaders, in the emigrants as well as those who stayed. Communities, families, churches, the spiritual life of individuals and groups, religious cultures and practices, relations between Protestants and Catholics in daily lives: these became the substance of the best of recent work.

Social analyses, however, have tended to submerge the question of fugitives' motivations at least as strongly as the state-centered histories they supplanted. A case in point is the work of Norbert Elias, a sociologist who later gained renown as an interpreter of court society and the civilizing process. Shortly after his own flight from Nazi Germany in 1933, Elias published a brief article on "The Expulsion of the Huguenots from France" in a German-language refugee journal published in Paris.[11] Elias situated the Huguenot emigration in a sweeping social context beyond individual faith and personal character. The anomalous term in the title—"expulsion"—holds the key to his meaning, for the Huguenot emigration was not, properly speaking, an expulsion at all. Unlike the action taken by the Spanish monarchs against Jews in 1492, the Revocation not only did not expel the Huguenots from France but even forbade their departure. Yet Elias saw in the Huguenots' fate an expulsion of a different kind. The French state did not expel the Huguenots; their communities—a "social constellation" stronger than law or royal will—did. In Louis XIV's France, dominant Catholics and minority Protestants faced off as competitors for diminishing resources in a situation of overpopulation. Huguenots, as the "group within that was perceived as most alien," became the scapegoats to be purged. Expelling a sizeable fraction of the population released the pressure created by unabsorbable numbers.

Elias' interpretation grafted onto the Huguenot emigration the structure of his own experience. In Louis XIV's France as well as in Nazi Germany, the fatal dynamics lay in established-outsider relationships. In later writings, Elias would enumerate the features of German society in the 1930s that explained its harassment of Jews: "a real bisection of the country"; a high awareness among the dominant groups of their power and the prospect of its increasing; a "distinguishable minority" that was yet strongly attached to the traditions of the community, "wholly embedded in the cultural flow and the political and social fate of the stigmatizing majority"; a "competition for social opportunities" between established groups intent upon closing ranks and outsiders who had proved remarkably successful in the sectors of activity left open to them.[12] All these had made their way into his Huguenot analysis, with French Catholics and Protestants substituting for German right-wing middle classes and Jews.

Elias' shifting of the crucial domain from the central state to the dynamics of grassroots communities opened new possibilities. It provided a rationale for examining the fate of Huguenots at the Revocation in the context of their everyday lives and personal relationships, rather than in statecraft. And yet his conception of the expulsion deprived Huguenots of what they took greatest pride and consolation in: that they were voluntary exiles moved by commitments of conscience. Here, by contrast, not only the Huguenots but also their adversaries were cast in the role of victims, acted upon by large impersonal forces. In Elias' explanation, the conflict was not a matter of religion at all, any more than the victimization of German Jews was a matter of either religion or race. And the Huguenots were every bit as indelibly fixed in place as the Jews would be. Their predicament was even greater than in Michelet's formulation, for even converting, even "saying the word"—"If he would but say one word, he would keep his properties and his homeland"—could not have saved them, for they could not stay. Their decisions did not matter; there was no decision to be made.

Over the years, then, whether for reasons of sentiment, ideology, or methodology, historians have scarcely asked of the Huguenot refugees questions about motivations that are routinely posed about other migrants. If perhaps a quarter of those who still professed Protestantism in 1680 in the Charentes and a nearly identical percentage in Poitou escaped from France during the decade of the Revocation, three-quarters stayed. Huguenots and their adversaries alike have commonly attributed the difference in behavior to the variable strength of religious conviction—"The most zealous risk all to gain all: that is to say, they seek to emigrate, despite the rigor of the Edicts"—and divided Huguenots into the true believers who left in order to preserve their faith and the less committed who compromised in order to stay: "exile for the committed Reformed or rallying [to Catholicism] for the tepid." Madame de Maintenon, the king's Charentaise wife, accepted but put a negative spin on this same association of firm belief with emigration. She who repudiated her own ancestors' Protestantism spoke the conventional wisdom when she identified those who left as those most zealous in their belief, most impervious to reasonable obligation: "These are the most obstinate and opinionated of the party, whom we have seen capable of renouncing their properties, their fatherland, their most essential duties, and even their legitimate sovereign, rather than submit to what was required of them."[13]

But how plausible is it, in light of historical evidence, that the decision to emigrate or stay turned solely on the strength of religious conviction? Were only those who left sincere in their belief? Can the decision to stay in France be taken as demonstrating the deficient "range and depth of lay religious commitment in early modern society"?[14] On the contrary, among those who remained in the kingdom, large numbers, perhaps the majority, did so without abandoning their Protestant convictions, either risking open defiance or shielding their clandestine Calvinism beneath a minimal Catholic veneer. The military engineer and reformer Vauban, who was among the very few who openly challenged the wisdom of the Revocation, told the king in 1692 that "of every hundred converts, perhaps not two are such in good faith."[15] Assemblies of the Desert began meeting within months of the Revocation, as early as the spring of 1686. Numerous Huguenots persevered and in so doing fashioned a bridge to a remarkable spiritual revival among following generations, from the second quarter of the eighteenth century onward.

Saint-Savinien, specifically, was a place where Protestants stayed through the Revocation and regrouped. The local curé, Bongirault, acknowledged: "I have many bad Catholics."[16] Claude Masse in 1717 reported this matter-of-factly to the king. "There is considerable commerce in this place, the large barques constantly coming up as far as Saint-Savinien. There are also many good merchants, but they are for the most part Protestants." In the very year of Masse's visit, a group of former Protestants who attempted, as the law now required, to satisfy their religious needs in the Catholic Church petitioned the Regent, complaining that their curé neglected his duties. When the "poor inhabitants" asked the curé to marry them or baptize their children, he refused, "saying that he was tired of it and that he would much prefer that they be Calvinist so he would have less trouble." Demanding the level of pastoral care they had learned to expect from the temples before the Revocation, they called the curé's behavior "scandalous to the public and particularly to a number of new converts who are in this parish."[17] By 1768, there would again be a temple in Saint-Savinien, though clandestine because the faith would not be legalized for another nineteen years. Indeed, the continuity of some Protestant families in Saint-Savinien stood the test of time, for after the temple was openly refounded in 1817, many of the family names of parishioners were the same as those of Protestants resident there in the 1680s. There was, however, no Isle or Robillard de Champagné.[18]

The persistence of Protestants within France after the Revocation has been examined in terms of the limiting conditions that rendered escape difficult—what made them not leave, as if it were a decision to stay that called for explanation. Peasants, for whom their lands were their only resource, could not leave as easily as merchants and artisans, whose skills and fortunes were portable. Those living in Protestant villages with strong confessional solidarities could not leave as readily as Huguenots who were scattered among Catholic communities, for in Protestant villages, "To leave, even with one's family, was to break bonds woven over many years, something of a betrayal among persons accustomed to living together."[19] Such inquiries have been at best uninformative and at worst deceptive, for they have neglected to ask: among artisans (or merchants or nobles or women or inhabitants of Protestant villages) with deep Protestant convictions, what made the difference between their leaving and staying? They were furthermore predicated on the assumption that Protestants desired to leave and were held back, or not, by certain identifiable social conditions. Emile Léonard made explicit the usually tacit assumption: "Those who could, went."[20] But his assertion is pure speculation. Is it not at least as reasonable to think that those who could stayed—that it is the decision to leave, rather than the decision to stay, that requires explanation? The more appropriate question is not what made some so fervent (or obstinate) in their faith that they left rather than convert, while others valued their established lives in France more than their religious creed, nor what made some Protestants unwilling to convert and others willing, nor what made escape impossible or possible. It is, rather, what made staying impossible or possible for those who were too committed to their Protestant faith to abandon it.

Individual decision-making or the operation of social forces? Religious or material motivation? Steadfastness or obstinacy? None of the observers' or historians' single-issue representations of the Huguenots' flight from France—nor, indeed, the Huguenots' own—seems capacious enough to accommodate even the salient outlines of the phenomenon. Faced with the Revocation and accompanying persecutions, many Protestants left and then decided to come back, sometimes with royal help and sometimes on their own. Many decided not to leave and then reversed course, so that though the emigration was most intense in the 1680s, it nevertheless continued through the first half of the eighteenth century. Many decided to leave but could not find the means to do so and devised second-best tactics for staying at home. Obviously, Huguenots under persecution made their choices among the options—conversion, a semblance of conversion, defiance (armed or peaceable), and escape—"in real time" and under shifting circumstances. The decision must often have been a close call and the result of negotiating numerous competing considerations. In the face of evidence that their decision-making was something other than one-dimensional and linear, it bears remembering that the question—"what made them leave?"—is, after all, an impertinent one. Could even the Protestants themselves have given full answers incorporating all the factors weighing on them?

Losing the Temples

If particular histories might redress some of the weaknesses in too-tidy ex post facto explanations, the case of the Robillard de Champagné is an unusually rich resource. Each member of the couple—Josias de Robillard and Marie de La Rochefoucauld—left a firsthand record of the decision-making that led to the family's leaving France. Josias composed letters to his children while he was preoccupied with coming to his decision. Marie wrote a memoir of the escape after all but the last baby had reached safe haven in Holland. Both Josias' letters and Marie's memoir reveal that their escapes had been anticipated and prepared over a considerable period of time and that the decision itself was a process rather than an event. Faced with the most consequential decision of their lives—and afterlives—they veered from one strategy to another, with the evolution of external conditions and the promptings of self-scrutiny, sometimes coming close to resolving to convert and stay.

Moreover, a close look at this case, in the detail its exceptional documentation permits, reveals a more complex set of intertwined motivations than any of the one-dimensional global explanations asserts. The religious and the socioeconomic, the spiritual and the material may be analytically distinct, but those making decisions could scarcely separate them in practice. The protagonists did not explain fully—perhaps could not have done so, either to themselves or to others—all the factors that impelled them to leave. But they touched upon them in their writings, and an alert reader can tease out the complexity of the decision-making from the clues they embedded in their texts.

The earliest indication of Josias' decision-making comes from a fifty-one-page letter he wrote to his children on July 15, 1685, three months before the Revocation, on the truth of the Protestant religion. It had already become difficult to be a Protestant in Saint-Savinien. When they moved to Berneré in 1677, the family found a Protestant temple in the center of town and in the center of town life. As persecution intensified and temples elsewhere were closed, the Saint-Savinien temple continued to serve the town's Protestants and welcomed worshippers from farther and farther away. Whereas an average temple among the 630 in France around 1660 had served some 2,000 worshippers, by 1681 Saint-Savinien's was serving perhaps twice that number.[21]

As Josias penned his letter to his children, the Saint-Savinien temple had been closed for more than three years. On November 23, 1681, Lucas de Demuin, the intendant, and Guillaume de La Brunetière, Bishop of Saintes, came to town to hear the preaching of the Capuchin monks whom the king had sent for the conversion of the heretics. The dignitaries noticed the proximity of the Protestant temple to the abbey chapel where the Augustinian monks celebrated their mass. Learning how greatly troubled the monks were in their devotions "by the singing of psalms by the three or four thousand persons who are sometimes in the said temple and by the sound of the bell that is above the door of the said temple," Demuin had the distance measured. As the intendant's secretary Bomier pointed out in the report of the proceedings he drew up before leaving town, Demuin demeaned the local congregation by obliging one of the elders of the Protestant consistory to hold the measuring tape. Twenty-four *toises* (about forty-seven meters) was the distance ascertained.[22]

Defense of the monastery was a fitting pretext for an aggression against Saint-Savinien's Protestants, for the Augustinians had been on the receiving end of Protestant attacks ever since the Wars of Religion. Calvinists largely destroyed the convent complex in 1568, just as they famously destroyed the magnificent Abbaye de Saint-Jean-d'Angély, of which it was a dependency. They threw eight of the thirty resident monks down a well; burned the church, cloister, and one of the two chapels; and occupied the vestiges until 1624, when the Parlement of Bordeaux ordered their restitution to the monks. In 1612, the proximity of the temple was set in stone when the Comtesse de Taillebourg leased to the Reformed inhabitants of Saint-Savinien the plot of land "familiarly referred to as La Chaulme." Thereafter, the temple raised on that site anchored the permanent presence of Protestants in the community that the Edict of Nantes had guaranteed them.[23]

The decision to destroy the Saint-Savinien temple was not quite so haphazard or spontaneous as Demuin's account suggests. The process followed illustrates well the way official treatment of Protestant congregations changed between 1664 and 1681. The Saint-Savinien temple had survived scrutiny by the two investigating commissioners (of whom one was Isaac Isle) in February 1664, though even then Colbert de Terron made his usual recommendation that the king outlaw the religious exercises and order the Saint-Savinien temple demolished within fifteen days.[24] It survived in 1664, with Isle's assistance, because it was able to argue that its exercise of the Protestant religion fell under the terms of the Edict of Nantes. Isle had saved numerous temples from such closing. In Cozes, in March 1664, Colbert de Terron tried to order the destruction of the local temple and forbid Protestant worship, "on pain of being declared disturbers of the public peace, rebels against the king and justice, and fined three thousand *livres*," on the identical grounds that their temple was overly close to the Catholic parish church. After Isaac disagreed, Protestant exercises were permitted to continue.[25] More than 250 temples in France were less persuasive and were officially suppressed by 1665. In Aunis, where thirteen Protestant temples were operating when the commission started its work in the early 1660s, only two (La Rochelle and Marans) survived the scrutiny and were operating down to the Revocation. Forty temples in Saintonge had already been closed by Demuin's administrative decision in the year preceding his visit to Saint-Savinien.[26]

At Saint-Savinien in 1681, the documents that had sufficed in 1664 to defend the temple's legitimacy and forestall closure proved inadequate, because the ante had been upped by the crown: the Edict of Nantes was now to be construed in the most uncompromisingly narrow terms. The congregation offered a baptismal record purportedly showing baptisms in 1597, but this was held insufficient to prove (as Article 9 of the Edict of Nantes required) "worship established and publicly held several and diverse times" in the town in both years 1596 and 1597. Nor were the documents accepted as proof that the baptisms had taken place in a temple rather than in secret or in a mere assembly, or that they were done by a minister rather than a layman, on the grounds that Protestant usage itself allowed baptism outside an established and public service. Nor was participation in a synod by a minister living in Saint-Savinien accepted as proof that the temple in the town predated the Edict. The authorities used these deficiencies as well as the temple's location to reinforce their conclusion that the exercise at Saint-Savinien should be prohibited, pursuant to Article 4 of the king's declaration of December 16, 1666, "that Temples built so close to the Church that they trouble the divine Service shall be demolished."[27] Scarcely six weeks after Demuin measured off the encroachment on the abbey, a royal *arrêt* dated January 12, 1682 ordered the demolition of Saint-Savinien's temple and prohibited any further exercise of Protestantism in the town. The temple was razed to the ground, for the purpose of the demolitions was to remove heresy from sight. The stones were to be used for enlarging the parish church of Saint-Savinien "that the Huguenots had formerly knocked down." Whether the Protestants were forced to destroy the temple themselves, as they often were elsewhere as a means of collective humiliation, is unknown.[28] Typically, the demolition of a temple was an occasion for ceremony and for conflicting emotions, so perhaps the Catholics of Saint-Savinien processed in celebration with the curé and other local dignitaries while Protestants shut themselves in their houses in mourning.

The bell was the only vestige of Saint-Savinien's temple that survived. Bells were too precious to destroy or discard—this one weighed 427 pounds—and so they often became objects of confessional competition. The illustration in the 1686 *Almanach royal* showing the demolition of the Paris temple at Charenton prominently features the bell as it is salvaged and carried off, no doubt for use in a nearby Catholic belfry. Saint-Savinien's temple bell was contested by the two confessions. Catholics claimed the bell had been stolen earlier from their own belfry, which is perfectly plausible, since Protestants had appropriated many from Catholic belfries when they pillaged churches during the Wars of Religion, though most of their temples did have specially made bells.[29] Even without a building to house it, the recalcitrant Protestants of Saint-Savinien would not give up the bell. Members of the Isle family took it home—surely in secret—for safekeeping on their coreligionists' behalf.

The Champagné, who had baptized three children in the now-closed Saint-Savinien temple, found it harder and harder to raise a Protestant

Figure 2.1 Demolition of the Temple of Charenton on October 29, 1685, following the revocation of the Edict of Nantes, from Louis le Grand la Terreur et l'Admiration de l'Univers, in the *Almanach royal* of 1686. Etching. By permission of the Bibliothèque nationale de France.

family. Infant baptism became increasingly inconvenient as temples closed. The Champagné would travel ten miles to Josias' ancestral church in Saint-Jean-d'Angély to have the pastor Jean Yver baptize their two-day-old baby Julie in September 1682. That church had been in place for most of French Protestantism's lifetime, having been built from stones of the abbey church destroyed by Protestants in 1569. It had been sacked in June 1621, at the moment of royal victory over the town, and the king had supplied the 100 *livres* needed for repairing the damage. But that same temple was closed down scarcely three months after Julie's baptism there. Five months later, in May 1683, the Saint-Jean-d'Angély Protestant cemetery was given over to the town's Catholics.[30] As at Saint-Savinien, reassignment from the destroyed heretic temples was a physical means by which the Catholic church renewed itself from the demise of its competitor.

Tonnay-Boutonne, the next closest temple to Champagné after the closure of Saint-Jean-d'Angély, was still open in 1683; it would be one of only four temples still standing in the entire *généralité* of Limoges at the moment when Louis XIV signed the Revocation.[31] But it was weakened in notable ways. It had limited financial resources: Charles de La Mothe Fouqué, future husband of Susanne de Robillard, was not paying the temple support he had promised, perhaps because of the "infinity of lawsuits in the Parlement of Bordeaux" occasioned by inheritance conflicts with his recently converted brother.[32] It lacked leadership. In 1681–1682, the congregation had no minister, assembling on its own for prayers and psalm-singing in defiance of an order from the lieutenant-particular of Saint-Jean-d'Angély that forbade the congregation meeting, on pain of a 300-*livre* fine. The new minister, Jacques Sanxay, would arrive from Saint-Jean-d'Angle in 1683 and stay until the Revocation, but he would spend six months of 1685 imprisoned for refusing to stop preaching when ordered to desist.[33] After leaving at the Revocation, he would welcome the Champagné children to Exeter, his new expatriate post, when they reached England in April 1687.

Nor were private services in nobles' châteaux as common a resource as they once had been. By May 1682, there were only three châteaux in the entire diocese of Saintes in which the seigneurs still held Protestant services: Le Douhet, Cravant, and Nieul.[34] To baptize a son born on April 20, 1684, Josias and the godfather, René de Culant, Seigneur de Saint-Mesme,[35] carried three-day-old René-Casimir nine miles southeastward from Berneré to the Château du Douhet.[36] Transporting the newborn over such a great distance suggests that the parents considered it important to rush baptism. Perhaps the infant seemed weak and likely to die. Or Josias may simply have been complying with the 1676 mandate from the Synod of Sancerre that parents present their newborns on the first Sunday after their birth "under pain of being grievously censured."[37] Or he may, defiantly, have acted to spare René-Casimir a Catholic baptism, as efforts were made to oblige Protestant families to use Catholic churches once local temples had been closed. According to Abraham Tessereau, "They ordered that all children born where there was no minister be baptized by the curé of their town, and three fathers who carried their children ten leagues from home for baptism were condemned and fined for contravening the order."[38]

Josias and Marie were fortunate that Le Douhet was still available in 1684, since it had barely escaped closure. In the course of attempts to close down the temple at Taillebourg in 1682–1683, the Syndic of the Clergy of Saintes argued that Le Douhet violated the terms of the Edict of Nantes permitting personal worship by nobles on their fiefs. The resident seigneur, Renaud de Pons, Marquis de Tors, "holds in the house of Le Douhet an exercise of the R.P.R. that is as public and as frequent as a local temple would be. The minister does not live at Le Douhet, he is supported not only by the said marquis de Tors but by the inhabitants who live in the parish of Le Douhet and others nearby. . . . Every Sunday the service attracts a great number of P. R., not only those who reside in the seigneury of Le Douhet but many others who come from neighboring parishes." The Syndic demanded that the Marquis de Tors close his private services to all but dependents on his estate and not allow outside ministers to officiate where they were not authorized to act.[39] No doubt because of that assault, pastor Audibert Durand in 1683 stopped signing the register as "minister of the locale" and became "minister of the château."

The Syndic's observations on Le Douhet's operations were correct. Because of the scarcity of places for Protestant worship and the urgency for Protestant baptism, not only René-Casimir but some 376 other babies from much farther away than Saint-Savinien were brought in the final years under the Edict of Nantes to Le Douhet's tiny chapel in a village that had only twenty-six resident Protestants from seven families.[40] Parents from coastal towns like Cozes, Marennes, and Saint-Seurin-d'Uzet that had lost their temples—sailors, carpenters, ships carpenters, apothecaries, agricultural laborers, coopers, shoemakers, merchants, salt-workers, and stone-carvers, as well as nobles like Josias—brought their infants for baptism by pastor Durand. Even Alexandre Beauchamp, Seigneur de Bussac, brought his son René for baptism in July 1684, no longer able to have services conducted in his own château, where many Robillard had been baptized a century earlier. At Le Douhet, in the home of Marie's distant cousin Judic de La Rochefoucauld, Marquise de Tors, the increasingly bereft Saintongeais Protestants would for a short time longer be able to bear witness to their faith.[41]

"Fundamental Reasons" of the Fathers

It was this faith that Josias laid out in his July 1685 letter from Paris to "my dear children."[42] Most likely, he had gone to Paris as a party in a law case before the Parlement. On August 30, the court would render its judgment against Josias, in favor of the Maréchale de Navailles' demand that the seigneury of Saint-Vivien be sold at auction to pay its seigneur's debts to her.[43] He may have been staying with his brother-in-law Casimir Prévost de Touchimbert, who was also involved in the Navailles case and whose presence in Paris was recorded at the Charenton temple in June.[44] Josias' remarkable letter, which was preserved for more than 300 years by his descendants, is the earliest surviving documentation of his protracted struggle to fashion responses to the situation in which the crown's assault on his religion had placed him. In the letter, three months before the Revocation, he stated his theological positions, evidently marshaling what his Protestant upbringing and his confrontations with Catholic missionaries had taught him, in hopes of saving both his family and himself.

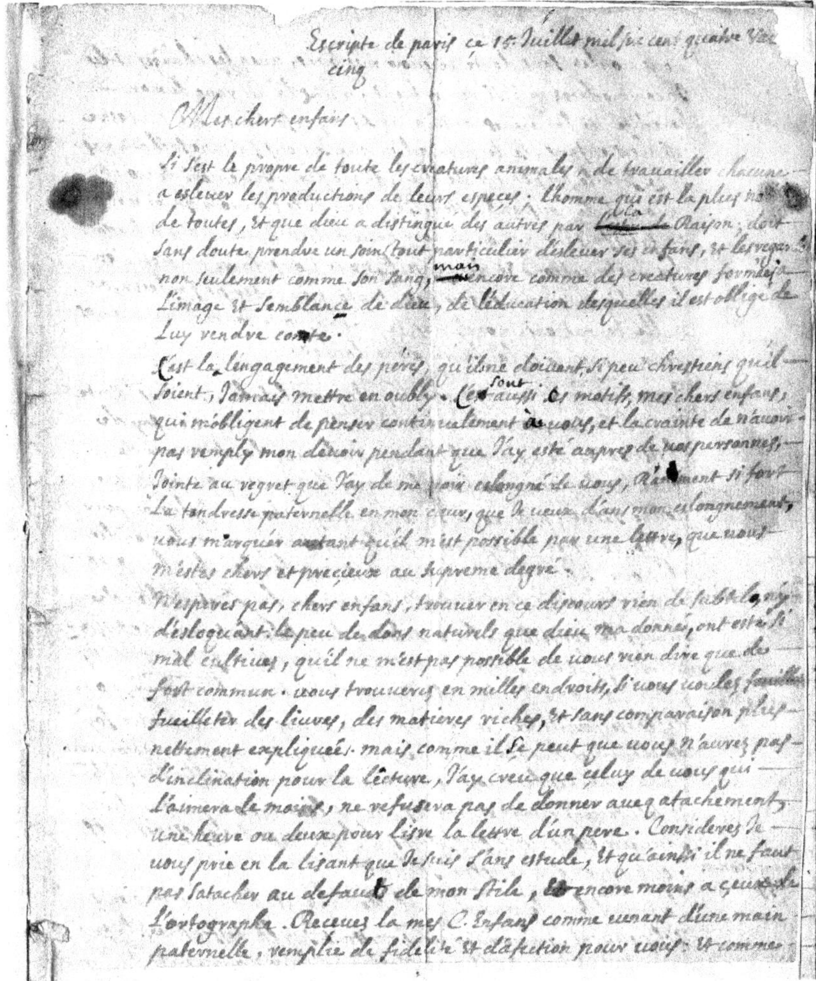

Escripte de paris ce 15. Iuillet mil six cens quatre Vingt
cinq

Mes chers enfans

Si Cest le propre de toute les creatures animales de travailler chacune
a eslever les productions de leurs especes; lhomme qui est la plus [illegible]
de toutes, et que dieu a distingue des autres par la Raison, doit
Sans doute prendre un soin tout particulier deslever ses enfans, et les regarder
non seulement comme son sang, mais encore comme des creatures formees a
Limage et Semblance de dieu, de leducation desquelles il est oblige de
Luy rendre conte.

Cest la lengagement des peres, qu'ils ne doivent, si peu chrestiens quils
soient, Iamais mettre en oubly. Ce sont aussi ces motifs, mes chers enfans,
qui mobligent de penser continuellement a vous, et la crainte de navoir
pas remply mon devoir pendant que Iay esté aupres de vos personnes,
Iointe au regret que Iay de me voir eslongné de vous, R[illegible]ment si fort
La tendresse paternelle en mon cœur, que Ie veux dans mon eslongnement,
vous marquer autant quil m'est possible par une lettre, que vous
m'estes chers et precieux au supreme degré.

N'esperes pas, chers enfans, trouver en ce discours rien de [illegible] ny
d'eloquant. le peu de dons naturels que dieu ma donnez, ont esté si
mal cultivez, quil ne m'est pas possible de vous rien dire que de
fort commun. vous trouveres en milles endroits, si vous voulez [illegible]
fueilleter des livres, des matieres riches, et sans comparaison plus
nettement expliquées. mais comme il se peut que vous n'aurez pas
d'inclination pour la lecture, Iay creu que celuy de vous qui
l'aimera le moins, ne refusera pas de donner avec atachement,
une heure ou deux pour lire la lettre d'un pere. Consideres Ie
vous prie en la lisant que Ie suis sans estude, et qu'ainsi il ne faut
pas satacher au defaut de mon stile, et encore moins a ceux de
l'ortographe. Receues la mes C. Enfans comme venant d'une main
paternelle, remplie de fidelité et daffection pour vous. et comme

Figure 2.2 Letter of Josias de Robillard to his Children, July 15, 1685, first page. Champagné Papers B4. Courtesy of the Department of Special Collections, Stanford University Libraries.

The theological positions Josias set out in his letter were the staples of traditional Reformed belief: *sola scriptura*, justification by faith, the Eucharist as spiritual nourishment and communion, the priesthood of all believers. "Holy Scripture is the basis and foundation of Christian doctrine . . . that ought to serve as a rule for the faith of Christians." And so, as Protestants were wont to do, he tested the principal "Roman"[45] dogmas that the Reformed did not share for their conformity with Scripture. Employing, by his own reckoning, "close to 180 passages of Holy Scripture, with all the fidelity that has been possible for me," he maintained that some Catholic doctrines and practices—fasts and feasts, transubstantiation, adoration of the Eucharist, veneration of relics, papal supremacy—were simply absent from the scriptural texts, while others—clerical celibacy, worship in a foreign language, and purgatory—directly contradicted the teachings of Christ and his apostles.

Familiarity with Biblical verses and facility in scriptural citation were expected of the Protestant faithful. Even so, the extent of Josias' religious learning and his ability to define and sustain a rigorous argument were uncommon. He was an earnest provincial Protestant layman, not a pastor, not even a particularly conspicuous member of his local temple, to judge by his absence from its parish registers. Yet he penned a document that is rich in evidence, systematic in organization, varied in its modes of argumentation, and always geared to the interests of his children who, he hoped, would read it and take it to heart. Perhaps he derived his taste for learning from his uncle Isaac de Mazières, Sieur de Marouillet, whose 1652 will left monetary legacies to Josias and his sister, and who bequeathed his Latin theology books to the consistory of La Rochelle. Alternatively, he might have been attracted to serious study by another uncle, Daniel de Mazières, who was a physician to the Duc d'Orléans.[46]

The raison d'être of Josias' letter was evidence, called for by the Huguenot conviction that whereas Catholics expected submission to authority, individual consciences were charged with deciding among competing doctrines, as Josias said, "what seems best to them." His fifty-one carefully constructed pages of evidence were to provide what his children would need in order to make their own religious decisions. He disavowed any paternal authority to prescribe: "It is for you to judge, my children. . . . I do not ask you to found your faith on my belief nor even on my instructions. I want you, after seeing them, to examine whether they are faithfully and solidly established and, following the invitation of our divine savior, study the Scriptures diligently to learn your salvation." Armed with "good sense," "common sense," the testimony of the senses, and the Bible, they would be capable of finding religious truth themselves. This emphasis on the choices of individual consciences was among the strongest stances Protestants could adopt for opposing a state that increasingly used force, bribes, intimidation, and appeals to authority to reestablish religious uniformity. It also had deep roots in Protestantism's theology of the priesthood of all believers. For both pragmatic and doctrinal reasons, then, it is not surprising to find that as persecution heated up in the 1680s, many theologians placed increasing emphasis on the claims of conscience, and Josias did likewise.

Josias' emphasis on scriptural evidence placed him squarely in the mainstream of Huguenot tradition. French Protestantism was distinctive among European Calvinisms in emphasizing intellectual assent to the truths of the Bible as the central act of the believer. Huguenot theological works concentrated on anchoring the doctrines of Calvinism in scriptural citations that corrected Catholic errors. Huguenot pastors trained intensively in exercises of controversy, and their sermons were typically concerned less with exhorting the congregation to godly living than with clarifying doctrine.[47] Published works for instructing the Protestant laity focused on equipping them to counter their Roman adversaries and paid less attention to the questions of practical morality or daily godliness that prevailed in Anglo-American Calvinisms and in early German pietism.[48] The most widely read of these works was the *Abrégé des controverses* (*Summary of Controversies*) published in 1624 by Charles Drelincourt, the great pastor of the Parisian temple at Charenton whose famous encounters with his local Catholic counterpart, the curé of Charenton François Véron, were the very model of Huguenot Scripture-based defense. The *Abrégé* summarized Roman doctrinal errors by juxtaposing extracts from Catholic controversialists and the Council of Trent to literal scriptural citation. The expatriate Pierre Bayle, in his *Dictionary*, credited Drelincourt with preparing the most ordinary of laypersons to defend the faith, "for with the arms he provided them, even those who had never studied could hold their own with monks and curés, and boldly take the fight to missionaries."[49]

Scripture-based defenses of religious truth were to the French Protestant laity what vigilant introspection and strict morality were to Puritans: a way of both enacting one's faith and securing signs of election. "The central drama of a Huguenot's life was not the progress from conviction of sin through conversion to the gradual movement toward full assurance. It was the demonstration of genuine conviction by remaining firm to the true faith in the face of pressure to abjure." Steadfast loyalty to the embattled minority church was seen as a sign of election, as "a strong presumption regarding the eternal salvation of the members of the 'little flock'... provided no too-dissolute conduct appeared to contradict it." "In France, being a Protestant meant *choosing to remain one*.... There was a voluntarist aspect to adherence to the E[glises] R[éformés de] F[rance], which involved a choice that was made afresh every day, even if subconsciously."[50]

Josias' letter to his children reflected both aspects of this distinctive Huguenot religiosity. Demonstrating the truth of Protestant doctrine through scriptural citation would make faithful adherence to it a sign and reassurance of salvation. Rational argument to prove the dogmas of the Protestant church would, by gaining their intellectual assent, keep his children in the true church. If they could persevere, all would be well, despite the persecutions they would endure. At the same time, Josias' scriptural citations were scarcely accompanied by anxiety over his own sinfulness and sins. The moral counsel Josias offers his children at the end of his letter consists of some very simple honesty. It is not perceptibly different from what a pious Catholic father might urge upon his own children, for it was not the Protestants' practical conduct that would set them apart from their compatriot Catholics.

Yet, if Josias' scriptural orientation placed him in the mainstream of Huguenot tradition, his letter reflected none of the newer controversial methods being developed by contemporary Huguenot theologians. By the time Josias wrote this letter, a mere three months before the Revocation, French Calvinism had experienced nine decades of intense, open controversy with Catholic theologians in "continuation of the civil war by other means."[51] Especially after midcentury, Protestant apologetics had moved away from literal scriptural reference in response both to increasingly intense offensives of the Catholic Reformation and to new secular philosophies of knowledge. Catholic theologians like Cardinal Richelieu pursued reunification of the faith by placing greater emphasis on Scripture, but with nonliteral readings of the text (inferences from "natural signs" embedded within it) that could be seen as corroborating Church dogmas such as transubstantiation that a Protestant's literal reading did not support. Only slightly later, critical textual analysis of Scripture, notably by the Catholic Richard Simon and the Jew Baruch Spinoza, undermined Protestant controversialists' reliance on the literal sanctity of the text and its self-evident clarity on fundamental points.

Both the malleability of the sacred text and the weaknesses made apparent by the "new skepticism"[52] shifted the central issue in Christian controversy from the content of particular dogmas to the criterion of truth or "rule of faith": "in what way one can distinguish, among all the Christian sects, that one where truth is to be found."[53] Catholic controversialists argued that Church tradition was fuller and more consistent than Scriptures alone and that the universal acceptance, over time and space, of Church theological tradition established its truth beyond the reach of skeptical doubt, as individual readings of the Scriptures could not do. The truth of the Church (as evidenced in its "marks" as "one, holy, catholic, and apostolic") was the warrant for the truth of its doctrines. Catholic polemics, then, came to focus not so much on arguing with the heretical dogmas of Protestants as on lamenting the fact of their schism. Catholic controversialists developed these arguments into a justification of the Revocation as the instrument by which schismatic Protestants could be reabsorbed into the universal church.

To counter Catholics' shifts in emphasis, Protestants reasserted their traditional reliance on Scripture as the rule of faith, but also countered claims that Catholicism was endorsed by universal acceptance and by history. Protestants' doctrines had enjoyed the assent of humanity, according to Pastor Claude, successor to Drelincourt at Charenton: "what [Protestants] believe has been believed everywhere, always, and by all. What they refuse to believe has not been believed everywhere, always, nor by all."[54] Protestant theologians increasingly supplemented Scripture with the works of the Church Fathers, whom their predecessors had tended to bypass in favor of Scripture alone, and with history to show the development of contradictions in Catholic practice and doctrine that betrayed the Scriptures. It was the Protestants who could root their religion in continuous history and permanent truth.

Pastors, though, scarcely modified the message, topics, or methods they employed in their sermons.[55] In this respect, what Josias wrote in his letter was closer to what was said from the pulpit than to contemporary theological discourse. He was still arguing the substance of doctrine, on the basis of Scripture alone, in point-to-point juxtapositions of Scripture and current Roman practice as he understood it, without allusions to new polemical strategies involving history or the Church Fathers. What is significant in his writing is not any form of theological innovation but simply the positions he, as a father and a teacher, felt suited the situation in which his family found itself.

With his children as audience, Josias meant the letter to secure transmission of a religion that not only held the keys to everlasting life but had also been integral to their family's identity across generations. The letter began and ended in direct dialogue with his children, and its pages were peppered with reiterated invocations of "my dear children." This seventeenth-century father imbued what he feared might be his last spiritual testament with his deep sense of duty to his children, his love for them, and his tacit acknowledgement that they might have a quite different relationship to religion from his own. He avowed thinking of them unceasingly and fearing that he "had not fulfilled my duty when I was with you." Pouring into the letter "the paternal tenderness in my heart," he assured the children "that you are dear to me and precious in the highest degree. . . . Accept it, my dear children, as coming from a paternal hand filled with fidelity and affection for you." He ended with a heartfelt prayer: "The tenderness I have for you has often obliged me to bathe with my tears what I am sending you. God by his grace give it a favorable outcome and lavish upon all of you his most holy and precious blessings, on your persons, on your families, and on your fortunes. Amen. Champagné."

Because the children might never master the literature as he had, "as you might not have a penchant for reading," their father extracted what he believed they would need. As practical instruction on how to handle the attempts at conversion he foresaw them confronting, he offered argumentation, Scriptural quotations, and advice on the demeanor to maintain when pressured. The letter seems to encapsulate his own experience of religious duress. What he tells his children to prepare for—the attacks they should anticipate, the answers they could make, the follow-up objections for which they should be poised—no doubt reflected the methods and arguments that missionaries had used in persuasion sessions with him. "Respond with modesty." Never respond in kind when Catholic missionaries say you are damned as a Protestant; Christ teaches us not to presume to judge, and besides, saying Catholics are damned would be to enroll among the lost "the king whom God established over us." The tone of his letter itself exemplified the calm, "modest" tone he counseled his children to adopt: for the purpose, he reined in the confessional passion and hatred that crescendoed in other Reformed polemics as the situation of French Protestants became increasingly desperate.

The children's immortal souls were at stake. But this does not exhaust the meanings of this father's gift or the skein of family present in the document. Also urgent in Josias' mind was a kind of retrospective validation of family heritage that needed continual reaffirmation. "We were born in the religion we profess . . . having suckled our religion with our milk." Examining once again the truth of Protestant doctrine was to ask anew "if [our fathers] had fundamental and solid reasons to separate from the Roman church." It was as if the Champagné's very righteousness and coherence as a succession of progenitors and heirs who became progenitors depended upon continued vindication of Protestant religion. Josias, as the current head of the family, was responsible for maintaining its Reformed identity for the sake of the long-vanished ancestors who, through their decisions of individual conscience, had fused Protestantism with the family heritage. Conversion of any type destroys the past. So in refusing to convert, Josias vindicated not only his religion but also his ancestral culture in the face of the government's mandate for a new commonality that would repudiate and efface it.

Josias expressed, then, a consciousness of fused ancestral and religious heritage and a pride in Huguenots' common history that have been said to date only from the post-Revocation era. Until 1685, purportedly, they were "a minority with a sense of shame, seeking to compensate for its eccentricity in religion by a high degree of political conformity, breaking with its past and preferring not to recall the Wars of Religion or even Saint Bartholomew." Seventeenth-century Protestants "recognized no link with preceding generations." Only after the Revocation did the confession acquire "an awareness of its own history . . . The minority which survived the reign of Louis XIV . . . had acquired a folk-memory. Henceforth there should be no more yielding, for this would be a breach of faith with family traditions and the 'founding father.'"[56]

Josias, to the contrary, on the eve of the Revocation, did invoke the example of his forebears and felt a deep obligation to vindicate them, to tailor his actions under persecution so as to perpetuate the correctness of what they had done in breaking with Catholicism. This responsibility to family, to private vindications, is far more prominent in Josias' confession of faith than the obligation of obedience to the king. To be sure, Josias warned his children not to malign "the king whom God has established over us." But he omitted any discourse of political obedience that might have provided the seeds for a decision to place obedience to the sovereign above fidelity to forebears by converting to the king's religion.

What Josias hoped for and argued for, at least implicitly, in his letter was continued coexistence in France among competing confessions. The duel of words and evidence might bring reconciliation in a reunified, truly Catholic and Reformed Christianity if the side with the weaker arguments (the Catholic) were induced to surrender voluntarily. Protestants could not do so. "We may, my children, and all the Protestants with us, ask the gentlemen of the Roman religion to give us solid scriptural proofs of the doctrines that they teach and that we contest, of which I am going to make a deduction article by article. If they do so, we are ready to join with them." Failing Catholic adoption of Reformed positions, however, "we cannot enter into [their communion] because they preach to us something other than what has been preached to us by our lord Jesus Christ and his apostles."

Coexistence, then, was a second best, and in settling for such religious pluralism, even as he maintained that truth was singular, Josias was adopting a position pragmatic for a confession that required pluralism in order to survive. It was, in effect, a rebuttal to the Catholic claim of universality and to the Catholic invitation to rejoin a commonality of belief, an invitation that proved appealing to many Protestants as the Revocation approached. Josias' position reflected an evolution in contemporary theological discussion—away from the uncompromising aspiration for triumph over Catholicism. But Josias was still some considerable distance from the advocacy of universal toleration that would soon flower in the Refuge, that "laboratory of the new rationalism."[57] Pierre Bayle and some Huguenot exile theologians, under the influence of epistemological skepticism and Cartesianism, would lose confidence in the powers of reason and proof (scriptural or other) to establish knowledge in either spiritual or material matters. Toleration on principle for diverse outcomes of honest examination would be the corollary they advanced. Josias, by contrast, argued more narrowly for nonpersecution of Protestants in a Catholic kingdom. Reformed religion was "innocent": it nurtured and sustained the faith of Christians and did no harm by omitting peculiarly Catholic practices that were human inventions not commanded by God.

More striking even than his distinction between core beliefs and optional applications is the extent to which Josias enlarged the zone of benign error for which the misguided need not be sanctioned, since "it does nothing contrary to the worship owed to God." Even, he said, if our belief is mistaken—even if, for example, the wine and bread of the Eucharist were the blood and body of Christ—so long as we worship God "with all humility, I maintain that nothing we do merits damnation even if he be in the sacrament really, for our adoration and our prayers are addressed to Jesus Christ, who is God of heaven and earth. He receives them without doubt just as well when addressed to him in heaven as if we addressed him in the sacrament, since we regard him always as our God and savior, sole and unique redeemer." Even if, as Catholics believe, good works were a means of salvation rather than, as Protestant doctrine holds, a mere sign of election, or even if purgatory were a way station to heaven in which sins were purged, our misunderstanding would do no harm. For "we teach that one must do good works for the love of God" and "we do not sin in giving to the blood of our Lord Jesus Christ the glory of cleansing us of all sin." Similarly, forgoing the intercession of the saints to go directly to Christ and confessing faults to God rather than through a priest neither harmed neighbors nor damned souls.

Josias' systematic argumentation for the Protestant religion and the benignity of coexistence with error would have been minimally persuasive with his Catholic adversaries, proceeding as it did from premises of individual inquiry and *sola scriptura*. He seemed unaware that no matter how coherent his presentation or how numerous his Biblical citations, his enterprise was hopeless—at least insofar as its intended audience might be the Catholics who had faced off against him. He was unyielding and inflexible in his convictions. Seeing him so fully enclosed in a Reformed mental universe, so locked into Reformed religious doctrine, helps to explain why the epithet the authorities most often affixed to Huguenots in the Revocation era was "obstinate." It also conveys how strongly and deeply religious was his motivation in this decision-making—whatever else may have been affecting his prospects at the same time. This seventeenth-century French nobleman, in crisis, sought solace and solutions in his religion.

Indeed, Josias would have recoiled at the thought that any worldly considerations might influence his choice among confessions. All things secular were outside the story as he told it. As a good Calvinist, he denounced conversion to Catholicism for worldly advantage: "all those who leave their religion in order to preserve their wealth and earthly honors are not of Jesus Christ." Any ways in which social considerations were shaping his future as a Huguenot seem to have been lost on him, though they were present as well.

Josias' Decisions

"My supposed entry into the Roman Religion will no doubt surprise you, my children, as well as all those who have seen the letter I wrote you from Paris on July 15, 1685." So began a second letter from Josias to his children dated June 15, 1686, again from Paris.[58] During the eleven months to the day since his first, long letter urging his children to remain in the true, Protestant religion, much had happened, and Josias had formed two new responses to the persecution that intensified as a prologue to the Revocation on October 17–18, 1685.

Josias abjured in the early fall of 1685, just months after his first letter, as troops and missionaries streamed into Saintonge and Aunis. Two occurrences on September 8 unleashed the twin pincers—force and persuasion—of the whirlwind conversion campaign that within weeks decimated Protestantism in the Charentes. First, the Marquis de Louvois, secretary of state for war, instructed the army commander in the West, the Marquis de Boufflers, to occupy Saintonge. Boufflers had been sent with two regiments of dragoons to Bayonne the preceding March, to prepare for invading Spain in response to anticipated Habsburg moves in the Low Countries. When that contingency passed, he marched northward to enforce the crown's orders against Protestants in Montauban, Périgord, and Bordeaux. On September 6, news of Boufflers' successes in Périgord and Bordeaux reached the court: "The king learned that more than fifty thousand Huguenots converted in the *généralité* of Bordeaux and told us that good news with great pleasure, hoping that many other persons will follow such a good example."[59] Louvois responded to the news on September 8 by congratulating Boufflers and extending his assignment: "The King has learned with great joy of the surprising success in executing the orders he had given you for employing his troops to procure the submission of the Protestants. . . . His Majesty leaves it to you to march toward Saintonge the number of infantry, cavalry, and dragoons you judge appropriate . . . for trying to do there the same thing you executed so well in these two *généralités*."[60]

That same day, eight days of public argument began at Saint-Jean-d'Angély between the pastor Audibert Durand—baptizer of baby René-Casimir a year earlier—and those charged with converting the Protestants of the town and region: the prior of the Abbaye de Saint-Jean, the curé, a Benedictine and a Capuchin controversialist, the lieutenant-general, the king's prosecutor, and town magistrates. Such debates were staged frequently as oral complements to the publications and private discussions that both sides used to convince readers of the truth of their particular dogmas. The missionaries who came in the early 1680s had tried debates in La Rochelle, without much success. But in Saint-Jean-d'Angély after a week of debate, on September 16, the pastor Durand abjured in the hands of the Bishop of Saintes—a conversion so remarkable that the *Mercure Galant* devoted thirty-eight pages of its October and December issues to celebrating it as testimony to the wisdom of the Revocation and the invincible truth of the Catholic religion.[61]

The pastor's abjuration was made into theater for the population. At two o'clock in the afternoon, a procession of judicial and ecclesiastical dignitaries left the Palace for the parish church flying the Cross and Banner. "During the procession, they continued to sing the *Veni Creator* that four cantors of the Abbey had intoned at the foot of the great altar, finishing it at the doorway of the Palace. There the Minister and the other *Religionnaires* awaited the bishop, who showed his joy at seeing them in such favorable dispositions and asked them if it was willingly that they resolved to abjure the heresy in which they had so long persevered. Then the Minister and all the others replied that they took this action without any constraint and more willingly yet since they had been convinced of the error in which they lived. That being done, the Bishop had them all kneel, and after they had abjured by the mouth of the Minister in a loud and intelligible voice, they were led with the body of the procession as they had been brought, all the while singing the Psalms *In exitu Israël, Super flumina Babilonis,* and *Miserere mei Deus.* The procession stopped at the great doorway of the church, and the Bishop of Saintes gave them touching words of exhortation before a priest intoning the *Te Deum* took them into the church. The other Prayers were sung in thanksgiving, and they all embraced each other, the Minister as well as the others, with extraordinary effusions of joy."[62]

During the week of the public debate, on September 14, Louvois had notified the intendant of Limoges, Gourgue, that the king wished to convert the Protestants through lodgings of troops. Gourgue went, as ordered, to meet with the colonel of dragoons d'Asfeld in Saint-Jean-d'Angély, where he congratulated the convert Durand and the officers who had won him over. Thereafter he "worked ceaselessly to reduce those of Taillebourg, Saint-Savinien, Tonnay-Charente, Tonnay-Boutonne, Matha, Fontenay-l'Abattu, and other surrounding places in his department." By September 19, he could report from Saint-Jean-d'Angély: "Four or five thousand have converted in the past five days on his route and at Saint-Jean and Taillebourg." That same day, the intendant Arnoul wrote that all but three or four families in Saintes and Saint-Jean-d'Angély had converted. Around September 20, news reached the court "that the cities of Taillebourg and Saint-Jean-d'Angély, which were scarcely inhabited by any but Huguenots, had entirely converted without it being necessary to send dragoons as in the other places, but solely through the exhortations of the Bishop of Saintes. . . . The conversions of the Huguenots continued in all these locations, and one heard about nothing but the ten or twenty thousand conversions in six weeks of time." On September 21, Colbert de Croissy thanked Gourgue for his report of conversions in Saint-Jean-d'Angély and Taillebourg and assured him: "Nothing you could do would please His Majesty more than contributing by your efforts to the conversion of his subjects of the R.P.R." On October 7, Louvois wrote from Fontainebleau that "The most recent letters from Saintonge and Angoumois state that all are Catholic."[63]

The dragoons of d'Asfeld continued westward with orders from Louvois to "cleanse the entire Aunis of *Religionnaires*," reaching La Rochelle and the Ile de Ré on October 12. Abraham Tessereau, drawing on eyewitness accounts, estimated the number of soldiers in the city of La Rochelle at 700–800. A Protestant sent word to Holland on October 12 that the city was so full of soldiers that commerce was at a standstill. Rochelais passengers disembarking in Amsterdam ten days later brought word "that the misery caused by the lodging of soldiers is indescribable." Conversions occurred so rapidly that a mere five days after the dragoons' arrival, the intendant Arnoul could find no more professed Protestants in the city on whom to billet them. On October 21, he reported that twenty-two of fifty-two gentlemen in the *généralité* had already converted and that he was sending dragoons to the homes of the thirty holdouts. A local schoolmaster who suffered the dragonnades and abjured under the pressure summed up the pain of the period: "Desolation was extreme for four months, September, October, November, and December [1685]."[64]

Tensions had been high even before the military moved in, due to rumors from the south about Boufflers' actions against Protestants along his route northward through Montauban, Bergerac, Bordeaux, Blaye, and Cozes. As early as July 24 (nine days after Josias' first letter) Arnoul had predicted as much, writing to Seignelay that the Protestants "are extremely rattled, and if they sensed the troops were ready to fall upon them as in Béarn, I have no doubt that most of them would decide to convert." In Béarn, the intendant Foucault reported that "Many abjured at the mere approach of the soldiers, without seeing them." So, too, in Saintonge conversions proliferated even before the arrival of the troops. One local nobleman named Boisrond, a cousin of the Culant who served as René-Casimir's godfather in 1684 and hence no doubt a friend of Josias and Marie, noted in his journal how Boufflers' actions provided incentive to convert early: "In the month of August we learned that the Marquis de Boufflers, who commanded a camp on the border of Béarn, had sown such fear in that province, which was densely populated with Huguenots and served so to speak as their nursery, that nearly all had donned the Roman scarf, so that the few holdouts who remained had been badly mistreated by the troops, the gentlemen equally with the others. From Béarn, the Marquis de Boufflers came into Guyenne and from Guyenne into Saintonge. I was notified of everything by my friends. As soon as he reached our border, I left to go to the court . . . to let the king himself know of my situation . . . Three days after my departure the entire province of Saintonge was covered with troops."[65] Like smallpox in the New World, abjurations infected the landscape ahead of the troops.

In addition to preemptive conversions, the mere prospect of the arrival of Bouffler's troops also precipitated emigrations. Arnoul wrote on September

15: "Not a day passes at present that a very great number of persons do not desert, from along the coast of the Bordeaux river and inland for three or four leagues, so alarmed are they by what was done at Bordeaux. And that is happening now at Saintes in open daylight and weapons in hand. They seize and carry off ships they find along the coast . . . leaving their houses completely furnished and their vines unharvested." On September 19, Louvois ordered Boufflers to raze the fugitives' houses and confiscate their belongings.[66]

Boufflers took personal charge of converting the noblemen in Saintonge, where numerous gentlemen, like Josias, were holding out. Boufflers and the bishop scheduled a group abjuration for September 20 and then deferred it briefly, at the nobles' request. It is likely that Boufflers conveyed the expectation of conversion to the nobles of Saintes as a matter of obedience, as he had done just days earlier to the notables of Bergerac: "they were told it was the King's will that they all go to mass and that if they did not obey voluntarily, one would be obliged to force them to it."[67] Before long the nobles abjured; Louvois let Gourgue know on October 6 that "the assembly of nobles that convened at Saintes had a better outcome than we thought, since sixty gentlemen abjured there or promised to do so in a few days." Josias would later speak critically of the bargains the gentlemen who complied at this assembly accepted: "more than forty gentlemen of this province had, once assembled, suddenly abjured or promised to abjure, on quite stringent conditions." Not all in Saintonge accepted the honor of abjuring with the king's man. On September 24, the Baron de Saint-Surin—close friend of Josias and future husband of the Champagné daughter Susanne—left his Château de La Grève near Tonnay-Boutonne and escaped to Holland, never to return.[68]

Remnants of Saintonge's Protestant nobility held out longer. The intendant Gourgue, believing that the people would be more likely to convert if gentlemen set a good example, kept a close eye on the progress with Protestant noblemen. On September 29, he reported that only fifteen remained unconverted in the *élection* of Saint-Jean-d'Angély and on October 6 that only a few gentlemen remained to be converted in all of Saintonge and Angoumois.[69] On the eve of the Revocation, Louvois suggested conveying to recalcitrant nobles "that they should expect no repose or gentleness as long as they stayed in this religion that displeases His Majesty. . . . Those who wish to have the asinine glory of being among the last may be on the receiving end of yet more disagreeable treatments if they insist on staying there." By January 1686, Gourgue could write that "conversions are continuing with success among the nobility of Saintonge. Only Olbreuse [brother of the Duchess of Zell] gives me trouble, as I have been unable to influence his thinking at all."[70] Indeed, Josias had converted long before.

In his second letter to his children, Josias relates the circumstances of his own abjuration. In late September, the intendant summoned Josias without warning three times in a single week, told him on the king's behalf that he must change his religion, and forced him to submit to long conferences with the intendant, the Bishop of Saintes, and several missionaries. Perhaps his private conferences were something like the give-and-take that Fénelon later orchestrated for Josias' holdout neighbor Olbreuse, in which Fénelon played the role of a Protestant, mouthing "all the most specious things the ministers can say," to which an abbé accomplice replied with good Catholic dogma.[71] If so, the cogency and erudition of Josias' first letter to his children would suggest that Josias could hold his own in such debate. But once the intendant realized that Josias could not be convinced by their arguments, he dispatched an army officer and four dragoons to Berneré: "with express written orders to remain in my home until I and my family converted. A few days later, he added the captain with all his entourage and gave the order to expand the garrison from time to time, threatening as well to take away my family."

Josias could judge the prospects from what was happening all around him, "seeing this storm across all of France and that it had carried away nearly all the Protestants, from the towns and country places, and particularly those of my neighborhood in Saintonge." The tiny village of Agonnay, just downstream from Berneré, recorded six abjurations during the last twelve days of September. At Saint-Mesme, seigneury of René de Culant, godfather the previous year to René-Casimir at Le Douhet, Protestants poured into the tiny parish church to abjure during the last week of the month: a family of five on the twenty-third, seven more from two families on the twenty-fifth, four on the twenty-sixth, and seven on the twenty-seventh, including the daughter of the Huguenot pastor. Culant himself abjured at Saint-Savinien on September 27, 1685, along with Auguste and Henri Guiton de Maulévrier, the Seigneur d'Agonnay and his younger brother, "in obedience to the orders of the King." They were not alone. In all of 1681, there had been but four abjurations in Saint-Savinien, and four again the following year. There were eighteen in 1683 and nineteen in 1684. In 1685, the Saint-Savinien parish register recorded 709 conversions of "heretics." No fewer than 571 of those occurred in the week of September 23–29. The Bishop of Saintes himself came to town on October 11— the last Sunday on which Protestant worship would be legal in France— to hear the abjurations and sign the parish register.[72] Before or after, Josias, at Berneré, agreed

> to capitulate . . . and sign the following written statement: I the undersigned declare that in obedience to the wishes of the king, I enter

> into the Catholic, Apostolic, and Roman Church, to follow all the dogmas and pure teachings taught there in conformity with the doctrine of our lord Jesus Christ and of his holy apostles, promising to adore and serve God there as he wishes to be adored and served and not otherwise, renouncing of my own free will all the errors that are contrary to the worship due to him. These are the terms of the written statement that I signed, which was approved and received in my chamber by the curé of my parish of Saint-Savinien, in the presence of the Sieur de Prade, captain of the dragoons, and the king's prosecutor from Saint-Jean[-d'Angély], who also signed.

The better part of a year later, as he wrote the second letter to his children, Josias reflected upon the extenuating circumstances of his conversion and his reasons for believing that the simple promise he signed might relieve him of being pursued by the authorities. The wording of his abjuration committed him to nothing, he said, other than the essentials of Christian belief to which Protestants themselves adhered: to adore and serve God as he wishes to be adored and served, to follow the pure dogmas and teaching that conformed to Christ's own, renouncing the errors contrary to true worship. Perhaps at the time he felt the formula presented to him, or even negotiated by him,[73] was no sin and a small price to pay for release from the pressures of civil and ecclesiastical authorities. But now, though his motives had been pure—he wanted his children to recognize "the good intentions that God by his grace has preserved in my heart since this unfortunate mayhem"—his conduct had brought him both guilt and shame. Calling his actions "criminal," he hoped to allay the "disagreeable effect on your minds" and put an end to the scandal among those close to him that those actions had caused.

As Josias later explained his decision, the unrelenting pressure had left him but two choices. He could save himself by fleeing France, leaving his family to be put in cloisters and prisons, or he could capitulate. The latter, he explained, would allow him to "put your persons and your consciences in a safe place. I confess that paternal tenderness for seven small children obliged me to agree to sign the statement. . . . I believed I could sign this statement as a means of protecting you from the storm." At least in retrospect, he says he equated their safety with not being put in cloisters or prisons, with staying together as a family. He must have envisioned the possibility that with his coerced and insincere abjuration as cover, they could live at Berneré as a family, a Protestant family, even after their religion had been proscribed.

Josias' abjuration, however, turned out not to be a solution in and of itself. Continuing threats forced him to attend Catholic mass. Nor were the children made safe by his simple abjuration. A royal edict registered by the Parlement of Paris on January 12, 1686, three months after the Revocation and four after Josias' capitulation, mandated that children of Huguenot families between the ages of five and sixteen be removed from parental authority within eight days and, at parents' expense, placed either in the custody of reliable relatives ("grandfathers, grandmothers, uncles, or other Catholic relations") or with persons named by the law courts, or, for children whose parents could not pay their maintenance, in the nearest *hôpital général*. Otherwise, Huguenot parents, the edict declared, would surely "abuse the authority that nature gives them for the education of their children."[74] In the shadow of this edict, the movement of the Champagné children to Catholicism began. The two oldest—eighteen-year-old Susanne and twelve-year-old Josias—abjured that same January at the Catholic parish church in Saint-Savinien. They signed their names in the parish register, professed the Catholic faith, and received absolution from the curé.

Another royal ordinance dated January 11, 1686 and registered by the Parlement of Paris on the twelfth prohibited Protestants and New Converts from employing servants who were Protestant. Employers were to turn them out within fifteen days. The penalty to the employer was 1,000 *livres* for each violation; male servants would be sent to the galleys, female servants whipped and branded with the fleur-de-lis.[75] This may explain why each of the Champagné children was accompanied, in abjuring, by one of Marie's domestic servants, twenty-one-year-old Gabrielle Cochonneau and twenty-five-year-old Margueritte Boujours. Gabrielle and Margueritte professed the Catholic faith and received absolution but stated they did not know how to sign.

It may be that the dragoons were then at Berneré; the regiments of Artois and Saint-Sylvestre were operating in Saintonge in January 1686. And the missionaries were right in Saint-Savinien. On January 16, between the time of Susanne's and young Josias' abjurations, Marie Prévost de Touchimbert, thirty-five-year-old sister of their uncle Casimir Prévost, abjured in the hands of a Capuchin missionary named Joseph de Thénars. Although she had been visiting Berneré from her home in Angoumois since October 31, 1685 and was back at Berneré by February 2, she was temporarily boarding (or being boarded because of her religion) at the home of Jacques Meslier, a Catholic merchant in Saint-Savinien. Suffering from "a paralytic nervous illness that rendered her incapable of traveling to the local church to make her abjuration there," she asked Father Joseph to come to Meslier's home and give her "absolution from the heresy of Calvin." Only the signatures of eight witnesses, her host Meslier, the curé, and the Révérend Père—not her own—confirmed that the incapacitated woman had made her peace with the king's church.[76]

During this winter of 1686, Josias was rethinking his beliefs, trying to decide whether he could reconcile himself to a sincere embrace of the Catholicism he had had to adopt in words. He asked himself whether he had been led astray by his devotion to the former church, "if my first impressions in the [Reformed] Religion had not bedazzled me." Succeeding in a sincere conversion would have had advantages both secular and religious. It would have permitted the family to stay at home, intact, and in safety. And it would have promoted a goal that both confessions hoped for: reunification of the Christian faith. Abjuring Protestants could at least console themselves, as three pastors from Châtellerault in Poitou did when considering conversion, with a sense "that there is no greater evil among Christians than being estranged from one another."[77]

There were Protestants who came to believe that they could make their salvation in the Roman church. Madame Catillon, mother-in-law of one of the Châtellerault pastors, was a New Convert in Paris, wife of a goldsmith on the Quai de l'Horloge. She wrote in the spring of 1686 to her son-in-law, who, after a few months in the Bastille, had fled to Geneva, leaving his wife and children behind in her parents' care. Madame Catillon found Catholicism, she told the fugitive pastor, not so bad as she had been taught to fear. She had not heard a word about praying to saints, had heard numerous edifying sermons and lessons drawn from the Gospels, and had been assured of justification by faith, just as Protestants believe it: "that we obtain nothing but by the unique merit of Jesus Christ and that we deserve nothing but by the precious blood of our Savior."[78] Reunion of the churches was manifestly God's plan, she had concluded, and good Christians could be saved within the Roman religion.

Reunion on the model of Madame Catillon was what Josias tried, precisely when she did, and could not sustain. By June 1686, when he wrote his second letter, Josias had decided that he could not subscribe sincerely to Catholicism: "I wish to live and die in the religion in which I was born, persuaded that I cannot be saved in the Roman religion." He had resolved upon a new response to the persecution, seemingly a return to the determination he had made in July 1685. Catholic missionaries promised both intellectual and emotional benefits to those who would convert,[79] but Josias found neither, and his continuing sense of intellectual wrong wreaked emotional havoc within him. The attempt to stay Protestant under a cover of religious conformity "forced me to dissimulate in ways unworthy of a Christian and abandon what I owe to God for the love of you, whereas I ought to abandon you for the love of Him." He felt stained by sin, his soul at risk of damnation. "I persist in all the sentiments I conveyed to you in my first letter."

Josias now envisioned two courses of action, both of which would afford him an open life as a Protestant. He hoped to be able to take the family into exile, that he would fairly soon "find opportunities to save you and myself with you." But if he were to prove unable to overcome the obstacles placed in the path of a family escape, or if such obstacles should delay escape too long, he had resolved "to abandon my goods and my homeland and yourselves, if I cannot save you soon; to go glorify Him and confess publicly my sin, in places where my religion is exercised. God grant me his grace and hold you, my dear children, in his holy protection." Josias obviously felt some considerable urgency to righting his own spiritual record. What is especially striking is that he did not make saving his children a sine qua non in his problem solving. Josias did not say his Christian duty was to save his children: it was his own spiritual safety, and for that he was willing, if necessary, to leave his children behind—not to mention his wife and the retainers who depended on him—in order to save himself.

The forced choice between one's own benefit and the integrity of the family may have been the most common decision that Protestant fathers had to face in the fall of 1685 and the ensuing months. A few other fathers in similar circumstances during the same months extricated themselves differently from the same painful predicament and, like Josias, left their children written explanations for the decision they came to. Pierre Lézan, an elder of the temple in Saint-Hippolyte (Gard), abjured by force in October 1685 and agreed to have his children raised in the king's church. Fifteen years later, he inscribed in his journal a letter to his six adult children that expressed his feelings about the religious course he and his family had taken. Lézan was resigned to being split between exterior observance of Catholic rites and interior adherence to Reformed belief. But he needed to record his subterfuge because he worried that his children neither understood nor valued the true religion the family hid. "To ensure that my children remember that the Religion we professed and into which they were baptized was all pure and holy, I am making them a very honest summary of what we profess in it and what we believe in it so that they will continue in this purity and that when God wishes to grant them the grace of drawing them out of the religion into which they have unfortunately entered, they will not turn a deaf ear to the voice of God that calls them, as he will not fail to do, as he formerly called his people of Israel after seventy years of captivity."[80] His exposition of Reformed truths was briefer than Josias': it focused on the practices of vernacular prayer, direct dialogue with God, and conformity of belief with the wording of the Bible, without elaborated discussion of doctrine. It was, however, as sincere as Josias' and as concerned that he be known by his children to be on the side of religious truth, after a decade and a half of clandestinity.

A third father, Pierre Garrisson, a lawyer in Montauban, abjured in early September 1685, during the operations of Boufflers' dragoons that preceded their arrival in Saintonge. Like Lézan, Garrisson kept his family intact and at home by doing so. Writing in the heat of the moment on September 6, he explained his own abjuration in a quite different emotional key than either Josias or Pierre Lézan. The dragoons, Garrisson said, had arrived on August 20. He was required to lodge several groups of them—the commander, five of his aides, nine cavalrymen, and eight foot soldiers, plus their horses—as well as to feed them and pay them cash allowances. The soldiers prevented him from making an appeal for justice to "our King, whose justice and magnanimity will doubtless not suffer such a direct violation of his edicts and those of his predecessors, when we are fortunate enough to make him hear our just complaints." Worst of all was the threat that his children would be taken from him and that his elderly father would be harassed as he had been. Confronted with all this, Garrisson veritably spat out his bitter decision: "I succumb." He gave in, he said, to power, to injustice, to "force and violence." In anger, he wrote to audiences named and unnamed:

> I Pierre Garrisson, doctor and lawyer, residing in the said Montauban, aged forty-six years, succumb under the weight of so many ills and so many fears. And after having shed a torrent of tears, I, in inconceivable grief, am going to declare that I abandon the Religion in which God had me born, where I was raised, that I have professed with great peace of conscience, and in which I hoped to live and die with confidence in the edicts of our kings and the protection of our great Monarch, who has so often spelled out his will on their observance. I pray God that he pardon me for such a great fault by his infinite mercy for the love of his son our Lord Jesus Christ and protest with sincerity of heart that if our sovereign Creator of Heaven and Earth, who holds the hearts of Kings in his hand and bends them as he deems fit, being appeased toward our poor sinners, sways the heart of our Monarch to hear our just grievances and restore us or maintain us in possession of his edicts without regard to the spurious declarations that force and violence extort from us, I will immediately, with the aid of God, profess the said Religion and repair the scandal that my weakness may have caused to the Churches that profess it, as the discipline of the said Churches shall require.
>
> And because I might be stopped by death before seeing this happy time, I write this to serve as evidence that I am aware of the fault I am going to commit and of my passionate desire to find myself in liberty to rejoin the Churches from which violence separates me.
>
> Done at the said Montauban the sixth of September 1685, signed in good faith by me, Garrisson.[81]

Garrisson inscribed his fury so that any who read this would know he was aware of the "fault"—not "sin"—he was committing. His writing would keep his abjuration from being misconstrued as either a sincere conversion or an effect of the self-serving cupidity often imputed to converts.[82] At the same time, it called out to God, as a prayer for pardon from God's infinite mercy. Perhaps most importantly of all, an address to himself served as a sort of prophylaxis mitigating the fault. Penning the private memoir beforehand made his self-declaration psychologically for him the real event, the signing of the Catholic register an anticlimax. By recording his motive and emotions before he signed the abjuration, he could also make clear that he was not caving in from simple cowardice or weakness or ex post facto rationalization. At the moment of decision, he had the strength to calculate rationally, explain persuasively, and lash out with a defiance that safeguarded his still Protestant heart.

Lézan's and Garrisson's testimonies illuminate the contrasting decision Josias came to in June 1686. Faced with the choice of abjuring or losing their children, Lézan and Garrisson chose their family rather than their religion. They believed they were purchasing with an abjuration the opportunity to convey to their children the same sentiments they held—that is, to raise them as Protestants privately, under the mask of conformity—to guide their conduct and to instill in them principles of virtue and honor. By contrast, Josias, in saying he would act to save his own soul, did not indicate what would become of his children after he had gone, or who would raise them, or how he imagined his first letter could keep them Protestant even if they subscribed to what he said therein.

During the months when dragoons were forcing Huguenot parents to these decisions in the capital city and provinces, Jules Hardouin Mansart, the architect of Versailles, and the sculptor Martin Desjardins were organizing a public space in Paris to celebrate the recent victories over the Dutch that brought the king to the height of his power in Europe and freed his military forces for anti-Huguenot service at home. By the time the Place des Victoires was inaugurated in March 1686, Mansart and Desjardins had put in the center of the space a gilt bronze statue of the king in his coronation robes being crowned by Victory with a laurel wreath as he stepped on the head of Cerberus, a symbol of religious heresy. Below the standing Sun King, amid scenes from Louis' wars and eight Latin inscriptions, they had affixed bronze medallions celebrating two of his domestic victories over forms of self-determination: one the abolition of (noble) duels and the other the destruction of heresy. The latter scene, set before a collapsed Protestant temple, showed Religion shielding two kneeling New Converts from the figure of unmasked heresy. Below the medallions, at the statue's base, Desjardins expressed in bronze, on the faces of four chained captives, the spectrum of emotions experienced by those whom

Figure 2.3 Statue to the Glory of the King in the Place des Victoires and the Ceremonies Held on March 22, 1686, in the *Almanach royal* of 1687. Etching. By permission of the Bibliothèque nationale de France.

Figure 2.4 Heresy Destroyed. Bronze by Martin van der Bogaert, called Desjardins. Louvre Museum. By permission of Erich Lessing/Art Resource, NY.

Louis had defeated in his recent military campaigns: Spain pleading and perhaps hopeful, Holland infuriated and defiant, the Empire bowed and resigned, Brandenburg grimacing in pain.[83] Had Desjardins etched instead the emotions experienced by those defeated in Louis' campaigns against Protestants, Garrisson could have modeled the fury and spite, Lézan the resignation, and Josias the pain.

In the event, though, Josias did not act upon his words. He would be not the first of the family to flee but the last. He remained at Berneré or Champagné until April 1688, two and a half years after the Revocation and his abjuration. What was behind his delay? Once the dragoons and missionaries departed, was he hoping that persecution and surveillance would not revive and again force him to violate his conscience? Had he been able to make his peace with practicing his Protestantism in secret, hoping perhaps that he could repair his fault in private devotion or with Protestant friends? For all his expressed determination to flee for his own salvation, even at the cost of cutting social and familial ties, he did not do so.

How can the timing of his eventual flight be explained? Why did he not leave for nearly three years after his first letter to his children, in which he says he might flee at once and alone? Does the time lag cast doubt upon the depth of his religious conviction? And why did he finally leave in the spring of 1688? Was he delaying in order to tend to his worldly affairs? What else, between July 1685 and April 1688, would weave itself into his decision?

3

Marie in Jeopardy

Like her husband Josias, Marie de La Rochefoucauld left behind a document that yields insight into the decision to flee. In January 1690, after settling in Holland, Marie inserted a brief narrative of the escape into her book of financial accounts. In her case, it was not a theological primer; Catholic errors and clerical coercion, which constituted Josias' main subject, loomed small in Marie's. Her memoir employed no Biblical verses: the story itself sufficed as proof of God's benevolence, for it was a story of saving and being saved. If, on the one hand, she mentioned her relief at no longer having to deal with "churchmen," on the other, in almost an ecumenical gesture, she used a peculiarly Catholic concept as a turn of phrase to describe her arrival in England after a difficult Channel crossing: "it seemed to us we were leaving what is called purgatory and arriving in paradise."

Marie was surely less learned in Reformed theology than Josias, though her exclamations leave no doubt that in exiling themselves the family sought "liberty to worship God openly." Perhaps because she wrote in the safety of Protestant Holland, where she did not need to fear coercion, her account lacked the edge of anxiety and anti-clerical bitterness that buffeted Josias'. For whatever reason, Marie's retrospective told a practical story, about how the escape was managed, primarily about people who had abetted and those who had needed to be gotten around. It placed the escape in a quite different context from Josias' letters, in a different sector of the complex of considerations that together determined their flight: not in doctrinal contests or in threats from priests but in struggles over the conditions of everyday life, in conflicts with civil authorities, neighbors, and kin for social and economic security—in other words, precisely in the material considerations that Josias wished not to admit. Although Marie's memoir ignores the question of motivation—she writes as if there had never been a need to choose or decide—it nonetheless illuminates the decision-making.

Marie remembered the Revocation in terms of a menacing military ("the dragoons"), an intrusive, controlling central state ("the governor"), and a judicial effort to strip her of Berneré ("at the Parlement of Bordeaux"). The dragoons who secured Josias' abjuration in September 1685 invaded Berneré more than once ("quartered at my house several times"). Marie in her memoir attributes their presence to her refusal to attend Catholic mass, so they may well have stayed on even after Josias complied in abjuring. They were probably there in January 1686, when in the space of two weeks five members of the household abjured: the younger Josias, daughter Susanne, two servants of Marie's, and the visiting paternal aunt Marie Prévost de Touchimbert. Marie de La Rochefoucauld says dragoons returned to Berneré after she relocated to the vicinity of La Rochelle, possibly in the spring of 1686, then withdrew after her whereabouts became known.

What the dragoons meant to Marie she did not say. The passage of any troops could be disastrous for a community, even when merely routine and unconnected to punitive or religious purposes. Older residents of Saint-Savinien would remember the two weeks in 1651 when Condé headquartered his rebel troops in the town, and they would remember with dread if the troops mistreated the Savinois as badly as they did residents elsewhere in the Saintongeais theater of the rebellion.[1] After the return of peace at home and abroad, in May 1682, the Duchesse de La Trémoïlle wrote from Paris to implore the intendant Lucas de Demuin to investigate reports that their town of Taillebourg, "which before the year 1668 was one of the prettiest in Saintonge, has since that time been desolated and rendered nearly deserted by the passage of soldiers." Lodgings certainly entailed material consequences: those upon whom soldiers were billeted were required to provide them with subsistence and free rein in the household. When the Marquis de Venours, Marie's future benefactor in Holland, was dragooned at his château in Poitou in 1681, he was forced to receive two captains, six lieutenants, a sergeant, and sixteen cavaliers, who turned the château into a "house of debauchery."[2] Stories of dragoon abuses are numerous and credible. More disciplined and less destructive cases of lodgings were also no doubt common, though underreported, so nothing exists to prove that Marie and her family were physically abused by the practice.

Still, they could well have been fearful of the worst, since Josias' cousin Gédéon Nicolas de Voutron was dragooned with disastrous effect at all three of his residences near and in La Rochelle early in the military occupation. As Abraham Tessereau would recount the incident after both he and Voutron were in exile in Holland, on October 2, 1685, four dragoons of d'Asfeld's regiment went to Coureilles, a country house belonging to Voutron close by the walls of La Rochelle at Les Minimes. The Dame de Voutron was there to complete the harvest. The dragoons took over the household; two days later they sold a flock of ninety ewes, four cows, several tuns of wine, and all the furnishings of the house. On the eighth, another five dragoons of the same regiment went to the uninhabited Château de Voutron, broke down the doors, and settled in along with their horses, taking meals at local taverns on Voutron's tab, and smashed the furnishings. On the fourteenth, fourteen dragoons came to Voutron's home in La Rochelle, where he was living with his family. The next morning at 8 A.M., six more came to join them. At two in the afternoon, twenty-eight more joined these twenty. "These new arrivals began to act like demons; they swore, they blasphemed, they spoke a thousand abominations, they threw out of windows whatever was carried to them, which other dragoons their comrades caught below and carried away; they broke windowpanes and tore apart furnishings, which lasted all night." Voutron complained to the governor, whose only response was: "Why do you not convert?" The lieutenant-particular of La Rochelle ordered Voutron to pay what these forty-eight dragoons were consuming in the local taverns, to which Voutron replied that if one would take into account what the dragoons sold in his other houses, he would pay any remainder. So the lieutenant-particular proceeded to sell everything in the La Rochelle house except one little bed. "We have to leave that for Monsieur and Madame, said he with a laugh."[3]

Beyond the financial cost and threat to personal safety, other meanings of dragooning may have had a deeply confounding effect on Marie and Josias. Lodging soldiers was an obligation of the French populace from which nobles were exempted on the grounds that they made their contributions to the realm's defense through personal service. One of the shocks of the original dragonnades against Protestants introduced in 1681 by the intendant Marillac in Poitou was that nobles—like Venours—were subjected to the practice along with commoners. The threat that dragooning presented was not, then, merely to solvency but to status—to the honor and esteem a family enjoyed in a society based on privilege and on face-to-face relations. Visiting lodgings upon nobles deliberately shamed them, implicitly imputing faults so grave as to annul noble privilege, even degrading them as of questionable nobility.

For some in Josias' and Marie's families, this implication of dragooning represented a particularly acute menace, for it converged with assaults in the Charentes on claims to nobility of municipal origin. When he was the intendant in Poitou during the 1660s, Colbert de Croissy lamented that nobility could derive from municipal offices (*noblesse de cloche*), at the very time when Colbert de Terron and Isaac Isle were jointly investigating the compliance of Protestants with the Edict of Nantes: "There are many nobles, who are not particularly illustrious, who originate with the mayors of Poitiers, Niort, and La Rochelle . . . the inhabitants, instead of devoting themselves to commerce, think only of attaining the offices of mayor and alderman in order to acquire a title of nobility for themselves and their children . . . which has made nearly as many nobles as there are citizens . . . [and] causes both ruination of commerce in the cities and oppression of the inhabitants of the countryside."[4] An *arrêt* dated March 5, 1685 set forth "very explicit sanctions and prohibitions on all persons of the R.P.R. who enjoy the privilege of nobility because their ancestors were mayors of the town of La Rochelle from continuing henceforth to have the status of nobles: they are thus excluded from the privileges attributed to nobility and will be assessed payment of the land tax and subject to all the other taxes like nonnobles for as long as they profess the R.P.R."[5] The intendant Arnoul declared *cloche* nobles nonnoble, subjected them to the land tax, and began lodging soldiers on them by July 24, 1685. At the beginning of September, he ordered all Protestant nobles to bring their proofs of nobility to be examined; those who did not comply were declared nonnoble. Later that month, he received precise instructions from Louvois on how to justify such derogations: "gentlemen whose nobility comes from letters granted by His Majesty or his predecessor kings to persons of the R.P.R. in which no clauses note that the king in granting them knew they were of the said religion shall be declared null without difficulty." On November 17, 1685, while soldiers may still have been at Berneré, Louvois informed the intendant Foucault that the king intended lodgings of dragoons on Protestant noble households to be punitive: "that the dragoons of d'Asfeld's regiment who are in the homes of gentlemen of the R.P.R. in Lower Poitou stay there until they convert, and that instead of living there in good order as they have until now, they be allowed to create the greatest disorder they can, to punish this nobility for its disobedience."[6]

The *arrêt* and the policy statements of Colbert de Croissy, Arnoul, and Louvois could have put the Isle at some risk. The decision upholding the family's nobility in September 1667 identified it as "issued from the office of mayor of La Rochelle." Lydie Pallet, the mother of Marie's cousin Isaac Isle, issued from the municipal nobility of Saint-Jean-d'Angély. Her grandfather had been the mayor of the city in 1549, and her father was ennobled as alderman of Saint-Jean-d'Angély in 1596. Lydie's brother succeeded their father as *échevin* in 1618 and held the office during the siege by Louis XIII in 1621.[7] The Isle line, then, had roots in the urban nobility.

The Champagné were not vulnerable to the same challenge, not apparently having emerged from municipal office. Christophe de Robillard, great-grandfather of Josias, was among the notables from whom testimony was solicited at Saint-Jean-d'Angély in April 1593, when the new king investigated the privileges of the city in the wake of the Wars of Religion. But Christophe was not on the list of gentlemen who owed their nobility to service in town government, nor on the list of town leadership.[8] Nonetheless, the Champagné and their kin were later threatened on their nobility. Josias' maternal uncles

Benjamin de Mazières, Seigneur du Passage, and Daniel de Mazières, Seigneur des Fontaines, were harassed by being declared nonnoble before seeing their nobility upheld on appeal. Even though Josias had gotten his letter of confirmation of his nobility on November 27, 1666 from the intendant d'Aguesseau in Limoges, the intendant's subdelegate, Rousselet, forced Josias in the spring of 1687—when the presence of dragoons at Berneré was fresh in their minds and just when Marie was preparing to escape—to provide proof of his titles to Champagné and his right to collect seigneurial dues there.[9]

The impact of the dragooning on Marie was strong enough for her to mention it in her memoir. It was not, however, during the dragooning itself—the moment of most intense physical coercion—that Marie left, but during what has been called "the Fénelonian pause": the respite from dragonnades that shifted conversion efforts to the putatively milder persuasion techniques of the famed missionary and future Archbishop of Cambrai, François de Salignac de La Motte-Fénelon.[10] Though the soldiers could always return, it must have seemed in 1687 that dragooning had passed. Perhaps Marie's decision to leave was made much earlier, even during the dragooning, for her memoir indicates that the escape was anticipated and prepared over a considerable period of time. She failed to find an opportunity in the first year and then was delayed further by an unexpected pregnancy. Still, the end of dragooning did not change her mind: whatever was fundamentally at play here continued after the soldiers had left the scene.

Sometime in the summer or fall of 1686, Marie had a run-in with the governor in La Rochelle. To this interaction she devotes more space in her memoir than to any other single event. The passage is most revealing of her personality, both in the stance she says she took vis-à-vis the authorities who had ordered her to convert and in her inclusion of this interaction in her retrospective. Apparently she was suspected (correctly) of living near the coast in order to flee the kingdom and was summoned to explain herself by a royal official whose identity gave the incident a special poignancy. Pharamond Green de Saint-Marsault, Baron de Châtelaillon, was a very newly converted former Protestant and close family friend of the Isle. His uncle was a kin advisor to Susanne Isle when she set up guardianship arrangements for her orphaned granddaughters. At the Revocation, local Protestants were taken aback by "the surprising conduct of the Baron de Châtelaillon, who having become the king's lieutenant for the province since his change of religion, did a thousand things against those whom he had just recently called his brothers that a man born Roman Catholic would not do."[11]

With thinly veiled pride at outfoxing the governor, Marie reported in her memoir that she was able to dissemble and convince him that her presence on the coast was merely a sojourn in one of the more convenient properties of her family. Here Marie played a double game that Huguenots prided themselves on not playing, but that often saved them. She denied her intention to leave. It was not, however, her only double game. Earlier, she, like Josias, had abjured, though the time and place are unknown.[12] People often abjured outside their home parish, perhaps to hide their shame from their Protestant neighbors. The thirteen abjurations at Agonnay, for example, in the four months after arrival of the dragoons in the area included seven outsiders: three from Saint-Savinien, and one each from Bors, Tonnay-Charente, Taillan, and Sainte-Bazeille in Gascony. So Marie could have abjured in any number of locations within a wide radius of her home at Berneré or her temporary residence in La Rochelle.[13] Marie's abjuration may have been late. She may have been among those to whom Boufflers alluded in a letter of April 27, 1686, stating that there were "several places in Saintonge . . . where hearts seem more hardened than elsewhere."[14] Even after abjuring, down to their escape, the Champagné played a double game as New Converts. If they went to mass or sent the children to catechism, they no doubt continued to read the Bible and psalms in the evenings at home, "destroying what the curé had said only hours earlier."[15] When confronted by the governor, Marie cemented the deception by posting surety through a friend who resided in La Rochelle—a supposed guarantee that she would not flee—and by having Josias pay a social call on the governor when he returned from defending their case in the Parlement. The impression her account creates is that intrusive government officials could be managed and neutralized. She represented them, then, as an obstacle to an escape that had been decided on for other reasons, rather than as a cause of her family's desire to escape.

"The Estate of Berneré, Which Belongs to Me"

Two remarks in Marie's memoir suggest that tensions with neighbors and kin were likewise involved in the family's decision to leave: "Monsieur de Champagné was at the Parlement of Bordeaux attempting to save the estate of Berneré, which belongs to me" and "Some people were envious of me." Josias' efforts at the Parlement were indeed a crucial backdrop to the Champagné's decision to leave France, for they ran precisely parallel in time with the climactic campaign against Protestants, from the late 1670s down through the family's escape. From 1678, when the end of the Dutch Wars freed troops and political effort for uses elsewhere, and from 1681, when the intendant Marillac's use of dragoons in Poitou opened the final phase of persecution, Protestants in France lived under increasing tension. Communities that until then had known peace between inhabitants of the two confessions began to fracture—gradually or, in some cases, precipitously—into opponents. The decision whether to stay or leave must be seen as being made within this context: not merely as a function of varying degrees of religious zeal or in terms of government actions (edicts or practice), but in terms of changes on the ground—in communities, in families, in networks—that were simultaneous with, sometimes exacerbated by and sometimes exacerbating, the government's determination to enforce religious conformity.

Thus, Susanne Isle's property division in 1677 coincided almost precisely with the start of French Protestantism's endgame. Her heir Marie de La Rochefoucauld would be working out the implications of that property division precisely during the period of escalating religious pressure. In intricate ways, that pressure over religion would influence the eventual failure of the property division itself and, together with that failure, provoke the departure of the Champagné family from France. The Champagné story, then, highlights vividly the intertwining of social and material with religious considerations that shaped Protestants' decision-making in the 1680s.

The fortunes of the Isle–La Rochefoucauld line would have been seen as sunny at the moment of Susanne Isle's property division. The Isle were succeeding, it seems, in maintaining family status from generation to generation. None of the La Rochefoucauld sisters was left, as Chateaubriand would later say of younger sons of younger sons, "with a share of a pigeon, a rabbit."[16] Marie de La Rochefoucauld, as favored heiress, seemed particularly well set up by the inheritances assigned to her: Berneré with all its farms (valued at 20,000 *livres*), a miscellany of adjacent lands, the lord's oven in Saint-Savinien, and half the furnishings at Berneré. Even taking into account the debts, amounting to 7,250 *livres*, that she assumed with the inheritance, the fortune was substantial. It was worlds away, to be sure, from that of her contemporary Elisabeth d'Orléans (daughter of Gaston, brother of Louis XIII) when she married the Duc de Guise in the very same year as Marie and Josias with a dowry of 2,444,500 *livres*—the comparative sums suggest the modest nobility of the Isle. Nonetheless, few women in the Charentes were so well endowed as Marie. The daughters of merchant families in La Rochelle in the half century after the siege of 1627–1628, of whom 90 percent were Huguenot, enjoyed dowries averaging 3,000–6,000 *livres*; only 5 percent received as much as 20,000 *livres*. Daughters of modest noble families in Aunis and Saintonge during the same years had dowries ranging from 2,000 *livres* to 15,000 *livres*; the upper sums accrued to orphans (like Marie de La Rochefoucauld) or widows. No dowry in nearby Cozes surpassed 5,500 *livres* in the last three decades of the seventeenth century.[17]

To all appearances, Berneré was working out well for Marie and Josias. Activity on the estate in the early and mid-1680s seemed routine. Marie was even able to effect some expansion of her landholdings, as Josias was doing at Champagné. In January 1686, the widow Elisabeth Gandouin signed over to Marie her sole asset: a meadow in the prairie of Berneré. In lieu of the rent Gandouin had been unable to pay, Marie accepted the land as full payment of the arrears "and expects the said meadow to remain united to the said seigneury."[18] Berneré, at the heart of Marie de La Rochefoucauld's inheritance, was sound. But the rest of Susanne Isle's estate was more tenuous. The web of her financial arrangements intersected at multiple points with the threads of others' finances, so in complex ways the provisions of her will both impacted and depended upon others. To an extent that, in retrospect, is easily lost sight of, the personal and familial solvency of a landed family like the Isle in this society, in which both wealth and status were based overwhelmingly upon land, depended upon the handling of cash.

Josias, too, was advantaged by Susanne Isle's property division, whose effects rippled across his own kin network. In January 1677, just weeks before Susanne's division, Josias traveled to Montalembert in Angoumois, his sister's residence, where he made a partial payment of what he owed her from their parents' estate. Rather than cash, he gave her the note of a loan their mother had made in 1660 to her nephew Pierre Le Coq, Sieur de Torsat. The note was worth 1,490 *livres* (1,000 in principal and 490 in accrued interest). It seems likely that Josias could not make the payment to his sister in cash; otherwise, Josias' brother-in-law Casimir Prévost de Touchimbert would hardly have agreed to accept Le Coq's note, for it was obviously already a bad debt. Nearly immediately, in February 1677, Casimir went into court to force collection, and on April 9 the court ordered Le Coq to pay the debt in full, plus court costs, within fifteen days.[19]

So in January 1677 Josias strained to pay something to his sister. But by April 1678 he would be able to pay off the remaining 6,000 *livres* he owed her by the terms of their 1662 division of inheritance. No doubt the distribution of Susanne Isle's heritage, in which he shared as recipient of Marie's dowry, played a role in his ability to pay Casimir Prévost, now widowed by Josias' sister's death, after owing the debt for sixteen years. Prévost in turn used the funds to make the final payment of 27,000 *livres* due on his principal residence at Londigny,[20] not far from Montalembert. What this chain of payments illustrates is the intertwining of family fortunes and the way the prosperity of any family member depended upon the solvency of others.

The year 1678 may have been the high point of Josias' solvency, for by the eve of the Revocation, Josias was again a debtor. In January 1685, he borrowed 2,400 *livres* from Charles Prévost de Touchimbert, Seigneur de Brassac, the brother of his sister's widower Casimir. When Josias failed to repay Brassac by May 1686, Brassac secured an order from the Parlement of Bordeaux for immediate repayment, under threat of confiscation of Josias' property, both movable and immovable. When, on 20 July, the debt was still unpaid, Brassac sent an official from Saint-Jean-d'Angély on horseback to Berneré to serve papers on Josias. In roughly the same months, Marie de La Rochefoucauld was similarly on the brink of insolvency with indebtedness originating in Susanne Isle's property division. On March 26, 1685, the Parlement of Bordeaux ordered her to pay the 1,066 *livres* 15 *sols* Susanne Isle had owed the local Augustinians since 1655, which she did in June.[21]

One challenge Marie de La Rochefoucauld faced was collecting the old debts that came to her with Susanne Isle's legacy and on which the very viability of Berneré as a landed inheritance depended. Some of these inherited collectibles eventually did accrue to Marie. The local cooper repaid his debt by indenturing his son. The miller Jean Oussineau had owed Susanne Isle 26 *livres*; by the spring of 1684, he owed Marie arrears of more than 74 *livres*, having paid her no dues for a windmill and meadows near Vaufraiche in the seven years since she became mistress of the estate, despite orders to do so from the judges at Berneré and Taillebourg. In April 1684, Oussineau brought Marie a partial payment and a promise to pay the rest in order to keep his lands. Similarly, in January 1686, when Josias took the land of the widow Marie Ponvert, that transfer perhaps repaid not only the 44 *livres* 9 *sols* Josias had loaned her to keep another creditor from her door but also the 118 *livres* she had owed Susanne Isle in 1677.[22]

The difficulties Marie experienced in collecting rents and dues on her lands were probably little different and scarcely worse than those facing other landowners of the day. Debts receivable often formed part of inheritances, along with land. And they might stay uncollected for generations, functioning, like *rentes*, as an interest-bearing security in a diversified portfolio also containing land, jewels, and other movables. Even if indebtedness was a routine part of life, though, it is still possible that more of Marie de La Rochefoucauld's fortune was tied up in receivables than was usual—or healthy. By the terms of the morning agreement, she had to have cash with which to pay her grandmother's pension for the remaining years of her life and subsequently to pay equivalent sums to her sisters. And she operated under time pressure, for, by the terms of the secret afternoon agreement, Marie had to collect certain of the old receivables in order to pay her aunt Madelene de Solière what Susanne Isle had reluctantly set aside as a 3,000-*livres* reserve against any remaining lien Madelene might claim on the Isle family fortune.

It seems clear that Susanne Isle intended that this sum not be paid to Madelene unless her heirs were forced to do so. This is why Susanne did not just pay off Madelene. All but 720 *livres* of the 3,000 *livres* put in reserve had been loaned out after Madelene married and was promised her dowry. All but

770 *livres* were loaned after Madelene made her first claim to more money from her mother in the late 1660s. So Susanne had had the resources to pay Madelene in full in cash. She had not faced the problem that would eventually defeat Marie: the inability to pay Madelene out of anything but real estate. Susanne could have paid Madelene in cash but elected not to do so because she believed her daughter was not entitled to it. This may also explain why, in 1676, when she wished to be reimbursed for the costs of raising Madelene's son Zacharie, Susanne Isle sued Madelene (or more precisely, the bankruptcy guardians for Madelene's estate of Soulignonne), rather than just crediting the sum against the 3,000 *livres* later held in reserve.[23]

Unfortunately for Marie de La Rochefoucauld, the gifting of March 8, 1677 began to unravel almost immediately. As early as the first anniversary of the original division, Josias was complaining to his sisters-in-law—as he would again in December and the following March—that he could not collect from third-party debtors the sum due to Marie by the original (morning) property division as offset to the life annuity that Marie was obligated to pay her grandmother or the sum stipulated by the afternoon agreement as the source of what she might have to pay to her aunt Madelene de Solière. Repeatedly, Josias would press upon Marie's sisters that no payments had been secured, though he had made "various demands" to the debtors and had resorted, on March 21, 1680 to requesting seizure of the debtor's property in the case of Catherine de La Valade. Josias complained to his sisters-in-law in May 1680 that all the expenses for this legal action were falling on Marie alone—she and Josias had paid 152 *livres* to the bailiff of the presidial court in the first year (1678) they tried to collect, even though the *rente* actually belonged to the sisters now that the grandmother was dead and by terms of the original division the sisters were to guarantee the sums to Marie in the event the debts she inherited were uncollectible. On the afternoon of May 7, 1680, the five surviving sisters and Josias met with the notary Fayet in Saint-Savinien to resolve the issue creating tension between them. Madelene, Susanne, and Lidie came from their Château de Bellay near Saint-Hippolyte, Elisabeth from the Château de La Thibaudière in Saint-Savinien, and Marie and Josias from Berneré.[24]

Marie's sisters conferred among themselves, got advice from their attorney, and decided on terms favorable to the beleaguered Marie. Regarding the house in Saint-Savinien for which Nicollas Pasturault and Judiq Gaultreau could not pay what they owed them, they agreed to sell or lease it to another if possible within twelve to eighteen months. Failing that, Marie's sisters agreed that their four-fifths of this 900-*livre* sum could be deducted from the 3,538 *livres* Marie owed them by the terms of the original property division. As for what they were owed by Isaac Guyent, Marguerite Ponvert, and the heirs of Jean Cadot the Younger, "given the difficulties in getting payment and that there might be expenses to no avail," the sisters stipulated that Josias and Marie should make the efforts they thought prudent for securing payment. If in six years' time—late spring 1686—these debts had not been paid, then Marie could return them to the community, and the sisters would, they promised, pay her whatever amount was unpaid or credit it against her part of the community at that time, principal as well as interest.[25]

Two complex cases illustrate how Marie's efforts to collect her grandmother's outstanding loans were impeded by the web-like structure of noble indebtedness: her dunning of Jean-Louis de Malesac and the legal competition over the assets of Catherine de La Valade, Dame de Chambon. The Malesac debt that Marie inherited in 1677 exposes the intertwining of debt-collection and family friction. Since 1672, Susanne had been pursuing 600 *livres* in fees due to her on a sale of property within her seigneury at Berneré. In this case, the Isle family itself was holding out on her. Claude Isle des Groies had owed Susanne the fees. His widow, Jacquette de Marbeuf, and her second husband Malesac were held responsible by the court in Saint-Jean-d'Angély for transmitting these funds to Marie after Claude's death, but half of the sums were due from the other heirs of Claude—his sisters Esther, Henriette, and Uranie. Now a widower himself, Malesac had been unable to get anything from the women with which to pay Marie, in part—or so he claimed—because Marie was withholding from him the papers relating to the debt and the law cases, which he needed in support of his demand against the Isle sisters. In a compromise dated July 17, 1686, Marie agreed to desist from pursuing Malesac for the entire 600 *livres* and to return the papers to him if he would pay her his half of the debt. In February 1687, Malesac paid Josias the 300 *livres* as his share in the litigation, and on March 11—days before sending her children into exile—Marie recorded receiving those funds from her husband.[26]

The fifteen years it took Susanne and then Marie to collect from Malesac were dwarfed by the thirty-seven years—from Marie de La Rochefoucauld's childhood to half a decade after she left for the Refuge—consumed in pursuit of the La Valade repayment. Susanne Isle had loaned the 3,187 *livres* 10 *sols* in 1655 on the understanding that they would be paid back in ten years, with interest paid annually at 6.25 percent. Despite legal action she took in 1668 and 1669, nothing was paid, and by 1678, when Josias first tried to collect, the arrears of interest alone had risen to 4,571 *livres*, and the total due had become too large for the family to repay. The Presidial of Saintes endeavored to sort out the family's financial affairs, in January 1678 ordering the defendant to furnish documentation of her property holdings within the fortnight. Josias travelled multiple times on horseback from Berneré to Saintes in pursuit of the payment due from La Valade, and on March 21, 1680, he formally requested judicial seizure of her property. Though his request for seizure of her estate was granted on May 25, 1680, the case dragged on.[27]

The details of Josias' efforts to collect the large La Valade debt illustrate the way the nobility, whose privileges and prestige rested upon landed estates, created among themselves networks of cash exchange that could variously prop up or undercut family finances, playing for each other the role that banks would later fill. In the web of competition with Josias for the La Valade properties was another local nobleman, Guy de La Blachière, Sieur de Coustiers. His money trail originated in 1650 when the Marquise de la Roche-Courbon loaned 4,500 *livres* to La Valade's husband. In 1655, the same year in which Susanne Isle made the loan to La Valade, La Blachière bought the promissory note from Madame de Courbon and began years of competing with another of La Valade's creditors, a Saintes merchant named Estienne Guénon, for access to La Valade's assets. In 1676, two years before Josias began pressing Susanne's claim, La Blachière was awarded 600 *livres* in interest from La Valade, a move that rendered it less likely that Josias would succeed in gaining repayment of the debt owed to Marie.[28] In 1681, La Blachière secured a court order to seize a large woods in nearby Saint-Sorlin-de-Séchaud that Josias and the judges who granted Josias the seizure on her property did not know La Valade owned. La Blachière had begun, then, to "jump the queue" on Josias. It was encouraging that in 1682–1683 the children of the debtor gave Josias a partial repayment. But they also came to an agreement with La Blachière whereby La Blachière would take the Chambon lands and assume responsibility himself for paying priority creditors of the family.[29]

This side-agreement with La Blachière, bypassing as it did the claims Josias was pressing, swung the La Rochefoucauld sisters into action. They sent to their lawyer at the Parlement of Bordeaux their draft of a petition he should submit to the court in their name objecting to the La Blachière–La Valade agreement. They did not recognize La Blachière's "alleged claims" and continually referred to him as the "so-called creditor." They considered the agreement a recipe for cheating them out of what the court had recognized when it attached the La Valade properties for them. In the end they won: the Parlement agreed in November 1685 that the woods and the wood cut there since the seizure could not belong to other creditors such as La Blachière, for this would infringe upon the rights of the La Rochefoucauld heirs of Susanne Isle.[30]

But nothing moved to fruition, even after the La Valade sons assumed responsibility for their mother's debt to the La Rochefoucauld sisters in January 1685 and promised to pay. The slowness of the process continued. On March 29, April 5, and May 9, 1687, just weeks before Marie's departure, Josias was in Saintes still pursuing the repayment of Catherine de La Valade's debt through seizure of her properties. Perhaps he was still away on May 16 when Marie gave birth to her twelfth child, Thérèse. Not until June 1692—after Marie was an exile in Holland and Josias was dead—would the various creditors of La Valade, still jockeying for position in the queue for her assets, be granted an order for an auction of her property, with subsequent division of the proceeds among them.[31]

These and other vexed assets that Marie de La Rochefoucauld inherited from her grandmother Susanne Isle became a burden on Marie's finances as well as a burden on Josias' time and energies. All the costs of collection fell upon Marie, all the work with the lawyers on Josias. In February 1687, Marie's sisters acknowledged owing Josias and Marie 439 *livres* 6 *sols* for the costs of the La Valade lawsuit and the income from a house they owned jointly in Saint-Savinien.[32] The sisters never did rescue Marie as they promised; rather, they too joined the line of persons who owed her money. Most serious of all, with the unraveling of the afternoon pass-through arrangement that was designed to allow Marie to pay off Madelene de Solière, if necessary, came the threat—eventually fatal to Marie's solvency and to Isle family solidarity—from Aunt Madelene herself. After her mother's death in December 1679, Madelene struck, denying the validity of Susanne's estate settlement in its entirety.

Aunt Madelene

Sometime before October 1681, Madelene de Solière initiated a case at the Parlement of Bordeaux, then in session at La Réole on the Garonne southeast of Bordeaux,[33] against Marie de La Rochefoucauld, claiming payment of 12,000 *livres* owed her by her late mother Susanne Isle. This brought into the open the Isle-Solière skeleton that the property division of March 1677 had endeavored to keep in the closet and from which the afternoon agreement attempted to protect the La Rochefoucauld sisters. All the participants knew at the time of the division that the potential for trouble was strong. Now Aunt Madelene would ruin everything.

Madelene de Solière was born in 1632, the year Bernerė became a seigneury for her parents. She grew up there, and it was her home until, at the age of twenty-seven in July 1659, she married Louis de Salbert, Seigneur de Soulignonne. Salbert's estate was a handsome one, not far from Saint-Savinien in the direction of Saintes. As his father had already died, Louis was its lord. The château, next to the village church, was a fourteenth-century fortification with a storied past, having figured in Bertrand Du Guesclin's wars against the English. The Salbert, like the Isle, were longstanding and committed Protestants, for generations intertwined with leaders of the Reform. In 1569, when the Huguenot forces retreated to Saint-Jean-d'Angély to regroup after their defeat at Jarnac,

Henry of Navarre accompanied his mother Jeanne d'Albret, Coligny, and Henri, Prince de Condé to Tonnay-Charente. "The princes and lords, and Sallebert, mayor of La Rochelle," assembled there to declare Navarre the new head of the party, succeeding his uncle Condé, and declare his cousin Condé his second-in-command. Later, the Salbert family provided two pastors for the Grand Temple in La Rochelle. Ennobled by the office of mayor, the family then joined the country nobility with the seigneuries of Romagné, Forges, and later Soulignonne.[34]

The marriage was an intralineal alliance. Louis de Salbert's mother, Léa de Bessay, after being widowed, had married Jean Isle, Seigneur de Beauchesne, first cousin of Susanne Isle, mother of the bride.[35] Madelene's nuptials, then, created a double marriage whose net effect would benefit the Isle lineage and place Madelene de Solière herself at risk. One common form of intralineal double marriage had two children of one family marrying two of another in such a way as to effect an even exchange of property. Another had a widow and widower marrying while the son of one married the daughter of the other. Here, Jean de Beauchesne did not have a marriageable daughter to pair with Léa de Bessay's son, so Madelene stood in for the Isle, her dowry making the Salbert solvent (it was hoped) without Léa's assets. Madelene's dowry made it possible to redirect Léa's fortune from her Salbert son and daughter to her children by Beauchesne, enriching and advancing the Isle.

The marriage contract reveals at once the generosity of Susanne Isle toward her daughter Madelene and the tenuousness of the financial situation in which the marriage would place the bride. Five years earlier, on December 24, 1654, Madelene had given her consent to a settlement negotiated by her mother with her elder sister's husband, Casimir de La Rochefoucauld. By its terms, Madelene would receive as her sole inheritance 12,000 *livres* to be paid to her by her older sister six months after her mother's death. In return for this promise, Madelene renounced all other "rights and claims" to inherit from her father and mother. In her own 1659 marriage contract, Madelene ratified and approved this renunciation a second time. Susanne, "in favor of said marriage," assumed the obligation originally assigned to her eldest daughter, now deceased, and agreed not to delay Madelene's inheritance until she herself should die, but rather advanced the payment of these 12,000 *livres* in order to help Madelene and her new husband establish a sound financial footing for their marriage. The 12,000 *livres* would be paid immediately upon the marriage ceremony: 2,000 of it in an IOU from the Sieur de Nanteuil, paternal first cousin of the bride, and the rest in cash. The sum was to be used for three purposes: to pay old debts of the groom's lineage, to provide *légitimes* for the groom's siblings, and (if any funds remained) to acquire landed properties. The newlyweds would be obliged to provide Madelene's brother-in-law

Casimir de La Rochefoucauld with receipts for each expenditure made with the dowry funds. To make this advancement feasible for Susanne, who had not reckoned on being without those resources during her lifetime, Madelene and her husband were to pay her mother annually, on Christmas Day, the sum of 100 *livres* as a life annuity—an exceedingly modest payout of less than 1 percent on principal. Louis and Madelene signed a notarized receipt in February 1662 at Berneré acknowledging that they had received all of the "twelve thousand *livres* promised by the said Dame de Lescure to the said dame Madelene de Sauliere her daughter in her marriage contract."[36]

The precariousness of the financial situation into which Madelene was stepping is evident in the fact that the bride's fortune had to go toward bailing out the groom's family. But families routinely used brides' marriage portions for the benefit of the groom's lineage, and Madelene's marriage contract protected her by stipulating that she would recover as dower, upon her husband's death, all she had brought as dowry. Still, there were further signs of fragility in the Salbert finances. Isle and Salbert monies had been mixed together in complicated ways by the marriage of the Salbert widow (mother of the groom, who acted as her children's "tutor and guardian") to Jean Isle de Beauchesne in 1639. A seventy-six-page inventory of Léa's possessions at the moment of her remarriage was designed to keep the lineage properties separate. But practice continued to confuse the affairs of the two families. In 1662, Louis' sister Sara ceded to Jean Isle and Léa all or a large part of her inheritance from her father,[37] and she renounced all claim to a *légitime* from her mother's assets, thus, in combination with Madelene's in-marriage, completing the detachment of Léa de Bessay's fortune from obligations to her first family. Moreover, after Madelene's husband and his sister came of age, they continued to entrust their stepfather Jean Isle with their financial affairs, "of which they have no knowledge at all nor the training for untangling them," assuming their stepfather to be "more capable of protecting them for having long had the management and disposition of the properties and affairs of the said late Sieur de Soulignonne."[38]

It seems likely that Madelene and Louis found the infusion of the Solière dowry insufficient to cure the Salbert lineage's financial woes and soon asked her mother to increase their inheritance. Susanne helped out repeatedly in the 1660s. In 1662, she gave Louis a *rente* collectible on her cousin Isaac Isle, Marquis de Loire. In 1666, she released Salbert "freely" from the obligation of paying her the 100 *livres* annuity agreed upon in the marriage contract. In one undated letter, Madelene thanked her mother for "the extreme generosity and friendship you have for me" and called her "a strong means for helping me pull myself out of the morass into which I have sunk. . . . All my life, good mother, I shall render you my humble obedience and recognize that I owe you everything." Later, this letter would be used against Madelene in Marie de La

Rochefoucauld's legal defense of Berneré, as is evident by the "*Ne varietur*" written in another hand across the upper border of its first page.[39] No doubt this letter was deemed useful as evidence that Madelene herself had recognized receiving from her mother the aid to which she was entitled and more.

At the point when Madelene wrote this letter, she and her mother appear to have been working together on their financial problems. Madelene promised to pay a visit in the next week to Madame de Chambon "since you wish it, and moreover I owe her a visit and will ask her for it in a good way," evidently for payment of the debt La Valade had owed Susanne since 1655. Madelene also let her mother know that her lawyer had recommended ways of proceeding "in your affair . . . I will send you his letter." But in 1667, Madelene went to court to seek an order reinstating her rights to the inheritance she had renounced in 1654 as well as in her marriage contract and annulling the receipt she signed in 1662 for the sums given her. Royal letters of restitution dated June 25, 1667 granted her request for a hearing, and the Parlement on June 3, 1669 ordered the parties to come plead their cases. But this order was allowed to expire, without action on Madelene's part, perhaps because of complications produced by the premature death of her husband, at the age of thirty-six, a mere week later.[40]

Madelene de Solière's experience of widowhood little resembled her mother's. Whereas Susanne Isle enjoyed secure possession of the Berneré estate and associated lands, Madelene, with Soulignonne heavily encumbered, had only a precarious hold on any home at all. Whereas Susanne Isle prospered within a matrix of kin held together by family loyalty and shared religion, Madelene suffered testy and hostile relationships with all those whose interactions with her were preserved in personal or official documents.[41] It may well have been a yearning to match—or surpass—the respect and status that she, as a child, had seen her mother enjoy that led Madelene to reach for a spectacular social promotion that seems in retrospect immensely foolish but was not unique among notable women of the province.

On May 29, 1672, Madelene de Solière wrote her mother from Paris.[42] Responding to her mother's inquiry about rumors that she was remarrying, Madelene confirmed to "my very honored mother" that "it is true that I have married, as you will see by the certificate I send you." She had hesitated to write before the ceremony because "I imagined it was a splendor to which I could not aspire . . . but at last the marriage is done in due form." A certificate Madelene enclosed had been prepared by one Lavergne, who signed as a priest, a doctor in the Faculty of Paris, and first almoner of the groom. It stated that Madelene had married in the church of the Franciscan Picpus Fathers in Paris on the day preceding her letter to her mother. The groom was "His Royal Highness Nicolas Leopol Ignace III of Saxony, Duke of Launambourg, Count of Aulbourg, Prince of Limbourg, Duke of Villistenne, Count of Lipsise, Marquis of the Empire, Prince of Fronuague, Perpetual Vicar of the Holy Empire, King of the Holy City of Hierusalm, Prince of the Saxons, Landgrave of Wirtambourg, Count of Tirol, Fribourg and other places." A fourth person, serving as a witness to the ceremony, signed as a priest.[43]

Madelene's letter, understandably, was effusive. She had found a match that honored and flattered her. Her new husband's rank implied princely privilege—"he is received in the company of the king of France, which is very advantageous to me." Out of tender regard for her, he would have her enjoy those advantages to the full. So now, on the morning after her wedding,

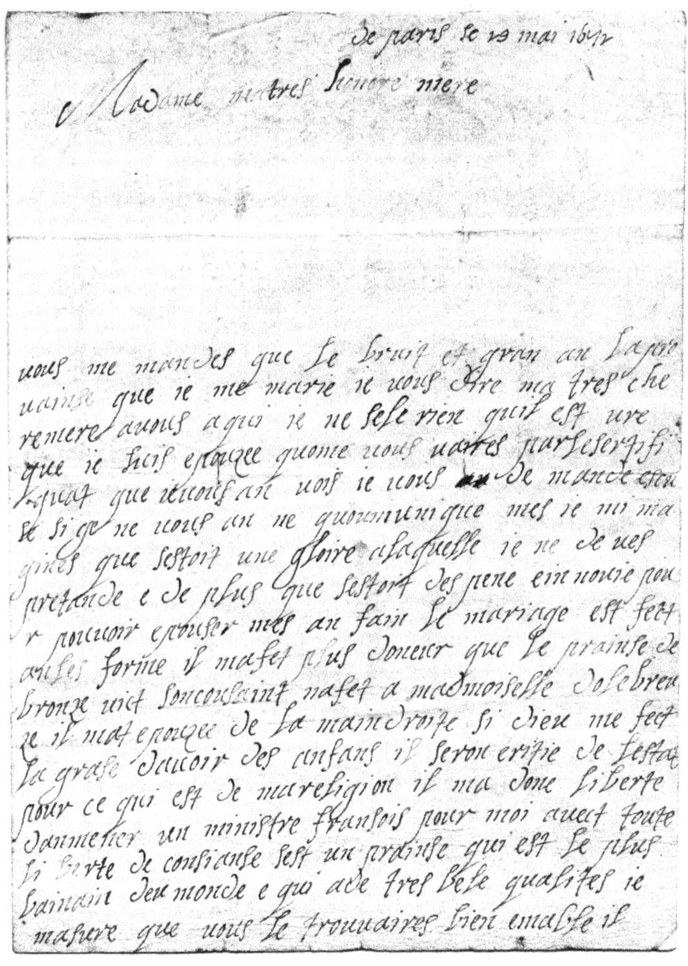

De paris le 29 mai 1672

Madame ma tres honore mere

vous me mandes que le bruit est gran an la pro
vainse que ie me marie ie vous dire ma tres che
re mere avous a qui ie ne sele rien quil est vre
que ie suis esposee quome vous vaires par le certifi
quat que ie vous an vois ie vous demande escu
se si ge ne vous an ne quommunique mes ie mi ma
gines que sestoit une gloire a laquelle ie ne de ves
pretande e de plus que sestoit des pene einnouie pou
r pouvoir espouser mes an fain le mariage est fect
an les forme il ma fet plus doneur que le prainse de
bronze vict son coulaint na fet a madmoiselle de lebreu
ie il ma esposee de la main droite si dieu me fect
la grase davoir des anfans il seron eritie de lestat
pour ce qui est de ma religion il ma done liberte
dammener un ministre fransois pour moi avect toute
liberte de consianse sest un prainse qui est le plus
hainain deu monde e qui a de tres bele qualites ie
masure que vous le trouvaires bien emable il

Figure 3.1 Letter from Madelene de Solière to her Mother, May 29, 1672, first page. Property of the author.

Madelene sketched out the prince(ss)ly household he wished her to have. Two of the sons of the late Monsieur de La Cour, she proposed, would come as pages to her court. Her sister Susanne's husband, Monsieur de Lestang, would have an appointment as duke that her new husband had previously envisioned bestowing on a man of quality in Paris whom he had already honored with "the collar of his [chivalric] order." Sister Susanne would be given a château. The prince wished her mother to come to Germany; Madelene herself confessed to anticipating "a great joy for me if I have the honor of spending my life in your company and serving you personally until my last breath or yours." As for the children of her late sister Marie, Madelene sent "a thousand kind regards to my nieces [the six La Rochefoucauld sisters]" but acknowledged that she could do nothing for her niece/goddaughter Madeleine because of her gender: "How I wish she were a boy." Madelene closed her letter by enjoining all to temporary secrecy: the prince did not wish the marriage to be divulged until she was appropriately outfitted, "since I have neither entourage nor furnishings."

The family and neighbors were spared the move, however, for Madelene was the victim of a hoax. The Picpus monastery stood indeed in Paris' Faubourg Saint-Antoine, established there in 1601 by the Pénitents réformés du Tiers-ordre de Saint-François. The young Louis XIII laid the first stone of its new chapel in 1611 and in 1621 took the convent under his personal protection. Its links with the world of the court persisted. The Picpus Fathers offered luxurious apartments to the ambassadors from Catholic powers, who lodged there before making their formal entry into the capital city via the Place du Trône (today Place de la Nation) and the Porte Saint-Antoine. And Picpus was the special object of charity of the *dévote* mother of Madame de Montespan, mistress of Louis XIV in the 1670s.[44]

But Nicolas Leopol Ignace, Prince of Saxony did not exist apart from the charade of chimerical titles. And so Madelene's "marriage" was an illusion and a deception. Who was this impostor groom? Nothing in Madelene's letter offers means of pursuing his identity or his motives. He may have been after money, sport, revenge, or winning a wager. He may have been a prankster who drew his inspiration from Molière's *Bourgeois Gentleman,* then all the rage on the Paris stage. The climax of this immensely engaging play staged the marriage of the daughter of the social climber Jourdain to a French bourgeois masquerading as the son of the Grand Turk. Sadly for Madelene de Solière, she was not privy, as Mademoiselle Jourdain was, to the groom's disguise nor, through it, united with her true love.

Or perhaps he was just a predator who saw the ease and irony of seduction that religious fragmentation offered him. A Protestant woman was the easier dupe, since she would be less familiar with the costume of clerics and the words of the Latin marriage mass, and perhaps unaware that a Catholic marriage required thrice-read banns, the presence of four witnesses in addition to the curé, and inscription in the parish register. This hoax may, then, have had an element of Protestant persecution. And what better place for humiliating a heretic? Picpus' very raison d'être was the defeat of heresy. The monastery boasted its own monuments of Catholic reconquest: in the chapel an Ecce Homo statue by Germain Pilon, sculptor of royal tombs, and in its library the collections of Jacques Davy, Cardinal du Perron, who, though born a Calvinist, devoted his career as theologian and diplomat to demonstrating the falsity of Protestantism. But weekly, on its own Sabbath, the monastery had to endure the spectacle of Protestants from the city streaming out the long rue de Picpus, through the Porte de Picpus (today Porte Dorée), en route to their great temple at suburban Charenton.[45]

Whatever the motives of the "groom," the story of Madelene's victimization is the sole source for understanding her frame of mind just a few years later as she initiated her effort to gain an enlarged inheritance at the expense of her niece Marie de La Rochefoucauld. The way Madelene told her story in her letter to her mother expressed the longing of a young, disadvantaged widow for an inversion of her social identity. She spoke of her match as conferring a social place in which she would no longer be the younger daughter pushed to the margins but the benefactor of her family: enhancing its network of connections, contributing to its social and economic standing, creating opportunities for kin and friends. Personal vindication, too, from the bad relationships she alluded to in her letter would come with her newfound fortune: "I would be much consoled to leave the province, for I am strongly persuaded of the little attachment my relations have for me. . . . I believe they are indifferent toward me. . . . Monsieur de Beauchesne declares war against me. . . . God free me from my enemies." Her chance to move to her German principality would both reward her favorites and spite those who had given her trouble.

Best of all, she, a daughter of minor provincial nobility, would henceforth be a princess. As foolish as Madelene's belief that she could be chosen by a prince may seem in retrospect, such a social promotion was far from impossible. Approval for marriage across ranks within the nobility of the sword was widely shared, both in Paris and in the Charentes. For a French squire's daughter, marrying a high nobleman was not transgressive; the French social ethos accepted, even expected, brides to marry as high as possible up the social ladder.[46] Madelene knew this from experience, for a misalliance of astonishing distance had already happened to a woman from her own province, her own generation, her own Protestant religion, and a family similar in stature to her own. North of Saint-Jean-d'Angély lay Olbreuse, the birthplace, in 1639, of Eléonore Desmier d'Olbreuse. The daughter of a modest, untitled country gentleman, Eléonore left the Charentes to become a lady-in-waiting in the entourage of the La Trémoïlle family in The Hague. There she met George-William, the reigning Duke of Brunswick-Zell, a small but significant North German state, who fell in love with her. In 1666, he made her his live-in companion, then in 1676 his wife and reigning Duchess of Zell. Their only daughter Sophie-Dorothée would marry her cousin George of Brunswick, who, in 1714, became George I of Great Britain, making the Charentais squire's daughter a progenitor to all of Europe's principal royal dynasties.[47]

The same atmosphere of possibility would soon spawn two more marriages of astonishing distance from within the milieu where Madelene de Solière was born and raised. On October 12, 1680, Uranie de La Cropte, daughter of an untitled nobleman from Périgord named Beauvais and former ward of Josias de Robillard's friend, neighbor, and future son-in-law Saint-Surin, embarked upon a fairy-tale life by secretly marrying the 22-year-old cousin and godson of the king, the Comte de Soissons.[48] The glaring disproportion of rank between the lovers provoked the consternation of all the groom's relatives, but Louis XIV himself approved and validated the match.[49] A few years later, this fairy tale would be repeated by the king himself with another daughter of the Charentes, Françoise d'Aubigné, a relation of Eléonore d'Olbreuse who was born in Niort in 1635. Like Madelene, Uranie, and Eléonore the daughter of a modest born-Protestant country squire, Françoise would secretly marry the greatest prince in Christendom, Louis XIV, in 1683 or 1684, as Marquise de Maintenon. In 1672 when Madelene wrote her mother, Françoise d'Aubigné was still merely the widow Scarron, and no one—least of all, Françoise herself—could have imagined her destiny. But the Duchess of Zell was well known everywhere. Indeed, Madelene referred to her in the letter announcing her "marriage": "[The prince] paid me greater honor than the Prince of Brunswick, his cousin, paid to mademoiselle d'Olbreuse. He married me 'of the right hand' [with full spousal privileges]. If God gives me the grace of having children, they will inherit the state."[50]

Madelene's reach for such a brilliant marriage—and her vulnerability to seduction by someone who promised it to her—ended in debacle. When she returned home, how did family and neighbors who had heard of the "marriage" first by rumor and then by her own report regard the returning Madelene? It must have been clear that she had fallen prey to her own naiveté. The old "enemies" from whom she hoped her marriage would free her may have tipped her reception back in the province to the rougher side. Certainly, a fund of hostility toward her would carry far into the future. The parish register of Soulignonne betrays—to a degree that is highly unusual for this type of source—local feelings about their seigneurial dame. In two places—dated September 1, 1679, and May 9, 1682—someone with access to the parish register defaced the book with remarks of utter disdain for her. Years later, when Josias' brother-in-law was locked in a custody battle with Madelene over the baby that Josias and Marie left behind, Casimir Prévost de Touchimbert would taunt her by producing in court the joyful letter of May 29, 1672. This letter only survives because he pulled it from the family files to embarrass her by making it part of the court record.[51]

Madelene de Solière returned to Saintonge as she had left it, as the widow of the Seigneur de Solignonne, not the Princess of Saxony. Her finances rapidly became desperate, and her relations with her mother deteriorated. No doubt both the timing and substance of Susanne Isle's 1677 property division were responses to the threat this deterioration posed to the rest of the family. Toward the end of the year in which she was tricked by the marriage, 1672, officers from the presidial court in Saintes invaded Soulignonne in an effort to enforce a 1670 collection order against Madelene. On one of half a dozen visits to the village, the court officer sent from Saintes entered the Château de Soulignonne, threatening to confiscate the furnishings in her home, and was astonished to find the abode entirely empty. A servant who would not give her name and a sharecropper named Antoine Chounet explained that all Madelene owned in the locality was the grain from the recent harvest, which was being stored in a nearby village. As soon as the icy roads would permit the passage of cart and horse, the court officers had that grain taken to Saintes for forced auction sale. Madelene never appeared, was declared in default, and the grain was sold on Christmas Eve. Even if she was away from home at the moment, this forced sale must have embarrassed her, for the officers made their presence obvious each time they visited Soulignonne, broadcasting aloud her indebtedness as well as the orders for confiscation and sale. In 1675, her seigneury was seized by the presidial court, which funneled the estate's revenues to Madelene's creditors by leasing it out to a merchant from Saintes. She would be allowed only to shelter her own dowry from the confiscation of the Salbert estate.[52]

Soon Madelene's impoverishment infected her family relationships. In March 1676, Susanne Isle, Madelene's mother, went to the presidial court in Saintes to collect "four hundred fifty *livres* for three years of arrears due her for the feeding, maintenance, and education of Zacharie de Salbert, son of the said Louis and the said De Solieres, together with one hundred fifty *livres* for the current year." Susanne won her suit for funds her daughter could not provide for her own son's maintenance; the sums she was awarded by the lieutenant-general were to come from those who had leased the lands of Soulignonne when they were seized for debt. Before long, Madelene's cousin Jean Isle, second husband of her own first husband's mother, would take her to the presidial court to force her to pay some forty-seven *livres* she owed him for five years of back-due fees and rents on a farm at Soulignonne.[53] The erstwhile Princess of Saxony, then, was alone, on bad terms with her family, relieved of custody of her own son, without an estate, and insolvent.

4

Aunt Madelene's Offensive

At some point in the drama of her "marriage," Madelene de Solière wrote another letter to her mother, this time begging for help.[1] The destitute Madelene piteously begged her mother to "send me some money, I have had to borrow to survive . . . in the name of God, mother, let me hear from you so I can decide whether to accept a miserable match relating to what I told you about, for I would have to die of hunger. I do not deserve that." Whether her mother responded with the generosity she had displayed in the early 1660s is unknown. Soon upon Susanne Isle's death on December 8, 1679,[2] Madelene set about redressing her financial situation at the expense of her mother's wishes for the family inheritance.

Madelene de Solière sued Marie de La Rochefoucauld and her sisters in the Parlement of Bordeaux in 1681 for what she saw as her rightful inheritance. Thus began a contest over the estate of Susanne Isle that would last for more than twenty-five years and would actuate the nightmare that the secret afternoon session on March 8, 1677 had endeavored to forestall. On the surface, the claims of Madelene de Solière seem patently unwarranted. As Susanne stated in her settlement of 1677, Madelene had been paid what was due her by the contracts she signed in 1654, 1659, and 1662. A closer look at the complexities of the law, however, and at the circumstances under which the law was applied between 1681 and 1710 makes Madelene's challenge and its outcome more readily understandable.

In 1681, Madelene's first suit against her La Rochefoucauld nieces made a relatively straightforward claim for repayment of her dowry. As the heirs of Susanne Isle, her mother and their grandmother, Madelene claimed, they were responsible for replacing the dowry Susanne had paid in 1662 but which had been lost to Madelene with the bankruptcy of her late husband's Soulignonne. Because of that bankruptcy, Madelene's dowry did not become her dower upon her husband's death, as a widow was entitled to expect. She claimed "guarantee against false use of her dowry." What Madelene claimed, then, was

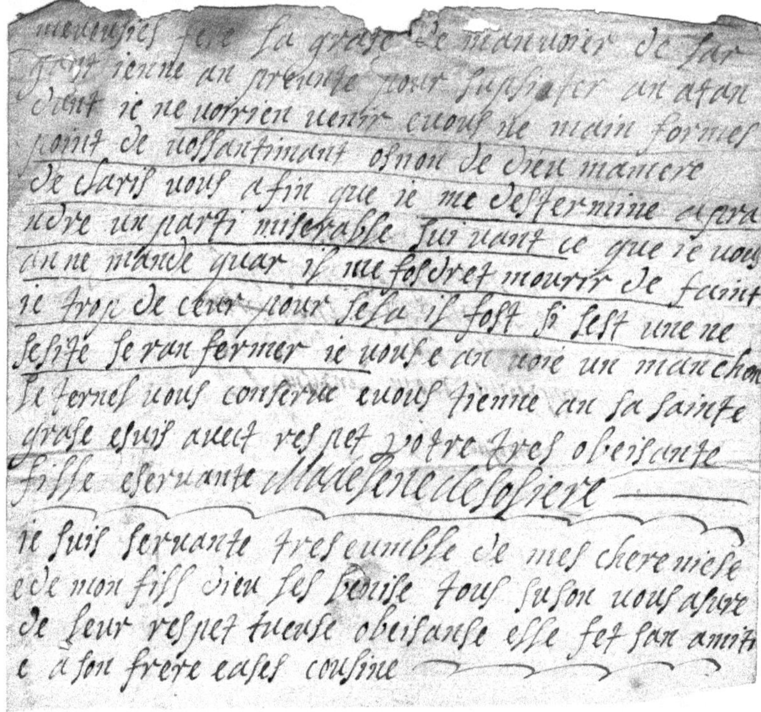

meuciensfies fere la grase de mannuoier de far
... ienne an prenute pour sussiafer an afan
dant ie ne norrien uenir euous ne main formes
point de nossantimant osnon de dieu manere
de Paris uous afin que ie me desfermine a pren
dre un parti miserable suiuant ce que ie uous
an ne mande quar il me fodret mourir de faint
ie trop de cher pour sela il fost si sest une ne
sesité se ran fermer ie uous e an uoié un manchon
le ternel uous conserue euous tienne an sa sainte
grase esuis auec respet uotre tres obeisante
fille eseruante Madelene de Solière
ie suis seruante tres eumble de mes chere niese
e de mon fils dieu les benise tous suson uous asure
de leur respet tueuse obeisanse elle fet san amiti
e a son frere e a ses cousine

Figure 4.1 Letter from Madelene de Solière to her Mother, undated, first page. Property of the author.

that she should be paid the original dowry amount of 12,000 *livres* once again, plus interest from the date of her husband's death in 1669.

In the factum they submitted to the court,[3] Marie de La Rochefoucauld and her sisters defended themselves against Madelene's demand that they pay her a replacement dowry by denying that they were Susanne Isle's heirs. What Marie de La Rochefoucauld and her sisters took possession of on March 8, 1677 was the estate of their deceased parents, not the few revenues that remained in the hands of Susanne Isle after she irrevocably gifted all her property to her daughter Marie in 1654. What she did have at her death had not devolved upon her granddaughters, for they had renounced any inheritance from her—driven to take this action, no doubt, by Madelene's suit itself. To make clear that not having inherited Susanne's assets, they were not liable for her debts, the La Rochefoucauld sisters gave Madelene all the personal property Susanne Isle left in Berneré at her death. Their hope must have been that if the judges were to find that Madelene had a just claim, they would also rule that it was Susanne from whom it was owed to her, so that all Madelene could collect would be the tiny amount of money and furnishings Susanne had when she died.

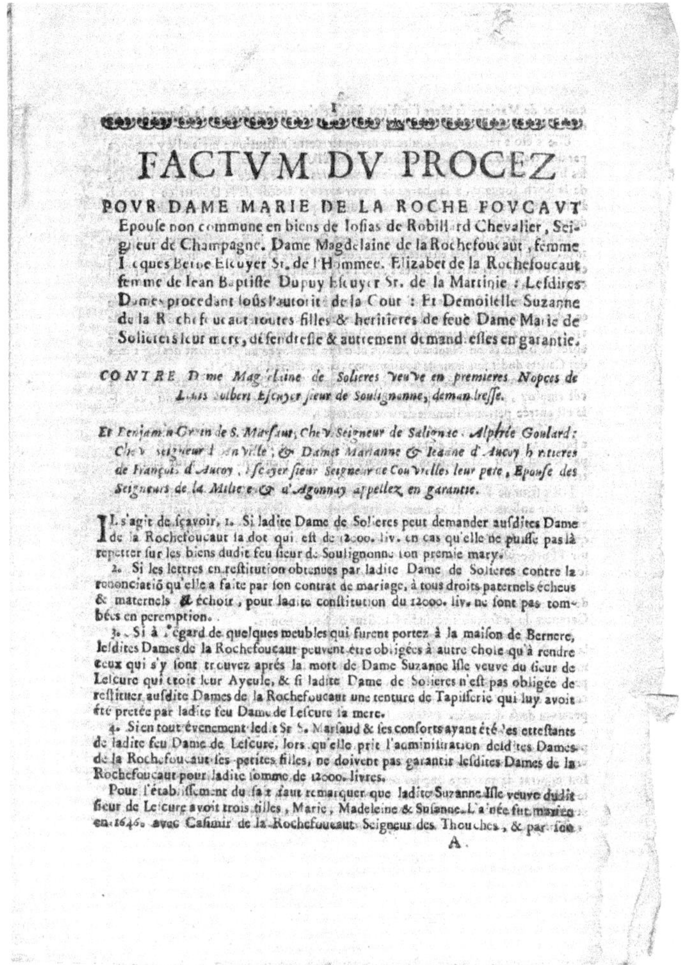

1

FACTVM DV PROCEZ

POVR DAME MARIE DE LA ROCHE FOVCAVT Epouſe non commune en biens de Ioſias de Robillard Chevalier, Seigneur de Champagne. Dame Magdelaine de la Rochefoucaut, femme Iacques Berne Eſcuyer Sr. de l'Hommee. Elizabet de la Rochefoucaut femme de Iean Baptiſte Dupuy Eſcuyer Sr. de la Martinie : Leſdites Dames procedant ſous l'autorité de la Cour : Et Demoiſelle Suzanne de la Rochefoucaut toutes filles & heritieres de feuë Dame Marie de Solieres leur mere, défendreſſe & autrement demanderesses en garantie.

CONTRE Dame Magdelaine de Solieres veuve en premieres Nopces de Louis Sulbert Eſcuyer ſieur de Soulignonne, demanderesse.

Et Benjamin Gruin de S. Marſaut, Chev. Seigneur de Salignac. Alphée Goulard: Chev. ſeigneur d'Anville; & Dames Marianne & Ieanne d'Aucoy heritieres de François d'Aucoy, Eſcuyer ſieur Seigneur de Couvrelles leur pere, Epouſe des Seigneurs de la Miliere & d'Agonnay appellez en garantie.

IL s'agit de ſçavoir, 1. Si ladite Dame de Solieres peut demander auſdites Dame de la Rochefoucaut la dot qui eſt de 12000. liv. en cas qu'elle ne puiſſe pas la repetter ſur les biens dudit feu ſieur de Soulignonne ſon premier mary.

2. Si les lettres en reſtitution obtenuës par ladite Dame de Solieres contre la renonciatiõ qu'elle a faite par ſon contrat de mariage, à tous droits paternels écheus & maternels à échoir, pour ladite conſtitution du 12000. liv. ne ſont pas tombées en peremption.

3. Si à l'égard de quelques meubles qui furent portez à la maiſon de Bernere, leſdites Dames de la Rochefoucaut peuvent étre obligées à autre choſe qu'à rendre ceux qui s'y ſont trouvez aprés la mort de Dame Suzanne Iſle veuve du ſieur de Leſcure qui étoit leur Ayeule, & ſi ladite Dame de Solieres n'eſt pas obligée de reſtituer auſdites Dames de la Rochefoucaut une tenture de Tapiſſerie qui luy avoit été pretée par ladite feu Dame de Leſcure ſa mere.

4. Si en tout évenement ledit Sr S. Marſaud & ſes conſorts ayant été les atteſtants de ladite feu Dame de Leſcure, lors qu'elle prit l'adminiſtration deſdites Dames de la Rochefoucaut ſes petites filles, ne doivent pas garantir leſdites Dames de la Rochefoucaut pour ladite ſomme de 12000. livres.

Pour l'établiſſement du fait faut remarquer que ladite Suzanne Iſle veuve dudit ſieur de Leſcure avoit trois filles, Marie, Madeleine & Suſanne. L'aînée fut mariée en 1646. avec Caſimir de la Rochefoucaut Seigneur des Thouches, & par ſon

A.

Figure 4.2 Factum du Procez pour Dame Marie de la Roche Foucaut. Property of the author.

Nor, the factum argued, could Madelene make a claim against the property the six La Rochefoucauld nieces inherited from their mother, for what their mother owed Madelene had been paid in full. After their parents' death, Susanne, as guardian of the six girls, had paid Madelene's dowry from their inheritances, thus satisfying the requirement that Marie de Solière as universal heir pay this sum to her sister Madelene. If Susanne acted improperly in her capacity as guardian and compensation was due for that, then the liability for damages should fall to those who were Susanne Isle's guarantors and advisors for the guardianship—those who vouched for her.[4] If Susanne was personally liable, Madelene should have to content herself with Susanne's small estate, which the sisters, by repudiating the inheritance, had already signed over to her.

Finally, Marie de La Rochefoucauld and her sisters held that if Madelene's dowry was not available to become her dower, it was the fault of Madelene and her husband. Madelene had simply mismanaged: "If the inheritance of the said Sieur de Soulignonne is insolvent, it can only be because the said Dame, the opposing party, has inappropriately initiated and pursued diverse lawsuits, has let the assets in the inheritance decline instead of safeguarding the properties, as she was responsible for doing, and has been allowed, by virtue of the favor she gained by converting, to skim off all the revenues of the estate of Soulignonne, for which without doubt the said Dames de La Rochefoucaut should not pay the price." To make this argument, the La Rochefoucauld sisters turned the arrow of blame against another of their kin: Jean Isle de Beauchesne. They entered into evidence the transaction of January 8, 1662 by which Madelene's husband and his sister authorized Jean Isle, their stepfather, to continue to handle their finances after they became adults, as he had done when they were minors.[5] They did this, the sisters' lawyer's annotation explained, to make it clear that Isle de Beauchesne was obliged to protect them. The proper targets for Madelene's suit were other family members and family friends, not Susanne Isle. Madelene herself, they pointed out, had seemed to recognize that Susanne was not responsible for her bankruptcy in that after Soulignonne was seized, Madelene went to court to appeal against the seizure but never made any such claim against Susanne.

On the contrary, "far from complaints against the said Lescure her mother, she expressed a thousand thanks to her in her letters." To show this, the La Rochefoucauld sisters' lawyer Dufaure de Lajarte entered into evidence the letter in which Madelene thanked her "very good mother," whom she called "a strong means for helping me pull myself out of the morass into which I have sunk." His purpose in making the submission is clear from the phrases he underlined in the text: "the extreme generosity and friendship you have for me. . . . My very good mother I found all my hopes on you. . . . All my life, good mother, I shall render you my humble obedience and recognize that I owe you everything."[6]

Dufaure de Lajarte's use of this evidence brought to the fore the ugly conflicts within the family, as did the rhetorical shaping of the factum prepared for Marie de La Rochefoucauld's case. The factum does not tell the story of a younger daughter given a lesser inheritance and sacrificed to an intrafamilial marriage for the sake of her cousins and to consequent poverty—the way Madelene might have related her own life—but of an overreaching daughter, a poor manager who squandered her inheritance, who concocted imaginary claims, was ungrateful for the repeated and generous assistance her mother

Susanne Isle gave her, and took advantage of her helpless elderly mother. Louis de Salbert and his wife Madelene, "taking advantage of the influence they had on the mind of the said Dame de Lescure, who was sixty-some years old and without anyone to lean on, obtained from her all the bonuses they wanted and her signature to them." The factum, then, employed two stereotypes of women: a wasteful woman driving her family into bankruptcy and a helpless old woman (which is unlike the picture of Susanne in other records). The factum's conclusion: nothing presented in the case "has given her grounds to demand a second dowry from the property Susanne Isle gifted to Marie de Solière and to ruin the La Rochefoucauld women on this pretext."

But Madelene had not exhausted her stratagems for recouping her finances from Isle resources. Sometime after 1681, she changed tactics. In addition to the still-pending suit for repayment of her dowry, she revived her claim, abandoned in 1669, against Susanne Isle's division of property among her three daughters. That is, Madelene asked for relief from the renunciation to inheritance she had made in 1654 and 1659, reviving the letters of restitution she had been granted by the Parlement of Paris in 1667 but had neglected to pursue. She now claimed that she had renounced under undue coercion. She also alleged undue coercion with regard to a second, smaller instance of disadvantaging to establish a pattern of deprivation. In 1649, Susanne Isle and Casimir de La Rochefoucauld made an agreement with the heirs of their neighbor the Sieur de Coulonge in which Susanne Isle acted as guardian for her two still-minor younger daughters, Madelene and Susanne de Solière. The agreement was that the 2,500 *livres* left by Coulonge as a legacy to Susanne Isle would be distributed to her three daughters in uneven shares: half to Marie, the eldest, a quarter each to the two younger.[7] This was consistent with the division Susanne Isle had made of her estate among her daughters at the time of her daughter Marie's marriage in 1646 and in retrospect equally unacceptable to Madelene.

The effect of Madelene's request for relief from her renunciation to inheritance, if granted, would be to give her a full *légitime*, a full one-third share of her parents' fortune, equal with her sisters Marie and Susanne, not limited to the settlement she had agreed to nor to the dowry she received in 1662. Madelene claimed that the 12,000 *livres* given to her by her mother as a dowry did not satisfy the obligation her sister assumed in 1654 to pay Madelene her share of the inheritance from her parents after their mother's death. These were two sums from two different payers. So Madelene stood again, she argued, where she had before 1654: entitled to her fully proportionate (1/3) *légitime* from the funds her sister had received as an inter vivos gift from their mother. With the death of her sister, the obligation passed to the sister's universal heir, Marie de La Rochefoucauld, from whom Madelene now claimed it.

This request for relief from her renunciation was a far more complex legal matter than her previous suit for a replacement dowry. It made explicit the grave danger that would have been clear to Marie de La Rochefoucauld from the outset of the legal contest: that what Madelene asked would effectively mean the transfer of Berneré to her. It could not be paid by Marie in any other way.[8] With Madelene's new claim to her *légitime*, Marie's hold on Berneré rested not merely on the legality of the dowry arrangements that Susanne Isle had made for Madelene in 1659 but on the justice of her decision to split the family inheritance into unequal portions for her daughters in 1646 and 1654. Not dowry law, then, but inheritance law came to center stage.

To this, Marie and her sisters made three responses. The first pointed to what would come to be called the statute of limitations on the letters of restitution granted in 1667. The *arrêt* of 1669 had ordered the parties to come plead their case, which Madelene never did. As Marie de La Rochefoucauld's factum pointed out, pursuit of letters of restitution expired if left in abeyance over three Parlementary sessions,[9] which had long passed. The factum also argued that there was no reason for releasing Madelene from responsibility for her renunciation: she had been an adult, aged twenty-seven, in 1659 (though she had been a minor in 1654), so she was responsible for the clauses in her marriage contract. Moreover, she personally signed the receipt for the dowry in 1662, when the sum promised in 1654 was paid, and in so doing she agreed to (or perhaps even requested herself) a change in the timing of the payment and in the uses prescribed. Her signature acknowledged receipt of the inheritance due her.

The third response from Marie de La Rochefoucauld and her sisters argued that the dowry payment made by Susanne Isle in 1662 was precisely the *légitime* owed to Madelene by their mother Marie de Solière. Susanne Isle had gifted her fortune to their mother and father irrevocably in 1654. She could not therefore have paid or have promised to pay Madelene a separate dowry, because she had no funds of her own. She paid the *légitime*/dowry from the deceased Marie de Solière's fortune. The dowry payments to Madelene de Solière in 1662 and to Susanne de Solière in 1663 fulfilled both women's *légitimes*, for in making those payments Susanne Isle was acting in her capacity as trustee of the funds she had given away in 1654, now that they had devolved, under her care, onto her six orphaned granddaughters.

The contest between Aunt Madelene and Marie de La Rochefoucauld played out, with increasing intensity and complexity, during the mid-1680s, precisely as the religious situation headed to its final and painful resolution. Madelene's suit began just as, in neighboring Poitou, the intendant Marillac implemented the first-ever dragonnades, which, copied around France, would be among the most effective means of persuading Protestants to abjure their heresy. It began just before the intendant and bishop visited the temple at Saint-Savinien, measured its proximity to the Augustinian abbey, and ordered it demolished. Madelene's hand was strengthened early on by her remarriage to Alexandre Roulin, Seigneur de La Mortmartin in Poitou, who was reputed to be quite rich. She moved to La Mortmartin to live with him there, and he became the strong hand in the case, acting as "legal representative both general and special for Dame Madelene de Solière his wife."[10] Marie's hand, by contrast, was weakened by her inability to realize from Susanne's debtors the funds assigned to her in both the morning and afternoon sessions in March 1677, and by her sisters' reluctance to rally to her side. Meeting on the afternoon of October 14, 1681 at La Petite Thibaudière near Saint-Savinien, Marie's four surviving sisters (without Marie present) hired the lawyer Dufaure de Lajarte to defend them in the case, agreeing to share with Marie the expenses incurred in the defense as well as the cost of any award assessed against her. The solidarity came from their shared recognition that the terms of the March 8, 1677 property division implicated them all in Madelene's putative claim if it should succeed. But Marie's sisters stated in the document setting up Dufaure de Lajarte's power of attorney that they were joining the defense after Marie threatened to take action against them.[11]

Might stresses among the sisters have involved an undercurrent of religious tension? At least one of the sisters was already a Catholic convert. La Petite Thibaudière was the Saint-Savinien home of Susanne Isle's cousin Elisabeth Isle, and Marie de La Rochefoucauld's sister Elisabeth also resided there. Sister Elisabeth abjured before Madelene's lawsuit even began, only months after Susanne Isle drew up her will. In the late fall of 1677, she, along with her cousin Elisabeth de Préault de La Thibaudière, traveled to Saint-Jean-d'Angély to take instruction at the Ursuline convent. Then, when "sufficiently instructed," the two young women made their abjuration on December 18 at the hands of a Jesuit priest in the Ursulines' chapel. Soon thereafter, Elisabeth de La Rochefoucauld, who had been baptized Protestant at Berneré, began to sign as a witness to the abjurations of others in Saint-Savinien's Catholic parish.[12]

For their part, Josias and Marie set to rearranging their financial affairs. First, they petitioned for a separation of their properties, which was granted by the royal authorities in Saint-Jean-d'Angély on November 14, 1682. Separating spouses' property was a relatively easy maneuver in France, compared, for example, to England, where there was no common law right to separate property or concept of lineage property. In England, "separate domicile was easier for women to obtain than separate property," whereas in France, petitions for property separations were almost always granted and separations of person or domicile rarely agreed to.[13]

Most often, property separations in France occurred because of the misbehavior of one spouse and were effected in adversarial court proceedings. When the debts run up by one spouse imperiled the other's possessions or threatened the family's subsistence, either spouse could petition for separation of property. But given the gender asymmetry in the control of property under normal conditions, it is not surprising that in practice the motivation for property separation was almost always the wife's fear that her husband was dissipating her assets or risked judicial seizure of his property. The effect of the property separation was to give the wife her dowry back: she could then control it and enjoy its income, though she still could not alienate it without special authorization by her husband during his lifetime or by a court judgment on her behalf. Separation could be quite threatening to a husband: being ordered at any given time to deliver her property back to her as liquid assets risked ruin for almost any husband. [14]

Why did Marie de La Rochefoucauld and Josias de Robillard separate their property? Could it be that Josias was spendthrift? It is hard to believe that he was a squanderer, given his own estate management, his careful organization of documents, and his financial actions. More likely the purpose in their separation was quite different: not an adversarial proceeding to wrest control from Josias but a mutually agreed reversal of the more common purpose, in order to safeguard his property from her creditors.

Then, as the threat from Madelene deepened, Josias and Marie, on April 26, 1683, went into Saint-Savinien, to their notary's study, and made a joint will.[15] Making a will is a more emotional experience than is often recognized. The tenor of a will's provisions can reveal a good deal to an attentive ear. In their will, Josias and Marie acknowledged "the great affection . . . a singular affection" that each had enjoyed from the other—Josias confessed "I have always loved her tenderly"—and their desire to be buried together, before turning to the disposition of their properties. Their religious clauses were marked by the spareness and reliance on family for which Protestant wills in this age were known. "We confide our Souls to God, our father and creator, and beseech him with all our strength, thoughts, and understanding, in the name and by the innocent merit of our sweet savior Jesus Christ his beloved son to pardon all our sins and offenses we have committed and might commit hereafter against his Divine Majesty, and that when it pleases him to separate our souls from our bodies, to place them in his holy paradise among the blessed, and after the glorious resurrection of our bodies on the last day to grant us the eternal happiness he promised for his beloved children." Burial of the first to die was left "to the discretion and good judgment of the survivor of us two, requiring only that it be done according to the practices observed in the R.P.R., which we have always professed"; they prayed their heirs "or those tending to our burials" to place the second to die next to the first "providing the place of our death is not so far away that transportation would be too difficult." They could scarcely have imagined what distance the coming years would place between them.

Marie's property declaration was one simple sentence: she wished Josias to enjoy all her property, movables and immovables, should she die first. Josias' clauses were more revealing of both the material and emotional situations in which they found themselves. First, he declared that if he died first, Marie was to have complete control over his property, including power to sell and power to withhold from any unworthy child, "without regard to any contrary custom or usage." His strictures here were strong: he wished there to be no restraints on her control, not even any requirement that she continually provide accountings of her use of property that was destined eventually for their children. Spouses were typically generous with each other in their wills. Still, Josias' giving Marie control of his property and power to decide how to split it among their children was not the only possible practice.[16] Josias' testamentary decisions showed his confidence in Marie.

Next, Josias declared that his property was to be safe from her creditors. Here was, no doubt, the real impulsion behind their recourse to the notary on this day. In a sense, this will was a parallel to their property separation and the inventory of their respective property holdings they drew up shortly after. Josias emphasized that the two sets of property were to be separate after his death as they had been held separate during his lifetime, "so that the creditors of my said wife, if any there be, may place no claims on the enjoyment of my said properties on the grounds that I have given them to her, for I have done so only with the express condition that the said creditors of my wife can have no more claim on them than they could have if the said properties had remained in my own possession." This, like the separation of property, was an obvious, and prudent, response to the pressure being placed on Marie's property by Madelene. There was an irony to it, though, for they themselves had, after all, been agents, in the case of the La Valade, of the catastrophe they were here trying to avoid for themselves. The La Valade debt they pursued from Madame de Chambon had come to her from her father in 1655, and because her assets and liabilities were held as community property with her husband, the debt ended up being paid by confiscation of her husband's estate.[17]

Other provisions that Josias inserted into his will offer a glimpse at the emotional toll exacted by the pressure from Madelene's suit. He developed at length, and in the most uncompromising of tones, the changes in provisions he wished to stipulate in the event that Marie remarried after his death. She would be required to give what she was exempted from submitting as a widow: an accounting within six months of her remarriage of the use she made of his property after his death. Thereafter, it should be considered as the children's property under guardianship. Most curiously, he "very expressly forbids and prohibits my male children from living with the man my said wife marries." They were to be put in boarding establishments or in the military or in some other situation appropriate to their quality, faculties, and ages. He "forbids with the same rigor, and annuls from this moment forward insofar as I can do so by paternal authority, all the agreements, conventions, or treaties of any nature whatsoever, whether direct or indirect without any exception, that my said male children may make with this husband of my said wife their stepfather." The daughters, having nowhere better to go, might stay with their mother in her second marriage.

Early modern husbands frequently made their widows' access to usufruct of their property contingent on her not remarrying, as a means of ensuring that the estate transmitted by the father could not be diverted into another household through the widow's remarriage. But why would Josias stipulate his sons' departure from the household? Stepparenting was very common in this period, and widows' marriage contracts frequently included the future husband's commitment to care for minor children of his wife's prior marriage.[18] Still, Josias may well have had particular reasons for concern about the perpetuation of his lineage and the vulnerability of sons upon the transfer of their mother's affection. He was witnessing the disintegration of a lineage—the descendants of Daniel Isle—and a disintegration caused at least in part by the absence of males. Moreover, he had witnessed what some would call the sacrificing of the young Louis de Salbert after his widowed mother remarried with Jean Isle de Beauchesne, who then controlled her children's finances. He surely knew other examples of such stepchild despoliation.

While the Champagné couple rearranged their finances through the separation of property and joint will, Marie was experiencing a third kind of challenge in addition to the religious and the financial—continuing childbirth. In the twenty years of marriage prior to her escape, she bore twelve children: four in the first five years of marriage, two in the second five-year period, three in the third, and three in the fourth. Except for the final birth interval of thirty-seven months and the unaccountably long thirty-five-month interval between children six and seven, her mean birth interval was a mere seventeen months.[19] When Aunt Madelene's lawsuit began in 1681, Marie was the mother of six living children, ranging in age from newborn to thirteen. She would bear another daughter in September 1682, just two months before she and Josias made their property separation. She would bear (and soon lose) a son, René-Casimir, in April 1684, just as the threat from Aunt Madelene took a turn for the worse.

In May 1684, one of Madelene's creditors, Claude de Belleville, Sieur de Coulon, filed suit in the Parlement of Paris claiming that Marie de La

Rochefoucauld and her sisters should pay him directly what Madelene owed him, since they owed Madelene money. Coulon's claim made it clear that the lawsuit of the impecunious Madelene for her inheritance exposed Marie de La Rochefoucauld to any and all of the persons to whom Madelene was a debtor. The Paris Parlement ordered the La Rochefoucauld women to provide a declaration of what they owed Madelene. So on May 18, 1684, Marie and her three surviving sisters, along with Josias, assembled at the Saint-Savinien office of the notary Bouyer to pursue their defense. The position they took was both substantive and procedural. Along with declaring that they were not debtors at all to Madelene, they claimed that if Coulon wanted to intervene, he could only do so where the case between them and Madelene was currently pending: at the Parlement of Bordeaux. They argued that he could not "draw the women involved out of their natural jurisdiction, for the purpose of making any declaration or affirmation of the claims and pretentions that they and the said Dame de Soulieres may have contested with each other."[20] And they hired a lawyer in Paris to carry their message to the Parlement and the plaintiff.

Marie gave birth to her last child, a daughter, on May 16, 1687. Three weeks later, on June 3, baby Marie-Thérèse was baptized in the Catholic parish church of Saint-Savinien by an Augustinian monk, in the absence of the local curé. Annet de La Martonie, a distant cousin by marriage on the Isle side from an old Catholic family, and Marie de Talleran de Grigneaux stood as godparents. Exceptionally, no one signed the parish register but the officiating monk. Did the father Josias or mother Marie attend the baptism of their only child born after the Revocation? Perhaps. Josias had seen all his older children baptized, and Catholic baptism was less traumatic for a Protestant family than other Catholic rites because it did not involve the Eucharist, which made the mass (and ceremonies like marriage that involved the mass) so offensive to Protestants. After the Revocation's closure of the last Protestant temples, Catholic baptism was the only way to establish a child's legal existence. But perhaps not. Parents usually did not attend forced baptism; some priests (though not the one who baptized baby Thérèse) stated the absence in the baptismal record, noting, for example: "The father of the infant did not wish to be at the baptism." Furthermore, "Thérèse" came neither from the repertoire of names used by the Robillard de Champagné nor from those adopted over and over again by the Isle. No name in the late years of the Catholic Reformation was more Catholic. One cannot imagine the Protestant Josias and Marie choosing that name for a baby they controlled.[21]

Twenty days later, Marie de La Rochefoucauld and her eldest son, Josias, were gone. Once she left, Josias had no claim on Berneré: his wife, who held the estate as separate lineage property, was a fugitive. Only the minor child, one month old, could be construed as having a legal claim to it. So on September

16, 1687, Josias turned over to agents of the crown the estate Susanne Isle had given Marie de La Rochefoucauld "forever" just ten years earlier. As was customary in such cases, the intendant appointed a caretaker for the property, a local named Rabillard, Sieur de La Bertramière (no relation to the Robillard). Josias continued to be involved in the working of the estate; evidently the crown took away control and authority but not management or even residence. Josias laid out funds for harvesting the grapes in the fall and pruning them in the winter, and paid for kindling to be used in the lord's oven. He distributed seed to the farmers and sharecroppers on the estate. But in the receipt he was given when he was reimbursed some 194 *livres* for these materials, the crown's agent pointed out that Josias had acted "on my orders."[22] It was only as guardian of the infant, who alone retained a claim on ownership of the estate, that Josias was permitted to continue to operate it.

Josias was still at Berneré on March 29, 1688, when he got his reimbursement from La Bertramière. But a week later, the authorities decreed a second, more serious de facto confiscation of Berneré. On April 8, the Parlement of Bordeaux issued an order, "sealed with yellow wax," demanding payment within a month of what Madelene de Solière claimed from Marie de La Rochefoucauld, acknowledging that Madelene's claim to the 12,000 *livres* had been granted by the letters of restitution in 1667. Paying was beyond Josias' power. On June 12, Madelene would go back to the Parlement complaining that Josias had not paid her, even though the requisite papers had been delivered to Berneré in such a fashion that he could not be unaware of the judgment. It seems Madelene did not know that weeks earlier Josias had left Berneré and two weeks after Madelene's complaint to Parlement, he would step into a new life—and early death—by joining Marie in Holland.[23]

Law or Favor? Religion? Gender?

How did Madelene do it? How did she succeed in using the arm of the law to overturn her mother's choices on disposal of the family estate? Was it favor or legal right that brought Berneré into her hands in opposition to the wishes that Susanne Isle stated clearly in her 1677 will? Did the concurrent religious conflict determine this result? Or did the law offer grounds for expropriating Marie de La Rochefoucauld's "estate of Berneré, which belongs to me"?

In the crucial decade of the 1680s, when pressure on Protestants was building across France, the competitors for Berneré faced each other across the religious divide. Sometime before February 1678, Madelene had converted from her family's religion to the king's, for at that date she—flatteringly described as "very respectable and very virtuous dame"—made her first appearance as godmother in the register of the parish church of Sainte-Geneviève in Soulignonne. A printed paragraph in the same parish register noted that on September 10, 1679, she gave the church the tabernacle on its main altar. From then on she appeared with some frequency in this Catholic record, often as godmother and occasionally as a sponsoring witness at abjurations of Protestants. In May 1682, when the Bishop of Saintes passed through Soulignonne and celebrated mass in the village church, he dined (as the parish register notes) at Madelene's seigneurial residence. The parish register records her second marriage with Roulin de La Mortmartin—this time authentic and blessed by the Church. No doubt as a sign of her distinction, the marriage was not celebrated by the mere local priest but by the curé of Notre-Dame-du-Puy in Saintes, who traveled out from the city by order of the bishop to bless the union. On September 9, 1685, at nearly the moment when Josias de Robillard was being pressured to abjure in Saint-Savinien, Madelene served as witness for a group renunciation of heresy by a dozen of her neighbors.

Susanne de Solière, Madelene's sister, had also become an active Catholic. On December 23, 1699, she and her husband, Louis de Lestang, would serve as godparents at the baptism of a new bell for the parish church in Saint-Aigulin, near Roche-Chalais on the Saintonge-Périgord border. Susanne de Solière's marriage, then, had circled her back, in new religious clothing, to the region where, a century earlier, her paternal grandfather had prospered with the Protestant forces in the Wars of Religion.

Marie de La Rochefoucauld, her sisters, and their descendants would charge that favor, not legal right, lay behind the decision to award Berneré to Madelene. Marie's factum claimed that Madelene was allowed to have the income of the estate "by virtue of the favor she gained by converting." When Marie's grandniece reopened the case in 1720, in an effort to regain Berneré, her factum would again charge openly that the authorities had promised Berneré to Madelene as her reward for converting.[24] Perhaps the authorities had done so: such quid pro quos were among the secret deals, pecuniary favors, and special dispensations that helped effect the Catholic "reconquest" of France. There is evidence from the courts themselves that justice was inflected by royal policy. First President Daulède of the Parlement of Bordeaux wrote to Châteauneuf after the Parlement condemned the pastor Vergniol to the galleys in perpetuity: "I must tell you that the proof was fragile and even defective on the main issue and yet the zeal of the judges bypassed the rules in order to make an example."[25]

There was reason for Protestants to suspect that the law itself and the authorities who applied it were tainted by religious bias. In 1679, shortly before Madelene filed her suit, the law courts in France were made all-Catholic and, as such, an arm of royal Catholic policy once again, as they had been during the Wars of Religion. Suspicion of royal justice had been a powerful sentiment among early French Protestants. One of the Reformers' first demands when war broke out in the 1560s was for impartial justice, a separate judiciary of and by Protestants, because they feared trials by Catholic judges. Precisely for this reason, the Edict of Nantes (Articles 30–65) set up new courts, the famous *Chambres de l'Edit* or *Chambres Mi-parties*—courts with a mixture of Catholic and Protestant judges—to hear cases involving Protestants in certain Parlements (including Bordeaux): "So that Justice be rendered and administered to our subjects without any suspicion, animosity or favor, that being one of the principal means for keeping them in peace and concord."[26] But the Parlements generally—strongly Gallican, anti-Protestant, and purged of Protestant members in their other chambers—resented the biconfessional courts, and they were abolished in July 1679 as part of the run-up to the Revocation.[27] Josias and Marie had to defend their possession of Berneré before Catholic judges, while Madelene, their adversary, had embraced the judges' religion.

Marie and Josias may well have seen this change in the judicial system as making it more difficult for them, as religious dissenters, to secure justice from the legal system even before their religion became illegal. In 1683, the Parlement of Bordeaux, before which the Madelene-versus-Marie dispute was pending, sent one of its judges into Saintonge to investigate, and remedy, alleged infractions by Protestants against royal edicts and declarations on religion. And this time the investigation was unilateral: there was no countervailing Protestant commissioner such as Isaac Isle had been in the 1660s. The face of justice in practice, then, was identified with hostility toward Protestants. This magistrate, Jean Duvigier, Baron de Saint-Martin de La Monzie-Saint-Laurent, arrived in Saintonge in September 1683 and soon proved himself "the most ardent persecutor of Huguenots." He ordered the ministers and consistories to provide an enumeration of their assets, as a preliminary to confiscating them, and eventually closed the remaining temples in the province. In doing so, he reversed the work of Isaac Isle two decades earlier. In Cozes, for example, when Colbert de Terron ordered demolition of the local temple in 1664 as violating the Edict of Nantes, Isaac Isle countered his arguments and succeeded in keeping the temple open. Without a Protestant commissioner to restrain his hand, Duvigier walled up the Cozes temple, in anticipation of its demolition, banished its pastor from the kingdom, and imprisoned the minister who claimed to succeed him.[28]

In the minds of Josias' and Marie's Protestant neighbors, what this magistrate from Bordeaux brought to Saintes was injustice: "iniquitous and tyrannical procedures, imprisonments, plunder, in a word all the unprecedented assaults by this alien commission." A petition sent to the king in July 1684 by the Protestants of Saintes laid out their "grievances against all the initiatives of the Sieur Duvigier, counselor in the Parlement of Bordeaux, who, on the pretext of the commission he claimed to have from the said Parlement, used a great number of irregular and violent procedures . . . under the appearance of justice." The Parlement itself was deaf to their appeals. "Petitioners can have no hope of justice from the local judges or from the Parlement of Bordeaux."[29] Indeed, that very month, Duvigier was advanced to a presidency in the Parlement, and it was the Parlement that would close the Saintes temple by its order on February 14, 1685, acting on "the criminal procedure adopted by the Sieur du Vigier, counselor of the King in the Court." The Protestants of Saintes were forced to "have recourse to Your Majesty, appealing to his justice and his goodness." They asked, as a remedy, that the organs of royal justice once again become biconfessional: "that he name two commissioners in the province of Saintonge, one Catholic and the other of the R.P.R., for receiving the grievances of the supplicants and those that might be made against them, to give their judgment, subject to appeal to Your Majesty and to his Council, forbidding the lieutenant-general of Saintes, the Parlement of Bordeaux, and all other judges to take cognizance of them on pain of invalidation, nullification, three thousand *livres* fine, and all expenses, damages, and interest, and the supplicants will continue their prayers for the health and prosperity of Your Majesty."[30]

Duvigier's actions alone would have sufficed to lead Protestants to conclude that justice had been contaminated. But from their perspective Duvigier stood for something even worse. Duvigier, the Catholic enforcer, was a former Protestant, newly converted. His great-grandfather had been a Protestant minister at Saint-Jean-d'Angély around the turn of the century, and his great-uncle, likewise a pastor in Saint-Jean from 1609 to 1667, appeared often as guest preacher in Saint-Savinien's temple. In May 1645, the young judge himself had stood with the wife of Charles de Villedon (Marie de La Rochefoucauld's aunt) as godparent for a son of the Seigneur de Champfleury, and in November 1647 he returned to do the same for the next son. He was linked by marriage to Josias, whose first cousin Judith and aunt Louise married into this Duvigier family. In the 1660s, Duvigier had even been Isaac Isle's counterpart for Protestants in Guyenne, alongside the intendant Hotman for the Catholics. As late as 1675, he had been a representative to the Synod of Basse-Guyenne, and until his conversion in 1680 he held Protestant services in his château. Duvigier had been in the now-abolished *Chambre de l'Edit* as a Protestant magistrate, in a seat he inherited in 1673 from his father and grandfather. Local Protestants, who knew that the office in the *Chambre de l'Edit* "had entered their family as recognition for the merit of a Saintongeais minister and upon the recommendation of the Temples in this province, could not deplore vehemently enough his becoming the destroyer of the same churches to which his family owed in part the [judicial] robe he wore."[31]

Gossip recorded in 1688 by the famous Protestant former officeholder in La Rochelle Abraham Tessereau charged that Duvigier lacked the probity of his ancestors. He was vain and ambitious: "Witness the haughtiness with which he treated the Reformed and their consistories, how he claimed they should call him *My Lord*." His conversion was mercenary: "Gambling was his great passion; he lost a lot, so it was said everywhere when he changed religion that he was thinking of covering his losses thereby, in hopes that the King would reward his change, for he changed at a time when conversions were being bought." The reward he reaped included "a considerable sum," which he squandered at the gaming tables, but also the office of president in the Parlement by virtue of which he was persecuting his former coreligionists in Saintonge. Indeed, when the Bordeaux magistrates met to compose and approve a letter to the chancellor suggesting ways he might enhance the prestige (and price) of their judgeships, they held up as a precedent for such a favor "the one obtained by the Sieur Duvigier in favor of his change of religion."[32]

Figure 4.3 Caricature portrait of Jean Duvigier, from *Les Héros de la Ligue: Ou, La procession monacale. Conduitte par Louis XIV, pour la conversion des protestans de son royaume* (Paris [Holland]: Chez père Peters à l'enseigne de Louis le Grand, 1691). Courtesy of the Department of Special Collections, Stanford University Libraries.

Duvigier was so notorious that he took his place among *Les Héros de la Ligue* (*The Heros of the Ligue*). This lampoon, published in 1691, contained a satirical poem entitled "Sonnet. Response of the Refugees to the Persecutors" and twenty-four caricature portraits of Catholic personages prominent in enacting or enforcing the Revocation of the Edict of Nantes, including Louis XIV, Bishop Bossuet, Louvois, and Madame de Maintenon. Each portrait was accompanied by an insulting verse. The one dedicated to Duvigier summed up his former coreligionists' sense of him as a man of injustice. "Du Vigier, Counselor in the Parlement of Bordeaux, who lost at gambling/all that he had gained against the Protestants./'The Huguenots made me one of their Commissioners,/I turned my back on them and from their defender,/I suddenly became their unjust oppressor,/And in that way, but for gambling, I would have made my fortune.' "[33]

Jurisprudence of the Parlement of Bordeaux

There was, then, immediate reason for Marie de La Rochefoucauld and her allies against Aunt Madelene's offensive to suspect that the law to which they would be subjected and the authorities who would apply it had been biased against them by religious partisanship, even in cases that, like Madelene's lawsuit, did not concern religious questions directly. At a minimum, their perception of contaminated justice may have helped them decide to emigrate even before the court's decision was handed down. But did the Parlement discriminate against Marie because of her Protestantism, rewarding Madelene for her conversion? Without direct records of the case,[34] the court's motives cannot be known. But the law itself can be analyzed as to whether it offered grounds for the decision that was made: that is, whether the decision in Madelene's favor can be accounted for by the provisions of jurisprudence and legal practice alone, without intrusion of religious partisanship.

The inheritance law that prevailed where Madelene de Solière lived and filed her lawsuit was the Roman law–influenced jurisprudence of the Parlement of Bordeaux. Its provisions could be strikingly different from those prevailing in areas of customary law in Western and Northern France—even divergent from the written (Roman) law followed in the neighboring jurisdiction of the Parlement of Toulouse. As Voltaire famously quipped, "So it is when traveling post to post in this kingdom; you change jurisprudence as often as you change horses."[35] Frequently, historians generalize about "French" law or "French law's" treatment of women on the basis of Parisian or Northern customary law alone. But the outcome for Madelene de Solière and Marie de La Rochefoucauld can be assumed to be a function of place—of Saintonge, not of "France"—of where they were located in the mosaic described by Voltaire. A view from the provinces offers an important corrective to the picture of women's condition in early modern France.

A basic geography of inheritance practices would divide France into two northern regions of provincial customary laws (*coutumes*), specifically Paris and the West (Normandy and Brittany), and the southern region in which Roman law prevailed. These three regions established three different ways of transmitting property based upon three different conceptions of family in three different socioeconomic milieus. In very broad terms, the three legal regimes approached inheritance as follows.[36]

The regime of the Paris *coutumes* tended toward equality in inheritance—it admitted no primogeniture, for example—but stopped short of mandating complete equality. Individual children could be given a "portion," either upon marriage or upon leaving home; this practice provided parents some limited discretion as to the size of inheritance each child would receive and the degree of equality among their children. At the death of the parents, the family pot was to be divided equally among those not already portioned. Children already portioned could not also be heirs but could choose whether to keep the portion they had been given and be excluded from further inheritance or return the portion to the family pot and receive an equal share of the combined legacy. Underlying this inheritance regime was a vision of the family as the household: the goal was to provide adequate resources for multiple successor households, rather than to keep the now-defunct family's holding intact for the lineage. As such, it reflected the precocious emergence of nuclear families as the primary social cell in this area of increasingly dominant towns and market economies. With respect to women, the Paris *coutume* is usually seen as unfavorable because it permitted disinheritance of the daughter; in practice, her dowry came to be treated as a nonreturnable provisioning that excluded her from the ultimate division of the family pot. She was "married off and no more was said about her."[37]

In the *coutumes* of the West (Normandy and Brittany), equality was the bedrock principle of property transmission. Any portions distributed before the parents' death must be returned at their death, to be distributed in equal shares. Neither parental wills nor heirs' choices could alter postmortem distributions: "The Normans killed the father. . . . *After me the equal sharing.*" The underlying concern here was not with the household but with individuals, principally males—with perpetuating "a superior class of free, independent men." It has been suggested that the "formidable egalitarian traditions" of this customary inheritance regime were "bearers of modernity": a source of the individualistic demands for equality that eventually, in the Revolution, toppled hierarchies. If so, it bore seeds of a modernity unfavorable to women, for in parts of the West—notably in Normandy—equality was only for males; daughters' portions did not return: they would have only their dowry and not share in the ultimate division of the estate.[38]

By contrast, the *coutumes* and Roman law prevailing in the South enabled, even encouraged, inequality, in the interest of preserving the holding intact for the benefit of the lineage, rather than for the household or the individual. These strongly inegalitarian inheritance regimes used the *préciput* and the power of the written will to concentrate property—not necessarily in the hands of the eldest male but in the hands of the heir chosen by the parent. There was no forced return as in the West, nor option for return as in Paris; one could both receive an inter vivos portion and inherit at the parent's death. Great discretion was afforded the parent, especially "the formidable figure of the sovereign father, so dear to jurists influenced by Roman law."[39] The concern was to preserve family property intact from generation to generation, reflecting the continuing importance of extended kin and the desire to keep lineage property in the hands of descendants who resided on that land. Yet even here there were limits on the extent of inequality among siblings; this was not England, where the power of the father over inheritance arrangements was virtually unlimited and total disinheritance his prerogative.[40] Every child had a legal claim on a fraction of the family fortune (a *légitime*). Here, therefore, more strongly than in the West or in Paris, women were entitled to a share of the inheritance. But the desire to concentrate property established hierarchies of gender and birth order that generally diminished women's interests, along with those of younger sons.

It was within this last inheritance regime that Madelene de Solière pressed her claims against Marie de La Rochefoucauld: her claim to repayment of her dowry and her claim to be released from the renunciation of future inheritance by which she had agreed to forgo her equal share in her mother's estate.

Madelene's dowry claim was a demand that she be paid a second time the dowry of 12,000 *livres* that her mother had given her in 1662. On the face of it, the claim was outrageous: families carefully calculated dowry amounts according to what they could afford to pay once, not twice. In any of the three law regimes outlined above, the dowry—paid once—might lawfully be all a daughter would receive. Yet three provisions of the Roman law in southern France opened the possibility of a second dowry: the daughter's entitlement to a dowry, legal protections for the dowry capital during the marriage, and the ongoing responsibility of the parents for the long-term solvency of the dowry. Madelene's case may have fit one or more of those provisions.

A dowry was an entitlement of daughters in the Roman-law south. In Paris and the West, parents were not obliged to give a dowry. "Don't give a dowry if you do not wish to" went the customary maxim of Paris. Norman custom asserted the same freedom to withhold dowry: "the father and mother can give their daughter movables without legacies or legacies without movables, and if nothing has been given to her, then nothing shall she have." But in Roman law areas, parents were so obligated, unless the daughter had proven herself morally unworthy or had married without consent. The entitlement had a moral basis, according to the Parlement of Bordeaux: it was "founded . . . on natural law, on the duty that nature imposes on the father to raise and set up his children, on the utility of the dowry for the family."[41]

The law provided elaborate protections for women's dowries, once paid, in women's own interest: "A woman dowered, a dowry protected." It was true that dowry funds were paid directly to the husband at the time of the wedding and that during the marriage he had control of them. Income from the dowry capital, whether real estate or movables, was his to enjoy. He could use this revenue to pay his own debts or as collateral for new ones, and his creditors could claim this revenue for his personal debts, even those he contracted before he received the dowry. But if the husband could manage his wife's dowry property and spend its revenues, he was also obliged to preserve intact the property itself—movable as well as immovable. The husband could not alienate the assets in her dowry without her consent, nor borrow against them or pay his debts from the capital of the dowry even with her consent. More specifically, a provision of Roman law in force down into the seventeenth century called the Velleien incapacity (or simply the Velleien) prohibited women from alienating—or agreeing to their husband's alienating—their own property for payment of the husband's debts. It, then, guaranteed the integrity of the dowry not only from a husband's depredations but also from a wife's agreeableness and weakness. In December 1686, an act in the Bordeaux Parlement stipulated "That during the marriage, the husband and wife cannot, either together or separately, make any agreement that might compromise the dowry." The husband retained his control over the dowry only so long as he was solvent. As soon as he risked falling into poverty, the wife could claim her dowry back from him.[42]

There were two reasons for this restriction on alienation of dowry assets. The properties a bride brought in dowry were intended to support the life of the spouses together and the well-being of the next generation. In this respect, the bride's dowry was to replace (or, hopefully, more than offset) what had already been lost, or would in the future be lost, in payouts for the dowries of the groom's sisters, so that the new couple's financial standing would be at least as good as his parents' had been. Moreover, the dowry was to become her dower. When she was widowed, she was entitled to take back her dowry property clear of the debts and liabilities her husband contracted during the marriage. So when Madelene's husband died, she had a claim on his estate for restitution of her dowry, and the law gave her claim priority ahead of his other creditors to whom he became indebted after he received her dowry funds.[43]

After Louis de Salbert, Sieur de Soulignonne died, Madelene did, in fact, try to recover financially by reclaiming her dowry directly from the remaining Soulignonne assets. Other noblewomen in the neighborhood succeeded in recovering their dowries free and clear of their late husband's debts. In 1678, Susanne Gombaud, widow of the Seigneur de Thézac, sued successfully for preferential access to his assets as a means of repossessing her 30,000-*livre* dowry. In 1681, Marie Gombaud, widow of François de La Rochefoucauld, Seigneur de Roissac, after marrying René de Culant, godfather at Le Douhet in 1684 for the newborn René-Casimir de Robillard, negotiated an agreement on the subject of her dower with others in the La Rochefoucauld family. The widow of the Isle cousin Frédéric Gommier de Frégonnière would negotiate a partial restitution of her dowry from the nephew and niece who were his heirs.[44]

Madelene de Solière, however, proved unable to collect her dower from her husband's assets, probably because they were attached by creditors whose claims antedated Madelene's marriage in 1659 and the payment of her dowry in 1662. Such preexisting debts had, after all, been mentioned in her marriage contract. The sister of Louis de Salbert's father, Madame de Boisroux, was already contesting her share of the Salbert inheritance before Madelene's marriage, and as late as 1693 Madame de Boisroux still held a judicial seizure on Soulignonne that Madelene could not overcome.[45] So instead, Madelene de Solière struck at members of her own family rather than at her late husband's.

A third provision of the Roman law assigned parents ongoing responsibility for the long-term solvency of the dowry and obliged them to replace any dowry that was lost to their daughter. An attestation in a 1691 case before the Bordeaux Parlement stipulated that if a husband were paid a dowry that was destined by the terms of the marriage contract for a specified purpose but alienated the funds in some other way, those who provided the dowry funds in the first place "will be held responsible for the insolvency of the husband, and in this case the wife is legally entitled to oblige them to pay a second time, despite the payment made to the husband." Likewise, if a widowed daughter had lost the dowry paid in her first marriage, the parents or surviving parent or other heir were obliged to constitute a new dowry for her remarriage. Such expectations of dowry repayment indicate how firm, under written law, was the daughter's entitlement to a dowry and to protection of the dowry once paid.[46]

At a minimum, then, the widowed Madelene could stake a claim against her mother, who had constituted her first dowry, in anticipation of her remarriage to Roulin de La Mortmartin. But there was a deeper problem than the loss by mismanagement of funds meant for Madelene's long-term support.

Given the law's care to protect the dower rights of married women, the very terms of Madelene's first marriage contract could well seem out of line. Her dowry, as specified in her marriage contract, would be used to pay debts of the Salbert family and the dowries/*légitimes* of Salbert's siblings. That is, it would pass through her husband's hands into someone else's, leaving him with no increase in wealth and no assets earmarked for her future dower. When he died, his estate no longer contained her property and was still riddled with debts. The law would have allowed Madelene to renounce her husband's inheritance and sue his estate for her dower, but doing so would have forced the sale of Soulignonne, thus depriving her son of his patrimony.

Madelene's marriage contract, then, seemed to violate the Velleien. The only exception to the Velleien prohibition on using dowry assets to pay the husband's debts was when "the obligation is obviously, in its effect, advantageous to the woman." Susanne Isle may have persuaded her kin and advisors in 1659 that the arrangement was favorable to Madelene. Or she and they may have been responding to the uncertainty of the Velleien's application in her day. The Velleien had never been universally observed. Some regions, such as Toulouse, rejected it entirely, allowing women to obligate themselves for their husbands. And women quite commonly renounced this protection by putting into a particular contract or into their marriage contract a clause renouncing the benefit of the Velleien. Moreover, the Velleien had been abolished by a Declaration of Henri IV in August 1606, and several ordonnances and declarations of Louis XIV extended this abolition, thereby authorizing women to obligate their dowry property during their marriage, on the grounds that "the liberty to mortgage one's own property 'is more in keeping with civil society and more favorable to family affairs.'" But this abolition of the Velleien had never been registered in the Bordeaux Parlement, keeping the Velleien in force there.[47]

It may be that the Bordeaux Parlement invoked the Velleien as grounds for paying Madelene a second dowry. A second aspect of her first marriage may also have inclined the Bordelais judges to decide in her favor. Hers was an intralineal marriage, matching Madelene with the son of a woman, Léa de Bessay, who, when widowed, remarried with Madelene's cousin Jean Isle. The infusion of dowry funds from Susanne Isle to bolster the shaky finances of the Salbert—the family of Léa de Bessay's first husband—could look like taking advantage of Madelene to free Léa de Bessay's considerable assets for inheritance by the Isle lineage. Both regional jurisprudence and royal policy frowned upon financial arrangements that moved assets from a first to a second marriage when there were children of the first. In Saintonge, Saint-Jean-d'Angély, and some other parts of the jurisdiction of the Parlement of Bordeaux, a remarrying widow was obliged to create a reserve for the children of the first marriage. Furthermore, a royal edict of July 1560 constrained what the remarried widow with children from a previous marriage could give to her subsequent husband.[48] Though the letter of the law did not precisely invalidate the way Madelene de Solière was treated in her intralineal first marriage, it is not impossible that the spirit underlying the regulation of the remarrying widow's assets might have combined, in Madelene's favor, with the laws providing for a second dowry.

In a similarly unexpected way, Madelene had the law on her side when she claimed she should have enjoyed an equal share in her mother's estate, rather than merely a fixed sum of 12,000 *livres* in dowry. Understanding this requires a look into the law governing renunciations of future inheritance.

In 1654 and again in 1659, Madelene de Solière renounced her rights to inherit paternal and maternal property, movable and immovable. In return, she secured for herself an inheritance of 12,000 *livres*. In the first agreement, she renounced in favor of her older sister Marie; in the second, at the time of her first marriage in 1659, she reaffirmed her renunciation, but that time, because of the death of her sister Marie, "in favor of her nieces, daughters of the said late [Marie de Solière]." Within a few years of marrying and receiving her dowry, however, Madelene appealed to Louis XIV for release from her renunciation of future inheritance. She was entitled to do so. Subjects who claimed to have good reason to be relieved from some engagement they had made—whether a contract or other legal act—could request letters of restitution from the king. A successful restitution would reinstate the situation that prevailed before the renunciation (or other contract) had been signed, including, when renunciation was being annulled, reinstating the appellant's entitlement to a *légitime*. When the voided contract involved income-generating assets, the income during the time of illicit possession had to be handed over to the legitimate owner.[49] The claim for release from her renunciation that Madelene pressed against Marie and Josias after her mother's death was a reprise of the request she made earlier and did not follow up on.

Renunciation was a bargain between parent and child by which the child (minor or adult) agreed to cede to another heir (usually a sibling) all claims on the family fortune other than a sum specified in the renunciation document that would replace the *légitime* and be paid during the parent's lifetime, usually upon the child's marriage. At the time of Madelene's original renunciation, the practice was new to the Southwest, and it entailed a break with both the provisions for inheritance in Roman law and those in the *coutumes*.[50] Roman law had not permitted advance settlement of inheritance because the amount of the *légitime*—an entitlement reckoned as a given fraction of the parents' estate—could not be calculated before the death of the parent. The new practice of renunciation of future inheritance overcame this prohibition, in the interest of earlier settlement of family fortunes. A child would be permitted to agree to a specified sum perhaps years before the estate-holder's death, despite its being impossible to say whether the sum settled upon was identical to what would eventually have accrued as a *légitime*.

As for the *coutumes*, the means they offered for concentrating the family fortune in the next generation was testamentary exclusion: total disinheritance, without cause, of children other than the heir chosen by the testator. The practice of exclusion had previously prevailed in the jurisdiction of the Parlement of Bordeaux and was the most rigorously unfavorable to daughters of any inheritance system. It came as close as any French inheritance regime to the "extreme testamentary freedom" of English fathers.[51] The new practice of renunciation differed in that there was no unilateral exclusion by the parent or other legator but rather a quid pro quo by which a child (minor or adult) received some specified payment from the family estate. In its greater inclusiveness, renunciation was more favorable to women than customary exclusion had been. Perhaps because the very term "renunciation" draws attention to what is given up in the act, obscuring the fact that the reciprocal gain in the exchange was a share of the wealth for the daughter(s), this comparative favorability of renunciation toward women has been widely misunderstood.[52] Overall, renunciation served to promote concentration of the patrimony in the next generation by allowing nonrenouncing siblings to claim a greater share of the family fortune than allowed under the regime of the *légitime*, without resorting to the harshness of customary exclusion.

Madelene's petition to the king has not survived, so the causes she alleged for rescinding her renunciation are lost. Madelene's age when she first renounced, seventeen, would not in itself have been a presumption for annulment. True, "the infirmity of their age" made minors incapable of decision-making; this was why minors were given guardians. But minors could make binding commitments and would only be released from them if damaged by them.[53] The probable grounds for Madelene's appeal and eventual success on the issue of renunciation lie more deeply in the ambiguities and intricacies of the jurisprudence of the Parlement of Bordeaux, which was only beginning to become clear in the decades of Madelene's renunciation and subsequent suit against Marie de La Rochefoucauld. Renunciation came into use in the Southwest before the supporting jurisprudence was fully developed, and numerous aspects of the new legal provisions were unsettled right down into the eighteenth century. The law of renunciation was—in the words of one jurist in 1679—"one of the most disputed at the bar." The lack of a body of coherent legal theory meant that cases arising from its use could be variously adjudicated depending upon the court hearing the case and the discretion of its judges.[54]

Susanne Isle unwittingly played into those unsettled questions by the way she arranged her daughter's renunciation. It is unclear how familiar Susanne was with the practice in the 1650s or how well advised she was by a lawyer about its complexities and its risks. She may or may not have been concerned about those, for arrangements enacted before a notary could often skirt the letter of the law and yet succeed in structuring experience as the maker intended, so long as no one contested them in court.[55] Susanne may simply have followed the lead of friends and advisors. One of Susanne's three advisors when she assumed guardianship of her granddaughters used renunciation himself to concentrate his legacies to his three daughters in much the same way Susanne did—and just as much in tension with the law. Benjamin Green de Saint-Marsault had his second daughter renounce her inheritance from her parents in return for a fixed dowry. In so doing, she allowed her older sister and younger sister to split the remainder evenly, the two of them together receiving four times as much as she. But she never complained as Madelene did—indeed, after her father died in 1688, she averred in a notarized document that she "was content" and repeated her renunciation.[56]

In five respects, any one of which might have offered grounds for nullification, Susanne Isle's compliance with the requirements of renunciation was tenuous at best. First, Susanne had her daughter Madelene renounce a decade before her marriage, by a separate act before a notary, whereas renunciation was normally accomplished as part of the marriage contract, in order to associate the husband in the renunciation.[57] The key consideration was that the renunciation needed to be close in time to the payment of the quid pro quo (usually the dowry), to assure expeditious receipt of the benefit by the renouncer. A second anomaly in Susanne's arrangements concerned the timing of Madelene's renunciation vis-à-vis her father's death. The practice was understood to be a renunciation of future inheritance, and so it could not be made after the death of a parent. Since her father had died more than a decade earlier,[58] the status of Madelene's renunciation vis-à-vis his property interest in Berneré was at best unclear.

A third anomaly was that Madelene's renunciation occurred so far ahead of the death of Susanne Isle. Division of the inheritance three decades before the parent's death opened uncertainties that may well have come to fruition in Madelene's case. If too great a disparity developed over time between the share the child would have received at the parents' death and the inheritance she received earlier through renunciation—either because the family fortune had increased after her marriage or because the number of her siblings had been reduced by death—then she could challenge the parents' wills upon their death by requesting release from renunciation.[59] A fourth weakness in Susanne's settlement with Madelene was—like the three already noted—an issue of timing.

One rule universally agreed upon was that renunciation was valid only if the beneficiary of the renunciation survived to the time when the quid pro quo (in most cases, including Madelene's, this meant the dowry) was constituted. If the beneficiary died before the dowry was paid, the renunciation—now deprived of its beneficiary—became null. And the beneficiary of Madelene's renunciation, her sister Marie de Solière, died before the payment of Madelene's dowry.

Still, would not Marie de Solière's six daughters, her heirs, succeed her as beneficiaries of Madelene's renunciation? This question raises the fifth, most damaging but also most interesting, anomaly in Madelene's renunciation, which concerned the gender politics of renunciation. To a man, jurists agreed that the purpose of renunciation was to consolidate a family's wealth, especially its landholdings, in the hands of a male heir. Male inheritance, the jurists agreed, was the very raison d'être of renunciation: "for conserving the name and dignity of families, which is conserved by males." "Renunciation by daughters is intended to serve the interests of males." "It being obvious that the sole reason and motive of the statute is the conservation of families by giving the property to the males and depriving of it the daughters, who would carry it to a different family." "Political considerations primarily were behind this innovation; preference for males was deemed essential for sustaining the state."[60] So while both females and males could renounce, they could do so only for the benefit of a male. Neither females nor males could make an act of renunciation directly in favor of a female, "which entirely overturns the natural order." "Renunciation by a daughter is null if there are only daughters at the time of the renunciation and at the time of the inheritance, because [renunciation] was introduced only to favor males and to support families."[61] So there could be no renunciation when there were no males. In other words, a family that had "fallen into distaff," like the Isle and Solière, could not exercise renunciation. Amid all the myriad uncertainties of interpretation and practice, this was agreed upon as clear.

In Distaff: A Mother, A Daughter

So how was it that Susanne Isle predicated her entire inheritance strategy upon the renunciations of two daughters in favor of a third? Renunciation had not been used in previous Isle generations. Susanne's parents used the customary division among their five daughters: preciputary advantage to the eldest and then equal division of the remainder.[62] Nor would the following generation—the six La Rochefoucauld granddaughters—be asked to make a renunciation. For some reason, Susanne innovated with her children—that middle generation of the three "in distaff." There were ways of dealing with distaff situations, ways of passing inheritance to daughters safely. But Susanne elected to use a new legal device—renunciation—in ways not recognized by its jurisprudence. Susanne seems to have been trying to make inheritance gender-neutral: to set up her first child just the way an eldest son was normally treated and to get renunciations from her younger daughters just as daughters normally deferred to their brothers: with the lion's share, including all the land (in this case Berneré), to one and less-than-proportional shares in cash to the others.

But Susanne faced a particular difficulty in doing so, a difficulty for which she likely thought renunciation was the remedy. Susanne's arranging renunciations by two of her daughters in favor of the third was presumably not simply a matter of personal favoritism. Certainly many people were less than fond of Madelene, as is clear in the Soulignonne parish register and as Madelene confesses in her letters to her mother. A more likely motivation was the desire to pass the family seigneury, Berneré, to the next generation intact. Doing so under the customary inheritance laws of Saintonge was not always easy. The fewer assets parents held other than the seigneury, the less able they would be to pass it intact to a single heir—unless they resorted to exclusion of the other heirs. Susanne's parents had had such extensive land holdings and cash assets—derived from the substantial inheritances both Daniel Isle and his wife enjoyed—that they could divide their legacies according to the *coutumes* without having to split up or sell the principal seigneury, Forgette. Except for the portion carved out as Berneré for Susanne Isle and Jean de Solière, Forgette passed intact to the eldest of the five daughters, and the other four (including Susanne) got other lands and cash, in conformity with the system of *préciput*. Later, the six La Rochefoucauld sisters would be able to inherit in the same way because Casimir de La Rochefoucauld brought many pieces of land with him into the marriage, which could go to the younger five daughters without compromising Berneré. But in the middle generation the disposition of resources was different, and Susanne may well have been unable to accomplish what her parents and her daughter Marie de Solière did. Berneré was a handsome holding, but Susanne Isle and Jean de Solière did not have a great deal more. Admitting all three of their daughters to the inheritance through the customary division would have meant breaking up or selling Berneré. So Susanne's case illustrates the problems created for modest noble families by inheritance regimes that assumed all children would inherit.

It is difficult to resist the tantalizing counterfactuals that Susanne Isle's case inspires within this gendered inheritance system. If Marie de Solière and Madelene de Solière had been males and their sister Susanne had renounced in Marie's favor, Marie's death would have given her inheritance (including Berneré) to Madelene as a male, because, as females, all six of Marie's children would have been ineligible to benefit from a renunciation. Instead, as Susanne designed her property division, Madelene was expected to watch from the margins as her parents' property passed to the daughters of her deceased sister.

By 1677, when she made her final property division, Susanne Isle may have been more alert to the problems she faced than she had been when she orchestrated Madelene's renunciation and dowry payment decades earlier. This may well be why she convened her kin advisors for the making of her will on that March morning and the reason for the secret afternoon agreement that set aside 3,000 *livres* as the estimated supplement that might—in a worst-case scenario—be required to top up the amount Madelene had received for her renunciation to the level she might claim as a full share of her parents' properties. For one thing, Madelene had already appealed for letters of restitution, though she had not followed through with her appeal after her husband died. For another, the perception that the law courts had tilted against Protestants was growing, and Madelene had put herself on the favored side by converting. Finally, in the intervening years since the marriages of Susanne Isle's daughters, renunciation had become a much-discussed issue in France. As she approached the making of her final will in 1677, Susanne Isle may very well have been following the protest, begun in 1674, by a distinguished noblewoman, Marie d'Orléans-Longueville, Duchesse de Nemours, against the renunciation her family had forced her to make. It was a case that "caught the public eye in Europe."[63]

Marie d'Orléans-Longueville was the daughter of the Duc de Longueville, a peer of France who held the rights to sovereignty in the principality of Neuchâtel. When both her half-brothers, in whose favor she had renounced future inheritance in her 1657 marriage contract, disappeared from the scene—one mentally incompetent and the other killed on the battlefield—she claimed reinstatement to the inheritance both of her parents' vast properties in France and of the Neuchâtel sovereignty. The legal case she pursued beginning in 1674, *Longueville v. Nemours,* challenged the exclusion of women from sovereignty in the state and from equal entitlements to property in the family. One of the most intelligent and learned women of her day, the Duchesse de Nemours scored a number of points against the procedure of renunciation that seemed persuasive to the facts of her case and could appeal to other women who had made similar renunciations. Her dowry was not proportionate to the family's wealth, she charged; the dowry did not draw upon the assets of both her father and her mother (who had died before the renunciation in question) as it should if it were a quid pro quo for renunciation to both their inheritances; her brothers the beneficiaries had been minors and were not present at the making of the contract; and the contract itself was null because it was effected without her free consent. When she renounced her father's estate in favor of her brothers, she said, she did so under coercion: not physical constraint, but "the effect of paternal authority [which is a power] akin to force" when "children naturally timid . . . fear to resist the will of a father." The gender discrimination inherent in renunciation law and practice violated the natural equality of men and women; it was "a corrupt act that takes away from children the quality of heirs that nature and law give them." Thus did the heart of Nemours' protest denounce not merely the facts of particular renunciations but the act of renunciation itself.

Nemours' case failed, but not before gaining wide public attention for her cause. The lawyer Gabriel Guéret published his extended account of the case in his *Journal du Palais* in the very year—1681—when Madelene initiated her suit, noting in his prefatory remarks that the case had "made a great splash in public." So it is not impossible that the celebrated Longueville case, running its course as Susanne Isle finalized her inheritance arrangements and Madelene de Solière prepared her challenge to them, influenced the obscure case in the hinterlands of Saintonge. If it is true, as historian Sarah Hanley suggests, that in *Longueville v. Nemours,* "judicial publicity generated from the courtroom circulated legal lessons to the public" and "taught the interested 'public' legal lessons on family strategies to emulate—or avoid,"[64] then Madelene de Solière may have been a most willing pupil and Susanne Isle a reluctant ear compelled to recognize the threat.

In her 1677 will, Susanne was exceedingly cautious, setting out her wishes much more legalistically and much more fully than she had in her previous will just two years earlier. Unlike in 1675, she explicitly named Madelene in her will as an heir, an obligatory nod to Roman law's insistence that all children be heirs. And with the afternoon session, Susanne put in place a contingency plan at odds with the will's assertion that Madelene had been wholly provided for earlier, no doubt because she was aware that the renunciation might not hold and Madelene might, after her death, come forward to claim a full *légitime.* Though the coyness of the language in the will and in the second agreement obscures the details of the motivation, the afternoon agreement appears to set aside a reserve in case Madelene would have to be compensated further, perhaps relying upon the clause in renunciation law to the effect that a defendant could forestall restitution by indemnifying the plaintiff.[65]

Susanne and her advisors may have come to realize that they were saddled with earlier documents whose imprecisions and ambiguities lent themselves to Madelene's further claims. In particular, those documents did not establish that Madelene's dowry and the *livres* specified as the quid pro quo for her renunciation to future inheritance were the same sum. Though it would have been reasonable to read the documents in that way, someone inclined against renunciations could also read both the marriage contract and the dowry receipt as indicating two separate sums. The marriage contract in 1659 repeated the promise embedded in the 1654 donation to the effect that Madelene would be paid her inheritance six months after the death of her mother by her sister and brother-in-law des Touches (an obligation that would devolve upon their heirs, their six daughters, when both parents died before Susanne). It points out that Madelene had, as an adult, approved the division of her mother's estate, including both the favoring of her older sister Marie and the limiting of her claim on her parents' property to her 12,000 *livres* inheritance, renouncing her rights to paternal and maternal property, movable and immovable. Marie de La Rochefoucauld's lawyer, Dufaure de Lajarte, underlined this clause on the copy of the marriage contract he submitted to the Parlement of Bordeaux.[66] But there was no clause for him to underline that clearly made the promised inheritance identical with the dowry. To the contrary, Madelene's marriage contract spoke of the dowry as coming from Susanne Isle, not from Casimir de La Rochefoucauld or his daughters, although proofs of its uses were to be given to him. This wording would lend force to the interpretation that the dowry was a gift separate from the inheritance that was to be paid by the La Rochefoucauld couple or their heirs. Madelene might reasonably have considered it such, or been misled to think so, when she signed.

This impression of two separate payments was reinforced by the wording of the 1662 dowry receipt. In this document, Madelene acknowledged receiving full payment from Susanne Isle of what her mother promised in the marriage contract. Still, it did not specify that this was the replacement, through renunciation, for the *légitime*. Again, the receipt stated that the 12,000 *livres* had been paid by Susanne Isle, not by her as guardian of the six La Rochefoucauld daughters, who, with their parents both dead, would be understood to owe Madelene that inheritance. Finally, though the 1662 receipt did not say what the source of the dowry was—whether funds Susanne gave away irrevocably in 1654 or Susanne's own funds at a later date—the impression that the latter was the case was strengthened by the fact that she required of Salbert and Madelene, in return, to give her a lifetime annual pension of 100 *livres* on the grounds that she was giving them funds she had counted on having for her own maintenance "for her entire life." Madelene never made a claim against her mother or against her nieces while her mother was still alive. Her nieces would try to use this fact against her, to discredit her claims by suggesting she dared not press an outlandish claim to her mother's face. But of course the funds she was claiming—those her sister owed her—were not due until after Susanne's death.

The story of the struggle over Berneré, then, between Marie de La Rochefoucauld and her Aunt Madelene was one deeply inflected by gender. Gender was embedded in the law, in the prohibition on renunciations in favor of women. But more than that, the story had a cast of only women. Not only were the plaintiff and the beneficiary of the renunciation women, so too were the will-maker and the beneficiaries of that will. It thus is hard to characterize either the law or the Parlement's decision in this case as pro- or antiwoman. But questions remain. Would the court have set aside Susanne's settlement so readily if she had been a man? Why did it pay more respect to a child's *légitime* than to a woman's preferences for disposition of her property? Is this, then, an illustration of how the weakness of the mother could be visited upon the descendants, one of the "ways patriarchal cultural practices circumscribed legal rights [of women]"?[67]

The legal grounds upon which the Parlement of Bordeaux overturned Susanne Isle's will cannot be known for certain. There would seem to be no grounds for assuming—as the La Rochefoucauld sisters and their descendants charged—that the authorities upheld Madelene's claims as a reward for her conversion to the king's religion. Though Huguenots in Saintonge suspected, as they told the king, that they could not get justice from the same Parlement whose emissary, Duvigier, led the persecution of their church in Saintonge, there were multiple ways of arriving at the court's decision on the basis of Bordelais jurisprudence alone, free of religious bias. Still, the case had a bearing on the Champagné family's decision to leave France after the Revocation, intertwining, in Josias' and Marie's experience, the economic threat and the concurrent religious struggle. The monetary award to Madelene de Solière—her unpaid inheritance plus accrued interest—could be paid only by ceding Berneré to her. The final court decree would not come for two decades after the Champagné family vacated the château for a life in the Huguenot Refuge. But Marie and Josias could see the faces on the cards by the time they left. It would be naive to think that the turmoil caused by the loss of their principal asset did not intersect with religious concerns in their decision-making about staying in or leaving France. In this way, the dissension within Marie de La Rochefoucauld's maternal kin became part of the Huguenot story.

5

Families Endure

What might a single case say about the experience of Huguenots in the era of the Revocation and the reasons why some of them emigrated while most stayed in France? The Champagné cannot be thought of as exemplary: their circumstances were not likely to have been replicated widely. Yet the profile of their lives does suggest that in-depth studies of individual and family situations might reveal a multiplicity of factors—personal and social, religious and material—that, in shifting combinations, incited some among the Protestant subjects of Louis XIV to leave his realm. The task is not to formulate a new global explanation for the emigration but to proliferate particular experiences—in a variety of locations, dates, social strata, and microcultures—from which common patterns might eventually be drawn.

The key is broadening the factors that might be involved in such decision-making. Refugees and their descendants characterized emigration as an act of religious faith that was taken without concern for, indeed at the sacrifice of, material well-being. Josias de Robillard, as was conventional among early modern Christians, divided the worldly from the spiritual and would have been displeased by the proposition that the two were intertwined in his own and his coreligionists' responses to the Revocation. Still, it is unlikely that material considerations were foreign to the decision-making process. Decisions on leaving or staying were made within the matrix of people's lives, subject to all manner of social and personal forces, and often over some considerable time during which the reciprocal effects of religious and material factors became clear.

Multiplying the considerations that conditioned choices does not diminish the sincerity of the emigrants' faith. On the contrary, it affirms the sincere faith of those who stayed, countering the impression, created largely by some leaders of expatriate communities, that true believers would have left. If the depth of conviction among the whole body of Huguenots, emigrants and the immobile alike, is assumed, is there another way to account for variations on how they and their families responded to the proscription of their faith? Did the dynamics of everyday life divide the emigrants from those who stayed, among those who were devout and devoted to their Calvinist faith? The Champagné case suggests one way in which the undermining of material and social foundations precluded their continuing as Protestants at home and so made emigration the path through which they could continue to practice their chosen religion.

The intendant Arnoul said the material motive for emigration lay in family finances. The Huguenots who emigrated, he said, were the insolvents. They left "to cover their bankruptcies." They left when their economic position in France was no longer viable, when their liabilities amounted to more than their assets or when their indebtedness was, at least, too high to be supported from the return on their assets. Arnoul's colleague in Languedoc, Basville, made the complementary accusation that Protestants with property stayed and converted in order to protect it: "For a long time now they have made their choice between their property and their religion, coming down in favor of the former."[1] The meanness of the accusations does not necessarily render them false.

While diversified agriculture and water-borne commerce in Saintonge and Aunis provided the foundation for regional prosperity, countless pitfalls could send individual families into deficit. Periodic agricultural collapses, like the one brought to Saint-Savinien by drought in 1681, created hardship across social divisions. Conjunctural trends—price inflation, depreciation of dues that had been converted to fixed cash amounts, stagnation of rents—exacerbated the challenge for modest nobles like Josias and Marie of maintaining their estates and the lifestyle expected of their rank, especially in places like Saintonge where inheritance law splintered family heritages with each generational transfer. As Josias and Marie discovered while endeavoring to collect what she was due from her grandmother's estate, overexposure to the solvency of others could upset the delicate, but otherwise viable, balance between credits and debits; one person's insolvency reverberated through whole communities and kin networks. The penalties imposed upon Protestants during the upheavals surrounding the Revocation aggravated the economic challenges for Protestants and Catholics alike. As early as the summer of 1687, Arnoul's counterpart in Limoges, Saint-Contest, wrote to Versailles that the *élection* of Saint-Jean-d'Angély "is reduced to misery . . . by the departure of the *religionnaires*." An official 1686–1687 survey of economic conditions in the same region noted that the conversion campaign had impoverished the inhabitants of Saint-Savinien specifically: "that has ruined them."[2]

To judge from the intendant's list of their property holdings in Aunis drawn up in 1689, Josias and other Huguenots who fled at the Revocation did have precarious finances. Of 109 property holders listed, 20 had liens against their property that exceeded the collateral property's gross valuation. Others were heavily in debt, though not in deficit. Alexandre Desmier d'Olbreuse, for example, held property valued at 14,680 *livres,* with liens against it of more than 13,223 *livres.*[3] These figures do not demonstrate that many or most of these emigrants were bankrupt, even if nearly a fifth of those who fled were in deficit and others near it. But they do suggest that financial pressure may have been among the mix of conditions in which families decided upon flight.

Both Josias and Isaac Isle were on this list, and both showed precarious finances. Isaac Isle was the third-largest landholder among the 109 fugitives. He left behind property valued at 55,000 *livres,* with liens against it totaling just over 36,062 *livres* (66 percent of its gross value). Nor was he alone in the Isle clan to have fallen into debt. His sister Elisabeth had declared herself without the means to repay debts totaling 2326 *livres* that she had borrowed in 1667, 1674, and 1681. His sister Marguerite had been in bankruptcy for nearly a decade.[4]

Josias was the eighteenth largest landholder on the list. His property in Aunis included Lisleau in the Agère marsh and three marshland cabins in Voutron, all inherited from his mother. Together they were valued at 19,000 *livres* and had been attached by a creditor, Simon Tayau, for 1,365 *livres.* At a mere 7 percent of the property's value, this indebtedness was far from showing Josias to be insolvent. It pointed, nonetheless, to his recourse to short-term debt in the years immediately preceding his emigration. The amount due included 65 *livres* in interest for one year at 5 percent and the 1,300 *livres* in principal remaining due from 3,200 *livres* Josias had borrowed in 1680: 1,200 *livres* he had borrowed in April 1680 from Marie's relation Louis Casimir de La Rochefoucauld, Seigneur de Fontcour, which La Rochefoucauld had signed over to Tayau nine months later, plus 2,000 *livres* Josias borrowed directly from Tayau in May 1680. Josias must have promised quick repayment and found himself unable to keep his word, for Tayau took Josias to court in La Rochelle in March 1683, winning an order requiring Josias to pay back the debt in full. Not until five years later, in the spring of 1688, did Josias pay down this debt by 1,900 *livres* in principal plus the interest to date. One of Josias' last acts before leaving for Paris to make his escape was to travel to La Rochelle on March 21, 1688 to pay Tayau. It must have been all he could afford to pay—he could not avoid leaving the country a debtor—but it is interesting that he paid the debt down at all on the eve of his departure, given his need for cash for his move.[5]

Living in unsettled times and caught in a web of uncollectible debts, Marie had, at the same time, to endure the conflict with her Aunt Madelene. Little wonder that Marie feared this conflict between kin would "thoroughly ruin" her family. Litigation of any kind was expensive; many a noble family in similar circumstances had been bankrupted by the routine legal expenses involved in collecting dues from tenants who might slip out of dependence on the lord entirely unless the payment of dues signaled their obligation. Costly, too, were the legal actions, nearly as routine, that expanded the domain. A legal action like Susanne Isle's property division in 1677 could cost many hundreds of *livres,* even if it were not disputed, as could an inventory after her death, not to mention the devastating blow of losing Berneré itself. Between the death of her grandmother in 1679 and her own flight in 1687, the reverses of the early 1680s upended Marie's standing, turning her from a creditor into a debtor.[6]

From one point of view, Marie could be seen as simply a bankrupt fleeing to cover her debts. She left without paying Madelene de Solière, without paying 1,730 *livres* 18 sols in *légitime* to her younger sisters, and without handing over to them their share of the loans she was collecting on behalf of Susanne Isle's estate. But the more telling economic reversal was the loss of Berneré itself. Even without that estate, Josias and Marie were far from destitute. The family would still have had Champagné as well as the holdings at Voutron and Agère. But in geographical areas of partible inheritance, it took two patrimonies from the two spouses in combination to constitute a viable family fortune. Josias had somewhat more than half of what his parents had possessed together, and Marie had her share of what her parents and grandparents had owned. But without the latter inheritance, Josias and Marie were undercapitalized as a noble family. There was enough of a financial dimension to the family's decision that Marie might have said, as her Poitevin neighbor Chalmot did upon fleeing: "His standing and his property having been taken away from him, he could not live in France. So he set off for a foreign land."[7]

Broken Solidarities

The economic havoc in the Champagné lives was grist for Arnoul's hostile generalization about "bankrupts." But the problem that faced the Champagné cut yet deeper. In their case at least, economic precariousness was a marker of something more serious and more fundamental: a renegotiation of relationships among kin and with the state that, through decisions some of her Isle relations made, would deprive them, if they persisted as Protestants, of the only means by which they could safely stay in France. Here, too, is where religious conflict came into the equation. What happened because of the crown's religious policy was much deeper and much more transformative than mere change of religion. Families were reconfigured. The loss of Berneré did not make the Champagné emigrate; rather, the loss of Berneré and the emigration were alike results of the collapse of the family as a solidarity. Family strife, partly caused by religious discord, removed the shield of relationships—those inherited and then cultivated through coresidence, coproprietorship, everyday face-to-face interactions—that might have made it possible for Marie's and Josias' family to stay safely in France as clandestine Protestants.

Pockets of protection for Protestants continued to exist within France (and specifically in Saintonge) after the Revocation. Some were the work of clerics who, unlike their persecuting brethren, opposed the violence and even came to the aid of their nonconforming neighbors. In other cases, local notables who had converted at least in appearance impeded efforts to pressure Protestants who remained in the community. In 1692, an alderman in Saintes notified the intendant that the mayor had committed numerous abuses of authority, having "supported the New Catholics and insulted the Old Catholics." Then, in April 1696, Pontchartrain learned that such protection was provided by a prosecutor in the Presidial and other officials: "As there are those who are protected by the leading people of the province, nobody dares say anything." In Marennes, Bégon wrote in 1693, the "heretics" were still in charge of justice, and police kept missionaries away from those still unconverted. An informant from near Marennes let Pontchartrain know in 1694 that new converts "controlled virtually the entire territory," keeping the unconverted Protestants apart and channeling resources to them.[8]

Such practices of community solidarity, alongside family cohesion, could keep a persecuted religion alive and allow those who refused to convert to persist in it with a degree of safety. Some evidence suggests that the crown treated those under family or community protection differently from those without it. In February 1687, the secretary of state for ecclesiastical affairs passed along the king's order that "With respect to those who, in dying, make such declarations [refusal of the sacraments] out of sheer obstinacy and whose relatives evidently disapprove, it is good not to raise the issue and not to prosecute. To this end, His Majesty wishes you to inform the clergy that they should not, on these occasions, call the judges so readily to act as witnesses, so as not to be obliged to apply the law fully." In such circumstances, clandestine Protestants could pursue a "little war of attrition": drawing up wills with Protestant language, eating meat on fast days, marrying secretly according to Huguenot rites, shunning mass and confession, refusing last rites, attending secret assemblies.[9]

In one way or another, the religious upheavals deprived Marie and Josias of those who might have formed a protective circle around them and should have come to their defense—to begin with, the advisors who stood as guarantors when Susanne Isle set up guardianship arrangements for her orphaned granddaughters in 1660: Benjamin Green de Saint-Marsault, Seigneur de Salignac; François d'Ocoy, Seigneur de Couvrelles; and Alphée Goulard, Seigneur d'Anville.[10] They and their children were now Catholic, and at least some of these converts took their places on the side of persecution.

The Green de Saint-Marsault, the oldest line of sword nobility in Aunis, had been among the earliest and staunchest Protestants in the Charentes. Daniel Green de Saint-Marsault, Baron de Châtelaillon commanded the Protestant troops at La Rochelle in 1622. His grandson Pharamond (Châtelaillon) was baptized in February 1633 at the Reformed temple at Salles, with Marie de La Rochefoucauld's aunt Marie serving as his godmother. As late as 1681, Châtelaillon was holding services in that temple, and his widowed mother was doing the same in her Château de Dompierre.[11] Châtelaillon's uncle Benjamin, who advised Susanne Isle in 1660, stood as godfather for his nephew's daughter in 1666, so at that date all were still Protestant. But Benjamin's daughter Marie abjured in 1685, and Benjamin converted before he died in September 1688.

So did Benjamin's nephew Pharamond, Baron de Châtelaillon, with far-reaching consequences for his own family, the Huguenots in the region, and particularly Marie de La Rochefoucauld. In the fall of 1685, during the same weeks when the dragoons, intendant, and bishop were working on Josias de Robillard, the intendant Arnoul applied pressure on Châtelaillon. He arranged for a former pastor who had secretly converted to work surreptitiously on him. He proposed that the king offer a monetary incentive: "He could perhaps be won over by according him some favor. He is a very respectable man and has two sons ready for the Navy. Perhaps if one were made governor of Fort Lupin, this post would flatter him. His conversion would be a grand example and I believe would have great consequences, particularly at this juncture."[12] Châtelaillon abjured on December 23, 1685, the very day before Arnoul would give up in exasperation at the refusal of Isaac Isle to convert: "the baron de Chastelaillon has given me his word; he is the first gentleman of the province and on his conversion depends that of thirty-two persons in his family, not counting the servants. He is presently working to bring them to heel; he promises me he will succeed in short order." Just months later, in May 1686, Châtelaillon was named governor in La Rochelle. It was he who summoned Marie de La Rochefoucauld to explain her presence near the coast in 1686. He was, then, a tantalizing example of the extent to which the religious policy of the crown was implemented through the fervor of converts or by, as the French would say, "a fresh convert still feeling the flames."[13]

With the intendant's help, Châtelaillon then worked on his own family. Arnoul requested a *lettre de cachet* from the king for putting one of Châtelaillon's own daughters in a convent for reeducation. Châtelaillon "is doing his duty very well in terms of religion and would like to make all his family do the same, but he finds he is not the master of it. He would like to have an order from the King to put one of his daughters in some convent; he can work with me on managing that in a way that will not make trouble for him in the city and will not apprise his family that it was he who requested it." In this way, the governor placed two of his own daughters into the Abbaye de Puyberland in Poitou as well as a niece into the Ursuline convent in La Rochelle. For the son of the governor, however, the consequences of the crown's religious policy were entirely different: well converted to the king's religion, Pharamond-Charles gained the honorific office of gentleman companion to the dauphin, son of Louis XIV.[14]

A contrasting response to compulsory conversion lost Marie and Josias the protection that might have been expected from François d'Ocoy or his family on the basis of his having served as a second guarantor for Susanne Isle when she set up guardianship arrangements for her orphaned granddaughters. Like the Green de Saint-Marsault, the Ocoy were longtime Protestants. François' father, Jean-Casimir d'Ocoy, was among the Protestant leaders who worked to merge religious resistance with the popular uprisings of 1643–1644, and François himself served as deputy to the national synod at Loudun in 1659–1660. François died years before the Revocation, but when his daughter and heir Jeanne married Auguste Guiton de Maulévrier, Seigneur d'Agonnay, she became not only kin and ally but also one of the closest neighbors to Josias and Marie at Berneré.[15] Jeanne's response to the Revocation illustrates the way protective bonds could be neutralized not by newly acquired Catholic militancy, as in the case of Pharamond Green de Saint-Marsault, but by one's own vulnerability while navigating the shoals of religious constraint. New Converts under suspicion themselves could scarcely provide protection for others.

The Revocation threw the Guiton de Maulévrier in Agonnay into turmoil. Both Auguste and his brother Henri abjured at Saint-Savinien around when Josias did, on September 27, 1685, doing so along with René de Culant, whom Josias had chosen as godfather at Le Douhet for his last-born son in the preceding year. Another brother and a sister escaped to Rotterdam in April 1686. Jeanne was planning an escape from France in the months when the Champagné were deciding whether to leave and struggling to save Berneré, but she never got out.[16] The parish register of Agonnay bespeaks the initial distance kept by this longtime Protestant family and then, after a change of generation, sincere accommodation to the mandated religion. For seven years after the Revocation, the family made no appearance in the local church, though two daughters were born in that interval. Only one of two children born in the 1690s was baptized there. Neither Jeanne nor Auguste ever served as a godparent there, which would be expected behavior for a local seigneur after the Revocation, nor would either of them be buried there. Only twice, in 1692 and 1716, would Auguste's signature appear on the parish register; Jeanne d'Ocoy's never would. Furthermore, the circumstances surrounding the baptism of their six-year-old son Henri-Alexandre in November 1703 testify to the parents' continuing resistance. Though both were still alive, neither parent signed the Catholic register on this occasion, and the baptism was noted as occurring "conditionally." A conditional baptism would be called for if it were unknown whether the child had been baptized before, an uncertainty only possible if the parents were not cooperating. Presumably, Henri-Alexandre was taking steps to a new religion as he neared age seven, the earliest age at which Catholic authorities could claim that a child wished to join the church of his own free will.

Only after this baptism (and indeed after the death of Jeanne d'Ocoy[17]) did the meaningful integration of the family with Catholicism begin. When daughter Gabrielle-Susanne died at age thirteen in July 1705, she received the last rites "in a manner most edifying" and was buried in the church. With the adulthood of the second generation, the family began to mark the milestones of their lives through the church. The eldest son and heir, Auguste-Alphée, abjured at last at age twenty-six in July 1709 in the hands of the Bishop of Saintes in his episcopal chapel, in order to marry the following year. Children Marianne, Auguste-Alphée, and Bénigne married in Catholic ceremonies and brought their children for baptism. They and their unmarried brother Henri-Alexandre all stood as godparents after 1706, as custom in ordinary times would expect the children of the seigneur to do. The next seigneur, Auguste-Alphée, stood as godfather for a new bell in Agonnay's parish church in 1722; when he died two years later at age forty-one, he was buried in the Church, having "received all the sacraments in an edifying manner and shown himself in every way a good and true servant of God."[18]

The Revocation, then, cut to the heart of Protestant networks that had once provided security for Protestant families, but did so no longer. The more they relied upon fellow Protestants in earlier years, the more bereft of support they now were. Josias and Marie were, likewise, no longer able to look for protection to the three guarantors of Susanne Isle's 1677 property division, who might have clarified Susanne Isle's actions and intentions. Isaac Isle was imprisoned immediately after the Revocation and eventually expelled from France. François de La Rochefoucauld, Seigneur de La Rigaudière and godfather of Marie's and Josias' eldest son, made an early bargain with the crown. As late as 1682, he was serving as an elder in the Tonnay-Charente temple and as its delegate to the synod of Barbezieux. But even before his religion of birth was condemned, he agreed to abjure in stealth. Days before the Revocation, Arnoul received from Versailles "the *lettre de cachet* monsieur de Rigaudière requested, to serve as a pretext for his conversion." Then three weeks after the Revocation, Arnoul reported that La Rigaudière was prepared to abjure. He converted on January 1 in the hands of the Père de La Chaise, the king's confessor, and would have his rewards. The intendant Arnoul was told to return to La Rigaudière the land that had been confiscated from his late wife (deceased three months earlier) on the grounds that she was Huguenot. Then in June 1689, while in Paris preparing his son to enter the army, La Rigaudière wrote to La Chaise, asking the good father to present the first of several petitions to the king. The petitions pointed out that the costs of outfitting his son for the king's service and instructing his daughters in the Catholic religion at Puyberland made it impossible for him to pay debts to his now-outlawed church that he had contracted before the Revocation. He took the liberty of approaching the king for assistance, he said, because he had been promised "at the time of his conversion to the Catholic faith that you would grace him with your favor." He hoped La Chaise could arrange all in secret, to avoid the inevitable scandal this would cause back home: "it is not so much in my own interest that I continue to importune Your Reverence in this matter as in the interest of the Catholic religion. What would those in my province say if they saw me acting in this manner? Do me the favor, my very Reverend father, of giving me your support before the King so this grief does not befall me." La Chaise took the request to the sovereign, who, before the month was out, "by his own hand" relieved La Rigaudière from paying the 1,350 *livres* he otherwise owed to the consistory of Saintes.[19]

The third of the 1677 guarantors, Charles de Villedon, was perhaps incapacitated by the collapse of his own standing. By mid-1681, he had lost his lands: his wife, an aunt of Madame de Champagné, referred in her May 19, 1681 will to "the deplorable state to which he is reduced by the loss of his fortune." But "considering the singular affection the said Seigneur de Magezy my husband has always had for me," she wanted him to have the usufruct of her property, should she die first; to secure that property from claims for repayment of his debts, she stipulated that if any creditors were to go after the usufruct, she revoked the donation. When Villedon died, some time before 1690, his widow turned over the seigneury of Magezy to his creditors and vacated the premises.[20]

Numerous other kin in the Champagné's protective circles had pulled out in one way or another. Marie's cousin Gédéon de La Rochefoucauld was imprisoned in Château-Trompette from 1685 to 1694. The lords of Le Douhet who had allowed Josias to baptize his infant at their château, Renaud de Pons and Judic de La Rochefoucauld, were imprisoned and then expelled from France. The same loss of support held true before long for two of Marie's three surviving sisters, whom the property division of 1677 should have made Marie's allies. Marie's sister Elisabeth abjured shortly after Marie's effort to recover her grandmother's debts began, on December 18, 1677. By February 1687, sister Susanne was also active in the Catholic Church; she and Elisabeth's husband Jean-Baptiste Dupuy de La Martinie stood as godparents at the Catholic baptism of Susanne Couillaud at Saint-Hippolyte-de-Biard on February 17, 1687.[21]

The defection of Elisabeth and Susanne de La Rochefoucauld was part of the deepest problem facing Marie and Josias. The splintering of the kinship network so evident in the struggle over Berneré was fundamentally what destroyed the Champagné's chances of staying in France as Protestants. In times of peace or war, feast or famine, the foundation of a family's safety in Old Regime France was the kinship group. The Isle had carefully tended their kin solidarity over the decades. Coproprietorship was one means of cementing solidarity that the Isle had used for generations. It was not uncommon for two or three or four men to call themselves simultaneously "Seigneur de Forgette" or "Seigneur de La Cave" because they took their inheritances in incompletely divided shares. In 1578, Susanne Isle's father and his two brothers, inheriting the estate of Coullon, decided to leave it undivided and enjoy it jointly. The three brothers also co-owned the lord's oven for a time. Shared holdings offered the social and economic advantage of keeping patrimonies intact, but dispensing with property division in this way presupposed clear agreements and the acquiescence of each to the functioning of the whole.[22]

This is the solidarity that broke down in Marie's case. The link in the chain constituted by the generation following Susanne Isle's snapped, threatening Marie's hold on the estate—Berneré—that was her inheritance and causing tensions with her sisters, who shared the remainder of the heritage. There were no more intra-Isle marriages, of which there had been several in the mid-seventeenth century, or shared seigneuries. Confessional differences ended such cooperative strategies for the sake of the kindred and scattered the kin. It was Marie's and Josias' sincere devotion to their religion that made it impossible for them to stay home by converting. But it may have been the disintegration of familial bonds that made it impossible for them to stay by dissembling. That would have required protection, and the kindred was no longer a cohesive protective circle. It is tempting to speculate that if clan solidarity had held, Marie would not have emigrated: she would not have had to do so in order to stay Protestant, and she would not have been permitted to do so by the ethic of the clan.

Instead, the Protestant Isle shattered into resisters and conformists. Isaac Isle was taken into custody by *lettre de cachet* in December 1685 for his refusal to convert and disappeared from the scene. He had been spared the dragoons in the fall—"in view of the fact that he is a man who served"—since crown policy exempted army officers from lodging soldiers. But as one might expect in the case of the former official defender of the region's Protestants, he was the object of other measures from the authorities. The intendant Arnoul characterized Isaac for Versailles as "this stubborn fool" and reported: "he has been appealed to in all sorts of ways, but we have been unable to win anything at all from him to date." Six weeks after the Revocation, at the end of November, Arnoul confessed to Seignelay that he had run out of ideas on Isaac: "I do not know how to get to him."[23]

Figure 5.1 Coat of Arms of the Isle Family. ADCM E274. Courtesy of the Archives départementales de la Charente-Maritime.

Arnoul prepared for possible failure by obtaining from the king a *lettre de cachet* to send Isaac away "into some distant province" if all conversion efforts should fail. The practice of sending incorrigibles from Aunis-Saintonge by *lettre de cachet* into internal exile had already been established: locals who were said to prevent people from converting and from going to hear the priests who had come to enlighten them were from time to time sent to Basse-Bretagne or Haute-Auvergne, "places where there are no *religionnaires*." Before executing the *lettre de cachet,* Arnoul would have one more resource to bring to bear on Isaac Isle. In mid-December, Saintonge received the young cleric who would make his reputation for sweet persuasion in this missionary campaign, and Arnoul made Isaac the first "put into the hands of the abbé de Fénelon." Arnoul had hopes of success, given his judgment that "Fénelon and his colleagues . . . have a manner of instructing and preaching that appeals strongly to New Catholics." But to no avail. On Christmas Eve, Arnoul reported that he had given Isaac an ultimatum and a deadline: "he has only tomorrow left for thinking about this, after which I will give him the *lettre de cachet.*"[24]

Isaac's companion under pressure was a Culant, cousin of the friend of Josias de Robillard who had stood as godfather to baby René-Casimir at Le Douhet in 1684. Like the Isle, the Culant descended from a Protestant dynasty; Olivier de Culant, Seigneur de Ciré, had been among the first won over to Calvinism and became one of the main leaders of the party in Saintonge; Jacques Culant, Seigneur de Landraye, was among the elders who received the king's order in February 1685 to turn over to the intendant the records, accounts, and funds of the already-closed temple of Ciré. Baby René-Casimir's godfather abjured in Saint-Savinien on September 27, 1685, and in so doing saved his descendants for France; his grandson would become Marquis de Culant and Chevalier de Saint-Louis. His granddaughter would marry a Green de Saint-Marsault, seneschal of Aunis and Baron de Châtelaillon. And the godfather's cousin, Isaac's Culant companion in prison, acceded to Arnoul's ultimatum. But Isaac proved to be "invincibly stubborn." So finally, on the last day of the year of the Revocation, Arnoul acknowledged failure: "I have been unable, in the end, to avoid giving the Marquis de Loire the *lettre de cachet* that I had for him, since he never was willing to give in."[25]

Isaac's friend Abraham Tessereau would later recount the treatment this officer and former Protestant commissioner received. Isaac was taken first to Brioude in the mountains of Auvergne "and thereafter he had to endure ordeals more brutal than those of exile. He was taken to the prisons of Clermont, where he was kept for fully seventeen months; after that he was shut up in the convent of the Carmelites in the same city. He endured it all, right up to the end, with much constancy; so that when orders came to the intendants in the provinces, in the first months of the present year 1688, to expel from the kingdom those prisoners for religion who were unwilling to change, he was put in the hands of a Prevôt from that region who, having been instructed to take him as far as the frontier, set him free within view of Geneva."[26]

Like Isaac, his siblings maintained the Protestant heritage of their branch of the family at great personal cost. Brother Charles escaped to England, joining Isaac in the Refuge. Sister Elisabeth was arrested trying to escape from France and on July 10, 1687—as Marie de La Rochefoucauld set foot in England—was sent to the convent of the nuns of Saint-François de Vezins, where she died just two years later. Sister Jeanne was arrested and placed in a convent in 1685. On the day the first group of Champagné escapees stepped onto their ship, Jeanne was in the convent of La Charité in La Rochelle. On the day Marie de La Rochefoucauld made her way onto the later ship, those incarcerated in the convent still included "the Demoiselle de Loire, sister of the Marquis de Loire, aged 50–60 years, who has not been willing to convert." The property holdings of Elisabeth and Jeanne were confiscated and given in 1688 to Isaac's children, who had, the grant document stated, become professing Catholics.[27] After years of confinement, in 1697, Jeanne was expelled from France.

Isaac's sister Marguerite, Dame de Treillebois, stayed in France and suffered from conflict—religious as well as financial—with her eldest son and among her children. Her eldest son sued her in October 1692 for access to revenues from the family's debt-ridden estates. She countersued in November, but her situation had long been precarious: as early as 1676, when she was the widowed guardian of her children, she had been pursued for debts in the presidial court.[28] In religion, too, the family group splintered. Marguerite's eldest son was under Arnoul's surveillance at just about the time his uncle Isaac Isle went into the hands of Fénelon. As the intendant wrote to Seignelay, there was a noble yet to convert "near La Tremblade named Treuilbois whom I am having spied on in order to arrest him . . . if he cannot be won over I believe it will be necessary to raze his home." Then on the very day on which he hit Isaac Isle with the *lettre de cachet* of banishment, Arnoul called off the proposed destruction: "I have won over the Sieur de Treillebois. . . . He confessed to me that one of his brothers was part of an intrigue and should be arrested and that he would let me know about it."[29] Alienation between mother and son, between brothers—how far this family had moved since the father sailed with the great Admiral Duquesne and his young nephew Duquesne-Guiton in such religious solidarity that Seignelay worried they would turn one of the king's vessels into a Protestant fief.[30]

Marguerite held out until July 28, 1694, when she abjured at the age of sixty-eight at Rochefort in the presence of the intendant Bégon, who even at that moment doubted her sincerity: "Two days ago I had the honor of writing to you to ask permission from the King to send the Dame de Treillebois to Holland, but she abjured yesterday, and so she is no longer in that situation. I see no sincerity whatever nor good faith in what she has done, but I am persuaded that her case should be suspended and she be given some time for getting instruction." She died in Arvert on September 18, 1696 and was buried in the parish churchyard the next day in the presence of the curé. In the end, three of her children by Daniel Vigier, Seigneur de Treillebois, left France, never to return from self-imposed exile. At least one of them would serve in the Dutch army with Josias de Robillard and in the English army with the younger Josias, and fall into such poverty that Lord Justice Galway (Henri de Ruvigny) petitioned William III to grant him a special pension.[31]

Isaac's cousin Henriette Isle de Quincé and her sixteen-year-old niece Esther Aymée de Laval, both residents of Saint-Savinien, left about the time Isaac was imprisoned. They did their *reconnaissance* on January 31, 1686 in the Savoy Church in London, and Henriette soon began to receive charitable assistance from the Royal Bounty. Henriette's sister Uranie Isle and her husband

Simon Bonniot, Seigneur de Boudon, escaped to England and had their property confiscated on May 17, 1688, because they had "abandoned the kingdom and gone to England in order to continue the said exercise of the R.P.R., which is contrary to the will of His Majesty and prohibited on pain of death." A third sister, Esther Aymée's mother Esther Isle, stayed behind. Henriette's and Uranie's shares as co-seigneurs of the Château de La Cave were reassigned to their New Convert sister. [32] Esther's son-in-law Annet de La Martonie would hold at Saint-Savinien's Catholic baptismal font the baby born to Marie de La Rochefoucauld after the Revocation, the baby who would be left behind by the departure of all the rest of the Champagné family.

While these several Isle—Isaac, his siblings, cousins Henriette and Uranie—persisted in their Protestantism and suffered for their persistence, others among the Isle kin became aggressively anti-Protestant and even helped seal the new religious regime. Within weeks of the Revocation, Hélène Mauchen, widow of Paul Isle, Seigneur de Quincé, surrendered to the Catholic church the 427-pound bell that had long summoned the Protestants of Saint-Savinien to worship and that the Isle had spirited away when the temple was closed. Protestant bells all over the Charentes were finding their way into Catholic belfries: Aulnay's to the Carmelites, Marennes' to the Capuchins, Mauzé's and La Rochelle's to local parish churches, Saint-Maixent's to the Cordeliers. In Bourcefranc, near Marennes, the bell hanging after 1685 in the Catholic parish church still bore its original dedicatory inscription: "I WAS CREATED TO SERVE THE REFORMED CHURCH OF SAINT-JUST IN THE NAME OF GOD. JEHAN FAVRE MADE ME IN THE YEAR 1604." In some places, the Protestants' bell stayed in hiding longer, symbolically keeping the rivalry between the religions alive. In La Baume-Cornillane near Valence, for example, the bell hidden in the home of an elder of the consistory when its temple was demolished in 1684 did not see the light of day again until the Revolution; in 1825 it was placed in the new temple.[33]

In Saint-Savinien, such rivalry ended early. There, on December 4, 1685, at the fourteenth-century church nearly adjacent to the Isle's Château de La Cave, the rescued bell was blessed and named—all Catholic bells bore personal names. The curé of Champdolent attended and signed the parish register, indicating that the ceremony was a notable event in the neighborhood. Was it to honor the donor that the bell was named Hélène and put under the protection of Sainte Hélène? Mauchen had abjured at Saint-Savinien on November 12, 1681, and since July 1682 she had been signing the parish register of Saint-Savinien's Catholic church as witness to the abjurations of her former coreligionists. Mauchen's handover of the bell symbolically sealed the Catholic victory in Savinois space but sealed as well the Isle's transfer of allegiance, as religious actors, to the king's church.[34]

So it happened that in June 1687, at the moment when Marie was crawling beneath the floorboards of an English ship off the Ile de Ré, the naval officer charged by the king with patrolling the coast to stop *religionnaires* from fleeing was a Saintongeais who had been bred a Protestant and baptized with the name of the Protestant leader who had doggedly defended the faith in the region. On July 8, 1687, as Marie stepped onto English soil, the intendant Arnoul sent the king a report that His Majesty had requested: a list of those New Catholics who were receiving pensions for their conversions annotated as to whether they deserved them by doing their duty. This man was receiving 150 *livres* and was reported to be doing his duty. He was the half-brother of Madelene de Solière's husband. He was Marie de La Rochefoucauld's second cousin. His name was Isaac Isle.[35]

This cousin of Marie's had been a fourth-generation Protestant in his mother's line as in his father's. His great-grandfather Giron de Bessay was one of the principal Protestants of Bas-Poitou during the Wars of Religion and commander of the Protestant infantry. His grandfather Jonas de Bessay was a frequent deputy to Reformed synods and assemblies who presided over the 1620 assembly in La Rochelle that called French Protestants to arms as Louis XIII bore down with his armies on Saint-Jean-d'Angély. When the naval officer's parents, Jean Isle de Beauchesne and Léa de Bessay, left their ancestral religion is not known. They were still Protestant at the time of their wedding in January 1639, but her brother converted that same year and made himself persecutor of his former brethren, obtaining an *arrêt* from the Conseil d'Etat in 1640 that outlawed the exercise of Protestantism on his lands.[36]

When this Isaac Isle assumed command of the frigate *La Sibille* in 1685, his specific orders were to stop Protestant fugitives in the waters off the coast of Saintonge. An additional coastal vessel (*traversier*) supplemented Isle's ship in July 1686; as Seignelay wrote Isle, "I believe that that will allow no ship to pass without your being able to visit it and that you will prevent any *religionnaire* or New Convert from leaving without permission." On March 22, 1687—just days before Susanne and the first party of Champagné embarked for England—the king sent Isle "a more powerful ship than the one you have. . . . I advise you to apply at all times a very great exactitude in the visiting of ships that exit from this river, so that you can answer to His Majesty that no person will pass against his intentions so long as you are there." In July 1687—the very month of Marie de La Rochefoucauld's flight to Exeter—he boarded two ships arriving at Saint-Georges and confiscated letters sent by refugees in Ireland. For this he earned Seignelay's praise: "I am pleased to tell you that you have done well." More tangible thanks came in February 1688, as Josias at Berneré finished preparing for his escape. They were explicitly a reward for one who had been raised Protestant and now was doing his anti-Protestant duty. Louis personally signed the parchment granting an annual pension of 600 *louis* to "the Sieur Isle, captain of a light frigate, New Convert."[37]

Most honorable thanks were yet to come. From 1693 on, this Isaac Isle pinned to his chest the same cross and ribbon the king affixed daily to his own, for within weeks of establishing a new and most prestigious chivalric order,[38] Louis XIV named this New Convert naval officer Chevalier de Saint-Louis. For "your services and the considerable wounds you have received," he was included among the thirty-two chevaliers to receive a pension of 800 *livres*. He knelt before the king (or his delegate) and swore the initiation oath: "You swear by God the Creator, on the faith to which you adhere, that you will live and die in the Catholic, Apostolic, and Roman Religion." As required, he provided "a certification from the archbishop or the diocesan bishop" (Article 12), for (Article 11) "none can be provided a place as knight in the Order of Saint-Louis if he does not profess the Catholic, Apostolic, and Roman Religion."[39]

That the younger Isaac Isle and Marie de La Rochefoucauld sailed the same waves as hunter and prey was the consequence of a process of family reconfiguration and implicit renegotiation with the king that arose independently of the Revocation but intersected with it and shaped the Revocation's impact on Protestants' lives. Louis XIV's decision to revoke the Edict of Nantes was an act of state-building. It sealed an alliance between church and state—among royal, ecclesiastical, and parlementary Gallicans—that would form the very foundation of Bourbon absolutism. It set in place a "social pact" or consensus on submission and discipline that helped to close the long period of rebellions that had plagued the crown since the Wars of Religion a century earlier.[40] The story of the Isle family illustrates how that "social pact" played itself out within families and communities, as the new exigencies of *une foi, un roi, une loi* (one faith, one king, one law) forced a rethinking of family traditions, loyalties, aspirations, and strategies for success—and often even a redistributing of family properties.

Some members of the Isle family, then, threw in their lot with the king, conforming to the king's religious requirements. There was wisdom in their doing so. After all, the set of penalties against Protestants was implicitly an offer of preferments for new converts. But the king also devised new patronage relations that redirected family aspirations toward the crown. By providing new opportunities for social and professional advancement, he could do for noble families far more than they could do for themselves. Their reorientation, at once religious and political, had its rewards. Two Isle girls, grandnieces of the naval officer charged with intercepting escapees, were admitted to Madame de Maintenon's prestigious school at Saint-Cyr. Their brother would be honored with a papal benediction. By the end of the eighteenth century, the descendants of Jean Isle de Beauchesne and Léa de Bessay, parents of the

Figure 5.2 Louis XIV, King of France in Royal Costume. Oil on canvas by Hyacinthe Rigaud, 1701. Louvre Museum. By permission of Erich Lessing/Art Resource, NY.

naval hunter, would include an archpriest of Pons, a canon of the cathedral in Saintes, numerous naval officers and dragoons, several graduates of the Ecole Militaire, and several Chevaliers de Saint-Louis. On March 27, 1789, just weeks before the outbreak of Revolution, the Marquis d'Isle climbed into the king's carriage and accompanied His Majesty to the hunt.[41] A family for whom, as for many landed nobles, Calvinism had been "at once a badge of independence and a means of maintaining it"[42] now prospered in the king's religion.

The dramatic face-off between Marie de La Rochefoucauld and her cousin, the younger Isaac Isle, is difficult to probe evenhandedly. Marie and her husband Josias left firsthand accounts of their reasons for remaining Protestant and emigrating; this younger Isaac Isle, so far as is known, did not record his reasons for taking the opposing course. Huguenots, then and since, were quick to fill in such a vacuum, attributing mercenary motives to the converts, whose actions were so often so beneficial to them in material terms. This is apparent in the accusations her nieces and their descendants leveled against Madelene de Solière as well as in the opprobrium the Saintonge Protestants heaped upon the magistrate Jean Duvigier. Tessereau noted ruefully the pattern of career advancement that followed conversion; after speaking of the Baron de Châtelaillon, he says he declines to speak more about the "false zeal of some New Converts like him, who entered judicial offices after their change of religion or who, being already in the military when they were Protestant, advanced further since they did as the others."[43]

Weighing Loyalties

Such attacks had been standard fare in the confessional conflict since its beginning more than a century earlier. But there is no reason to assume that the decision-making process of those who abjured and conformed was any less complex or vexed than that of the Huguenots who decided to flee. A source that reveals some of the complexity on the abjuring side, as well as the way an honest religious choice could yet be tied to sociopolitical change, has come down from a neighbor of the Isle: René de Saint-Légier de Boisrond. He was the Protestant-born nobleman who recorded the arrival of Boufflers' troops in the fall of 1685. His maternal aunt was a sister of the Green de Saint-Marsault who served as a guarantor for Susanne Isle in 1660, and his cousin was baby René-Casimir's godfather René Culant. In 1649, he had purchased from Jean Isle de Beauchesne, father of the naval officer, the portion of the seigneury of Saint-Xandre that had previously belonged to the father of Madelene de Solière's husband Louis de Salbert. He was, then, likely among the Isle's and Champagné's social set, and his thinking may have been something like that of the younger, abjuring Isaac Isle.[44]

Boisrond told the story of his life from 1675 to 1690: that is, precisely the years when he faced and resolved the dangers his Protestantism had come to pose for him.[45] He leavened the narrative with tales of his exploits: never heroic, sometimes bawdy, often frivolous. At one point, when he ran into the Chevalier d'Aubeterre passing through Poitou, he joined him in his carriage for a spontaneous "voyage of debauchery" to Paris. Entire years passed in "my little amusements, either in hunting or in bagatelles." In other years, "I had hardly any occupation but my ordinary follies and seeking things that could give me pleasure." Perennially "I threw myself, as is my naughty penchant, into relationships with women." He painted himself, then, as a provincial nobleman of the old school. But he had spent some time in Paris as a young man and had in particular frequented the Hôtel d'Albret, where, he recalled—now that she was first lady of the realm—he had renewed his childhood acquaintance with another young noble from the Charentes, Françoise d'Aubigné.

It was to this same Françoise, now Marquise de Maintenon and wife of the king, that Boisrond took recourse just before Boufflers' dragoons entered Saintonge in 1685. At this critical moment, he laid before her his thoughts about the situation in which he found himself and the issues—religious and political—that faced him as a Protestant. Later, he would extend his ruminations on the issues involved in his conversion by recording his conversations with another key political figure who had been his patron, the now elderly Prince de Condé—a man whose forefathers led the Reformed armies in the Wars of Religion before converting with their cousin Henri IV and who himself had led rebel armies in the Fronde before submitting in obedience to Louis XIV. In both the scenes with Maintenon and those with Condé, Boisrond told his own story as a passage from autonomy to obedience.

By Boisrond's account, he rode off from his estate in Saintonge to the court at Fontainebleau toward the end of September 1685. When admitted to Madame de Maintenon's apartment, he found her having her hair combed. While her attendants dressed her, he laid before Maintenon the question that troubled him: "whether a gentleman can honorably change his religion at sword-point and with troops in his home." This extraordinary phrasing of the religious question in terms of noble honor and monarchical force rings of an old-style understanding of governance and social standing, as does the entire procedure of riding to the court to beg protection, through an intermediary patron, from the king. Boisrond claims he first asked Maintenon to beg the king to permit him to leave the kingdom in order "to reflect in liberty upon my conscience." She demurred, daring not, she said, ask that of the king. But she volunteered to ask him to grant Boisrond safety for a period of time sufficient to think through the issue: "to protect you from what you call sword-point, to give you time to examine whether your conscience can permit you to make yourself Catholic, during which time you will receive no harm either in your properties or in your family." Boisrond responded with gratitude, but his was the gratitude of a dependent tinged with the assertive, autonomous "moi" of an aristocrat: "But remember, if you please, that I commit myself only to instruction in which I am the master." In relating the events of the next day, when he learned that he had been granted three months in which to come to a decision, Boisrond again evoked the notion of "honor," in an evident effort to establish (for his readers) that his motives were honorable rather than mercenary. Maintenon, he says, made him a profitable offer: "Come to your decision while you are here and make your abjuration; I promise you that that will bring you a pension of [3,000 *livres*]." To which he says he replied: "I have spoken with you in good faith, Madame; I have not yet given thought to the matter. I accept the time that the King would give me as a man of honor and place higher value on the honor of your esteem than on a pension of a thousand *écus*."

As he subsequently sifted his options, Boisrond framed his situation in terms of his political understanding rather than his religious convictions. He understood that a change of religion could "save me, as well as my family, from public calamity, in fulfilling the intentions of the King and those of my protectress." But he was not yet among "the Protestants who cede to authority." By the time he reached home, however, "I had already resolved to obey the King." Before the year 1685 was out, Boisrond had an audience with the king: "as soon as the Duc de Noailles, who presented me, had said my name, the King, turning graciously to my side, said to me, I know the decision you have come to and I am very pleased by it. Sire, said I to him, I have fulfilled the intentions of Your Majesty."

That scene—the contented king, the nobleman pleased to satisfy the intentions of the king—encapsulates the process by which some Protestant-born nobles and the monarch in Versailles reached mutual agreement, after the Revocation, on a new form of governance. What Boisrond articulated and enacted in his conversion was, then, what has been called "the Indian summer of feudal ideology": an updated noble ethic that melded the individualism of the knight with the enhanced claims of the king's will, preferring and privileging future advancement over family memory.[46]

Boisrond would return to Saintonge and work in concert with royal officials to further the crown's objectives, attached as they now were to his own interests. The king would leverage central control at the grassroots level on the "credit" of local elites who, purged of dissidents, could be relied upon to be loyal to the king and his vision of governance for the realm.[47] The dynamics of the Revocation, then, promoted "absolutism"—not by simply imposing the royal will but by crafting a set of constraints and enticements that persuaded those who had acted in decentralizing ways that their interests and ambitions would best be served by joining the king in his program of central authority. Far from destroying local hierarchies, cultural practices, and patterns of sociability, as Tocqueville would later charge, Louis reoriented them. In one sense, Huguenot emigrants, including the Champagné, refused the replacement of private noble patronage by royal generosity and left France in order to remain within traditional networks elsewhere.[48]

The accommodation Boisrond reached was, however, a "hard pill for my wife to swallow, good Christian and ardent Huguenot though scarcely knowing why." His description of the drama with his wife made his rallying to the king most evident. When she left home and went into hiding—"My wife got away from me, I do not know where she is"—he petitioned the king for "a *lettre de cachet* for finding my wife and putting her in a convent" and received it from the hands of the Bishop of Saintes. When he received a letter from his daughter informing him that she and her mother had reached London, he forwarded the letter to Boufflers as proof that he was aligned with the authorities rather than with his kin. "I informed him so he could judge whether I continued in the right path." In May 1686, Boisrond traveled to Holland, with the king's permission and with a grant of 100 *pistoles* from the royal treasury, to try to persuade his wife and daughter, who had fled from his household and from the kingdom, to return with him to France. He was not well received in the refugee community. "Everyone took me for an emissary from the French court, come to suborn the refugees." As with his own conversion, so with his break from the refugees, he framed his response in terms of duty and obedience to the king: "I replied that I had a good master whom I would never deny and whom none should dare to defame in my presence. . . . Everywhere the refugees scandalized me with the license they took in speaking of the King and of the State. . . . I had a great altercation in the ship with a French minister whom I did not know at all. This man spoke of the King with unexampled impertinence; I did my duty and did it so well that the insolent fellow told me I could regret it. I treated him the whole time with ridicule, leaving him extremely angry and the crew of the ship astonished to see a Frenchman in that country speak as I did."

Boisrond's account of his experience illustrates well how religion had become one of the tests in a larger shakeout in which families either reoriented themselves to the absolutist state or fell by the wayside. Kin networks were central to the operation of Louis' state. As the state became stronger, "the familial character of the network of power" became even more pronounced. One need only recall the contest between clans that split the ministries in the early years of Louis' personal reign. Colbert and Le Tellier both filled offices with their kin, Colbert frankly declaring "I burn with the desire to see our family rise."[49] But kin networks needed to be integrated with the monarch's interest and purged of the solidarities independent of the king that had made them (among the nobility at least) rise up periodically in opposition to royal power.

This purging of family networks did not target only Protestants, nor did it begin with the Revocation. But Protestantism had been one of the solidarities independent of the crown, and the remaking of families is one of the contexts in which Louis' persecution of Protestants should be viewed. Kinship networks—like the ship of Duquesne and Treillebois—were dangerous if they were Protestant. The elder Isaac Isle had exemplified the independence and solidarity of Protestantism, as he faced off against the state in defense of his coreligionists. Families that wished to compete for success in Louis XIV's state could not afford to stay Protestant, and the New Convert

Isle family became—and remained—deeply involved in royal institutions. The Revocation culled out from previously strongly bonded kinship networks those who were compliant and made them the new families of favor.

It would be too much to say that family policy drove the Revocation, that Protestantism was outlawed in order to purge families. Nonetheless, the Revocation accomplished something in this domain that the crown must have welcomed. The measures Louis took to resolve the split between religious parties provoked a split among the dissidents, a breaking-up of family solidarities that isolated hardline opponents of conversion. Pressure from the crown broke the psychological hold of the family's shared religion, freeing those who were willing to change religion to redefine the family's interest.

Nor could one claim, on the basis of a single family's experience, that a pattern of family crisis generally underlay the emigration.[50] In principle, everyone who abjured had Protestant kin. Many, if not most, of the families who were Protestant up to the time of the Revocation became divided along religious lines. Future studies will test the extent to which family crisis contributed to the emigration decision. Did families that preserved their solidarity by protecting their still-Protestant kin keep them in France by doing so? Did those, like the Isle, who did not place family solidarity above religious division see their relatives leave the kingdom for exile abroad? In a sense, the hypothesis that family crisis underlay emigration focuses attention on a subject Huguenot scholarship has been loath to address: those who abjured, their motivations, family values, and actions toward their nonabjuring kin. What made the difference in their minds as they prioritized family solidarity and religious conformity? What made some families protect their nonabjuring kin and others abandon them, even hunt them down—the younger Isaac Isle with his ship, Châtelaillon and Boisrond with their *lettres de cachet*?

The significance of the Champagné case can be usefully juxtaposed with the contrasting experience of the Lacger of Castres, a family remarkably similar to the Isle. Both were substantial provincial noble families whose distinction had originated in judicial and civic offices, though the Lacger continued an urban professional profile long after the Isle moved to the country and to sword occupations. The Lacger's family seat was some 200 miles southeast of the Isle's, in another of the southern French regions that were heavily Protestant from the beginnings of the Reform. They, like the Isle, had been Protestant from at least the 1560s, though not all the Lacger went over to the Reform during the Wars of Religion. One brother, Antoine, turned Protestant while the other, Jean, stayed Catholic: "The two brothers, Jean and Antoine II, maintained a close cooperative relationship despite the religious differences that had emerged by the mid-1570s. Throughout their regular and considerable correspondence—there was an average of one letter per month—the occasional quip about one or another's 'party' does not appear to have lessened the amiable bonds between them. They possessed a powerful sense of family interdependency and worked together for their mutual advantage. The ties of kinship and sociability overcame religious division."[51]

Remarkably, that same primacy of kinship prevailed again a century later when the Revocation confronted French families with a terrible decision. At that point, the Protestant line of Lacger, like the Isle, split: some abjured, some remained Protestant. The pattern of Lacger responses seems to bear out the mix of material considerations and conscience that was evident in the Champagné case. Lacger men whose financial and social standing rested upon royal posts (magistrates, military officers, civil officeholders) had little choice and so converted, perhaps not entirely enthusiastically. Those who could sustain themselves from landed wealth alone withdrew from public life and continued to live quietly as Protestants.[52] That the landed estate was the sine qua non for the modest nobility's remaining in France as clandestine Protestants confirms the meaning of the Champagné departure when they lost Berneré.

Religious division within the family had entirely different consequences, however, for the Lacger than for the Isle. While the young Isaac Isle was earning his Cross of Saint-Louis by his "services" against Protestants, the Lacger New Converts were protecting their Protestant kin, in continued family solidarity and amity. "Religious divisions were simply not permitted to shatter family solidarity.... The bonds of family affection overcame confessional rifts.... A sense of what was best for the family's future governed the whole." Both sides of the Lacger had their reasons for cultivating solidarity. On the Protestant side, continuing amity was perhaps easier after the Revocation than it had been earlier in the history of the Reformation. In the late sixteenth and early seventeenth centuries, all decisions to abjure seemed to be a voluntary betrayal of the cause, an opting for gain. After 1685, many were more sympathetic to the predicament of those who abjured because they did so under constraint rather than voluntarily. As for the Lacger whose conversions allowed them to continue in judicial and military offices, they were, perhaps, impelled by guilt or shame to take care of their more faithful (Protestant) relations. At the very least, their positions "enabled [them] to watch over the safety of [their] Protestant kin. Though these officers had not been able to remain Protestant themselves, they could improve the situation of, and in some ways protect, those in the family and the larger community who remained faithful to the Reformed tradition."[53]

So the Catholic Lacger "found ways to assist—especially financially—those cousins who had maintained greater constancy in the commitment to Protestant beliefs." Two Catholic cousins ensured the continuing prosperity of the Protestant line through the disposition of their estate when they died without children. Both François and Jean-Jacques de Lacger converted in the era of the Revocation, practiced Catholicism, and requested burial in the parish cemetery of Notre-Dame de La Platé. Both were lieutenant-colonels in the army and Chevaliers de Saint-Louis. François gave the greater part of his immense estate, including his seigneury of Navès, to his eldest Protestant cousin, while leaving a small grant to a Catholic cousin. Jean-Jacques left roughly 40 percent of his estate to a Protestant nephew with whom he lived in his old age as well as roughly half to a Catholic nephew. So with the wealth they amassed in service to the Catholic monarch who persecuted the religion into which they had been born, the Catholic Lacger acted to "dramatically reinvigorate the [economically weaker] Protestant lineage."[54]

To a person, the Protestant Lacger stayed in France, enabled to do so precisely because differences of confessional adherence did not shatter their family solidarity. The Protestants, protected by their Catholic kin, drew their own local confessional network even closer than it had been before the Revocation. Now religiously outlaws, they intermarried, cooperated economically, and served as godparents for each other's children; in short, they acted as the Isle had before the Revocation rent them apart, forming an integrated kindred tied together by their common religious culture.

With the help of kin, they avoided persecution. None of the Protestant Lacger had their children taken from them. Familial protection could be effective against the other most dangerous threat for insincere New Converts: mortal illness. On their deathbeds, Protestants who resisted confession and administration of last rites by the curé risked having their goods confiscated and their corpse dragged on a hurdle and tossed on the garbage dump. In families where solidarity survived religious division, kin could hide an illness from the curé, who would otherwise intervene with the law on his side. As one curé of Sedan opined: "As they are always surrounded by their *religionnaire* relatives who turn them away from the last sacraments by their prayers and threats, and do not notify us, we only learn of this misfortune after the persons have died."[55]

Families "Survive"

How might such persisting priority of family solidarity over religious division be explained? Personalities and other intangibles surely played their part. But the Lacger's biographer singled out one contributing factor that resonates with the contrasting Champagné case. The Lacger had the great advantage of never lacking male heirs—never falling into distaff—and having strong, long-lived patriarchs dominating the family. Successive strong-handed decision-makers determined "the Lacger's accomplishment—their long-term survival."[56]

It may be that survival was in one sense their great triumph. When the Old Regime was swept away, there were still Lacger. There were still Isle, too. But the very concept of "family survival" is an odd one whose meaning ought to be probed. Did families as a whole survive? Did the members of the family survive? Or only certain members of the family? Did some survive at the expense of others? The story of the Isle family reveals meanings of "survival" that are usually overlooked. Families like the Isle and Champagné endured hardship, internal conflict, and tragedy during the crisis of the Revocation. They also endured through it: some of their members left, but the family endured, obscuring the violence through which it "survived."

In the years when Isaac Isle was working to defend the Protestant temples of Saintonge, the king began to require nobles to present paper proofs of their noble status. Isaac and his cousins duly presented their papers in the 1660s and 1690s. Thereafter, families came to devote more and more attention to what constituted de facto their identity papers, systematizing them into genealogies.[57] Many of these would be published, in official collections such as those of students admitted to Madame de Maintenon's Saint-Cyr or later to the Ecole Militaire, or in collections pieced together from notarial archives and family attics.

But genealogies trace a line, not a family, and lines move male-to-male. The proofs of nobility required for admission to Saint-Cyr or to the Ecole Militaire, for example, traced a retrospective line from the pupil applicant to the father, grandfather, great-grandfather, and great-great-grandfather. The woman married to the male ancestor in each generation (like all her progenitors, male and female) was irrelevant: no line stretched upward from her. Such irrelevance of the wives was a key to the modernization of the Old Regime hierarchy, since "misalliance" in the form of marriage between a nonnoble (perhaps wealthy) woman and a noble man did not compromise the noble status of the family. Also irrelevant to proofs of nobility were all the sisters in the successive generations of sires, who might appear once in their group of siblings, only to disappear without a downward line being traced.

Wives and sisters were not the only ones to disappear from this retrospective tracing of family lines: the fathers who had only daughters disappeared, too, since no male descendant would ever trace a genealogy leading back to them. So it was with Casimir de La Rochefoucauld, father of the six sisters including Marie de La Rochefoucauld, and with Daniel Isle, father of the five sisters including Susanne Isle, with whom the multigenerational distaff line began. Casimir is listed in *La France Protestante* as "died without posterity." Beauchet-Filleau did not know where to locate Daniel in the Isle genealogy; Filleau linked Daniel to his parents in his sibling group but was unsure who his children might have been.[58] This disappearance from the future of a family that "survives" is part of what "falling into distaff" meant for men. Fathers with only daughters were lost, as mothers were lost simply by virtue of being born female and hence unable to transmit family "survival" in the form of the family name. Casimir de La Rochefoucauld and Daniel Isle, then, were only progenitors of a ghost line as far as family "survival" was concerned.

The family line, simplified by the shedding of females and the fathers of females, survived, too, generation to generation, through the sacrifice of certain members whose contribution to family survival fell from memory—families, like nations, forget selectively in order to remember a narrative of continuity. Such were persons disadvantaged in inheritance like Madelene de Solière, and her case is instructive precisely because she did not agree to play her assigned part as younger sister when new political and religious stresses eroded the family solidarity that could have made her do so. In matters of inheritance, family "survival" presupposed not only uneven portions but willingness on the part of those disadvantaged to accept their limited portion for the good of the house. Most often, decisions made by parents and their kin advisors were accepted by the children whose futures they prescribed; even a discontented heir would under usual circumstances feel constrained to accept an arrangement in the face of family consensus. If no one on the receiving end took exception and complained to a court, even arrangements not wholly consonant with the law could take effect. Strong discipline within families could make them, in internal matters, almost a self-regulating community that eschewed the machinery of the state, especially if shared religion fed the solidarity of the kindred.

Several factors converged in the era of the Revocation to undermine both ready acceptance of disadvantage and the ability of families to regulate themselves. Some were nonreligious. More generous inheritance practice—through increasing use of renunciation rather than exclusion, for example—meant that more children (especially daughters) shared in the family's wealth. In order to give more children appropriate portions, noble families had to find a way to increase their wealth in each generation at a rate faster than a preindustrial economy could provide. Hence they turned to an alliance with the king's purse. The same trends made enforcing inequality more difficult. The need for reinforcement from political power to defend against less-advantaged heirs increased the dependency of noble families on royal favor and on the courts. Moreover, the decreased ability of the family head to enforce family decision-making may have been most acute when the family head who was prescribing arrangements was a woman. In Saintonge, inheritance law put discretionary power in the hands of the parent, permitting the parent to prescribe unequal inheritances. The woman who headed a household had full legal authority to run its affairs. But her decisions might still have been more vulnerable to challenge than those made by a patriarch such as, for example, the Lacger.

Still, royal religious policy, culminating in the Revocation, did play a role in undermining family solidarity and all that depended upon it. Contrary choices made in the face of persecution and rewards deprived formerly Protestant kin of the religious solidarity that had reinforced family unity. Loss of religious solidarity had the power to turn ordinary family quarrels, which typically honeycombed Old Regime affairs, into fatal ones. The case of Madelene de Solière exemplifies the poisonous cocktail produced when religious division mixed with endemic family stresses. At another time, her attitude might have been merely a smoldering resentment perhaps commonplace in a province where the inheritance regimes disadvantaged daughters and younger sons. Instead, Madelene turned her back on the expectation of filial loyalty, stoking family discord and provoking the contest over Bernerė that contributed to the departure of Josias and Marie.

The Revocation also reshaped "surviving" families by creating emigrant ghosts. Unlike the Lacger, who stayed intact and protected their clandestinely Protestant members, divided families like the Isle, riven with stresses both religious and material, failed to protect their persistingly Protestant members, who, deprived of protection, fled or exposed themselves to punishment. The importance of protective networks, familial or local, in permitting Protestants to remain in France is borne out by community and geographical differentials among fugitives. As is well known, emigration varied with the density of Huguenots in communities.[59] It has been estimated that 40 percent of Huguenots fled from the North of France, where Protestants tended to be few and scattered. By contrast, in the Cévennes, "where communities formed a close-knit society attached to land that they could not and would not abandon," the rate of fugitives was as low as 5 percent. Similarly low numbers emigrated from the Southeast, which enjoyed "a familial tradition of resistance that emigration and repression scarcely made a dent in."[60] Emigration rates also varied with the readiness of local nonemigrants to conform. The areas from which emigration was heaviest were also those with least open resistance and fewest secret Protestants because of strong pressure from the Catholic majority.[61] Could the same be said of families—that numerous or willing conversions, by establishing a new familial norm, triggered departures by marginalizing the obstinate, while opportunistic or forced conversions, by not infringing the old solidarity, accommodated plural religious identities?

It is not hard to see a civil war playing out in some once-Protestant families through means placed by the state at the disposal of the converted. *Lettres de cachet* strengthened the hand of the New Convert paterfamilias—like Châtelaillon and Boisrond—who wished to reestablish religious uniformity among kin. The crown dispossessed those whose broken family bonds made them flee and reassigned their properties to kin who stayed and conformed. It seems impossible to separate the effects of monarchical centralization, religious unification, and family purges. The king's mandate of Catholicism forced French Protestants to choose between the king's will and their own religious heritage, undermining lineage solidarity when individuals and branch families made contrasting choices.

Yet the notion that the monarchy attacked families or promoted the disintegration of lineage solidarity sits uneasily with the ideological intertwining of absolute monarchy and patriarchal family. "The crown did not seek to weaken paternal authority. It sought, on the contrary, to reinforce it, guided perhaps by a new conception that regarded harmony inside the family as the basis of social harmony; but also by a venerable principle according to which protection of families was one of the fundamental duties of the monarchy."[62] The state relied on family units to discipline, to enforce laws and social norms, to keep order: why would it risk weakening them? As with prevention of escapes, there was a wide gap between pronouncement and practice. Legal empowerment gave officials the discretion to infringe paternal power when they judged that helpful to their objectives, but did not mandate application in every case. Many more children were left with suspect families than were taken from them. But to judge from the rolls of interned youngsters, thousands of children were taken from their parents—certainly enough to place in every Huguenot parent's breast the fear of losing their children. In its drive for religious uniformity, the crown did not so much seek to enhance paternal authority over children as to direct it and even co-opt it when the king's interests and the father's interests were at odds.

Crown actions testified to the power of family and to the perceived need to align families with state interest, by force if necessary. Working through families and replacing families were alike based upon an understanding of the family's dual potential: as the building-block of an orderly state or as a bastion against government influence that needed, under certain circumstances, to be broken up. The Revocation involved a shift or intensification in the way the state worked to control the family, going beyond empowering fathers to do its work in areas where their two interests converged to imposing its will when interests diverged.[63] The family might be a natural institution, but it was one the king would shape and (as required) prune, like a bush at Versailles.

In France, crown policy against Huguenots helped to alter fundamental patterns of loyalty at the heart of Old Regime society by eliminating certain families, but without attacking kinship itself. The king needed strong families, but he had no incentive to care who the incumbents were, no interest in who composed or headed a family, so long as they were loyal. The destruction of particular families such as the Champagné is not anomalous once one understands that the crown's objective was not supporting the families in place but ensuring that families offering reliable support became the constituent parts of the state. That is why the properties of their departed or resistant kin were redistributed to those willing to break with family religious tradition and why the conforming paterfamilias was furnished with letters of private justice for recreating religious uniformity within reconfigured families.

The Revocation set against each other members of the kin group that could go forward only in cooperation. In Marie de La Rochefoucauld's case, resolution of intrafamilial conflict that erupted in the years leading up to the Revocation was taken from the family itself, as the king's justice annulled the decisions made by Susanne Isle and her kin advisors. The bonds that had been created by social interaction and deepened by shared religion over the course of generations broke apart. Without the help of a coherent kin group to provide them with protection, the Champagné—and others who resisted conversion—could not safely stay. A catalyst to the Huguenot exodus may well, then, be found in the microsocial dynamics of families and communities rather than in the sweeping macro/structural forces such as population growth and competition for land. Shifts in social embeddedness, the remaking of "social figurations," fluctuations in "the interdependencies, close or remote, perceived or invisible, within which individuals are 'chained,' "[64] led some, but not most, of France's committed Protestants to leave the realm.

PART TWO

ESCAPING FROM FRANCE

6

Preparing the Escape

Once they decided to leave, the Champagné merged into a migratory wave that would sweep upwards of 150,000 subjects from Louis XIV's France in just a few years. The pattern of the Champagné escape—division of the family into multiple escape parties, emigration of some children but abandonment of others, separation of spouses—was common among the Huguenot refugees. Families rarely emigrated intact.[1] The ship that carried as contraband Jacques Fontaine, a ministry student from Saintonge, left La Tremblade for Appledore in November 1685 with Fontaine's own party of four (himself, his niece, his fiancée, and her sister), two boys from Bordeaux, and six young girls from Marennes. The twenty-five fugitives sailing from La Rochelle to Brielle in April 1688 with Jean Migault, a schoolmaster from Poitou, were two married couples, one with their youngest child in tow; three fathers bringing seven children among them; a widow and a lone mother, each with a daughter; one woman alone; and five men alone.[2]

Many considerations—some shared, some particular to a family's circumstances—separated children from parents, temporarily or permanently. Marie de La Rochefoucauld's pregnancy and Josias' need to wrap up the fight for Berneré at La Réole forced them to stay behind and send children on ahead. More commonly, one or more parents left children behind because of the physical rigors of travel or the limited availability of willing transport. Madame Collot, mother of a provincial noble family remarkably similar to the Champagné and linked to Marie in the Refuge, left her youngest child, aged three, with a friend in France because he was too young to endure such a hard journey. The captain first consulted for the escape of Madame de Puychenin, a Rochelais acquaintance who would help arrange Marie's departure, would let her bring her eldest son but not the younger ones. Others lost their children by royal action. The Comtesse de La Rochefoucauld-Roye, when she left by special permission in May 1686, was allowed by Louis XIV to take only three of her children, her other seven remaining in the convents and schools where he had placed them.[3] Even pastors who accepted the king's offer of licit emigration within the fortnight following the Revocation were coerced into splitting their families; the fourth clause of the Edict of Fontainebleau permitted them to take only those of their children who were under the age of seven.

Separation of spouses, too, could be coerced by royal action. Madame du Parc d'Archiac escaped to Plymouth while her husband, a cousin of Marie de La Rochefoucauld, was in custody.[4] Or it could be an act of spousal defiance. Madame de Boisrond hid from her husband until she could flee with her daughter and refused to return from Holland when he tried to fetch her back to France. Yet other couples who persisted together in the faith separated only to facilitate the escape with the intention of reuniting in the Refuge.

Marie de La Rochefoucauld's departure in advance of her husband exemplified both collaborative strategizing and spousal defiance. The fact that she and Josias eventually reunited in Holland as well as the affection with which she spoke of him in the memoir she wrote after his death suggest that the family's three-part escape was to some extent a collaboration of the spouses. Indeed, Marie's departure was made possible by a network of Josias' kin and friends—some in the Charentes and others in the distant Refuge. Escape memoirs, including Marie's, characteristically slight the prior arrangements that made exit possible, focusing rather on the journey between home and Refuge. This has created an impression that finding a ship or an overland guide was an individual matter of serendipity, worked out on the spot as fugitives rushed to leave.[5] Some Huguenots were indeed forced to improvise their flight across the border with little or no advance notice. But the Champagné escape was long anticipated and collaboratively arranged.

Marie mentioned in her memoir a few respects in which she relied upon help from others. When the governor questioned her, suspecting—correctly—that her move to the coast was preparation for departure, the monetary bond he required from her was provided by a friend whose identity she declined to divulge even in her private writing three years after the event and hundreds of miles away. She did, however, upon arriving in Holland, name two persons who helped her in La Rochelle: Madame de Voutron and Madame de Puychenin. The first was the wife of Josias' first cousin and slightly older contemporary Gédéon Nicolas de Voutron.[6] The daughter of a merchant in La Rochelle and residing in the Voutron house in the city, Marie Thauvet, Dame de Voutron probably provided Marie and her children with a place to live while waiting to escape. She was unlikely, however, to have been the same person who pledged the bond for Marie, since, though she herself had newly abjured, the surety would have had to come from someone considered a reliable Catholic, and her husband was in prison for his refusal to convert. Never willing to abjure, Gédéon Nicolas, Seigneur de Voutron, remained imprisoned at La Rochelle from November 1685 for more than two years, except for a month's respite over New Year's 1686, until he was eventually expelled from the kingdom. Madame de Voutron gestured sufficiently in the direction of abjuring that she was granted a pension, but before long, "because she fulfills none of the duties of a Catholic," Châteauneuf decided to withhold payment of it.[7]

Marie's second collaborator on the ground in La Rochelle, Madame de Puychenin, was Marie Henriette Chateigner, daughter of a family residing in the seigneury of Cramahé outside La Rochelle.[8] She was the local contact for the overseas transit—the ship, the pathway, and the welcome—which was put together by her in La Rochelle, her husband in Rotterdam, and Charles de La Motte Fouqué, Baron de Saint-Surin, a close friend and neighbor of Josias in Saintonge who would marry the Champagné daughter Susanne in The Hague in 1692. Saint-Surin had left his home in Tonnay-Boutonne on September 24, 1685,[9] perhaps the very day on which Josias abjured under pressure, settling for more than a year in Holland and then proceeding to Exeter in England. There he negotiated with English ship captains to go to France to pick up Protestant fugitives. When a captain agreed to do so, he would notify Puychenin in Rotterdam to arrange the financing and draw up the list of persons to be included in the escape. The role Madame de Puychenin assumed back in La Rochelle was to serve as a mail drop and intermediary with those whom relatives and friends in the Refuge had placed on the list for inclusion in the escape. Her husband gathered mail in Rotterdam and loaded it on shipboard to her in France. A ship captured in May 1687 on the Seudre was filled with letters addressed through her to would-be escapees. The addressees were arrested, and dragoons were sent to the home of Madame de Puychenin's aunt in Ré, who was suspected of abetting escapes. But no punishment for Madame de Puychenin was recorded in connection with the incident. Madame de Puychenin herself had tried, unsuccessfully, to leave France as early as August 1686 and was still seeking a captain at the end of December 1686, but she ended up staying longer than Marie and her children.[10]

This three-point network—Exeter, Rotterdam, La Rochelle—arranged escape vessels at the time of the Champagné children's escape and at the time of Marie's escape. By the beginning of April 1687, three ships were in place for loading escapees and ready to leave; one at La Rochelle and two at Ré "are to leave soon with numerous refugees who will meet up in La Rochelle two or three days before the departure and several of whom have already stashed their effects in said vessels. These people or their effects can be found at the home of the aunt of Puychenin, who ordinarily lives on the Ile de Ré but may well be in La Rochelle at present, where she has property."[11] It seems certain that the advance party of Champagné children was on one of these ships: the *Tiger,* under Captain Thomas Robinson. Port records for Falmouth list an arrival for the *Tiger* that accords to the smallest details of timing and cargo.

Daughter Susanne's memoir of the escape notes that their captain emptied wine casks to make room for the fugitives, and the *Tiger* arrived in England with three wine casks for which no duty was paid because they were empty.[12] Upon entering Exeter early on a Sunday afternoon, the Champagné children proceeded directly to the home of the pastor Sanxay, whom their family knew well since he had been the Reformed minister at Tonnay-Boutonne, and met up with Saint-Surin. Susanne got word of their safe arrival to her mother before she left Berneré for the last time, perhaps through the intermediacy of the two Puychenin in Rotterdam and La Rochelle.[13]

Then, toward the end of June, while Marie was hiding in La Rochelle awaiting passage, Saint-Surin hired an English ship commanded by an English captain "so the vessel will leave in a few days from where it is now. It is not known precisely where it will go, but there is a strong appearance that it is La Rochelle." This was no doubt the ship that carried Marie de La Rochefoucauld to England, to a reunion with her children and Saint-Surin in Exeter. With two groups of Champagné safely abroad, it remained only to bring out Josias and the baby. In September 1687, while Marie and her children were resting in Exeter, Saint-Surin told Puychenin he had arranged for another English captain to sail for La Rochelle, this time to pick up Madame de Puychenin, her children, and her aunt, as well as a number of persons integral to the Champagné story: perhaps Josias himself, the infant Thérèse, and her nurse, if Josias was not still in La Réole (which he was); the family of Monsieur de Ciré (brother of René Culant, baby René-Casimir's godfather); the son of Monsieur de Bussac (in whose château chapel many earlier Champagné had been baptized); and Monsieur de Magezy (Charles de Villedon) and his daughter.[14]

Collaborative strategizing between spouses, then, created the Champagné's escape through a tight transnational network of Josias' friends and family. Still, Marie's early move toward emigration may also signal a never-explicit friction between the spouses. Throughout the period of preparations, Marie's determination moved the emigration forward in the face of multiple obstacles, including Josias' ambivalence about leaving. Josias had abjured his ancestral religion just before the Revocation and was trying out Catholicism during Marie's initial sojourn in the La Rochelle staging area. Josias mentioned in his June 1686 letter to his children that his abjuration had caused a scandal among those close to him; it seems reasonable to think that he referred to an estrangement between him and Marie. Josias' renewed commitment to Protestantism, conveyed in the same June letter, may have played a role in bringing her back to Berneré that summer for harvest tasks. It seems likely that she became pregnant on this harvest-time visit to Berneré, since the baby born on May 16, 1687 would have been conceived around mid-August. Soon after the harvest, Marie returned to La Rochelle. She and the children resided once more with

Madame de Voutron, drawing monies as well as supplies from the lands Josias' mother bequeathed him in the nearby marshes of Agère and Voutron.[15]

The moves back and forth between town and country may have provided some cover for the intention to escape, since the authorities in the city could assume that any missing family members were in the country and vice versa. But these separations, as well as Marie's willingness to take herself away from Berneré for extended periods of time in a fashion that made her dependent on others, may also bespeak a distancing from Josias, as do certain of her financial dealings in this period. The fact that it was not until March 11, 1687 that she signed at Berneré for funds Josias had collected in a transaction dated January 20, 1687 suggests the length of the interval during which she separated from him by residing in La Rochelle. Moreover, on December 30, 1686, she signed a power of attorney for Josias, no doubt so he could manage her properties in her absence; he could not do so without such authorization, since the two had legally separated their estates. But before leaving, she gave a second power of attorney, with or without Josias' knowledge and approval, to a neighbor residing on the Boutonne near Champagné, a cousin of Jean Yver, the former minister in Saint-Jean-d'Angély. Someone other than Josias was to handle her affairs in her absence.[16]

Financial Arrangements

Marie's move to the coast with the children early in 1686 marked the beginning of the planning—just as the governor suspected it did. The length of her preparations—lasting more than a year—mirrors the experience of others and helps explain why, in the aggregate, the number of Huguenot departures from France would peak not in the year of the Revocation or the next, but precisely in the year of Marie's departure, 1687, and that following.[17] It was not enough to free the bodies and souls from Babylon: fugitives would need both funds to cover the cost of the escape and capital for resettlement abroad.

The escape itself was not inexpensive, and, as is usual with clandestine commerce, charges could vary significantly. Transporting Huguenots was lucrative for ship captains, but they pursued this profit at their peril; if caught in the act, they were liable to be sentenced to imprisonment in French galleys, and, in cases of foreign captains, not even intervention by their ambassador with the French court could effect their release. Colbert de Croissy turned down one petition for grace from the Dutch ambassador, "since an example should be made against the Dutch who every day transport fugitives, which is intolerable." The risk that willing captains ran kept the price high. Marie's memoir says passage from La Rochelle to Exeter for three persons cost her 473 *livres* and the crossing from Topsham to Rotterdam by sea for "my entire family" another 40 *écus*. Susanne's memoir noted that the ship's captain charged 200 *livres* for each of the persons in her advance party. Jacques Fontaine's party paid 10 *pistoles* (110 *livres*) each to be taken from La Tremblade to Appledore by John Dennis, master of the *Industry* of Barnstaple. The intendant Arnoul said the agreed cost for passage was 12 *louis d'or* (132 *livres*) per person—the same for children as for adults.[18] To put this level of expense into perspective, the charge for room and board in a very fine convent cost on average 150–200 *livres* per year.

Overland was even more expensive. The famous guide Pierre Le Duc would take parties from Paris to Holland for 20 *louis d'or* (220 *livres*) apiece. There could be other expenses, notably payments to the intermediaries who brokered ships or the guides and other personnel who accompanied those escaping overland. The Poitevin noble Josué Robineau de La Chauvinière—a distant relation of Marie de La Rochefoucauld through the wife of Isaac Isle—paid an intermediary in January 1687 about 150 *livres* in *louis d'or* for each of the persons in his party; two on the same boat who negotiated with the captain directly paid 120 *livres* apiece. Jean Migault discovered that 35 *livres* of the 75 *livres* per person fee he was offered on an English vessel would go to his intermediary and only 40 *livres* to the captain.[19]

Bribes could also be an expense. Arrivals in the Refuge retailed stories about the role of "gratifications" in their escape. Anne de Chauffepié claimed in her memoir that the fugitives on the boat taking them out to their English ship were able to bribe the guards from Ré who boarded and found them. After a payment of 100 *pistoles*, they were let go. But then the same contingent of guards reboarded the ship, took them all plus the captain prisoner, and looted their belongings. A crafty escapee from Cognac named Le Brun and his son were stopped by some cavaliers who were garrisoned at the home of the Isle cousin du Gua de La Rochebreuillet. Searching Le Brun, the cavaliers found 800 *francs*. But Le Brun had worked out the power dynamics of the situation and told the cavaliers: "If you take me, I will sign [an abjuration] and you will be obliged to give me back my money. I will leave it with you if you give me my liberty." The ploy cost him what he had in his pocket, but the soldiers allowed him and his son to continue their flight.[20]

Of course the funds required to support a new life abroad were vastly greater and more challenging to amass. The 200 *écus* that Jurieu estimated each refugee brought on average would not customarily be lying about in cash. It took Pierre de Cosne, an orphan in possession of the family estate at La Bletterie in Sologne, nearly two years to amass the "considerable sum to help him leave the kingdom and live where he was going until he found some means of subsistence." By the time Pierre Changuion escaped in the summer of 1686, carrying out as much gold as could fit between the soles of his shoes and a purse containing more, he had "already worked for a long time to put his affairs in order and convert to cash the most liquid things he owned, whereas for the other properties, like lands, meadows, vines, house, and so on, nothing could be drawn from them." Indeed, having one's wealth invested in land, normally an effective means of both social advancement and financial stability in France, could be a source of poverty in exile. Jacques Cabrit lamented that his mother's dowry had been used to buy land, for that led to their destitution "when we were obliged to leave France, for otherwise we would have been able to carry money with us."[21]

Still, assets could be transferred successfully. At the moment the Champagné departure began, Bazin de Bezons, intendant in Bordeaux, told the controller-general that fugitives had taken out so much in movable assets that southern Saintonge was drained of wealth and "those who remain are quite miserable." Harlay, intendant in Burgundy, reported that Protestant "deserters" took with them "all the money, movable property, grains, forage, and livestock from the region, which were only too well received in Geneva or in Switzerland." Champagné family financial records hint at transactions they undertook specially in preparation for flight, though they can be difficult to distinguish from the routine acquiring and disposing of assets that were an ongoing activity even for those, like Josias and Marie, whose fortune was primarily landed—and especially for a couple whose finances were as hard-pressed as theirs were.[22]

Perhaps Marie carried away in July the 550 *livres* that Josias turned over to her in March from the sale of wood; escapees often did carry liquid assets on their person. Five of the fugitives arrested with Robineau de La Chauvinière on an English boat at the mouth of the Loire in January 1687 carried cash amounts ranging from 36 *livres* to 1,373 *livres* (illustrating the complexity of currency, La Chauvinière carried the largest sum in the form of 57 Spanish *pistoles*, 45 *louis d'or*, 16 gold pieces worth 2 *pistoles* each, and 27 silver *écus*). Refugee wills in England often mentioned pearl and diamond ornaments, suggesting that more than a few emigrants managed to salvage this easily portable form of capital. Robineau de La Chauvinière tried to carry out turquoise, diamonds, pearls, and other jewelry valued at 200 *livres*. Marie de La Rochefoucauld, too, may well have carried jewels with her as she lay beneath the deck of the ship taking her to England, since a clause in her daughter Susanne's 1692 marriage contract in The Hague said the bride's dowry consisted of rings and jewels estimated by relatives and friends who witnessed the marriage contract to be worth 3,000 *livres*."[23] Marie's daughters Julie and Marianne would receive similar jewels when they came of age. The high value of precious stones, compact in size, made them perfect for the escapee's purposes.

But how could moneys reach refugees abroad if they were not carried as cash or jewels on one's person when attempting an escape? Numerous refugees, including the Champagné, piggybacked the export of their funds on routine commerce. Marie de La Rochefoucauld had assets waiting for her when she arrived in Holland, for a letter Josias sent her while she was en route urged her to look into opportunities to "invest the money you have in that country [Holland] in such a way that you can withdraw principal when you like, or in two or three months." Just how these particular funds had been sent to Holland cannot be said. But three methods of transfer emerge in the Champagné records: fictitious loan repayments, deposits with trusted intermediaries, and the trade in brandy.

On March 21, 1688, shortly before he left for Holland, Josias went personally to the chambers of the notary Rabusson in La Rochelle to record his payment of 1,900 *livres* to Sieur Tayau, a lawyer at the Presidial of La Rochelle.[24] Ostensibly, Josias was repaying a loan, and if that was truly the case, he was remarkably conscientious to clear his debts on his way out of the country. But might the payment have been a subterfuge? Tayau was also Josias' confidant in legal matters, and one of the common methods for exporting funds without carrying them on one's person was just such a deposit, under the pretext of loan repayment, to be forwarded after the depositor's arrival abroad. Without the ruse of a loan, any handoff of funds to Tayau could have drawn unwelcome attention from the authorities, who knew well that "those who left drew up fraudulent bills and promises in private transactions in favor of persons to whom they had no real debts, with a view to safeguarding their effects and having the sums declared as owed to false creditors sent to them in foreign countries."[25]

Using a trusted intermediary back home, without the documented fiction of a loan, was a relatively easy but sometimes risky vehicle for moving funds into the Refuge. Josias learned how risky in his second maneuver, which involved his sister's brother-in-law Charles Prévost de Touchimbert, Sieur de Brassac and which a nineteenth-century Champagné descendant would call "a very sad transaction deeply tinged with premeditated swindling." During Holy Week 1688, just days before his departure into exile, Josias left Brassac 800 *livres* in cash that were too heavy to carry with him plus a gray brood mare for Brassac to sell on his behalf. "I left him all that on his good faith."[26] Brassac never deposited the funds with Monsieur Heraud, the banker in La Rochelle from whom Josias intended to retrieve them in absentia.

Huguenots with greater resources than Josias were also swindled by those to whom they entrusted the transfer of assets. "The Marshal Schomberg on his arrival in Lisbon was extremely surprised by the bankruptcy of the man to whom he sent his money, who had left, alleging reasons of religion, with several others to go to Brandenburg. This marshal wrote to the King [of France] to beg him to interpose his authority with this Elector, to give him some satisfaction. His Majesty agreed." Still, Josias' reliance on Brassac showed poor judgment to begin with, for the two of them had just two years earlier contested a debt in court. Brassac's betrayal may be attributable simply to Brassac's chronic need for cash to pay his own debts.[27] Even so, his perfidy also reflects the extent to which family disintegration preceded (even helped provoke) the move into exile.

Looking back, Josias saw the collapse of the deal with Brassac in moral terms, as a betrayal of friendship, honor, hospitality, and religion. During the three months he spent in Holland after his escape, as he reviewed his finances and set his affairs in order before departing with the army of William of Orange, Josias reflected upon his relations with Brassac and left a memo explaining how he had been duped—a four-page lament that is the closest thing to an escape memoir from Josias' pen. Josias had taken Brassac into his confidence in the midst of a threatening situation, revealing his escape plans to him after Brassac "came to assure me that he was my faithful friend and would render me any service he could and that I could confide in him." In Josias' marsh-land residence at Lisleau in October 1685, at Berneré in November 1686, at his cousin Madame de Fontpastour's house in December 1687, and at Champagné in April 1688, Josias "revealed all his affairs to him." When Brassac offered to pay Josias interest for the time the funds were in his hands, on the grounds that they would be useful to him, Josias declined, linking his own well-being to his friend's by assuring Brassac that "I would be delighted if he made a profit from them." Upon his leaving for the last time, "we exchanged thousands of assur-ances of friendship." For Josias, then, it was not just the ethics of the market-place that were violated in this affair, but the bonds of kinship and friendship. "That is what came of the grand offers of service he gave me. . . . This is the pure truth of the matter, God pardon him for the wrong he did to a fugitive family in a foreign land that was not able to sell an inch of land before departing."[28]

The third and most important maneuver the Champagné used for moving funds into the Refuge exploited the trade in brandy that, right through the Revocation period, sustained a flow of Dutch and English ships, factors, and moneys into the Charentais countryside. New Converts who continued to reside in France were able to move in and out of the kingdom in pursuit of their business affairs. They were likewise able to move money out of the kingdom easily under the cover of this trade. The way this facilitated emigration was not lost on contemporaries: "The New Converts are practically the only ones who ship cargos: they send brandy to their brothers, their relatives and their chil-dren who are refugees in foreign lands, and it is certain . . . that trade in this city is nearly all in the hands of those men, while the old Catholic townsmen do hardly any of it." Numerous refugees from the Charentes used the commerce in brandy to support themselves and their families in Holland. The pastor Masson, formerly at Cozes and now in the Refuge, "has at Cognac in Angoumois 1,800 *francs* worth of brandy that are to be taken to the town of Cha[rente]. Jean Faneuil, a merchant living in Rotterdam instructed his sister Madame Dubois, who lives in the said town of Charente to load this brandy on the first vessel for the account of the said Faneuil, fearing that the creditors of the Sieur Masson would confiscate them." Champagné family friend and transport-arranger Saint-Surin likewise transferred funds through the wine trade, leaving thirty-five units of brandy with his brother to be collected, upon their arrival in Holland, either in kind or in cash.[29] So did the Champagné.

In a letter he sent to Marie on November 2, 1687, as she made her way from Exeter to Holland, Josias instructed her on how to make the most of the commercial merchandise they had sent from Berneré to Amsterdam ahead of her arrival there. She must quickly familiarize herself with the business world of Holland and advise him of her findings "as soon as you have learned a little about trade." In particular, she must take care of the brandy she had there: not selling right away but waiting for higher market prices, in the meantime having it tended often to prevent it from leaking. Storage, he knew, would be expensive, but she should nonetheless find the cheapest way to warehouse the brandy, as the meager 1687 harvest in the Charentes boded well for a rise in prices: "There is wine around Bordeaux, but everywhere else there is less than last year, and the wines are not so good, so there will be much less brandy than last year." Josias was, then, conveying to Marie the way Charentais seigneurs like himself had learned to play the vagaries of the market.[30]

In these instructions lay the seeds of the transformation of Marie de La Rochefoucauld into an investor in the Refuge, the dual metamorphosis—from passivity to activity, from landed economy to trade—of a woman who seemingly participated little in the financial affairs of the estate in France but became the party responsible for the family fortune in a world of commerce.[31] In the near term, however, the task was to transfer funds from France to Holland, so she needed to send Josias information on conditions in her new location that would help him back in the Charentes make the best possible transfers. She was asked to let Josias know who her dealer was to be, the location of accounts to which he could send items from France, "what can be expected in that country for old and young wines," and the actual movement of wine prices so he could decide how to proceed. This last request suggests that Josias and Marie envisioned the export of brandy as a means of continuing financing, not just a short-term expedient.

The Champagné, then, a noble landed family, used market capitalism to effect their relocation. As such, they were connected to what has been called the "Protestant International," trading networks linking Protestant merchants and financiers on the eastern and western seaboards of the North Atlantic and peopled by a business emigration independent of persecution both before and after the Revocation.[32] For the Champagné, the trading networks dominated by French Protestants in La Rochelle and its hinterland were a facilitator, and their move into the Refuge might have been impossible without that commerce. Their decision happened to fall into a precise commercial conjuncture: after Charentais brandy was well established as an export to Amsterdam, demand rising in the second half of the seventeenth century, but before the Dutch turned to domestically distilled gin and centered their brandy taste on the superior-quality "cognac" produced upstream in and around the eponymous city, to which the brandy from the hinterlands of La Rochelle was a poorer cousin.[33] Still, the Champagné family did not emigrate for business reasons; their move resulted from pushes out of France (familial, religious, financial) rather than from any commercial pull into a location with superior prospects for profit.[34]

What Possessions Would They Take Along?

In 1696, Jan Luyken, the Dutch Mennonite poet and artist, published an influential engraving of Huguenot refugees leaving France for their place of asylum. Luyken was a publicist, a newsman who alerted a broad audience of readers and nonreaders to current and recent events. His engraving conveys the drama of the migration, the broad canvas suggesting both the event's scope and its historic importance. But Luyken's rendering of the refugees suggests more about the way their hosts perceived the Huguenots arriving among them than about the migrants' actual experience as recorded in their memoirs and in official records. His refugees appear in very large numbers, as if actors upon an enormous stage, embarking on very large sailing ships, and together form a highly visible wave of diverse beings. Yet fugitives made their way from France in small groups, on small ships, and in secrecy. The combined effect of hundreds of small disembarkations in Holland may simply have made the hosts imagine a tsunami. Similarly, the evident prosperity of some refugees may account for Luyken's imagining that refugees arrived with their assets—driving pigs and cattle, riding horses, accompanied by dogs.

The opposite picture emerges in Huguenots' own stories of the emigration, which emphasized the impossibility of bringing property into the Refuge and figured the emigrant as descending into poverty. New arrivals in London—silkworker or tailor or midwife—needed small handouts to buy the most basic necessities: a coverlet or a child's pair of shoes or burial costs. Even the banker

Figure 6.1 The Flight of the Reformed Out of France. Etching by Jan Luyken, 1696. By permission of AKG Images.

Samuel Bernard, perhaps the richest man in Europe, cited poverty as a reason for his reluctance to leave France rather than conform: "Besides the nearly insurmountable difficulties of the passage, being under surveillance as I am, it is dreadful to abandon more than 200,000 *livres* of property in houses and *rentes* to go beg for one's bread in foreign lands with a wife and children. I know one must abandon all for God. One must pray that he give us the strength and the means for life with only a bit of bread in foreign lands and the ability to do so."[35]

This clash of representations raises the question: what could or did refugees take along? Like migrants generally, Huguenots who defied the king by leaving the kingdom against his orders had to make decisions about what to take with them. Given the ambiguity about prospects of return, they must have taken both what they would need in exile and what they would need if they were someday able to return. But since—unlike most emigrants—they had to escape undetected, how limited were they as to what they could carry?

There were ways of sending goods out, though how frequently they were used is unclear. Madame de Puychenin, who helped organized the Champagné escape, sent ahead of her own attempted escape in August 1686 "a coffer to her husband filled with clothing and 70 *écus* in silver." Traces of the cargos that actually accompanied Huguenot emigrants as they fled can be found both in official records and in the escape memoirs that Huguenots would later write down in exile. Jacques Cabrit, leaving from Languedoc, sewed "10–12 gold *louis* into my culottes, at the spot where the stockings are rolled" and took a sack of "necessities" that was so heavy and fatiguing after a single day of walking that he hired a soldier for a *sol* a day to carry it for him. Anne de Chauffepié's memoir notes that her jailers in the Citadel of Ré confiscated her scissors, knives, and books, including "those with prayers and meditations by Le Faucheur and Du Moulin . . . [and] our Bibles." Robineau de La Chauvinière carried not only his 1,373 *livres* in cash and 200 *livres* worth of gems, but also silver tableware valued at 500 *livres* (including six dozen spoons and forks), a box of ribbons, several lace headdresses, two fans, four brand-new muskets, three pairs of pistols, six swords (brand new and very valuable), and "some very important papers."[36]

Indeed, it is the cargo of papers and books that finds its way remarkably often into escape memoirs—frequently enough to suggest that saving or losing books and papers held special meanings for those leaving home. In preparation for his escape, Tessereau's great friend Elie Bouhéreau traveled from La Rochelle to Paris, where he persuaded the English ambassador to send his library of books and manuscripts to England, giving him a receipt of purchase as if the ambassador had bought them. Jacques Cabrit's father, a pastor who was preparing for his legal departure, took his library, "composed of a great number of good English books," out to their country home by night and buried it in a stable. "Most likely all that has been moldy and rotted for years." One book, though, Cabrit carried with him when he escaped: a book of psalms that he used to identify himself as a Huguenot wherever it was expedient to do so along the way.[37]

It is not surprising that, as people of the Book, Huguenots would take books with them and mention their doing so. Papers, though, had a different importance that is even more suggestive. There were papers religious and papers secular. One type of religious paper was the certificate of conversion, fraudulent or real, that could protect escapees under interrogation en route. Cabrit carried the "certificate of reunion" that a complacent curé in a neighboring village had given him without much questioning in return for his signature on a simple renunciation of theological errors and a gratuity of five *sols*. Two would-be escapees from Poitou caught walking near La Rochelle told the authorities interrogating them that they were to identify themselves to those who would shelter them in the coastal staging area and to the ship's captain by showing their *témoignage* from Saint-Maixent. *Témoignages* found on captured fugitives were considered damning evidence of guilt because "no one embarks without their attestations, so the deserters will be received in the foreign lands."[38]

As for secular papers, the passport—authentic or fake—could mightily smooth an exit. Pierre Changuion was able to secure one from the governor of Sedan that allowed him to go to Liège in the guise of a merchant with business there. The Dutch ambassador's secretary in Paris was known to issue passports to Protestants withdrawing to Holland, for which offense Louis XIV instructed his ambassador in The Hague, the Comte d'Avaux, to demand his recall by the States General. But other documents of personal identity could be much more crucial than the passport for transferring social capital into the Refuge in the longer term, and some managed to bring them along. Daniel Collot carried with him the 1675 royal act recognizing his family's nobility "that I was able to save as by a miracle" and the pension letter by which the king awarded him 200 *écus* per year after he lost an arm in battle as well as an inventory listing all the family papers that were left behind in the possession of a cousin—"by which you have seen who you are," as he told his children. One of the fugitives from Caen caught in Bayeux in July 1687 carried only two half *louis d'or*—a pittance—but in his pocket had a small bundle of papers that included two certifications of release from the admiral under whom he had evidently served "and other useless receipts."[39]

What may have appeared "useless" to the official who inventoried captured items could be of critical importance to the persons who chose to carry them, rather than other possessions, when leaving home. Early modern families were obliged to furnish their own material confirmation of social identity, and so they would have at home "a coffer of notarized family contracts and deeds." Refugees who lost in their flight from France the lineage documents that bore their family's tangible identity would endure the lack of credence in the Refuge that made integration difficult in concrete, material ways and aggravated the trauma of displacement. For them, exile became "civil death" or "yet another form of persecution" unless they could document themselves through replacement papers they created (memoirs) or collected (*témoignages*) to rematerialize their identity.[40]

Marie de La Rochefoucauld does not indicate in her memoir what she took along or left behind when she escaped, but another of her documents confirms that she took very little other than the few jewels her daughters later received. On October 9, 1690, three years after arriving in Holland and almost precisely a year after her husband's death, Marie left her quarters on the Lauriergracht in Amsterdam to go to the office of the notary Jean Hoekebak and draw up an "Inventory of the effects in her hands at present, to serve her and her children as appropriate until such time as Divine Providence puts them in a situation to make a fuller inventory, if it pleases God to reestablish them in their properties." She was obliged to do this by terms of her husband's will, as guardian of their children. She showed the notary various papers, documents, titles of nobility, and property, which he proceeded to list. The final pages of the inventory purported to cover the "furnishings presently in the house where the said Dame de Champagne resides, situated on the Laurier Gragt, and which is all she may have in her possession." The residence contained bed linens and table linens, two chests, an oak cabinet, twelve straw chairs, tableware, cooking utensils, a fireplace andiron, two Bibles, and two volumes entitled *Les Consolations contre les frayeurs de la mort* (*Christian's Defense against the Fears of Death*).[41] Such a sparse material environment lends credibility to Susanne's statement in her memoir that the advance group of Champagné children took with them only the clothing on their backs. Most likely, none of the household items were carried by Marie on her escape. The Bibles and devotional books may or may not have come with them from home; both the Geneva Bible and Charles Drelincourt's *Consolations* (1651) were readily available both in France and in Holland.

Josias' baggage, though, carried most or all of what the inventory listed other than the household furnishings. As he made his way, first overland via Paris and then by ship from Dieppe, his saddlebags and trunks—the "two large, well-stocked trunks" that one of his valets delivered overland to Marie in Voorburg or the "large suitcase" Josias took himself by sea—bulged with papers and parchments he thought important enough to bring along, despite the fact that they increased the risk of capture. If he were stopped and searched en route, the cache of documents would betray his intentions to leave the kingdom without permission. What were these documents? Why did Josias bring them? What can they tell us about the family's concerns as they left France? And how did they shape the story told in the Refuge about their family? The answers to these questions can be found by juxtaposing what was available to bring—the papers that were at Berneré and Champagné before the family departed, as listed in an inventory Josias drew up on the eve of his departure and took with him to Holland—to the papers Josias chose to bring—those listed on Marie's Amsterdam inventory in October 1690 and then inherited by their British descendants (the manuscripts known as "the Champagné Papers").[42]

In January 1688, after all the family had left except himself and the now eight-month-old Thérèse, Josias sat down to inventory the "titles and papers" belonging to him and his absent wife. It must have been a grinding task over many days to gather, read, summarize, and annotate in tiny script 112 documents on 15 folio-size pages. It must also have been emotionally wrenching, especially in Josias' fragile state of mind. An inventory scarcely lends itself to the expression of emotion, but at one point the voice of the man who sat writing this one comes through in a manner that touches those he could never have foreseen would be reading it. After describing the division of inheritance with his sister, as he had almost finished reviewing the documents he presented to prove his ancestry, he blurted out: "'Tis I who am this Josias de Robillard who writes the present inventory." The assertion is a signature, a voice crying out to identify himself as the man at the end of the trail of the preceding documents, as the scion of this race.

Josias wrote the inventory, he says, "to serve as clarification and to be useful to my children after my death." This statement of purpose merely envisions the same transfer between generations that settled families faced, not even hinting that Josias was on the verge of leaving. But other features of the inventory suggest that his intentions in compiling it had as much to do with the family's future standing in the Refuge as with their past business in Saintonge. Of the seventy-two items concerning Berneré, Josias had the option of loading only fifty-five into his Holland-bound saddlebags, since, as he would say in a marginal note added in Holland, the other papers that would normally have been at Berneré were at the Parlement in La Réole in connection with Madelene de Solière's lawsuit against Marie. Of these fifty-five, he chose to bring with him into the Refuge only fifteen. He left behind the records of everyday operations of the estate (local justice, small-increment land purchases, land-letting), other people's land management (the La Rochefoucauld sisters' affairs at Saint-Hippolyte), long-concluded transactions concerning the lord's oven, and contentions with friends or relations (Chambon, Malesac).

What he selected for transfer from Berneré into the Refuge were those documents that identified the family, the lineage, the standing of the family in French society. Josias selected for Marie those documents that demonstrated her lineal identity, those closest to the titles of nobility that Josias and other male heads of family submitted in 1666 and whenever the crown asked them to do so. Six documents described what Susanne Isle inherited from her father and mother, in doing so stating the "qualities" of her parents and brothers-in-law. The three recounting how Berneré was carved out of Forgette for her and Jean de Lescure were not just land deeds but proofs that they held the rights of justice and homage that only a noble could exercise. The marriage contract of Marie de Solière with Casimir de La Rochefoucauld, the documents confirming payment of what was due to that Marie as Susanne Isle's daughter and heiress, and the set of four agreements among the six La Rochefoucauld sisters in implementation of their grandmother's will were, as Josias wrote in the inventory, "important for the settling of our rights."

The documents Josias brought from Champagné had a different character—they were the man's documents, those of the eldest son of an eldest son—but Josias' selection here was similar. Josias left behind all the estate management documents from his own time as Seigneur de Champagné: a sack of land purchases, documents concerning justice on the seigneury, records of tenancies and leases, all the accounts of his management of the lands at Agère and Voutron that were his maternal inheritance, his reckoning of the taxes he was obliged to pay at Rochefort (as of 1688, he was paid up only through 1671), and a 1687 order from the subdelegate Rousselet confirming Josias' authorization to collect dues from those who resided on his estate at Champagné. He left his sister Marie's 1657 marriage contract with Casimir Prévost de Touchimbert, perhaps for use by their children, who eventually became heirs to Champagné.

What Josias took to Holland from Champagné were twenty-one of the forty inventory entries, precisely the documents he had presented to the *recherche de noblesse* in 1666 plus the documents on his own generation that his children would need for proving their nobility. He carried away the records of vital events dating back to a land purchase in 1482 by "Jean de Robillard, squire," a man at arms in the company of Jacques de Luxembourg; the succession of inheritances from Jean de Robillard's son André in the 1520s, then settled at La Grange near Saintes, where the family would continue to reside until it acquired Champagné late in the century; property divisions in 1572, 1619, 1626, 1640, 1641, 1662, 1663, 1669, and 1677; André de Robillard's reporting for military duty and the "march of the gentlemen" in 1557; the wills of grandfather Christophe in 1611 and father Josias in 1652; the marriage contract of Josias' parents in 1639 as well as his own with Marie de La Rochefoucauld in 1667; his and Marie's mutual will of 1683; and the certificate dated November 27, 1666, signed by the intendant d'Aguesseau at Limoges acknowledging that these records proved his nobility.

As a consequence of Josias' selections—coupled with the fact that everything concerning the lawsuit over Berneré was unavailable and would remain so because Josias left just as the Parlement rendered its judgment in favor of Madelene—the papers and parchments Josias and Marie could produce in their exile and bequeath to their children depicted a stable noble family. In stable possession of La Grange for two centuries and Champagné for one, seigneurs of a Berneré carved out from Forgette and explicitly assigned to Marie de La Rochefoucauld, they could be presumed to have been wrenched from their home only by the religious upheaval of the Revocation. Marie's memoir of her escape, written in January 1690, mirrors this in that it, too, omits all discussion of the Berneré lawsuit, and only the most discerning can catch from the memoir any whiff of conflict in family and community. So it is not surprising that when Champagné descendants, and others who used the family's archive, wrote the story of the escape, they celebrated a stable noble family settled on its estate that gave up everything for the sake of conscience.[43]

Only remarkable luck has permitted a fuller picture of this family's history. The documents left behind at La Réole were eventually returned to the archives at Berneré, where they mixed with the papers of the eighteenth-century owners of the château. At some unknown point they were sold and made their way into the hands of a local historian in the Périgord, not far from the origin of the Solière de Lescure family. The documents left behind at Champagné remained there and mixed with the papers of Josias' Prévost de Touchimbert nieces, who took over the property after there were no more Robillard de Champagné in France, and then mixed further with the records of the two neighboring estates belonging to the person to whom André du Rousseau de Fayolle sold Champagné in December 1784. Eventually, this combined cache of documents joined the collections at the Archives municipales de Saintes.[44] The revised picture of the Champagné and, through them, of the Huguenot emigration results from supplementing the papers Josias carried into the Refuge with the two sets of papers left behind at Berneré and Champagné.

Passing the Frontier

The Saintonge and Aunis coast, from La Rochelle south to the Gironde, lent itself particularly well to escapes. Unlike the long coast of Brittany, it had no rocky shores, and unlike Normandy few cliffs. Numberless bays, inlets, and stream mouths accessible by fishing boats and small cargo vessels surrounded the large commercial and military harbors where surveillance of maritime traffic was concentrated. Migrants from its hinterland had long floated out the Charente and the Seudre, making La Rochelle and Rochefort the principal departure points south of the Loire for French emigration. Even Saint-Savinien played some role in the overseas export of persons, since oceangoing ships pulled right up to its quais, scarcely a few miles from Berneré. When Huguenot fugitives infiltrated these well-established outward flows, some may have boarded right at Saint-Savinien; they certainly boarded at Tonnay-Charente, just downstream, where most ships carrying brandy to England and Holland were loaded.[45]

Marie had good reason not to do so. A party of ministers leaving legally from Tonnay-Charente on November 14, 1685—among them, the pastor Sanxay, who would greet the Champagné when they arrived in Exeter—illustrates why. The distance from Tonnay-Charente overland to the sea was only some twelve miles, and yet it took their *La Montagne de Lievre*, captained by Robert Simon and headed for Rotterdam, nine days to reach the sea because of bad weather. The anonymous memorialist aboard describes the ship's threading its way among the warships in the river, including one large sailing ship filled with men and cannons "to prevent the passage of those without certificates and to guard the coast."[46] A clandestine passage that could take longer through Saintonge than across the Channel and via river waters more thickly patrolled than the open sea would make little sense.

The first two Champagné contingents left instead from La Rochelle, using ships brought there by the export trade in wine and salt. Susanne's party of seven replaced part of a cargo of wine that was stowed atop a bed of salt for transport to England. The loss of the contents of the casks would have been amply compensated by the 1,200 *livres* that the replacement cargo of six children paid for their passage. Marie's party of three was likewise stowed on salt. As the authorities knew well, such escapes were made easier by the fact that virtually all the masters and crews of ships plying the salt trade from the Saintonge and Aunis coast were themselves Protestants: Huguenot, English, or Dutch.[47]

For Huguenot escapees, accessing ships in the bays and inlets of the Charentes' seacoast involved a network of safe houses scattered through the environs of La Rochelle. This network of hiding places led would-be escapees to secret frontier crossings. Some were quite close to the old port. On October 21, 1686, Frédéric Baudouin de La Bruchardière walked with his wife, three-and-a-half-year-old child, and servant to their embarkation point "near the Saint Nicollas gate, across from the first mill that touches the cliff," from which an English twenty-five-tonner would carry them away the next morning. The members of Elie Bouhéreau's family came separately to a house on the shore outside La Rochelle "where all Protestants that could make their escape us'd to meet; they go in the front door and out the back to board ship."[48]

Susanne indicates that her group stole off late one evening from the Château square in La Rochelle to a house by the embankment, apparently quite close to the city. There they entered the back door and climbed silently, in the dark, up to the attic, where they awaited their 2 A.M. rendezvous on the shore with four sailors who carried them to the ship. Marie had to trudge considerably farther to board her ship. On her first, unsuccessful try, she left her hiding place in the city at night, walked two leagues out and two leagues back, retracing her steps. On the second, successful attempt, two leagues one-way sufficed. She connected "by the grace of God" with the sloop that took her party out to a ship at sea off the Ile de Ré. By late morning, they were away from shore and out of sight of "all the enemies of truth."

Given the distances Marie mentions and that she was headed to a ship anchored north of Saint-Martin-de-Ré, Marie probably escaped via the stretch of shore from La Repentie to l'Houmeau that the intendant Demuin described in 1681 as sprinkled with Huguenot escape houses. From Madame Ruault's house in the parish of Saint-Maurice or Monsieur de Chalais' house at Portneuf (both well inside the city today) fugitives made their way to Pampin. That was a five- to six-hour walk from La Rochelle—roughly what Marie said she walked on each of her attempts at escape—out through open country covered in vines, where one could easily skirt the few isolated farms and villages, to avoid detection. At Pampin, escapees waited for a ship. From there to the shore took less than half an hour on foot through the salt marshes. Because there were no harbors or coves sufficient for seagoing vessels, one took a rowboat or dinghy out to a ship anchored in the Pertuis Breton.[49]

The possibility that one or both of the two Champagné escapes from La Rochelle used Pampin as their safe house is strengthened by the identity of its owner, Daniel Green de Saint-Marsault, Seigneur de Dompierre. His father, from an old Huguenot family, had served as one of the guarantors for Susanne Isle's guardianship of Marie and her five sisters. Dompierre was already suspected of actively colluding in escapes at Pampin. In 1681, he was imprisoned in the Saint-Nicolas tower in La Rochelle "on grounds that he assisted in the escape of certain persons of the R.P.R. who passed into foreign lands."[50] Still, Pampin continued to serve would-be escapees, and the Champagné would certainly have known that. How revealing it is of the complexities facing would-be escapees that this Dompierre, who abetted the Champagné escape, was the cousin of the New Convert governor, Châtelaillon, who summoned Marie to explain why she moved her family to the coast and worked to foil her plans to leave.

Once ferried from the safe house to the ship, emigrants' joy at leaving behind "all the enemies of truth" was certain to have been tempered by the arduousness of the passage. Even in good seas such as Susanne's group enjoyed, the passengers were too queasy to eat the food the captain supplied (biscuits, peas, salted meats) on the seven-day crossing to Falmouth. Marie, by contrast, did not report that the sea voyage was eventful, simply that they spent eight days at sea "not without fear and many perils." Others elaborated in their memoirs on the kinds of problems a sea escape could present. Baudouin de La Bruchardière had smooth sailing to England, but the subsequent crossing to Holland was terrifying: "[we] believed we would perish at any moment." The most affecting description, because the writer kept the record in real time rather than reflecting later upon the experience, was the diary of the anonymous minister on that ultra-slow boat from Tonnay-Charente in November 1685. He let the weather provide the storyline and the drama for his party's departure. Everyone, he says, got seasick except the sailors and the pastor Sanxay's wife. "The same stormy wind blew with a terrible force . . . it seemed at every moment that it would upend us . . . for four nights and three days, death was present before our eyes and there seemed no way to avoid it."[51]

In addition to the miseries of sailing—a new mode of movement for many escapees—a departure by sea afforded fugitives less control over their directions and destinies than they might have had on land. The captain and crew had the upper hand. Susanne says in her memoir that her party was not taken to the destination she and the captain had agreed upon (Topsham near Exeter) and that only because she appealed to the authorities in Falmouth, where the captain wanted to leave them, did he take them farther. Still, he dumped them at 9 P.M. on a deserted shore outside Salcombe, from which they had to walk to Exeter. Much more serious was the vulnerability of passengers to the power the crew held over their possessions and even their lives. Baudouin says that the sailors on his harrowing crossing from Harwich to Scheveningen ran off in the lifeboat at the height of the storm, leaving them stranded until some Dutch sailors picked them up and deposited them on shore but stole all their belongings. Legends tell of crews throwing defenseless refugees overboard once the ship was out to sea. Foucault, intendant at Caen after serving in Poitiers, prosecuted a group of sailors who drowned the fugitives they had locked belowdecks.[52] Many fugitives must have wished, during their sea journey, that they had opted for an overland escape.

Josias did make the decision to travel by land, via Paris as far as Dieppe, though the rest of his family had left by sea. Several routes would have been possible; overland escape routes were as varied as their starting points. Saint-Surin reached The Hague in November 1685 after almost two months of steady movement—nearly every day in a different town—via Autun, Geneva, Zurich, Heidelberg, and Frankfurt, rather than heading straight north on what he took to be the riskier routes through Flanders. The Collot, starting from near Blois, traveled eastward to Basel, the father and mother on horseback with four children aged six and under riding in panniers on a horse that a valet led by the bridle. Paris became a primary staging point for Protestants heading overland to the northern frontier, but few emigrants from Saintonge and Poitou took the northern overland route, to judge from the domiciles of fugitives caught at the northern border.[53] Susanne explained her father's choice of route by saying he thought he would be under less close surveillance in the capital than back home, where it was already known that his family had left the kingdom. Yet surveillance in the capital was heavy; the first group the newly organized Paris police learned to spy on were the Huguenots. Escaping northward was difficult, even after one left the dense surveillance in the city.

Josias somehow threaded his way through the traps in northern France—neither he nor Marie left any record of his experiences en route—and his success in doing so suggests that his choice of route was a wise one. He may have thought he could carry more out on horseback than by ship. He explicitly thought he could make his way as far as Paris without difficulty, for he wrote to Marie on November 2, 1687: "if need be I can go to Paris, for I have business that could give me an excuse for going there."[54] Whatever his reasons for choosing his route, Josias left Berneré at Easter, left Paris about six weeks later on the last day of May, and arrived in Holland after three weeks en route. Before boarding a ship in Dieppe for the final leg of the escape, he sent on ahead overland the two valets who accompanied him from Paris; they reached Marie first, with most of Josias' baggage, and let her know he was coming.

7

Chancing Escape

The Champagné had never been certain that their escape would succeed, no matter how long and thoroughly prepared. Both Marie de La Rochefoucauld and her daughter Susanne wrote that they escaped at great risk of being caught and prosecuted. Marie reports in her memoir that French soldiers boarded and searched the boat on which she, the younger Josias, and the servant were hidden. Susanne writes that her group was visited on board three times without being found. Both Marie's and Susanne's memoirs imply that their escapes succeeded because they managed to outwit authorities intent upon catching and punishing them. Then, as each group reached safety, fears for themselves ceded to apprehension about the rest: the children already in Exeter "feared that all would be discovered and that I would be put in prison. . . . I was in terrible fright of learning by each post that [my dear husband] had been put in prison."[1]

Last to leave, and hence longest suffering from the uncertainty of escape, was Josias. He may have sensed an irony in his situation: he had feared earlier that he would have to go off first, leaving his family behind. Instead he was the last at home and alone with baby Thérèse. In the fall of 1687, Josias and Marie corresponded, she from England and he from Berneré. Like the escapes themselves, the correspondence was an exercise in deception. Since Josias felt himself under surveillance, Marie had to use forwarding addresses in order to prevent her letters being intercepted. She sent her October letter in care of a "postmaster," from whom Josias was able to collect it. In the future, Josias told her in November, she should send letters in an envelope bearing no name but only the requisite stamp, alternating among three intermediaries: via his lawyer (perhaps meaning Tayau), "to the merchant I trust the most," or "by the great city," the last no doubt designating a resident in La Rochelle they had previously agreed upon as secure. For his part, he would send letters in care of a certain merchant in Amsterdam, with only the letter "C" on the envelope; she should let the merchant know that anything arriving with that mark would be for her. The precautions Josias and Marie took with their correspondence were wise. The crown alternately spoke of the sanctity of private mail and violated it. Seignelay admonished the lieutenant-general in Normandy that "the decision he made to take letters of *religionnaires* and New Converts is contrary to the intentions of His Majesty and would do great damage to commerce." But Madame de Puychenin's correspondence had been seized, and Pontchartrain would write Bégon about a case in which certain Protestants in La Tremblade were corresponding with refugees outside France, ordering him to keep them under surveillance and if possible seize their letters.[2]

To prevent identification in case a letter fell into the wrong hands, Josias and Marie kept their news very general and omitted both their own names and the names of kin and friends. She had to write in the manner of a business letter without signing: "You must treat me in your letters as I treat you, without using either 'tu' or 'toy' nor any other familiar term." Fearing to mention his children, Josias alluded merely to "my nearest relatives." He referred to baby Thérèse in commercial terminology, as if she were a package or produce: "the merchandise you have in this country that you desire so ardently." Josias wrote, then, under the mask of affectless language whenever any subject might help a captor of the letter identify the writer or recipient.

On November 2, 1687, as Marie moved on from Exeter to Holland, Josias wrote his wife, "my dear companion," a poignant letter expressing his psychological pressures. The letter was a long mix of news about what was transpiring around him and a deeply sad expression of how the troubles were personally affecting him. The quality of the harvest, prices on the brandy market, outrages against local Protestants, his own health and feelings—all these braided through the letter as if Josias could not disentangle the disparate forces that, together, threatened to destroy him. Part of the toll on Josias came from fears for his own safety and sorrow over punishments to his friends, part from fears of his own weakness, and part from the trauma of separation.

A number of their friends and kin—unnamed in Josias' relation—were in prison. Marie's La Rochefoucauld cousin Du Parc d'Archiac was in the Château-Trompette in Bordeaux. Mademoiselle de Saint-Surin, sister of Susanne's future husband, had been put in a convent in La Rochelle, then in a prison in Lyon, then moved to the Bastille and the Château de Nantes.[3] Josias' own family had been hit even harder. Two first cousins on his mother's side were in prison. Gédéon Nicolas de Voutron, whose wife helped Marie escape, had been imprisoned soon after the Revocation. Another Voutron had been arrested trying to flee with a brother of Madame de Puychenin, the other accomplice in Marie's escape, both disguised as peasants. They had tried to reach a ship off the Ile de Ré but were arrested at La Repentie, near Pampin, imprisoned, and told by the governor "that if they did not obey the will of the King they could not avoid being condemned to the galleys." The two Voutron and the Sieur des Roches-Cramahé were all held at the Fort de La Prée on the island that the younger two had been trying to reach during the months when Josias was alone.[4]

These cousins and neighbors were no doubt among those whom Josias felt he had a moral obligation to visit, without being able to make himself do so. "I was obliged at the time of my strongest anxiety to see persons of my acquaintance in prison and elsewhere who wished it. . . . I did it less often than I should have and I have used weakly the talents people want to persuade me that I possess. And the storm that thunders over my head has made me go cowardly to work, human weakness being so vast in me that the fear of earthly punishment prevents me from fulfilling as I ought the duties of charity." He was ill: "I am still so weak that I can leave the bedroom only for a quarter of an hour." He had tried one of Marie's remedies, but it "did me no good. I do not know if it is too old or poorly mixed, but in a word it did so little good that it has been useless to me." As in his two earlier letters to his children, he showed himself here to be deeply introspective and deeply concerned about his ability to measure up to the expectations of the God who was ever-present to him. Most ominously, he was unsure, he admits, that he would prove strong enough to hold out indefinitely against the pressure to convert. "I fear the temptation and distrust myself so strongly that I fear falling into the greatest fault in saying I want to do good." At the same time, he wanted Marie and the children to know that his belief in the Reformed religion was unshaken, that he remained committed to what he had written in his second letter to his children. His peace lay in God's grace: "amongst all these troubles God's grace has given me abundant consolations and taken all upon His providence."

In gloom and self-doubt, he spoke of another fear: that "our separation that my spirit has had great difficulty enduring and from which I fell ill" might become permanent. "I have resolved that if it is the will of God I should even see you never again. And in case that happens, I pray you in his name as well as my dear nearest relatives to take comfort in it." As if to help Marie, in what he guessed might be her need for reassurance, he added to his words of farewell words of hope and commendation, reminding her of the nobility of what she had done in departing. If we never meet again, he told Marie, you and the children must console yourselves with the knowledge that "You have left everything behind to go in search of the pearl of great price. Look back only as much as God allows: that is to say you should not ask Him for what you have left except insofar as He judges that right. You have by a special grace from God, at the peril of your lives, put your souls in peace. Make good use of that in the future, and show that in leaving your goods and your homeland your principal goal has been to wear the livery of our lord Jesus Christ and to follow His light everywhere." Then this defeated, self-absorbed man, this austere

Huguenot whose writing more closely hewed to the theologian's rhetoric than to the poet's, elided his despair over their separation and his obsession with God's ever-presence into a hymn to his love for her—a conceit so lovely that she kept this deeply moving letter, alone of all those he wrote her, for the rest of her life: "The separation of intimate friends cannot occur without suffering, but they should console themselves with the union of their hearts. And when I think that you present your prayers for me to God at the same moment when I do so on my side for you, I am persuaded that we are together, by the union in this meeting of our prayers before his holy tribunal."

Josias' November letter, then, was as checkered as the life he was leading, careening among continuing religious persecutions, business matters as a landlord, efforts "to save the estate of Berneré," and personal terrors. No doubt all these shaped Josias' thoughts as he weighed his future at the turn of the new year 1688. In January, he compiled the inventory of the papers located at Berneré and Champagné that eventually went into the Refuge with him. In his commentaries on the various papers, he spoke as if he expected to stay and, more than that, expected the children in exile to return. The papers included Marie's and "those that concern my separate property that I make to serve as clarification and be useful to my children after my death." These were not the words of someone who was confident that he was about to leave forever.

As Josias waited—caring for baby Thérèse, fighting Aunt Madelene's lawsuit for Berneré, collecting debts, and preparing what he needed to take along or send ahead—he could have found increasing support for remaining in France as a clandestine Protestant. In late 1687 and early 1688, a layman named Magnan from the village of Gascougnolles in Poitou, formerly an elder of the temple at Mougon, had been corresponding with refugees in Holland, defending those who stayed behind. To refugees' imputations that those who remained in France violated their faith, Magnan defended the viability and utility of clandestine worship. In secret assemblies, he said, Huguenots bore witness to their faith, repented their abjurations, and repaired their fault in one another's presence. In addition to the religious benefits secret assemblies brought to individual believers, their staying in France was in the very interest of the religion. "What would have become of so many beautiful churches in France that God established by his grace if our fathers had fled from persecution? . . . Today perhaps God wishes to use us to revive his devastated church!" It was against Jurieu's condemnation of those who stayed that Magnan pressed his arguments. The great pastor in Rotterdam used his earliest *Pastoral Letters* to preach against "Nicodemism": interior adherence to truth beneath a dissembling exterior. Even if one's conscience could endure the falsehood of not bearing open witness, the stain of abjuration, and the shame of the mass, Jurieu wrote, one was summoned to flee from Babylon. "So, my brothers, do not look for some reason not to imitate this great number of your brothers who, sundering all the ties attaching them to their homeland, went searching the entire earth for a homeland more humane."[5]

In the winter of 1688, as the legal proceedings on Berneré neared their conclusion in La Réole and the ostensible reason for Josias' staying behind promised to disappear, his indecisiveness about leaving was brought to a head. He would hear of the tragedy at Grand-Ry, the culmination in violence of the conflict over enforcing religious conformity within the kingdom. On February 22, 1688, in the broad meadow adjoining a noble residence that a fugitive family had abandoned near Aigonnay (Poitou), just thirty-eight miles from Josias at Champagné, a crowd of Protestants assembled in secret worship. The gathering was ambushed by soldiers who fired from the surrounding trees. Of the 800–1,800 reportedly present, some dozens were killed and wounded on the spot, several dozen or several hundred taken prisoner; the intendant Foucault reported that six were hanged, thirty-one sent to the galleys, and two women lashed.[6]

Word of the assault at Grand-Ry reverberated widely. Within weeks, the story had reached the refugees in Holland and been incorporated into the *Pastoral Letters* Jurieu wrote in Rotterdam to be smuggled back to Protestants still in France. Jurieu took heart from the revival of resistance that Grand-Ry exemplified and began to sense, as Magnan already had, that such revived resistance might be the means for forcing reestablishment in France of the liberty to worship. "My very dear brothers, a month ago we advised you to withdraw from places of persecution as promptly as you could. But today I wish to give you different advice and much more important. . . . I showed you a road to salvation, which is flight; today I open for you another which far surpasses the first. It is courage, resistance, rebuilding, and determination to worship God and to praise him openly to men's faces in assemblies private or public." The news from Grand-Ry, then, provoked a major shift in the counsel Jurieu offered Protestants in France: those who stayed, he now said, could yet be the ones to secure the victory of the true church as well as their own salvation.[7]

News of Grand-Ry surely sped toward Josias as it did toward Jurieu in Rotterdam. Was Grand-Ry the last straw for Josias? It was for another Protestant residing near the site, a schoolteacher in Mauzé named Jean Migault. In the memoir Migault wrote after reaching safety in Holland, he dwelt upon the raid as the last persecution he experienced in France. For Migault, and no doubt for others, what Grand-Ry signified was the failure of a strategy of staying in France as clandestine Protestants. Ironically, Migault and Josias decided to leave just as Jurieu was redefining Protestants' duty from fleeing to staying. After the raid at Grand-Ry, Migault planned his escape, spending the next two months looking for a ship, and then left with most of his children on Easter

Monday of 1688. Josias (but without his remaining child) set off on nearly the same day.[8]

Once Josias determined to leave, how much danger did he run in escaping? How much danger had Marie run? And the children? Was it the case that, as a relative of one captured fugitive related, "The bridges and roads are guarded so tightly that only birds can pass through without a passport"? Was Jurieu's report correct that "the seaports are guarded with great exactness . . . their prisons are filled with poor fugitives—women, girls, and men—condemned to be tortured for attempting to flee the raging persecution"? Or has it been "ridiculous to believe in all the atrocities the Huguenots claimed. . . . History does not confirm these allegations. . . . It must be admitted that the violence was not great"?[9]

Law, Practice, and (Hi)Story

The stage had been set in the late fall of 1681 for pursuit and punishment of would-be escapees. When the intendant Marillac introduced the dragonnades in Poitou, with troops furnished by Louvois, crowds of displaced Protestants flowed to the seaside near La Rochelle. Many gathered at Pampin, the château of the Sieur de Dompierre that probably provided Marie's safe house six years later, and several parties of substantial size were caught at the moment of setting sail on English ships. Departure without permission from the kingdom was already forbidden, upon pain of incarceration and property confiscation, but, as this unanticipated flood would demonstrate, officials had not yet worked out how to deal with violations of this law. Seignelay merely passed along general instructions from the court: "to prevent the said *Religionnaires* from leaving the kingdom, see to it that none of them embark in the area of your jurisdiction."[10] Six days before he met with the Bishop of Saintes in Saint-Savinien to close its temple, on November 17, 1681, the intendant Demuin impressed upon Secretary of State Châteauneuf the seriousness of this episode of attempted departures and improvised response. As Demuin understood, the onset of direct violence against the Reformed was a turning point in Huguenot relations.[11]

This 1681 incident is noteworthy as well for generating competing narratives from the two adversaries in the struggle for survival or elimination of Protestantism in France. Abraham Tessereau included it among the tales of dangerous escapes and cruel oppression that made up his *Histoire des reformés de la Rochelle*. Tessereau told of heroic steadfastness by large numbers of captured escapees. "The prisons were filled with all these people as was the tower called 'The Lantern'; the aged, pregnant women, sick persons of both sexes, all entered there." The guards robbed them of their money and of their *témoignages*, the latter of which they particularly regretted since they feared that reprisals would be taken against the ministers who issued them. Officials even confiscated, and redirected to the *hôpital général*, part of the victuals sent to prisoners by the charitable people of La Rochelle. The failed escapees were assaulted "by arguments and continual threats, so that at the same time as their bodies were deprived of the nourishment they required, it became more difficult to keep up their spirits, which likewise were weakened by forced fasting." The prisoners stood firm, despite their suspicion that their constancy would perpetuate their imprisonment.[12]

By contrast, the official report sent by Demuin to Châteauneuf emphasized that the escapees were released without punishment. If any were detained, it was only a few of the men who were put in prison "to make an example." Demuin released the thirty to thirty-five men, women, and children found hiding in a ditch north of the city, "whom we have ordered to go back to their homes." The 300 or so "strangers, men, women and children of diverse qualities and conditions" found at Pampin were dismissed in a similar fashion. The police took down their names and domiciles, then "told them they had to return home, where they would receive no ill treatment and that to this end they could come back to La Rochelle en route, where they would be suffered to lodge for one night." Guards who stayed behind "in the said house to exhort them to obey the said declaration of the king" (prohibiting departure without permission) left the scene at nightfall.[13]

How were the people intercepted at Pampin in 1681 dealt with? Which version of the event is credible? Each of the competing narratives has a certain internal consistency. Each author has clear motivation to tell the story as he did: Tessereau to discredit the authorities whose threats would soon force his own flight, Demuin to vindicate his own handling of the situation. Each let his recent experiences color his report. Tessereau, the Protestant scholar, had spent the summer of 1681 collecting evidence from all over Poitou about the atrocities committed by Marillac's dragonnades.[14] He inevitably saw the November events in La Rochelle through the lenses of indignation and suspicion he had acquired in the preceding months. Just as he collected only negative stories in Poitou, so he credited only unhappy accounts in his home city.

Demuin, for his part, told the court what he thought it wanted to hear, construing the treatment he described in his report—release of would-be escapees rather than imprisonment—as what the king and his ministers expected. Seignelay had ordered Demuin to prevent embarkations, and the intendant could claim to have done so by reversing the flow of fugitives back to Poitou, without mentioning any mass incarcerations such as Tessereau described. Moreover, Demuin had a second reason to shade his story in the direction of leniency. Two years earlier, Colbert had scolded Demuin for excessive severity in his treatment of a Protestant officer, and in the very summer of 1681 Demuin was reprimanded from Versailles for the "indiscreet and ill-controlled zeal he frequently shows towards those of the R.P.R., and His Majesty is pleased to inform him accordingly that he desires the conversion of his subjects of the said Religion at least as much; but that he does not wish on that account to do injustice in the routine affairs they have among themselves or with Catholics."[15] It is scarcely possible to adjudicate between these two accounts—one inclined to magnify the violence and the other inclined to downplay it—only to note that the Protestant story enjoyed longer and more public play than the official report and was far more influential in shaping history. It is often said that history is written by the victors, but here, posterity has taken its cue from the defeated.

The contest over Protestantism in France played itself out in a clash of arms and disputes over doctrine, but also as a competition of narratives that the state was not well positioned to win. The Champagné story exemplifies this in relation to the imprisonment of Josias' cousin Gédéon Nicolas de Voutron, who would become, in a sense, the poster boy of Huguenot imprisonment for the publicists in the Refuge. In his pastoral letter from Rotterdam dated January 1, 1687, Jurieu placed Voutron at the head of the section relating news from France that regularly followed his theological lessons. Voutron fell into the category of "our martyrs" in Jurieu's taxonomy, which was comprised of prisoners who, when threatened with imminent death, welcomed it with courage. "Monsieur de Voutron, gentleman from around La Rochelle, recently gave us a grand example of this kind of constancy. For a year now, he has suffered the cruelest prison one could imagine," suffering hunger and thirst, thrown into a black hole in leg-irons, without light or fire in the winter and without any nourishment other than a ration of bread and water scarcely half of what his sustenance required. His jailer, the governor of the Citadel of Saint-Martin, told him the king had ordered the death penalty for all religious rebels, the gentlemen to be beheaded and the others hanged, and "he had only one step to take to save himself, to gain paradise and establish his fortune and that of his entire family." Voutron believed what the governor said and welcomed the alleged execution, saying: "it pleases me and consoles me for all my troubles in prison since that will bring them to an end and I will bask in the sight of my God." The governor's threat was a ploy to scare the prisoner into abjuring, but Voutron came out ahead. He was released from solitary confinement two days later, returned to the main prison, and permitted henceforth to see his relatives and friends.[16]

Jurieu's account of Voutron's treatment was published while the protagonist was still in prison on the Ile de Ré. Not until after his transfer to

Château-Trompette in June 1687, however, did Ré's governor Bernard Dolton, Comte d'Aubarède, learn of Jurieu's narrative. Aubarède responded with indignation, a formal denial of Voutron's charges, and a wholly contradictory account. "Jurieu is very ill informed about how the Sieur de Voutron was treated in the Citadel of Saint Martin. . . . COMPLETE IMPOSTURE, NOT A WORD OF TRUTH IN WHAT JURIEU SAYS." His conversations with Voutron were always correct, he claimed, until he determined that the prisoner only pretended to be considering conversion; then the governor spoke to him no more. As for the amenities, Voutron had his bed and bedroom, with as much fire as he wanted. When he asked to be moved to the south side of the fort where it was warmer, it was done. He always got whatever food he wanted, fixed the way he requested. His wife was free to visit him and to send whatever he wanted. She had biscuits and jams made for him, which he savored. He ate little because he was subject to gout, but that decision was solely his. He was allowed to talk with whomever he desired. As for the irons he complains of having put on his feet, no such thing was ever yet seen in the citadel; "that fool would like to be a martyr for his religion at little cost. . . . I really wish he were at the Citadel, I would teach him TO FORGE LIES."[17]

This gentleman from Aunis, Josias de Robillard's first cousin, was, then, made into an example on both sides: by the authorities, who intended his imprisonment to punish him and strike fear into like-minded holdouts, as well as by the leaders in the Refuge, for whom his story publicized at once the viciousness of the persecution in France and the Huguenots' steely resolve in facing it. Again, as in 1681 at La Rochelle, the Huguenot version of events portrayed a darker experience, the official's testimony greater leniency. Again, the Huguenot telling of Voutron's imprisonment succeeded in setting the mold of its history. Jurieu's narrative was public and widely disseminated, Aubarède's disclaimer was private and impotent to make the anti-Huguenot point that the French did not mistreat their people.

Whether Huguenots had the more accurate story or not, they seemed to have a better understanding of the power of stories and how to tell them for maximum impact. Tessereau explained his lengthy description of Voutron's ordeal by observing that "It has been necessary to enter into this long detail in order to show, on one of the subjects the Protestants of La Rochelle believed they could take pride in, how far men's patience was tried in that region." Detail such as the number of soldiers escorting Voutron on each change of prison and the name of their commander, the condition of the premises in each prison, and the treatment meted out in each locale made the stories plausible and moved their audience to sympathy. As did a passionate tone, the stories of persecution strung together in Elie Benoist's *History of the Edict of Nantes* in particular "relying on the fiery indignation which possessed him to give force to his narrative." So did the naming of names, which helped readers imagine individuals' suffering. Voutron, Mazières, Le Goux de Périgny, Roches-Cramahé, Marquis de Loire, Marquis de Tors, Demoiselle de Loire, Demoiselle de Chauffepié, Demoiselle Pyniot [Puychenin], La Largere [Puychenin]—these were the men and women of reputation among the friends and relatives of Josias and Marie whom Benoist offered as "distinguished persons [who] offered great examples of courage" when treated with violence: "[the nobility] pillaged; sent into exile; imprisoned, dragged from dungeon to dungeon.... Gentlemen who made piety their principal duty."[18]

Tessereau's purpose with his stories—as well as Jurieu's and Benoist's when they repeated Tessereau's accounts or compiled their own—was, in part, to facilitate exiles' resettlement by proving to the various rulers and host communities upon whose goodwill they would henceforth be dependent that theirs was a just cause: they had left for good reason and were not rebels resisting a royal father of his people. Stories of persecution and courage were their weapons, worked into vivid texts whose cumulative power obscured their selectivity. It was not their job to give a balanced account or to admit contrary incidents of leniency; it was, rather, to seize the narrative in order to vindicate their own actions, lay the blame upon the French authorities, and express bitter resentment over their treatment.

Like the events at La Rochelle in 1681 and Voutron's imprisonment, Grand-Ry, too, became a focal point of competing narratives. The event was read as a clash of religious beliefs, as a police action against sedition, as a summons to martyrdom, and as a simple massacre. Several who were arrested and sent to the galleys for attending Grand-Ry said that they had gone there to testify to the truth of the confession by repenting their forced abjuration. In opposition, the *Journal* of a local abbey decried the assembly and condoned the attack as necessary to preventing the spread of heresy. The intendant who carried out the raid, Foucault, characterized Grand-Ry in his memoirs as a police action against rebellious subjects whose threat forced him to order the troops to fire. In the same vein, the crown authorized even harsher suppression in the future: if further assemblies were held, "the dragoons are ordered to kill the greatest number of Protestants they meet, without sparing the women, in order to intimidate them and prevent others from again falling into a similar crime."[19] The pastor Jurieu, in Rotterdam, as one would expect, framed the attack on his fellow Protestants as martyrdom. "These poor faithful gathered like lambs in a meadow" were attacked by dragoons and archers who "fired the way one fires on a flock of pigeons." He made welcome news of it, though; in this slaughter of innocents, Jurieu saw the beginning of triumph. "Suddenly, zeal and courage are reborn, like a blaze emerging unexpectedly from amidst a great heap of ashes." If Protestants still in France would resolve to martyr themselves, as those sacrificed at Grand-Ry did, continued persecution would become impossible: "the need to hang an infinity of men and depopulate the kingdom will disarm the king's justice and incline him to clemency."[20]

Such clemency, however, would never come, at least not from Louis XIV, and Huguenots would remember Grand-Ry not as the beginning of their rescue from persecution but as the great tragedy of the early "desert" period. The long-term victory of Grand-Ry would be its setting of the historical narrative, for the event would be remembered in the terms in which Jurieu had framed it: for saving Protestantism within France. Grand-Ry became in Poitou "the most authentic shrine of its Huguenot history."[21] In 1951, a plaque put up at the site of the massacre fixed the meaning of the story in bronze: "In this place, especially from 1688 to 1706, assemblies of the "desert" gathered. One of them was surprised on February 22, 1688. Of 200 prisoners, 31 were condemned to the galleys and 15 martyred. Grand-Ry was razed. In remembrance of those who made it possible for us today to worship God in peace."

Josias may possibly have put his hands on Jurieu's April 1 letter before he left later that month, for "all the houses of New Converts are filled with these letters that are titled 'pastorals' and read with as much devotion as their prayers." Or he may have picked up the story of Grand-Ry in the simpler form in which it reached a local plowman named Jacques Bonnet, who a few years after the event wrote down the eyewitness accounts he heard circulating in oral tradition. In this version of the tale, the raid was simply a massacre: "the dragoons began to swoop down quickly on this poor people; with muskets in hand and unsheathed swords hanging from their arms, and blasphemies in their mouths, they cried in unison: Kill! Kill! . . . All that could be heard were shots from rifles and pistols being discharged across the crowd."[22]

Competing narratives were part of the context in which Huguenots, like Josias and Marie, tried to decide upon a plan of action—whether to leave or stay—and calculate their chances of success, should they decide to escape. Officials did their best to fashion a nontextual narrative that warned against trying. What set the story on the officials' terms was the practice of exemplary punishment: highly visible condemnation of selected malefactors designed to convince others that every such infraction met similar treatment. When Bernard du Vignaud and two young women from Ruffec in Angoumois were caught escaping at Coutances in Normandy and imprisoned there, the intendant of their home region, Bernage, asked that they be returned for a show trial in Angoulême, "as their escape was widely known here and nothing would more effectively stop these types of flights in the future than the example one could make on this occasion." When the Sieur Barreau outfitted his daughter with a horse and guide overland to Holland and prepared to send her money via his commerce in wine, the intendant Bégon "believes it appropriate to

Figure 7.1 Commemorative Monument at Grand-Ry, Poitou. Photo by David Gilman Lougee.

make an example" in prosecuting him and his wife. When Louvois learned in January 1687 that New Converts in Poitou had held an assembly, he instructed the intendant Foucault "that if that was true, I should promptly punish those who assembled so severely that the example made of them would restrain the others." When the king placed the cruiser commanded by Marie's cousin Isaac Isle on the Saintonge coast, he described its purpose as exemplary rather than comprehensive: this show of force against the Huguenots would last "long enough to make them lose the spirit of desertion."[23]

Prominent persons made especially useful examples, as in the case of Voutron. Exemplary justice can make an impression through the staging of the ordeal (a trial, a public apology, an execution), through the nature of the crime alleged, or through the identity of the victim. When exacted against someone of stature, exemplary punishment reverberates through a hierarchical social system because it reverses the principle on which social organization rests: punishing the privileged drives home the lesson that no one can challenge power with impunity. So Josias was at some risk, given his standing in the community. For a notable like Josias to stay home without sincerely converting may have been at least as dangerous as attempting to leave, especially while he was visiting prisoners, corresponding with persons in the Refuge, and making his financial and physical preparations for departure. This vulnerability may have weighed on him as he lingered alone at Berneré. But the great threat, unbeknownst to Josias and Marie, was actually in the place of safety they were trying to reach.

The Escape through the Eyes of a Spy

The communication channel between the Refuge and recalcitrant Huguenots back in France that prepared and operated the escape routes for Marie de La Rochefoucauld, among many others, was paralleled by an equally secret information chain that preyed upon it. This second network linked private communication within the Huguenot community to French government efforts to prevent illicit departures. Intelligence gathered abroad was relayed to ministers at Versailles and by them to royal agents in the local areas from which Protestants might attempt to escape. At the nexus of this chain during the immediate post-Revocation period, when the Champagné and thousands of others were preparing or effecting their escapes, was a spy run by the Comte d'Avaux, the French ambassador in The Hague, a man who called himself "Sieur Tillieres."[24] This expatriate from the Charentes was both a key player in refugee decision-making and, for nearly three years at the height of the emigration, from October 1685 to August 1688, Louis XIV's eyes and ears in the heart of the Refuge. At least weekly, and even more often when urgent information had to reach French officials, this informant sent d'Avaux letters that allowed the French authorities to monitor what the refugees abroad (and would-be refugees back in France) were up to. The work of this spy yields insights into the crown's ways of dealing with its defecting subjects that invite a rethinking of the Revocation chapter in Huguenot history.

Tillieres' early letters reveal that he was a volunteer: he simply slipped d'Avaux a note at the end of September 1685 offering his services to the ambassador and the king. D'Avaux at first was skeptical, the king reluctant to engage and pay him on the grounds that whatever he might report could not be of great value, given "the small number of persons of the R.P.R. who remain in my kingdom." But the informant soon convinced d'Avaux that he could provide reliable and usable information. When the Secretary of State Seignelay asked in March 1686 how many fugitives there were in Holland, for example, d'Avaux looked to Tillieres for the answer: "He is devoting all his efforts to obtaining a secret book of the Amsterdam Consistory in which the names of those who are in that city and those who passed through it are written down. I believe, though, that it is something that will be hard to come by." By the end of the month, Tillieres had succeeded.[25]

From time to time Tillieres would accept such a particular commission from the ambassador. But for the most part, he simply circulated among the refugees, picking up whatever information he could, especially about the escape plans of would-be fugitives and their accomplices at home and abroad. Monsieur Borgasse, a banker in Paris, had arranged with a merchant in Antwerp who traded laces and other finery in Paris to take himself, his wife, and their children out of the realm for 4,000 *francs*. Monsieur Lardy with his wife and a child of eight or ten years were waiting to escape with the guide Pierre Le Duc "in rue Guenegaud on the second floor in the last carriage gate on the left when coming from the Pont Neuf." The sister of the galley slave Marolles awaited escape with her children "in the street adjoining Bourg L'abbé . . . at the second carriage gate. . . . They never open the door of the house before pulling a cord to raise a small wooden frame that makes an opening through which they see who is at the door; they do not open for any they do not know, or the servant comes onto the stoop to say no one is home."[26]

Tillieres proved able to uncover, remember, and deliver stunning detail on Huguenot escape plans. His ability to do so indicates that this informer not only moved freely within the refugee community but had its trust. His sources were numerous, but two groups stand out among them. The first was the women, especially those who were in Holland without their husbands. He made a practice of meeting them upon their arrival, when they were most in need of assistance from the community. He must have been a man whom women wished to have around and whose apparent sympathy made them feel that he was on their side. One can only imagine the way he manipulated their vulnerabilities in order to gain confidences he could betray. Madame de Pardaillan, a widowed cousin of Saint-Surin who would be among Marie's intimate friends in the Refuge, was one of his unwitting victims. She shared with Tillieres details of her own and her relatives' escapes that could seriously compromise both the refugees' own well-being and the futures of their accomplices in France. Tillieres was able to tell d'Avaux that Madame de Pardaillan had left silver valued at 15,000 *livres* in Paris as well as other valuable items in the Château de Jarnac and in Tonnay-Boutonne with Saint-Surin's brother, who knew where the Paris silver was stashed. Within months the spy could be more precise: she had left her silver tableware with the Maréchal de Duras.[27]

The second group that welcomed Tillieres into their midst on a continuing basis and confided readily in him was the French refugee ministers. Tillieres met with them daily, and they regularly filled him in on the news as it arrived from France as well as on the initiatives born among the refugees themselves. The depth of the ministers' confidence in Tillieres was evident in March 1686 when Le Moyne, formerly minister in Rouen and now in Leiden, and Guilbert, formerly minister at Caen now in Amsterdam, arranged for a commercial vessel to sail to Rouen to pick up friends. Le Moyne's brother took Tillieres aboard and showed him two of the hiding places built into the ship, one of which could hold fourteen persons beneath the captain's chamber. The spy was, as always, careful to protect his masquerade: there were on the ship "several hiding-places that he had not dared ask to see for fear of rendering himself too suspect."[28]

Tillieres' position in the refugee community allowed him to report to d'Avaux, and through him to the court, the escape intentions of numerous Huguenots, including a stunning number of Josias' and Marie's kin. In the summer of 1686, he learned of the plans of Marie's cousin who had served as a guarantor at the rewriting of Susanne Isle's will in March 1677: "Monsieur [de La Rochefoucauld] de La Rigaudière, a gentleman from Saintonge who changed religion, is trying to leave France, but he is not certain whether he will go by way of Switzerland or not." He reported at the same time that Josias' brother-in-law Casimir Prévost de Touchimbert intended to leave: "Monsieur de Touchimbert, who lodges at the Black Head in the rue de La Harpe in Paris, goes often to see Mademoiselle de Saint-Surin, who is in a convent. He would like very much to be in Holland, according to the letters I have seen. It seems that his intention is not to remain in France." He learned of the impending escape of Touchimbert's daughters from the pastor Yver. He had already reported the previous March that Mademoiselle de Saint-Surin, the sister of the Champagné friend who arranged their first two escapes from his post in Exeter, was in Paris waiting for her opportunity to leave.[29]

Later, he reported escape plans in the family of Josias' maternal cousin Voutron. This Voutron was the prisoner in the Citadel of Ré whom Jurieu publicized, in January 1688, as the paradigmatic victim of official French fanaticism and whose wife abetted Marie's escape from La Rochelle. Tillieres reported on July 30, 1688, that a letter from France assured "that his two eldest sons and the youngest are disposed to leave; I believe the first has a naval employment." The minister in Versailles who received d'Avaux' dispatch to this effect forwarded the information to Seignelay on August 13. Tillieres' July 27 dispatch had even more pointedly targeted a second Voutron cousin of Josias, using him as an identifiable would-be escapee who, if put under surveillance, could allow the French authorities to foil the imminent escape attempt of "a troop that is to leave France shortly. I am told it is of considerable size." This person was "a man named Voutron du Passage. He was formerly a Cornette in France, and his brother who is in Holland was long a prisoner in the Citadel of Ré. I do not know any others, but I hope that those I name here might uncover the rest."[30]

Tillieres also compromised Marie. He identified the Champagné as intending to escape long before they did so. He knew some details of Marie's impending escape even before she boarded the ship that took her out of France. In the last week of June 1687, while she was in hiding in La Rochelle awaiting passage abroad, Tillieres gave d'Avaux the information about the ship Saint-Surin was sending from England to pick her up; Saint-Surin's addressee in Rotterdam, Puychenin, had obligingly told him the contents of Saint-Surin's letter. He was able to track Marie's progress. On September 9, 1687, just weeks after her escape to England, Tillieres informed d'Avaux that "Madame de Champagné has just crossed into England with seven of her children. Only fifteen days after giving birth, she took to the road and walked for four leagues, leaving her husband and newborn behind in France." Tillieres knew this because on September 1, Saint-Surin wrote the news from Exeter to his cousin Madame de Pardaillan in The Hague, and Madame de Pardaillan showed the letter to Tillieres.[31]

Tillieres was able to provide even greater advance notice of Josias' intentions. Like Marie, Josias was already in the spy's sights before he left France. As Tillieres reported on September 9, 1687, in the same dispatch that announced Marie's arrival in England: "It will not be long before the husband follows her; he is only waiting for an opportunity to embark with his infant and a nurse." In Saint-Surin's words, as Tillieres repeated them: "Her husband and more than thirty gentlemen with their entire families are soon to do the same; we are expecting this entire company to arrive in three English vessels." Again a week later, while Marie and her children were resting in Exeter, Saint-Surin wrote Puychenin that he had arranged for another English captain to sail for La Rochelle, this time to pick up Madame de Puychenin, her children, and her aunt as well as a number of persons integral to the Champagné story: Monsieur de Ciré [Culant] and his family, the sons of Monsieur de Bussac, and Monsieur de Magezy and his daughter. "I believe that Monsieur de Champagné and others will be among the group."

Later, in the dispatch dated December 8, 1687, the spy suspected that Josias' escape was imminent, if not already underway, for he had read a letter from Josias to Marie. He paraphrased the contents of Josias' letter, including the code language that seemed to him to mean that Josias would leave soon—"Do not write to me for a month or six weeks. I am going to take a trip from which I will only return then"—and added his own interpretation: "so there it is, Monsieur, word for word what is in Monsieur de Champagné's letter about his travels lasting a month or six weeks; it is not difficult to figure out where he intends to go." On February 28, 1688, Tillieres further reported to d'Avaux that Josias wrote Marie saying "that were it not for an illness he would already have left. Here are some of the terms of his letter. I would wish to take with me the younger son of Du Parc d'Archiac; I do not know if I will succeed in that, but in any case I will certainly have another of our relatives to keep me company." The authorities, then, had been warned by mid-December 1687 that Josias was an imminent flight risk and at least six weeks before Josias actually left had details of his emigration plans and his intended companions. Finally, Tillieres gave one last alert designed, he hoped, to catch Josias. On June 16, 1688, he reported: "Yesterday evening, one of [Monsieur de Champagné's] lackeys arrived at Madame de Champagné's home in Voorburg, reporting that his master is in Paris and will come overland on horseback led by a guide to whom he has lent a horse. The guide is to take him as far as Mons. The lackey came by sea with two large and well-stuffed trunks; the master retained a bulky valise that the guide is to carry behind him."[32]

Did Tillieres' espionage put Marie de La Rochefoucauld and Josias de Robillard de Champagné at risk of being apprehended, as he intended? Tillieres' report included not only the alert to Marie's intentions but also a suggestion as to how she could be caught. "In any case, you can observe the wife of Puychenin [who was still in La Rochelle], who will certainly be kept informed, and in this way discover the vessel and treat it like the others." As soon as d'Avaux received the spy's report, he alerted Versailles, and the crown forwarded the information to Arnoul, the intendant of La Rochelle, who was responsible for interdicting escapes from Saintonge and Aunis between 1684 and 1688.[33] In her case, the timing of the specific alert worked in Marie's favor: d'Avaux did not know until June 30 that the planned escape would be from La Rochelle rather than from the Seudre, his dispatches took four days to reach Versailles unless they were sent by two-day express courier, and even the fastest turnaround among the ministers with an express dispatch to Arnoul would not have allowed Arnoul to intercept her July 2 sailing, even if he had been highly motivated to do so.[34] But in Josias' case, Tillieres notified d'Avaux months before his eventual escape that he was an imminent flight risk, so nothing prevented the authorities from stopping his departure. It seems they were not motivated to do so.

Both Marie and Josias, then, in their successful escapes, eluded snares laid for them by communication between the region from which they were fleeing and the neighborhood they targeted as their new home. Tillieres, at the nexus of this communication, concluded from the success of the Champagné and others that those snares were weak. To Tillieres' eye, the border was porous, and escape was not difficult. Ship after ship, he reported, left without difficulty. "A vessel just arrived from La Rochelle with fifteen refugees who left without the slightest opposition." "It is reported from England that quantities of refugees are arriving who are allowed to leave the kingdom very easily." "I have heard from several refugees, and I have even seen letters from France that indicate that all those who wish to leave get to do so for a few *louis d'or*."[35]

Tillieres complained when his information was to no avail. "It upsets me greatly that despite all my efforts, everything passes: gold, silver, people, and ships. I am sure the ship La Roze will come and go like the others." When he thought (erroneously) that the Nieul neighbors of the Champagné had made it to Holland, he complained: "I deplore the fact that these people go and come after warnings so faithfully given; I fear that the other ships I have warned about will pass in the same way." And again, "I am devastated that this vessel sailed despite twenty warnings I gave you about this departure." The party of six from Villiers le Bel, near Montmorency, had arrived in March 1686, led overland by their three guides "as I had reported . . . it is surprising that people escape after the warnings I give." Just days after Josias arrived in Rotterdam, Tillieres told d'Avaux he was happy that Monsieur and Madame de Coutières had been arrested trying to flee, but "if I had been believed this way with respect to many others, there would not be so many of them in this country." This porosity Tillieres imputed to lax efforts on the part of officials. He doubted that the authorities were serious about capturing escapees. "I report things to you as they happen; if, as I have no doubt, they do escape, it will not be my fault."[36]

Tillieres' sense of the reason why even some of his fullest and timeliest information did not result in captures is compelling. Easy departure comports better with the fact that some 150,000–200,000 people escaped from France than common claims that "The king's orders, faithfully executed, closed all the passages; visits to the ships were so exacting that it was virtually impossible to hide."[37] Might there have been some truth to Tillieres' sense that the French authorities cared less than assumed about preventing people from leaving?

The word of a spy—a character whose very posture was deception, who masqueraded on a daily basis, hiding the truth about himself—may seem an unlikely basis for rethinking the Huguenot experience of the Revocation. But d'Avaux found Tillieres credible, and the king came to agree. When Louis XIV expressed skepticism about Tillieres to d'Avaux—"You should watch closely to see if this informant tries to make himself valuable with falsehoods as well as with truths"—the ambassador defended his spy: "It seems to me, Monsieur, that this informant works in good faith and that he applies himself as much as he possibly can to uncovering the plans of the refugees of the R.P.R." "I am the more inclined to have faith in all he says of these ships that go to pick up the French because I know how very often they arrive here by sea." Because he found Tillieres' accounts credible, the ambassador recopied them (finding Tillieres' own hand barely legible), encoded the most sensitive sections, and sent them on to Versailles. He did not edit them; as he explained to the Secretary of State for Foreign Affairs Colbert de Croissy: "I would have liked to send you only extracts, but I believed that you would prefer to have the entire letters because there might often be in them something that I would not think of consequence and that would be."[38]

Because he believed Tillieres' reports, d'Avaux, with the king's permission and the king's specially appropriated funds, rewarded Tillieres handsomely. By June 1686, he had already received a total of 3,000 *livres*. In July 1686, d'Avaux gave Tillieres no less than 1,000 more, followed by another 600 *livres* at the end of August "to motivate him to continue to work assiduously."[39] Tillieres' accounts are credible to the historian, as they were to the ambassador, because his life and livelihood in Holland as well as his future prospects if he returned to France depended upon the accuracy of his intelligence. Can Tillieres' perception of lax enforcement, of weak intent to intercept escapes on the part of French authorities be confirmed? Were Marie and Josias in less danger than they may have thought? Were they able to leave France because the authorities did not care enough to stop all departures, including even those they had credible advance knowledge of?

Escaping from Saintonge, 1687–1688

The moment at which the Champagné escaped, 1687–1688, was the high point of departures. A wave of mass sailings took fugitives away from Saintonge at the end of February 1687. Four large ships left from Mornac, one from Chaillevette, and three or four from La Tremblade. A mass departure in full daylight from Royan (ten barques carrying as many as 500 people) succeeded, even though the ships could be seen from the town as they awaited higher tide. The authorities could only watch them go, since the tide on which they could ride out was but two hours away and soldiers would require three hours to reach them. The intendant Bazin de Bezons wrote to the controller-general over the course of February–March 1687 to report mass departures all along the Seudre. On March 11, he reported that the mouth of the Seudre had been barred—Marie's cousin the younger Isaac Isle took his place aboard his frigate there—but on March 22, Bazin had to admit that more than 600 people had left in the latest desertion.[40]

These successful mass departures must have encouraged Marie and Josias as they prepared their own and their children's escapes. But success was mixed. On January 18, 1687, the seneschal of Nantes arrested Robineau de La Chauvinière—kinsman of the wife of Isaac Isle—and his party as they hid between decks of an English boat at the mouth of the Loire. Two cousins of Josias, Marguerite and Marie de Caillaud, whose mother was godmother of the younger Josias, were also arrested at Paimboeuf on the Loire at the moment they embarked for Holland. Just days after Susanne's escape, two ships were stopped on the Seudre filled with New Converts; 2,500 *livres* in cash taken from the fugitives were distributed to the officers making the arrest, and goods valued at 3,700–3,800 *livres* were to be distributed to the various soldiers taking part in the capture. The ship carrying the mail that implicated Madame de Puychenin would be caught on the Seudre on May 13, 1687.[41]

The consequences of capture were also mixed. Some of those caught were treated according to the rigors of the law—incarceration in convent, prison, or galleys—while others went unpunished. Marie and Josias had seen the severest punishment meted out to Josias' Voutron cousins and their neighbor Chateigner de Cramahé, who were in prison as Marie prepared her escape. They knew of the famous imprisonment of Anne de Chauffepié, daughter of the pastor at Champdeniers, because Voutron's cell was next to hers. But they could not but also know of other fugitives who, when captured for the same offense of deserting the kingdom without permission, were merely sent home. Robineau de La Chauvinière returned home and gained the king's support for restitution of his confiscated property after a brief detention with his wife in their own quarters of an inn near where they were captured—this even though he was so well known as "the most obstinate" of Poitou Protestants that the king had ordered him imprisoned just the year before.[42] The would-be fugitives caught off Mornac in February 1687 were released and sent home with a portion of the property they had carried with them. On April 12, 1687, within days of the first Champagné contingent's departure, the seneschal of Jarnac notified the intendant Arnoul of an escape from his town:

> I had my foot in the stirrup to go alert you that a dozen New Converts from this town, whose names the bearer [of this letter] will have the honor of telling you, left last evening and the evening before. But since some of their relations promised to take me where they had gone, which is, according to them, to Pons, Gemozac, and Cozes, I am going to follow them to bring them back if I can through gentleness or arrest them in case of resistance.

The seneschal asked Arnoul to keep an eye out for them. In the letter's margin, in Arnoul's handwriting, is a notation of the case's outcome: "found the people, whom I sent back to their homes." Between the departure of the Champagné children in April and Marie's in June, a case of escape very close to them had precisely the same outcome. The Sieur de Nieul, brother-in-law of the Seigneur d'Agonnay, Berneré's next-door neighbor, had purchased a ship and hired a crew of twenty-five to thirty Protestant sailors to take Agonnay's mother and sister as well as himself to Holland. They were stopped at the point of boarding their ship: the ship was confiscated, sold at auction with its contents, and the master sent to the galleys. But the passengers were told by the authorities simply to go home. The return home was such a standard ending to captures of escapes that it was even woven into the story Isaac Isle's daughter Henriette-Lidie would tell her fellow nuns of her family's attempted escape; the guards who discovered them aboard their ship had simply sent them home.[43]

The view the Champagné could have had of the chances of escape was, then, a hodgepodge of inconsistent official responses that could only leave them uncertain about what they risked in departing. Indeed, the uncertainty might have been among the nerve-wracking aspects of the escape for the Champagné. Even as some deserters were exempted from the letter of the law forbidding departures, the law itself and the punishments it prescribed were reiterated without attenuation, the only amendments being elaborations of prohibitions or penalties. So in March 1687, following the mass departures from Mornac and La Tremblade, as the Champagné children were about to leave and Marie arranged her affairs at Berneré one final time, Seignelay directed the Admiralty to republish the edicts against departure, redouble surveillance, and reject the pretexts known to be used by Protestants for leaving.[44]

But if they tried to gauge the probabilities of success, rather than just leaving as soon as they could, the Champagné may have been able to detect some variation over the course of 1687–1688 in the determination of officials to intercept fugitives. In early January 1687, the king ordered the intendant Foucault to withdraw the frigates and guards patrolling the coast north of La Rochelle, which he gradually did. This and contemporaneous redeployments of the coast guard gave many the impression that the effort to stop departures was waning or had even been abandoned. Foucault noted that the withdrawal of frigates and guards led *religionnaires* to believe that the king was easing off and would tolerate their departure. An observer of the escapes from the coast south of La Rochelle noted: "Rumor has it that at La Tremblade, at Mornac and Royan word spread that anyone could withdraw if he wished and that the King granted the liberty to do so." Feydeau de Brou, the intendant at Rouen, told the controller-general on June 1, 1687 that a recent group tried simply to depart openly, "persuaded as they were that since the raising of the coast guard there was no order at all from Your Majesty to obstruct their passage." The unsuccessful fugitive La Chauvinière told his interrogators, when asked why he was leaving, that "having learned His Majesty wished passage left free for everyone, having had the guard lifted on the coasts, he believed that he could leave freely without contravening the orders of the King."[45]

There are several explanations for this variable enforcement of the prohibition on Huguenot emigration. First of all, a policy of exemplary punishment is by definition a policy of inconsistency: some will be punished and others ignored or absolved; certain conditions will call for more punishments, others for fewer. As such, it fit perfectly with the predicament in which the crown found itself by 1687—hoist on its own petard in problems more intractable than it anticipated when making the law. Once the criminalization of departures was decreed on the Revocation document, the authorities had little room to maneuver in the face of massive departures. Explicitly relaxing or discontinuing enforcement would undermine the authority of the king, making him look weak, as if he were ceding to the claims of Protestants and criticism from abroad. The king had no choice but to support the law publicly with sufficient harshness to obtain a respectable result but little enough to minimize damage. Inconsistency resolved the predicament that Huguenots' insistence on emigrating imposed upon the authorities.

Inconsistency was not necessarily a policy choice rather than simply the result of limited ability to come up with a solution when persisting Protestant resistance exposed the contradiction at the heart of the Revocation: that coupling mandatory conversion with prohibition on departures simply trapped disobedient subjects inside the kingdom. It may be that Louis XIV's style of governance was unequal to the task of formulating a consistent response. "You are looking for a model of lofty strategy, maneuvering, all of a piece? A waste of time." Louis XIV "never sought to remedy the confusion that marked its [the Revocation's] execution" because in his mind it was merely one among numerous ever-shifting political considerations that he managed not through strategic planning but through piecemeal reactions as issues arose. Enforcement of the Revocation rested, in practice, on "hesitations, contradictions . . . scraps of plans that did not mesh, movements that clashed with one another, collisions and conflicts."[46] It may even be that within the matrix of aspirations that Louis XIV harbored—embellishment of his own glory; establishment of his own authority; gains vis-à-vis the Empire, the Turks, and the Papacy; and the coming of war with William of Orange—enforcement of the Revocation was too low a priority to command his consistent attention and action.[47]

Still, in the years immediately following the Revocation, there are some indications that Louis did devise a resolution to the dilemma by prioritizing the elimination of Protestantism within France over prohibition of departures abroad. In January 1687, just before the Champagné escaped, the French ambassador in The Hague, d'Avaux, wrote to Versailles expressing his concern about official policy toward Huguenots back in France. He believed that the persecution of Protestants in France and the consequent formation of a large and vocal Huguenot community in Holland were damaging French foreign policy. Their presence in the Refuge and their propaganda gave William of Orange ammunition for winning over to an anti-French posture the hitherto pro-French States General, Amsterdam merchants, and public opinion.[48] It was because he perceived a need to forestall the growth of the expatriate population and their poisoning of Dutch opinion that d'Avaux worked to funnel to Versailles information for checking Huguenot escapes. Without question, for many Huguenots escape from France was rendered more difficult, or even impossible, by the actions d'Avaux took in Holland, often on the basis of intelligence provided by his star mole within the Huguenot refugee community.

Yet d'Avaux did not believe that intercepting departures was the critical move the crown should make. D'Avaux delicately suggested to the king that the best way to stop emigration would be by reducing harassment of Protestants and New Converts within France. On the basis of letters from France that his informant had seen, he believed Huguenots would not flee if they were not obliged to attend mass and imprisoned for failing to do so. The numbers arriving fell off, he said, whenever there was "greater liberty in France and persons there are not forced to practice Catholicism." "I have even been told recently by a reliable source that many refugees have declared that if the rumor proved true that henceforth those in France would not be forced to take Catholic communion nor attend Catholic mass, they would return to the kingdom. They all say generally that not a quarter of those who came here would stay." The ambassador sent his most candid warning about the dangerous course the French government was pursuing in indirectly forcing emigrations: "I believe I would be shirking my duty and falling short in the loyalty I owe to Your Majesty if I did not report what I learn when it concerns the good of his service." In response, the king directly rejected the suggestion that pressure within France be relaxed, and, interestingly, expressed a lack of concern about the emigrations: "The desertions of my New Convert subjects are the effect of a damaged imagination, and the remedy that could be applied might perhaps be yet worse than the harm done. We must look to God's beneficence for cessation of this disorder, which He may have suffered to happen only in order to purge my kingdom of disobedient and uncontrollable subjects."[49]

Indeed, following the exchange of views with d'Avaux, Louis instituted a policy more in line with his own sense of the disorder than with his ambassador's recommendation, infringing or at least downgrading the prohibition on departures. On February 16, 1688, the Marquis de Dangeau recorded in his journal a new royal policy for dealing with "disobedient and uncontrollable subjects": "The King has resolved to send out of the kingdom all those persons of the Religion who remain there; he confiscates their property and gives them permission to withdraw wherever they like; he will have them conducted out of the kingdom." A month later, following the assembly and massacre at Grand-Ry, the Marquis de Sourches recorded the same royal decision, this time making explicit a hierarchy of punishments that subordinated concern over loss of subjects by emigration to the primary goal of eliminating Protestant worship within France, as had occurred at Grand-Ry. It distinguished among prisoners who simply refused to convert (whom the king would "chase from his state") and those who had relapsed or taken actions to keep their religion alive in the kingdom (whom he kept locked up), the severest punishments to be reserved for those who had taken up arms in revolt, namely those of Poitou, "who had even fired on Monsieur Foucault, their intendant."[50]

Seven days later, on March 19, 1688, Josias' cousin Gédéon Nicolas de Voutron was sent abroad "for being steadfast in refusing to abjure the R.P.R." Anne de Chauffepié learned in the same month "that the prisoners for religion were being sent out of France and that I should prepare myself to depart shortly." She left her convent at Arcisse on May 24, sailed out of Dieppe on June 1, and arrived in Rotterdam on June 3, just before Josias. The fifty-five expelled Huguenots who petitioned the States General of the United Provinces for monetary assistance on August 17 included twenty-five from Poitou-Charentes, notably Voutron, Cramahé, Vasselot, Béjarry, and Legoux de Périgny (formerly an elder of the La Rochelle temple). Marie's cousin the Marquise de Tors, heiress of Le Douhet, would be ordered expelled along with her husband and daughter in September 1688.[51]

The king was not alone in thinking the departure of Huguenots might be salutary. After all, the objective of religious uniformity could be served indirectly by flight. Some in authority spoke their opinion that there would be advantages if it were so. Fénelon, the missionary most intent on converting the Huguenots of Saintonge (including Isaac Isle), wrote to Seignelay opposing the relaxation of the coast guards, but also pointing out that permissible departures might alleviate the difficulties of conversion by removing malcontents and by thus decreasing the numbers to be served: "Those who desert will perhaps facilitate by their flight the instruction of those who do not leave." In the same vein, Bégon thought when he arrived at Rochefort that departure of the most obstinate would make conversion of those remaining easier. Even the intendant most renowned for his anti-Huguenot severity, Lamoignon de Basville, would later speak against efforts to keep Huguenots from departing: "After these first escapes, which received more attention than they deserve, after eight years of an intense and bloody war, does the country noticeably lack men to cultivate it or defend it? France has its own internal resources, and if the most obstinate leave, it is a gain to lose rebellious subjects. Nothing is more fortunate than to see this multitude of factious and restless people scatter and the tranquility of the state be strengthened by the conversion of the ones or the escape of the others." Louis XIV would not have agreed with all of Basville's view; he worried about the loss of soldiers and sailors, and about reports he heard from other intendants about the decline of agriculture and industry caused by the flight of Huguenots.[52] But the sense on the part of these servants of the crown was that the primary objective of converting those who stayed within the kingdom might be well served by decreased attention to the subsidiary objective of preventing departures of those who opted to take their obstinacy elsewhere.

Closer to home for the Champagné, tension between the formal prohibition on departure and an additional reason not to enforce it pervaded the work of the key official in the Charentes. The intendant Arnoul was responsible both for intercepting escapes from Saintonge-Aunis and for promoting prosperity in one of France's great maritime regions. Like d'Avaux, he shaped his actions and recommendations to the realities he saw on the ground far from the eyes of the court where policy was made.[53] Like d'Avaux, he recognized that forced conversion pushed people to leave, but unlike d'Avaux he doubted the wisdom of stopping emigration, for he believed that intercepting departures posed a threat to his region's prosperity. "With respect to the expedients one could propose," he wrote to the king, "one finds hardly any that, to oblige the new converts to do their duty, do not give them the desire to depart . . . one can scarcely imagine any that, in order to prevent escapes, do not harm commerce, and that is what accounts for the fact that what is proposed is not always without difficulty. . . . What I believe is that escapes cannot be prevented without great damage to commerce." The commerce that fueled French strength was precisely the commerce that permitted easy and routine circulation of persons, ships, and money between France and the countries that welcomed Huguenot refugees.

Arnoul's preference for open commerce over a closed coast drew a rebuke from Seignelay: "I tell you frankly that you are wrong about the persons who leave the kingdom when you say that the harm is not great and that that does not reduce trade. You need to know that the greatest harm that can happen to the State is the loss of a great number of subjects who left taking their industry into foreign lands, enriching them at the expense of this Kingdom, and that is what you should prevent with all your strength across the entire extent of your department."[54] So Arnoul continued by casting himself as obedient executor of the king's policy—"I will spare neither my care nor my efforts and would dedicate my life to it if necessary"—and keeping the spotlight on his assiduous efforts: "all possible measures are being taken to prevent desertions." His punishments of Protestants served the theatrical function that exemplary justice required. He imprisoned escapees. On occasion, he would have the corpse of a convert who relapsed into heresy dragged on a hurdle, smoke the holds of departing ships to catch Protestant stowaways, and order recalcitrant Huguenot women to be shaved by the public hangman.

But he also let people go—among many, the Champagné's Nieul-Agonnay neighbors and the group from Jarnac, whom he sent home. Arnoul's papers in the Bibliothèque Nationale contain a pack of *lettres de cachet* sent to him by the king, signed but with a blank where he could fill in the malefactor's name. That Arnoul did not use all he was issued testifies to his views outlined here. The persecutions he did visit upon Huguenot subjects could, cumulatively, be stitched together by outraged refugees to create the most horrific of pictures. But Arnoul was inconsistent in applying crown policy toward fugitives—alternately severe, mild, and indifferent—because he worried about the incompatibility of maritime commerce and the policy of religious coercion formulated far inland. An accurate historical account of his treatment of Huguenot fugitives would contain cases of his indulgence as well as his severity.

Perhaps Arnoul decided to ignore Tillieres' warning and let Josias go in 1688 because royal policy had shifted to expulsions or simply because of the low priority he placed on intercepting escapes. For whatever reason, Josias, who had long been tagged as an imminent fugitive, left France, as he told Tillieres upon arrival in Holland, with no difficulty whatsoever. Josias' escape in a season of tolerated, even encouraged or forced, departures is aptly symbolized by his fortuitous pairing at his *reconnaissance* in Rotterdam with a man from La Rochelle who had been expelled. Two spaces below Josias' was the signature of one of the rare persons on that register from his part of France—Pierre Legoux de Périgny, from La Rochelle. Périgny had been expelled as a recalcitrant Protestant after being imprisoned in the Saint-Nicolas tower at La Rochelle, in Vermenton in Burgundy, in Noyers, and for seven months in the Château de Nantes.[55] Those passing into exile by choice in secret, like Josias, and those ejected publicly against their will came together to form the Refugee community.

Although it was intended to facilitate elimination of Protestantism inside France, inconsistent enforcement of the Revocation's formal prohibition on emigration ironically created both the Refuge and clandestine Protestantism within France. Escape from the Charentes was tricky to orchestrate, but the odds of succeeding were high, particularly in certain periods, and the possibility of benign treatment if caught was not insignificant. The French borders were, after all, open enough to allow some 150,000–200,000 escapes. But formally prohibiting departure surely reduced or slowed the flow outward: more would have left had it not been so expensive, complicated, and vulnerable to punishment. Bezons said as much: "I am persuaded that if no frigates and traversiers were preventing the escape of those who remain, many would leave, though they claimed the contrary to me." If that is so, it was the attempt to curb emigration—as lax and spotty as it may have been—that guaranteed a future for Protestantism in France: "Saintonge lost, it is said, 100,000 Protestants, a contestable number. It kept as many, if not more. These renegades became the hotbed where the faith reignited. The State, in opposing flights as strongly as possible, worked effectively at the same time to conserve these latent germs of the R.P.R."[56] There would be a future for Protestantism in France, though without the Champagné, except perhaps Thérèse.

PART THREE

THOSE WHO STAYED

8

Thérèse's Guardian

The network of Protestant nobles that endured in Saintonge down to the Revocation was, then, torn by the departure of neighbors and kin. For a generation or two, Protestant or once-Protestant families who stayed in France would be aware that persons they had known as adults or children would never be seen again because, in the crisis of the Revocation, they had made the hard choice to relocate to the Refuge. Now, with reduced numbers and in a transformed political environment, they would have dramas of their own to surmount: holding together their reconfigured kindreds, renewing their religious and social identities, redefining their relations to power. These were the challenges facing, among many others, the Prévost de Touchimbert, Mazières, Voutron, and Isle.

And Thérèse. The baby born to Marie de La Rochefoucauld five weeks before the departure of her mother never reunited with her family. The plan had been for her to escape with her father; as late as November 1687, Josias anticipated arranging an escape that would allow him to bring the then six-month-old infant with him. But he arrived in Holland with only valets in tow. How much Marie de La Rochefoucauld would ever know about her lost child is unclear. Other than Josias' November 1687 letter, only one item in the Champagné Papers refers to Thérèse: a handwritten extract from a 1691 ruling by the Parlement of Bordeaux that must have been sent to Marie in Holland by those caring for the child.[1] Otherwise, she disappears from their records. Her Catholic baptism is not mentioned with the baptisms of her siblings in the family's private papers, and she is omitted even from Marie's autobiographical memoir. The life history of a child is the most difficult to resurrect. Unless elders for some reason record it, only the child's context will leave traces, so it alone yields clues to understanding Thérèse's life without her family in Saintonge.

When Josias left home at Easter 1688, he had several choices for a guardian with whom to leave his daughter. Three of Marie's sisters lived nearby, but he chose not to give Thérèse into their care, very likely because they had converted to the religion Josias wanted above all for his children to elude. His only sibling, his older sister Marie de Robillard, had died, but her widower was still living in his Château de Londigny just across the provincial border in Angoumois. Casimir Prévost de Touchimbert's ties to Josias and Marie ran deep. His mother, Jeanne de La Rochefoucauld du Parc d'Archiac, was a first cousin of Marie's father. His father had been godfather for Marie's sister Madeleine. Casimir himself had presented the newborn younger Josias for baptism at Champagné. He and Josias had come to an amicable final settlement in 1678 of their respective claims to the inheritance from Josias's parents. Josias and Marie de La Rochefoucauld were hosting Casimir's sister Marie at Berneré in the months surrounding the Revocation, when she fell under the influence of missionaries and abjured. Casimir's brother Brassac was so completely trusted by Josias that he was able to embezzle the funds Josias counted on to finance his escape and resettlement. It was to this Casimir that the departing Josias entrusted Thérèse. Who he was and what transpired while he was guardian for Thérèse is the only story that can be told about her.

Casimir Prévost de Touchimbert

The Prévost were a large, old, and prominent noble family of Poitou.[2] The proofs of nobility Casimir drew up in 1686 traced his lineage back eight generations to 1370. But other genealogies located progenitors in Poitou as early as the twelfth century and identified a line of distinguished officers that stretched across the middle ages, including a Bishop of Poitiers in 1217. Toward 1500, before the Reformation introduced seeds of new dissension into the realm and into its kinship networks, three sons of Casimir's seventh ancestor established the three branches of the family that would make their mark in Old Regime history. All three branches stayed in the vicinity of Salles-de-Villefagnan, in the "threshold of Poitou" between Angoulême and Poitiers that was very familiar to Calvin and where, early on, Calvinists became numerous.[3] The seeds of religious conflict planted in this locality would estrange the three branches of the Prévost family from each other for more than a century.

The Prévost de Sansac branch of the family settled in the Château de Sansac near Confolens in Angoumois. In the mid-sixteenth century, one younger son was Archbishop of Bordeaux, while his oldest brother served as governor of Angoumois, Gentleman of the King's Bedchamber, and Grand Falconer of France. The latter and his son, governor of Bordeaux, "were found gloriously mixed up in all the wars and military enterprises taking place in their day," including the major battles against the Huguenots in the Wars of Religion. The family archives retain letters from Henri II, Henri III, and Catherine de Médicis addressed "To my cousin le Sieur de Sansac." A second branch, Prévost de Traversay, settled at the Château de Civray and later at the Château de Traversay between Civray and Melle. This family line, too, was Catholic and enjoyed unbroken royal favor down to the end of the Old Regime. Jean-François rose to become a ship's captain and governor of Saint-Domingue. Four of his sons were admitted to the Ecole Militaire; the eldest rose to eminence in royal employ and, as an émigré from the Revolution, became Grand-Admiral of the Black Sea Fleet and Minister of the Navy for Catherine the Great, Paul I, Alexander I, and Nicholas I of Russia.[4]

The third branch, called Prévost de Touchimbert after a seigneury the family had held since at least 1466, made little perceptible mark on national affairs but was well endowed with patrimonies and local eminence. After Casimir's great-grandfather converted to the Reformed faith and joined the troops of La Rochefoucauld in the Wars of Religion, the Seigneurs de Touchimbert became influential in Protestant affairs. Their fortune increased substantially in 1668, when Casimir's father inherited three estates from Jeanne de La Rochefaton, Duchesse de La Force, wife of Armand Nompar de Caumont, Duc de La Force. In 1671, these lands were split between Casimir and his four siblings. François, as the eldest, took Saveilles, whose château was among the loveliest in Angoumois. Charles, Seigneur de Brassac et du Tour, took La Salle-Duretal in Poitou and relocated to Le Rétail near Saint-Hilaire- sur-l'Autize. Casimir took Montalembert in Angoumois, which was perched atop a long ridge overlooking the plains through which the old Roman road led from Poitiers to Saintes. He occasionally resided at Montalembert, though he continued to be named for his holdings at Londigny (two miles away) and Lisleau.[5]

The Revocation would send the three Touchimbert brothers their separate ways. The youngest, Charles (Brassac), abjured before the Revocation, on October 1, 1685, but François and Casimir actively contested the king's mandate of conversion. François was already at loggerheads with the crown over the religious prerogatives attached to his inheritance of Saveilles. When an *arrêt* of the Council of State dated June 8, 1682 prohibited Protestant worship in Saveilles, François continued holding the services and countered that as a seigneur with rights of high justice he was entitled to do so under the Edict of Nantes. As heir to Jeanne de La Rochefaton, he paid the local consistory the 3,000 *livres* she earmarked for it in her will, only to see the Saveilles temple suppressed almost immediately and the legacy redirected to the *hôpital général* at Ruffec.[6]

Casimir probably fell under suspicion as early as June 1685, when he was among the "outsider Lords" spotted at Paris' Charenton temple for the Protestant burial of Diane de Poligny, wife of Jacques Du Bois, Sieur de Saint-Mandé. Sensing a threat in the occasion, the king ordered La Reynie, head of the Paris police, to discover "the names of the outsider Lords who were at Charenton, and send me the list of them."[7] Casimir, like François, had dragoons in his house during the late summer and fall of 1685, when dragoons were likewise at Berneré. At the end of October, Louvois asked the intendant Gourgue about Casimir, whom the minister identified as one of the "*religionnaires* most distinguished by their obstinacy," and then two days later, having read to the king Gourgue's report on Casimir's behavior, he relayed the king's order "that if it is true that the Sieur de Londigny said what you say he said, then his intention is that you have him arrested." The intendant was offered two alternatives for Casimir's incarceration: "One that the Sieur de Londigny be sent away to Langres and the other that he be imprisoned in the Château d'Angoulême, according to how bad his conduct seems to you from the information against him sent to you by the lieutenant-general of Angoulême."[8]

Neither, though, would be Casimir's fate, for the arrest order crossed the path of the brothers Casimir and François as they headed to Versailles to meet the king. Riding to court to appeal to the king was a venerable tradition for those who thought the king was mistaken, misled, or ignorant of wrongs being carried out in distant provinces under his name. The notion of the king as upholder of the law, righter of wrongs—good Saint-Louis hearing grievances and rendering justice beneath an oak tree in Vincennes—remained particularly strong in the minds of Huguenots, whose protections under the Edict of Nantes had come precisely from the king. But for them the venerable tradition was no longer a viable one. During the first dragonnade in Poitou in July 1681, the Marquis de Venours, a leading Protestant nobleman from Poitou and a future patron of Marie de La Rochefoucauld in the Refuge, met Louvois at Fontainebleau to submit petitions and other documents that he swore contained true reports of the violence being meted out to Protestants in Poitou. After showing the materials to the king, Louvois turned on Venours in anger: "I blushed with shame at having brought your request to the King, because His Majesty told me that he was well aware that your petition is filled with falsehoods." As late as 1704, a Huguenot nobleman from Uzès in Languedoc, Aigaliers, recorded in his memoirs how he rode to Versailles to persuade the king that the prudent way to end the violence and establish peace was for his subjects "to be allowed to serve God according to the sentiment of their conscience. . . . I had made the decision to make those things (killings, burnings, condemnation to the galleys or to exile) known to the King, hoping that if His Majesty knew them, he would give us justice." After meeting with the king, Aigaliers fled the country, disgraced "for having professed my religion in front of His Majesty."[9]

The Prévost de Touchimbert's mission to the king may well have originated in the assembly of more than 100 Protestant gentlemen of Poitou who had gathered in a field near Luçon earlier in October. Even as the gentlemen and the intendant Foucault addressed each other there, both sides had their eyes on the king. What Foucault told them may have been the same remarkable nesting of conscience within obedience that he would convey to a further assembly of Protestant gentlemen he convened at Poitiers on November 2: "It is a delusion that can only come from intentional blindness to wish to distinguish between the obligations of conscience and obedience that is due to the king, on an occasion when these two duties are inseparable, since His Majesty acts only for the interest of religion." The intendant claimed to ventriloquize the king, warning of "the calamity threatening you . . . take advantage of the final warning the king gives you from my mouth." For their part, the gentlemen selected a deputation that would bypass the intendant and carry their message directly to the king, to complain to him that the dragoons violated the Edict of Nantes, according to which they were not to be molested in the exercise of their religion, and to ask the king's permission to leave the kingdom if the persecution were not to cease.[10]

The Touchimbert brothers may have been named to that deputation or they may have determined independently to undertake a personal appeal to the king. Their petition matched closely that of the Luçon assembly. They invoked the services of their ancestors and of the one son who had just recently entered naval service. They described the violence done to them and their properties by the dragoons sent not by the king but "by a subdelegate of the intendant of the province who uses your authority." They claimed that both their nobility and the Edict of Nantes protected them from such injury. They begged for "liberty of conscience and preservation of their honor" but for "liberty to withdraw to a foreign land with their families" if it were the king's desire that their conscience be violated and their honor degraded. The petition was respectful; it opened with the brothers throwing themselves on the king's mercy and closed with their wish "to continue their prayers for the prosperity of Your Majesty." Yet there is in it something of the understanding of the nobility's relation to the king that Boisrond articulated before his agreement to convert: a sense that nobles derived entitlements from lineage over time ("they are descended from a very ancient noble family"), an expectation of justice through due process ("they were the object of exceedingly dishonorable treatment to which they would have believed they could be subjected only after being tried in court"), and an assumption that the king ruled within the bounds of his promises (given that "they act in accord with the Edicts under which they were nurtured . . . the supplicants cannot believe that the violence done to them before the Revocation of the Edict could have been ordered by Your Majesty").[11]

Prospects for their venture to Versailles were not propitious. A month earlier, Louvois had notified Foucault that the king would not hear complaints brought by delegates from the provincial churches. Just about the time the brothers left home, Louvois sent word through d'Asfeld, who was in charge of the dragoons in Poitou, that a petition from the nobles of Poitou had arrived and that he had "not the slightest intention of reporting its contents to the king for fear of procuring them a considerable punishment and that they would be well advised to refrain from such conduct in the future." Then, on November 7, Louvois wrote Foucault that any further delegations would be punished, according to "the order I received from His Majesty to have the said gentlemen arrested as soon as they appear."[12] Indeed, upon reaching Paris, François, Casimir, and three other delegates from Poitou were arrested without being allowed to approach the king. Louvois notified Foucault on November 9 and Gourgue on November 11: "I thought I should let you know that the Sieurs de Touchimbert, Protestant gentlemen and brothers from the province of Angoumois having come here to present their protestations to the King, His Majesty ordered that they be sent to the Bastille."[13]

Imprisonment at the Bastille was not always oppressive, but in these cases, the conditions of incarceration were strict. Le Tellier notified the jailer, Besmares, that the five prisoners were to be separated and prohibited from communicating with one another or with anyone else, in writing or orally, until further orders. Even letters from the prisoners' wives required special permission from the king and were not secure: "His Majesty approves of your delivering them and wants you to send me the responses." The crime for which François and Casimir were arrested was not their attempt to reach the king but their continuing adherence to a forbidden creed. Their sentence was of indeterminate length: however long it would take for them to agree to convert. Within eight weeks of arriving in the Bastille, the other three Poitevin deputies had made the required promise to convert and were released.[14] But there had been no movement on the part of the brothers Prévost.

A routine piece of family business yields a glimpse of them between November 1685 and February 1686. On Christmas Day of 1685, Louvois allowed the brothers to speak with an agent of Monsieur de Soubise, who had business to transact with them. At issue was the Touchimbert's suit for payment of 7,102 *livres* owed by Louis de Rohan-Chabot, Duc de Rohan, for the seigneury of Pougnes that Casimir, his two brothers and two sisters had sold to François de Rohan, Prince de Soubise in 1668. Final settlement was made before notaries of the Paris Châtelet on the afternoon of January 10, 1686, at Rohan-Chabot's *hôtel* on the Place Royale. Brassac had come from his residence in Poitou and was lodging in the rue Hautefeuille, parish of Saint-André-des-Arts. Sister Madeleine had come from her home in Poitiers on her own behalf and with a power of attorney signed on October 31 by her sister Marie, who was living with the Champagné in their Château de Berneré in

Saint-Savinien. François and Casimir, imprisoned, missed the event.[15] It was more than a financial transaction that they missed—indeed, it was a veritable acting out of the endgame of Protestantism in France. The Rohan were heirs and descendants of the two great warriors (Henri, Duc de Rohan and Benjamin de Rohan, Duc de Soubise) who led the final Protestant armed resistance at the siege of La Rochelle in the 1620s. The Rohan-Chabot and the elder line of the ducal Rohan family had made their religious accommodation well before the Revocation; a generation back was Protestant rebellion, ahead the famous Cardinal de Rohan. While the brothers Touchimbert were imprisoned for refusing the compliance through which the Rohan prospered, the Princesse de Soubise was a senior lady-in-waiting for the Queen and sometime mistress of Louis XIV. Soubise before long would turn the Hôtel de Clisson in the Marais section of Paris into the spectacular Hôtel de Soubise.

Whether the Touchimbert brothers and sisters appreciated the symbolism of the event is unclear. But within two weeks the imprisoned brothers moved fairly rapidly to compliance. They were allowed as of January 13 to confer with each other and as of January 15 to be visited by Brassac, who had converted months earlier and whose frequent visits Louvois believed might contribute to softening his brothers' resistance. The release orders for the brothers, "after promising to become Catholic," were signed by Louvois the first week of February, and the prisoners left together on the ninth or tenth, promising in writing that they would abjure within the following fortnight. Their release was a victory for family solidarity: all five siblings would once again be united in religion. Madeleine, who does not seem to have visited her brothers in the Bastille, joined Brassac in vouching for the sincerity of their promise to convert. And on the sixteenth, though no one in Paris knew it, a related drama had played itself out in Saint-Savinien; sister Marie had abjured, making her profession of Catholic faith and receiving absolution from a Capuchin missionary priest.[16]

Casimir returned home and abjured there on February 20, 1686, the Père de La Chaise presiding, along with six of his children: Casimir, Marie, Angélique, Diane, Julie, and Sylvie.[17] Then he quickly returned to Paris, where he pursued personal and legal business under watchful official eyes. He visited two Protestant prisoners in the Bastille, one of whom, Sainte-Hermine, was closely allied with the Champagné, as well as the sister of Saint-Surin in the convent where she was detained. From August 1686 to March 1687, he was in court defending his noble title to Montalembert and his consequent exemption from certain taxes. The spy Tillieres reported on June 1 that Casimir was lodging at the Black Head in the rue de La Harpe; a police report dated December 20, 1686, listed among the New Converts lodging there "The Sieur de L'Islot

Touchimbert also a gentleman from near La Rochelle who was in the Bastille and who abjured at the hands of the Père de La Chaise."[18]

Both Casimir and his brother François would continue to be objects of official suspicion, even fifteen years after their coerced conversions. In April 1692, Casimir's name appeared on a list of fourteen noblemen who, the intendant in Poitiers told the king, "would be capable of undertaking something"; the king ordered them to be arrested "at the slightest suspicion about their conduct." In 1700, "Touchimbert" was under surveillance by Maupeou d'Ableiges, intendant in Poitiers, to whom Secretary of State Barbezieux wrote on New Year's Day: "The King wishing to be informed of the conduct of Monsieur de Touchimbert, gentleman of Poitou, New Convert, I beg you to tell me what I need to know in order to report to His Majesty."[19]

For a decade and more, then, Casimir Prévost de Touchimbert endured the kind of pressure that so depressed the spirits of his brother-in-law Josias de Robillard during the brief post-Revocation period preceding his flight. Why did he not leave? Casimir may at certain times have been intent on leaving. The brothers' petition in October 1685 had asked permission to leave. Within months of his release from the Bastille, Casimir led those already in the Refuge to believe that he would join them soon, for in June 1686 the king learned from the spy Tillieres that Casimir "would like very much to be in Holland, according to the letters I have seen. It seems that his plan is not to stay in France." Within a year, the Touchimbert were reported to have moved "a great deal of wealth out of the Kingdom and to have more than 14,000 *francs* in London." Moreover, his daughters Marie and Angélique and his son did move into the Refuge. Marie de La Rochefoucauld noted in her escape account that upon her arrival in Holland in the late fall of 1687, she stayed with "my Touchimbert nieces," who, with a relative (most likely father Casimir's sister Marie, who had abjured in Saint-Savinien in 1685 while a guest with the Champagné at Berneré), had made their *reconnaissance* at the Rotterdam French Church on March 19, 1687. A year later, on March 22, 1688, Casimir's son Casimir made his *reconnaissance* at the French Church in The Hague.[20]

Here again was an escape well warned of in advance that was not stopped by the authorities. Soon after their arrival in Holland, the Prévost women told Tillieres that more Touchimbert had wanted to come with them but could not do so at that time: "they will leave as soon as they can." The marginal note inscribed at Versailles on Tillieres' report indicates that this intelligence was forwarded to Saint-Contest, intendant at Limoges, who did not intercept further Touchimbert departures; young Casimir escaped afterwards, during the same lax period in which Josias left without difficulty. But why, if escape was an option, did father Casimir, who had expressed his intention to leave,

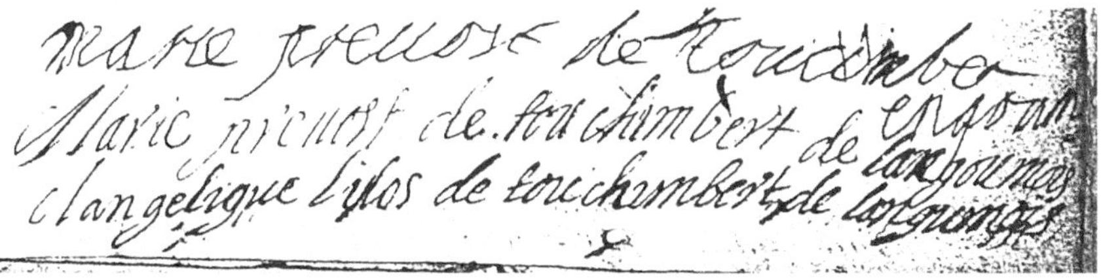

Figure 8.1 *Reconnaissance* by three women of the Prévost de Touchimbert family, March 19, 1687, at the Waals Hervormde Kerk te Rotterdam. Courtesy of the Stadsarchief Rotterdam.

remain in France as one after another of his family departed? What set of circumstances made him decide—by contrast with Josias de Robillard and Marie de La Rochefoucauld—to stay in France despite the suspicion that his persisting Protestantism imposed upon him? Casimir did not leave because after his release from the Bastille he could not do so without leaving behind his youngest children. The December 1686 police report that placed Casimir on the rue de La Harpe noted that he "has three daughters who entered the house of Madame de Maintenon near Versailles"[21]—that is, the Maison royale de Saint-Louis at Saint-Cyr, the famed pet project of Madame de Maintenon. This information offers an unexpected insight into Casimir's decision to stay and convert—and, no doubt, into the decisions of other "obstinate" Protestants who did not emigrate in the period of the Revocation.

The Matter of Saint-Cyr

Some genealogies of the Prévost family list the fugitive son and two daughters of Casimir Prévost de Touchimbert and Marie de Robillard, Josias' sister, while others do not. They generally, however, do list four of their children, all girls: Diane, born in June 1672; Julie, born in July 1674; Esther-Silvie, born in January 1676; and Marie-Anne-Susanne, born most likely in 1675. These four daughters were old enough by the date of the Revocation to choose to abjure Protestantism on their own, according to royal declarations setting seven as the age for religious consent,[22] but probably too young to be considered by their father ready to be left on their own. It is not surprising, then, that Casimir joined his fate to those of his younger daughters in the years surrounding the Revocation, seemingly not by choice. In the summer of 1686, three of the younger four entered the school at Saint-Cyr.

The Maison royale de Saint-Louis at Saint-Cyr was a renowned and formidable institution that had opened its doors only a few months before the Prévost daughters arrived there. Founded by Françoise d'Aubigné, Marquise de Maintenon just about two years after she became the morganatic second wife of Louis XIV, Saint-Cyr's stated mission was strengthening the French nobility through the education of its daughters and future wives. Informed by a vision of aristocratic reform most eloquently articulated by François de Salignac de La Mothe-Fénelon and by the pedagogical prescriptions he set out in his 1687 *Treatise on the Education of Girls,* Saint-Cyr has been understood as a secularizing, nationalizing, and modernizing institution of the Old Regime.[23]

Figure 8.2 Françoise d'Aubigné, Marquise de Maintenon with her niece Françoise-Amable d'Aubigné (future Duchesse de Noailles), before a view of the Maison Royale d'éducation de Saint-Cyr, ca. 1688. Oil on canvas by Louis Elle the Elder. Châteaux de Versailles et de Trianon. By permission of RMN-Grand Palais/Art Resource, NY.

Over the years, the school had its critics. Enemies of Maintenon satirized it as her ego trip. Crown officials who were hard-pressed to fund it later in the eighteenth century lamented how stale its education had become in an age of Enlightenment, sometimes proposing that its endowments be redirected to more useful charitable or governmental purposes.[24] The Revolution closed the school in 1793 on the grounds that it had become just another convent, despite its founder's desire to avoid turning out nuns. But in the nineteenth century, the first comprehensive histories of Saint-Cyr celebrated the school as an institution so effective in enhancing the marriageability of its graduates, and so needed as a charitable subvention for noble families who must devote family resources to their sons' service in the king's armies, that noblemen flooded the king with requests for admission, and most of the families clamoring to gain this favor for one or more daughters inevitably met with disappointment.

The Prévost de Touchimbert case gives the lie to this characterization of Saint-Cyr, complicating retrospective understanding of the school's purposes and operations in the period of religious reunification. Perhaps the anti-Huguenot purpose should have been obvious from the start. The coincidence of dates was not lost on the memorialist Saint-Simon: "The magnificent establishment of Saint-Cyr followed closely upon the revocation of the edict of Nantes."[25] Fénelon, after all, won his early renown as missionary to recalcitrant Protestants like Isaac Isle in the Charentes homeland of Maintenon, the Prévost, and the Champagné. As superior of the Nouvelles Catholiques on the rue Sainte-Anne in Paris, from 1679, Fénelon oversaw the examinations of converts and presided over their abjurations. One of the eight Latin inscriptions on the pedestal of the king's statue in the Place des Victoires joined Saint-Cyr to Louis' defense of Catholic orthodoxy in 1686: "He has built more than five hundred Churches that he has endowed with considerable revenues, and he has established the maintenance of four hundred young Demoiselles in the magnificent Maison de S. Cir."[26]

The connection between Saint-Cyr and the assault on Protestantism was a focus of anti-clerical, Republican polemics in the nineteenth century. The historian Jules Michelet wrote that to Saint-Cyr "were brought the prettiest and most docile of the New Catholic girls, after being subdued by the rigor in provincial convents or won over by Fénelon at the house in Paris." Camille Sée, principal author of the 1880 law secularizing girls' education, painted the blackest possible picture of Maintenon when he learned that her writings were being introduced into schools designed to be free of religion. Far from being modern, he charged, Maintenon and Saint-Cyr produced nuns, snuffed out natural feeling for family, prepared girls to be submissive, and targeted Protestants. "Saint-Cyr, the convent of convents, this jail for young Protestant girls abducted from their families and whom one tried, after their forced conversion, to make nuns."[27]

Neither Michelet nor Sée offered evidence for their characterization of Saint-Cyr as a prison for Huguenots or cases of Protestant girls who had been reeducated there. Participation of Saint-Cyr in the catholicizing mission of the monarchy continued, therefore, to be obscured by the celebratory histories that made the school a focus of French memory by abstracting it from the context of confessional conflict and playing up the school's aristocratic reform objectives. Even the Protestant biographers Eugène and Emile Haag, who blamed Maintenon mercilessly for the Revocation and excoriated the defects of her character, spoke of Saint-Cyr with admiration, as a project of "her tireless charity for the poor."[28]

The experience of the Prévost de Touchimbert and other kin and friends of Josias de Robillard and Marie de La Rochefoucauld provides evidence reinstating the anti-Huguenot dimension of Saint-Cyr's purpose. In July 1688, just as Josias de Robillard was arriving in Rotterdam, a neighbor of Casimir's in Angoumois sent a letter to a refugee in Holland who showed it to Tillieres, who in turn reported to Versailles: "The other letter is from a man in the valley of Ruffec who writes in nearly the same manner and says that a gentleman of that place named Lileau Londigné, who has two daughters in the cloister of Maintenon and whose other children are in Holland except for one young daughter, is preparing to leave for England; he only waited this long to leave because he hoped his two daughters in the convent would be returned to him, but they do not want to give them to him." A recipient at court noted in the margin to the spy's report: "it must be the convent of Saint-Cyr being spoken of here."[29] Evidently, Casimir Prévost de Touchimbert determined not to leave France without the daughters who were being held against his will in a royal school that claimed to admit only the daughters of families keen for their inclusion.

What makes this surprisingly documentable Prévost case so interesting is the light it sheds on one of the pivotal figures of Louis XIV's late reign, Madame de Maintenon. The Prévost girls' enclosure in Saint-Cyr speaks to the perennial question of Maintenon's role in the formulation and implementation of her royal husband's religious policy, which has usually focused on the influence she may have had on the king's decision to revoke the Edict of Nantes in October 1685. Chronology alone suggests a link. The years of intensifying persecution leading up to the Revocation were the very years of her growing favor with the king. Their marriage occurred during the year preceding the Revocation.[30] Saint-Cyr was conceived and designed in the months preceding the new Edict. Furthermore, Maintenon's family background had made confessional reunification a personal concern for her. She was born and baptized Catholic in

Niort (Poitou) in 1635,[31] the granddaughter of Agrippa d'Aubigné, a fiercely Calvinist ally of Henri IV who expatriated himself to Switzerland toward the end of his life. Her father had married a Catholic. One of his Protestant sisters, Madame de Villette, raised Françoise in her Huguenot household along with her own four children for perhaps ten years, until her parents took her briefly to the Antilles. Upon their return, her mother placed Françoise first in the Ursuline convent in Niort and then in the Ursulines on the rue Saint-Jacques in Paris, where she began to practice Catholicism devoutly.

Maintenon's religious background and early life have been widely misunderstood largely because those close to her fictionalized them, no doubt employing fictions Maintenon conveyed personally to them. The "Notice biographique" that Marie-Claire Des Champs de Marsilly, Marquise de Villette wrote around 1730 for the nuns at Saint-Cyr stated that Maintenon was "baptized in the temple of Niort." The nuns themselves wrote that Maintenon was converted to Catholicism through a series of competitive multiday conferences in which a pastor and a Catholic theologian vied for her soul, very like the one Josias de Robillard tried to prepare his children for in his pre-Revocation letter. Such a story of conversion after being born and raised Calvinist—more intriguing than the truth of a Catholic girlhood largely spent in a Protestant home—reinforced Maintenon's chosen representation as strong-minded, intelligent, loyal to her own and her family's commitments, but able to recognize true religion. It also drew attention to her family's nobility and link to royalty by recalling that she was a granddaughter of Agrippa d'Aubigné, companion of Henri IV. In addition, falsifying her religious origins made her, in a sense, an insider to the Revocation project: as the kingdom replicated her personal journey from heresy to orthodoxy, her past experience of conversion uniquely qualified her to play the converter.[32]

Numerous persons over the years have assigned Maintenon some degree of responsibility for Louis' shift to the criminalization of Calvinism. At the time of the Revocation, her sister-in-law Madame (wife of the king's brother), who disliked her so much that she called Maintenon "the old trollop," said Maintenon must have been responsible for the new policy direction because Louis was too ignorant in religious matters to have come up with it himself. "If she had died thirty years ago, all the poor Protestants would still be in France and their Temple in Charenton would not have been razed. The old witch, along with the Jesuit Père La Chaise, has been the cause of it all."[33] The compilers of the satirical *Héros de la Ligue* featured her portrait and her putative voice in their gallery of the Revocation's villains: "I ought indisputably to be joined to The Ligue./I built convents and Saint Cyr shows it./From widow of Scarron I became wife of a King:/And if I succeeded, it is solely through intrigue."

MAD.E DE MAINTENON.
Veuve de Scarron.
Ie dois ſans contredit être iointe à la Ligue.
I'ay basti des convents. et ſaint ſire en fait foy.
De veuve de Scarron. ie ſuis ſôme d'un Roy:
Et ſi j'ay reussi. c'est par ma ſeule intrigue.

Figure 8.3 Caricature portrait of Madame de Maintenon, from *Les Héros de la Ligue: Ou, La procession monacale. Conduitte par Louis XIV, pour la conversion des protestans de son royaume* (Paris [Holland]: Chez père Peters à l'enseigne de Louis le Grand, 1691). Courtesy of the Department of Special Collections, Stanford University Libraries.

Recently, however, scholars have been more inclined to hold that Madame de Maintenon had no part in the decision-making process. Issues of domestic and international statecraft beyond the ken of the wife incited the Revocation—developments within the Gallican church, the need for a shared Catholicism that could provide the kingdom with ideological coherence, and Louis' desire to place himself at the head of a Europe that seemed to be recatholicizing with the accession of a Catholic to the English throne and the defeat of the Turks by the Empire. If personal factors were involved in the decision, they were likely to lie in the king's turn to devotion as he aged; his personal shift in the direction of Catholic piety was perhaps the common root of his compatibility with Maintenon and his prohibition on Protestant heresy, rather than one leading to the other. Much ink has been spilled on the question whether Louis XIV would have consulted Maintenon on this policy matter, or any other, in the early years of their marriage, though she seems to have become a more frequent counselor in the 1690s and beyond.

What is known of Maintenon's later views on Huguenot policy suggests that she was a moderate—a pragmatist, perhaps, like Arnoul, who considered the cost of the measures required for the Revocation's full implementation too great. In 1697, Maintenon commented, at Louis XIV's invitation, on a proposal to permit Huguenot fugitives to return to France. In retrospect, she wished they had adhered to the original terms of the Revocation—including its final clause preserving liberty of conscience—over the intervening dozen years, "working with patience and gentleness to convert them by persuading them of the truth." The monarchy had miscalculated: "The Père de La Chaise promised that it would not cost a drop of blood, and Louvois said the same." As Elisabeth Labrousse has written: "the entire anti-Protestant religious policy of the Court was based upon the conviction that it was very easy to make of a Huguenot—already a Christian—a Roman Catholic."[34] In these circumstances, Maintenon wrote, the prudent course would be to revert to the original terms of the Revocation, without issuing any new declarations or revoking any of those that have been issued: that is, not allowing refugees to return but attenuating the measures taken against them in France; not requiring them to practice Catholicism until they believed it but forbidding public exercise of their religion; no longer exposing them to such public humiliations as dragging on a hurdle but continuing to exclude them from honors and offices.

The moderation of the view Maintenon expressed in this instance may support the view that any advice she gave Louis XIV at the moment of the Revocation might have been quite different from what he decided to institute. Yet there was another dimension to Maintenon's actions with respect to Huguenots and the Revocation that must be placed beside her expressions of moderation in matters of policy, which the Prévost de Touchimbert case helps illuminate. Whether Maintenon influenced the making of religious policy in 1685, in 1697, or at any point at all, she played a role in carrying it out. Her method of religious reunification was to see that children—whatever the religion of their birth—were raised Catholic. If the children could be won, then when the adults had passed from the scene, all would be Catholic: "their children will at least be Catholic, even if the fathers are hypocrites." "If God preserves the King there will not be a single Huguenot in twenty years." But how to win the children while leaving the adults more or less alone? Taking away the children "with much discretion" was Maintenon's contribution to the implementation of the Revocation: "to consider this matter as one of the principal affairs of the State, to take concerted and consistent measures to separate youngsters from their family, sparing neither care nor money to find them the necessary subsistence outside their home. . . . By proceeding in this way, one would succeed in annihilating Protestantism in France and delivering her from an evil she has long suffered."[35]

Both in her own family and in the school at Saint-Cyr, Maintenon applied "concerted and consistent measures to separate youngsters from their family." From well before the Revocation, she pursued religious unity within her own family by forcing the conversion of her Protestant kin. Maintenon had been raised with four Villette-Mursay first cousins: Philippe; Aymée, Dame de Fontmort; Madeleine, Dame de Sainte-Hermine de La Laigne; and Marie,

Dame de Caumont d'Adde. Of these four, one (Aymée) had turned Catholic, and the other three were still Protestant on the eve of the Revocation. Maintenon tried to persuade the Protestant Philippe to convert himself and his children: "I admit that it would be a great joy for me to see you in a position to make both your fortune and your salvation." When Philippe refused, she turned to his children. In 1680, Maintenon arranged with Seignelay to send Philippe on a two-year voyage to North America, and while he was gone she took possession of his eldest son, who converted in a matter of weeks. Flush with her success, she then took possession of Philippe's nine-year-old daughter, Marthe-Marguerite de Villette-Mursay, in an action she herself called an "abduction."[36]

With one cousin's son and daughter in hand, Maintenon turned to the children of her other two unconverted cousins. One son and one daughter of Madame de Sainte-Hermine and the daughters of Madame de Caumont d'Adde were sent to her by their parents, upon Maintenon's promise that she would not tamper with their religion. To get control of the second Sainte-Hermine daughter (whose nickname was "Minette"), Maintenon enlisted the help of her brother and exploited the king's capacity for arbitrary justice. "You must have her write to me that she wishes to be Catholic. You will send me that letter, and I will send you a *lettre de cachet* with which you can take Minette into your home until you find an occasion for her to depart." The outcome was that all the children of Philippe converted, as did all four children of Madame de Caumont d'Adde. By contrast, the children of the Dame de Sainte-Hermine de La Laigne did not convert. The boy and two girls resisted and refused, and after three months with Maintenon in Paris they left. Maintenon wrote to her brother: "I am persuaded that they will repent of it." Indeed, they paid dearly over many years for their refusal to convert. When they returned to their home in Poitou, they found it occupied by dragoons.[37] In the ensuing years, as dragoons and other measures brought abjurations by the thousands, Maintenon would vent her exasperation with the holdouts among her kin: "I tell you, I do not like to have to answer to God, nor to the King, for all these delays in conversion [in her own family]." "I believe no Huguenots will remain in Poitou but our relations."[38]

Maintenon's conversion activities within her family, and her commentaries on them, offer a useful entrée into the meaning of terms such as "gentleness" and "persuasion" among Protestantism's adversaries. Maintenon did not use physical violence. But she used carrots and was severe in her expectations for bestowing them. She was unbending in her perception of her own rightness. Above all, she assumed that Huguenot lost sheep could be brought back to the fold through education. This orientation placed her among the moderates, but her determination to effect religious unity also placed her firmly among the enforcers of the Revocation.

Maintenon's conversion activities within her family have been known; they were used by her enemies during her lifetime to depict her as pitiless, as keen to exercise force in the interest of her own power and standing. Less well known are the conversion activities she pursued through Saint-Cyr. How many girls were taken to Saint-Cyr against the will of their Protestant parents, as the three Prévost de Touchimbert were? How many parents of Saint-Cyr pupils were suspect New Converts like Casimir Prévost de Touchimbert from whom the girls were to be kept away? How many girls were Protestant upon entering Saint-Cyr and Catholic upon leaving? Answering these questions requires a new investigation of the Maison Royale and its students.

The proofs of nobility drawn up for each Saint-Cyr pupil by the royal genealogist d'Hozier show, at a glance, no fewer than ten Huguenot demoiselles in the opening years of the school: the three Prévost de Touchimbert girls from Angoumois, Jeanne de Chievres-Salignac from Saintonge, Geneviève-Elisabeth de Culant-Ciré from Aunis, Charlotte-Lucrèce de Ramesai from Beauce, Anne-Catherine d'Orte-Fontaines from Champagne, Sara de Dompierre-du Bocage-Moussoulens from Lorraine, and Julie d'Hemeri-La Borde and Marie-Claire Des Champs de Marcilly from Ile-de-France.[39] Whether all of them entered involuntarily in the manner of the Prévost girls is not clear, but several did. Marie-Claire Des Champs de Marcilly came to Saint-Cyr from the convent of the Miramionnes, in which she had been placed as a recalcitrant Protestant.[40] Anne-Catherine d'Orte-Fontaines was caught trying to escape with her parents at the age of seven and, after a stay in the Ursulines in Metz, was put in Saint-Cyr in 1687, just before her ninth birthday. As late as the 1740s, Saint-Cyr could still be used for reeducation of Huguenot girls; the youngest daughter of the Sieur Maravat—a "headstrong Calvinist"—was assigned to Saint-Cyr by Louis XV, against her father's will, when the two elder daughters, aged eighteen and twenty, were in the Ursulines of Auch.[41]

In addition, the number of family names that appear both on the Saint-Cyr pupil roster and on lists of Protestants suggests that the dimensions of the phenomenon were larger than the small number of girls who can be positively identified as placed in the school for reeducation: Green de Saint-Marsault, Belcastel de Montvaillant, Cosne and Cosne-Chaverney, David, du Carel, Durfort-Duras, Geneste, Goulard, Marconnay, Sainte-Hermine, Toulouse-Lautrec. The extent of forced conversions cannot be established solely from the matching of family names, because Saint-Cyr had a dual role in the Revocation story. Some girls were put into Saint-Cyr for reeducating because their families were obstinate Protestants. Others were admitted to Saint-Cyr as a reward for the prior conversion of their family. The daughters of families among the Champagné's family and social set for whom admission to Saint-Cyr was a sign of advancement following conversion include Anne Madeleine and Marie-Anne-Angélique Isle de Beauchesne, great-granddaughters of Jean Isle de Beauchesne and Léa de Bessay;[42] Angélique de Lestang-Rulles from Sigogne, kin of Susanne de Solière's husband; Marie-Marthe Saint-Légier d'Orignac, descendant of Boisrond; Hélène de Polignac, an heir of Uranie Isle;[43] Catherine Coullaud du Vignaud, a niece of Casimir's second wife; and Marie-Elisabeth Prévost de Touchimbert, Casimir's daughter from his second marriage.

Beyond Saint-Cyr, Maintenon created and employed a web of women and convents that served both as antechambers to Saint-Cyr for Protestant girls and as alternative conversion locales parallel to Saint-Cyr. Maintenon used this web to lead several women of the Isle family to Catholicism through her close friend Madame de Miossens and the Visitation convent on the rue Saint-Antoine in Paris.[44] Another thread in this web completed the emptying out of Casimir Prévost's family—removing the fourth and last of his nonemigrating children by his first wife, sister of Josias de Robillard—that began in 1686 through Saint-Cyr. In September 1689 came the "order of the King to withdraw from the Convent of Port-Royal the demoiselle de Touchimbert and conduct her to the house of Madame de Miramion."[45]

Marie Bonneau, Dame de Miramion, had been a friend of Maintenon's since the early 1660s. Widowed at the age of sixteen after only a few months of marriage, Miramion turned to pious good works and founded the Filles de La Sainte-Famille, known as the "Miramionnes," in 1661.[46] For her new community she bought two contiguous grand *hôtels* on the left bank of the Seine, almost directly facing the Fort de La Tournelle, a vestige of Philip Augustus' wall where convicts, including recalcitrant Protestants, were imprisoned while waiting for the chain gang to deliver them to the galleys in Toulon or Marseille. There the Miramionnes gave free schooling to girls, nursed the needy, trained teachers to go into the countryside, and offered a place of spiritual retreat for laywomen. Endowed with Miramion's own fortune and occasionally drawing upon subventions from the king, the house also had a mission to convert heretics.[47] Miramion's house had many similarities, on a more modest scale, to the Saint-Cyr of Madame de Maintenon. Both institutions educated girls, and both housed many daughters of good family—the Miramionnes gave preference to noble pupils and nuns, while Saint-Cyr required nobility. The two convents were also mutually supportive. When asked to do so by Maintenon's confessor, Miramion interceded with the king in 1688 to secure the release from the Visitation convent on the rue Saint-Antoine of the famous mystic Madame Guyon, where she had been "placed for penitence."[48] Guyon became a protégée of Maintenon at Saint-Cyr until the Quietist controversy forced her removal from the school in 1693. In the other direction, Miramion's admiring biographer, Alfred Bonneau, notes that Maintenon "conducted several young Protestant girls to the Miramionnes."[49] But he says nothing more about that issue.

More could have been said by Maintenon's cousin Madame de Sainte-Hermine, whom Maintenon had sent to the Miramionnes in 1686 when her daughter was placed in Fénelon's Nouvelles Catholiques, or by the proprietors of the Château du Douhet, where the Champagné baptized their last child René-Casimir in 1684. In 1688, a few months before Marie's neighbor and distant cousin Judic de La Rochefoucauld, Dame du Douhet; her husband Renaud de Pons, Marquis de Tors; and their daughter were expelled from France, their daughter, whom authorities hoped to "overcome by taking her away from her mother," was sent from the Nouvelles Catholiques to Miramion.[50] Or the Prévost de Touchimbert, whose daughters disappeared into the network of women animated by Madame de Maintenon, just as Casimir stepped in to care for the remnant of Josias' and Marie's family in France: the baby Thérèse.

9

Caring for Thérèse

During Casimir Prévost de Touchimbert's difficult years of uncertainty about emigrating and inability to repossess his daughters from Saint-Cyr and the Miramionnes, Josias de Robillard left to join his wife in Holland, and Casimir assumed responsibility for the property and person of his year-old niece Thérèse de Robillard. The responsibilities as guardian would add to his burdens, bringing him into a no-holds-barred struggle with the child's maternal great-aunt Madelene de Solière, who had already contributed to the departure of Thérèse's parents. For all his efforts to care for the child, her life would end in tragedy where the king ordained that she reside, rather than at Berneré with her suspect paternal uncle.

Casimir was named guardian of the baby and her property in Saintonge rather soon; the first time he went to court against Aunt Madelene, in August 1689, the Parlement of Bordeaux addressed him as such. He seems to have moved his family into Berneré, rather than moving Thérèse to Montalembert or Londigny; his two daughters (Marie Elisabeth and Jeanne) by his second wife were born and baptized at Saint-Savinien in 1692 and 1694, and a daughter by his late first wife, Josias's sister, was married there in 1698. For a decade, he would be swept into the maelstrom of legal battles that had preoccupied Josias before his departure—notably, the protracted aftermath of the Parlement's decision to reassign Berneré to Aunt Madelene. The crown's decision to use custody of Protestants' children as a means of ensuring that "there will not be a single Huguenot in twenty years" opened a second front of contention for Casimir: a tug-of-war over Thérèse first against Aunt Madelene and then against the bishop backed by the king. The two-front competition illustrates a further way—along with dragonnades, closure of temples, and civil disabilities for Protestants—in which the monarchy's religious policy advanced the disintegration of Protestants' social and familial bonds, this time with the children as pawns and convents as instruments.[1]

It seems surprising that Casimir could be recognized as guardian of a child orphaned by the flight of her parents into the Refuge. The various declarations and proclamations relating to the properties abandoned by fugitives and the children to be taken from Protestant families all emphasized that the new owners or guardians should be good Catholics. Casimir, of course, was not this; for the entire decade of his guardianship he was viewed by the authorities as an obstinate and possibly dangerous Protestant. The same can be said of the relative who was named guardian of the lands in the coastal marshes that Thérèse would inherit from her father, her paternal cousin Philippe-Benjamin de Mazières. Holders of fugitives' property were to present a certificate of Catholicity in La Rochelle within two weeks of being awarded custody of property, and Mazieres satisfied the order relating to Thérèse's properties. But Mazières was far from a reliable Catholic.[2]

The designation of Mazières and Casimir illustrates the quandary in which the abandonment of properties and persons sometimes placed the government. On the one hand, exceptional cases aside, officials preferred to follow standard rules of inheritance in the reassignment of properties—that is, to hand them over to the closest kin. Given that entire kinship networks often shared the proscribed religion, the nearest kin of refugees could be Protestants or New Converts whose compliance with royal policy was suspect. The family basis for property reassignment, then, aligned material reward with religious conformity, as the law mandated, much more imperfectly than did other measures for advantaging Catholics such as the reallocation of offices. In Thérèse's case, at least, the family tie was allowed to trump religious reliability.

The burden of Thérèse's legal and financial problems cannot have been welcomed by Casimir. He was starting a second family with a new wife. He had quarrels of his own and property disputes to manage. Under these circumstances, Casimir's dogged defense of Thérèse's hold on Berneré must have been motivated by friendship for Josias and a sense of family responsibility as Josias' brother-in-law and Marie's second cousin. He had no material interest in the court contests he would have to pursue as her guardian. Under no circumstances would either he or his children gain anything in them; he was only the widower of Josias' sister, an aunt of the child. The only claim his line could possibly have on any of the properties abandoned by the Champagné would apply to Josias' holdings (Champagné, Agère, Voutron). For the moment, Thèrèse's title to them was clear: the inheritance from the parents of Josias and Casimir's late wife had been amicably settled years before.

The battle over Berneré had still a long time to run,[3] and before it was finished, it would damage numerous descendants of Susanne Isle. The court had ruled that Madelene's renunciation of her parents' inheritance was null and void, "and that thus she has a special lien for the said sum plus interest on the said Berneré estate and other properties of the said Dame Isle her mother, not only for the said sum of 12,000 *livres* plus interest but also for her rights to a supplement of her *légitime* and other rights that she had been made to renounce in her marriage contract." That this ruling, if sustained, would require relinquishing Berneré to Madelene was clear. The court, however, wished to look more closely, before issuing a final order in Madelene's favor, at the way her 12,000-*livre* dowry had been used to pay Salbert family debts; that is, at how it had been indirectly invested in the estate at Soulignonne. Over and over again, the La Rochefoucauld sisters would interject flatly that "the Dame of Soulignonne was dowried and paid, and gets no redowering or supplement of *légitime*," but not until the situation shifted tragically in 1699 would the main question of Berneré be directly addressed again.

Skirmishing over investigation of the Salbert financial accounts and other side issues delayed the final order on Berneré for more than a decade. The Parlement ordered Casimir and the La Rochefoucauld sisters allied with him to provide Madelene with everything she would need in order to press her case for restitution. Casimir redirected his efforts to focus on Jean Isle de Beauchesne, cousin of Susanne Isle and second husband of Louis de Salbert's widowed mother, Léa de Bessay, who had handled Louis de Salbert's finances both before and after his majority. No doubt Casimir harbored the hope that if Madelene were indeed due a second dowry it could be paid from funds that had been released to Léa and to Louis de Salbert's sister Sara, Dame de Cellettes, by the diversion of the first dowry to cover Salbert debts, rather than from confiscation of Berneré. Casimir summoned Beauchesne's heirs and Sara to provide the court with evidence on Salbert finances. They never did so. Casimir submitted proof that he had done everything the court asked of him, but Madelene nonetheless blamed him and the La Rochefoucauld sisters for obstructing the Salbert investigation so that the court's ruling could not be finalized, leaving her, she complained, "high and dry without any resource at all."

While the Salbert angle of the case stalled, the four defending parties—Casimir, representing Thérèse, along with the three surviving sisters of the fugitive Marie de La Rochefoucauld (Elisabeth, Madeleine, and Susanne)—expended their energy and their venom on the stratagems Aunt Madelene drummed up for squeezing subsistence out of her three nieces and her grandniece Thérèse. They treated Madelene's claims to her mother's estate with disdain and Madelene herself with a distinct lack of sympathy. Casimir accused Madelene of creating her own problems through her spendthrift ways, through "the design the said de Solière has to continue a licentious life while oppressing her benefactors and her closest relations." The La Rochefoucauld sisters asserted, in response to Madelene's call for payments from them, that she was not the one in need of financial assistance: "As part of this claim she insinuates that she has been stripped of all assistance, while in fact she enjoys the estate of Soulignonne, she receives the rents therefrom, she appoints the judges, and, last but not least, she currently resides in the Château de Soulignonne while the [La Rochefoucauld] women are reduced to subsisting each on a single small farm . . . each possessing only one poor swatch of meadow . . . that gives them not 50 *livres* of revenue and suffering extremely from their indigence."

In this, the La Rochefoucauld sisters were half right. Their own situation was indeed precarious. In January 1686, Madeleine de La Rochefoucauld and her husband Jacques Berne, Seigneur de l'Houmée, then living in La Rochelle, sold all the buildings and premises of Bellay, her inheritance from Susanne Isle's 1677 property division, to a merchant living in their parish of Saint-Hippolyte-de-Biard. Of the 4,550-*livre* sales price for Bellay, Madeleine de La Rochefoucauld and her husband were to receive only 350 *livres* "in silver *louis* and circulating currencies." The rest would go directly from the purchaser to the creditors of her husband's father and mother. Ironically, Madeleine de La Rochefoucauld found herself—partly because of pressures from Madelene de Solière—in the same situation that had caused Madelene's problems in the first place: what she brought to her marriage paid off debts on her husband's patrimony. Worse yet, the debts the purchaser assumed in buying Bellay turned out to be greater than he bargained for, and he threatened to sue Berne over them.

What the La Rochefoucauld sisters were wrong about was Madelene's hold on Soulignonne. For many years, Soulignonne had been under seizure for debt, but Madelene managed to continue living in her home even as the estate's revenues were diverted to her creditors. Her entitlement to Soulignonne was, however, only provisional. She was able to hold Soulignonne during the minority of her son. But he became an adult by 1694, took possession of the estate, and asked her to leave. As a consequence of her inability to restore the Salbert finances, she found herself evicted from the estate that her dowry funds had helped the Salbert family retain. The La Rochefoucauld sisters suggested that Madelene negotiate with her son or ask the court for a share of Soulignonne's revenues rather than dunning them for money. But the court turned down Madelene's claim for income from Soulignonne, not having the documentary evidence that she was entitled to that.

Alongside the continuing dispute over Susanne Isle's estate, Casimir and Madelene jousted over custody of the person of Thérèse. Though the courts continued to recognize Casimir as the child's guardian, once Madelene sued for custody in 1690, the Bishop of Saintes Guillaume de La Brunetière, who had known Madelene in Paris, arranged for Thérèse to go live with her great-aunt, "who raised her very well."[4] Casimir asked for a court order directing Madelene de Solière to return the child to him and authorizing him, if Madelene should refuse, to seize Thérèse wherever he might find her. Madelene responded with her strongest and most insidious move: playing the religion card. She argued that she was the fitter guardian because she had made a sincere conversion to Catholicism fifteen years earlier, and that the bishop had confided Thérèse to her after persons of the first dignity informed him of her longstanding religious conformity. She alleged moreover that her conversion was the source of all her troubles, it having brought the hatred of her strongly Protestant family upon her. In part, appealing to religion was a tacit explanation for the weakness of her situation in general; having no allies within her family, her long struggle for her inheritance was a lonely one. Citing the religious divide opened up by her conversion could deflect attention from any responsibility she might bear for her alienation from her mother and nieces. But Madelene's religious claim was also the craftiest possible ploy in the post-Revocation environment. The court knew that guardianship could be taken away from suspect converts, and Casimir—still under suspicion despite his 1686 abjuration—would have known it, too. Madelene alleged that assigning Thérèse to Casimir would place the child among heretics. Rather than arguing her own qualifications to educate Thérèse, she exploited the heartbreak of the Prévost family: the Dame de Lisleau, Casimir's new wife, she told the court, was deemed by the king unfit to raise Thérèse, for he took away the Prévost daughters, to be raised in cloisters.

Casimir did not defend the sincerity of his own conversion or address the injustice of his daughters' removal to Saint-Cyr and the Miramionnes. Rising to Madelene's bait would have acknowledged that his character and his wife's were fair game in the custody contest. Rather, Casimir pointed out that he was chosen by the child's relatives, and he contradicted Madelene's contention that all Thérèse's relations were Protestant by citing her Catholic kin, who included Lestang, the husband of Madelene de Solière's sister Susanne, and Elisabeth de La Rochefoucauld's husband La Martinie, "and several others it would take too long to discuss in detail."

And he attacked Madelene's character, unleashing raw moralistic insult and misogyny that likely drew not only upon a lifelong acquaintance with Madelene but also upon a consciousness of the irreversible damage she had done to the family for whose remnant he now served as guardian. Casimir brought into the courtroom what must have been the greatest humiliation of Madelene's life. Noting that she had identified herself to the court as the widow of the late Sieur de Soulignonne, he wondered why she did not mention the marriage celebrated between her and His Royal Highness Nicolas Leopol Ignace III of Saxony in 1672, a marriage proved by her letter to her mother and the accompanying certificate of marriage that Casimir entered into evidence. Just to rub in the humiliation, he lavished upon the stamped paper of his petition enough of the phony bridegroom's phony titles to create the echo of a Molière farce.

Casimir used the fictitious marriage not only to question Madelene's self-identification before the court but also to challenge her authorization, as a woman, to take part in court proceedings: she could only do so if she were a widow or were authorized to participate by her husband. "It is very just," he wrote, that Madelene either provide the court with proof of this prince's death "or get authorized by him. . . . It is settled law established by the Court that a married woman cannot legitimately proceed without that. . . . She is still considered under the authority of this husband and as a consequence obliged to get authorized." Furthermore, not only was she addressing the court fraudulently as an unauthorized wife: she was by her own admission a polyandrist. She admitted to remarrying with Alexandre Roulin, Seigneur de La Mortmartin, now deceased, but she submitted no proof of the death of her second husband, the prince. In the eyes of the court, Casimir insisted, "this polygamy will remain a fact in the case until such time as the said de Solière demonstrates the contrary."[5]

Casimir's mischief seems to have been ignored by the court, which in subsequent rulings spoke of Madelene simply as the widow of Salbert and Roulin.[6] But his attack on her character accelerated to the point of accusing her not only of immorality but, eventually, of capital crimes. "She appears every day and into the night with her bosom exposed, her face painted, and with dress more suggestive of the courtesan than of a fifty-nine-year-old widow of three husbands . . . her extraordinary conduct, proved such by the letter dated May 29, 1672 [in which she informed her mother of her "marriage"], incurred the disdain of her relations, and her inappropriate shenanigans toward a variety of persons have earned her numerous censures." Casimir's accusations of immodest dress and language unbefitting a woman echo cultural stereotypes often marshaled against women in French court cases: the disorderly, unruly woman whose sexual license scandalizes and whose extravagance bankrupts her family; the weaker sex who cannot manage a patrimony or tell a true groom from a false. "Suffice it to say that this sincere conversion and this alleged capacity for educating a minor are hardly embellished by the fact that . . . on Sundays she went right to the foot of the altars in the church of Soulignonne, in the presence of the curé clothed in his priestly garments, and uttered numerous words unbefitting her sex." It was part of Madelene de Solière's burden as a woman in early modern France to be vulnerable to gendered insults to her honor and character in sexual and moral terms whenever she asserted her own interest, as she did in the court cases against Josias de Robillard and Casimir Prévost de Touchimbert. Casimir in his disdain for Madelene constructed her from misogynistic materials ready to hand: a picture of a woman not so much dangerous as incompetent, unsavory, indecent, and easily led astray.

Madelene de Solière had the particular misfortune of crossing a number of persons who dealt disrespectfully with her in everyday interactions. In 1692, as both the Berneré suit and the custody battle dragged on, an altercation between Madelene and one Antoine Mollet interrupted mass in the parish church of Soulignonne. Mollet blocked her way as she and her niece walked to their pew. When she asked him to let her pass, he replied (according to Madelene's complaint) with "words disrespectful to the said Dame, to whom he owes respect" and by lifting his head several times "lifted the said Dame by the nose." Whether Madelene kicked Mollet while he was on his knees praying or he kicked her so hard she thought she would fall to the ground was a matter to which four locals from Soulignonne testified when the Presidial held hearings on Madelene's charges.[7] Though Mollet, who hailed from nearby Corme-Royal, claimed to have been innocently passing by when he decided to have a prayer in the Soulignonne church, he had an ongoing grudge with Madelene de Solière. She had previously testified in court against him "for similar injustices and insolences." This time, Madelene claimed, "his indecent behavior in a holy place, his premeditated plan to knock the said dame to the ground," and the fact that he disrespected "the very Dame of the place in the presence of all her tenants merited nothing less than an exemplary punishment."

Madelene crossed another neighbor who had the means to leave an unflattering written record of her in which later readers might perceive the weaknesses in her character or, perhaps more sympathetically, the hostile environment in which she tried to make her way as a single woman of limited fortune. This was the curé at Soulignonne, Bernard Richard, whose church of Sainte-Geneviève lay just across the road from the château.[8] The two neighbors were on unfriendly terms, and their face-off was asymmetrical in that the curé controlled the parish register. In 1696, two nobles prominent in the parish, the Seigneur de Nieul and Madame de Ransanne, had a new bell cast with their names engraved on its side to replace the "small cracked bell that sounded like a kettle." Madelene demurred, thinking "that the other names on this bell were prejudicial to her," no doubt because it was the Seigneur de Nieul who had had the estate of Soulignonne seized for her debts and who in this way threatened to take over as seigneur of the village and patron of the church.[9] Madelene sued and obtained permission to have the bell recast in a different foundry, with her name and that of the bishop engraved upon it. She promised as part of the deal to pay for the bell and to reimburse Richard for the money he had personally spent on the first one.

To Richard's obvious resentment, "the said Dame de Soulignonne mocked the said curé" by claiming the right to have the bell in his own church blessed by another priest. The curé de Plassai, sent out by the bishop for the purpose, was unable to go through with the ceremony because the bell was still too hot and not yet paid for. At that point, curé Richard decided to pay for the bell himself if the founder would rub out the names of "Madelene de Solière and Zacharie de Salbert, who call themselves the lords of this place, because it was not just that these sorts of people be honored when I am the donor of this bell." When the bell was mounted in the belfry of Sainte-Geneviève, the poor curé was smarting at having had to give up for it all his personal assets—"177 *livres* not counting a pair of heavy chains, a mortar weighing eight pounds, a chandelier, three large pewter plates, a bell-pot for cooking slop, and 3 *livres* in other fees, so that it cost me 230 *livres*." In short, concluded the weary curé, "that has only aggravated and prolonged further the hatred that the said Dame de Solière had formed against me, which troubles me little, as I place all at the foot of the cross and fully accept what our lord Jesus Christ wills, asking him to pardon me if there is any error in this testimony." It seems unlikely that this parish bell rang in mourning for forty days when Madelene de Solière died in 1707, as it would for the death of the new seigneur in 1737.[10]

Perhaps it was after the incident of the bell that curé Richard decided to retroactively change entries that predated his 1689 arrival at the church. Two entries in the book are in oversized printing characters that dwarf the much smaller handwriting of successive curés. Both entries occurred shortly after Madelene's conversion, during a period when she may have been working to establish the dominance in the parish that was typically exercised by the local seigneur, and both featured Madelene de Solière prominently. On the first printed inscription, the revisionist Richard impugned Madelene's honor, striking across the text and inserting beneath and in the left margin a repudiation of Madelene de Solière's claim to have donated to the church a tabernacle on the main altar: "Whoever printed these words has lied; we in the parish spent five years collecting the funds to pay her for it, even though it had been donated by a virtuous lady from Pons." On the second printed entry, Richard impugned Madelene's social identity as well as her personal honor, reinking "Magdelaine de Soliere Dame of the said place" so that it read "the broken-down Magdelaine de Saliere, so-called Dame of the said place." "Saliere," as a corruption of Solière, would literally mean salt cellar but figuratively calls to mind "sale" (filthy, foul) or "salaud" (bastard, louse). The addition of "so-called [ditte]" before her title implied unjustifiable pretension to authority in the locality, which would of course raise the specter of her losing her estate and social position, as the lawsuits against her for debt were currently threatening to effect.

Curé Richard's emendations and his general way of using the parish register made the text much more than the record of births, deaths, marriages, and abjurations that both church and civil law required him to keep. He used the register to shape the events in Soulignonne to his perspective and interest.

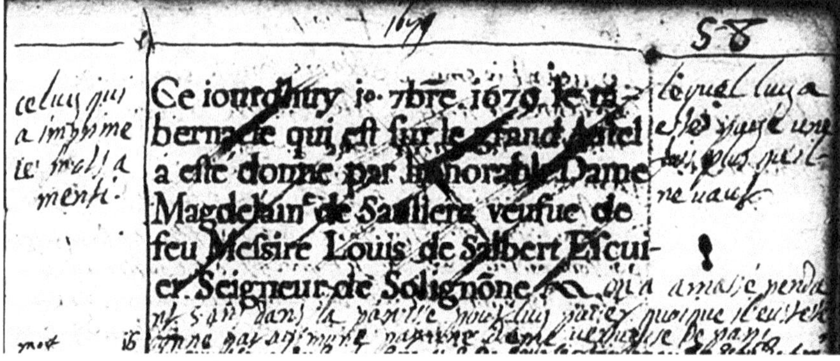
Ce iourdhuy 1o. 7bre. 1679. le ta-
bernacle qui est sur le grand autel
a esté donné par honorable Dame
Magdelain de Salliere veufue de
feu Messire Louis de Salbert Escui-
er Seigneur de Solignône

Figure 9.1 Parish Register of Sainte-Geneviève Catholic Church, Soulignonne, September 1, 1679. Courtesy of the Archives départementales de la Charente-Maritime.

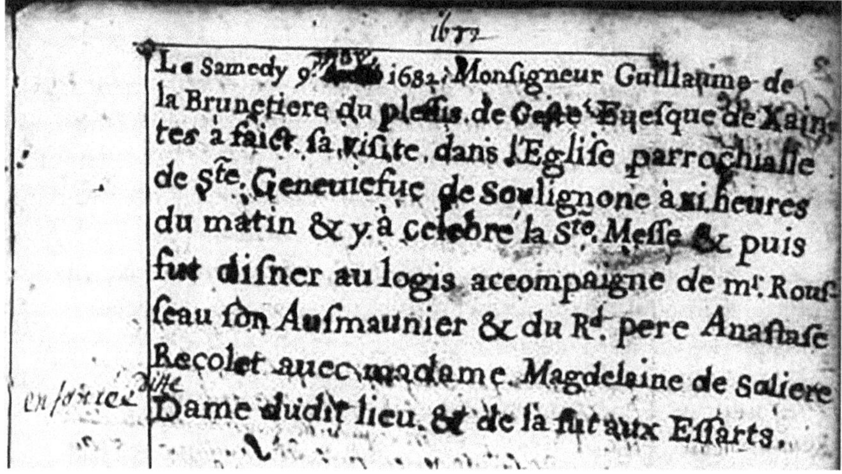
Le Samedy 9 1682. Monseigneur Guillaume de
la Brunetiere du plessis de Gesté Euesque de Xaintes a faict sa visite dans l'Eglise parrochialle
de Ste. Geneuiefue de Soulignone à xi heures
du matin & y à celebré la Ste. Messe & puis
fut disner au logis accompaigne de mr. Rousseau son Ausmaunier & du Rd. pere Anastase
Recolet auec madame Magdelaine de Saliere
Dame dudit lieu. & de la fut aux Essarts.

Figure 9.2 Parish Register of Sainte-Geneviève Catholic Church, Soulignonne. February 9, 1682. Courtesy of the Archives départementales de la Charente-Maritime.

When a local history society published excerpts from the Soulignonne parish register in 1891, the editors expurgated the text, with an implicitly disapproving nod toward Richard: "We did not think we could repeat the often slanderous words this vindictive curé inserted throughout the parish registers."[11] But doing that strips the text of much of its historical meaning, as a record of a contest between the two authority figures—secular and religious, woman and man—in a seventeenth-century village. On her side, Madelene tried to use the church to bolster her authority as seigneur and did so clumsily. Having grown up as a Protestant, she perhaps brought no mental model of seigneur-curé relations with her to the village church after she converted. Perpetually insolvent, she was time and again unable to live up to promises of largesse through which she hoped to shore up her weakening hold on her late husband's estate, her last remaining source of social standing.

Whether out of carelessness or from arrogance, Madelene de Solière offended curé Richard, and he retaliated in his parish register with a picture of her that converged with the one drawn for the court by Casimir Prévost de Touchimbert. Was Madelene the self-serving, irresponsible, unruly woman they made her out to be? Or does an unmasking of the two men's motives—one competitive in court cases, the other in a locality—delegitimize the hostile characterizations they prepared for magistrates and posterity? There may have been independent proof of Madelene's deviance. Casimir claimed he could furnish the Parlement with legal documentation that she had been convicted of abusing her son and arrested for complicity in the murder of her husband Roulin de La Mortmartin (nonchalantly inserting recognition of her "marriage" to the prince by calling Roulin her third husband). Perhaps the best evidence that the charges against Madelene by Casimir and the curé were not baseless is that the Parlement of Bordeaux in August 1691 ordered Madelene to return Thérèse to Casimir.[12] The court did not decide the custody conflict on religious grounds but awarded custody even to a religiously suspect uncle over a long-converted aunt. There were old-Catholic relatives available—Casimir had named some of them in court, in response to Madelene's accusation of familial heresy—who were as close kin to Thérèse as Casimir was. This decision on Thérèse's custody is a useful corrective to generalizations about the inability of New Converts to prevail before the courts in the post-Revocation years.

Thérèse, however, never reached Casimir, because another authority—the king with his Gallican church—had intentions at odds with those of the Parlement. By the end of 1691, the four-year-old child was living in a convent at Saintes. The story of how she got there and what became of her there illustrates the crosscurrents of family authority, royal policy, and competing decision-makers that rendered the impact of the Revocation on Huguenot families so exceedingly complex.

Thérèse's Convent

As an ecclesiastical city, Saintes had no shortage of convents that received young girls. The royal geographer-cartographer Claude Masse wrote of the city that "It would take an entire volume to report the details on all the various orders of priests and nuns." The most distinguished was the Abbaye-aux-Dames. This royal convent, far more venerable than Saint-Cyr and more storied, had been founded in 1047 by Geoffrey Martel, Count of Anjou, and his wife Agnes of Burgundy and had been protected by Eleanor of Aquitaine, whom the nuns continued to call their "mother and teacher." The abbesses had "always been high-born ladies,"[13] and the abbess serving since 1686, Charlotte de Caumont-Lauzun, sister of the Duc de Lauzun, was a relation of Casimir's.[14] Thérèse had links to this convent. The legendary abbesses of the preceding centuries had been La Rochefoucauld women: Louise from 1544 and then Françoise, who persuaded their Calvinist brother not to destroy the abbey when Condé ordered him to do so during the Wars of Religion, and then their grandniece Françoise de Foix, who rebuilt the abbey in updated baroque style after the great fire of 1648. On Thérèse's paternal side, one of the eighty-six nuns in the Abbaye-aux-Dames was her second cousin, Gabrielle de Robillard, whose family had been Catholic from at least her father's generation.[15]

But Thérèse was not placed in this storied community. She might have been, since the education of girls was among the nuns' occupations. Their most famous pupils had been the three Rochechouart de Mortemart sisters from nearby Tonnay-Charente: Madeleine-Gabrielle, later abbess of Fontevrault; Gabrielle, later Marquise de Thianges; and Françoise-Athénaïs, Marquise de Montespan and predecessor of Madame de Maintenon in the king's affection. But the Abbaye-aux-Dames held itself fairly aloof from involvement in the conversion activities surrounding the Revocation. The young girls who entered this abbey tended to be permanent residents, future nuns unless their lives were cut short by an elevated childhood and adolescent mortality rate.[16]

Another convent in Saintes housed another of Thérèse's second cousins, a sister of Gabrielle. Sister Agathe de La Passion Robillard de Champagné (Jeanne de Robillard) took her vows at Sainte-Claire de Saintes in 1675, when she was twenty-one; in 1697 and several times thereafter, down to 1732, she was the abbess.[17] It might have made sense to place Thérèse in Sainte-Claire; the authorities liked to group the unconverted with their securely Catholic relatives, distancing them from the unreliables among their kin. But Thérèse was instead placed in the Filles de Notre-Dame in the parish of Saint-Vivien. The Compagnie de Marie Notre-Dame was an institution that sprang specifically out of the circumstances of the Reformation in southwestern France, having originated in Bordeaux in 1607. Its founder, Jeanne de Lestonnac, was a niece of the writer Michel de Montaigne and, like him, came from a family that was split internally on the matter of religion. Perhaps impelled by her experience of religious division, she created the Compagnie de Marie Notre-Dame specifically as an institution for reconciling the two divisions of Christianity through a syncretic spirituality of Calvinist and Jesuit influences that would encourage conversions to Catholicism.[18]

The convent of the Filles de Notre-Dame in Saintes was authorized by Pope Paul V in 1618,[19] and its purpose-built facilities were occupied in 1626. Claude

Masse found their premises impressively vast and endowed with a lovely view.[20] In keeping with the original intent of Jeanne de Lestonnac, the Filles de Notre-Dame in Saintes specialized in the education of girls and the conversion of Calvinists into Catholics. Their seal perfectly expressed their purpose and activities: the Virgin holding the baby Jesus in her right hand symbolized the educational mission, the fleur-de-lis or scepter in the left the commitment to France, and the crescent of flames underfoot the purification from heresy.[21]

So the Filles de Notre-Dame sprang authentically from the objective of the moment, as the venerable Abbaye-aux-Dames did not; it also sprang from the locality, in that the small community—with thirty-one nuns, only about one-third the size of the Abbaye—gathered together women from Saintonge whose families were neighbors, friends, and sometimes kin. Several of the nuns among whom Thérèse came to live would have known the Château de Berneré, her family, and the circumstances of her family's religious life. Anne Guiton de Maulévrier came from the longtime Protestant seigneurial family at Agonnay, just next to Berneré. Another nun, Gabrielle Acarie Du Bourdet, a distant cousin of young Thérèse and neighbor at Crazannes, would become superior of the Filles de Notre-Dame during Thérèse's residence there, in 1698. In addition, at least three of the girls put into the Filles de Notre-Dame as Protestants when Thérèse was there were her kin. Two du Gua de La Rochebreuillet children, granddaughters of Isaac Isle's sister, were put there because their parents were fugitives. Nineteen-year-old Céleste de Voutron, a daughter of Josias' first cousin the fugitive Gédéon Nicolas, was put into the convent in 1694.

Figure 9.3 Seal of the Compagnie de Marie Notre-Dame. Reproduced in "Les Notre-Dame," *AHSA* 23 (1894): 114.

To add irony to tragedy, none other than the wife of Duvigier, New Convert Protestant-punishing magistrate in the Parlement of Bordeaux, was detained in the Filles de Notre-Dame. The Secretary of State Châteauneuf, the intendant Bégon, and the Bishop of Saintes had put Madame Duvigier there with the collusion of her husband, and she would remain there, despite her pleas for release, until she decided to "have herself instructed, with a sincere desire to know the truth."[22]

It was not the Parlement's decision that landed Thérèse de Robillard in the Filles de Notre-Dame de Saintes, however. Throughout, Casimir appealed to the court, while the Bishop of Saintes appealed to the king. When the Parlement awarded custody to Casimir, the bishop explained, he, "in order to obstruct the outcome of this lawsuit," moved her to the convent under military auspices. "I asked the Marquis de Sourdis, who commands the troops in these provinces, to have her put in the convent of the Filles de Notre-Dame, where she is now." As soon as Casimir found where she had been taken after the Parlement's order in his favor, he sued to reclaim her. The bishop then wrote to both the Père de La Chaise and the royal advisor Colbert de Torcy, asking that the king override the Parlement's decision to return her to her uncle. Casimir, he pointed out, was a particularly inappropriate guardian for the child: he "is one of those New Converts who fail to evince any great attachment to the Catholic Church . . . who is not Catholic in the slightest." Like Madelene, the bishop cited Casimir's sad history of losing his own children to Saint-Cyr and the Miramionnes to justify pushing him aside: "he was not allowed to educate his own daughter. . . . A girl cannot be better off than in a convent such as the one where she [Thérèse] is, nor worse off than in the hands of Monsieur de Lisleau, who, according to what we are told, does not live as a Catholic." Over against the law court, the bishop explained to Colbert de Torcy, "we have only the authority of the King for leaving this poor little girl in the asylum that has been procured for her, where she can be raised Catholic. I beg you very humbly, Monsieur, to obtain an order from His Majesty to keep her in the convent where she is very well cared for and well instructed."[23]

Apparently, the royal order was sent, as Thérèse stayed in the convent. For at least three years, Casimir trekked to Saintes to press his claim to repossess Thérèse.[24] His petition to the court in 1694 laid out two principal issues—who had the authority to decide where Thérèse would reside and, if in a convent, at what cost—but not before accusing Madelene de Solière of contempt of court: "It is also very true that Madame de Solière plotted with the said opposing party of nuns; instead of obeying the court order and returning this child to her guardian, she gave her to them, thereby undercutting the court order and subverting execution of this provision."

Nearly three years after the Parlement awarded custody to him, he stood before the very same court to ask that it order execution of its August 29, 1691, decision over the opposition of Claude Ozias de La Brossardière, superior of the convent. Casimir failed to see on what grounds the nuns could pretend to set aside the court's order granting custody to him and how the nuns could have been permitted to address themselves to the bishop and the intendant after the Parlement had ruled. The nuns responded that they had received an order from the king to the effect that Thérèse must stay with them, "that they would not even be permitted to release her." So Casimir attempted to ally family claim with Parlementary authority on the one side against an order from the king and the zeal of the Catholic party on the other: "which has obliged the petitioner to emphasize the authority of the court, to whom he has shown that he had obeyed its orders, executing them to the letter." He hoped to win his court case, then, by casting himself as a stronger defender of the court's authority than even the court itself.

Casimir was not the first to try to exploit the unstable relationship between the logics of law courts and the royal court in order to obstruct reassignment of Protestant children from family to convent. In 1686, Marie d'Albret, Comtesse de Marsan, longtime friend and ally of Madame de Maintenon, founded the Nouvelles Catholiques convent at Pons, which became one of the principal houses for reeducation in the Southwest of France. The roster of its resident children included, alongside the majority indication that the girl was put in "by order of the king to be instructed in Catholic religion," a number attributing incarceration to an "order of the Comtesse de Marsan."[25] The petition to the king from Protestant inhabitants of Saintonge in July 1684 that complained so sharply about their treatment by Duvigier[26] also contested Marsan's authority as seigneur to remove the children of her Protestant "tenants and vassals" from their families, "which obliged many private persons to appeal to the said Parlement of Bordeaux for permission to testify and to obtain the liberty of the abducted children and put an end to these great vexations."[27] Two months earlier, inhabitants of Pons, the residence city of Marsan, had indeed written to the Parlement detailing cases in which girls were put in the convent in Pons "by order of the said dame de Marsan" and asking the court to enjoin her from such activities. The receiving magistrates were unsure how to proceed, not knowing whether some secret authorization had perhaps been given by the king for this sort of action. The president Grimard wrote the chancellor requesting guidance and deferring to the royal will: "I shall accept what you kindly prescribe for me." The doyen of the Parlement, Du Sault, wrote the same day to the secretary of state asking "if some order from the king permits seigneurs and dames to take youngsters of both sexes away, to have them raised in the Catholic religion, for if not, seeing that the assaults one uses for this can only be blamed and condemned, the practice, under the vain pretext of doing good and converting the children of heretics, seems likely, if not corrected, to incite public violence in their seigneuries. This way of acting is not apostolic and cannot produce anything good. . . . we are informed that other seigneurs and dames also do the same."[28]

Implicitly, the law of the law courts—not to mention the ethical sense of the doyen—only had effect in the absence of a royal order to the contrary. It was because they recognized this that in July the Saintongeais addressed their plea for the privileges of families directly to the king: "As the supplicants were unable to obtain anything by [appealing to Madame de Marsan], nor by addressing Parlement, they hope that Your Majesty, in accord with the sentiments of his justice and his royal generosity, will take pity on the desolation to which they find themselves reduced by the violence and assaults perpetrated against them."[29] It was probably because Casimir, too, recognized that the royal will trumped judicial judgment that he came to rest his case for custody of Thérèse on insult and injury rather than on the high ground of legal theory.

Casimir asked if the nuns were permitted "to insult the said gentleman guardian in the most sensitive matter of his honor." He accused the nuns of slandering him when the legal grounds for their claim to Thérèse proved weak and turned their slanders back upon themselves, to question their fitness as educators of children: "they have vomited atrocious insults against the said gentleman supplicant, on August 12, 1694 speaking of him as a rebel against the orders of his prince, which is the most serious accusation that can be made against a person of his quality who has never had any stronger inclination than serving the king and proving himself to be one of his most obedient subjects, but because he does what the law court's orders tell him to do, what his minister enlists him to do, and what the kin of the minor have advised in the matter of her maintenance payment in the convent. When the nuns saw their greed checked, they let loose by accusing him of rebellion against the king's orders; the law court will undoubtedly judge from this how good an education they give the girls under their control."

On the issue of the payment to the convent for Thérèse's maintenance Casimir played two games: pitting different communities of nuns against each other and marshaling the rhetoric of the old Protestantism (and of contemporary sexism) against the character of nuns. The Filles de Notre-Dame demanded what he called "a fat pension" of 300 *livres*, but Casimir had negotiated an agreement with the Religieuses de La Propagation de La Foi in Saint-Maixent to house Thérèse for only 80 *livres* a year. If the Parlement would not execute its earlier order to return Thérèse to him, he would agree to leave her with the Filles de Notre-Dame at the 80-*livre* rate. When the nuns in Saintes refused to accept that bargain, the Parlement referred the matter to the relatives to decide where Thérèse should reside and at what cost. Casimir convoked the relatives in the presence of the seneschal of Saint-Jean-d'Angély in December 1693. The family agreed with Casimir on the contract with the nuns of Saint-Maixent. But the Filles de Notre-Dame refused to go along: "on the contrary, they continue to insist on having both the minor and her property; their only grounds are without doubt an avarice that is scarcely compliant with their position and their profession."

Was it avarice that prompted the Filles de Notre-Dame to ask such a payment? The typical charge per head for pupils in convents in the late seventeenth century was closer to 150 *livres* than 300 *livres*. Nuns have been characterized as profiteers of the Revocation, exploiting Huguenots for their own enrichment. The amount they charged was whatever they could get away with, "arbitrarily fixed, always very heavy, and often ruinous. . . . Seeing the multitude of these pious incarcerations, one must conclude that the Huguenots of the wealthy or well-off classes were trapped and systematically fleeced."[30]

On the other hand, the very purpose for which houses like the Filles de Notre-Dame were established brought them financial fragility. They were to receive the girls and women the king assigned to them without sure means of covering their cost. The king would pay some charges himself or allocate income from properties abandoned by fugitives or try to get families to pay the charges if there were any prospect of their being able to do so. Asking parents to pay for the education they did not want for their children was, indeed, one of the cruel practices of the post-Revocation era. The father of one incarcerated New Convert observed sarcastically: "Those who are so anxious to instruct my child in your religion will surely have the charity to wish to pay her pension." Nor could payments be relied upon by convents that needed them. The Filles de Notre-Dame's sister house in Poitiers lamented that "Our lords the Intendants . . . have these last years placed in our hands and confided to us several women and girls, both Huguenots and new converts, of whom ten or twelve have not paid any pension." Of thirty-four Protestant women and girls living in the Nouvelles Catholiques on rue Sainte-Anne in Paris in 1702, the convent of which Fénelon had been superior, the nuns received income from only two. During the time when the superior Claude Ozias and Casimir were sparring over Thérèse's pension, on November 11, 1692, Ozias was also in court suing the guardian of the two du Gua de La Rochebreuillet daughters, Thérèse's cousins, to collect their maintenance arrears.[31]

For the Filles de Notre-Dame, moreover, internal funds could not cover the costs when the authorities or the families failed to pay. Just before she began jousting with Casimir Prévost, superior Ozias provided sworn testimony on the financial condition of the convent. Ozias' balance sheet suggests that as a relatively new institution, the Filles de Notre-Dame of Saintes had not been acquiring for ages the capital that generated regular annual payouts, as the royal abbey in the town had.[32] Their landed income was small—perhaps 120 *livres* a year. They needed, as Ozias said, to bring in "pensions from lay girls whom they instruct in Christian piety and good manners in the said monastery" and to charge the full cost or more (including a portion of the general overhead of the convent) for the room, board, and education of the children they housed. In short, the convent was pressed financially, rather than vainly avaricious, as their superior squared off against Casimir Prévost de Touchimbert over Thérèse's fee. They needed boarders, though it does not necessarily follow that they needed Protestant girls brought to them by force, nor that they encouraged this practice.[33]

The response of the Parlement to Casimir's arguments against Claude Ozias and the Filles de Notre-Dame can only be inferred from the result: Thérèse de Robillard stayed in the convent to which the bishop, with support from the king, had delivered her. Nothing can be directly known about her experience there. There were cases of ill-treatment of incarcerated Protestant girls. Bishop Bossuet wrote to Madame de Tanqueux, Superior of the nuns of La Ferté-sous-Jouarre in 1687, to reprimand them for gagging the Protestant girls sent there. Fourteen-year-old Françoise d'Aubigné (later Madame de Maintenon) had once written to beseech her aunt, Madame de Villette, to release her from the Ursuline convent in the rue Saint-Jacques: "Life there has been worse than death for me. Ah! madame and aunt, you cannot imagine the hell this so-called house of God is for me and the abuses, hardships, and cruel treatments from those made guardians of my body and of my soul."[34]

On the other hand, some Huguenot girls—even among those forced to enter—were appreciative of their convent experience. Anne de Chauffepié, who was imprisoned in the Citadel of Ré before being moved through a succession of convents and eventually expelled from France, recorded in her escape memoir the kindness and compassion toward her of the Ursulines of Niort: "They had no fear of letting me partake of all those small pleasures I could find in that place, by walking in their garden and by living freely with the nuns and the boarders with whom I ate."[35] A striking number of the girls even found the convent so congenial that they decided to stay. One of the early students at Saint-Cyr who was born Protestant and placed there involuntarily became an Ursuline at Poissy—none other than the Demoiselle Orte who had been caught escaping with her parents and put in Saint-Cyr in 1687. A daughter of Isaac Isle who was put by Madame de Maintenon in the Nouvelles Catholiques chose to spend her life in the convent of the Visitation in Paris. Her sister, Isaac Isle's other daughter, was placed involuntarily in several convents but eventually became a nun at Puyberland. Céleste de Voutron, Thérèse's cousin, whose father had been famously expelled from France after long imprisonment, lived alongside Thérèse for four years as an involuntary New Convert at the Filles de Notre-Dame in Saintes,[36] having had "the misfortune of being born in the Calvinist religion. She was put by order of the King in our house at the age of nineteen, still headstrong in her religion," but she abjured at twenty-one and then at age thirty took her vows as a nun in the same house she had first entered against her will.[37]

Probably the most consequential aspect of Thérèse's experience in the convent was her age. She was only four when she arrived, which was both against the rules and exceptional, though not unknown. Female orders set five or six as the minimum age at which girls could be admitted to their houses, while at Saint-Cyr the minimum entry age was seven. Elizabeth Rapley found cases of future nuns who arrived at ages three or four in four convents of the Filles de Notre-Dame and two Ursuline convents, and there were surely more such cases of early entry both among future nuns and among temporary boarders. The refugee doctor from La Rochelle Elie Bouhéreau noted in the margin of his diary that his youngest daughter, left behind at age six months with a nurse when he escaped in 1686, died in a convent at age four in May 1690. But such early arrivals were likely not very numerous, even among girls entering involuntarily for reeducation. At the Nouvelles Catholiques in Pons, out of some thousand inmates between 1682 and 1789, only five entered under the age of six.[38] Interestingly, Casimir seems not to have made the age argument when, early on, he claimed that Thérèse should be with him rather than in a convent.

Thérèse de Robillard de Champagné did not survive the tutelage of state and church. She died at the convent of the Filles de Notre-Dame in Saintes just two weeks before her twelfth birthday, on April 29, 1699.[39] Putting her in the convent certainly lowered her life chances, since until the medical revolutions of the nineteenth century offered sanitation and controls on contagion, coresidence in enclosed communities was not safe. Putting her in the convent at such a young age compounded her vulnerability, for the "seasoning" of new arrivals was harsher at younger ages, and mortality rates generally declined as children grew. Some have contended that the death of Huguenot girls in convents was an indicator of their mistreatment. However, Catholic girls died very young in convents, too. It would be difficult to produce a comparison of the death rates of New Convert girls and Catholic girls in convents. Perhaps the most that can be said is that psychological factors (homesickness, depression) seem likely to have played a role in such deaths for girls of both confessions.[40]

The tragedy of Thérèse's life and death is deeply moving. She was more than the title to property, which is the only guise in which she can be remembered. One hopes she was comforted as she lay dying and that she found consolation in whatever religion she believed at that moment. Her death reminds posterity that the entire Revocation story was a human tragedy. Lives were lost, lives were ruined, turned away from the comforts and certainties their societies had every capacity to give them. Bodies, communities, aspirations, friendships, families disappeared. Rather than the more common focus on the roots of the suffering in the motivations—personal and political—of its agents, this story bares what their targets faced and the decisions they came to for living—or dying—through it.

Whither Berneré?

Once Thérèse died, there were no more Champagné in France. Since all Thérèse's siblings were fugitives, her properties would be split among her nearest paternal and maternal kin, according to the estates' varied provenances. Her father's properties fell to the daughters of Casimir Prévost de Touchimbert and Marie de Robillard. Berneré—still encumbered by Madelene de Solière's long battle to recover her dowry and *légitime*—went in the short term to her mother's sister, Elisabeth de La Rochefoucauld, who had married Jean-Baptiste Dupuy de La Martinie in 1686.[41] But the contest for Berneré would drag on for nearly half a century longer.

In January 1705, Madelene de Solière won an order from the Parlement of Bordeaux prohibiting Elisabeth from cutting timber at Berneré, on the grounds that she could not degrade the value of property on which the Parlement had recognized Madelene's legitimate claim. At last, in July 1706, Madelene de Solière gained the final ruling in the long-running case, which annulled the renunciation of inheritance she had signed decades before and in effect placed the parties once again in the situation predating Madelene's marriage, with Madelene entitled to 12,000 *livres*, plus interest, from the holdings of her long-deceased sister, mother of the La Rochefoucauld sisters.[42] Madelene de Solière savored her vindication only briefly, for she died the following year.[43] Her heir was Susanne de Lestang, daughter of Madelene's sister Susanne de Solière.[44] Lestang obtained an *arrêt* in 1709 from the Parlement ordering payment to (the heirs of) Madelene de Solière of the inheritance her mother, Susanne Isle, had never given her: the original 12,000 *livres* plus 24,000 *livres* in interest. Elisabeth de La Rochefoucauld, having no other means of paying the swollen inheritance as the court ordered, ceded Berneré to Susanne de Lestang on January 12, 1710.[45]

In the end, then, Madelene's struggles availed herself little and accomplished only the transfer of her parents' estate from one set of her nieces to another: from the daughters of her eldest sister, whom parental preference had designated for the larger legacy, to the daughter of her younger sister, who, as third-born, had accepted a minor portion without demur. By disputing the property division that Susanne Isle elected, Madelene contributed to the abandonment of Thérèse by the emigration of Marie de La Rochefoucauld and the rest of the Champagné.

Even then, Berneré knew no closure. Two years after Elisabeth's cession, Berneré formed part of the bride's dowry when Susanne de Lestang married Benjamin Maichin, Seigneur de Bessé et de Trézence, a cavalry captain.[46] But even the Lestang-Maichin possession of Berneré did not close the case beyond appeal. In 1707, three years before she ceded Berneré to Susanne de Lestang, Elisabeth de La Rochefoucauld had married her daughter Marie Dupuy de La Martinie—one of three daughters, yet another generation in distaff—to her second cousin, a returnee from the Refuge, further entangling Berneré history with the Huguenot story. Louis du Gua, Seigneur de Saint-Coux, had left France with his father and an older brother in 1687. He did his *reconnaissance* at the French Church of The Savoy in London on February 27, 1687, at the age of fourteen. He returned from the Refuge in 1701, as a younger son who had recently reached the age of majority, to abjure and retrieve the properties of his father.[47] A number of the children of Marie's and Josias' friends and kin did the same. Isaac Isle's son returned around the same time as Louis du Gua.[48] Geoffroy Culant, first cousin of the godfather of René-Casimir de Robillard de Champagné, returned from Holland, abjured Protestantism, and repossessed the patrimony.[49] Return was much more common than has been noted in Huguenot histories. Of the thirty-four girls and women residing in the Nouvelles Catholiques on the rue Sainte-Anne in Paris in 1702, for example, no fewer than six were taking religious instruction in the convent after returning from exile in England.[50] Much of the ambassador d'Avaux's time in Holland was consumed by requests from Huguenot refugees who wished to return even at the cost of abjuring.

The returning refugee Louis du Gua repossessed the du Gua family estates and had a daughter by his wife Marie Dupuy—another successive generation in distaff—before Marie died in 1708. In September 1720, the widower du Gua set out to take Berneré back from Susanne de Lestang. Du Gua argued that he (and through him, his daughter Marie-Susanne-Françoise du Gua) was entitled to Berneré because his and Marie's marriage contract included Berneré in the half of Elisabeth's fortune assigned as her dowry. Furthermore, du Gua argued, the Parlement's *arrêt* mandating transfer to Madelene de Solière's heirs stated the sum due her as 36,000 *livres* and ordered that it could be paid "in land or in cash." Du Gua claimed that therefore Madelene's heir, Susanne de Lestang, was understood to be holding Berneré only as collateral for future payment of the debt, until the sum could be paid in cash. On September 16, 1720, du Gua borrowed 35,000 *livres* and the next day offered them to Susanne de Lestang and her husband as debt repayment. When they refused, he countered with an offer of 18,000 *livres* for half of Berneré. They refused again, and his attempts to reclaim Berneré came to naught.

In 1727, however, Marie-Susanne-Françoise du Gua married into the La Vie family of *parlementaires*. Her husband Jean-Charles de La Vie, a counselor in Parlement, tried to use his knowledge of the intricacies of the law to take up his father-in-law's attempt to reclaim Berneré. When Elisabeth de La Rochefoucauld ceded Berneré to Susanne de Lestang, she kept the documents relating to the lawsuit by which they lost it. From those papers, her son-in-law crafted a meticulous legal argument for the reversion of Berneré to the descendants of Elisabeth de La Rochefoucauld.

La Vie developed the three principal arguments du Gua had put forward in 1720 to reverse the 1710 cession and added a fourth. First, he argued the inviolability of marriage contracts: "the donations made by fathers and mothers for the purpose of procuring the marriage for their children . . . [are] inalienable without the express consent of those who have received them." Next, La Vie took up du Gua's argument that Susanne de Lestang held Berneré simply as collateral—the estate was "given as collateral . . . and not otherwise." Third, he argued that the 1710 cession could not under any circumstances have been a sale, since having constituted Marie Dupuy's dowry to include Berneré, Elisabeth de La Rochefoucauld had no authority to cede it to the Lestang. Finally, he argued that the entire legal contest, from the 1660s on down, was illegitimate: Madelene de Solière had simply perpetrated a remarkable fraud.[51] La Vie's arguments were more elaborate but no more successful than du Gua's had been. The descendants of Susanne de Lestang—she, too, had only daughters—continued to live at Berneré; Jacques de Rousselet, husband of her daughter Marie-Anne-Henriette Maichin, assumed its lordship in 1754. Their direct descendant, Monsieur de Chastenet, sold the property in 1857, ending more than two centuries of Isle-lineage proprietorship since the Château de Berneré was built for Susanne Isle in 1633.[52]

The first century of the Château de Berneré, then, was a story of repeated loss. Both the first heir Marie de Solière and her husband Casimir de La Rochefoucauld died young. Their daughter Marie de La Rochefoucauld lost Berneré and emigrated, a departure that was provoked at least in part by the aggression of her aunt, Madelene de Solière, and which in some measure contributed to the loss of Thérèse. Aunt Madelene's continuing aggression eventually also caused Marie's sister Elisabeth de La Rochefoucauld and Elisabeth's daughter Marie Dupuy in turn to lose the estate. The wreckage caused by Madelene de Solière never advantaged her. Only the Lestang family, which had stayed on the sidelines during the long conflict, came out ahead.

10

Cousins

Once Thérèse de Robillard died in the Filles de Notre-Dame, the Robillard de Champagné existed only outside France. But most who were Protestants in France when Louis XIV signed the Revocation stayed, and most of the friends and allies with whom Josias and Marie de La Rochefoucauld built their lives at Berneré became Catholics in the decades following: Prévost de Touchimbert, Mazières, Voutron, and Isle. The immediate successors of those who actively resisted the Revocation joined the king's religion and in so doing positioned themselves and their families for social and professional advancement. Officials hostile to Huguenots such as the intendants Arnoul and Foucault had predicted that material rewards would bring venal Protestants to obedience: the king had taken "a sure route to assuring the conversion of gentlemen, by giving them pensions and placing their children."[1]

But the manner in which some nobles handled full conversion suggests that healing the religious divide offered benefits beyond the pecuniary. The Prévost de Touchimbert were able to rebond, through newly shared religious rites, the branches of the kindred that the Reformation had estranged. Two Isle daughters found spiritual solace after losing their ancestral religion by taking vows as nuns. Others found that so long as they could preserve the family solidarity that their Protestantism had once undergirded they could maintain whatever religious practice they chose by exploiting inconsistencies within royal policy and contentions between royal officials. The Mazières gave the king the outward compliance he enforced and no more. Some Voutron complied, while others pushed the boundaries of royal tolerance, evading full compliance for decades, and were met with persistent pressure gentler than the letter of the law would lead one to suspect.

Casimir's Families

Casimir Prévost de Touchimbert lived for nearly three decades after the Revocation, dying in the summer of 1712. The years during which he could not save himself as a Protestant by leaving France must have been the low point of his life. Nearly sixty years old at the Revocation, widowed, and soon stripped of most of his children with the late Marie de Robillard, he must have felt his life was behind him and the possibilities of new beginnings were nil. Some of his children had left the country, and the rest had been taken away. He would never see his refugee children again. His daughter Esther-Silvie, the youngest of the three girls who were taken to Saint-Cyr, died at the school in January 1689 at the age of thirteen.

Suspected at least into the new century of being an insincere—even dangerous—New Convert, Casimir lived in an increasingly Catholic context, public as well as familial. Not that Protestantism disappeared from its Poitevin heartland. Pastor Viala reported about his clandestine travels through Poitou in the summer of 1740: "I would never have believed that the Protestants were so numerous there, especially in the countryside of Haut-Poitou. Entire parishes have no Roman Catholics . . . except the curé and his sacristan." But Viala also identified one feature of Protestantism that had changed: "There are few rich persons among them; they all live by the labor of their hands."[2] Noble leadership had disappeared in the half-century following the Revocation.

Commitment to the faith of his fathers had motivated Josias de Robillard to refuse the king's command to convert; his experience and that of his family illustrate the Revocation's degrees of failure. By contrast, whatever his own sentiments might have been, Casimir de Prévost's family transitioned, and their religious redefinition illustrates the Revocation's degrees of success. The three children of Casimir and Marie de Robillard who, staying in France, survived Saint-Cyr and the Miramionnes were Catholic. Royal favor, their own reeducation, and their marriages rooted in Catholicism the abandoned patrimony they inherited from their fugitive Robillard de Champagné cousins. Then a second marriage and second set of children for Casimir furnished a new foundation for a conformist Prévost de Touchimbert family.

When Julie and Diane finished at Saint-Cyr and Marie-Anne left the Miramionnes, they were Catholic, in line for royal favor, and marriageable. Conversion had widened their available marriage pool, bringing in Catholic families with whom they would never have intermarried before, but they also maintained connections with longstanding allies through marriages with New Converts like themselves. The timing of the marriages into families with varying religious histories—first with Catholic, then with Protestant—may well have been strategic, Casimir's way of confirming the bride's and her family's conformity. Julie left Saint-Cyr, as the regulations stipulated, at her twentieth birthday in 1694, and she received royal pensions toward her future maintenance.[3] The first of the sisters to marry, she wed Jacques de Volvire-Magné, from a family of "fanatical Catholics," in January 1697. Marie-Anne, the youngest, married second at Saint-Savinien on August 6, 1698, with the son of a Catholic family that was open—in this and the next generation—to alliances with New Converts: Pierre du Rousseau, Seigneur de Fayolle. A year later, when Thérèse de Robillard died at the Filles de Notre-Dame in Saintes, Marie-Anne took possession of Champagné. Diane, the eldest, married third on February 11, 1705, with a descendant of Huguenots: Simon Dreux, Seigneur d'Aigné et d'Heuil. Months after being widowed in 1714 she married Charles-Bernard-Donatien Tiercelin d'Appelvoisin, Marquis de La Roche-du-Maine, from a New Convert family that had been Protestant from at least 1588 until the Revocation. By virtue of Thèrèse's death, Diane took possession of Josias' estates at Agère, residing herself in her husband's grand Château de La Roche-Magné, which was the last in Poitou to be constructed in high-quality Gothic style.

Four years after the upheavals of the Revocation and his imprisonment in the Bastille, Casimir remarried with Marie Coullaud and began a new, demonstrably Catholic family. One daughter of this second family, Jeanne, became a nun. Another daughter, Marie Elisabeth, who had been baptized in the Catholic church at Saint-Savinien, followed in the footsteps of her elder half-sisters by going to Saint-Cyr—this time, no doubt, a voluntary admission sought by the parents. Saint-Cyr functioned consecutively, then, for the Prévost de Touchimbert in both of the ways it could serve the once-Protestant French nobility: first as conversion institution, and second as reward for consonance with the religious demands of the monarchy. Sadly, Marie Elisabeth died at the school in July 1706 at the age of twelve, as her half-sister Esther-Silvie had seventeen years earlier. The three sons of Casimir and Marie Coullaud made military careers that led to court circles and social distinction. The eldest, Auguste, was a musketeer in the king's guard; another son, Jean, was a lieutenant in the dragoons in Guadeloupe; the third, François, was a captain in the regiment of Champagne. Auguste's son would be a page in the king's Grande Ecurie, Marquis de Touchimbert, cavalry captain, and Chevalier de Saint-Louis. Auguste's daughter Thérèse would become in 1749 the fifth of Casimir's descendants to attend Saint-Cyr and the third to survive it; she became a nun.[4]

Brother Charles' line became Catholic more gradually, despite his own early conversion. He was still struggling in 1698 to convert his wife, Catherine de La Rochefoucauld, and three daughters: Charlotte, Gabrielle, and Marie. The intendant ordered the daughters into a convent for reeducation but was forced by their family's limited resources to leave them at home with their father, who, after all, had shown his good faith by converting even before the Revocation and urging his Bastille-imprisoned brothers in 1685–1686 to follow his example. Charlotte married a New Convert, Gabriel Vasselot, Seigneur de Reigné, in 1713 and left her mark on the glorious fifteenth-century Château de

Reigné—literally inscribing her name and the date 1722 on a stone lintel on the terrace—when remaking its north facade and gardens. Daughter Gabrielle inherited the seigneury du Tour and was living there in 1724; she took vows as a nun in 1727 at the Union Chrétienne in Poitiers. She would serve as superior of this house that had been established for the reeducation of Protestants.[5]

The family of Casimir's eldest brother and Bastille companion François worked their way gradually to religious conformity and social eminence. Fifteen years after his release from the Bastille and abjuration, François died as a Catholic and was buried not at Saveilles, where he had fought to continue holding Protestant services on the eve of the Revocation, but in the parish church of Salles-de-Villefagnan. Both his sons converted while serving in Louis XIV's navy. But as a New Convert the younger son, Isaac, came up against the concern to regulate New Convert marriages that was a prominent part of the crown's religious policy. In December 1700, Isaac asked permission from the king to marry Elisabeth de La Rochefoucauld, a first cousin of both Marie de La Rochefoucauld and Josias de Robillard. The two families had long intermarried: for the third generation in a row a son of the Prévost de Touchimbert would marry a woman of the Parc d'Archiac branch of the La Rochefoucauld.[6] Perhaps out of suspicion that old family alliances could import competing loyalties into the new religious landscape, reinforced by the fact that the proposed bride was still unconverted,[7] the king at first withheld his consent, tightened surveillance on the young naval lieutenant, and threatened to transfer him in order to rupture the bond between the proposed spouses: "have this officer informed that if he leaves his quarters to go see this woman without the permission of Monsieur Du Magnon, you have orders to stop him, and if from what you learn of his attachment to this woman you believe he can only be turned away from it by being sent to a different department, let me know so I can send him the order." But François—probably by now well converted—intervened with the king on his son's behalf, and permission for the marriage was granted shortly thereafter.[8]

François' elder son François, like his brother Isaac, married a New Convert, Marie Chitton de Montlaurier, a very close neighbor of Saveilles in the same parish of Pliboux. Of all the New Convert Prévost de Touchimbert, he made both the most visible religious conversion and the most successful pivot from suspicion to royal largesse. A scant year after father François' death in 1701, the son François requested, and received, permission from the Bishop of Poitiers to build a chapel at the corner of the grand courtyard of the Château de Saveilles. From 1237, when René de La Rochefaton took Saveilles in marriage, down to the Reformation, when the family became Protestant, the La Rochefaton proprietors of the château had attended the village church in Paizay-Naudouin, where two side chapels dedicated to Sainte Catherine and Sainte Marguerite belonged to the family. After the La Rochefaton (and then the La Force heirs by marriage) became Protestant, those chapels must have been empty, as the family held their own services at home in the château without the formal chapel that Protestant worship did not require. So the building of a Catholic chapel at the Château de Saveilles was a performance of the family's sincere and entire reconversion. The consecration of the chapel and the blessing of its bell on March 9, 1703, in the presence of five local priests and a great gathering of local nobles, announced the family's return to the Catholic fold. So did the placement, at the same time, of a six-foot seigneurial pew in the newly rebuilt village church. At the Revolution, the chapel in the château was disaffected and stripped of its ornamentation; the pew in the village church was taken out and burned. In 1806, the chapel was turned into a bakery.[9]

By then, the chapel had done its work, rendering tangible in stone the family's alliance with church and monarchy. When it was only a few years old, in 1711, the chapel changed hands: from its builder François, now deceased, to his only child, a daughter whose education and marriage marked the apogee of Touchimbert de Saveilles fortunes. Marie-Susanne may have been a student at Saint-Cyr, for on January 31, 1712, Madame de Maintenon honored her with a personal letter approving her marriage to Henri, Marquis de Bourdeille, Comte de Matha. By her marriage on February 26, 1713, Marie-Susanne carried Saveilles—with its chapel and family pew in the correct religion—to one of the kingdom's most eminent and most faithfully Catholic lineages. Bourdeille was the fourth-generation descendant of the seneschal of Périgord who commanded the royal troops in the region during the Wars of Religion and whose younger brother, the famous courtier Abbé Brantôme, so ridiculed Jean de Solière's father. Before Marie-Susanne, Comtesse de Matha, retired to Port-Royal in 1764 and died in Paris in November 1773, she would serve as lady-in-waiting to the Duchesse d'Orleans. She would see her second son become Bishop of Tulle and then of Soissons, and her elder son Henri-Joseph become first baron of Périgord, Comte de Bourdeille, Seigneur de Saveilles, and Gentleman of the Bedchamber to the Duc d'Orléans.[10]

Once all the children of the Prévost de Touchimbert line of the great noble Prévost family had joined the king's religion, a new family cohesion emerged: the three branches of the kindred that had split at the Reformation bonded together in the performance of Catholic rites. Jean-Pierre Prévost, Seigneur de Traversay, of the senior, old-Catholic branch of the family asked Casimir's descendants to stand as his babies' godparent: in 1723, Auguste Prévost de Touchimbert for his daughter Marie-Anne Prévost de Sansac; in 1731, Auguste's wife for Madeleine-Charlotte; and in 1743, Louis-Charles du Rousseau, Seigneur de Fayolle, and his wife for Charlotte-Marianne. In 1748, Jean Prévost de Puybottier married Thérèse de Vassselot-Reigné, granddaughter of Charles Prévost de Brassac—a cross-branch marriage that could not have taken place without religious reunification. When the future Russian admiral was baptized at Traversay in 1759, the signing witnesses included Duquesne de Fayolle, Charlotte du Rousseau, and Diane du Rousseau—all from the Londigny branch of Prévost de Touchimbert—and Thérèse de Vasselot-Reigné. In 1779 at a Prévost de Traversay marriage, Pierre du Rousseau, Chevalier de Fayolle, was a witness, and André du Rousseau signed as an advisor to the groom under the title "Seigneur de Champagné."[11] In this way, the entire Prévost kinship network recaptured through their newly shared religion the kind of cross-branch solidarity that the Isle had enjoyed when they were all Protestants but that unraveled in the run-up to the Revocation.

The Mazières and Nicolas de Voutron

The Prévost de Touchimbert, then, did not slip unobtrusively into Catholicism but gave strong signals of inclusion. By contrast, Josias' maternal cousins complied incompletely and reluctantly, pushing the boundaries of accepted behavior before conforming in varying degrees. They found a way to replicate, even tighten, the family solidarity they had enjoyed before the Revocation and used it to cushion the impact of forced conversion.

Josias' slightly younger first cousin Philippe-Benjamin de Mazières (and caretaker of toddler Thérèse's marshlands until her death) illustrates the extended pathway—from resistance to grudging compliance and at least minimal safety—taken by one who stayed. Philippe-Benjamin abjured not long after the Revocation, on February 28, 1686, before the parish curé of Voutron, declaring that "in obedience to the will of the King, I join the Catholic, Apostolic, and Roman Religion." For him, abjuration meant temporizing rather than sincere conversion. At the beginning of 1689, he was living at the Hôtel de Thou near Saint-André-des-Arts in Paris when the police discovered his name in the papers of Paul Cardel, a pastor expelled from France at the Revocation whom they arrested when he returned to Paris to minister to Huguenots. The police apparently did not move to apprehend Mazières at that point, and the next year, when holders of fugitives' property were ordered to present a certificate of Catholicity to the lieutenant-general of La Rochelle, "Philippe Benjamin de Mazières du Passage as guardian of Marie Thérèse de Robillard" satisfied the order.[12] Yet he cannot have been anything but suspect. The royal endorsement of his capacity as custodian and the religious abjuration that made it possible merely illustrate how difficult it was for officials to find reliably Catholic relatives to take over the properties of Protestant fugitives.

Despite the indulgence of authorities in the region, Philippe-Benjamin's cover did not last long after his escape from the Cardel affair. In January 1692, he went to Paris on account, as he alleged, of a mill that belonged to his father-in-law and other domestic affairs.[13] On February 11, while residing at the sign of the Black Horse in the rue de l'Hirondelle, he was caught by the Paris police, along with a group "from the Religion or pretended New Converts," in "a house in Paris where they hold worship services of the R.P.R." Philippe-Benjamin was treated far more gently than many who were apprehended at Protestant assemblies, not suffering consignment to the galleys as the law prescribed. He was first taken to nearby For-l'Evêque, the royal prison situated between the Châtelet and the Louvre that still bore the title of the ecclesiastical proprietor from whom Louis XIV had taken it away. After interrogation on February 14 by the police chief Gabriel Nicolas de La Reynie himself, Philippe-Benjamin was sent by Pontchartrain's order into the Bastille. It took six months for Pontchartrain to grant him the liberty of the courtyard that allowed him to be visited by friends.

The exit from the Bastille on January 20, 1693 that Pontchartrain designed for Philippe-Benjamin suggests how the crown envisioned bringing to heel a New Convert whom they for some reason chose not to prosecute by the letter of the law. Having received assurances "of the good dispositions in which he is at present," Pontchartrain ordered Mazières transferred to the Oratorians' seminary of Saint-Magloire, "where he is to be instructed for changing religion, and to remarry in our Roman Church." The first phrase declares insincere the abjuration he made at Voutron in February 1686; the second declares inauthentic the marriage he and Esther Guillaudeau, a New Convert from a longtime Protestant family of La Rochelle, had celebrated perhaps as long before as 1690, when their marriage contract was drawn up.[14] The wording of Pontchartrain's order suggests that they had been married, but in a ceremony not fully consonant with the strictures of Church and state. Philippe-Benjamin and Esther illustrate, then, a new form of clandestine marriage in the years following the Revocation—marriage by former Protestants outside their own Catholic parish before a carefully chosen and undemanding curé—as well as the crown's focus on marriage in the conversion process. What this Mazières was required to do in order to free himself from royal control was make a confession of faith that would so persuade a priest in the church militant—not merely one he could resort to on his own terms—that he could be admitted to the sacrament of the Eucharist and thereafter be married according to standard Catholic rites.

The remarriage that took place after he entered the Oratoire evidently left Philippe-Benjamin in grudging compliance. When his second son was baptized at Voutron on June 14, 1696, not a single family member attended, though they were at home. A handwritten note accompanied the six-day-old infant to the church and was filed in the parish register near the baptismal notice: "The name of the infant is Pierre de Mazières, son of Monsieur Benjamin de Mazières, chevalier, seigneur chesnier de Voutron and Dupassage and Ester Guillaudeau, father and mother. The marriage of the said Sieur and Dame du Passage was ratified at Saint-Jacques-du-Haut-Pas in Paris in the month of February 1693."[15] At least two of his other children's baptisms took place an unusually long time after their birth—unusually long both in former Protestant practice and by Catholic doctrine. The first son, Philippe-Henri, was held from baptism for nearly six months in 1693–1694, Susanne-Héleine for eight weeks in 1702. This delay might bespeak a reluctance to participate, a lack of zeal for what was offered, a desire to search somehow for an alternative. So, too, might the noticeable lack of a settled parish; the baptisms of the children rotated through La Rochelle's Saint-Barthélemy, Voutron, and La Rochelle's Notre-Dame-de-Cougnes, the parents not committing to a single religious center where their compliance could be monitored.

Philippe-Benjamin used the protective circle of family to cushion the impact of the forced religious change. He and Esther Guillaudeau limited participation in their children's baptisms and marriages to New Converts, especially to the same set of kin who worshipped with them as Protestants before the Revocation. Unlike the Prévost de Touchimbert, who managed baptisms and marriages in ways that bonded New Converts with old Catholics and reunited family lines that the Reformation had sundered, Philippe-Benjamin's preference was to tighten the circle. Those present for the baptism of daughter Susanne-Héleine on December 21, 1702, were the father; the infant's sister Ester de Mazières; the godfather Gédéon Nicolas de Voutron, naval officer and first cousin of Philippe-Benjamin; the godmother Susanne Duquesne, daughter of Gédéon's sister Marie-Marguerite; and two additional sisters of Gédéon and Marie-Marguerite, Henriette and Céleste de Voutron. At the baptism of daughter Héleine on August 4, 1701, the circle was even tighter: the godmother and godfather were the newborn's brother Philippe-Henri and sister Ester, even though they were but seven years old and younger. For the May 14, 1694, baptism of the eldest son, Philippe-Henri, the witnesses and participants were New Converts well known for their difficulty in converting. Olympe de Cailhault, widow of Philippe-Benjamin's uncle André and godmother in 1673 for the newborn son of Josias de Robillard and Marie de La Rochefoucauld, signed as a witness. Olympe's husband Jean Gabaret, the godfather, had spent a decade struggling to keep his naval offices despite his Protestant past. As an admiral, he could operate at the highest levels of the Navy; on February 13, 1692, "at four o'clock, the king took counsel with the king of England, Monsieur de Pontchartrain, Monsieur de Tourville, the Chevalier de Château-Renaud, d'Amfreville, and

Gabaret on what our fleet ought to undertake this year." But just six days after Gabaret's performance at the Mazières baptism, Pontchartrain reported that Gabaret was not attending mass. Earlier, on September 17, 1688, Seignelay had written Gabaret to complain that his new wife performed "no act whatever of Catholicity": "His Majesty is all the more dissatisfied because such conduct on the part of a general officer who heads a corps of the Navy in the department of Rochefort cannot but provide a very bad example and one of dangerous consequence . . . I tell you frankly that if you neglect to correct this matter, His Majesty will do so himself by having her put into a convent."[16]

Philippe-Benjamin de Mazières prospered through the years of his religious transition. He built an updated château at Le Passage with techniques used for the nearby Corderie royale at Rochefort. He added properties from his neighbors' misfortunes. He purchased l'Houmée in 1703 from Jacques Berne, the heavily indebted husband of Marie de La Rochefoucauld's sister Madeleine. He never stopped being questioned on his religious conformity, but before the end of his life his children would provide the answers. In 1717, Philippe-Benjamin found someone to assume his late wife's one-third share in a large, rundown house in La Rochelle whose rebuilding would otherwise be ruinously expensive. To conclude this transaction, he had to petition the king, because his deceased wife had been Protestant more than three decades before. The Comte de Chamilly, then commanding in Aunis, Saintonge, and Poitou, forwarded the petition with his assurance that the family had demonstrated its conformity with the king's orders on religion: the Mazières children "have been raised in the Catholic religion and profess it."[17] The next generation was, as Maintenon foresaw, Catholic "even if the fathers are hypocrites."

Josias' Voutron cousins made up the third side of the triangle of close kin with the Champagné and the Mazières. Gédéon Nicolas de Voutron was the martyr whose incarceration in 1685 drew the anger of Jurieu and Tessereau, and whose wife, Marie Thauvet, helped Marie de La Rochefoucauld and her children escape from France. Expelled from the country in 1688, Gédéon never returned to France; he died in England after only a few years of exile. His wife stayed behind, never saw him again, and struggled to stay out of the hands of the law until her death in 1694. She abjured soon after the Revocation and was rewarded for doing so. But when she failed to follow through on her promises, Châteauneuf revoked the favor "because she performs no duty as a Catholic."[18]

Their children scattered across the full spectrum of possibilities for proscribed Protestants: two emigrated, two complied without drama, three became nuns in the houses to which they had been involuntarily consigned for reeducation, and one openly resisted conversion. The eldest son, Pierre, joined his father in the Refuge shortly after his departure.[19] The third son, Philippe, abjured in the spring of 1686 and served in the French navy for a decade more, and then left for Holland.[20] The second son, Gédéon, converted, like his brother Philippe, in the spring of 1686, and took the Château de Voutron when his father and elder brother emigrated. His sentiments as he transitioned to Catholicism may have paralleled those of his "nearest relation" and business agent Philippe-Benjamin de Mazières, though he left fewer traces of them. For nearly three decades after the Revocation, his appearances in the Voutron parish registers were rare; unlike Madelene de Solière and Hélène Mauchen he did not readily assume the religious role traditional for a seigneur in the parish of his seigneury. He was as exclusive as Philippe-Benjamin with respect to the witnesses included in his children's baptisms: consistently limited to his siblings, those of his wife, and the Duquesne husband and children of his sister Marie-Marguerite. Like Philippe-Benjamin, he found that his own and the family's past in the wrong religion never ceased to dog him. As late as 1698, when the Bishop of Saintes asked the king to grant a pension for Voutron, the king declined, though satisfied with his services and appreciative of his conversion. Gédéon nonetheless built "an honorable career, though without particular luster" as a naval captain and Chevalier de Saint-Louis, and founded a dynasty of naval officers.[21]

All five Nicolas de Voutron sisters were placed in convents in 1694, by the king's order and at the king's expense, "to be instructed in the Catholic faith": Marie-Marguerite (Madame Duquesne) and two others in La Providence in La Rochelle; Céleste in the Filles de Notre-Dame in Saintes, where seven-year-old Thérèse de Robillard was an orphan ward; and one in the Nouvelles Catholiques in Pons, creation of Maintenon's friend the Comtesse de Marsan.[22] For three years, Céleste distinguished herself in Saintes "by her stubbornness," setting "a very bad example by her obstinacy."[23] But then she converted "with much understanding and edification," and the Bishop, at the suggestion of her brother-in-law Duquesne-Guiton, entrusted her with guiding toward conversion two of her sisters whom he brought from La Providence to join her in the Filles de Notre-Dame.[24] By springtime of 1698, the three sisters were all reportedly "doing their Catholic duty very well," and on Christmas Eve of that year, after four years in custody, the last of them were released.[25] Three of the five daughters of the Gédéon Nicolas de Voutron who was martyred for his Protestant faith became nuns: Anne Sara and Susanne at the convent of the Soeurs hospitalières in La Rochelle, Céleste at the Filles de Notre-Dame in Saintes. When Céleste died of apoplexy in 1736, her sisters in religion composed an affectionate outline of her life:

> This dear Mother had the misfortune to be born in the Calvinist Religion. . . . God, who had given her a great soul and an amiable

> character with all the qualities of mind and heart, did not allow her to be a prey of the Devil. . . . Our dear mother after her conversion served as a mother to her brothers and sisters, whom she converted through her good counsel, and deferred her own establishment until they were all settled. By her gentle manner she made several of her sisters nuns: she herself crowned the great work by dedicating herself to God in our House, where she had had the good fortune of receiving the Faith."[26]

The nuns' telling of Céleste's story, pairing her own conversion with her involvement in that of her sisters, pointed to the way the sibling group of Voutron and Mazières who stayed in France faced the Revocation. Siblings who converted and those who refused, those who professed the religious life and those who changed for pragmatic reasons, all involved themselves in each other's lives and supported each other, sharing a commitment to family more akin, perhaps, to the solidarity of the Lacger than to the fragmentation of the Isle.

While three Voutron sisters became nuns, a fourth, Marie-Henriette, returned to live with the family, and the fifth, Marie-Marguerite, refusing to abjure, remained a focus of royal conversion efforts for many years, both before and after she married into the famed and formerly Protestant Duquesne family. Abraham Duquesne-Guiton, her husband, was a nephew of the renowned admiral and Seigneur de Belesbat, just down the Boutonne from Champagné and down the Charente from Saint-Savinien. He converted in the very week of the Revocation, aligning his religious practice sufficiently to continue serving as a naval captain.[27] His appointment made his marital plans a concern for the king and even gave the king a weapon he could exploit for bringing Marie-Marguerite to heel, but it also created a delicate situation for the king, who wished both to retain Duquesne-Guiton's services and make his royal navy an exemplary all-Catholic institution.

Early in 1692, the Bishop of La Rochelle refused to marry the couple on the grounds that Marie-Marguerite was, as Bégon reported, a "badly converted Huguenot . . . it is believed that the Demoiselle is going to settle in some other diocese where she will finds things easier." Sometime that spring, the couple reportedly traveled, along with one of her sisters, in search of a priest less strict than those in the diocese of La Rochelle and found one in Toulon, perhaps the same one who indulged Duquesne-Guiton's cousin Duquesne-Monnier when he was stationed in Toulon and married there without difficulty. Like Philippe-Benjamin de Mazières, Duquesne-Guiton and Marie-Marguerite had recourse to a new type of clandestine marriage, the Revocation having created a new reason for would-be spouses to marry outside their home parishes.[28]

During the months Philippe-Benjamin spent at the Oratoire being instructed in religion with an eye to correcting his irregular marriage, his cousin Marie-Marguerite and Duquesne-Guiton pressed their case for recognition of the irregular marriage they had made, with one important difference between the cases: whereas Philippe-Benjamin found himself in a binary situation—he vis-à-vis the king—Duquesne's case proceeded in a triangle, the crown officials in Rochefort and in Versailles putting themselves in a position of negotiating between Duquesne-Guiton and the Bishop of La Rochelle. To Duquesne-Guiton the crown officials were always formally peremptory. When he appealed from the uncooperative bishop to the king, he was told: "You must observe the formalities prescribed by the Church." Two weeks later the word from court was even clearer as to the dangers that a marriage short of full compliance with Catholic practice could pose for the captain: "Since the letter I wrote you on the subject of your marriage, the King has been informed that it was contracted in a manner that cannot be sustained without putting your family at very grave risk and rendering the standing of your children very uncertain, and as it is in your interest to redo it according to the formalities prescribed by the Church, His Majesty expects you to follow what the Bishop of La Rochelle has told you about that. He wants you to do that. I beg you personally to take care of this matter so that the King hears no more about it."[29]

Yet if the mandate of compliance was enunciated in unambiguous terms, behind the scenes intendant and minister were more indulgent of their naval officer and less than supportive of Church norms. On April 1, 1692, Bégon confided his misgivings about the Duquesne-Voutron affair to a friend, linking it with that of his incarcerated cousin. "I knew what happened to Monsieur Du Passage [Philippe-Benjamin] and I have often discussed with [the Bishop] of La Rochelle what you write of. He bases his position on the canons of the Councils and on the thinking of most French bishops, among them the Archbishop of Paris and Monsieur de Meaux [Bossuet], who have told him that they did the same in their dioceses. I have given an accounting of this to the king's ministers, who judged it was not appropriate to have His Majesty interpose his authority, even though they are well persuaded that it would be for the good of the state to find some adjustments that could facilitate the marriages of New Converts. [The Bishop] of La Rochelle agrees that confession is not necessary for the validity of the sacrament of marriage, but that is not the heart of the matter, which comes down to knowing whether any curé can be considered the curé of a person who does not profess the Catholic, Apostolic, and Roman religion."[30]

Bégon's concern was much wider than the Mazières and Voutron-Duquesne cases. A few years later, Bégon would make a policy statement of his opposition to the Church's too-strict practices on marriage of Protestants. "All the faithful subjects of the King perceive with indescribable sadness that the rigorous ordinances of the bishops on the marriages of New Converts drive them away from our religion and sap the State at its foundations." Marriages between Catholics and Protestants, he wrote, were among the best and gentlest ways to bring the latter into the Catholic religion: "The spouse who professes it insensibly draws the one who does not into his camp." What Bégon argued against was the bishops' requirement that both bride and groom be Catholics in order to marry. Severity—requiring both to confess and to take communion in advance—made would-be spouses prefer concubinage or adultery, even celibacy, and it encouraged emigration. Facilitating marriage would promote willing integration into Catholicism and reverse the depopulation of France (Bégon believed the diocese of Saintes had lost 25 percent of its people in a decade). The issue required urgent correction; Bégon suggested that the king call an assembly of the clergy as soon as possible to examine this issue, which, to his mind, was crucial "for the general good of the State."[31]

Perhaps for similar reasons, the royal minister, even as he insisted on full compliance in his letters to Duquesne-Guiton, expressed support for the naval officer in his exchanges with the bishop. He warned Duquesne again of the risks the couple ran as long as their marriage was not according to the forms: "If you were to die, one or the other of you, in the situation where you now are, your family would fall into a most disagreeable predicament. It is very important for you to establish order at the earliest possible moment, and to this end you must persuade your wife to get instructed, after which, the rest will not be considered important." On the same day, he assured the bishop of his confidence that Duquesne-Guiton would conform to the king's orders and asked the bishop to lean as far in the direction of Duquesne's needs as he could: "as the said du Quesne is a fine officer whom I would like to please, I would be very obliged to you for easing his release from this affair as soon as possible. . . . I ask you, in this case, to treat him as gently as you can and to ease his way to fixing his marriage, in order to secure the repose of his family."[32] For all the officials' efforts at accommodation, the Bishop of La Rochelle continued to refuse to recognize their marriage or regularize it until Marie-Marguerite demonstrated her good faith in religion.

Within months of this exchange of letters, Madame Duquesne was put by order of the king in the Convent of the Religieuses de La Providence in La Rochelle. Almost immediately, Duquesne requested her release, bypassing the question of her religious sentiments to base his request on two other grounds: that she was ill "and besides, that she must take care of the harvest." The minister easily saw through the husband's claims and turned down the request. Bégon was ordered to transfer her to the Hospitalières de La Rochelle, but Bégon himself suspended the order, after which the crown canceled it in

December 1694, on the basis of reports "that the Dame du Quesne appears to want instruction in good faith." She was released from the convent of La Providence on January 9, 1695, having promised to become Catholic.[33] The promises that secured her release she would not keep. In March 1698, the minister, his patience seemingly exhausted, threatened Duquesne: "His Majesty granted permission for her to leave the convent where she was put in the hope that she would get instructed and that you would get her to conduct herself as you have done. He has been extremely displeased, and I must tell you that if in one month she does not get instructed and you do not find a means to oblige her to do it, the King will withdraw your pensions and will no longer have you in his service, not wishing to have an officer in his service who himself and whose family are bad examples for New Converts; His Majesty may already have made this decision with respect to you, without consideration for your past services. It is up to you to act on this."[34]

Duquesne was not cashiered, and the drama of his resistant wife dragged on beyond the lifetime of the king who demanded her submission. The couple had the parish curé baptize their daughter Henriette Madeleine in the chapel at Champdolent on May 9, 1700, but by year's end Pontchartrain remained disillusioned and at wits' end with both of the spouses. Bégon was instructed to warn Marie-Marguerite directly: "Make her understand that if she does not change her conduct on the matter of the Religion, His Majesty may decide to have her put in a convent." A second child, a two-week-old son, was brought to the parish baptismal font on October 28, 1701. But baptism was the least persuasive evidence of conversion; it was the sacrament that Protestants had agreed to have performed, as necessary, in a Catholic church. So Marie-Marguerite was once again placed in a convent in June 1703: "Based on what His Majesty has been told of the obstinacy of Madame Duquesne in not fulfilling her Catholic duty, he has directed me to send the attached orders to put her in the Nouvelles Catholiques in La Rochelle."[35]

Duquesne would go on to be named admiral for Provence in 1705 and eventually lieutenant-general of the king's navy as well as Chevalier de Saint-Louis. But his wife would never be considered reliable and never cease to be a factor in his professional relations with the crown. Early in 1714, Duquesne-Guiton asked, with the support of the intendant Beauharnais de Beauville, to be named governor-general in the Antilles. Twenty-nine years after his conversion, he was made to understand that his former religious adherence was still a factor in his professional prospects. "The religion you formerly professed would have been an obstacle if His Majesty had not learned from me that your conversion was sincere and that you fulfill all the duties of the Catholic religion." A warning was nonetheless in order. "You should have in mind when you are in Martinique that you must provide an example to the people there and that therefore you will have to take renewed care not to do anything that might raise the slightest doubt about the sincere conversion you have made." Then Duquesne-Guiton was summoned to come to Versailles as soon as possible to speak with the minister.

Duquesne-Guiton had acknowledged in his request for the office that his wife "was not well converted," and that, he contended, was his "greatest sorrow." Accordingly, he preemptively assured the king that he would leave her in France and go alone to the islands.[36] That summer and early fall, Duquesne-Guiton's planning for departure demonstrated both his intention to leave his wife behind and his sincere satisfaction of the "duties of a Catholic." On July 15, in Rochefort, he drew up a power of attorney for Marie-Marguerite that accorded her sweeping discretion to manage and dispose of his property without exception before any tribunal and in any of a long list of types of transactions, including consent to the marriages of their daughters or "putting them in religion." The will he made on September 17, in view of "the dangers of the crossing he is going to make to his governorship," expressed his desire to be buried according to the observances of "the Roman Catholic Church. . . . As a true Christian he recommended his soul to God the Lord of Heaven and Earth, praying that by the merits of the death and passion of His dear son Jesus Christ and the intercession of the Virgin Saint Mary his mother He will deign to have mercy upon him."[37]

But Marie-Marguerite Voutron was not to be so easily set aside. Duquesne-Guiton could hardly break the rules directly or renege on his promise to the king that as governor-general in the islands he would forgo the pleasure of his wife's company. So family solidarity stepped in. In May 1715, after Duquesne-Guiton had been in Martinique for the better part of a year, Marie-Marguerite's brother, the naval officer Gédéon Nicolas de Voutron, asked the king to permit her to rejoin her husband. His arguments were many. The separation caused the couple double expenses and deep personal pain. "Monsieur Duquesne (despite his silence) feels the separation from his wife so keenly that if he loses hope of seeing it come to an end, he will not live long. This would be the most extreme misfortune for his family." Marie-Marguerite's religion should present no difficulty, for she "will live without scandal in his house in Martinique as she does in Saintonge." Her daughters, who were good Catholics, would take her place in church. Besides, this permission might even effect her conversion by removing her from the many relations and friends who fortified her resistance and encouraged her to think of her obstinacy as heroic. In the islands, she would see and hear learned clerics every day who in friendly conversation could weed out the roots of her stubbornness, which at any rate were already much weakened. In sum, this was the only way to induce her to convert. And "if after she has spent a year in Martinique she deceives his expectations, he will be the first to ask not only that she be made to return but also that she be once again confined in a convent."[38]

At this point—thirty years after the Revocation and less than two months before the death of the king—Versailles orchestrated an approach to the case of the still-Protestant Marie-Marguerite de Voutron that speaks volumes about the way royal officials cherry-picked the Revocation decade after decade, working to realize the religious uniformity that the law decreed without resorting to the punishments that the law prescribed. The Comte de Chamilly was to confer with Voutron in the hope that the brother might suggest means to defeat his sister's obstinacy. Then Chamilly should visit Marie-Marguerite in her home at Belesbat, to ferret out as best he could her real sentiments and the chances of her coming around on the matter of religion. He was to read to Marie-Marguerite a letter from the king.[39]

The letter was a masterpiece of tightly crafted, insidious persuasion that oscillated manipulatively between reinforcement and threat.[40] It opened with flattery for Marie-Marguerite in courtly language that implied that she and her virtues were known to the king. "There would be nothing more to wish for from Madame Duquesne if, to all the good qualities with which she is endowed, she would let herself be persuaded of the truths of religion, which it is most essential that she do." It then described how close she already was to Catholic piety. His Majesty was aware that she loved prayer, loved holy readings, and observed frequent fasts—none of which, the letter noted, were customary among Protestants—so a merely small step would take her to the true faith: "His Majesty knows well that she is not far from it." Pivoting to the negative, the letter revealed that this all-seeing king who knew her so well also knew more than she did about her own standing among those close to her, about her own personal failings, and about the isolation they brought in their train. "She is only kept [in her errors] by a pride that is not condoned in any religion and for which she is blamed by the persons in her entourage who she believes admire her steadfastness." Sheer vanity isolated her from the tender regard of her husband and family as well as from her king.

Once having blamed and isolated her, the letter invoked the magnanimity of the king who opened his arms to his wayward subject. If His Majesty could think that allowing her to go to Martinique would, by separating her from those who led her astray, induce her to accept this last chance to satisfy her husband, her children, and her king, he would gladly give his permission. If she would agree to convert, the ingrate could be redeemed by "the good wishes that [the king] has for this Dame, even though she has never done anything he desired from her." But royal indulgence had its limits: "this good will and this gentleness would only go so far and ultimately it could not last forever." Time was of the essence with respect to the king, as it was with respect to her husband's well-being: "I do not want to think about what might happen, and not long from now, in terms of the sorrow that Monsieur would feel about that and which would be capable of putting him in his grave."

Chamilly's follow-up reports, dated August 3 and August 13, recommended that Madame Duquesne be given permission to join her husband without imposing any conditions on her and without any time limit. Pontchartrain congratulated Chamilly for his skill in dealing with her. "I consider this lady convinced by your reasonings." But she had not in fact converted; she was permitted to join her husband in Martinique on the mere hope that she could then be convinced to convert. A letter dated August 9 informed Voutron of the king's decision to allow her and her children to go to Martinique at their convenience on a merchant ship. A letter of August 21 let Beauharnais know that the king had decided to let her go with her daughters whenever she wished without any opposition or conditions. Enclosed with this notification was a letter Beauharnais was to give to the captain of the ship on which she would travel, a letter that the captain was to give directly to Duquesne-Guiton upon arrival and under no circumstances allow to fall into the hands of Madame Duquesne. That letter informed Duquesne that his wife indicated to Chamilly during his visit to Belesbat that she would soon do her duty on religion. But if she did not do so in the year of her stay in Martinique, the king wanted her sent back to France. The royal governor would of course bend his efforts to making her conversion a reality, thus not merely satisfying the king but preventing a further separation of the couple. No one had yet leveled, though, with his wife. "Madame Duquesne does not know of this order from His Majesty; you will let her know of it when you believe it necessary to do so."[41]

Whether Marie-Marguerite de Voutron ever went to the Antilles and whether she ever converted is unclear. Certainly, her ability to resist conversion for more than three decades after the Revocation, and in the face of royal insistence, rested upon the family's solidarity, the protective acquiescence of her husband and brother in her religious commitment, even to their own discomfiture. Duquesne-Guiton returned to France at the end of 1715 and reassumed his position as admiral on March 1, 1716.[42]

The Isle

The Mazières and Voutron became Catholic, then, gradually, facing royal coercion, testing repeatedly and for some years the determination of the crown to force their conversion, aided by the patience—even indulgence—of officials who exercised discretion that the letter of the law did not grant them. Their more or less unobtrusive entry into a new religion contrasted with the Prévost de Touchimbert's strong actions and strong signals of inclusion in the king's church. A similar pattern of strong action marked the move into Catholicism by the Isle who stayed in France, in particular the children of Isaac Isle. The family left behind in France by the expelled former defender of Protestantism in Saintonge and Aunis scattered along four of the paths opened at the Revocation to those who had been raised Protestant: lasting refusal, rapid conversion, resistance and eventual accommodation, or exile and return. His wife never made a sincere conversion, but the three surviving children accommodated sooner or later to the king's religion.

The eldest daughter, Henriette-Lidie, took the path of rapid conversion, abjuring a few months after the Revocation, on February 4, 1686, just after her father was sent into detention in Auvergne. Then on August 17, 1691, she became a novice at the Filles de la Visitation Sainte-Marie on the rue Saint-Antoine in Paris "of my own volition and without any constraint." A year later, on August 21, 1692, she took solemn vows as a nun in that house.[43]

The premises in which Henriette-Lidie would spend the remaining thirty-two years of her life were among the most beautiful buildings in all of Paris. The interiors were graced with luxurious furnishings and splendid artistic décor, as befitted the convent chosen by some of the kingdom's most eminent

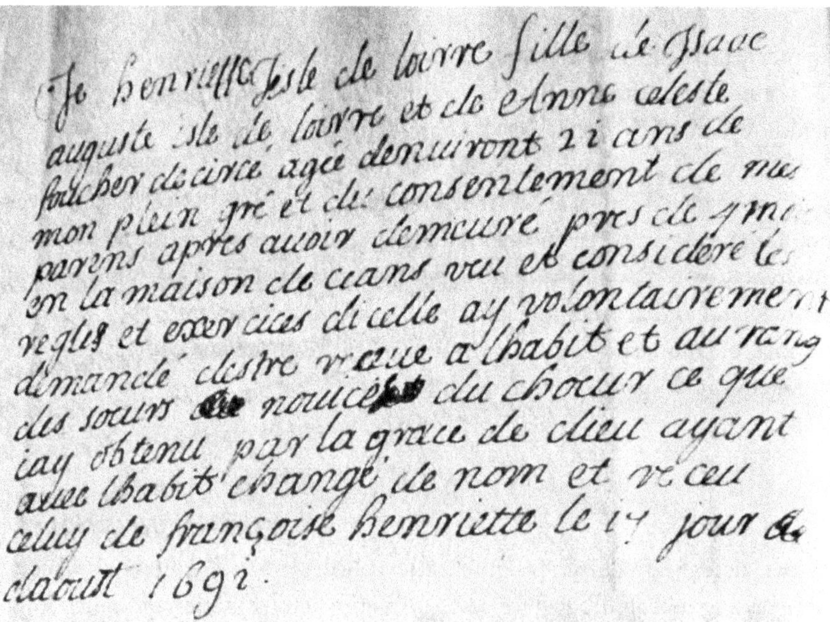

Je henriette Isle de loirre fille de Isaac
auguste isle de loirre et de Anne celeste
foucher de circé agée denuiront 21 ans de
mon plein gré et du consentement de mes
parens apres auoir demeuré pres de 4 mois
en la maison de ceans veu et consideré les
regles et exercices dicelle ay volontairement
demandé destre receue a l'habit et au rang
des soeurs novices du choeur ce que
iay obtenu par la grace de dieu ayant
auec l'habit changé de nom et receu
celuy de françoise henriette le 17 jour de
daoust 1691.

Figure 10.1 Vows of Henriette-Lidie Isle (Soeur Françoise Henriette), from Archives des monastères de la Visitation (Paris), *Livre du Noviciat*, n° 202. Courtesy of the Religieuses de la Visitation Sainte-Marie, Paris.

families for the education and professions of their daughters, the retreats of their widows, and their own funerary chapels. The convent's baroque chapel was designed by François Mansart and housed the tombs of the Frémyot, Coulanges, Sévigné, Ormesson, and Rabutin-Chantal families, and of the Superintendent of Finances Nicolas Fouquet. It was a great social privilege to become one of the three dozen choir nuns in this Visitation house, in an order founded in 1610 by Jeanne de Chantal and François de Sales.[44]

How did the daughter of a minor provincial nobleman make her way into such an exclusive convent in the capital? She may have been brought to the attention of the convent's superior by her maternal aunt, the Marquise de Circé (at least this is the claim in the obituary written for her years later at the convent).[45] Her mother's family, the Foucher, had gained significant court connections through the 1669 marriage of the Marquis de Circé, brother of Henriette-Lidie's mother, with Marie d'Angennes. The bride's paternal cousin was Julie d'Angennes, lady-in-waiting of the Queen, wife of the Duc de Montausier, governor of the dauphin, and daughter of the famous salon hostess the Marquise de Rambouillet. The bride's maternal uncle was the abbé Claude Le Clerc du

Figure 10.2 View of the Eglise des Filles Sainte-Marie, Rue Saint-Antoine, Paris. Etching by Israel Silvestre the Younger. Condé Museum, Chantilly. By permission of RMN-Grand Palais/Art Resource, NY.

Tremblay, almoner of the king; her great-uncle was the famed Père Joseph. Such connections could have laid the groundwork for Henriette-Lidie's entry into the Visitation on the rue Saint-Antoine.[46]

An irregular aspect of her profession there—her dowry—suggests, however, a court connection even more significant than the ties of her Foucher kindred. Payment of dowries by new nuns' families was expected to accompany their vows: Roger de Rabutin, Comte de Bussy, paid 12,000 *livres* for the entry of his daughter Jacqueline Thérèse in 1660, while the widow Marguerite de Maulévrier would pay 10,000 *livres* in 1697 for her daughter Madeleine Françoise Colbert.[47] Where could Henriette-Lidie have procured such funds? Her father was in exile in Holland, and her never-converted mother can hardly have been ready to step forward with a dowry. The king himself—"wishing to favor the pious plan that the Demoiselle Isle de Loire has devised"—filled the void left by the disintegration of the family that his own religious policies had provoked. On the day before her novice vows, he accorded her the 400 *livre* life annuity that made possible her entry into this highly regarded and highly visible convent. Behind this grace—perhaps also behind Henriette-Lidie's conversion—can be discerned the hand of Madame de Maintenon. One witness at her taking of the veil was Charles d'Aubigné, brother of Maintenon; the other witness was Abbé Milon, almoner of the king, who was one of the priests handpicked by Fénelon to accompany him on the mission sent to Saintonge and Aunis in November 1685—the very mission that tried and failed to convert the new nun's father.[48] When Henriette-Lidie signed her vows with the new name she adopted in religion, "Françoise Henriette," was it to honor Françoise d'Aubigné, Marquise de Maintenon that she did so?

Henriette-Lidie, daughter of the man who had led the defense of Protestant congregations in the Southwest, was a prize catch for Catholicism. At her death, the narrative written by her sisters in the convent and sent around to other houses of Visitation nuns made her life a Catholic exemplary tale. The young Henriette-Lidie was a *femme forte* (strong woman); well schooled in Protestant theology by her family and with a prodigious memory, she resisted with great fortitude and learning the ablest attempts to convert her. "The late Bishop of Saintes, after three hours of dispute that only the coming of nighttime terminated, could not help but admire the vivacious spirit of Mademoiselle de Loire, even as he bemoaned the deep darkness enveloping her." When consigned to a Paris convent after being caught attempting to flee the kingdom, she steadfastly refused, for many months, to question the faith in which she had been raised. But eventually, daily conversations with Abbé Fleury and study in the writings of Bishop Bossuet allowed her to see "how little good faith and uprightness those of the [Protestant] party possessed."[49]

After abjuring in the hands of Fleury, she became not only Catholic but, according to her obituary, an emotionally committed Catholic. "It can be said that the zeal of the House of God consumed her and that her only reason for living was to see the triumph of the Church. . . . Innumerable were the prayers and good works she did for this purpose and the tears she shed on this subject." She particularly loved those features of her new faith that Protestants specifically abhorred: frequent use of holy water and indulgences; the cult of saints, especially the Virgin; the presence of Jesus in the Eucharist; the pope as Jesus' vicar on earth; and Jesuits, one of whom was her special confidant for twenty-five years. "In a word, she created in this House the very model of the New Catholic, which she brought to life with pious and holy works."

Her family, "very zealous defenders of the Calvinist heresy," reacted with cruelty to her conversion. Her mother took away "her pearls and diamonds and all the ornaments appropriate to her social standing, gave her [to wear] a simple commoner's dress and let her lack for necessities." Her mother fed her only forbidden meats during Lent, so she spent her long weeks of penitence "practically without nourishment." Her father disinherited her and, fleeing to Geneva, would not see her again. One day when her maternal grandfather the Marquis de Circé came to visit, "she threw herself at his feet and said to him: *Without you my Father, without you I shall perish.*" The grandfather and aunt alerted the king, who moved Henriette-Lidie to the Nouvelles Catholiques in Paris. Madame de Maintenon offered her a splendid marriage, which she declined in favor of a religious vocation.

Despite her parents' cruelty, Sister Françoise Henriette remained faithful to them and was devastated that both remained in error. Her father was upright, courageous, and loving, though blindly unyielding on religion. Her mother played the villain in the piece, but Sister Françoise Henriette grieved to find her abjuration not to have been genuine.[50] Eventually, Sister Françoise Henriette's sorrows regarding her parents broke her temperament; "she was attacked by a complex of infirmities and by a languor that changed her natural gaiety into melancholy." A family broken apart by heresy turned on itself and consumed its finest part.

Death notices like that written for Sister Françoise Henriette were included in the circular letters that Visitation houses sent each other as a means of maintaining unity across the Order and of edifying each other with the inspirations occurring in each house. Such circular letters were mandated by the Order's founding documents; they were to be simple and exact narratives, respectful "without exaggerating," and "containing nothing that might be found risible by lay persons if they were to fall into their hands."[51] Because of her death notice, Sister Françoise Henriette's usefulness to the faith continued long after her death. In the spiritual literature published by the Visitation late in the nineteenth century, her story continued to make her a face of Counter-Reformation triumph. The order's *Année Sainte* suggested taking inspiration every November from the example of Henriette-Lidie's ordeal in heresy and her virtues in saving herself and others from it.[52] The differences between the two versions put out by the Visitation are inconsequential, easily explicable by the change of audience and period. But the differences between the Visitation narrative and the historical record on her life and her family are at once major and instructive for an understanding of story and history, in particular of the form in which both emerged from Louis XIV's persecution of Protestants.

The Visitation story relates that after the Revocation the Isle de Loire family attempted to flee to England on a merchant vessel out of La Rochelle, Henriette-Lidie in disguise as a sailor. In preparation, she learned to scale the riggings of ships with remarkable agility, much to the pride of her parents. The attempted escape failed because "he who watches over Israel had thoughts of mercy and peace for our dear Sister: the King's troops arrived at the port of La Rochelle at the very hour of the embarkation." A friend's inadvertently calling her "Mademoiselle" in their presence defeated her disguise and the family's plans for flight. Yet there is no other evidence that the family ever tried to escape. The correspondence of the intendant Arnoul provided a real-time tracking of Isaac Isle's behavior in the fall of 1685, without mentioning an attempted escape, and there was no time between the Revocation and Isaac's being taken into custody when such an escape attempt could have taken place.

Nor was the role Isaac Isle was made to play in the narrative one that he was allowed to play in his life. The obituary states that he "withdrew" to Geneva after disinheriting Henriette-Lidie because of her conversion and that he died in Geneva three months after (and ostensibly because of) her taking of vows. Yet he was imprisoned immediately upon the Revocation and then forcibly expelled from the kingdom in 1688, several years before his daughter settled upon her religious vocation. He did not have the power to disinherit her both because the law forbade Protestant parents from disinheriting their converting children[53] and because, having been banished from France, he had no property to convey or withhold. He did not die in Geneva but in Holland and not until 1695.

The Visitation narrative likewise reworks the story of Henriette-Lidie's conversion, setting it on Christmas Eve 1686 in a Paris convent under the aegis of the Abbé Fleury. Yet her abjuration took place at an earlier date in a different place and among different witnesses—on February 4, 1686, at Rochequairie, a property in Poitou of the Robineau family, in another of whose residences, La Vergne in the parish of Beaufou, she was then residing. Her absolution came from the curé of the parish of Saint-Etienne-du-Bois; the witnesses included François Chevalier de Saulx, a doctor of the Sorbonne who was well known for his success as a missionary in Poitou and would soon join the re-Catholization missions that strove, by converting the Protestants in the heart of the Cévennes, to forestall the rebellion of the Camisards.[54] The context, then, for her actual conversion was familial. The Robineau were allies and neighbors of the Foucher. Both families were formerly Protestant, now Catholic. Henriette-Lidie's grandfather, Jacques Foucher, had abjured around 1650 or 1660; her uncle Abimelech, who was baptized Protestant, abjured sometime between January 12, 1668, when he served as godfather at the baptism of Henriette-Lidie's brother Abimelech in the Saint-Savinien Protestant temple, and August 3, 1669, when he married in Paris. The grandfather could well have played the role in removing Henriette-Lidie from her mother's control that her death notice accords him, for he lived until 1686.[55] Very likely the Foucher were the "relations" whose consent Sister Françoise Henriette noted in her 1691 vows, given the absence of her father and the opposition of her mother. Like the Isle, both the Foucher and Robineau were families with deep Protestant roots that splintered at the Revocation, some individuals actively opposing their previous religion and some remaining in it. The boatload of escaping Protestants intercepted near Nantes in January 1687 carried a cousin of the Robineau with whom Henriette-Lidie was living.[56] But Daniel-Alexandre Robineau, with whose family Henriette-Lidie resided, was Catholic. Céleste Foucher lost her daughter Henriette-Lidie to the abjuring members of her own family before losing her to the Visitation.

The reworking of Henriette-Lidie's abjuration allows omission from the account of her entire sojourn among the Robineau, which included a puzzling episode: the possibility that she married and had a child. Documentation in the parish archives states that around the time of her abjuration Henriette-Lidie married Germanic Robineau, son of the family with whom she was residing at the time. He died on August 13, 1687, eighteen months after she abjured, suggesting that his death may have either ruptured plans for the marriage or made Henriette-Lidie a very young widow. A second item suggests the latter. The same parish archives state that a daughter of Germanic and "Lydie Ille de Loire" later married and named her own child Thérèse-Marguerite-Lydie;[57] use of the name Lydie—absent from previous Robineau namings but common in each generation of Isle, including a sister of Marie de La Rochefoucauld—seems to confirm the place of Henriette-Lidie Isle de Loire in this ancestry. The dates of Germanic's death are compatible with the date of Henriette-Lidie's move to the convent in Paris; she could have left the Robineau after Germanic's death. Whatever did happen was entirely omitted from the convent narrative of her life.

The Visitation account of Sister Françoise Henriette's life also made no mention of her siblings—an odd omission, since they both resisted conversion long after Henriette-Lidie entered religion, and the inclusion of a recalcitrant sister and brother would only have accentuated the brokenness of the heretical Isle de Loire family as well as her uniqueness within it. The omission of the siblings itself bespeaks the partial truth the narrative would tell.

The revision of Sister Françoise Henriette's story may have originated with her as she refashioned herself as a Catholic and strove to align her life with her new faith. Those who wrote the narrative no doubt had to rely on what they had heard from Françoise Henriette over the years. The effect of the narrative reworking was of course to give a Catholic meaning to Sister Françoise Henriette's life and through her life to establish a certain representation of the Revocation. Adding the attempted escape rendered the Isle de Loire parents disobedient toward the king as well as mistaken in religion. Emphasizing their daughter's independence, strength of mind, and intellectual gifts confirmed the power of the Catholic truth that could overcome such principled resistance. Moving her abjuration from the bosom of her maternal family to the convent made it an intellectual, rather than a worldly, conversion and, importantly, one effected by royal policy—the Revocation itself. The narrative pointedly identifies the catalyst with the king: "l'Abbé Fleury, later Precepteur of the Princes and then the King's Confessor." Leaving out her father's imprisonment and expulsion shifted coercion and persecution from the royal to the heretic side. Suffering was the work of family, from whom the convent, the king's actions, and royal personnel rescued her. In particular, then, the refigured story confirmed the wisdom and necessity of royal policies that removed children from Huguenot parents. All in all, it memorialized Louis XIV's Revocation as "an undertaking worthy of his religion and of his piety."

Finally, the reconfigured story reminded readers that the conflict was a matter for the present, 1724, not simply for the past. Céleste Foucher, the nun's mother, was evidence that the task was yet unfinished, for at the moment of the writing she was still alive and still lost to religious truth. "She still today maintains the dogmas [of the heresy] with an obstinacy that removes any hope of a return [to the Catholic Church].... Let us join together ... to obtain the conversion of a person who has indeed some very respectable qualities and whose example would be so useful for the edification of the holy Church." So the obituary became a call for renewed efforts vis-à-vis Huguenots. It was perhaps not coincidental that the obituary was composed precisely at a moment when royal pressure on Huguenots was more intense than at any time since the turn of the eighteenth century.[58] So powerful is ever the need to tell a story that, while ostensibly about the past, fits present circumstances.

None of the other Isle de Loire family members could have furnished such an exemplary tale—at least not until very late in their lives. Céleste Foucher and her youngest daughter Marie-Anne abjured soon after the Revocation, but without convincing the authorities of their sincerity. Early in 1693, the king asked "my cousin the Comtesse de Miossens" to take custody of thirteen-year-old Marie-Anne, removing her from her mother's care "on account of the bad education she might give her on the matter of the Religion." Reassuring Miossens that the child would not be a burden—she "will not be an expense for you, since she has some property for supporting herself"—Louis declared himself persuaded "that you will be agreeable to raising this Demoiselle at your side."[59]

"My cousin the Comtesse de Miossens," Marie-Elisabeth de Pons, was a great friend of Madame de Maintenon and part of the network of women—also including Miossens' first cousin Madame de Marsan—who worked with Maintenon on the conversion of Protestant daughters.[60] Miossens herself was from a long-time Protestant family. Down into the 1680s, she sponsored Protestant religious services in Bourg-Charente and in the environs.[61] She was also a familiar figure in Saint-Savinien. She had stood as godmother in the temple of Saint-Savinien in April 1667 beside the godfather Claude Isle des Groies, cousin of the man whose daughter she was commissioned to convert. Maintenon had been keen to have Miossens' conversion, writing from Versailles in August 1685: "Every effort must be made to convert Madame de Miossens." On January 30, 1686, Miossens made a court spectacle of her own conversion, abjuring in the hands of Bishop Bossuet in the chapel of the Château de Versailles and receiving a pension of 4,000 *livres* as a New Convert.[62]

What followed Marie-Anne's assignment to Miossens seems to have been a mix of microscopic attention from the crown, disorganization, and flight. In March 1694, just a year after the original order to take the child in hand, the king wrote again to Miossens asking her to explain why the girl was not with her. Bégon had delivered her the preceding year to Miossens, but now the superior of the Ursuline convent in Saint-Jean-d'Angély had written to Madame de Maintenon that the child was back with her mother, "a very bad Catholic." Where, the king wanted to know, was the girl now, and how had this happened when there had been no subsequent royal order permitting the child to leave Miossens? A month later, armed with responses from Bégon and Miossens, the crown ordered the mother placed in "the nearest Nouvelles Catholiques"—which turned out to be the Convent of La Providence in La Rochelle—and the daughter in a convent in Cognac. The mother was released after only three months, "well converted," though her conduct was to be under continual surveillance. She requested her child's return the following year, assuring the king that there was no longer any danger to her religious education. Four years later, though, Marie-Anne was still being held and remained an object of the king's attention; he approved the child's release from Cognac to her (Foucher) maternal grandmother in July 1697, so long as she was escorted directly into the grandmother's hands by "trusted persons"—no doubt to prevent a detour into the hands of her mother—and agreed that the child could collect the 300-*livre* pension she inherited from the family estate at Loire.[63]

Two years after her transfer to her grandmother's custody, Marie-Anne could be found in a convent in Saumur. Someone wished to transfer her to the Filles de Notre-Dame de Puyberland, which, with royal subsidies, specialized in the abjurations of daughters from Protestant noble families. The king declined the request, but one way or another Marie-Anne did make her way to the elite convent in Poitou, where, by some lengthy process of resolution, she not only came to terms with Catholicism but became a nun.[64]

Marie-Anne Isle de Loire entered the novitiate at Puyberland in 1704 and took full vows on March 5, 1706. She paid a dowry of 4,000 *livres*, an additional 3,000 *livres* for her own personal needs, and a further 1,000 *livres* to live in a comfortable private room with a fireplace, cabinet, table and chairs, and luxurious bed rather than in the dormitory. Where did these funds come from? From inheritance left to her at the death in 1705 of her only brother, Isaac-Auguste?

Figure 10.3 Portal of the former Convent of Puyberland. Photo property of the author.

Or from her still-Protestant mother, who did not pay the dowry for her sister at the Visitation in Paris? From her Catholic grandmother, who periodically took custody of her? The Foucher did have a special relationship to the Puyberland convent: Marie-Anne's second cousin Sophie-Elisabeth Foucher de Circé would be the last of the convent's abbesses, the one who turned the house over to the Revolution in 1791. Or from Madame de Maintenon, who had arranged her sister's dowry? The convent's abbess was the daughter of Maintenon's godfather, its founder may have been a cousin of Maintenon, and the convent had adopted many of the educational methods established by Maintenon at Saint-Cyr. The most remarkable aspect of Marie-Anne's comfortable sojourn in the elite convent was that she left it, at her request, for a stricter and less worldly order. In 1712 she petitioned the Bishop of Poitiers:

> That a short time after she had the good fortune to renounce the heresy of Calvin to enter into the bosom of the Church, she found herself inclined to embrace the religious life in a reformed community of the order of Saint Benedict. But her affairs did not allow her to fulfill that desire, which nonetheless increased in proportion as God let her taste the sweetness of the monastic life. She made her religious profession in the hands of His Excellency at the monastery of Puyberland, in the confidence that God thereafter would accord her the grace to fulfill her first designs. That she has suffered since then terrible pangs of conscience that could never be quieted by all the important and solid things that have been said to her in favor of staying with her prior commitment. On the contrary, she has always been, and still is, persuaded that her salvation is at risk if she delays obeying the voice that calls her to a more reformed order.

The bishop granted her request, and she left for the Trinité of Niort in July 1712.[65]

While Céleste Foucher refused to abjure, Henriette-Lidie made a rapid conversion, and Marie-Anne resisted but eventually conformed, the only surviving son of Isaac Isle went into exile and then returned to France. As late as 1695, Céleste Foucher was still identifying her son as "Izaac Auguste Isle, chevalier, Seigneur Marquis de Loire, gendarme in the Royal Guards" and as residing in Paris. But Isaac-Auguste had long since gone abroad. In April 1692, he begged for financial assistance in Geneva from the Calvinist community's Bourse Française, saying that he had left military service in France, where he was a naval officer, without bringing funds to support his voyage to join his father in the Refuge. He boldly asked for more than the usual handout and was given an especially generous six *Escus blancs*.[66] He would later receive help in Frankfurt-am-Main. When he passed through Berne, the English envoy's secretary Elie Bouhéreau, who had known Isaac Isle as a fellow Protestant in La Rochelle, issued a "Passport to Monsieur Jacob Île, who is leaving France, where he was an officer, to go, on religious grounds, to join Monsieur the Marquis de Loire, his father, in Holland or England." Son and father reunited in Nijmegen. Later that summer, Bouhéreau visited with Isaac in Nijmegen. Perhaps it was during this visit that Bouhéreau formed the opinion of the younger Isle's character that led him to insert a marginal note next to the passport record: "He is a Cheat."[67]

Father and son apparently stayed together in Nijmegen: in 1695, Isaac-Auguste joined the refugee church of which his father Isaac had been a member since his arrival in 1689. Father Isaac died in 1695, and the son returned home a few years later with the help of the French king after making an escape that mirrored in reverse those that he and other Protestants had hazarded from France. Pontchartrain informed the intendant Bégon in December 1703 that "The son of the Marquis de Loire from Aunis and another young man named Alain, originally from Jersey, escaped from the English fleet when it was in the harbor at Leghorn and have come from Toulon to Paris with the intention of proceeding to La Rochelle. The King is paying for their trip, and they are to depart immediately. They seem to have good intentions both concerning religion and for His Majesty's service. He ordered me to alert you to their departure and to keep an eye on them. I ask you to make an effort to let me know what becomes of them and what they end up doing so that I can report to His Majesty."[68]

In April 1704, Isaac-Auguste petitioned the Parlement of Paris to permit him to access income from his father's estates at Loire. The court recognized him as Marquis de Loire and as heir of his father, the predecessor Marquis de Loire, and granted him 400 *livres* as a subsistence allowance to be taken from the court-ordered leases imposed on his father's former properties.[69] He then died in Saint-Savinien without posterity the following year at the age of thirty-one and was buried in the tomb of his ancestors. His mother, Isaac's widow, Céleste Foucher de Circé, never left France; she remarried after Isaac's death in exile and outlived all her children.[70] Isaac's line of the Isle family came to an end; in 1715, when Claude Masse visited Loire, the seigneur was Le Moyne de Sérigny.[71]

PART FOUR

RESETTLING ABROAD

11

Into the Refuge

Josias' first act, upon reaching his destination, was his *reconnaissance*. Even before seeing Marie and the children, from whom he had been separated for more than a year, he wanted to put himself right with God. "He wrote me from Holland—the place of safety, as he called it—because he wished to make his *reconnaissance* before being distracted by the joy of seeing his family, which was very dear to him." Josias signed the register at the Rotterdam church on June 27, 1688, in a steady and precise hand that bespoke much practice with writing. Arriving refugees often hastened to make their *reconnaissance*, sharing with the receiving congregation their reasons for abjuring in France as well as the ordeals and sufferings they had steadfastly endured, performing in this way their own righteousness, commitment to religious truth, and eligibility for admission to the rites of the Church. Susanne made hers in Exeter a week after her arrival.[1] Marie made hers in Dartmouth as soon as she stepped onto English soil, delaying her reunion with her children in Exeter to do so. Reclaiming the religion they had been forced to renounce back in France was one way of bringing familiarity into an alien and disorienting situation. Another was reknitting networks of kinship and friendship.

In Holland, in particular, the Church that functioned as the exiles' portal to the Refuge replaced the Reformed community whose destruction in France had deprived them not only of religious expression but of social base. Immigrants from French-speaking Flanders a century earlier had established a network of Walloon churches across the Northern Netherlands. In them, the Huguenots' language was spoken, the liturgy and governance structure were similar to the ones they knew, and charity from the congregations could be drawn upon by needy arrivals. Furthermore, from its origins in flight from repression within the Spanish Empire, Dutch Calvinism had drawn a "theology of exile," a sense of "Dutch Israel" as God's chosen people in which Huguenots could find echoes of their own travails in Babylon. Because of this, and because Dutch individuals and government bodies offered them generous support, material as well as ideological, "the French emigrants quickly felt at ease

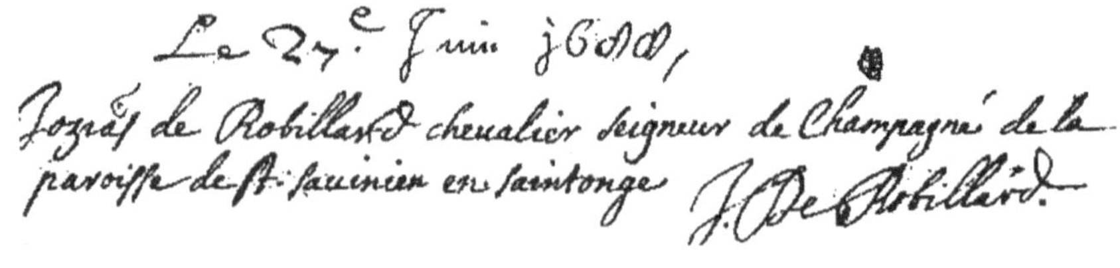

Le 27e Juin 1688,
Josias de Robillard chevalier seigneur de Champagné de la paroisse de St Sauvinien en Saintonge J. De Robillard

Figure 11.1 Reconnaissance by Josias de Robillard de Champagné, June 27, 1688, at the Waals Hervormde Kerk te Rotterdam. Courtesy of the Stadsarchief Rotterdam.

in the United Provinces and less out of their element than elsewhere."[2] Their refound churches allowed the 35,000–50,000 Huguenot arrivals in the era of the Revocation to feel, in religious terms, even more at home than they had recently felt in France. Françoise de Beringhen, an associate of Marie de La Rochefoucauld in exile, expressed this verbally and materially when she donated "several pieces of silver that she held from the late Madame de Beringhen of happy memory" to The Hague's Walloon Church and a silver baptismal basin to the Rotterdam Walloon Church "in appreciation for receiving from God the grace to hear his word and participate in Holy Communion there for the first time after leaving France in 1688."[3]

Marie de La Rochefoucauld moved through the network of Walloon churches during the three or so years when she was searching for a permanent home. At first she must have briefly associated herself with the temple in The Hague, while staying there with her Touchimbert nieces. In the late spring of her first year abroad, though, a new French church was established in a village just outside The Hague, Voorburg, to which she had moved with the nieces and their brother. The pastor of the new congregation was the younger Jean Yver, son of the pastor in Saint-Jean-d'Angély who had baptized several of the Champagné children. Then, on July 3, 1689, while Josias was in England, about to go with the English army to Ireland, Marie was received a member of the French Church in Amsterdam. It was there that she would learn of Josias' death and write her escape memoir. As late as October 9, 1690, when she drew up a notarized inventory of her possessions, she was living in a house on the Lauriergracht in the section of Amsterdam called by the refugees *Le Jardin* and today known as *Jordaan*. But her stay there was brief; she closed the circle of her wanderings by returning to The Hague in 1691, this time permanently. The family settled there; the three youngest children joined its French church as they came of age: Gédéon in April 1695, Marianne in October 1695, and Julie in July 1699.[4]

The network of Walloon churches served Huguenot refugees as a liminal space between the land of arrival and the land of origin, an alternative to being immersed without ballast into a culture at once familiar and alien. In some respects Dutch culture would have seemed congenial. It maintained a court society, which was familiar to French nobles such as Marie, and an "anti–Louis XIV state of mind" incubated by its war experiences in the 1670s may have comforted refugees betrayed by their king. On the other hand, Dutch society was far more open, egalitarian, and commercial than even the trading cities of France. It had a history of welcoming and sheltering persecuted minorities—Mennonites, Quakers, Lutherans, Anabaptists, Socinians, Puritans—and so Huguenots like Marie de La Rochefoucauld found themselves in a society more diverse than they had ever known. The United Provinces were a decentralized republic, a loose federation of seven provinces and quasi-independent towns in which multiple provincial and municipal corporations and elites shared power. The Stadholder was unlike a king, an ambiguous figure of the Union: head of the military establishment but without judicial or fiscal powers, "more an arbiter than an initiator in political matters." The cultural similarities and differences meant that between the refugees and the Dutch "brotherhood was expected, but remained uncertain."[5]

Like the network of Walloon churches, the dense colonies of fellow French into which refugees clustered created a space in which new arrivals could regulate their relationship to the familiar-unfamiliar land of welcome. Unlike the network of Walloon churches, though, networks of friends and kin were not ready-made in the Refuge; they needed to be constructed by the refugees themselves, often from connections that back home had been distant, indirect, even mere hearsay. Escape narratives often describe the welcome and hospitality given upon the author's arrival by refugees from back home. Susanne's memoir noted the reception her advance party received in Exeter: "numbers of our other brothers, like us come out of France and of our acquaintance . . . welcomed us with so much pleasure and generosity that I believed I already enjoyed the delights of paradise." Jean Cabrol was welcomed in Geneva by "many people I knew," including an aunt and an old neighbor from Nîmes. Jacob Babault's memoir conceptualizes his trek across Holland and up the Rhine as a relay from acquaintance to relative to former neighbor.[6]

Similarly, Marie de La Rochefoucauld expressed wonder in her memoir that though she came out of France knowing only one name in Rotterdam—that of "Monsieur Faneuil"—she was immediately surrounded there by persons to whom she was known. Monsieur Puychenin, who had helped arrange Marie's escape, and Mesdemoiselles de Martel were quickly found for her by Faneuil. She was taken in at The Hague by "Mademoiselle de Touchimbert and my nieces" and then at Voorburg by these nieces and their brother. The former neighbor Saint-Surin had of course joined the Champagné in Exeter before they continued on to Holland. A Mademoiselle de Mazières had come with them out of France. The two pastors Yver had left France for Amsterdam in the weeks following the Revocation. Marie is sure to have known before she left Berneré that friends and relations would be at her destination to greet her when she arrived.

These assorted greeters lent, indeed, a veneer of continuity to Champagné lives before and after emigration. Yet the individuals whom Marie mentions most often in her journal and those participating in the milestones of the Champagné family in Holland were not for the most part refound friends and kin from Berneré; her most consequential sociability and support networks were in a real sense new, only in outline echoing those formerly enjoyed in the home country. The Isle were absent; Isaac Isle was in The Hague when Marie arrived, receiving charity of 31 *florins* 10 on April 3, 1689, from the French Church there, and lived on in Nijmegen but outside Marie's ongoing circle.[7] Isaac's son Isaac-Auguste came to join his father in Nijmegen but never appears in Champagné records. Isaac's nephew Treillebois des Rabesnières appears once in Marie's account book, but only once. So does "Mademoiselle de Monlevrier," a sister or aunt of Berneré's neighbors at Agonnay. Pierre Vincent Nicolas de Voutron turned up in 1714 at the wedding of Champagné daughter Henriette-Silvie; the young Nicolas de Lisleferme, a cousin of the Nicolas de Voutron, appears once in Marie's account book. Renaud de Pons de Tors, Seigneur du Douhet and husband of Marie's refugee cousin Judic de La Rochefoucauld, reconnects with the family as godfather in 1693 for Susanne's firstborn son. The Prévost de Touchimbert disappeared from Champagné records after the earliest days, the women apparently moving to England and the brother leaving in 1688 with the army of William of Orange.[8] The Puychenin and Chateigner who helped in the escape appeared no more. Mademoiselle de Mazières dropped from sight.

New names came to dominate the Champagné milieu in the Refuge. Madame de Pardaillan, Madame de Villars, and Mademoiselle des Roches are named in the section of Marie's journal devoted to her financial affairs after Josias' death.[9] Susanne's memoir names the Comte de Soissons. Witnesses to the marriage contract of Marie's daughter Henriette-Silvie included Henriette de Passac and no fewer than seven individuals from the intermarried *parlementaire*-financial clan of Le Coq, Beringhen, Muysson, and Rambouillet. Witnesses at Susanne's wedding and godparents for her children included Princess Henriette d'Anhalt, Charles Bonnard du Marests-d'Antoigny, Charlotte de Venours, Henri Boisbellaud de Montacier de Lislemarais, Du Fay de La Taillée, Henri de Boisse de Pardaillan, Mesdemoiselles de La Primaudaye, and Angélique and Louise Martel—presumably the same "Mesdemoiselles de Martel" who were among Marie's first greeters in Rotterdam. The absence of former associates and the prominence of names not included in the

Champagné records back in France lend a veneer of unfamiliarity and rupture to the refugee experience.

Looked at more closely, the group formation visible in Marie de La Rochefoucauld's case was something between continuity and rupture, a sort of hybrid network structurally similar to those enjoyed back in France but drawing together previously unknown individuals from previously known lineages. These individuals were, like the Champagné, shards from formerly Protestant kindreds that shattered under the pressure of the Revocation, carrying most of the kindred into the king's religion.

The Martel refugees exemplify this process of group formation in the Refuge. The history of the Martel in Saintonge began during the Wars of Religion, when the great Protestant Pons family fell into distaff and the heiress Anne de Pons married François Martel, son of a noble family in Normandy. Their grandson Gédéon, Comte de Marennes, fought alongside Saint-Surin's father at the Siege of La Rochelle and married his sister Elisabeth, which linked the Martel to the Champagné's social set. When the granddaughter of Gédéon and Elisabeth, Uranie de La Cropte, was orphaned in the 1660s, Saint-Surin, the child's first cousin and future husband of Susanne de Robillard, was named her guardian, and the family council gathered together a roster of persons from the Champagné story: Renaud de Pons, Marquis de Tors and Seigneur du Douhet; Charles de Villedon, Seigneur de Magezy; the child's distant cousin Louis de Bassompierre, Bishop of Saintes; Saint-Surin's brother Hector de La Motte Fouqué, Seigneur de Tonnay-Boutonne.[10] When Saint-Surin and his wife Susanne de Robillard decided not to return to France after the death of his elder brother Hector, Uranie, now married to the Comte de Soissons, inherited the barony of Tonnay-Boutonne, which would have belonged to Saint-Surin if he had not emigrated and then to the three sons of the widow Susanne.

These Martel so well known to the Champagné were not, however, the Martel who welcomed Marie to Holland, for those in France had become Catholic at or before the Revocation. Saint-Surin's aunt Elisabeth, Madame Martel, was unflinchingly Protestant,[11] but her daughters abjured and joined the Martel's more famous and powerful relations the d'Albret[12] in court circles deeply invested in conversions. Daughter Judith Martel lived with her d'Albret cousins at the Paris home of the Maréchal and Maréchale d'Albret, whose closest companions were the Duchesse de Richelieu and the widow Scarron, later Madame de Maintenon.[13] She lived, then, with the woman who in 1680 would found the Nouvelles Catholiques at Pons for reeducation of Protestant girls (the Comtesse de Marsan), the woman who would facilitate the conversion of a daughter of Isaac Isle (the Comtesse de Miossens), and the woman who may have played a role in the move of Marie's own daughter Thérèse into the convent of the Filles de Notre-Dame (Madame de Maintenon).

It was, rather, kin of kin or kin of friends with whom Marie de La Rochefoucauld formed a bond in Holland: descendants of the Martel de Saint-Just to whom the Normandy holdings of the family fell when the heiress Anne de Pons drew François Martel away to Saintonge.[14] The famed Norman refugee Isaac Dumont de Bostaquet mentioned the Martel family in the lengthy listing of his relations that begins his memoir: "Some children of the baron de Saint-Just left, Monsieur Martel and Mesdemoiselles his sisters, two of whom took refuge with him in Holland along with Mademoiselle de La Taillée, daughter of the eldest sister of the said [baron] Martel, who was a prisoner in a convent in France for reasons of religion."[15] This succinct sentence unlocks the dynamic by which Marie de La Rochefoucauld found a new sociability network in the Refuge: Martel to Du Fay de La Taillée and then from La Taillée to Bonnard du Marest d'Antoigny, Gourjault de Venours, Gourjault de Passac, and Olbreuse. The aunt of the three Martel refugees married Louis Du Fay de La Taillée, whose two sisters married Bonnard du Marest d'Antoigny and Gourjault de Passac. Their first cousin was Eléonore d'Olbreuse, Duchess of Zell. This matrix of individuals whom Marie de La Rochefoucauld had not known in France would henceforth be vital to her family's prosperity. Bonnard served as godfather to Susanne's son Henry Charles Frederic in 1701 and took as his second wife in 1712 Marie's daughter Henriette-Silvie. A Passac daughter stood godmother for one of Susanne's children, and Charlotte de Venours, known as madame de Villars after her 1701 marriage at Celle to Gabriel de Malortie de Villars, became one of Marie de La Rochefoucauld's closest allies. The Martel in Holland connected the Du Fay and all their alliances to their first cousin Eléonore d'Olbreuse, Duchess of Zell.[16] Marie's closest associates until her last years in the Refuge were the Martel, Bonnard, Du Fay, Venours, and Olbreuse; Susanne's continuing livelihood and the futures of her sons also came to depend upon this new matrix of friends stitched together in the Refuge.

By comparison with her life at Berneré, then, Marie now drew her contacts from farther away, both geographically and socially, from friends of former friends or distant kin of kin. These individuals were, moreover, shards of previously intact families splintered by the Revocation: a Bonnard here, a Du Fay there, a few Martel-Saint-Just. Like the Champagné, they were refugees not only from religious persecution but also from broken families. Elisabeth Bretinauld, Madame de Pardaillan, a cousin of Saint-Surin, nicely illustrates this. The Bretinauld had been Protestants from the time of the Wars of Religion, alongside the La Motte Fouqué, Martel, Robillard, and Isle. Elisabeth's marriage in 1668 and her brother Henri's conversion to Catholicism in 1677 trapped her in a two-front conflict—one with her brother and one with her in-laws—in which religious difference became intertwined with competitions for property. Her brother first tried to use religion to enhance his hold on her property and subsequently tried to wriggle out of the religious framework for the same purpose when Madame de Pardaillan's situation changed. Well before the Revocation, as heir of their parents, the brother was charged with fulfilling the terms of her dowry, but he withheld the funds, claiming that because of his conversion his mother had increased his sister's share of the inheritance and reduced his, which would violate the king's decrees. After her escape, her brother claimed all her property and was awarded it on October 30, 1687.[17] Madame de Pardaillan had been equally estranged and under attack from the family of her late husband Henry Escodéca de Boisse, Marquis de Pardaillan Mirambaud. They would circulate the news of her departure in language that reeked of disdain for her and her "thoughtless zeal": "What she is blamed for is having undertaken this voyage to England knowing the prohibitions from the king and how important it is to obey. . . . We may well thank God at seeing heresy banished from France without a drop of blood being shed. Blessed and praised be He forever!"[18]

The sociability network Marie enjoyed in the Refuge illuminates the dynamics of Huguenot resettlement abroad, particularly the extent and pace of assimilation—loss of one identity and adoption of another. While Marie's new network embraced individuals previously unknown and persons who had lost the kin contexts they had once enjoyed in France, it was as exclusively noble as what its members had left behind. No nonnobles other than pastors, financial brokers, and notaries found their way into the pages of Marie's journal. Her adaptation to exile did not, then, bear out the claim that the Refuge was socially modernizing in that it effaced class divisions and incubated shared national feeling.[19] Nor did the Dutch enter her pages, with the exception of these local professionals and a few contacts Marie says she gained early on at the Orange court, primarily to help advance her eldest son. Her alliances preserved status distinctions and stretched laterally beyond Holland's borders, to England and Germany, rather than into Dutch society. The refugee cocoon seems to have enclosed Marie de La Rochefoucauld as fully within a Dutch city as separate Huguenot colonies did in Prussia or Huguenot towns did in Ireland. Marie de La Rochefoucauld would live very nearly as long in Holland as she had lived in France, but her memoir and account book give precious few indications of her connecting with it.

Such a process of group formation—between individuals previously unknown broken off from kindreds known—depended upon refugees' ability to make clear their own identity and to learn the identity of others. The prominence of genealogical information in Huguenot escape memoirs responded to this need to let other refugees know who one was so that appropriate new social groups could connect the shards of the old. Dumont de Bostaquet, for example, devotes the opening section of his memoir to detailed listings of his French properties and to extended namings of military colleagues and the families—aristocrats and nobles of Normandy and Paris—with whom he had connections or "friendships"—that is, to mapping his status, his place, his identity in Old Regime society by dropping the names of the persons with whom he belonged. This was partly for professional reasons, to demonstrate his social standing and hence eligibility for employment in William of Orange's army. It was also a means of reaching out for connections with new individuals in the Refuge who were kin or friends of his extended kin back home, of identifying himself to others with whom he might forge a new social matrix.[20]

This shuffling of social matrices from pieces of old ones, with the attendant need to broadcast and recognize identities, made the Refuge a confusing place. The French ambassador d'Avaux found it so, repeatedly being hoodwinked by persons misrepresenting their identity, their religious affiliation, or their desire to return to France. "Most of the refugees invent and put out so many different things that many people find it impossible to believe there is not a kernel of truth in them." In return, pastor Jurieu warned the faithful against the falsities of Catholics: "It is necessary to be on guard on all sides when dealing with Popery; it can be said that in this religion lying is everywhere . . . for anything goes when seducing . . . a dreadful tissue of fables, lies, false facts, suppositions, frauds, double-dealings, fake news, all tending to seduce and to get them to step into the trap."[21] No wonder that Marie de La Rochefoucauld, too, succumbed to the impostures of the Refuge.

Two Stories Untold

He claimed to be from Angoumois and to be a relation of friends and kin. He said his first cousin Boismolé married the aunt of Madame de Pardaillan. He said he was related to the Maulévrier, who were more or less next-door neighbors, at Agonnay, to the Champagné back in Saintonge. Perhaps it was these claims that made Marie de La Rochefoucauld believe the Sieur de Tillieres was someone she could rely upon when she arrived in Holland without Josias toward the end of 1687.

Tillieres wrote d'Avaux that when Marie reached Holland after several months of recuperation in Exeter, he was among the first to greet her. He hoped, he told the ambassador, to establish a relationship that would allow him to exploit her: "Madame de Champagné, newly arrived as I informed you, told me she wished to come live in this place with her seven children. I am searching for a house in my neighborhood for her, and I hope that that will prove useful to us." Immediately he was able to get information from her: about friends and relatives who wrote from back home that they were preparing to escape; about the person in Saintonge who served as intermediary addressee for letters the refugees sent to friends and kin back home; the identity of the person in La Rochelle who had abetted Marie's escape, an identity Marie would decline to name even in the memoir of her escape she would write in her private journal. Marie's revelations allowed Tillieres to tell Versailles many months before his escape that her husband Josias was preparing to leave.[22]

Tillieres' efforts to stop Josias' escape failed, despite the information Marie unthinkingly furnished to him, but Tillieres did succeed in turning Josias from a target into an informant. When Josias rejoined the family in Holland seven months after Marie's arrival, Tillieres learned the details of his trip from Josias' own mouth, for Tillieres was among the first persons to whom Josias paid a visit. On the very day following Josias' *reconnaissance* in Rotterdam, Tillieres wrote d'Avaux that Josias had come by ship, from Dieppe, "from which close to three hundred persons have left in the past month carrying incredible sums, crowds arriving there from all sides seeking to embark. He went to a clandestine service and to various assemblies that are held in the town in broad daylight. He says that Psalms are sung aloud and all the other exercises of the R.P.R. are performed there." Three days later, Josias visited Tillieres again, continuing their conversation in Tillieres' home. Josias related—and Tillieres reported—a second description of his escape: that he had embarked at Dieppe on June 15 with fifty-six persons on a Dieppe ship bound for Rotterdam: "that he had his boxes and a valet put on board without the slightest difficulty. There was in this vessel nearly a hundred thousand *francs* in cash, which have been put in the hands of various merchants in Rotterdam. He also told us that this ship was to return to Dieppe at the first opportunity." Once again the spy's intent—catching the escapees—was clear, and again he suggested how the authorities back in France might effect the capture through the information Josias provided: "he did not tell us the name of the vessel or of the captain: I should hope that the day of its departure will make that known."[23]

As Tillieres tapped the circles of family and friends to which Marie de La Rochefoucauld belonged, Josias continued to serve as a source of actionable information for him. Tillieres reported that a minister in Bourg-Charente named Loaquet, who had ostensibly converted in order to stay in France, was secretly still Protestant and still exercising his ministry. "I got this bit of news from two persons of whom one was the Sieur de Champagné." Others whom Tillieres cited as his duped informants included Madame de Pardaillan, her son, Renaud de Pons, d'Olbreuse, Treillebois des Rabesnières, and the Touchimbert sisters. Jean Yver, too, formerly the pastor in Saint-Jean-d'Angély, fell into Tillieres' trap. He showed Tillieres a letter naming those in his old parish who were ready to leave. He also told the spy where he had hidden his library in Saint-Jean-d'Angély when he could not bring it along, a nugget of information that Tillieres passed on to d'Avaux with suggestions as to how the books might be seized. Yver let Tillieres know the name of a merchant in Bourg-Charente who served as the middleman for letters between dozens of refugees in Holland and their families in the environs of Jarnac, and also transmitted funds for them into the Refuge.[24]

Ministers like Yver and lay persons like Marie de La Rochefoucauld knew Tillieres as a person who day in and day out worked in the religious and secular interest of the refugees. Tillieres took the lead, for example, in establishing the first new French church set up in Holland after the Revocation, Marie's church—briefly—in Voorburg. On February 14, 1688, "the Marquis de Tillier and de Bassompierre" addressed a meeting of the town council of Delft, asking permission to establish a French Church in Voorburg to serve the refugees settling there. In exchange for the permission, Tillieres offered to cover all the costs of a church for ten years, guaranteed that the refugees would not request any assistance, and promised that charitable donations collected during services would provide relief for the village's poor. He further proposed the younger Jean Yver, the twenty-seven-year-old son of the Champagné's former pastor, as founding minister for the new church. Then in the very month when Marie de La Rochefoucauld's memoir notes with some pride her move to Voorburg—"I was the first French woman to take a house there, and six months later we numbered sixty refugees of good family"—the Delft authorities approved, the Synod meeting at Campen appointed Yver, and he took up his duties in the new Voorburg French Church. With respect to the aftermath, however, Marie's candor was constrained, for the summer of 1688 was a season of premature ends.

The Voorburg church collapsed due to young Yver's personal indiscretions—and, one can presume, the death of the congregation's sponsor and funder. The banns for young Yver's marriage were read in Amsterdam on June 18, he married there on July 8, and the precocious birth of his first child in August led the Synod to depose him in September "for a grave transgression." The congregation dwindled; in less than two years it had virtually no members. Religious exercises were suspended by the Synod in August 1690.[25] The refugees had moved elsewhere; even Marie had moved off to Amsterdam.

And Tillieres had been killed. At 5 A.M. on the morning of August 19, 1688, as William of Orange gathered forces for an invasion of England, as French officials scrambled to decipher the prince's intentions, and as Josias prepared to join the invasion, a dozen Dutch guards sent by the Court of Justice presented themselves at his home. Invading the courtyard, they confronted Tillieres, sword in hand; he took his stand in the doorway and cried out that he would never be taken alive. Before the sun rose, and after a quarter-hour melee in which two archers were wounded by his sword, Tillieres lay dead of a gunshot.[26]

Who did him in? The timing of the assassination raises suspicions: just weeks earlier, Tillieres had requested to come in from the cold, to be allowed to return to France with royal permission. Had his French handlers lost their need for the spy? Or had Tillieres perhaps requested repatriation because he sensed his cover was unraveling and then simply delayed too long to escape the retribution of those he betrayed? D'Avaux disclaimed any hand in the death but noted that rumors circulated by the Prince of Orange's men were linking the spy to him, as a way of discrediting their enemy's ambassador. He speculated, with relief, that the guards had not found any papers that would incriminate the French operation, since he continued to hear support for his spy from the French community: "it is not known yet how and why he came to be suspected, and most of the refugees still said after his death that no one had welcomed them or assisted them more than he."[27] The refugees' historian Elie Benoist would later write that he knew of Tillieres' betrayal of the community. Indeed, Benoist claimed, from what seems to have been his inside knowledge, that the Huguenot community itself lay behind the murder of the spy.

> This man, who had never had any religion, played the Protestant in Holland. He accorded all the refugees a welcome that made them think of him as their father. He gave money to those who needed it: he procured positions for them that were appropriate to their social standing. He founded a sort of colony at Voorburg, a convenient and agreeable place situated between The Hague, Leyden, and Delft. There he drew together a church and in this way gained the confidence and esteem of all the refugees. But it was soon surmised that he only affected this appearance of piety in order to commit his blackest betrayals more easily. . . . When enough proofs had been gathered of the betrayals of this villain, who hoped, no doubt, by these new crimes to obtain pardon for his old sins, the State gave the order to arrest him. The Grand Provost went to Voorburg to seize him and had him killed before his eyes, because he had set himself up to resist arrest. The Provost was believed to have had a secret order to have him killed rather than taking him alive, for fear that it would be more awkward to try him in court and thereby give France an opportunity to claim him or retaliate in some damaging fashion, whereas nothing could result from the death of a man killed while resisting the Ministers of justice with a sword and pistol in his hands.[28]

Benoist noted the impact of this incident for the refugee community, "who, after having been so shamefully betrayed by a villain who seemed to desire nothing other than helping them, no longer knew whom to trust."[29]

As someone both "welcomed" and "assisted" by Tillieres, Marie de La Rochefoucauld may have been quite affected by the unmasking and death of a man who had made himself her confidant. In the memoir she wrote two years later, Marie did not mention him, naming instead the Martel and Touchimbert as her first greeters in the Refuge. But he was there at her arrival, and her omission of Tillieres from her family's story of escape and resettlement was a tacit denial of what by the time of her writing she knew had been a grave fault. Equally a denial was her claim in the memoir that she had kept everything she heard close to her chest: "I did not dare tell anyone because there are spies everywhere; when anyone asks me for news, I pretend not to know any."[30] Marie's claim of caution was an implicit self-exoneration that erased from her story the role she had played in providing the spy with reportable information on the escape plans of Josias and others who communicated with her. She left her misplaced trust a story untold.

The Death of Monsieur de Champagné

That same summer of 1688, within weeks of making his *reconnaissance* in Rotterdam and reuniting with his family in The Hague, Josias de Robillard enrolled in the Dutch army, which was preparing to descend upon England. Marie noted Josias' departure in her memoir and repeated what pastor Jean Yver relayed to her a year later of his death: "He fell ill at Belfast, where he was attended by Monsieur de La Garde, a minister, who confirms what many people tell me and especially Monsieur de La Melonière, who has never seen anyone make such a beautiful end or say such edifying things as my dear husband said to him." Whether because she did not know more or because she did not wish others to know what she knew, she left Josias' death a story largely untold.

The Stadholder welcomed into his invasion force several hundred refugee army officers, who offered him both physical and symbolic benefits: both much-needed manpower and a sharpened self-image as defender of the international Protestant cause against Louis XIV. Rather than creating specifically French regiments, William took several dozen refugee officers into his own Life Guards and attached others to the Red and Blue Dragoons on the Dutch establishment. Two French colonels enrolled refugee volunteers: L'Estang in the cavalry, La Melonière in the infantry. The ambassador d'Avaux notified Louis XIV on October 19: "I have had the honor, Sire, of telling Your Majesty that all the French officers who were here went off with the Prince of Orange, even some of those who never served before embarked with the fleet." According to the ambassador, Orange's invasion force would include some "556 infantry officers distributed in the battalions, 180 cavalry dispersed in the squadrons, and 60 volunteers like Glatigny, La Caillemotte, a son of Monsieur de Beringhen, and others like them who are not attached to any corps."[31]

Why Josias enrolled is puzzling. He was more than forty years old. Unlike Isaac Isle, he had no known experience in the military. Moreover, during the year he spent alone at Berneré, he had been unwell, dispirited, and reluctant to leave. Why, in the aftermath of depression, illness, and longing for his wife and family, would he have left again so soon, in an unfamiliar role on a mission certain to be physically demanding? Marie's memoir offers no clues whatsoever. The two lines separating his *reconnaissance* and his departure were notably terse, withholding, tight-lipped: "My dear husband made his *reconnaissance* on Sunday, after which we went to meet our children in Voorburg, where we lived together until September 13, when the Prince of Orange left The Hague to go to England. My dear husband was made an incorporated captain in the regiment of Monsieur de Scravemour, a Dutch nobleman and friend of the Prince." Did tension between the spouses push Josias to depart? Hints of tension had appeared earlier, but Marie expressed great joy upon his arrival in Holland and at the end of the diary deep sadness about his death. Why did she not say more about the motives for renewed separation? Why, if her children were her intended audience, did she not provide them with an explanation for the loss of their father? Did she assume that the elder children already knew the reasons

Figure 11.2 William's Departure from the Netherlands in November 1688. Etching by Romeyn de Hooghe, 1688. Courtesy of the Cantor Center for Visual Arts, Stanford University.

and yet not wish to enlighten those who were too young to understand at the time but would read the diary later?

Josias may simply have been keen for employment. He and Marie did not arrive in the Refuge destitute, but the prospect of supporting a large family indefinitely without additional income may have been intimidating. The Dutch authorities had been forthcoming with subventions for refugee officers, granting three sets of pensions for them in the two years following the Revocation. The three "promotions" of 100,000 *florins,* 50,000 *florins,* and 30,000 *florins* made the military men, according to one refugee, "the most fortunate after the ministers . . . they live in ease." But by the summer of 1688, it was greatly uncertain whether another "promotion" would be forthcoming. "It is feared that after this promotion the door will be closed, and there will be no new one. Only the places of the dead will be filled by those arriving."[32] William's buildup in anticipation of the invasion of England provided what the refugees asked and more—but for many, in the end, far less than they would have hoped.

Still, military service imposed up-front costs that might or might not be recouped over time. Dumont de Bostaquet, the Norman gentleman who penned a detailed memoir of the expeditions to England and Ireland, noted "the heavy expense I was obliged to make" when he enlisted. And little personal honor was on offer: too many humiliations of rank and pay attended Josias' enrollment for that. The lesser status of those like him who lacked French army service affected morale: "These officers who came directly from French service were preferred to the others who had not served for some time. That elicited jealousies and murmurs." As an incorporated officer he might get a bounty when he signed—Bostaquet received one in Holland—but he would have no command, belong to no company permanently, and be paid only when on active service. Huguenots often reported that they were the last to be paid even when on duty. Bostaquet describes how he, as an irregular officer, was shuffled from outfit to outfit and how, "depending upon the corps where they were, [the incorporated officers] had the misfortune of always being lodged last and nearly always very badly."[33]

Perhaps Josias felt some social pressure to join up, since so many French noblemen were doing so. Marie speaks of his enrolling "with all the other French men," as if it were an expectation. Few former French officers found places in the Dutch army immediately after the Revocation, but, according to Bostaquet, as soon as it became known that William intended to go to England, "The refugees carrying the sword, officers and others, generally went to The Hague and gave their names to be enrolled in this holy war. . . . Their numbers were very large, and the aged as well as the youngest prepared to follow this liberator." Holy war: the dispirited, homesick Josias may well have thought the family's best hope of return to France lay in William's victory over Louis

XIV and envisioned enrollment as his only way of contributing to that return. Jacques Fontaine wrote in his journal that his friends enrolled "imagining they would conquer France and reestablish their religion there, against the wishes of the great persecutor Louis."[34]

Whatever his reasons, a mere four months after the fugitive Josias sailed from Dieppe to Rotterdam, the Dutch volunteer officer Josias retraced his route through the English Channel. The paradoxes into which the Revocation had thrown the expatriate Huguenots came vividly to some minds in transit: "We detected Dover and the coasts of Boulogne. I confess that I could not see our ungrateful homeland without emotion and without reflecting on the attachments I had there in my numerous family who stayed there; but as our fleet was not to work for their deliverance and we saw England closer, we had to turn our thoughts to that coast, until God should put it in the heart of our hero to rescue our homeland, which groans under oppression. . . . Many in our troop from Poitou wanted us to go invade their coasts."[35]

When the fleet arrived in Devon on November 5, 1688, it landed on the same coast where the ships of the Champagné children and Marie de La Rochefoucauld had landed slightly over a year earlier, between Falmouth, at which Marie landed, and Exeter, where both groups of fugitives settled briefly. Josias was in a sense, then, retracing the trip he did not take with his family in 1687. When the army proceeded, as the earlier Champagné parties had done, to Exeter, Josias perhaps took part in a ceremonial entry that could not have been more different from his family's arrival, the army flaunting 200 English cavaliers "richly mounted on Flanders Steeds," 200 Blacks from Dutch America in furs and plumes to attend the Horse, 200 Finlanders "in Bear-Skins, taken from the wild Beasts they had slain," 50 Gentlemen and 50 Pages attending and raising the Prince's banner inscribed "God and the Protestant Religion," 50 horses led by 100 grooms, all preceding the Prince of Orange on his "milk-white Palfrey, armed cap-a-pee, a Plume of white Feathers on his Head, in bright Armor," flanked by 42 footmen and followed by 200 mounted gentlemen with their pages, 300 Swiss, 500 volunteers with 250 horses, and 600 captains and guards "armed cap-a-pee. The rest of the Army in the Rear, his Highness with some principal Officers enter'd the Town, where they were not only received, but entertained with loud Huzza's, Ringing of Bells, Bonfires, and such Acclamations of Joy, as the Convenience of the Place and their Abilities could afford."[36]

A week's pause in the town allowed the Dutch troops to recuperate and regroup, and allowed William to rally English allies for the march on London. Josias may have used the respite to visit the French church that had sheltered Marie and the children and see its minister, Jacques Sanxay, who had been the pastor just miles from Champagné at Tonnay-Boutonne. Bostaquet recounted that an Anglican service he attended during his sojourn in Exeter astonished him by so closely resembling Catholic services—"all the exterior of popery remained there. . . . very contrary to the simplicity of our Reformation. I was not the least edified by it"—before he discovered the French Church and connected with the expatriate community there. He was delighted to find a tailor from back home and a bourgeois from Dieppe. Others, too, found shards of home there; Treillebois des Rabesnières, Marie's Isle cousin, reunited at Taunton, when on patrol out of Exeter, with Jacques Fontaine, his former neighbor in Saintonge.[37]

The rapid conclusion of the English campaign offered Josias the opportunity to return home quickly. On December 18, William of Orange rode into St. James's Park in "a small Callash, drawn by four Bay Horses" to meet the Sheriffs of London and Middlesex, and "Marshal Schomberg sate at his left hand."[38] On February 13, Parliament named William and Mary joint monarchs of England and Ireland, and on April 11 they were crowned in Westminster Abbey. Some Dutch regiments were sent back to the Netherlands, but William invited the French soldiers to continue in English service and gave them permission to travel back with the Dutch troops to visit their families in Holland—or even relocate them to England—during the hiatus before the next campaign.

Dumont de Bostaquet spelled out in his memoir the decisions facing Huguenot officers at this juncture with respect to their location and their relation to their families. He professed to love Holland and miss his family. Moreover, the patronage links that had found him a place in the initial Dutch invasion force might better support him in the long term than a transfer to English service. "Besides, I considered the military establishment in Holland more stable, the kingdom of England not maintaining any foreign troops except with great aversion." But his personal loyalty to William—the same traditional way of thinking about obligation that had for generations attached French military men to foreign rulers, even when fighting against their fellow French—determined him to stay in English service. "Since I had followed the prince, it was just that I obey him, he being my king and my benefactor."[39] As for returning temporarily to Holland to visit or fetch their families, there were risks if the men were absent during enrollments for the next campaign or when back pay was distributed to those on site. Probably few did return to Holland, for Bostaquet remarks that The Hague was deserted when he returned there in February 1689 after a five-month absence: there was little entertainment, he said, with all the French officers still across the Channel. At the end of March Bostaquet moved his wife from The Hague to Greenwich, where he stayed until he left for Ireland in midsummer, immediately after accompanying the body of the Marquis de Ruvigny, former deputy-general and spokesman of the Protestant churches in France, to his grave on August 7.

Did Josias also go back to The Hague in February? Did he propose relocating his family to England? Probably not. Marie's memoir implies that he remained in London without interruption between campaigns and specifies that he attended the coronation in April. Whether he was kept in London by the promise of back pay or by a desire to secure a place in English service or—what seems unlikely—by a lack of interest in seeing his family, he made a fateful decision by staying. In March, Schomberg was authorized to raise four regiments of French soldiers for the coming expedition to Ireland: one of cavalry and three of infantry, to be drawn largely from the Huguenots who had come from Holland in the Dutch army, in William's own guards, and as volunteers. These would be the first units composed of foreign soldiers ever fully integrated into the English army, which had typically scattered foreigners through native regiments out of mistrust of their loyalty when grouped.[40] The general himself commanded Schomberg's French Horse, which was largely composed of officers who had served in the Blue and Red Dragoons for the invasion of England. Three colonels appointed on April 1, 1689—Isaac de La Melonière; Pierre Massue, Comte de La Caillemotte; and François du Cambon—raised and commanded the three French regiments of foot, each comprised of thirteen companies, a major without a company, and twice as many irregular officers as commissioned officers.[41] Expectations were high: the Huguenot regiments were "without exaggeration the very finest in the army. . . . I believe we could have boldly gone up against the phalanxes of Alexander and the Roman legions."[42]

Josias joined La Melonière's Foot. Marie wrote with a touch of pride about Josias' equipping himself anew: "He had to spend a great deal. They dressed in scarlet cloaks and justaucorps lined in black velvet with silver braid, a blue jacket also with silver braid. He bought himself three horses and had two valets and all that was necessary for his own use." She took even greater pride in the story she was told at his death: that he had stayed behind to render his fellow refugees a great service when the troops left London for Chester in mid-July: "a few days before leaving, he was delegated by the corps to go to the court to request funds to include a great number of officers who had no means at all. His request was granted, which gained him much respect and thanks from these poor refugees."

Schomberg left London on July 17, arrived at Chester on July 20, and spent the next twenty-six days assembling the men and supplies for the invasion of Ireland. Scravemore, Maistre de Camp General, preceded him by two days and began setting up camp to the south of town, just above the River Dee.[43] By the end of the month, two Dutch regiments, numerous English ones, and a French one were in place at Chester, "and more every day, for they lye round the Country within twenty Miles of this place, and can be here in a day or two's warning." "There is likewise expected in here this morning a Regiment of French Cadees [gentleman volunteers], which all here expect to be a very fine sight. The Conflux of People hither to see the Camp from all parts of the Countrey is so great, that this Town might be almost taken for England's Metropolis."[44]

At Chester Josias rejoined his company, having come on his own in the post coach, a trying and uncomfortable four- or five-day journey from London. Marie suspected, knowing Josias' precarious health, that his act of beneficence toward the poor refugee soldiers compromised Josias' chances of survival: "What I fear this honor cost him in fatigue." He probably had little time to recuperate in the River Dee camp, for he was surely with his regiment when it embarked for Ireland. By August 8, Schomberg was aboard ship at Hoylake near Chester with 12,000 men, ready to sail to Ireland. After four days aboard waiting for favorable winds, Schomberg set sail on August 12, accompanied by eight English infantry regiments, a Dutch regiment and battalion of guards, four French companies of cadets, and three French regiments, including La Caillemotte's and La Melonière's. The next day they landed in the Bay of Carrickfergus, seven miles from Belfast. On August 14, they marched to Belfast, "the Enemy flying before us in great confusion; the Men are all well, and very Courageous." They recuperated and regrouped for a week before marching on August 21 the eight miles to Carrickfergus.[45] By the end of August, Carrickfergus had been taken by troops including the Huguenot regiments, at some significant cost: among the deaths was the son of the Marquis de Venours,[46] who was a patron of Marie de La Rochefoucauld in Holland.

Marie states in her memoir that Josias died at Belfast and that her pastor Jean Yver notified her on October 28 on the basis of a letter to him from Charles Moreau, paymaster of Schomberg's troops in Ireland. Given the difference in calendar (Britain's Julian calendar lagged behind the continent's Gregorian calendar by ten days, so Marie was notified on October 18 in the English style) and the time a letter took to reach The Hague from Ireland (approximately two weeks), Josias must have died around the first of October (English style). If Josias had died during the first (August 14–20) or second (August 28–September 2) pause in Belfast, Marie would have known of it earlier than October 28. More likely, he died during the "unparalleled havoc of disease among the troops of Schomberg in the camp of Dundalk," a catastrophe "probably unexampled in the military annals of Britain."[47]

Dundalk, on the coast some fifty miles south of Belfast, was Schomberg's choice for encampment as he moved his forces from the success at Carrickfergus toward the ultimate goal of Dublin. The troops set out for Dundalk on September 2 and marched for a week in rain and wind. Supplies were inadequate because the retreating Jacobites had removed the livestock and burned the fields, and the English army had too few horses to pack provisions. Schomberg sent some of the horses back to Belfast for bread, but his main hope was that supplies could be brought by ship to Dundalk once the troops arrived at the camp on September 9.[48]

Crisis befell the troops at Dundalk, indeed even as early as the march to Dundalk from Belfast, when a notable number of soldiers died. As early as the second week of September, deserters from the English forces were informing King James "that Schomberg's Troops were very much diseased, and already in want of provisions." By the end of the month, further deserters reported that "Four-score a day at the least were sent from the Enemies Camp to the Hospital, and that all their Horses were turned out to Grass for want of Hay and other necessarie Fourrage." Indeed, the muster on September 25 showed the ranks had thinned "by reason of the distempers then beginning to seize our Men." Illness accelerated around the turn of the month: more fell sick and more violently. At the muster on October 1, a quarter of those in camp were sick, and the 1,914 soldiers "absent" no doubt included many who had already died.[49] Josias likely died in this acceleration. When Schomberg finally abandoned "fatall Dundalke" on November 9, James' troops reoccupied the site of the Williamite camp. "Besides the infinite number of graves a vast number of dead bodies was found there unburied, and not a few yet breathing but almost devoured with lice and other vermin. This spectacle not a little astonished such of our men as ventured in amongst them, seeing that raging with hunger some had eaten part of their own flesh and having yet their speech begged as a charity to be killed."[50]

The mortality crisis at Dundalk was a perfect storm of converging menaces: bad weather and topography, food shortage, and pestilence. Bostaquet spoke of the illness as particularly Irish: "for from the moment we first entered this island, we were attacked by winds and rain. It rarely suffers harsh winters but is almost always hit by winds and rains. Our camp was on the edge of a marsh that was covered on one side by horrible mountains that emitted continual vapors like a furnace." Others blamed food shortages brought on by inefficient logistics. Troops suffered hunger or ate stuff that sickened them. "Six French soldiers from La Melonière's regiment ate a root they found in a garden and took to be carrots. They fell ill from it and lost their minds."[51] Starving men grabbed at stray sheep, which "cast a great many into fluxes." Jean François de Morsier, a Swiss in La Caillemotte's regiment, linked his nearly fatal dysentery to his diet of gruel and stagnant bogwater: "I grew so sick that I could not stand upright; moreover, I was tormented by a burning fever from which my only relief was to rest my head and brow against the tent sodden from the incessant rain. . . . My fever did not abate and this ill health made me long for home."[52]

But there was more sickness in the camp than just "the flux." George Story, chaplain of the Earl of Drogheda's regiment, thought at the time that the fever distinct from dysentery that entered the camp was "the Irish ague" or malignant typhus. "Many of them when they were dead, were incredibly lousie. . . . There were several that had their Limbs so mortified in the Camp, and afterwards, that some had their Toes, and some their whole Feet that fell off as the Surgeons were dressing them." "For the continual rains over their heads, and a boggy camp under their feet, together with the want of necessary cloathing, food and physick, and a perpetual duty, brought the disease of the country upon them, and the stench and corruption of that, a pestilential fever, which robbed them of their senses first, and then their lives. That this was a camp-plague, appeared by the blisters, and their carcasses turning immediately black, and stinking as a gangrene, and by the lice and vermin which issued out of their plague-sores."[53]

It was most likely here that Josias de Robillard fell ill, leading to his death in Belfast days later. Chaplain Story estimated that of the 14,000 troops at Dundalk, more than 6,300 died: 1,700 at the camp, 900 more on ships heading to Belfast for treatment, and 3,762 in hospital at Belfast. Josias was far from the only French officer to die; Bostaquet mentioned several others, including the Sieur de Sainte-Hermine from Aunis, who was a distant cousin of Josias through the Mazières and one of the three Sainte-Hermine children who rebuffed Madame de Maintenon's conversion efforts in 1680. Sainte-Hermine fell ill after very little time at Dundalk and died at Chester.[54]

When Schomberg ordered a survey of conditions at Dundalk on October 18, the very day on which Marie de La Rochefoucauld learned of her husband's death, the three French regiments gained relatively high marks. La Melonière's was "in pretty good order, well clothed" with experienced officers.[55] They suffered, though, two disadvantages. Many of them were not being paid, either because they were farther down on the payment list than available moneys reached or because the faulty recordkeeping of the Paymaster did not have them on the list at all.[56] Investigators noted of La Melonière's regiment: "Their health is also good, excepting the incorporated officers who have somewhat suffered in consequence of arrears of pay." The large number of incorporated officers in the three French infantry regiments, indeed, had higher morbidity rates than those reported for the army as a whole. In La Melonière's, 40 percent of incorporated officers had already fallen ill and 4 percent had died in the five weeks since their arrival in camp at Dundalk. Josias, then, served and died in Ireland in the riskier rank of French incorporated officers.[57]

The mortality crisis at Dundalk was characteristic of early modern warfare, if more severe; when the battle was won, the chances of death did not disappear. It was characteristic of Ireland as well. From Henry II's invasion

Figure 11.3 Major Josias de Robillard de Champagné. Oil on canvas. Copy after an earlier painting, ca. 1700, by the British (English) School. By permission of the National Trust.

in 1172 down to Cromwell's, Schomberg's, and ever since, "there is hardly an instance of military operations by the English [in Ireland] unattended with sickness among the troops."[58] Josias' odd foray into the military life ended in a tragic, exceedingly painful, and lonely death. "A great many of them died miserably. . . . So great was the Mortality, that several Ships had all the Men in them dead, and no Body to look after them whilst they lay in the Bay at Carrickfergus." "Our men died like rotten sheep."[59] The picture Moreau and La Melonière offered Marie of Josias's "beautiful end" allowed her to tell an upbeat story of the death in her memoir. It allowed her and their children to remember the Josias whose belief in a loving God and redeeming Savior had ever been foremost in his heart, without suspecting the depths of the desolation and squalor in which he passed away.

There may be truth in Marie's suspicion that the fatigue of the journey from London left Josias unable to endure the travails of the Irish expedition, rendering him especially susceptible to the scourges of weather, hunger, and disease. Ironically, if it contributed to his death, the good deed Josias did in London for his fellow French soldiers is the one incident in Josias' military adventure that fits with the personality of the Josias evident in his letters on theology for his children and his loving, sentimental letter to his absent wife. Josias's death ended his life prematurely and changed the lives of all his family. La Melonière gathered together Josias' money and equipment "to be passed on to me, which he did and with the utmost kindness asked me for my son." Young Josias joined the regiment in time for the march on Dublin in the summer of 1690 via the Boyne. When he retired from his military career, he settled as a neighbor to Dumont de Bostaquet and many other veteran officers of William's wars on the spoils of Huguenot victory in the Irish town of Portarlington.

12

Experiencing Exile

On January 10, 1690, ten weeks after Pastor Jean Yver informed her of her husband's death, Marie de La Rochefoucauld wrote a memoir of her experience of the Revocation, the escape, and the resettling of the family in Holland. Marie's autobiographical account would have, exceptionally, a twin—an account of the same emigration by her eldest daughter Susanne de Robillard de Champagné, later Madame de La Motte Fouqué (Saint-Surin).[1] While numerous Huguenot refugees wrote memoirs of their escape and resettlement, in no other known instance was a single escape recorded in two different memoirs. Susanne wrote her version of the escape either while still in Holland or after her definitive move around 1702 to Celle in Brunswick-Lüneburg. The two escape accounts were passed down in different branches of the family—the Irish and the Prussian—that lost touch with each other. Separately, they are only moderately notable, for each alone seems somewhat routine, emotionally flat, and unreflective. But reading the two accounts comparatively and in context restores to the texts their masked emotional charge and discloses deeper meanings, especially insights into what the emigration meant to families and how women experienced expatriation or exile.[2]

Huguenot memoirs have usually been read as more or less straightforward descriptions of the events they recount, and the history of the emigration has to an important extent been written from information in those accounts. Marie's and Susanne's, however, reward a reading from the perspective of how they tell their story, proceeding from textual clues to experiential revelations.[3] Within the memoir of the mother, the clues lie in the silences of her narrative—known aspects of her situation that she declines to mention—as well as in the structure and language of what she tells. Establishing that the memoir's audience is not the one it at first appears to address yields insights into the tenor of life in the Huguenot expatriate community and teases out Marie's unspoken ways of understanding her experience in terms of her gender, her religion, and her class. Within the memoir of the daughter, the clues lie in the way she revises her mother's tale and in the generic form she gives to her narrative. These point to the surreptitious expression, by the younger woman, of the pain of exile, to the familial crisis engendered with that pain, and to the reasons why the two generations of women experienced their flights and resettlements in quite different ways.

Marie, the Mother

Marie's account of the family's emigration fills the first six and one-sixth pages of the forty-three she eventually inscribed in the parchment-covered notebook she would use to record financial transactions for the next twenty-seven years. By placing her retrospective at the opening of an unmarked book, Marie expressed her consciousness of embarking upon a new and unprecedented phase of her life. By fixing her signature ("m de la rochefoucauld de champagné") at the bottom of each page, she pinned her very identity to the "present narration"[4] she was offering of her past. By affixing the date January 10, 1690 to the opening sheet, Marie indicated precisely when she wrote and so identified the moment that influenced her act. She thought she had ended her long migration, having settled among Huguenots in Holland. After several years of decision-making in her husband's absence or incapacity while de jure a wife, she had become at age forty-two unequivocally head of the family. She took up her pen and wrote her life upon becoming a widow.

The pairing of memoir and financial accounts also suggests what Marie believed she was doing with the memoir. Marie writes her escape account itself with a financial eye; twice in her telling she specifies the costs of the escape, thereby investing the monetary amounts with meaning as elements in the story. Marie's entire memoir is in a sense her accounting for her use of non-monetary resources, a record of her success in acquitting the duties asked of her, as she understood them. Overall, then, hers is an account book in both its parts, of which the first is simply expressed through narrative.

Marie structures her memoir by the succession of contexts through which she and the seven children moved in emigrating: Berneré, La Rochelle, Falmouth, Dartmouth, Exeter, Rotterdam, Leiden, The Hague, Voorburg. Once she reaches Holland, her story proceeds within the Huguenot refugee congregations and among friends. The church guides through its rituals (worship, *reconnaissance*, admission to communion), and fellow refugees offer orientation, companionship, and charity. Except in The Hague, where she mentions aristocratic Dutch ladies with whom she has been able to establish connections, the only persons she cites by name are expatriate Huguenots. Only once—in Exeter—does she mention unnamed locals, in this case to acknowledge their kindness. For the rest, it is within the Huguenot community—rather than

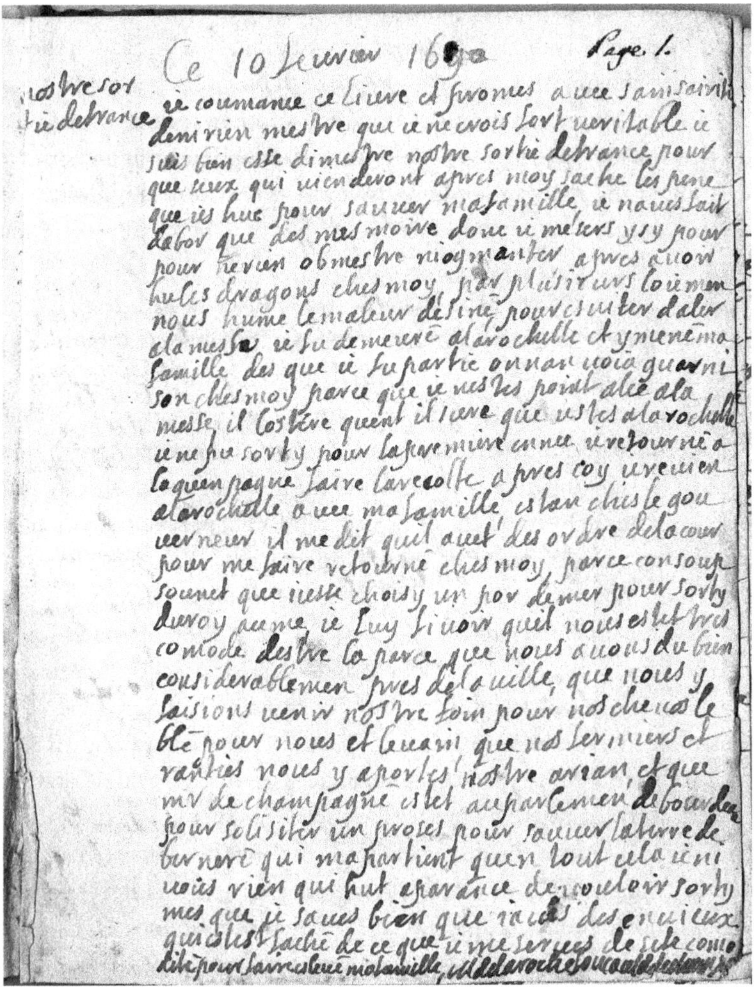

Figure 12.1 Journal of Marie de La Rochefoucauld, January 10, 1690, first page. Champagné Papers A59. Courtesy of the Department of Special Collections, Stanford University Libraries.

between it and the host environment—that, in her account, the social dynamics of emigration run.

This manner of telling her story accords with the lasting pattern of her interactions in the Refuge. The notaries, financial agents, and friends through whom Marie would manage her fortune were almost to a person fellow Huguenots. Marie and her children passed their lives within Huguenot milieus. Lifelong immersion in the enclaves of the diaspora was unexceptional. What Marie's memoir confirms is the difference this practice of settlement in Huguenot expatriate communities made to the way refugees experienced emigration: how effectively it could shield them from the dissonance of cultural encounter, mitigate the shocks of displacement, and neutralize the consciousness of loss. The pervasive placidity of Marie's narrative—strikingly at odds with the chaos of escape and the anguish of exile—is possible precisely because no matter how distant the Huguenot outposts from one another or how disparate their host environments, the migrant could move through geographic space as if within a single and familiar community. Even as she wandered, Marie could sustain the consciousness of an expatriate rather than descending into that of an exile.

The diaspora's crafting of the narrative runs, though, still deeper, for in a sense those Marie encountered in the successive Huguenot communities participated in its shaping. No doubt Marie recorded her story for "my dear children," whom she invokes with these words in the final paragraph of her narrative. She intended her children to have it, as they would someday have the family capital she was tracking in the remainder of the account book. Writing private memoirs for reading by one's children was traditional in seventeenth-century France, among women as among men. Noble families like the Champagné, whether Huguenot or Catholic, recorded the events of their lives in "yellowed notebooks, their lines covered with violet ink, that they intended for their children and that languished at the bottom of desk drawers or in attic crates, and that were often destroyed by an indifferent heir." Inscribing the story at least postponed its tumble into oblivion: "To tell a story is to take arms against the threat of time."[5] More than this, in a society where individuals' status and values were ascribed by their lineage, such accounts served as exhortations to descendants to live up to the duties of the patrimony they inherited at birth.

The story Marie tells is, in subtle ways, ill adapted to the children for whom she writes it down. Only in the final lines of her account does Marie address the children, and nowhere does she speak as if she envisions her audience as participants in the events she narrates. Other memorialists of the Huguenot migration, such as Jean Migault and Jacques Fontaine, wrote to their children directly and located them within the story. Migault recounts his escape for his children as a common experience, using the "we" voice and even addressing "you" as fellow voyagers and fellow rememberers: "You remember, and will always remember, even to little Olivier, how much you suffered during the nineteen days [of voyage to Holland from La Rochelle]." Similarly, Fontaine in his memoir speaks to his children directly as "you" and refers to his wife as "your mother."[6] Marie, by contrast, tells a story of "I" in which her children appear among the supporting cast but not in dialogue with the storyteller.

Moreover, having been part of the escape, the Champagné children knew already the contents of the account. Unless their mother was going to share her emotional experience of the events—which she does not do—what new could she tell them? Indeed, they knew much that the memoir does not reveal. They knew that though Marie exults about being reunited in Exeter with "my children . . . all my family," Thérèse was still in France at the moment of the story's recording and the object of a custody battle among her relatives. Why does Marie write as if no child of hers was left out of the family's salvation? Because she was indifferent to the child she knew only briefly—perhaps she was inured to loss, four of her earlier eleven children having died young? Or did she leave Thérèse out precisely because her loss was painful? Whatever her own feelings about this infant daughter, a story omitting mention of her was ill assorted to the hearing of the missing child's own siblings. Marie's children knew, too, more than she mentions about her husband. They knew—because he wrote long letters to "my dear children" on the subject—that he was not with them in the escape at least partly because of his own apostasy and his vacillation about leaving. They knew that the family had lost Berneré because their Solière and Isle kindred had lost its coherence. The story Marie tells, purportedly to her children, does not acknowledge issues that must have weighed heavily on her—and their—thoughts and emotions.

The issue is not whether Marie tells a true story. The "autobiographical pact" that Marie makes explicitly at the outset of her memoir defines her own truthfulness: "I begin this book and promise sincerely to put nothing there that I do not believe entirely true." She lives up to her promise in the quite precise form in which she gives her vow: all that she puts in the account is true, but not everything is put in. Nor is the issue that Marie offers a selective story—every autobiographical memoir is selective. The issue is, rather, on what grounds were her decisions of inclusion or omission based and whose needs or expectations—those of what implied audience—constituted for her "the constraints of acceptable discussion"?[7] To understand the dissonance between the story Marie tells and the audience she claims in her writing requires separating the audience for whom the narrative was shaped from that for whom it was written down, the act of composing from the act of inscribing. If her children were the audience for whom the account was recorded, they were not the one for whom it was crafted. A shadow dialogue with an unnamed audience lies nearly hidden at the story's heart.

The first clue to the audience of composition is the conversational quality of Marie's prose: its unadorned style, its rhythms that approximate speech. That women's writing style tended to be straightforward and close to conversational has been noted, in particular with respect to prominent Huguenot women.[8] But Marie's case is conversational in more than its lack of adornment. The autograph manuscript of the memoir is crucial evidence in this respect, because it shows that Marie, even when holding a pen in her hand, was formed more by oral experience than by written. Her spelling is entirely phonetic, she uses no periods or paragraphing to format a page visually, and the units of sound are run together or separated in keeping with the rhythms of speech rather than in the typographical units of words on a printed page. For this reason, only the reader who listens to the sequence of sounds, either by reading aloud or in the mind's ear, rather than visually deciphering the alphabetic icons can understand Marie's verbiage. Though it is not uncommon to find variant spellings in early modern manuscripts, Marie's case is extreme and points to her lesser familiarity with written communication, her immersion in the oral.

It seems likely that the memoir is so close to orality because—rather than composing the escape account as she wrote—Marie actually composed it orally as she told it and retold it to live audiences. The audiences were quite likely the very Huguenot communities through which she passed in her migration and whose succession provided the framework of her story. Telling their escape was the Huguenot fugitives' rite of passage: the passage being the escape, the rite the telling. The Church itself got them talking. Refugees' first obligation after escaping from France—before they could be readmitted "to the peace of the Church"—was the *reconnaissance,* according to which new arrivals had to testify before their coreligionists—"in the presence of the whole troop"—concerning the circumstances of their lives and faith before, during, and after their flight. On the basis of their narration, they would be formally accepted, or not, back into the fold. Marie says she made her own *reconnaissance* in the first community she reached after escaping, Dartmouth. No records for that parish have survived,[9] but the formula recorded on March 22, 1688, for the group in The Hague that included her nephew Casimir Prévost de Touchimbert suggests the requirements of the *reconnaissance* and the expectations with which the refugee's story would need to accord: "After they presented themselves before this Company to recognize the fault they committed by signing in France and to ask pardon from God, and at the same time the peace of the Church, in view of the testimonies of their repentance, their request has been granted them, after they promised to lead holy lives and submit to the discipline established among us."[10]

The *reconnaissance* obliged each fugitive to become a storyteller and perhaps planted a taste for telling one's own story and hearing those of others. Subsequently, those refugees who moved from congregation to congregation found themselves repeatedly in situations that invited retelling the same story.[11] Thinking of the emigration memoir as being composed for congregation-based tellings makes sense of certain features of Marie's story. It explains her chronology—why she begins with the arrival of the dragoons in her home in Saintonge—because it is not her life story but only the episode of escape and relocation that was appropriate for telling to that succession of congregations. Thinking of Huguenot communities as Marie's audience for composition may also help explain the configuration of silences in her account. On the one hand, certain silences were permitted by the very character of this audience. If they were strangers to her, they were also in a sense insiders, people who themselves had experienced a version of what was being related. So, for example, the audience did not need her to spell out the persecution, or the meaning of dragoons, or the grounds for deciding to flee rather than convert. These silences define the assumptions shared between the teller and her listeners, fellow refugees.[12]

At the same time, other silences might well have been enforced by this audience. The *reconnaissance* rite was highly prescriptive and judgmental: the burden was on the postulant to satisfy the expectations of the church. The less formal storytelling in groups one passed through in later stages of the migration path would have implicit expectations, too; the new arrival seeking integration would have every incentive to conform clearly to community norms and to avoid issues that might raise disagreement or uncertainty—such as the abandonment of baby Thérèse, the ambivalence of Marie's husband Josias, or the part that nonreligious factors such as family dissension and material loss may have played in the decision to leave.[13] The telling would be an activity of social bonding and community creation.

The genre of the escape account would be invented in these interchanges. Later, published accounts would become well known and may have served as models for escapees who wrote their memoirs later in their lives, at some distance from the escape. But in the early days of the diaspora, there was as yet no written genre. The nearer in time it was composed to the escape itself, the more fully a memoir would have been shaped by the oral sharing and hence by the values of listeners, and the more its storylines would bear the marks of the collectivity. These ostensibly "individual" stories bob and weave in implicit dialogue as the tellers, intent upon connecting with the community, incorporate into their story some of the community's experiences and expectations. As a consequence, each orally composed escape story incorporates and mirrors the Huguenot migration more broadly.

As much as the expectations of the congregations hearing it may have shaped the story Marie told, she also had her own motives for composing and her own need for telling her story in a certain way. Storytelling confirms for the teller what she considers her true identity. "The shape of our lives often distorts who we really are . . . autobiography is the story of an attempt to reconcile one's life with one's self." The spine, then, of the tale, to which the writer perhaps unconsciously makes the narrative conform, is not the life course itself—what a fully informed observer might consider the facts of one's life—but one's self-conception, one's narrative truth and personal myth.[14]

Marie's narrative truth is that she is a good mother. The only identity she gives herself in the escape memoir is mother/wife; the only set of duties she feels concerned to show herself acquitting is her familial vocation. Implicitly her entire memoir says that she has played well the important part a woman has to play in the success of the family through her own strength, initiative, and self-reliance. To be sure, hers are not the housewifely responsibilities of making clothes, cooking, and so on, which she never once mentions carrying out. They are, rather, orchestrating a successful escape, stewarding the family patrimony, securing patronage, setting up the children, winning pensions, collecting payments. Her role may be only the mother of a family, but it is expansively defined as refounder and head of the family, decision-maker. She is far from being subsumed in the family; rather, her self-presentation resonates with an egoistic pride—always "I" rather than "we"—that suggests an aristocratic ethic converging with her familial vocation. She represents herself doing these actions herself: they are the pains "I" took to save "my" family, not the effect of solidarity or cooperation. They are the fulfillment of her personal duty; she does not represent herself in relational terms and is not the slightest bit self-effacing.[15]

This rigorously personal story—told in the first person—is neither intimate nor developmental nor explicitly religious. Her own life is her storyline, yet the times and her interior life scarcely intrude. For the most part—excepting her effusiveness over her husband's arrival and her perhaps inadvertent betraying of her preference for her second son—she makes her argument that she is a good mother by pointing to her actions rather than by expressing her sentiments. So if autobiography is by definition introspective, then this is not autobiography in the modern sense.[16] Marie's progression from place to geographic place is not paralleled by interior transformation.

Nor is this a spiritual autobiography, the story of her progress in perfection or faith, or of God's working in her life and her soul. In suppressing change and withholding her inner life, Marie's writing contrasts with some other notable Calvinist narratives. Her memoir does not allegorize the terrain she traversed. Spare with words, she makes no use of religious rhetoric or biblical narrative as vehicles for structuring her experience.[17] Not a single scriptural text, no prophetic or apocalyptical vocabulary, no metaphors of pilgrimage or chastisement grace her pages.[18] Even the closest reading detects little resonance of the New Testament or inspiration from the Psalms. Nor does she convey a sense that God was clearing her path or make God a continual presence, bringing him in only at the end of the account when she states the lesson that God saved her for her children. She does not tell her story of escape as a religious account.

That Marie does not tell her story of escape in overtly religious terms may seem surprising in the memoir of one going into exile for the sake of religion. Alternatively, it might be construed as evidence that religious motivation was less important in the Huguenot emigration than has usually been thought.[19] In Marie's case, the absence of religious language reflects, rather, the means

Marie chooses for establishing her piety: not through words of devotion but by indirect demonstration. In the financial accounts that follow the escape story, she shows herself preserving the family and its social identity, advancing the interests of the family line and of its particular members. In so doing, she implicitly argues that she is a good Christian without overtly claiming so, for Protestantism lent the halo of vocation to precisely the role she shows herself playing. By narrating the drama of "my family," she implicitly justifies herself in God's sight and claims the personal satisfaction that comes from living up to one's calling.

Susanne, the Daughter

The escape account written by Susanne is a different story. Nearly twice as long, it is more literary—more polished in its expression, crafted to entertain as well as to inform, and patterned at least in part to a recognizable generic form. Lacking the conspicuous signature and date that so precisely situate her mother's account, it leaves indeterminate its origins as well as the audience it addresses.[20] In sharpest contrast, the daughter shapes her account to a polemical end. All of its previous editors were fooled on this score, misled by reading this one text in isolation into characterizing it as a "naïve story . . . not a literary work but a naïve revelation of the Huguenot character" and depicting its author as narrating "with childlike simplicity."[21] Rejoining the mother's and daughter's accounts bares the younger woman's filial rebellion: Susanne crafted her story precisely to counter the representation of the emigration left behind by her mother.

Susanne had, without doubt, seen her mother's memoir before writing her own, for she structures her account in the same way—as a progress from congregation to congregation, site to site. In all probability, she had heard her mother spin and respin the tale of their escape in those very congregations and absorbed her framework in the hearing. But details common to the two accounts more likely came from reading than from hearing. For example, she probably read, then appropriated, her mother's dating—which is precise but mistaken—of the departure of William of Orange's armies for England in 1688.[22]

She would have seen what her mother wrote, at the latest, in 1722, when she returned to Holland from Celle to meet her siblings and divide up the family inheritance. The character of Marie's account book virtually guaranteed that it would have been displayed on that occasion, for that family reunion was the book's manifest destiny. This was the moment and the task for which the accounts had been kept, and there was consequently concrete reason for the

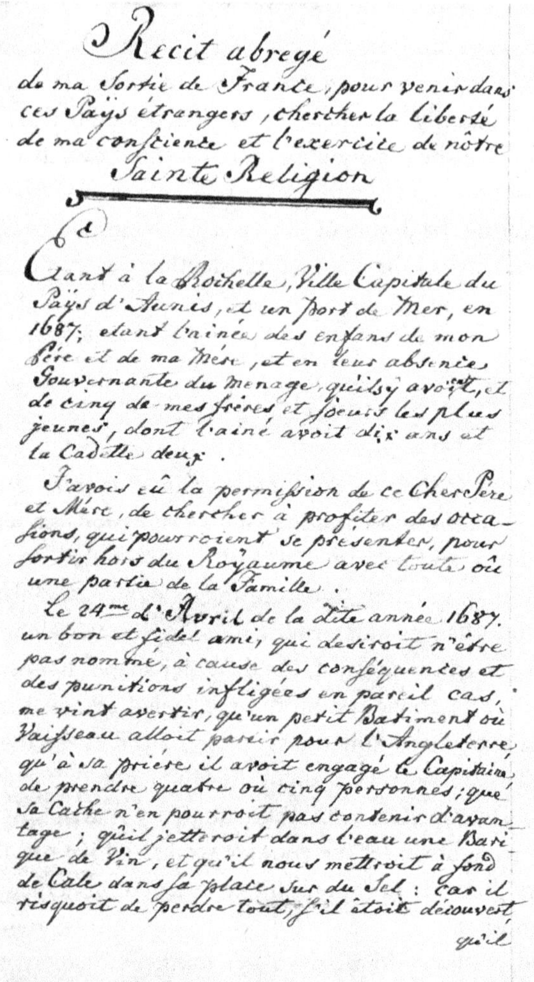

Recit abregé
de ma Sortie de France, pour venir dans
ces Païs étrangers, chercher la liberté
de ma conscience et l'exercice de nôtre
Sainte Religion

Etant à la Rochelle, Ville Capitale du
Païs d'Aunis, et un Port de Mer, en
1687; etant l'ainée des enfans de mon
Pére et de ma Mére, et en leur absence
Gouvernante du menage qu'ils y avoient, et
de cinq de mes fréres et soeurs les plus
jeunes, dont l'ainé avoit dix ans et
la Cadette deux.

J'avois eû la permission de ce Cher Pére
et Mére, de chercher à profiter des occasions, qui pourroient se presenter, pour
sortir hors du Royaume avec toute où
une partie de la Famille.

Le 24me d'Avril de la dite année 1687.
un bon et fidel ami, qui desiroit n'être
pas nommé, à cause des conséquences et
des punitions infligées en pareil cas,
me vint avertir, qu'un petit Batiment où
Vaisseau alloit partir pour l'Angleterre,
qu'à sa priére il avoit engagé le Capitaine,
de prendre quatre où cinq personnes; que
sa Cache n'en pourroit pas contenir d'avan-
tage; qu'il jetteroit dans l'eau une Bari-
que de Vin, et qu'il nous mettroit à fond
de Cale dans sa place sur du Sel: car il
risquoit de perdre tout, s'il étoit découvert,
qu'il

Figure 12.2 Susanne de Robillard, Récit de La Sortie de France de Madame de Thonnay-boutonne en 1687, first page. Courtesy of the Universitäts- und Landesbibliothek Darmstadt.

book to be brought out and shown to the children. Until then, her accounts were Marie's alone. Susanne might have seen them by chance or by permission at one time or another in the 1690s, when she was still living in The Hague with or near her mother, before she moved to Celle around 1702. But Susanne had no need to know and Marie no need to show them.

The years in which Susanne could have composed her own account stretch, then, over as many as five decades—from her young adulthood in the 1690s to the years yet to be lived by the fifty-four-year-old woman who attended the reunion. Situating the memoir in time might reveal the circumstances that provoked the telling and disclose whether it expresses the consciousness of a young adult or of a "woman of a certain age." Textual clues to the date of composition are equivocal. In the final paragraph of her account, Susanne says she wrote her memoir in her youth, while caring for her siblings in Holland. The latest events related in the text itself, though, undermine this dating. She left her natal family in December 1692, when she married Saint-Surin—an event that, interestingly enough, she does not mention. But her brother Josias' appointment to a company, noted in the text, occurred only in 1695.[23] It may be that Susanne herself distinguished between composition and inscription, the account having been composed in her mind and emotions as she lived the experience in her youth and written down later. If so, both mother and daughter composed and wrote in separate acts—Marie composing orally, Susanne mentally. Marie's story circulated before it was written down, her writing remaining strictly private down to the twentieth century; Susanne's circulated in manuscript, almost certainly during her lifetime.[24]

Perhaps because it was meant for circulation, Susanne gave her story its literary polish. Though she covers the same span of time as her mother, she elaborates on the incidents she recounts, often with mischievous wit and a sense for the dramatic. She writes, with a twinkle in her eye, that when they were secreted in the ship's hold their bodily fluids continued secreting. She avows wryly that on their meals-included voyage they were too seasick to cost the captain much. She turns the escape into an adventure story, her battle against the reneging captain into a crusade for justice, and her tiny sister's inclusion among the escapees into a cliff-hanger. Susanne does not say whom she intends as her audience, only who they are not: her family. She begs for forgiveness from her family if they should ever happen to read her memoir. And she would have had reason to hope it would not fall into their hands.

Susanne's account is so expressly modeled on her mother's, yet so divergent in factual points and emphases, that it constitutes an assertion of her own claim to tell the story in place of her mother. Among the altered details, Susanne redates the escape from April 10 to April 27. An earlier commentator who saw both accounts assumed that Susanne was supplying accuracy where her mother had erred: "Marie was not on the spot at the time."[25] But it seems certain that Marie's is the correct date, since port records for Falmouth list an arrival that accords to the smallest details—even to the three wine casks for which Captain Thomas Robinson of the *Tiger* paid no duty because they were empty—with the date Marie gives and list none on or near Susanne's.[26] It is not obvious, however, why Susanne would make this change, for it adds no particular rhetorical punch to her account. More obvious in intent is her revising the makeup of her escape party. Whereas Marie said the seventh person was her (adult) cousin Mademoiselle de Mazières, Susanne makes the seventh the children's governess—which, by obscuring the presence of the adult cousin, inflates Susanne's own role in the escape. Another change has the same effect: she understates her age and that of each sibling, presumably to magnify the prodigiousness of her feat. She was just short of her twentieth birthday, not sixteen as she says. Her siblings who accompanied her in the escape ranged in age from four and a half to twelve and a half, not from two to ten, the range she specifies in her text.

A pattern of exaggeration in the memoir is, indeed, one of the means by which the story is reshaped from a Marie-centered one to a Susanne-centered one. Susanne substitutes her own "I" story for her mother's. Whereas Susanne scarcely figured in Marie's account, in her own telling she is in charge and responsible for the escape's success. All the escaping siblings except Josias, who left with his mother, owe their salvation to her. She has been left to her own initiative in La Rochelle to find and take advantage of opportunities for escape. She makes the arrangements, and the escape succeeds because of her capability (negotiating with the captain), her craftiness (dissembling at the Château square), her resourcefulness (catching fish to eat), and her assiduous caring for her siblings wherever they alight. Lest this seem no more than the inevitable effect of a change in perceiver, other subtle points in Susanne's text point to deeper meanings of these and other alterations.

Having seized the narrator's voice and recentered the story on herself, Susanne arrogates to herself the persona that Marie assumes for personal vindication: the good mother. "I"—Susanne, not Marie—"served as mother," she asserts, for it was she who gave shelter, nourishment and nurturing, protection, religious education, and emotional solicitude. It was she who saved the children—even the tiniest, as Marie did not. Indeed, the highly dramatic and otherwise puzzling story she tells about persuading the reluctant captain to add her toddler sister to the escaping coterie at the last minute may be a subtle barb aimed at a mother who left her own youngest behind. The opposition comes out clearly as Susanne vaunts her own doing without a maidservant and follows this so quickly by the seemingly offhand observation that her mother arrived with a maidservant that the "with" echoes the "without" in reproach. Implicitly Susanne defines good motherhood differently from Marie. Over against Marie's vindication of herself as a matriarch, Susanne celebrates herself as a mother-caregiver, a homemaker. This is what she said the Exeter folks acknowledged by nicknaming her "the mother of the little children"—all that her mother was culpable for not doing.

It was the mother's lack of appreciation or recognition that gave the daughter an emotional need to write her own account. Her efforts, prodigious as they might be, fail to evoke the words of appreciation Susanne needs to hear her mother say: "Thus have I always done my best to be helpful and agreeable to her . . . [my mother] seemed to me to be content." The daughter writes her escape account the way little girls play dolls: acting out in the world of their imagination the tenderness they wish their mother would lavish upon them. The deep estrangement between daughter and mother that Susanne expresses through her escape account is, of course, "an old, conventional story, every eldest daughter's tale," as the adored new child supplants her on the mother's lap—or in the family's aspirations. An older contemporary of Susanne's, the famed writer of fairy tales the Comtesse d'Aulnoy, framed her memoirs quite overtly with the same theme of familial abandonment that Susanne surreptitiously weaves into hers:

> It was the first of my misfortunes that I was born too soon. . . . I was lookt upon as Heiress of my Father's Estate. . . . With these Fancies I was flatter'd all along; and I had already attain'd Eleven years of Age, when my Mother was brought to bed of a Boy. But no sooner was this Son and Heir come into the World, but my Grandmother began to lavish out all her Affection for me, upon him; my Beauty was no longer flatter'd. No more talk of my being a Princess or a Dutchess at least: No—I must stifle all those gaudy Expectations: My Brother had bereav'd me of all those great Advantages.[27]

For Susanne, writing the memoir that supplants her mother's is a way both to express and to rectify her own sense of bereavement. Through the rescripting, she places herself again at the center from which her mother's own persona and her mother's own favorite child (or children) had pushed her in her mother's account.

The theme of bereavement and estrangement comes out strongly through an idiosyncratic turn that Susanne gives to her lone biblical citation, Psalm 27: "The Lord is my light and my salvation." This psalm is one of the staples of Calvinism and a perennial recourse of exiles, a comfort to those under attack, feeling alone, and unable to count on anyone's loyalty.[28] It is not surprising that Susanne would have used it for teaching spiritual lessons to her sisters and brothers, and the large ink stain on the page bearing this psalm in the seventeenth-century psalter among the Champagné family's papers would seem to confirm that this page was indeed much used. But what is the meaning of the remark—"[That psalm] which, in my view, suits me extremely well"—that she interjects immediately following her mention of the psalm? In what sense did this psalm have a particular pertinence to Susanne but not, for example, to all her siblings as well? The answer may well lie in the verse on which the ink fell: "If I had neither father nor mother,/ My God would be for me, no matter what." The glosses to this verse in the margin of the Calvinists' Geneva Bible—the Huguenots' own, of which Marie had two copies in her possession in Holland—suggest that it pertains not merely to cases in which physical distance or death have separated parents from child but also to cases of an even more agonizing separation: abandonment by parents, who, by the order and laws of nature, ought to care for a child.[29]

That this is the verse Susanne thought especially appropriate for her is confirmed by the movement of her narrative from the psalm to her mother's aloofness and her now-deceased father's appreciation of all the daughter did for "his family." Clearly, her father is the object of her deepest emotional bond. She grieves that he is no longer with her and cherishes above all else the letter in which he recognized the "pains I took to save his family." And yet, if he is identified as her emotional bedrock, he is elusive in her narrative, always absent from what drives it. The absence of both parents at the outset, which Susanne signals in the first sentence of her account, provides the very condition of her own heroism, of her independent action in their stead. And the turning point in her story—and beginning of her pain—occurs when her mother rejoins the children but her father—the one person she could have counted on to dote on her—does not. This sense of lost vindication from an absent father

PSEAUME XXVII.
Partant aussi dedans sa maison sainte
Chanter, offrir, sacrifier lui veux.
Puis que je viẽs, ô Seigneur, te prier
Soit ma requeste entenduë de toi:
Puis qu'au besoin tu m'entens écrier,
Je te suppli' avoir pitié de moi.
¶ J'ai dedans moi apperceu mon courage [ainsi,
Comme en ton Nom m'avertissant
Employe toi à chercher mon visage:
Tu vois, Seigñr, que je le cherche aussi.
De moi helas! ta face ne soit loin:
[illegible] ne chasse en fureur, ô mon Dieu
[illegible] favorable en maint lieu,
Dieu mon Sauveur [illegible] laisse au besoin.
¶ Quand je n'aurois pour moi pere ni mere, [soit.
[illegible] Dieu sera pour moi, quoi qu'il en
[illegible] partãt, ô Dieu mõ Pere,
[illegible] chemin bõ & droit.
[illegible] suis par plusieurs ennemis,
Et [illegible] qui en leur bouche n'ont
Sinon

PSEAUME XXVIII.
Sinon l'outrage, & le tort qu'ils me font:
Las! ne permets qu'à leur plaisir sois mis.
¶ Certainemẽt n'eust esté l'asseurãce,
Qu'ici bas mesme avant que voir la mort
Des biẽs de Dieu j'aurai la jouïssance
Sous un tel faix déja je fusse mort,
Or donc atten toûjours patiemment
Le Seigneur Dieu: soustien jusques au bout.
Dieu te viendra asseurer [illegible]
Or donc atten de Dieu [illegible]
PSEAUME XXVIII.
O Dieu [illegible]
que mon [illegible]
soin te taire: Aut[illegible]
Sinon à ceux me comparer, Qu'on veut au
D

Figure 12.3 Psalter belonging to the Champagné Family. Champagné Papers III:B:5. Courtesy of the Department of Special Collections, Stanford University Libraries.

she expresses not only in an explicit paragraph but through the subtly implied genre—the fairy tale—that gives allusive mythic form to her entire testimony.

The first soupçon of a fairy tale is the tragicomic scene of lost children wandering in the wilderness of Devonshire, their captain having failed them, the town governor's command having failed them, and now their French language failing them. Susanne's resourcefulness and her few words of Latin lead them out. But on their arrival in Exeter, the break in Susanne's life becomes clear. She turns from an adventuress-heroine into a domestic toiler, doing "coarse tasks to which I had not been raised at all": sewing her brothers' undergarments, pinching pennies, shopping, cooking, making the fire. Once the leader of the successful escape, she is no longer powerful but only dutiful, a workhorse. Her drudgery deepens through the story as the field for effective action constricts and possibilities for recognition fade. At last, in the concluding paragraph, the picture of her fixing her sisters' hairdos for their parties allows the reader to recognize Susanne as Cinderella. She is the child who, though most meritorious of them all, is sacrificed for the benefit of her siblings. She is the deserving young woman abandoned by the parents who should have cared about her well-being but did not.

With just these few unmistakable cues to the well-known fairy tale, Susanne calls into her reader's mind the rest of its elements: strains between the women in a family, maltreatment by an older woman of a young one who proves herself meritorious when tested, triumph and sweet revenge worked out by a fairy godmother, exoneration of the father who (absent without explanation) is absolved of responsibility for his daughter's suffering. Contemporaries knew the tale well. When Charles Perrault included Cinderella among the family-drama fairy tales he published in 1697, it took on a new popularity among readers and became all the rage in the salons.[30] But the story itself was more than twelve hundred years old and was current in folk telling, so the themes Susanne called to mind were a shared stock everyone knew, and she could cue her reader to envision in the same mold the story she was telling.

The fairy tale trope allows Susanne to imply an interpretation of her life that she touches on only at key points without narrating it fully. More than this, using the fairy tale authorizes her to tell the story from her own point of view, for the lowly genre was understood to be told by women. "Mother Goose," the governess in the nursery, the two French writers (Marie-Jeanne L'Héritier de Villandon and Marie-Catherine le Jumel de Barneville, Comtesse d'Aulnoy) who first recorded them: all were women. What the genre allows the woman's voice to do is to complain. Through the generic framework she can dare to express anger, pain, resentment, and jealousy about the hierarchy of affection and power within the family that would be too explosive if expressed in straightforward fashion.[31] Even in the face of complaint, the fairy tale, by associating the protagonist's own situation with a woman's predicament as the genre universalizes it, invites the audience to take the protagonist's side, identify with her ordeal, and be attracted to her virtues.[32]

Finally, the fairy tale form allows Susanne to convey disappointment. The genre sets up an expectation of a triumph, whose absence in the end conveys to the reader the protagonist's dashed aspirations without her having to spell out what her dreams or expectations had been. The mere absence of a happy ending effectively evokes her own unhappiness. Cinderella, after all, is a tale of female wish fulfillment. Cinderella triumphs in the end—gaining the love of a prince, revenge on those siblings who were preferred over her, and the place in life that fits her merit—and her vindication sounds the moral of the tale: that hard and patient work pays off. Susanne suggests for herself neither the fulfillment of her dreams nor the vindication. Implicitly, hers is a lament for promises unfulfilled, for loss, for merit left unrewarded. Hers is a tale of exile rather than of expatriation. Susanne has turned the escape drama into an expression of intrafamilial conflict, into a family romance.

The hidden dialogue between daughter and mother embedded in Susanne's escape account makes her memoir a particularly precious addition to the still rare "scraps of emotional evidence which have come down from pre-modern times."[33] It gives a picture of mother-daughter emotions seldom even hinted at, while saying something about the Huguenot emigration, especially the experiences of its women. Through the hidden dialogue and especially through her use of the fairy tale's mythic form, Susanne tells her story in a way that bares her emotions, especially her pain and her anger, her deep feeling of being passed over, her longing for the appreciation she feels she deserves but her mother will not give, her grief over losing the father who—she feels sure—would have given her the recognition she craved.

Susanne's pain expressed her perception of a double asymmetry of loss in the experience of emigration: asymmetry vis-à-vis her brothers and vis-à-vis her life in France. Her mother was the key figure in both, once as an agent and once as a model. Marie held not merely the pen but also the purse strings. In part because she had her own holdings independent of her husband and in part because she was widowed, she controlled the family's fortune. She alone held the power over any gifts Susanne might receive during her mother's lifetime, her dowry, and ultimately her inheritance. Marie could give or withhold, unconstrained—and here is a concrete result of emigration—either by the law codes of the French province from which she came or by other family members who might have overseen the disposal of heritages back home. Although Marie did not exclude Susanne from the family fortune as thoroughly as she did from her history of the escape, her inter vivos gifts to Susanne were smaller than those to her brothers. In November 1701, when Susanne was in dire financial need, Marie remade her will to increase brother Josias' portion of the inheritance.[34] Perhaps Susanne's correction of the narrative was the only action she could take in her own defense, in the face of unequal distribution of family resources.

More than this, Susanne's exclusion from her mother's memoir and bounty—and, as Susanne sees it, from her affections—triggered feelings about her larger exclusion from social place. What is significant is not so much that Susanne rejects her mother, but rather that she does so in conjunction with, and through, the story of emigration; the linkage signifies her loss of social world and discloses the pain she suffers from the fact of exile. Loss of social place—along with the socially defined rights and obligations that accompany that role—was, of course, a risk refugees incurred. That Susanne was among those who did not have in exile what she had enjoyed in their homeland is evident in the circumstances of her marriage at age twenty-five to a sixty-seven-year-old friend of her father, Saint-Surin. The couple's economic precariousness was such that her husband at least twice petitioned the States General of the United Provinces for charitable assistance. His lands were confiscated by the French crown soon after his emigration in September 1685, as were those of his sister when she was imprisoned in the Château de Nantes. At the death, without posterity, of their only brother, all the lands that would have belonged to Susanne's husband passed to two cousins, the Comtesse de Soissons (Uranie de La Cropte) and the Marquis de Langallerie.[35] Letters to those cousins in the mid-1690s as well as to the estate agent in Tonnay-Boutonne who tried to get them some financial support from Madame Duquesne-Guiton at Belesbat (Susanne's cousin Marie-Marguerite Nicolas de Voutron) were to no avail.[36] In 1697, noting "the sad state to which he is reduced," Saint-Surin implored the States General to "grant me the substance required to keep me alive and raise my family. . . . I do not ask them at all to render my status equal to the one I could have in France, where I left behind the first and most considerable barony of the province." On December 19, 1700, writing to thank them for the pension they had given him (at first 400 *francs* a year, later increased to 600), Saint-Surin begged for peace of mind at his time of death: "Weighed down by infirmities, by gout, gravel, and frequent illnesses, seventy-five years old and soon to be called to God, and in mortal worry about what my wife will subsist from after my death, she who left her homeland as I did and her properties for the sake of the Religion, with her two children and several months pregnant . . . and without anything for their subsistence or to give them after my death."[37]

On the fifth day of her widowhood, October 7, 1701,[38] Susanne herself was reduced to petitioning the same States General for charity on behalf of "herself and three boys whom Providence caused to be born your subjects in less than six years, the youngest of which is at her breast. . . . She presently has no means of providing her sad family with the bread it needs daily, nor even to bury her poor husband in the simplest manner. And though they have more than twenty thousand *livres* in cash from rents in France, they have not received a *sol* of it for sixteen years."[39] For Susanne, the widow's weeds were a far cry from what she had been promised in her marriage contract in 1692 (and would presumably have been hers in France): that at her husband's death her carriage and horses would be dressed in mourning at his expense and that she would get to live in whichever of his seigneurial houses she should chose.[40]

That this time of need—the intensive days of young motherhood and deprivation—was the moment when Susanne composed her memoir is suggested both by the financial transactions attached to Marie's escape memoir and by the action Susanne took nearly as soon as she was widowed. At the time Susanne and her husband were petitioning for charity, her mother held substantial capital investments, including bonds on the very States General they were importuning. Just weeks after Susanne was widowed, Marie, ill in bed, made a new will that reduced Susanne's portion of her inheritance by reinstating Josias, Susanne's brother, to the portion from which Marie's earlier will had excluded him and specifying that in the event of her death all her daughters should live with Susanne.[41] Within a year Susanne would move to Celle, leaving behind not only Holland but also her sisters—and her mother. There she lived out her days as genteel companion to more distinguished noblewomen, including Madame de Villars and Madame von Bülow, in the retinue of the Duchess of Zell and the Princess of Aldenburg.[42] Because of the Revocation and her family's flight from France, Susanne could not have the life that the women in her lineage had led, that Marie had led, that Susanne wanted and no doubt had her whole life long expected to have as an adult, despite the fact that she felt she would be better at it than her mother. Her expectations of social place collapsed. Exile for Susanne was "the place where the fairy-tales failed."[43]

Susanne was precisely an exile rather than, like her mother, an expatriate. Whereas Marie conveys a sense that she has not been changed by the experience of emigration, Susanne laments—and resents—that exile has redefined her very identity. Marie's account conveys little or no sense of loss—to be sure, she has lost her husband, but not her status, rank, or conviction of superiority. Her story's placid matter-of-factness downplays tribulations, rules out grievance, and gives a sense of continuity, of confidence, of being on a sound footing. She tries to carry out traditional expectations despite having lost the context in which they were rooted. She continues, as she says, to live among French families. By contrast, Susanne's account reeks of tribulation and loss. Whereas Marie seldom encounters any but good people, Susanne continually confronts challenges, obstacles, and injustices. More conscious than her mother of being newly an outsider, she laments that they had "abandoned our properties, homeland, friends." Susanne perhaps displaces onto her mother an anger she cannot allow herself to express about the disappointment of new circumstances. Angry that her mother has abandoned her or that she continues to be dependent on her mother when she wants to be in charge, she responds with the only power she holds in her hands: by refusing to be merely a bit player in someone else's narrative.

Family, Memoirs, and Memory

The escape accounts of the Champagné, like those of other Huguenots who fled France at the time of the Revocation, have been read as much for inspiration and celebration as for insight into the experience of flight and resettlement. A reader of Marie's wrote that it "makes me feel great respect for the energy and courage of those fine people who never allowed themselves to go down . . . those galant old Huguenots." A reader of Susanne's memoir christened it "a monument to genuine Huguenot devotion to God, prudence, and determination."[44] But when read closely, these memoirs add a new dimension to the turbulence of the emigration. In the Huguenot diaspora, the lines of contention ran not only between refugees and the French monarchy or between refugees and their new host society but within families themselves.

The multiple ways in which the Revocation menaced families—as communities were torn apart by rivalries within France, in persecutions, in flight, in exile—have yet to be fully appreciated. Some families disintegrated trying to save themselves. The daughter and son-in-law of Pastor Du Bosc, who ministered to the Rotterdam flock when Josias made his *reconnaissance* there, set out from Normandy with their three children to rejoin him at Rotterdam. "Of their three children, alas! the youngest had been arrested at the border, taken to Caen and thrown in the Nouveaux Catholiques; the two others died during the voyage of fatigue and hunger."[45] Even the families whose members reached the Refuge together or who, escaping in fragments, reunited there could not always be put back together again.

The emigration was a crisis point for the family as a unit as well as for each individual composing it. The case of the Champagné suggests that the experience of exile may have led to a questioning of authority relations in the family as fully as it did in the state when refugee intellectuals such as Jurieu contested monarchy. Emigration reshaped the dynamics of kin and family life, as families changed their composition and behavior in their new contexts. It also affected individuals differently by virtue of their gender and age—more precisely, of the stage in their lives at which the event occurred.

The experience of emigration and exile emerged from the convergence of three "times": the time of the event (emigration), family time (the point in the family's life course at which the event occurred), and personal time (the point in each individual family member's life course).[46] At emigration, the Champagné family unit had reached the point of the loss of the father and transition to being headed by a female. For every individual in the family, then, the pain of losing the father was overlaid on the emotions of exile. More than this, strategies for preserving the family unit were made more complex and difficult to implement by having a female head just at the moment when uprooting aggravated stresses already present or added new ones particular to resettlement. As for "personal time," at the moment of emigration several children in the family were nearing the time for leaving home: the moment of their own separation and effort to replicate the family they had grown up in.

Exile changed the algorithm by which the family's needs constrained or promoted individual aspirations. All three sons probably left home earlier than they would have in France. By contrast, Susanne probably left home later than she otherwise would have. The escape put her into a state of suspended animation, for she had the misfortune of reaching marriage age—or at least the age at which her mother had married—just when the escape was being planned and carried out. For this reason, emigration extended the period in which mother and daughter lived together and—especially after the departure of her older brothers—the period in which the family's need for a caretaker of young children took precedence over Susanne's need to found her own family. It was because they were positioned differently with respect to the convergence of the three times that Marie and Susanne responded differently to emigration: Marie rose with confidence to the challenge of family leadership, bolstered by the resources and experience of maturity; Susanne was undermined by bitterness and the uncertainty of a shattered "life plan."[47]

The two escape accounts of Marie de La Rochefoucauld and Susanne de Robillard, so opposed in purpose, illustrate the ambivalent relation between the writing of memoirs and the family in the seventeenth century. Marie wrote in the spirit of lineage, to provide a new mythic basis of identity for "my family," which, in exile, had been dispersed and was no longer held together by the landed patrimony of their ancestors. Susanne, by contrast, substituting her own for her mother's story, brings to mind the observation that among the French nobility "because the family's continuity and development required the sacrifice of individuals' desires, family life inevitably produced tensions and rebellions."[48] Yet her narrative suggests that a third term might well be added to the binary of lineage spirit and individualist rebellion. Far from rejecting the patriarchy, "his family," or asserting her independence from it, Susanne continues to make family the frame in which she places herself: the story she writes responds to her perception of her own sacrifice by claiming the family rather than seeking individuality outside its bonds. It is precisely for saving it, preserving its unity, that she craves credit.

The story of the saving of the Champagné family resonated differently in future generations after the dueling escape memoirs separated with the two women who composed them. Marie took hers to Ireland, along with the dozens of parchments that Josias had smuggled out of France as the family's tangible identity. Her story remained well known to her descendants, who continued down into the twenty-first century to tell the Champagné story as she had told

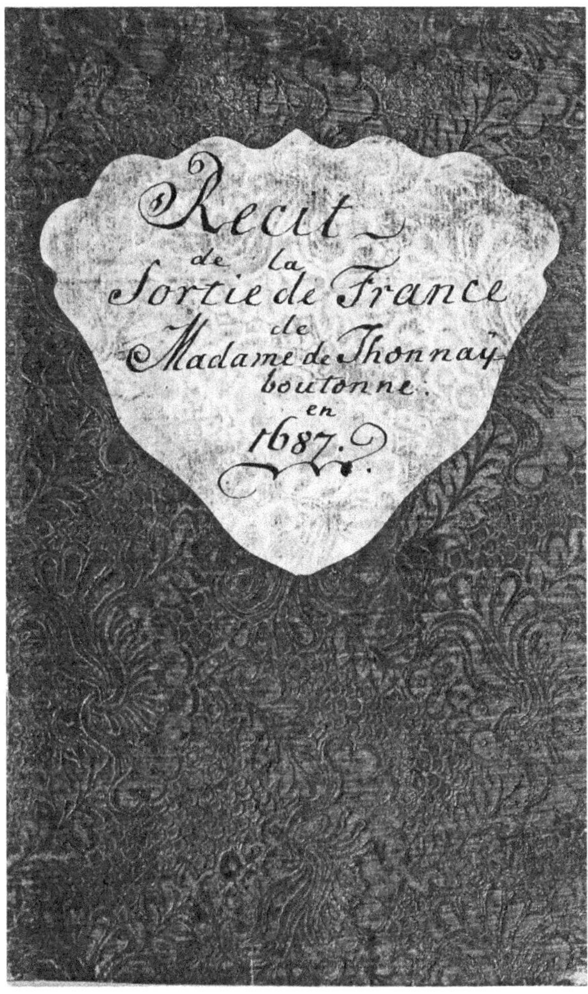

Figure 12.4 Cover of Susanne de Robillard's Récit de La Sortie de France, as presented to Princess Marianne of Prussia. Courtesy of the Universitäts- und Landesbibliothek Darmstadt.

it. Susanne's memoir, like her, ended up in Germany, where her descendants continued to hold and evidently prize her text, for in 1827 they presented a manuscript copy to Princess Marianne of Prussia.[49] Yet probably because the stature they achieved in their new homeland rested on exploits military and male, they would learn to tell their family story without Susanne's testimony, her persona, or even her side of their ancestry.

Susanne's great-grandson, the poet Friedrich Heinrich Karl, Baron de la Motte Fouqué, would, like Susanne, script fairy tales—in his case the renowned *Undine* (1811), a part of the romantic revival of folk literature in Germany that also involved the Grimms. Perhaps his Huguenot heritage inclined him to this genre; the Grimms themselves collected many of their stories from Huguenot descendants who were still telling French tales in their family circles.[50] But neither Susanne's narrative nor the fairy tale genre would shape Friedrich's telling of his family history, which he would recompose in the guise of a biography of his grandfather, Susanne's second son, the famed Prussian general and friend of Fredrick the Great.[51]

In rescripting, the poet did not so much counter Susanne's narrative as just ignore it. She figures in his version merely as part of the love story and then as the aggrieved widow who was drawn (passively) to Celle "where she presumably was recommended to the members of the British royal house who resided there." He imagines his lineage as a rags-to-riches tale: having been robbed at the Revocation and possessed of nothing at the outset of their exile, the family a century later had regained eminence in Germany. His is a story of the men in the male line, of their spirit, the courage they inherited from generation after generation of noble warriors. Among the fugitives themselves, the key figure was Saint-Surin, who experienced the exile as an adventure: "The memory of his noble ancestors, their courage and their sword he took with him. . . . Perhaps it was not without gaiety that he faced danger in his new wandering life in baffling foreign lands." In the next generation, "the poor, virtually abandoned refugee son rose with honor to one of the most distinguished posts in the army and government, and was able through the noble generosity of his friend the king to see the circumstances of his three children well founded. And he left behind himself a name that in his new Fatherland, through him, has become well known and honorable, just as it had been for centuries in their Frankish homeland."[52] The rescripted tale by the poet, fabricator of fairy tales, was not, then, a fairy tale of women's aspiration but an epic, a male tale—a family memory in which women had no identity or contribution to make, no voice, and no power to tell the story.

13

Marie at the Head of the Family

During her eleven months in the Refuge preceding Josias' arrival and for the three decades following his departure, Marie de La Rochefoucauld was in charge of the family finances. How she managed them is recorded in the later pages of the same parchment-covered notebook in which she wrote her version of the family's escape. Marie had not prepared for this responsibility at Berneré, having ceded the handling of her fortune to her husband, as was both customary and mandated by the law. Josias had undertaken the collecting of the loans Marie inherited from Susanne Isle and orchestrated the defense against Aunt Madelene's assault on Berneré at the Parlement in La Réole. The occasional leases to which Marie affixed her signature in France were minor matters, the rental of a farm or indenturing of a debtor's son. By contrast, Marie became a decision-maker in the Refuge, from age forty until nearly seventy-five, when her son Josias fetched her to Ireland and, for the most part, reinstated male control of her finances. One of the astounding aspects of the Champagné's transplantation into the Refuge is the way this woman, who grew up in the economic world of the modest landed nobility, came into her own as an independent steward of the family fortune and as an investor in financial instruments that were laying the foundation for future capitalist markets.

Huguenot expatriates played a notable role in promoting the rapid innovations in public finance and private investment that would incubate modern international banking at the end of the seventeenth century. Protestants who had been financiers in France brought to the Refuge "the skill that can make money breed money," experience with systems for government finance developed in service to the French kings, and continuing contacts with kin and former colleagues dispersed across the diaspora in what amounted to a "Huguenot International." These immigrating investors seem to have moved with greater ease and alacrity into publicly traded investments than their English and Dutch contemporaries, who "might perhaps more readily put their surpluses into land or mortgages, into loans to individuals on bond, or even . . . keep them in a strong box in the house."[1] Accordingly, they became a principal source of the sums that flowed into English government funds and private stock transactions in the years following the Glorious Revolution of 1688. Capital that Huguenots had moved into the Refuge by piggybacking on routine maritime and overland commerce that governments dared not interrupt came to finance that very commerce and those very governments. "What in the beginning was perhaps an arrangement for getting capital out became a powerful banking and exchange network."[2]

Marie de La Rochefoucauld brought capital into the Refuge, but she was not an experienced investor, nor would there be any reason to believe that she understood how money could breed money. Her transformation from a landed economic base to a capitalist one was also not a facet of a larger mutation in the family. The Belesaigne in Amsterdam, for example, centered their family and social lives on their business, using marriage alliances, inheritance, and placements of the children to craft a "family network" that worked together to raise their capital and extend the reach of their financial ventures.[3] Marie's family context in the Refuge was, by contrast, entirely traditional. Every professional and personal decision made by her or her children kept them in the same military-nobility orbit they would have lived in back in France. The transformation of her finances was an anomaly within the overall pattern of her life in exile.

This anomaly makes Marie's case particularly valuable for understanding the economic and financial effect of the Huguenot emigration, which could only assume the importance claimed for it in the countries of the Refuge if participation went beyond the few families of enormous movable wealth who have gotten most attention because their records, like themselves, were rich. Marie's records offer a portrait of an ordinary investor at the turn of the eighteenth century. Not a titan like Adrienne-Marguerite Huguetan, daughter of the Huguenot financier in Holland Pierre Huguetan, a woman who in 1733 had capital totaling 338,084 *florins,* nearly one-third of it in 4,000 shares of the English East India Company and 3,000 new annuities of the South Sea Company. Rather, someone ordinary in the modest size of her stake. From Marie's account book emerges, moreover, the overall portfolio of this ordinary investor, not merely single investments as they appear piecemeal on separate company listings. Perhaps the pattern of her holdings reveals something of her personality, ways of thinking, and values.[4]

The bulk of the fortune available to Josias for investing and, after him, to Marie was in their possession at the start of their exile, whether through the shipment of brandy, the carrying of jewels in pockets, or otherwise. Marie did, though, along the way collect some funds other than those Josias had to hand during his months in The Hague. As widow of one of William of Orange's military officers, she received a pension from the new King of England.[5] She also continued Josias' pursuit of three old personal loans. The chance of repayment from the scoundrel Brassac was so remote that Marie did not even mention it. Nor could she ever figure out whether Josias had collected, when in London in 1689, from one Mr. Tayaut (perhaps the same who may have helped Josias get money out of France in 1688) the 200 *francs* Josias loaned him "on his good faith," so nothing materialized in that matter. But she did collect from the New Convert Lardeau back in France as well as from fellow refugees Sanxay and Guion. A sum of 3,000 *livres* that the fleeing Josias confided to Lardeau when passing through Paris eventually arrived, but Marie netted only about 2,000 *livres* when her son-in-law Saint-Surin traveled to Rotterdam to collect it for her "because of the loss in currency exchange and money devaluation, but there is no remedy for it: that was common for everyone. . . . It is a misfortune that was felt." Jacques Sanxay, formerly the pastor at Tonnay-Boutonne, repaid in full in 1695 the £100 Marie had loaned to one of his parishioners when she was resting in Exeter. As for the fellow refugee Isaac Guion, she collected from him the "thirty-five pounds sterling and a few shillings" she claimed she was owed, even though she did not have the paperwork supporting the collection. "Since I do not have the loan document and judgment to give back to him, I signed an act with a notary in which I promise him that if the said papers are found in France and his payment had already been made, I would refund him the same sum."

Did Marie receive other funds from back home? New Converts often sent funds to their relatives in the Refuge, especially when the French assets of the exiles had accrued to members of the family. Some felt a moral obligation to do so and valued such payments as a way of maintaining family bonds across the distances of the diaspora. Samuel Majou, a slightly older contemporary of Josias in Bas-Poitou, left a record in his will of the funds he sent regularly to his children at Balk in Friesland and Celle in Brunswick-Lüneburg as well as an eloquent admonition to his children who remained in France to continue this practice as an obligation of family solidarity. "Love each other wholeheartedly; rush to help each other . . . never allow yourselves to be divided. . . . If God does not make it possible for our dear children, La Vaslinière and his poor wife and children, to come back to this kingdom, then when you split up the inheritance, give them what belongs to them as to one of you others, and get the revenue to them where they are; and not only that, but some of yours as well if they need it . . . we have from time to time sent them the income from their property. . . . And as for our movables, we want their share to be set aside for them in the same way and sent to them in ready money."[6] Did Casimir Prévost de Touchimbert send money while he was guardian of Thérèse, or Philippe-Benjamin de Mazières while he managed Josias' former lands in the marshes of Voutron? Did Elisabeth de La Rochefoucauld do so after Thérèse died, in the interval before the Parlement's final award of Berneré to Aunt Madelene? Marie's account book does not indicate so, and no known record suggests as much.

But stunningly, without ever noting this revenue in her account book, Marie also received officially sanctioned income of 500 *livres* a year from the estate she abandoned in France, a type of transfer specifically prohibited in law. Each year, the French government collected the revenues from lands left by Protestant fugitives. At least four times, and possibly much more often, given that the payment to the Champagné was inscribed in the government's lease agreement with the temporary manager of the estate, a significant part of the revenues from Berneré was approved by the intendant Bégon for transmittal to Marie in Holland. "That of five hundred *livres* also received from Pierre Isambert, the court-appointed farmer of the estate of Berneré abandoned by Josias de Robillard and dame Marie de La Rochefoucauld, his wife, fugitives, for one year of the farming . . . by terms of the lease drawn up, which mentions the subtraction of half the price of the said lease in favor of the Sieur and Dame de Robillard, by your orders."[7]

Unlike kin-to-kin transfers, which were both illicit and common, this kind of official transfer was rare. Marshal Schomberg was permitted to collect revenues from his lands in France, by special grace of the king, for some time after his departure from the kingdom, as were the Princesse de Tarente, the Marquis de Ruvigny, and his son the Earl of Galway.[8] The Le Coq—three of whom were signatories to the marriage contract of Marie's daughter Henriette-Silvie in The Hague in 1714[9]—received monies from France with permission. François Le Coq, a financier and counselor in the Parlement of Paris who was expelled from France in 1688 as incorrigible, received a pension of 4,000 *livres* directly from Louis XIV. His sister-in-law Françoise Beringhen collected income from assets in France for several years after her expulsion in 1688 and was able to use Dutch political influence as well as the French legal system itself to confirm her right to do so for as long as she lived.[10] Was this more common than previously thought? These few instances of official permissions contrary to the letter of royal law invite rethinking of the practices of the government vis-à-vis those who defied the king's decree of religious conformity by leaving.

The totality of the Champagné patrimony, both what was transferred to Holland with the exiles and what was collected later, Marie de La Rochefoucauld managed after 1688 in a way that took her far from her Saintongeais rural roots: moving exclusively into intangibles, concentrating in English credit markets, and inclining to innovative financial instruments.[11] It is not surprising that the holdings of this formerly landed noble family came to rest in intangibles. Marie's resources in exile were too meager to permit acquisition of landed property. She may also have developed a "migrant preference for semi-liquidity,"[12] and cash transactions would not have been entirely unfamiliar to her, since some of what she inherited from Susanne Isle was in the form of outstanding loans. But neither she nor her grandmother invested in the *rentes* that French noble families typically owned in addition to their real property. In the Refuge, Marie's entire fortune was in intangibles—invisible assets, secured at best by mere paper and often simply by certificate numbers. The risk with an intangible went far beyond the vagaries of landed income; if a stock price collapsed or a loan was uncollectible, there would be no next harvest or next collection of dues from tenants to replenish the family coffers. No wonder that, on occasion, Marie appended to her descriptions of investments that existed only on the account books of her brokers in London an expression of the anxiety that intangible wealth may engender. A letter from Des Clouseaux in London, she noted in 1699, was "the sole knowledge I have of my sum and what it has been placed in. . . . May God bless the thing."

Under Marie's stewardship, then, the Champagné veered in exile in the direction opposite from the typical French trajectory by which liquid income was recycled into status through purchase of land. Marie moved the family fortune not merely to intangibles but to intangibles far from her own location. Though continuing to reside in Holland, she came to concentrate her investments in England. Before her husband died, the couple's portfolio was Dutch. Just days before he left The Hague in October 1688 for the invasion of England, Josias and Marie together lent 5,000 *florins* to the States of Holland at 4 percent interest. When Marie first began managing the patrimony alone, she invested all the funds in Holland. Ten months after Josias' death, she purchased 300 shares in the Dutch East India Company. A year later she loaned 2,000 *florins* to the King of Spain at 5 percent return, a loan guaranteed by the States of Holland; in April 1692 she increased her holdings on the King of Spain with a further 2,000 *florins*, this time at 6 percent. In the early 1690s, her first years of widowhood, she patterned her financial management on the safe, fixed-return investments in Holland that Josias had shown her before his departure. The one salient departure in these years was Marie's purchase in 1692 from Pels, the leading banking house in Amsterdam, of a life annuity for herself and contracts on the lives of the four daughters who resided with her in The Hague.[13]

In 1695, Marie shifted her financial management dramatically from the types of activities that had occupied Josias to a wholly new nexus of credit markets centered in England. Could she have been well enough informed to be encouraged by a sharp rise in the value of the *guilder* vis-à-vis pounds sterling in 1694–1695 that enhanced her transnational buying power for investments carrying higher rates of return?[14] Or might son Josias, who was serving in the English army and who colluded in at least one transaction with Des Clouseaux, have had a hand in the shift?[15] Whatever lay behind it, the shift in Marie's investing both tied her to a historic turning point in European financial history and bespoke her state of mind as an investor. From 1695 on, she placed all her capital in English assets, doing so at virtually the first moment of the "English financial revolution." In this she was one of the thousands of Huguenots who bankrolled the public funds that underwrote the stability of the English crown and arguably produced that country's success in the eighteenth century, including its decisive advance ahead of France.[16] The effect of her shift in investment pattern was that Marie took on a new cosmopolitanism of economic interests that her family had not had before. This in turn involved her in ongoing transnational exchanges of funds and reliance on networks of international dealers and bankers: a fact of her life came to be the notarized powers of attorney, letters of credit, and conversion fees that such exchanges entailed.

The particular English intangibles in which Marie placed the family fortune were innovative and untested; that she went for them suggests Marie's personal comfort with the new. To this point, she had been quite conservative, as was typical of the Huguenot community's investing habits.[17] She favored stolid assets: the Indies, the bonds on the States General and the King of Spain, and personal loans. From 1695 onward, she purchased only tallies on the English public debt and English lottery tickets. Several of those were eventually converted by the sellers into 5 percent South Sea Company stock, transforming short-term debt into long-term equity and catching her up in the greatest stock boom and bust occurring during her lifetime.

Figure 13.1 Wax Seal of Marie de La Rochefoucauld on the power of attorney she signed for collecting dividends on her South Sea Company stock, May 23, 1724. British Library. MS Add. 15,945. The left half of the seal bears the lizard of the Robillard de Champagné, the right half the La Rochefoucauld chevrons with ducal coronet. By permission of the British Library Board.

The flow of her monies tells the tale. What she received in February 1691 from the sale of her brandy first financed her two purchases of bonds on the King of Spain in 1691–1692 and then moved—half in 1695, half in 1699—into tallies at 8 percent. The funds that had underwritten the very traditional face-to-face personal loan to Pastor Sanxay's parishioner in Exeter she parlayed into her first purchase of tallies, 100 pounds sterling worth on paper and parchment at 8 percent in 1695. The 5,000 *florins* she and Josias had loaned to the States of Holland in 1688 she sold in 1699 and put the proceeds into tallies on salt. The funds that had been in Indies stock all went into tallies on coal and leather at 8 percent and 7 percent. By the end of the 1690s, she had no more of the traditional investments Josias had shown her.

Substituting tallies for more traditional bonds bespoke her inclination to trust in the new, as did her investment in tickets on state lotteries and in tontines on her daughters' lives. Tallies were short-term loans to the Exchequer against designated tax receipts already authorized by Parliament but not yet collected. They often needed to be discounted from face value, since the date of repayment was uncertain. Depending on the discount from face value (which raised the actual rate of return), they could be very lucrative. For example, Salt Tax tallies after 1700 would trade most often at par, but until 1700 they traded 6–36 percent below par; in the period when Marie began buying them, then, they carried a windfall yield. State lotteries were a form of government loan in which purchase of a ticket netted a variable interest for a stated period of time with a chance of winning annuities of various values. In each lottery, some tickets—to provide "the added excitement of quite large prizes"—would carry interest rates far higher than the market average. "The unrealistic generosity of the terms offered made the lotteries highly popular. . . . [They] tapped the general rage for gambling. . . . In the harsh and uncertain conditions of eighteenth-century life the state lottery was a perennial way of escape into wealth and leisure—if only in the imagination." And yet "the lottery projects of this period represent far more than just a gamble on dreams of wealth . . . a solid form of investment and a method by which the investor of limited means could gain an entry into the public funds."[18]

As for tontines, they were long-term survivorship loans according to which subscribers continued to receive a pro rata share of earnings only so long as their nominee was alive. Pro rata shares of survivors increased in value as other nominees died until one subscriber (or a specified small number of subscribers) would, in a windfall, receive all the capital. First practiced from the 1670s in the United Provinces by both municipalities and private syndicates as a speculative form of annuity, their advantage over regular annuities was the possibility that the annual payout would increase over time, but like all life annuities they were also vulnerable to total loss for those whose nominee died. In the early years, tontines were not always calibrated to the age of nominees, so they would have been an especially attractive bet for youths and young adult nominees, as in the Champagné case.[19]

Marie's shift in 1695 was from Josias' choices to her own. She did not become aggressive in the credit markets; she selected and traded with an eye to yield, she drew dividends and interest by holding for longer terms rather than playing the market for capital gains. But she was not timid in her choices of investments or in her relations with her brokers. Her English holdings were experimental instruments suited to the investor avid for the upside risk. At least once she encumbered her largest single holding, her Dutch Indies shares, for cash she invested elsewhere in an operation that amounted to extended-term margin investing. She traded actively, not simply empowering her investment advisors or her son Josias. To each of her agents in London—Moreau, Des Clouseaux, Huguetan, Hermitage—she sent funds and instructions on what to do with them. In August 1695, as she began to dip her toes into English instruments, she sent Hermitage funds with instructions to enter her in the lottery. When he replied that he "did not find that appropriate," she instructed him to buy her blanks, and he bought her seven on the Parliament's lottery with a return of 12 percent.[20] Moreau bought her tallies on salt in April 1699 "per my order." That August, when she sold her Indies stock, she sent 1,100 pounds sterling to Des Clouseaux "to place for me in London," and he told her he did "as she wished." Again in 1711, she asked Des Clouseaux to buy three billets on the new lotteries at 10 pounds each, which he did. She even corrected Des Clouseaux's year-end statement in December 1705, which, by her own reckoning, was off by a pound.

The investments Marie chose gave her a comfortable living, though nothing approaching what she had enjoyed at Berneré. It is difficult to calculate her net worth, both because her account-book notations were rather more incidental than comprehensive and because she often failed to distinguish in them between currencies: French *livres*, Dutch *florins*, and English pounds could all be listed as *livres*. But combining her fragmentary income notes for 1700 and 1701—two years in which she did no buying or selling—reveals the English investment payouts that supplemented her pension income of 40 pounds sterling and her annuity income of 700 *francs*. From English investments of at least 2,256 pounds sterling, she received a minimum investment income of 168 pounds sterling, an overall return of at least 7.4 percent and an enviable sum at a time when a respectable English family could live comfortably on 200 pounds a year.[21] Her tontine investment paid off even more spectacularly for the Champagné patrimony. Son Josias would note in his account book after Marie's death (about 1737) that the tontine's capital (originally 15,435 *florins*) was now 24,900 *florins* and the family's share (originally 735 *florins*) now over

3,000. So while the capital had increased in value by 61 percent, the family's share had more than quadrupled in forty-five years. At that point, if daughter Susanne were to survive just five more of her co-nominees, the family would receive a capital payout of 8,000 *florins* (a return on investment of nearly 11:1).[22]

A second transition in Marie's relationship to liquid capital was apparent early in the new century—a transition that bespeaks both her capacity to adapt to new circumstances and the trust she inspired among the Huguenot exile community: Marie became something of a petty banker herself, especially for her women friends. It was not common for women to handle other women's monies, though Huguenot women did often handle their own investments.[23] Marie would not have done so in France, but now her contacts and the capital markets in which she was involved were cosmopolitan. As early as 1701, Marie collected pensions and interest from Des Clouseaux and Huguetan in England for Mesdames de La Primaudaye, Vervillon, Pardaillan, and des Roches, to whom she then passed along "to each one what belonged to her."[24] Later, Collot d'Escury funneled these women's payments to Marie: "he gave me the money, which I distributed to each in proportion to what each was owed." She exchanged money from several Huguenot women in Holland for money in her own London account and sometimes advanced interest payments to those for whom she had yet to receive the funds from London. In 1704, she collected income in Holland and forwarded funds for tally purchases through Des Clouseaux in London "for the account of Mademoiselle de Monlévrier," formerly her neighbor at Berneré. When Nicolas de Lisleferme (cousin of the Nicolas de Voutron and hence of Josias) sent 2,200 French *livres* to his refugee son, the funds passed from Bordeaux to Pels in Amsterdam through Marie in The Hague. She reimbursed herself for costs incurred and remitted the balance to the young Lisleferme: "I acted at the request of Monsieur Moreau; I am owed about an *écu* in postal fees for the letter, which is to be deducted from the payment."

At least from 1708 onward, several Huguenot women kept funds on deposit with Marie. Madame de Villars left in Marie's hands 382 *livres* "that I promise to pay her when she pleases." Until at least 1712, Madame de Guiran deposited a 2,000-*florin* Holland government bond with Marie, who collected the interest and forwarded payments to Guiran's creditors. "I promise to collect the interest and pay it to the said dame or to whomever she specifies. I likewise promise that I or my family will return the said bond to the said dame when she wishes or to her heirs or to the executors of her will." In 1711, she received three bonds belonging to Monsieur de Mirande, 3,000 *livres* "that I promise to return to him whenever he wishes; this is for collecting the interest, which I remit to him upon his request, as he asked me to do." In 1711, Des Clouseaux in London was holding in Marie's account eight tickets on the lottery, of which four belonged to her own family, two to Madame de Villars, and two to Madame von Bülow. In a sense, then, Marie acted, informally, as a kind of early women's bank; all her agents were men, all her "clients" but two were women.

Placing the Children

Marie de La Rochefoucauld's conscious purpose as she stewarded the family fortune was not merely to support herself but to make a future for her children. She closed her escape memoir, in the midst of her grief on losing her husband of twenty-two years, by expressing her sense of vocation as matriarch and mother: "I would never have believed, my dear children, I could survive after such a blow, but God has sustained me in a manner that has surprised me. Apparently, this is in order to take care of you. I declare to you that this is my intention and that nothing is so dear to my heart, asking God with all my soul to acquit me well of it."[25] The capital she traced in her ledger was the patrimony that, as she conceived it, belonged to the children together: "My intention is to leave my children all the instructions I can and that I believe necessary regarding their property and to show them the use I make of it." From the outset of her stewardship, then, she crafted her accounts and the transactions themselves with the goal in mind of preserving the family and its social identity across generations.

The very nature of Marie's account book bespeaks this. It does not record current expenditures, household provisioning, or routine domestic management. Only once—the very last entries in the accounts, in 1717—did she jot down a noncapital outlay, a reminder that she had paid the rent on a summer apartment in Aix-la-Chapelle and bought daughter Marianne a scarf. Nor was the accounting her way of checking her cost of living against her means. It offers no indication of how frugally or luxuriously she lived. Her concern was not her "universe of possessions," which would become so important in account books as social capital later in the eighteenth century. Nor does the book offer any sense of the Huguenot sociability and hospitality in the Refuge that the spy Tillieres made so vivid in his dispatches. The very religion and spiritual life for which she emigrated appear nowhere. Unlike the private journals with which Marie would have been very familiar, it does not register family milestones such as the marriages of children and births of grandchildren.[26]

It was, rather, a tracking of the patrimony, pointing toward the day when she would die and the patrimony be split. As a widow with progeny's inheritances to oversee, Marie had been put in a situation somewhat similar to what Susanne Isle experienced during her own widowhood after the death of her eldest daughter and her La Rochefoucauld son-in-law. And yet widowhood in the Refuge was different. No kin advisors oversaw Marie's choices. The constraints enshrined in French law did not apply. A fortune entirely in movables and the variegated financial markets open to her gave Marie a field of play vastly larger than Susanne Isle's.[27]

Because Marie was comparatively so little constrained, the choices recorded in the account book can reveal some of her values and personality: her independence, her comfort with the new, her expectations for her children. Recent studies of eighteenth-century women's account-keeping have endeavored to sketch how the very activity of account-keeping helped incubate modern personalities: "the ways numbers represent and constitute the self; specifically the ways numbers in financial accounts were used in the eighteenth century to record experience and create subjectivity . . . as a means of individuation, of creating and articulating personality, and—not to be underestimated—to establish private ownership."[28] It is hard to see this in Marie's account book: her activity was not sufficiently dense, her entries not sufficiently frequent—sometimes once a month, often never in one or more years—to have shaped her so deeply. But her account book had, nonetheless, meanings beyond the financial for Marie.

Like the escape account that precedes it, Marie's account book was a narrative: a story and a performance. The move from the first to the second section of the parchment-covered notebook drops the autobiographical, as if Marie did not deem her life after Josias' death worthy of inscribing. Still, the separation between escape account and financial record in the shared volume is not complete, for the investment transactions she jots down are the medium through which she implicitly narrates the unfolding of the family's future. In this respect the format of her account book is informative. It is not in ledger style, as her son Josias' books would later be. Each entry is a prose paragraph rather than a numerical line item divided into columns for income and outlay that are susceptible of being added up, brought to a bottom-line balance, and verified. Her authorial voice tells a brief story of each transaction, the persons involved in it, and often the process through which it occurred. This makes her account book a display of her capacities and virtues, her ability to order and keep in control, for herself and her children.

As such, her accounts reveal not the creation of modern personality but the confluence of older and newer ways of thinking in a context embracing older and newer types of property. Over time, the diversification of forms of wealth—the shift from wealth concentrated in land to intangibles and consumer possessions—would create new ways of thinking, including the emergence of individualistic subjectivity and its expression in consumer practices and account books as well as in novels and autobiographies. But Marie, like others in transitional generations, lived neither in one world nor in the other.

In the Refuge, she abandoned the older conception of land-based property but hung onto the traditional values of family and patrimonial investment that she had learned in an earlier social and economic matrix. She foreshadowed the new by investing exclusively in movables, but perpetuated the old by seeking through them to build patrimony rather than elegance or comfort. In her account book narrative, her attention to the placing of the children and her continuous planning for the ultimate division of the patrimony bespeak the very traditional segment of the diaspora in which she sought to reestablish the family and the continuity with their earlier lives in France that she wished to realize in the Refuge. Her circumstances and her financial instruments were new, but her personal and social values were not.

Almost immediately upon arriving in Holland, Marie began to use her contacts through former neighbors and patrons for the purpose of setting up the children. By the time she finished, the familial diaspora she created from her new home in The Hague would stretch the breadth of Northern Europe. The youngest sons went first. Even before father Josias rejoined the family in The Hague, Marie sent her thirteen-year-old second son, François-Auguste, to become a page at the court of the Princess of Anhalt, a favor granted her by Mademoiselle de Venours, a refugee noblewoman from Poitou.[29] Shortly thereafter she sent her third and last son, twelve-year-old Gédéon, into the Dutch navy.[30] Sending her young children away may have been one of the costs of emigration, for the practice with the Isle and other nobles in Saint-Savinien had been to keep them at home until adulthood. Her pain at losing her sons rings through her description of the first departure, François-Auguste, "whom I escorted as far as Orde [Hörde? Gouda?]. I outfitted him well and paid for his journey. He left in March 1688 with numerous letters of recommendation. He was very well received at the court and was well taken care of. God bless them with his holy grace and make my son worthy of the honor they do him. I pray God for this with all my heart."

The eldest son, Josias, fourteen years old at his arrival in Holland, was able after the family's move to The Hague to pay his court to the Princess of Orange and frequent her festivities, pursuing, as Marie wished, the possibility of a position as page. Such a post was infinitely more prestigious and advantageous than the one in a minor German principality given her second son. Ironically, the success of the Dutch expedition to England in November 1688, in which the elder Josias was a participant, dashed this hope. "My son often went to court, attending the morning ceremony and dinner of the Prince and the circle of the Princess, by whom he had the honor of being known. He had a sure place as page in the household of Her Highness the Princess for the new year, but their elevation to the English throne no longer allowed taking them from other nations." Son Josias' establishment came from a different source:

upon Josias' death in October 1689, La Melonière, the Huguenot commander in whose French regiment of Schomberg's army the elder Josias had served, "with the utmost kindness asked me for my son," whom he made an ensign in the Huguenot troops that completed the defeat of Louis XIV and James II in Ireland.[31]

The four daughters left home later and older. One daughter, Julie, would be placed in the Society of Harlem at age twenty-one. The Société des dames françaises de Harlem, founded in 1683 by the Marquis de Venours in premises provided by the magistrates of Harlem and with financial help from the Princess of Orange, was designed as an asylum for thirty noble French widows and demoiselles "without family and often without resources."[32] A second time, for Julie, it was to the Venours family that Marie was indebted for a child's future. Another daughter, Marianne, neither married nor settled in a community like the Society of Harlem; she would live out her days with her mother and, alternately, with her brother Josias in Ireland and her sister Susanne in Celle.[33] Two other daughters married refugee noblemen. In 1714, thirty-three-year-old Henriette-Silvie became the second wife of Charles Bonnard, Seigneur du Marest d'Antoigny, a military officer from the Touraine. Susanne was much younger, only twenty-four, when she married Charles de La Motte Fouqué, Baron de Tonnay-Boutonne, on December 28, 1692 at The Hague. When widowed in 1701, Susanne moved—again, through contacts initially made among the Huguenot nobility from Poitou-Charentes—to the household of Madame von Bülow in Celle.

Within a generation, then, Champagné family members dispersed across Western Europe, the children settling permanently in Ireland, the Netherlands, and Germany. By the middle of the eighteenth century, when Marie and the children had all passed from the scene, the four surviving grandchildren made their homes in Ireland, Celle, and Brandenburg-Prussia.[34] The Robillard-Champagné had, then, become an illustration of "the international nature of the Refuge."[35] Josias' and Marie's progeny became a European family.

The family radiated from its center in The Hague through a chain of patronage relations, a logic of the old European regime that can be pieced together from various sources. In her memoir written in 1690, Marie de La Rochefoucauld gave a religious inflection to her reasons for continuing on to Holland rather than stopping in her first post-escape destination: "I left England because I had a large family, especially boys to place. I was not at all willing to put them in the service of a Catholic king, having taken them out of France for reasons of religion. I thought no place was better or safer than Holland." The significant element in that statement is her avowal that patronage possibilities shaped her decision-making. The Hague was the northwest European nexus of a chain of patronage relations that stretched in every direction. As the peripatetic soldier

Baron von Pöllnitz would write a few decades later: "The Hague is the best Place in Europe for a Foreigner to make a good Acquaintance with the greatest Ease, because of the many Societies or Assemblies, public Spectacles and Walks. If a Person appears ever so little in public, he is presently known."[36]

Huguenot refugee memoirs from this period often laid out their patronage connections at length. Jean Migault did so in his autobiographical account of his escape from France; Dumont de Bostaquet did so in his.[37] Likewise, in her escape memoir and account book Marie brought into view parts of the networks to which she belonged in The Hague: the military patronage (La Melonière, Scravemour, Venours) and the women who entrusted her with some of their financial dealings (La Primaudaye, Vervillon, Pardaillan, des Roches, Guiran, von Bülow, Martel, Villars). Both the military links and the female friendships can be fleshed out by information in other documents to show that the Champagné negotiated their new circumstances in exile by connecting themselves to their lives back in France and to the conventional social usages they would have pursued had they stayed there.

Trans-European traditions continued to be exploitable in the Refuge. When Susanne and her husband Saint-Surin (La Motte Fouqué) sued, successfully, for subventions from the States General of the United Provinces in the late 1690s, Saint-Surin's petition invoked the earlier European experience of his father, who fought with the Prince of Orange's army for Dutch independence and was killed by a Spanish cavalry assault at Maastricht in July 1632.[38] In this way Saint-Surin sought to locate himself in the minds of his Dutch hosts among the legions of military officers whose service had routinely crossed political boundaries, a traditional and still vibrant cosmopolitan orientation for European noble families. Louis XIV had forbidden his subjects leaving the realm without explicit royal permission as early as 1669, largely out of concern over loss of military resources. The Huguenot emigration, in defying Louis' prohibition, rejected the nationalization of persons that the forces of modernization advanced.

Perhaps the traditional, cosmopolitan future of the Champagné can best be read at the baptisms of Susanne's children between 1693 and 1701 in The Hague. The godparents for the four baptisms were a mix of the family's past and the family's future. Friends known directly or indirectly back home included Renaud de Pons, Marquis de Tors; Henri de Boisse, Marquis de Pardaillan; Angélique-Perside de Martel; and Charlotte de Venours. A new protector was "Her Most Serene Highness Henriette Catherine, Dowager Princess of Anhalt, born Princess of Orange," who served as godmother in 1695 for Henri-Charles and then in 1698 for Henri-Auguste, the future famed Prussian general La Motte Fouqué. Marie, of course, had already used the Venours and Anhalt connections to place her son François-Auguste. Susanne would again avail herself of these patronage ties after she was widowed in 1701, first following Charlotte de Venours to Celle, where this daughter of the Marquis de Venours married Gabriel de Malortie de Villars. A short time later, she sent her seven-year-old son Henri-Auguste[39] as a page to the court of the Princess of Anhalt-Dessau, a favor originating either in the patronage of his godmother or in the influence of his uncle and namesake François-Auguste or both.

In Celle, Susanne moved into the patronage orbit of Eléonore d'Olbreuse, Duchess of Zell and a former neighbor of the Champagné in France. The well-known case of Eléonore exemplifies the importance of transnational patronage networks in structuring the Refuge. Eléonore Desmier d'Olbreuse was born in 1639 at the Château d'Olbreuse, located between Niort and La Rochelle. Her father was an ordinary seigneur from a military family whose genealogy stretched back to the days of William the Conqueror but whose influence was only local. Her forebears had joined the Reform early on, fought in the Wars of Religion alongside Henry of Navarre, and maintained their Protestant faith after the new king abjured. "This simple girl from the Pays d'Aunis or Saintonge"[40] had left France because of the patronage position she held with the La Trémoïlle, the overlords for the Robillard-Champagné estate back in Saintonge. Eléonore first served as maid of honor to Marie de La Tour d'Auvergne, dowager Duchesse de La Trémöille and then, upon the dowager's retirement in 1662, moved to Holland as lady-in-waiting to the Princesse de Tarente.[41] The princess had married a son of the Duc de La Trémoïlle, Henri Charles, who relocated to the Netherlands, where his religion did not disqualify him for a military commission. It was a characteristic move in this period for a daughter of modest nobility to join the entourage of a greater aristocratic woman, just as her brothers would become apprentice soldiers in the armies or households of greater aristocratic men. And just as the men's military pathways often crossed borders, so did the marriages and patronage appointments of the women.

Great aristocrats typically served as marriage brokers for their entourage, offering the modest nobility among its members more extended marriage opportunities than they would have had at home. Eléonore, in the entourage of the Princesse de Tarente, gained a leap of social advancement that was normally known only in fairy tales and was perhaps unrivalled except by Louis XIV's second wife, Madame de Maintenon. "By this one should notice how God, when He wishes, raises up a person. She was not very good looking, but agreeable in face and mind, very poor and of a noble family of Aunis." Eléonore formed a liaison with the Duke of Zell (George-William of Brunswick-Lüneburg) that blossomed in The Hague; the two settled as a couple in Celle, where they eventually married and which became, under the Duchess's influence, nearly a French town.[42] In Celle, Eléonore gathered around her French expatriate nobles, especially but not exclusively Huguenots. She created a Frenchified sociability deep in Germany, featuring balls, comedies, fireworks, theatre, fêtes, French-language conversations, and a superb orchestra put together by Eléonore that spread French music in northwestern Germany.[43] The denizens of the Celle court depended heavily upon the resources the duchess made available to them. As she would write to her cousin La Taillée back in Poitou, "I have an infinity of refugees in Holland I support, including your aunt Mademoiselle Martel. I have the same in this country who live only through me."[44]

The Celle court harbored a concentration of personages from the Charentes, particularly those who had had connections with the Olbreuse or with the La Trémoïlle. Many of them had direct or indirect pre-emigration links to the Champagné. Notable among those who came were the brother of the duchess, Alexandre Desmier d'Olbreuse, and his wife Madeleine-Sylvie de Sainte-Hermine de La Laigne. When Susanne de Robillard arrived in Celle, she became the live-in companion to this sister-in-law of Eléonore, by then widowed and known after her remarriage as Madame von Bülow. Susanne's attachment to Madeleine-Sylvie connects the Champagné story not only back to the pre-emigration networks of Saintonge but very specifically to the conversion activities of Madame de Maintenon.[45]

Madeleine-Sylvie de Sainte-Hermine de La Laigne—Madame d'Olbreuse, then Madame von Bülow—was the daughter of Maintenon's Protestant first cousin Madeleine de Villette, Dame de Sainte-Hermine de La Laigne. She was one of the three Sainte-Hermine children whom Maintenon enticed to Paris in 1680 but who left without ever agreeing to convert.[46] Of these obstinate youngsters, Maintenon wrote when they departed, "I am persuaded that they will repent of it," a prediction she had a hand in bringing to pass. Shortly before the Revocation, in the spring of 1685, Madeleine-Sylvie became the second wife of Alexandre Desmier d'Olbreuse, and the Duchess wrote admiringly to her brother of her new sister-in-law: "her merit is known to me, and I have long known how she resisted the advantages offered her by Madame de Maintenon on condition that she leave her religion. The steadfastness she demonstrated in that encounter gained her the esteem of all who knew of it; for me, I gave her mine from that time on, and I love her without knowing her." For a while just before the Revocation, the Château d'Olbreuse was a kind of safe house where Protestants fleeing persecution or en route to exile could hide. Jean Migault wrote of hiding himself and his children at La Laigne and Olbreuse before their escape via La Rochelle. Anne de Chauffepié wrote that she, her sister, and a friend hid from the dragoons at Olbreuse in September while her aunts hid at La Laigne. But "in November, Monsieur and Madame d'Olbreuse were informed that Madame de Maintenon did not approve of their keeping us at their house, and Madame d'Olbreuse wrote [Maintenon] a letter filled with good will toward us, begging her to let us stay with her, knowing that she could easily do so if she wished. But her severity could not be softened on the matter, and without writing herself, she had one of her brothers tell Madame d'Olbreuse that she should send us away if she did not want her house filled soon with dragoons, from which she had until then been exempted at the request of the Duchess of Zell."[47]

In April 1686, just a year after their marriage and six months after the Revocation, the Olbreuse couple were permitted to emigrate, "on the recommendation of the Duke of Zell." By the same royal order that released the two Olbreuse, the remaining four Protestant Sainte-Hermine de La Laigne were taken into custody: the mother and father, a daughter, and a son. Madeleine-Sylvie's sister Anne-Marie-Françoise ("Minette") was placed in the Nouvelles Catholiques on the rue Sainte-Anne in Paris, where Madame de Maintenon paid her maintenance and gave the orders concerning who was permitted to see her. She remained in custody for ten months until she abjured; she then enjoyed a fine marriage to the Comte de Mailly in the royal chapel at Versailles in July 1687, a handsome pension from the king, and appointments that kept her at the heart of the court until her death in 1737. Their mother was placed "in the house of Madame de Miramion," the institution closely allied with the conversion activities of Madame de Maintenon. She was released after abjuring in April 1687, though Maintenon's continuing complaints that she never took Catholic communion suggest that the accommodation was purely expedient. The father died in prison in December 1687 without ever abjuring. The brother Philippe, whose 1685 request to emigrate had been turned down by the king, endured the Bastille from March 1686 to February 1688, where he was not permitted visits from his family and where missionaries were sent to work on him. He and Madeleine-Sylvie were the only two of the Sainte-Hermine children never to abjure. Along with Isaac Isle, Gédéon Nicolas de Voutron, Renaud de Pons and Judic de La Rochefoucauld, Anne de Chauffepié, François Le Coq, and others, he was declared incorrigible and expelled from France in the spring of 1688 (at the moment of Josias' escape). Like Josias de Robillard, he joined the forces of William of Orange to fight in England and Ireland. He fell victim to the sickness at Dundalk alongside Josias and died at Chester.[48]

Susanne de Robillard spent the final four decades of her life as companion to this Madeleine-Sylvie, now known in her second marriage as Madame von Bülow. Madame von Bülow died in Celle on December 21, 1739, and Susanne in Celle just months later, on September 29, 1740.[49] Living at court with one of the Duchess's closest relatives must have given Susanne at least a glimpse of some of the period's most consequential personal dramas. Eléonore has often been compared to Madame de Maintenon. Both were born near Niort in the

1630s into modest noble families, and both married sovereigns in pairings that defied social norms and could only be explained by the personal qualities of the woman and the susceptibility of the sovereign to those qualities. Both were influential in their respective courts and have been subjected to diverging judgments about how decisive their interventions might have been on their prince's policies. Both were often slandered and satirized. The two consorts engaged actively on opposing sides in rival religions, using levers of political influence to fight the battle on the level of families, where much of the battle of the Revocation was fought.

Eléonore's realm was of course infinitely smaller than Maintenon's, but in a twist of fate she left the larger legacy. Maintenon was nearly fifty when Louis XIV married her and never was queen, never was publicly recognized as his wife, never had children by him. Eléonore, by contrast, allied with the duke in her twenties, became regularized as duchess through marriage, and saw their daughter, Sophie-Dorothée, legitimated and married at sixteen to her first cousin Duke George of Hanover. By the time Susanne arrived in Celle, Sophie-Dorothée had already been declared guilty of adultery with the dashing Count of Koenigsmarck, deprived of her fortune, and imprisoned in the fortress of Ahlden, where she would stay in captivity for thirty-two years, until she died. But Susanne would have seen the departure of George of Hanover—with his sons but without his wife—for the throne of Great Britain in 1714. She would have seen the marriage of Eléonore's granddaughter, Sophie-Dorothée's daughter (also named Sophie-Dorothée), to Friedrich Wilhelm of Prussia in 1706. This nexus of dynasties made Eléonore a progenitor of all the monarchs of Britain and Prussia, as well as of myriad minor princes across Europe. Living close to Eléonore's court gave Susanne's children opportunities to show their Champagné and Saint-Surin mettle. For her son Henri-Auguste, it opened the door to more than twenty years as an officer with Leopold I, Prince of Anhalt-Dessau, known as "the Old Dessauer" (who in Europe's pantheon of military figures was reputed second only to his ally Prince Eugene, brother of the Comte de Soissons),[50] nearly fifty years of close friendship with Frederick the Great, and renown as a Prussian general during the Silesian and Seven Years' Wars.

Traditional aristocratic clientele networks, then, distributed the Robillard-Champagné family geographically. The Huguenot diaspora teemed with transnationals that crossed religious boundaries as well as political borders and that were maintained through correspondence, shared sociability, intermarriage, professional migrations, commercial exchanges, and travel between sites.[51] The best known of the border-crossing networks was the interchanges of finance and trade that have been dubbed the "Protestant International."[52] But other networks ran from congregation to congregation,[53] between pastors, among intellectuals and artists, through the readership of publications,[54] and, among the nobility, between kin and from client to patron.[55] This last, the nobles' "plane" of the diaspora, rested upon long-standing cosmopolitan patronage networks that predated the Revocation, having long circulated military men and marriageable women through what were just beginning to become more and more impermeable national frontiers. Saint-Surin's father had been killed at Maastricht serving in the Dutch army in 1632. Abraham Duquesne, later Louis' most famed admiral, served four years with the Swedes during the Thirty Years' War. Josias' fellow Huguenot Saintongeais noble Boisrond knew what his ultimate recourse was when his childhood friend turned royal enforcer Duvigier coerced him to convert: "I knew well how to hide the little property I had and that the sword I carried would always earn my bread in whatever kingdom where I might carry it." Skilled artisans were not alone in carrying their capital in their own bodies. The leader of James II's troops in Ireland was a German serving in the French army, Comte de Rose (von Rosen); the leader of William III's troops, the Duke of Schomberg, was born in the Palatinate of an English mother, served Charles II and then Louis XIV, becoming marshal of France in 1677, served the Portuguese crown in its resistance to Spain, entered Brandenburg service after the Revocation and then joined William of Orange. Louis XIV remarked in October 1688, when learning from d'Avaux that William of Orange, with Schomberg at his side, was about to depart for an invasion of England: "Do you not find it very extraordinary that Monsieur de Schomberg, who was born German, had himself naturalized Dutch, English, French, and Portuguese?"[56]

When the Revocation denied free movement, violating the period's norms and several treaties that guaranteed free relocation for religious purposes, it asserted a new and drastic form of nationalization that enforced not only religious uniformity within the territory but enclosure of the national population. Huguenots who went into exile were vindicating with their feet the disappearing range of free movement in a prenational world. Ruvigny's emigration exemplified the assumptions that created the Refuge at the time of the Revocation: it was "neither more nor less than a total switch of personal allegiance from Louis XIV to William III and could almost be compared to a great noble bringing along his vassals in his train to serve a new master."[57] To this extent, the Huguenot emigration was a premodern or even antimodern phenomenon. Refugee populations, migrations, and diasporas have become so prominent in the contemporary world that it is tempting to regard them as distinctively modern. Seeing the expatriate Huguenots as anticipating modernity—as "'elite' precursors of modern thought and sensitivity, the vanguard of 'progressive' trends in Western civilization, from capitalism, to individualism, to democratic socialism"[58]—has been a strong bias in Huguenot studies: their Republic of Letters was an intellectual modernizer, an organ of

Enlightenment; their claim to their own religious freedom was a precursor to modern religious toleration; their trading networks were the vanguard of capitalism, and so on. These characterizations are not without their truth. But it is wise not to overlook quite traditional social features in the creation and operation of the Huguenot diaspora. Migration was a normal process of the premodern world, and well-established transregional networks provided the pathways structuring it.

As a consequence, the dynamics of migration in the era of the Revocation may be most fruitfully conceptualized not as a binary passage from French nationality to assimilation in a new national culture but as a three-way negotiation among available sets of bonds, loyalties, and identities—French, cosmopolitan, and the new homeland—even as each of those evolved in contact with the others. More histories of patrons and clients might recapture the networks that Huguenot refugees negotiated. More families' diaries, letters, account books, patronage practices, and genealogies might uncover the choices refugees made, as well as the ways of thinking and the values those choices imply.[59] Marie de La Rochefoucauld's negotiation was clear. Her family was *in* the Netherlands but never *of* the Netherlands, even as it was no longer *in* or *of* France. By the time she went to live with young Josias in Ireland in 1722, only Gédéon among her six surviving children was in Holland, and only he had taken a Dutch spouse. François-Auguste, Marianne, and Susanne were in Germany and Josias in Ireland; Susanne and Henriette married in Holland but with other refugees. Marie's experience of exile is clarified by recognizing that she used the financial "International" to preserve the patrimony but chose the nobles' "International" for her children's futures.

Dividing the Patrimony

As her children scattered along the patronage networks of the Refuge, Marie de La Rochefoucauld recorded in her journal, alongside investment changes in the patrimony, her inter vivos payouts to the children, which she intended to be subtracted from their individual inheritances at her death. Susanne's marriage cost Marie more than 100 *pistoles* for trousseau and other expenses. Marie gave her "a bedstead with a feather mattress, twill cover, and accessories, six bed sheets, two dozen napkins, six chairs, a table, and other small items for her household." Their value, Marie wrote, "I believe equals the share of the movables that she could claim in my estate. I gave her a string of pearls and a ring, which is likewise what she could wish for as her share of my jewels." Julie and Marianne each received a string of pearls at age sixteen; without saying so, Marie presumably recorded this for the same reason she recorded Susanne's necklace and ring: that for each girl this was "what she could wish for as her share of my jewels."

To the sons, Marie gave what they needed for entering their careers when they needed it. In 1699, she paid 1,200 *florins* to buy Gédéon a lieutenancy in a Zeeland regiment commanded by the Baron Sprat. "When my estate is divided, he will acknowledge this sum to his brothers and sisters." In 1708, she sent François-Auguste 100 pounds sterling toward the setup costs for his company of dragoons: "that will be counted against what belongs to him after my death." But the first, most frequent, and most generous payments she gave to her firstborn son, Josias, quite probably because as the eldest son his distinction would be the strongest definer of the family's social standing. Her indulgence with Josias, her high expectations, and her disappointments in him, as recorded in the accounts, reveal her persistence in traditional ways of thinking even in new circumstances.

Josias and his mother seem to have seen each other rarely during the thirty-two years separating his departure for Schomberg's army early in 1690 and the reconvening of the children in The Hague for settling her affairs in 1722. He did attend Susanne's wedding in 1692 and sign her marriage contract. Nonetheless, even in his absence his draws on his mother's purse were persistent. When he was twenty, in 1693, Marie sent 100 *pistoles* to his cousin Des Rabesnières in London "to purchase an employment for my son." But rather than buying Josias a commission, Des Rabesnières gave the money to Josias, who spent it: "He gave him the money, which he lost. So I want that taken into account by his brothers and sisters when they divide my estate." In apparent exasperation, she rewrote her will, reducing the inheritance Josias could expect when she would die. But two years later she sent him another 1,000 *livres* when he was given an infantry company in an English regiment; he was obliged to equip the company, recruit into fourteen vacancies, and get naturalized, "which he found very expensive." This sum, too, would be debited toward his eventual inheritance: "He should not complain about paying too much; I proceed as judiciously as I can."

Four years later, out of evident satisfaction with his advancement in the English army, she reversed her earlier reduction of his inheritance and reinstated his claims to what they would have been in Saintonge: "I wish and affirm that my eldest son will still take the *préciput* [one-fifth] of what remains after my death, as his father wrote down; I reconfirm it and wish it to be so." For two years, until she wrote a new will in November 1701, her account book alone spoke her desire for her son. His reinstatement took on new formality when she—"lying in bed sick"—had her notary Samuel Favon in The Hague write down what she must have suspected would be, literally, her last will.[60] In it, Marie broadened the resources and discretion of her firstborn son, expressed concern for her youngest daughters, and in an odd formulation attempted to co-opt daughter Susanne into the caregiving role she herself would be vacating. Josias would have the favored inheritance: "In conformity with the intentions of her late husband, Josias de Robillard her eldest son, squire, Sieur de Champagné, captain in the English Army in Ireland, shall take as preference legacy the fifth part of all her assets and other movable effects remaining after her death, whether in the nature of bonds or otherwise."[61] He would in addition have a one-seventh equal portion with the six other children and was to have complete liberty in its use, including possible gifts to his sisters.

In the same will, Marie expressed a mother's desire for peace and goodwill among the children. She named Josias guardian for any minor children and François-Auguste successor guardian. Then she sketched out a coresidency plan for the daughters that would place the caregiving burden on Susanne without according her the financial control or decision-making powers to be held by the male guardian: "Recommending in general to all her children to live together in peace, friendship, and union as they were raised and maintained up to now, in particular to her daughters to live together after her death with their eldest sister Dame Susanne de Tonneboutonne in one household and the same house, until they are entirely provided for and set up." Implicitly, giving the choice for coresidence to the sisters Susanne would care for rather than to Susanne, upon whom the burden would fall, expressed the same sense of distance, even estrangement, between mother and daughter that pervaded their two competing escape memoirs. Susanne had just lost her husband Saint-Surin, had three sons aged six, three, and four months to care for with few resources, and was on the verge of leaving The Hague for Celle.[62] Perhaps Marie had reason to fear that her younger daughters would scatter if she died and so phrased her proposal of coresidence as a request to them. It seems possible, even so, that Marie here committed toward Susanne the one truly unkind act posterity can know from her.

Marie recovered her health, and Josias continued to draw funds from his mother. Her 1701 will stated the sum already advanced to him that was to be subtracted from his inheritance as 2,000 *florins* "that she was obligated to provide for his establishment and advancement at various junctures." In January 1705, she sent him 50 pounds sterling against his inheritance, and thirteen months later another 500 *florins*. In April 1709, Josias borrowed 1,000 *guilders* at 6 percent interest from his brother François-Auguste in Germany. When the division of Marie's property was eventually made, in 1722, Josias took little back with him to Ireland, since he had already received in subsidies and loans most of his allotted inheritance. As he lamented in a letter to brother François-Auguste: "I consumed my wheat before it ripened."[63]

Marie's practice of noting her inter vivos payouts was her free choice, tied to her conviction about how the patrimony she preserved should be divided among her children. Sitting in Holland, cut off from her old home in France, with her investments and children scattered in at least three different countries, she was not required to keep track of her gifts or to stipulate that they be subtracted from the recipients' future inheritance. She did so because she chose to distribute the patrimony as if it and they were still in Saintonge and as if it were still lineage immovables rather than intangibles. Apart from the one interlude of pique when she disinherited spendthrift Josias, she adhered in her successive wills to Saintongeais traditions governing division of landed properties, which were not legally binding on her, and declined to partake of the testamentary freedom those same traditions offered for disposition of a fortune, like hers now, consisting of movables.[64] If a Frenchwoman's will can be seen as her self-portrait,[65] then Marie painted herself by remaining true to old family agreements rather than exercising all the discretion her new location allowed to her.

Marie might, alternatively, in the family's changed circumstances, have used her testamentary discretion to leave the patrimony all to one child as a way of helping at least one branch of the family maintain some status—a strategy perhaps appropriate to a downwardly mobile family—or have limited inheritance to those with progeny. Instead, she adhered to the relatively egalitarian spirit of the Saintonge law codes. Perhaps she did this as a way of smoothing over the rupture of emigration by treating her children as she would have in Saintonge. Perhaps she deemed this the best way to avoid replicating the kind of intralineal antagonisms that had helped drive them out of France or stoking those internal tensions that, each in its own way, had been exacerbated by emigration: between husband and wife about whether to emigrate; between daughter and mother over who deserved credit for the successful escape; between mother and eldest son over his spending; between Marie and Marianne, the last unmarried daughter living at home, whose personalities were incompatible.[66] Perhaps the strongest source of solidarity for the siblings was adherence to a set of values they brought with them from the only place where they ever lived all together. For whatever reason, Marie de La Rochefoucauld expressed in her choice of inheritance principles her own fundamental conviction about what equity was for her family as a whole.

Marie de La Rochefoucauld made a future for the Champagné by implementing a family strategy that used new financial instruments in the service of old familial values and exploited traditional patronage networks to simulate inherited status in new locations. The change in her personal circumstances had been nearly complete: from France to Holland, from landed fortune to movable, from wife to widow. The Refuge in which she would live more than half her life was incubating a future in which the life she had lived in France would eventually be unknown. But that life was still being lived in France by her former coreligionist kin: the Prévost de Touchimbert, the Mazières, the Voutron, and the Isle. When she began her financial accounts, Marie summoned up the possibility of a return to France, no doubt envisioning such an eventuality through a policy change by Louis XIV—forced by William of Orange or not—rather than through their own abandonment of the religion for which they emigrated. But did she ever regret or lament their decision to relinquish the lives they might have lived where they were born? Was it precisely her regret that they had had to leave for their immortal souls that kept her wedded to the familiarities and values she brought with her when she came?

In 1722, when Marie de La Rochefoucauld was seventy-five years old, her children gathered in The Hague—Henriette-Silvie and Marianne nearby, Susanne coming from Celle, Josias from Portarlington, and Gédéon from Flanders. Only François-Auguste missed the family reunion, because of ill health in Dresden. The means by which they divided the patrimony into their respective portions expressed Marie's disinclination to impose her favoritisms upon them: they drew straws. Then Josias took his mother to his home in Portarlington, where she would live out her days. "The cruel circumstances in which I found my mother and my sister de Champagné [Marianne] on account of their clash of temperaments and the decrease in my mother's income that no longer allows her to live on the same footing as before, which in my view is very small, made me decide to suggest that she come with me to Ireland next spring. The understanding I believe I have of her principles and of her temperament and those I know my wife to have assure me that with the care I can give her we will all work together for each other's happiness. If God blesses my plans, I will fulfill my duty and gratify my own sentiments."[67] Marie de La Rochefoucauld died in Portarlington eight years later at the age of eighty-three. Who in Saint-Savinien before the Revocation could ever have imagined that she and her husband Josias would end their lives far from Berneré, both in Ireland, 150 miles and forty-one years apart?

It was within their respective national contexts—rather than in the cosmopolitan Refuge—that succeeding generations of Champagné emerged fully as a history-making family. The only children of Marie de La Rochefoucauld and Josias de Robillard de Champagné who had living issue[68]—Susanne and Josias—established lines of descendants in Prussia and Britain. Both lines became far more distinguished in their new nations than they had been in France—a remarkable long-term success effected by the same combination of military profession, patronage, patrimony, and family solidarity through which the Champagné had managed to maintain their place in the risky but all-important Revocation generation. From childhoods in Celle, two sons of Susanne and Saint-Surin made their way to the center of Prussian power. Henri, third son, joined the circle of friends around Prince Henry, younger son of Frederick William I of Prussia and Sophie-Dorothée of Hanover. A military officer and frequent habitué of Henry's Rheinsberg, he retired to Celle unmarried and childless. The second son, Henri-Auguste, became a close friend of Fredrick II and a noted general during the Silesian and Austrian wars. General La Motte Fouqué's grandson was the esteemed romantic poet, author of *Undine*.

On the British side, son Josias married Lady Jane Forbes, daughter of the Earl of Granard, in 1705. Their only child, Arthur, was Dean of Clonmacnoise

Figure 13.2 General Heinrich August de La Motte Fouqué. Oil on canvas by Antoine Pesne, 1745. Stichting Huis Doorn. By permission of AKG Images.

in the Church of Ireland's Cathedral Church of St. Patrick, Trim. Two of the Dean's sons became British generals; in one of the last letters the Dean wrote to his cousin in Prussia in October 1776, he shared his pride in the courage and ambition of his two sons who were young officers in America, both of whom wrote in July to tell him they would soon "bring the rebels to recognize their duty and their submission to the Mother Country."[69] More fortunate in victory were the Dean's descendants through his daughter Jane. She became Countess of Uxbridge[70] and mother of the first Marquess of Anglesey, a prominent Tory and one of the richest peers in Britain, who was dubbed "the Waterloo Marquess" because he commanded the Anglo-Belgian cavalry at Waterloo in Wellington's decisive defeat of Napoleon.[71] Two Uxbridge children married into the Stewart, Spencer, and Hamilton families. Through them, the refugees Marie de La Rochefoucauld and Josias de Robillard de Champagné became ancestors both of the statesman Sir Winston Churchill and of Prince William, heir today to the British throne.[72]

Conclusion

History and Story

This history of the Champagné is a book about stories: about Josias' letters to his children on his changes of religion, his implicit story in the documents he carried into the Refuge, Marie's and Susanne's memoirs of the escape, the malicious fictions of Aunt Madelene's seducer, Jurieu's and Aubarède's tales of Voutron's imprisonment, Tessereau's and Demuin's narratives of 1681, eyewitness reports on Grand-Ry, Boisrond's account of his conversion, the edited history of Saint-Cyr, the commentary on her family and conversion that Henriette-Lidie Isle gave her companions in the cloister, Josias' beautiful death. It is at the same time a book about retelling: about shifting the boundaries between the told and the untold once the original reasons for selectively shaping the story have passed away. The stories told by Josias, Marie, and Susanne, emerging from the trauma of persecution and expatriation, provided them with a way of understanding what had happened to them so unexpectedly and, by casting the blame on their French persecutors, a way of vindicating themselves and justifying their decisions to leave. Like them, the many refugees who inscribed their experiences in autobiographical accounts soon after their flight from France framed their memoirs with a vivid picture of the devotion to religious truth that made them unable to comply with the king's religious directives, the violence that drove them to flee, the dangers they faced in escaping, the personal courage that brought success in the escape, and the outsized costs they suffered from the move.

These stories shaped the way the Huguenot story came to be told in general: as a story of crushing persecution within France, the deeper religious commitment of those who left, the tight borders and severe punishment of apprehended deserters, the individualism of these martyrs for religious choice that made them harbingers of modernity. Historical studies of Huguenots have repeated the throbbing litany of negative cases that Tessereau, Jurieu, and Benoist publicized for polemical purposes, seamless exposés of seemingly continuous actions that downplayed or even excluded the contrasting cases of official laxity, the authorities' decisions not to act or to act at odds with the letter of the law. Elie Benoist compiled and publicized firsthand testimonies from escapees as they arrived in Holland, hot with a rush of relief at having made their way, in many cases without knowing whether they had been pursued. In his pages, hundreds of victims described the sufferings of their families and neighbors at the hands of Louis XIV's dragoons and government agents. Benoist's history was not factually inaccurate; he examined carefully the stories offered to him, and his volumes provide much precious documentation not available elsewhere. But Benoist's selective inclusions were those that helped establish the Huguenot story as one of unmitigated persecution and unalloyed religious heroism.

Setting aside a story hallowed by repetitions over generations is a challenge.[1] Perhaps a retelling of the Champagné story that sifts critically the narratives assembled by exiles and supplements them with historical records that reveal the story untold can yield a more precise picture of Huguenot experience and provoke new investigations. A host of new or revisited questions may lay bare the points connecting the Huguenot story to the main lines of French history, as well as the ways in which that larger story cannot be told well without a fresh and fuller understanding of what happened at the Revocation. The Champagné do not offer a new model of experience: their particular case cannot be taken as typical, paradigmatic, or representative of the larger group. But neither does it illustrate merely "the quirky eccentricity" of one family.[2] It is, rather, on many points the black swan to the standard story, the contrary case that calls into question generalization after generalization about what Louis XIV did to the Protestants in his kingdom and about his subjects' responses to his policies and actions.[3] It brings into the analysis of decision-making by individuals and families as broad a range of contextual experiences as surviving documentation allows. It traces the full trajectory of the family story from well before the decision to leave through the resettlement in new territories in order to reconsider each phase and expose the extent to which new circumstances provoked new thinking or traditional values persisted in unprecedented situations. It brings into its field of vision an entire social network, looking comparatively at migrants and nonmigrants to illuminate the consequences of leaving or staying. It demonstrates that the Huguenot experience worked out on the ground and inside families the large shifts in practices and assumptions that historians generally approach at the top.

The Champagné's decision-making when facing the Revocation—a lengthy and untidy, even confused, process whose outcome was deeply influenced by the actions of others—does not support a conventional categorization of this exodus as a phenomenon apart, one in which the strength of religious commitment alone separated migrants from nonmigrants. Mixed motives not so dissimilar from those provoking earlier and later mass emigrations—social, economic, local and familial, as well as religious—split Protestants of steadfast faith into individuals and families who moved abroad, where they could worship in peace, and those who remained in France, where their devotions were forced underground by royal determination to universalize Catholic practice.

Nor does the escape emerge from the Champagné story as quite in line with the conventional story. Escape was indeed a distinctive part of the Huguenot emigration. Like émigrés from the Revolution a century later and dissidents who would flee twentieth-century totalitarian regimes—but unlike the overwhelming majority of modern migrants—Huguenots who decided to leave France had to get out in secret. The numbers of persons who ventured escape have been taken as testifying to the strength of Huguenot commitment and resolve. Soon after the Revocation, the refugee pastor Pierre Jurieu predicted a special place in Huguenot history for the escape: "It is certain that in the history that may be written of our persecution, the chapter on the escapes should be one of the most beautiful." Jules Michelet later framed the fate of French Protestantism in a similar vein: "It is glorious for human nature that such a great number of men sacrificed everything in order not to lie, passed from wealth to poverty, risked their life, their family, in venturing such a difficult flight."[4] But like the motivations for departure, the circumstances of the escape have been more assumed and alluded to than scrutinized, in part because the refugees' framing of the issue was so convincing. As a clandestine act, the escape transpired outside the ken of observers and so could best become history through the escapees' own telling. Jurieu's *Pastoral Letters* and Elie Benoist's *History of the Edict of Nantes* dramatized the dangers of the escape and the moral qualities it both required and demonstrated. In these accounts, royal authorities exercised tight surveillance, they targeted their resources on would-be fugitives, and they retaliated with rigor, even brutality, whenever they caught someone in the act.

This picture of the escape was credible for two reasons in addition to its refugee origins: it matched the letter of the law, which criminalized departures from the kingdom without permission and prescribed merciless sanctions for any transgressions, and it matched a certain picture of Louis XIV's reign as the apogee of absolutism, built upon the efficacy of royal will, control from the center over the local, and subjection of the nobility by the king's men. Ironically, this view of the reign that fit so well with the Huguenot picture of the escape was the one propagated by the king himself and woven by his propagandists around the defeat of Protestantism. When the almanac for 1686 depicted the grandeur and power of "Louis the Great, Terror and Admiration of the Universe," half of the underlying medallions celebrated the king for subduing foreign rivals and half showed the king's religious triumphs: the demolition of the temple at Charenton, the repair of Catholic churches, the missions dispatched to convert the heretics, and the thanks rendered to the king by his grateful clergy.

Perhaps the revised and now-dominant picture of Louis' reign as much less centralized in policy formulation and much less capable of implementing its will from the center permits a new questioning about the escape. Government documents, spy reports, and personal records suggest that both fugitives' strategizing and government responses were more complex than the

Figure C.1 Louis le Grand la Terreur et l'Admiration de l'Univers, in the *Almanach royal* of 1686. Etching. Louvre Museum. By permission of RMN-Grand Palais/Art Resource, NY.

conventional picture suggests. How did those who determined upon emigration manage their escape? How difficult was it to elude the obstacles that officials put in the path of those who wished to leave? How strongly did officials oppose them anyway? How consistently did they punish would-be emigrants with galley prison and "confiscation of body and property" as the letter of the Revocation mandated? Did the crown recognize that departures enabled it to subdue Protestantism more easily than it could have done with 150,000–200,000 resisters on the ground within France? And what do the answers to these questions say about the reign of Louis XIV?

The prospect that a new look at the Huguenot experience might reverberate upon the main interpretive lines of Louis XIV's France appears also in what the Champagné story reveals about the Protestant nobility and about the centrality of its relations with the king to its decisions on converting. Protestantism is often thought of as a religion of urban elites and workers—bourgeois and artisans. Yet French Protestantism found its early sponsors among the nobility, and at the moment of the Edict of Nantes in 1598 the nobility remained the movement's backbone. Successes of the Ligue in the North during the late phases of the Wars of Religion largely stripped the new faith of its nobility and reduced Protestantism there to an urban "bourgeois" base, but in the Southwest—the home region of Henry of Navarre and the Champagné—nobles retained their adherence to Protestantism well into the new century. At the time of the siege of La Rochelle in the 1620s, some 60–70 percent of the landed nobility in the diocese of La Rochelle were still Protestant. In the South, then, "Protestant communities constitute social pyramids similar to those of the population at large, that is, incorporating a mass of peasantry, craftsmen, bourgeois, and lesser nobles." Nearly down to the Revocation, it could still be said of southern regions that "French Protestantism is not an urban, but rather a rural, phenomenon. Its best leaders were found among small nobles tied to the land."[5]

The story of seventeenth-century French Protestantism is in part the story of how it lost its hold on the French nobility that had founded it, fought for it, and sustained it into Louis XIV's *Grand Siècle*. Three events have seemed key in that loss: the crown's defeat of the Protestant party in the siege of La Rochelle, the loyalty of Protestant nobles in the Fronde, and the conversion of Turenne in 1668. The loss of great nobles like Condé, Rohan, La Trémoïlle, and Turenne weakened the Reformed cause from the top down. And yet the Champagné and the network of noble families of which they were a part reveal that the transition in Protestantism's social base, if underway from 1629, was far from complete by 1668. As late as 1664, the intendant Colbert de Croissy estimated that in Poitou-Charentes half to three-quarters of the nobility were Protestant.[6] When the Revocation outlawed Protestantism in 1685, it exacted an agonizing decision from the many nobles who were still Huguenot. The

Revocation era, then, remains an important point for examining the movement of nobility from sponsors of a suspect faith to converts in the king's religion.

French memory has not been kind to the Protestant nobility. "Historians have been virtually unanimous in pointing to their [the nobility's] greater tendency simply to convert to Catholicism rather than struggle to retain their religion in the face of increasing pressure from their peers and the crown." This observation echoes a general suspicion about tepid Huguenots at the Revocation. Jon Butler, for example, in his classic *Huguenots in America* argues that the disappearance of Protestantism reveals how shallow the Huguenots' "spiritual commitment" was in the late seventeenth century and how strong was "the ability of coercion to reshape religious belief, practice, and allegiance in seventeenth-century and eighteenth-century Europe."[7] The Champagné story counters this view through its focus on Protestant nobles who persisted in their religion down to the point of the Revocation and then branched off in different directions. Some among them (like several of Marie's cousins in the Isle family and her Aunt Madelene) changed religions. Some (like several of Josias' cousins) openly defied the king's orders. Some (like Josias' brother-in-law Casimir Prévost de Touchimbert) conformed with great difficulty. And some (like the Champagné themselves) fled. The deep interweaving of identity, family, and faith that sustained French Protestantism down to the Revocation disintegrated, as Louis XIV intended, and was reconstituted in new forms after those who clung to the old vision departed. This study of one family, then, helps convey the continuing strength of noble Protestant networks and the vulnerability of families in at least one locality right up to the end, the variety of nobles' responses to the Revocation, and the consequences of switching to the king's religion or deciding not to do so.

The Champagné suggest that what the Revocation provoked was a watershed in loyalties. Subtle differences on the issue of obedience to the king seem to have shaped the decision to stay or leave. Juxtaposing Josias' letter refusing conversion with Boisrond's narrative of his conversion exposes contrasting senses of obedience and obligation, and suggests the salience these may have had in the two men's divergent decisions. Obedience—rather than doctrinal truth, which they left to the missionaries and clergy—was the note the authorities consistently sounded in demands for religious conformity. On his way to Saintonge with his troops in late August 1685, Boufflers spoke to the assembled notables of Bergerac in terms of obedience and paternalism, informing them "that it was the King's will that they all go to mass." Abjurations in Saintonge frequently included the phrase: "This is for obeying the will of the king." The notables in Saint-Jean-du-Gard agreed in October 1685 to "re-enter the bosom of the Roman Catholic Church in order to give satisfaction to His Majesty." Governor Hincelin in Guadeloupe noted after the Revocation that Protestants on the island were more likely to respond to assertions of authority than to theological arguments, perhaps because "in fact this is work reserved to the king's authority, for he alone can put them on the path to salvation."[8] In the same vein, Boisrond's memoir frames his conversion to Catholicism as a process of redefining obedience: through successive conversations with noblemen and churchmen, he moved from a sense that his honor as a gentleman was independent of, and perhaps in conflict with, the king's sovereignty—expressed in his interview with Madame de Maintenon—to acquiescence in an obedience that could meet both his own needs and the king's.

Josias de Robillard de Champagné professed respect but did not sound the note of obedience to the king in his letter to his children. Can the contrast between Boisrond and Josias mean that the decision to stay or leave turned upon notions of obedience, on conflicting visions of the king's authority? The well-known republicanism and resistance theory incubated in exile by religious leaders such as Jurieu, and often identified as the legacy of the Refuge to Enlightenment political thought, might lead to this conclusion. But no easy correlation can be drawn between obedience theory and responses to the Revocation. Elie Merlat, the pastor in Saintes until 1680, published his treatise mandating unconditional obedience to the king while in exile in republican Lausanne. Pierre Bayle, who himself defended royal sovereignty and wrote that the absolutist doctrine of his friend Merlat was "very common among Protestants,"[9] lived out his life in exile in Holland.

More likely, the basis of the contrast between Boisrond and Josias lies in the note Josias did sound and on which Boisrond was silent: the obligation of loyalty to family, to his forebears. Both Boisrond and Josias descended from ancestors who had been among the earliest standard-bearers of Protestantism in Saintonge, but only Josias mentioned ancestral religious heritage and obligation as a consideration in his thinking at the moment of the Revocation. "We were born in the religion we profess . . . having suckled our religion with our milk." Examining once again the truth of Protestant doctrine was to ask anew "if [our fathers] had fundamental and solid reasons to separate from the Roman church." The Champagné were a transgenerational line, a succession of progenitors and heirs who became progenitors, and Josias, as the current head of the family, felt he must be loyal to long-vanished ancestors who, through their decisions of individual conscience, had fused Protestantism with the family heritage. Inhabiting their houses, stewarding their lands, bearing their name, Josias was obligated, for the sake of the line, to recommit to Protestantism. His, then, was a traditional conception of family and familial solidarity, a traditional—perhaps archaic—sense of family: a vision of intertwined kin, generations, and religious rites, precisely the style of integrated bonds that the Isle family had exemplified in midcentury.

The kin and colleagues who left their ancestral religion set aside this vision of family in favor of an alliance with the king that offered new opportunities for social and political advancement. The family that redirected its aspirations toward the king was not a network of "old lineage solidarities"—common origin, descent, ancestors, history, or continuity over time—but the living social group created by "associational ties established within each new generation."[10] These converts were no less family-oriented than their predecessors or than those who decided to honor family tradition in the face of the Revocation. Family endured as a value, but with different definitions of family and family interest.

The turning of families from traditional family obligation to redefined obedience, with an eye to future well-being, has been castigated as shameful in the standard Huguenot story, as a sign of venality and weak religious belief, of choosing material advancement over religion. Yet secular and religious motivations cannot be neatly parsed. Social advancement, family solidarity, political loyalty, and religious choice were multiple simultaneous processes layered upon one another so closely that a decision in any one drew upon and redounded upon them all.

Family interest reverberated on the process of religious choice because the crown attacked Protestantism at its family roots. It implicitly sponsored a shift in definitions of family interest by encouraging adults to break with their family past as well as by reeducating children (by force if necessary) in ways of thought and belief not held by their parents. It did so because promoting the willingness of Protestants to disentangle family interest from family religious heritage was key to the erosion of Protestantism in Louis XIV's France. Across the century, "as public institutions such as guilds and police courts became thoroughly Catholicized, and the public face of the Reformed church itself became increasingly tightly regulated, the Reformed community of La Rochelle came to depend more and more on the private institution of the family for its survival . . . [on] inter-weavings of religious attitudes with family strategy in an age of escalating discrimination."[11] But family units bonded together by their shared Protestantism must have seemed to the king something like the ship the Admiral Duquesne piloted with his coreligionists Treillebois and Duquesne-Guiton, the ship that made Seignelay so nervous: a piece of royal sovereignty at risk of acting as an independent fief. So cutting the family tie of loyalty to Protestantism was a prerequisite to implementing the crown's policies not only on religion but on much more. The limited success in doing so, in the end, not only led to the loss of tens of thousands of emigrants but left intact the family and local solidarities that would eventually become the source of Protestant revival and legalization. The centrality of family both to crown efforts at eradication and to Protestant survival renders the crown's offensive to reconfigure families and the dynamics of families as they faced the Revocation indispensable terrain for historians who wish to understand the fate of Protestantism and of absolutism in France.

Josias de Robillard de Champagné and Marie de La Rochefoucauld—buffeted by financial stress, the loss of Berneré, and disintegration of the Isle kin network—took their family into exile rather than cut the family tie of loyalty to Protestantism as demanded of them. The irony was that Josias and Marie had to leave the landed patrimony in order to honor the religious patrimony and to exit the milieu of kin in order to save their nuclear family alone. In the Refuge, they would structure their lives according to a backward-looking vision of traditional fidelities—familial, noble, and cosmopolitan—that they left France in order to preserve. Once having decided to escape the Revocation drama, they and their descendants built new lives and prospered in ways more traditional than modern.

Years ago, Nancy Roelker, the late scholar of Huguenot history, described for colleagues the two commemorations of the 300th anniversary of the Revocation she had attended in London and Paris. In London, she reported, discussions centered on Huguenot families who took refuge abroad after the Revocation. In Paris, discussions focused on the king's motives for the Revocation as a legal and political decision. These diverging approaches to the Huguenot past persist, but the case of the Champagné argues for merging the two discussions: mining family histories to attain a decentered view of royal practice that might help reconceptualize not only the fate of Protestantism in France but also the nature of Louis XIV's state itself.[12]

Multiple single-family histories can offer a breadth and depth of detail on decision-making about confessional adherence in the site—the family—where religious decisions were made. French Protestantism was outside the "magisterial Reformation"; that is, French persons became Protestant by personal choice rather than by mandate of the ruler, as in England and parts of Germany. In France, personalities, personal ties, fortunes, laws, interests, aspirations, deceptions, animosities, and friendships intersected to become the circumstances that pushed definable families and individuals toward Protestantism or Catholicism, and, at the Revocation, toward staying or leaving. Compressed into the human dimensions of the household, these become not abstract "factors" or "trends" but the very stuff of personal and interpersonal lives. In particular, a family focus can bring into view women's experiences. Marie de La Rochefoucauld's family is extraordinarily valuable in this regard, since the principal personages in her drama turn out to be women in four generations: Susanne Isle, Madelene de Solière, Marie de La Rochefoucauld, and

Susanne de Robillard. This succession of women reveals in its full operation what Jonathan Spangler has called "the matriclan": the mother's network of relations, which, as Spangler argues, is crucial to full understanding of family experience.[13]

A family focus fits Huguenot history, moreover, because both church and state made the family a central battleground in the religious contest. The ideology of Louis XIV's rule was based upon patriarchal principles; his religious policy attempted to build upon paternal power and family unity, relying upon the paterfamilias to convert his family unit and (in apparent violation of his own patriarchal principles) authorizing removal of the children to convents for reeducation, or to the homes of Catholic kin when conversion through the fathers failed. The oft-debated role of Madame de Maintenon in the Revocation lay precisely here. It was on this battleground that the morganatic wife of Louis XIV made her contribution to the Revocation, both through Saint-Cyr and through her seemingly ubiquitous intrusions into Reformed families.

As for individual Protestants, family loyalties and kinship ties—strong or weak—shaped their responses when the king willed that they convert. Historians of Huguenot experience have presented evidence of a "state of cooperative coexistence" between Catholics and Protestants—neighbors, kin, and strangers alike—while the Edict of Nantes was in force and cross-confessional solidarity even when the Edict was revoked.[14] Such solidarity was indeed one among various familial responses to internal religious divisions, as religious choice came to be prohibited in public law. There is some evidence that families that were internally harmonious in ways other than their religious divergence could ride out the chaos of the Revocation safely within France. In other cases, however, when Protestant families rent by tensions and animosities other than religious became split between the two religions by the conversion of some but not all of their members, the fate of its nonconverting members could be sealed by what a recent observer in Bosnia has termed "intimate betrayals."[15] The successes and failures of the anti-Protestant policy that Louis XIV believed crucial to his wished-for transformation of governance rested, that is to say, on family lives, personal emotions, and private decision-making as lineages of faith and fortune faced the Revocation.

Afterword

RETELLING THE CHAMPAGNÉ STORY

The Champagné's world offered some easy answers but many unclarities, many masks covering pretenses and impostures. As an upright Huguenot, Josias de Robillard agonized over the need for transparency, eventually going into exile because his conscience would not allow him to pretend to adhere to the king's religion in which he did not believe. Yet his family's story turned, over and over again, on betrayals and impostures that seem to come out of the pages of a novel: a sham marriage that duped a provincial woman visiting Paris, a spy who befriended and betrayed Marie de La Rochefoucauld, embezzlement by a neighbor in the Charentes of funds Josias had saved for exile, forced consignment of a toddler to a convent, a royal school ostensibly for the benefit of noble families that converted children against their parents' wishes, and unending judicial wrangling between competing narratives of justice. All these betrayals and impostures bespeak a texture of uncertainty and vulnerability that were integral to life in the early modern world. Ambiguity and duplicity bedeviled decision-making, as the signs by which one could ferret out intentions, predict consequences, and define priorities were often remarkably unclear. It is ironic that a religious quarrel about truth, which had to be one and identifiable, played itself out so often in a world of fantasy and falsity.

The possibility that the historian's retrieving and retelling of the Champagné family story might be just the latest in this line of betrayals began to worry me as soon as I realized that I would not accept the story as the protagonists themselves told it. The need for a fuller story took me by surprise—struck as I originally was by the consonance between the story told in the Champagné Papers and the standard Huguenot narrative. I gradually came to see, with accumulating outside sources, that what I had found not only filled out the family story but implied a new Huguenot history. On the one hand, I believe that a historian has a special responsibility when dealing with individual lives rather than with abstract themes or public policies: an individual deserves to have her story told undistorted by a historian's interests or limitations. On the other hand, all the issues raised by autobiographical memoirs apply to historical cases where people have explicitly or implicitly told their own story. Huguenot memoirs in general—not merely Marie's and Susanne's and Josias'—cannot be taken as straightforward recordings of what actually happened. The memoirist crafts the story s/he needs. Huguenots writing in exile had to edit memory, to agree on what to forget and what they must remember, in order to live with themselves and with each other. In the end, the historian writing of individuals has to believe that telling a fuller story from a multiplicity of perspectives complements and respects, rather than violates, the self-generated story. Juxtaposing the story received and the "story not told" exposes the needs that generated the selected remembrances and forgettings in the first place, as Huguenot refugees composed their story for themselves and their community.[1]

My project had in fact begun in this terrain of memory and forgetting. In a search for seventeenth-century women's autobiographies, I stumbled upon a 1928 reprint of Marie de La Rochefoucauld's memoir. The intrinsic interest of the text was amplified by the suggestion in an associated article that family papers, including the manuscript of the memoir, were still in the hands of the family.[2] I knew from earlier work how much was to be learned from original manuscripts, rather than even the most scrupulous reprints, and the value of embedding an autobiographical text in at least a modicum of biographical information. Finding the family that currently held those papers therefore became the first of several detective missions this project would compel me to undertake. With the help of the Huguenot Library at University College London, I was put on the track of the descendant in whose hands the papers had resided in 1928: Sir Eustace Dixon Borrowes, 11th Baronet Borrowes. Then-librarian Derek Wright was able to tell me that Borrowes had died in 1939 while residing in Saltwood, Kent. My letters to the Kent County Record Office and the Centre for Kentish Studies at County Hall, Maidstone netted me no records but only the advice to consult the Royal Commission on Historical Manuscripts. Meanwhile, my colleague Paul Seaver advised me to contact the Principal Registry of the Family Division at Somerset House, which gave me my second big break in the case: a copy of the will Borrowes had drawn up in Dublin in 1932. The heirs named therein—his wife, Margaret Lady Borrowes, and then "such of the children of my sister Mrs. Parry-Jones as shall be alive at my wife's death"—were the two slim reeds on which my search would henceforth rest. The trust office address given for Lady Borrowes in the will was the first I tried to exploit: she would surely not be still alive, but perhaps the bank had a forwarding address or knowledge of her heirs. No response.

The second slim reed was the surname of the lineage into which, with her marriage, the sister had been absorbed. Time and again in the project I would learn how difficult it is to find sisters/daughters and their children, because married women change their surnames and because genealogies are customarily drawn in the paternal line alone. Time and again the difficulty would arise when nature gave only daughters in a generation. But in this case, as I would later learn, manmade war, rather than nature, had created a family in distaff: the only child, Kildare, of the 11th Baronet was killed at Jutland in the First World War. With the death of young Kildare in 1916 and the death of his uncle, Walter, in a submarine also in 1916, there were no other heirs to the baronetcy.

Searching for Mrs. Parry-Jones with the single clue of the surname more than sixty years after the date of the will called for stratagems little used by professional historians. Paul Seaver, while on sabbatical in Britain, took a stab for me at the London phonebook and sent me the address of every listed Parry-Jones—with and without hyphen. My letters to each of the London addresses only netted me several letters of kind wishes from persons who regretted having no knowledge of the woman I was searching for. *Burke's Peerage* surely occurred to me more tardily than it would have to a Briton, but it eventually did occur to me, and it turned out to be more informative than the telephone book. In it, I found a Parry-Jones, a retired officer in the Royal Fusiliers, whose wife was indeed the inheriting sister. Returning to the Registry at Somerset House, I procured a will drawn up by Mrs. Parry-Jones in Valparaiso, Chile, in 1951 that named as her heirs her husband, Montagu Martindale Parry-Jones, and after him her three daughters. The 1970 Registrar's attestation of Mrs. Parry-Jones' death in February 1968 gave current addresses, as well as married names, for two of her daughters. Here again, I would experience the difficulties posed by the rarity of women's appearances in the historical record. If the peerage could have passed to a sister in 1939, the 11th baronet would not have been the last in a 300-year-old line, and one of his nieces would have been listed in *Burke's*. Instead, I had only addresses more than twenty years old to go on. I posted letters. I tried to phone into the village listed for one daughter—"Operator, please ring just anybody in Byfield"—but the anonymous voice who answered in a local pub was unacquainted with my prey.

Perhaps further attempts by mail and telephone—in those pre-internet days—to contact either of the daughters by way of the old addresses would eventually have borne fruit. But at this point, and by sheer chance, I stumbled upon what I was looking for in a place I could have reached without the previous searching. Serendipitously, the Huguenot Society of Great Britain and Ireland published a new membership roster in which one listed person was identified as having an interest in the Champagné. Here was someone who knew where the Champagné papers were—her husband being a descendant of Marie and Josias through the son who settled in Ireland—and who was willing to ask their holder, on my behalf, whether I might consult them. That connection at last led me to a small office adjacent to a garage behind a charming North Yorkshire cottage inhabited by one of the Parry-Jones daughters.[3] Here were the papers themselves that it had taken me so long to find.

In France, the pathway to the documents I needed was equally subject to caprice and as blessed with the friendships of generous persons. By chance, on my first visit to Saint-Savinien I landed in the bed-and-breakfast accommodation of a couple who knew the current occupants of the Château de Berneré and who, upon learning of my project, arranged for us to have tea with them in the very premises Marie and Josias left, never to return, in 1687 and 1688. The history of the château was imperfectly known to the new occupants, who were unrelated to the previous owners, for one simple reason—the documents on the château's founding were in Yorkshire. The proprietor's face showed every bit of his surprise when a woman from California told him that the château's history he began to tell me was incorrect. He had not known that the château did not originate with Marie de La Rochefoucauld's sister Elisabeth nor that its builders had been Huguenot nor that the couple who were its third occupants—Marie and Josias—had gone into exile at the Revocation. But in return for what I told him—and which I seem to have told in sufficient detail to make my story credible—he told me of a bookseller who some time before had contacted him with the opportunity to buy a dossier of documents relating to the family who built the château. Not being a descendant, he had had little interest in the offer, but I knew instantly the potential importance of that information to my project and rejoiced, several weeks later, at receiving from him the bookseller's name and address.

Then began a hunt for this source that became protracted beyond all expectation. The easy part was phoning the bookseller. He remembered the dossier of documents but also recalled that he had sold it a decade earlier. He declined, on grounds of client confidentiality, to reveal the purchaser, but when I told him I was writing a book on the family and how desperately I needed the dossier, he promised to look up the information in his files and let me know. After waiting a year without word from him, I contemplated my options: perhaps hiring a private detective to find the purchaser—though I did not know exactly what a hired hand might be able to do that I could not—or engaging a research assistant to canvass archives and libraries on my behalf (I had already tried the Archives privées at the Archives nationales in Paris, to no avail).

By the end of the second year, I decided instead to exploit the power of money. I wrote to the bookseller, reminding him of my earlier request and proposing that he serve as my agent for finding the dossier of documents. Half his fee was enclosed, and the other half would be sent as soon as he found the dossier and secured access to it for me. The remainder of the fee had no time to burn a hole in my pocket: the bookseller's response was immediate. I received the business card of the person who had the dossier and assurance that I would be welcome to consult it at his residence.

But my expectation of soon seeing those documents failed to reckon with the discrepancy between my sense of urgency and the low priority commanded in others' lives by my writing project. Letter after letter to the holder, over the course of several years, lay unanswered. Then one day, while playing around with the newfangled Internet, I impulsively typed in the holder's name and, to my surprise, found an e-mail address. It is a testimony to the change the Internet has made in our lives that I had an immediate response to the message I sent him through the new technology. Of course, he assured me, I would be welcome to come consult the documents; to this end, he would retrieve them from his archives.

My first trip to Périgord to consult the documents, with my husband at the wheel, was a personal success. We discovered Bourdeilles, a favorite place to which we return whenever possible and which also figures in a minor way in the Champagné story, but the dossier of documents eluded me. The holder had been unable to locate them in his massive archive of document collections on local history. A second trip was as pleasurable but as empty in outcome. At last, one February, the holder alerted me that he had found the dossier and it was at my disposal. It took only one more trip to secure it, and then a fourth to secure a second, smaller dossier of related documents that he came across while sorting through his holdings. These were the papers from the legal contests over Berneré and young Thérèse that profoundly transformed the Champagné story.

This continuing emergence of new documentation has made it difficult to find the best moment to call a halt to the research and publish. New sources continue to come to light. The Isle descendant who holds its family archive contacted me and sent his very detailed Isle genealogy long after I had written the sections on that family's experience of the Revocation. There are other sources that have eluded me, some despite very extensive commitment of time and ingenuity. I have never confirmed the self-identification of the spy who was such a traitor to Marie personally and to the Huguenot community in Holland generally, though I have looked in half a dozen archives, visited half a dozen towns and villages bearing the name he gave for the location of his home, and enlisted the help of genealogists and genealogical associations in Angoumois, Saintonge, Poitou, and Anjou. On the English side, there are portraits and photographs yet to discover, and perhaps a few trinkets that belonged to Marie. As late as 1948, portraits of the Champagné refugees were still in the hands of descendants, but the identity of their purchasers in that year was lost shortly thereafter in a fire at the auction house that handled the sale. In Germany, the original manuscript of Susanne de Robillard's memoir has never turned up; copies possessed by Princess Marianne of Prussia and by Susanne's children have had to suffice. Nonetheless, the documentation secured to date allows the telling of the history in its principal elements; one day, some other enterprising researcher may make it yet more complete.

In the course of this long research project, I have incurred debts I can never repay except with personal gratitude. Stanford University faculty research funds supported numerous trips to European archives. A year as Violet Andrews Whittier Faculty Fellow at the Stanford Humanities Center offered time for writing. The staffs of the libraries and archives in France, England, Ireland, Holland, Switzerland, and Germany were invariably forthcoming, even though my requests sought the proverbial needle in their respective haystacks. In the end, Michael Keller, University Librarian at Stanford University, made it possible to bring the Champagné Papers to a place where they will be preserved, organized, and joined to the other family-related manuscripts I was able to procure in Périgord. In Special Collections at Stanford, these materials will be more easily accessible to those who wish to study them than they were to me: future scholars will not need to go through the prolonged detective adventure it was my pleasure to pursue.

The special joy of the project, however, has been the personal relationships that enriched my life as much as my research. J'aimerais remercier tous ceux qui m'ont aidée dans mes recherches et à la rédaction de cet ouvrage par leur amitié et par leurs précieuses contributions. Leila Scott made me welcome in her home and set me up in a workroom by the garage with a space heater, a light, a table, and the trunk of Champagné papers whenever I could make it to Yorkshire. I have fond memories of our lunchtime excursions and teatime conversations; it saddens me that she did not live to see the scholarly fruits of her warm and gracious hospitality. Her role in my project goes beyond our direct associations, however, for it was she who preserved the family papers at a critical moment. In the 1960s, at a time of personal and political crisis, Mrs. Scott travelled to Chile to bring her mother back to England. As they prepared her belongings for the trip, Mrs. Parry-Jones dismissed the trunk as not worth lugging back: it only held old family papers. But Mrs. Scott refused to abandon the family history, and it was the trunk from Chile that continued to hold the papers in the Yorkshire garage to the end of her life. Except for the manuscript original of Marie's memoir, which Mrs. Scott always kept in a dining room drawer, sensing its exceptional value even though she—who did know French—could not read it.[4]

In Holland, two residents of The Hague, who, like Mrs. Scott, did not live to see my project come to fruition, befriended and helped me immensely. Kees Geervliet, an amateur genealogist and retired merchant seaman, guided me to the notarial collections in the municipal archives and introduced me to the Rijksarchief. Corinne Pardede, barones van Boetzelaer, of the Collot d'Escury Stichting, granted me access to the Collot d'Escury archives on deposit in the Rijksarchief, welcomed me into her family, and strolled with me in the rose gardens of Scheveningen. She would have loved to see her ancestors, the Collot d'Escury, who resembled the Champagné so very much, occupy a larger place in this emigration story. In France, Jenny and John Elmes along with Guy and Christiane Bardol were as warm in their welcome as the abundant Saintonge sunshine. Patrick Esclafer de La Rode welcomed me into his Château de Montclar and provided me with documents that made this study possible. In Ireland, Petra Coffey, meeting with me in Yorkshire, Bangor, London, Charleston, and Dublin, and taking me to Portarlington, helped guide this historian of her children's ancestors and became a friend.

Appendix

FAMILY TREES

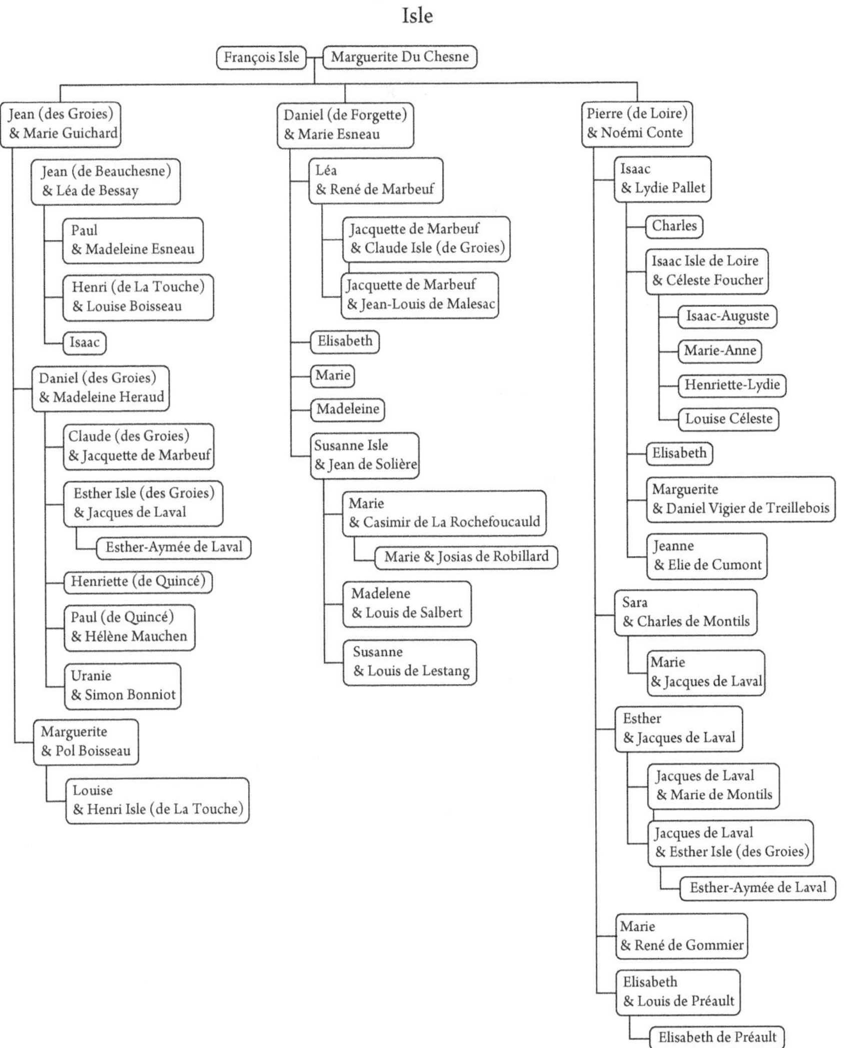

Isle
François Isle
Marguerite Du Chesne
Jean (des Groies) & Marie Guichard
Jean (de Beauchesne) & Léa de Bessay
Paul & Madeleine Esneau
Henri (de La Touche) & Louise Boisseau
Isaac
Daniel (des Groies) & Madeleine Heraud
Claude (des Groies) & Jacquette de Marbeuf
Esther Isle (des Groies) & Jacques de Laval
Esther-Aymée de Laval
Henriette (de Quincé)
Paul (de Quincé) & Hélène Mauchen
Uranie & Simon Bonniot
Marguerite & Pol Boisseau
Louise & Henri Isle (de La Touche)
Daniel (de Forgette) & Marie Esneau
Léa & René de Marbeuf
Jacquette de Marbeuf & Claude Isle (de Groies)
Jacquette de Marbeuf & Jean-Louis de Malesac
Elisabeth
Marie
Madeleine
Susanne Isle & Jean de Solière
Marie & Casimir de La Rochefoucauld
Marie & Josias de Robillard
Madelene & Louis de Salbert
Susanne & Louis de Lestang
Pierre (de Loire) & Noémi Conte
Isaac & Lydie Pallet
Charles
Isaac Isle de Loire & Céleste Foucher
Isaac-Auguste
Marie-Anne
Henriette-Lydie
Louise Céleste
Elisabeth
Marguerite & Daniel Vigier de Treillebois
Jeanne & Elie de Cumont
Sara & Charles de Montils
Marie & Jacques de Laval
Esther & Jacques de Laval
Jacques de Laval & Marie de Montils
Jacques de Laval & Esther Isle (des Groies)
Esther-Aymée de Laval
Marie & René de Gommier
Elisabeth & Louis de Préault
Elisabeth de Préault

Susanne Isle and Jean de Solière

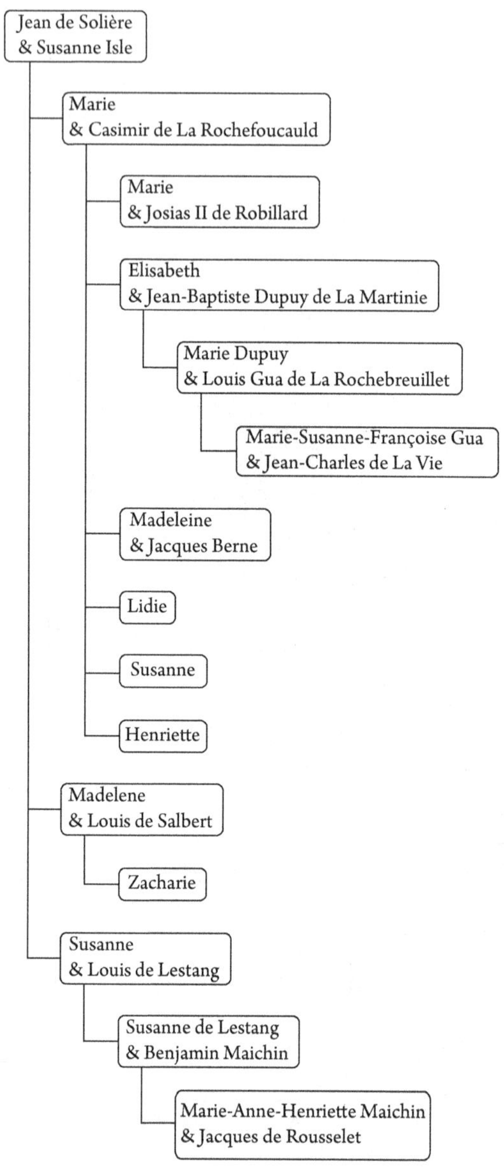

Jean de Solière
& Susanne Isle
Marie
& Casimir de La Rochefoucauld
Marie
& Josias II de Robillard
Elisabeth
& Jean-Baptiste Dupuy de La Martinie
Marie Dupuy
& Louis Gua de La Rochebreuillet
Marie-Susanne-Françoise Gua
& Jean-Charles de La Vie
Madeleine
& Jacques Berne
Lidie
Susanne
Henriette
Madelene
& Louis de Salbert
Zacharie
Susanne
& Louis de Lestang
Susanne de Lestang
& Benjamin Maichin
Marie-Anne-Henriette Maichin
& Jacques de Rousselet

La Rochefoucauld

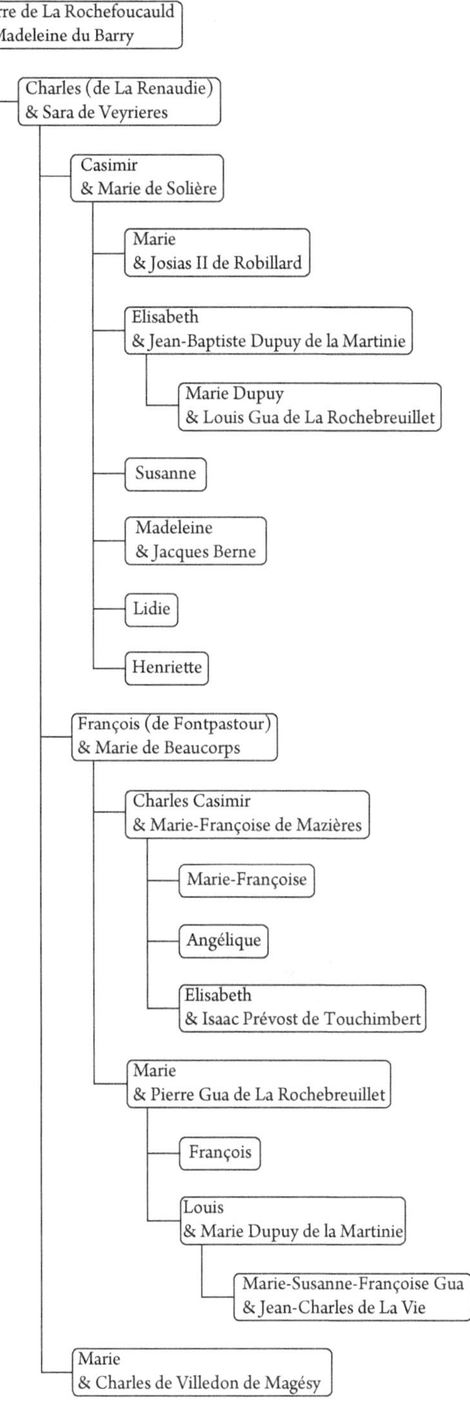
Pierre de La Rochefoucauld
& Madeleine du Barry
Charles (de La Renaudie)
& Sara de Veyrieres
Casimir
& Marie de Solière
Marie
& Josias II de Robillard
Elisabeth
& Jean-Baptiste Dupuy de la Martinie
Marie Dupuy
& Louis Gua de La Rochebreuillet
Susanne
Madeleine
& Jacques Berne
Lidie
Henriette
François (de Fontpastour)
& Marie de Beaucorps
Charles Casimir
& Marie-Françoise de Mazières
Marie-Françoise
Angélique
Elisabeth
& Isaac Prévost de Touchimbert
Marie
& Pierre Gua de La Rochebreuillet
François
Louis
& Marie Dupuy de la Martinie
Marie-Susanne-Françoise Gua
& Jean-Charles de La Vie
Marie
& Charles de Villedon de Magésy

Robillard de Champagné

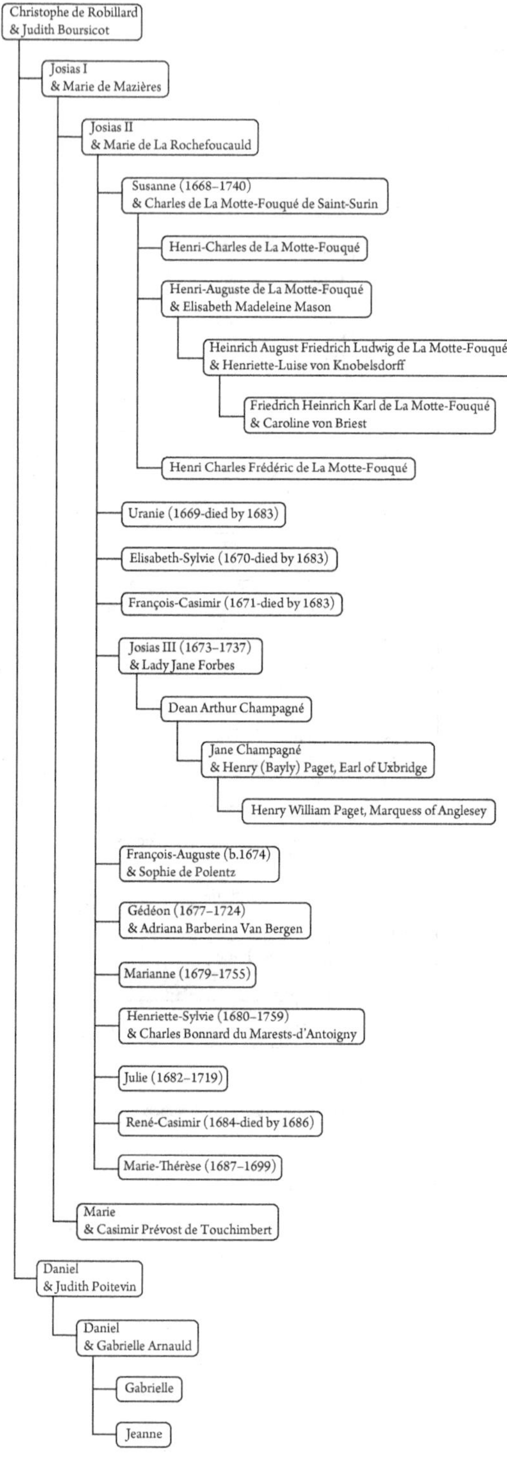

Christophe de Robillard
& Judith Boursicot
Josias I
& Marie de Mazières
Josias II
& Marie de La Rochefoucauld
Susanne (1668–1740)
& Charles de La Motte-Fouqué de Saint-Surin
Henri-Charles de La Motte-Fouqué
Henri-Auguste de La Motte-Fouqué
& Elisabeth Madeleine Mason
Heinrich August Friedrich Ludwig de La Motte-Fouqué
& Henriette-Luise von Knobelsdorff
Friedrich Heinrich Karl de La Motte-Fouqué
& Caroline von Briest
Henri Charles Frédéric de La Motte-Fouqué
Uranie (1669-died by 1683)
Elisabeth-Sylvie (1670-died by 1683)
François-Casimir (1671-died by 1683)
Josias III (1673–1737)
& Lady Jane Forbes
Dean Arthur Champagné
Jane Champagné
& Henry (Bayly) Paget, Earl of Uxbridge
Henry William Paget, Marquess of Anglesey
François-Auguste (b.1674)
& Sophie de Polentz
Gédéon (1677–1724)
& Adriana Barberina Van Bergen
Marianne (1679–1755)
Henriette-Sylvie (1680–1759)
& Charles Bonnard du Marests-d'Antoigny
Julie (1682–1719)
René-Casimir (1684-died by 1686)
Marie-Thérèse (1687–1699)
Marie
& Casimir Prévost de Touchimbert
Daniel
& Judith Poitevin
Daniel
& Gabrielle Arnauld
Gabrielle
Jeanne

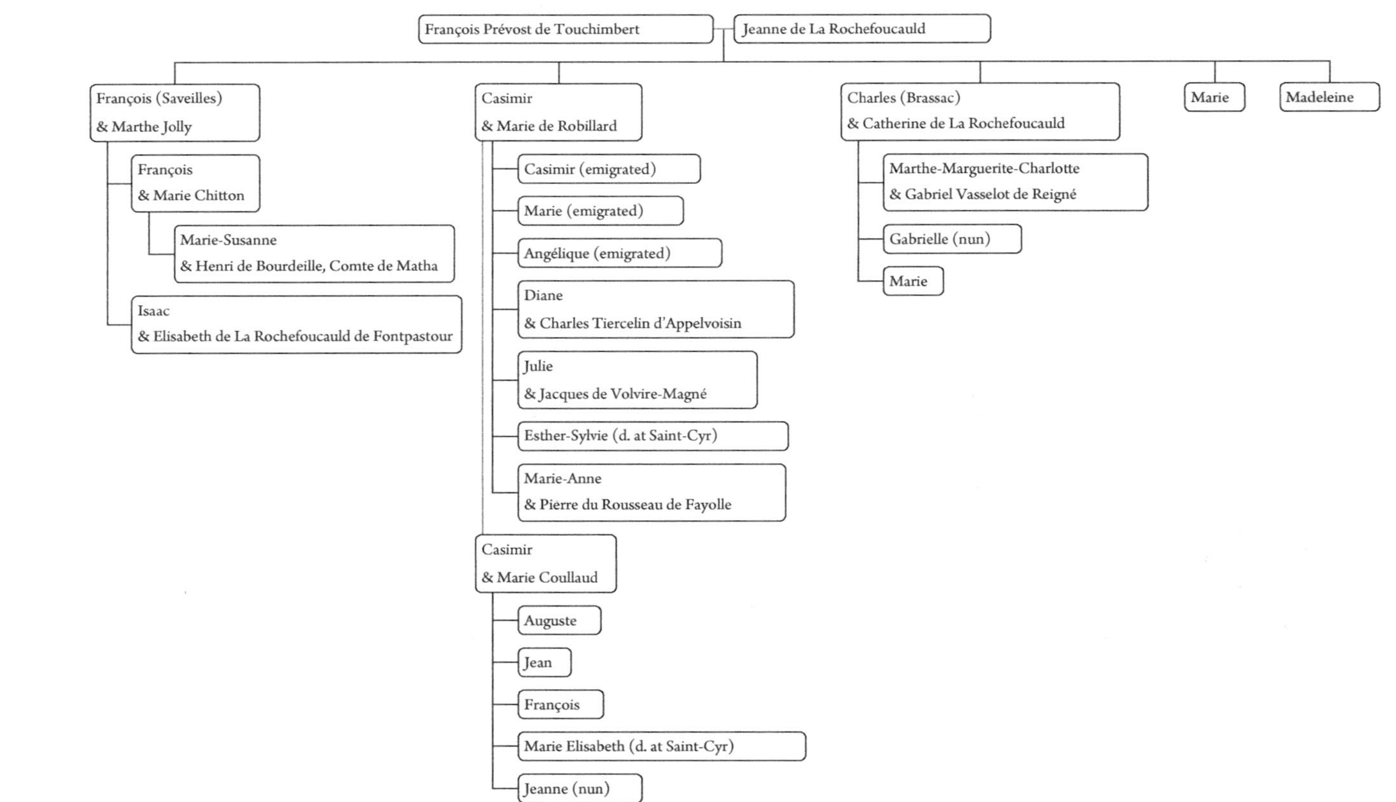
Prévost de Touchimbert
François Prévost de Touchimbert
Jeanne de La Rochefoucauld
François (Saveilles)
& Marthe Jolly
François
& Marie Chitton
Marie-Susanne
& Henri de Bourdeille, Comte de Matha
Isaac
& Elisabeth de La Rochefoucauld de Fontpastour
Casimir
& Marie de Robillard
Casimir (emigrated)
Marie (emigrated)
Angélique (emigrated)
Diane
& Charles Tiercelin d'Appelvoisin
Julie
& Jacques de Volvire-Magné
Esther-Sylvie (d. at Saint-Cyr)
Marie-Anne
& Pierre du Rousseau de Fayolle
Casimir
& Marie Coullaud
Auguste
Jean
François
Marie Elisabeth (d. at Saint-Cyr)
Jeanne (nun)
Charles (Brassac)
& Catherine de La Rochefoucauld
Marthe-Marguerite-Charlotte
& Gabriel Vasselot de Reigné
Gabrielle (nun)
Marie
Marie
Madeleine

Mazières-Voutron

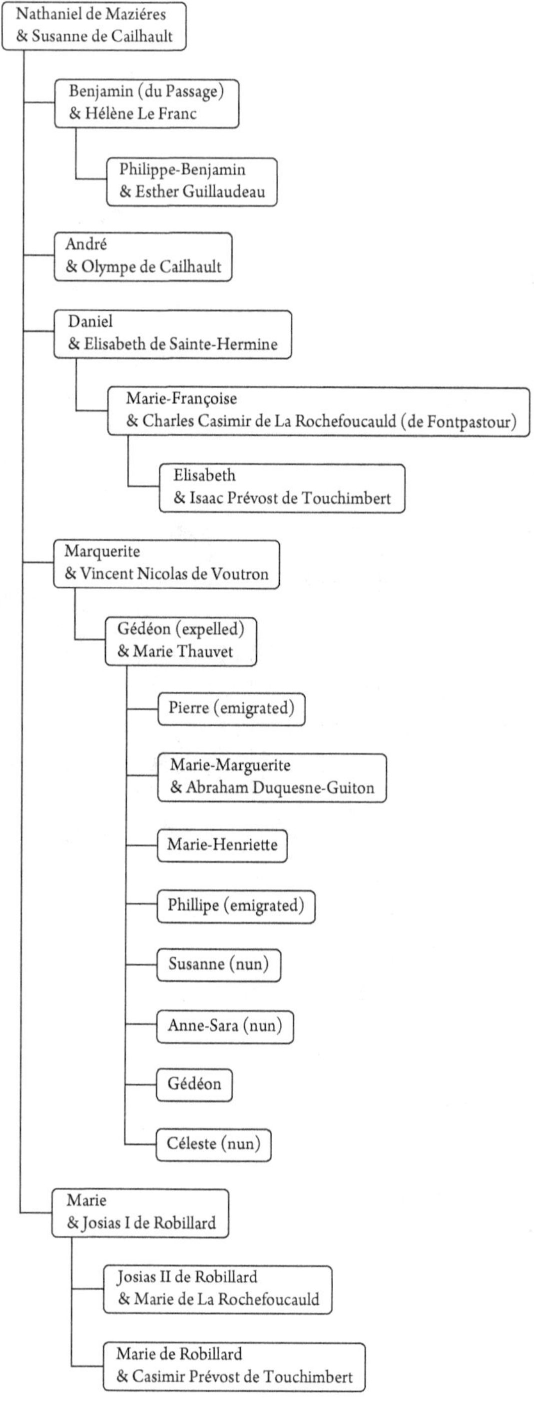
Nathaniel de Maziéres
& Susanne de Cailhault
Benjamin (du Passage)
& Hélène Le Franc
Philippe-Benjamin
& Esther Guillaudeau
André
& Olympe de Cailhault
Daniel
& Elisabeth de Sainte-Hermine
Marie-Françoise
& Charles Casimir de La Rochefoucauld (de Fontpastour)
Elisabeth
& Isaac Prévost de Touchimbert
Marquerite
& Vincent Nicolas de Voutron
Gédéon (expelled)
& Marie Thauvet
Pierre (emigrated)
Marie-Marguerite
& Abraham Duquesne-Guiton
Marie-Henriette
Phillipe (emigrated)
Susanne (nun)
Anne-Sara (nun)
Gédéon
Céleste (nun)
Marie
& Josias I de Robillard
Josias II de Robillard
& Marie de La Rochefoucauld
Marie de Robillard
& Casimir Prévost de Touchimbert

Aubigné-Olbreuse

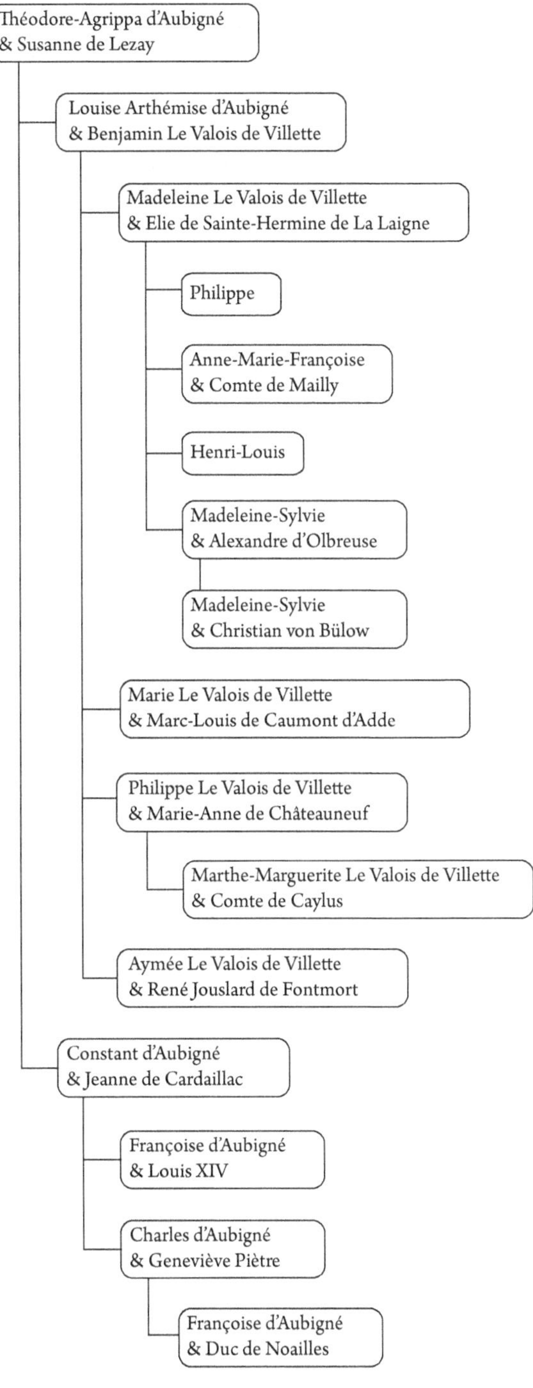
Théodore-Agrippa d'Aubigné
& Susanne de Lezay
Louise Arthémise d'Aubigné
& Benjamin Le Valois de Villette
Madeleine Le Valois de Villette
& Elie de Sainte-Hermine de La Laigne
Philippe
Anne-Marie-Françoise
& Comte de Mailly
Henri-Louis
Madeleine-Sylvie
& Alexandre d'Olbreuse
Madeleine-Sylvie
& Christian von Bülow
Marie Le Valois de Villette
& Marc-Louis de Caumont d'Adde
Philippe Le Valois de Villette
& Marie-Anne de Châteauneuf
Marthe-Marguerite Le Valois de Villette
& Comte de Caylus
Aymée Le Valois de Villette
& René Jouslard de Fontmort
Constant d'Aubigné
& Jeanne de Cardaillac
Françoise d'Aubigné
& Louis XIV
Charles d'Aubigné
& Geneviève Piètre
Françoise d'Aubigné
& Duc de Noailles

NOTES

Abbreviations

ADC	Archives départementales de la Charente
ADCM	Archives départementales de la Charente-Maritime
ADD	Archives départementales de la Dordogne
ADDS	Archives départementales des Deux-Sèvres
ADG	Archives départementales de la Gironde
ADV	Archives départementales de la Vienne
AHSA	*Archives historiques de la Saintonge et de l'Aunis*
AMAE	Archives de la Ministère des Affaires Etrangères (Paris)
AMAE Cp.H	AMAE Correspondance politique. Hollande.
AMB	Archives municipales de Bordeaux
AMS	Archives municipales de Saintes.
AN	Archives nationales (Paris)
ANOM	Archives nationales d'outre-mer (Aix-en-Provence)
BA	Bibliothèque de l'Arsenal (Paris)
BCEW	*Bulletin de la Commission de l'histoire des églises wallonnes*
BibSHPF	Bibliothèque de la Société de l'histoire du protestantisme français (Paris)
BL	British Library
BMLR	Bibliothèque municipale de La Rochelle (Médiathèque Michel-Crépeau)
BNF	Bibliothèque nationale de France
BSA	*Bulletin de la Société des archives historiques de la Saintonge et de l'Aunis*
BSHPF	*Bulletin de la Société de l'histoire du protestantisme français*
BASS	*Bulletin des Amis de Saint-Savinien*
BCEW	*Bulletin de la Commission de l'histoire des églises wallonnes*
CP	Champagné Papers, Stanford University Libraries, Special Collections
FHS	*French Historical Studies*
HGA	Haags Gemeentearchief (The Hague)
E/L	Esclafer/Lougee Manuscripts, Stanford University Libraries
NAI	National Archives of Ireland (Dublin)
NA/PRO	National Archives/Public Record Office (London)
NA/AR	Nationaal Archief/Algemeen Rijksarchief (The Hague)
PHSL	*Proceedings of the Huguenot Society of London* (title varies over time)
RSA	*Revue de Saintonge et d'Aunis* (title varies over time)
SHD:TV	Service historique de la Défense. Armée de Terre. Vincennes
SHD:MR	Service historique de la Défense. Marine. Rochefort
ULD	Universitäts- und Landesbibliothek Darmstadt

Introduction

1. French women retained their birth name throughout their life, not adopting the surname of their husband. The memoir is CP A59: Marie de La Rochefoucauld, Ce 10 Ienvier 1690.
2. Christian Jouhaud discusses "how practices of commemoration lead to the absence of the very past they recall" in "Camisards!" Walter Benjamin explained that it is not neglect or forgetting that marginalizes a story but its "enshrinement as heritage. . .. There is a tradition that is catastrophe. . .. [Such phenomena] are saved through the exhibition of the fissure within them." Benjamin, *Arcades Project*, A 473.
3. Whelan, "Persecution and Toleration," 22, 32. Recent publications that approach Huguenot experience not as a history apart but as an indispensable window on the Old Regime as a whole include Monahan, *Let God Arise*; Luria, *Sacred Boundaries*; Cabanel, *Histoire des protestants en France*; Garrioch, *Huguenots of Paris*; and Mentzer and Van Ruymbeke, eds., *Companion to the Huguenots*.
4. Chernin, *In My Mother's House*, viii. The author's Foreword to the 1994 edition is a brilliant rumination on "telling stories, and their transmission" and on "that tyranny, the written." (xi)
5. On approaches to migration, see Benmayor and Skotnes, *Migration and Identity*; Buechler and Buechler, eds., *Migrants in Europe*; Moya, *Cousins and Strangers*; Green, "Politics of Exit."
6. Cadier-Rey, "Exode," 121.
7. Dangibeaud, "Mission du Marquis de Boufflers," 217.

Chapter 1

1. Two of Duquesne's principal companions in arms (Treillebois and Duquesne-Guiton) were closely related to the Champagné. Isaac Isle's sister Marguerite married Daniel Vigier de Treillebois. Duquesne-Guiton, who accompanied the admiral in all his combats until the admiral's retirement in 1686, would marry Josias' first cousin Marguerite Nicolas de Voutron in 1692 and settle in the Château de Belesbat at Champdolent, near Berneré. See chapter 10.
2. Archives communales de Saint-Jean-d'Angély. E Supp. 1303: Sommation faite par le corps de ville, 1344; Clédat, "Château de La Cave"; Beauchet-Filleau et al., *Dictionnaire*, 5:142–53; AN 1AP: Archives de La Trémoïlle. Chartrier de Thouars 2127: 11/7/1: Aveu rendu. The Isle's acts of *foi et hommage* for their various fiefs and seigneuries are 11/6/10ter-34, 11/7/1-6, 11/9/8.
3. SHD:TV Fonds du Génie MS 503: Claude Masse, Recueil des Plans de Saintonge, 94. On Forgette, see the notice by Frédéric Chasseboeuf in Floris and Talon, eds., *Châteaux, manoirs et logis*, 153, 464–65.
4. AN 1AP: Chartrier de Thouars 2127: 11/6-9: Contrat de baillette and Aveus rendus; CP A46: Summary of the Feudal Tenure of Berneré, undated. The rights of high justice (capital punishment) for Berneré were confirmed by the Parlement of Bordeaux in September 1656. CP A56: Estat et inventaire sommere des tiltres et papiers que J'ay tant de ceux trouvez apres le despart de dame marie de La Rochefoucauld mon espouse pour s'en aler en les pays estrangers, que de ceux qui concerne mon bien particulier que je fais pour servir desclaircisement et valoir apres mon deceps a mes enfans ce que de raison fait au mois de janvier 1688, Item 29.
5. Frédéric Chasseboeuf's notice on Berneray in Floris and Talon, eds., *Châteaux, manoirs et logis*, 148, 463; Crozet, *Châteaux de Charente-Maritime*, 28.
6. CP A56: Estat et inventaire sommere, Item 47.
7. By one estimate, no more than 20 percent of women widowed over the age of forty remarried. François Lebrun, "Amour et mariage," in Dupâquier et al., *Histoire de la population française*, 2:316.
8. CP A24: Marriage Contract between Casimir de La Rochefoucauld and Marie de Solière, November 6, 1646; CP A32: Division of Property by Susanne Isle, March 8, 1677. The

universal heir was the person who received the remainder of the estate after all legacies and debts had been paid.

9. CP A56: Estat et inventaire sommere, Item 24; Beauchet-Filleau et al., *Dictionnaire,* 6:66. Susanne Isle traveled to Angoulême at the end of December 1674 to meet with (and settle up with) her daughter Susanne and the family of her own late husband. In the three-way settlement, the Lescure de Nanteuil gave Susanne Isle a *rente* to discharge what was owed to her husband from his own family, which she then gave to her daughter as final settlement of the dowry promised at her marriage eleven years earlier. The daughter acknowledged having received full payment of her dowry from her mother. Then the daughter ceded to the Lescure de Nanteuil several accounts receivable she had received from them at her marriage. CP A56: Estat et inventaire sommere, Items 25–28.
10. The six girls had been baptized as follows: Marie between August 1647 and January 1648, Elisabeth on November 8, 1648, Madeleine on January 18, 1651, Susanne on October 16, 1652, Henriette on December 31, 1657, Lidie unknown. AMS MS 1065: Registre des baptêmes de l'Eglise Reformée de Saintes 1570–1627, Le Douhet, Tonnay-Boutonne, Aulnay, Saint-Jean-d'Angely et Saint-Savinien, Taillebourg (extraits) 1673–1685, 520. Unless indicated otherwise, information from parish registers (Catholic and Protestant) comes from the pertinent Archives Départementales.
11. Bégon, "Mémoire," 119. This is the report prepared in response to the king's famous call to the intendants for detailed descriptions of all the provinces of France for the edification of the Duc de Bourgogne.
12. Coustures, *Nobiliaire,* 381–82; Nadaud, *Nobiliaire,* 4:281; AMS MS 74 (1688): Contrat de mariage, November 9, 1648; NA/AR. Eerste Afdeling. Staten-Generaal. Liasse Requesten, inv. nr. 7540, May 3, 1689; SHD:TV Fonds du Génie MS 185: Claude Masse, Mémoire géographique sur partie du Bas Poitou, Pays d'Aunis et Saintonge (1715), 748; Boutin, *Breuil Magné et Loire.*
13. Diefendorf, "Women and Property"; Hanlon and Carruthers, "Wills, Inheritance and the Moral Order." Robert Forster linked this expectation that the patrimony would be divided among the children to the general economic fragility of the Saintongeais nobility and its need to engage actively in estate management. "Provincial Noble," 683. Further discussion of these legal issues is found in chapter 4.
14. "It is said that *A House has fallen into distaff,* to say that A Daughter has become its heir; and it is said of Kingdoms and States where daughters are called to the succession, that *They fall into distaff. The Kingdom of France does not fall into distaff." Dictionnaire de l'Académie française,* 2:354. Madelene de Solière had a son, Zacharie, who survived to adulthood but only briefly outlived his mother and seems to have had no progeny.
15. An estimated 60 percent of families had a male heir, 20 percent no heirs at all. Wrigley, "Fertility Strategy"; Goody, "Strategies of Heirship," 16–18; Smith and Oeppen, "Estimating Numbers of Kin."
16. In this adage, the lilies refer to the French crown (*fleur de lys*), which is preserved from female rule by the Salic Law. The adage echoes Matthew 6:28–29.
17. André Burguière and François Lebrun, "One Hundred and One Families," in Burguière et al., eds., *History of the Family,* 2:92, 75. The burden on the patrimony was especially heavy when dowries were paid in cash, as those of both Susanne Isle's younger daughters were. Less onerous for the patrimony were dowries that could be paid over time out of current income (such as *rentes*) so as not to deplete working capital.
18. Maréchal Gaspard de Saulx in the 1570s, quoted in Forster, *House of Saulx-Tavanes,* 4.
19. Beauchet-Filleau et al., *Dictionnaire,* 1:594, 5:147–48, 6:460.
20. ADCM E268: Famille Isle. Contrat de mariage, September 29, 1685. The groom was the son of Jean Isle de Beauchesne and Léa de Bessay, a half-brother of Madelene de Solière's husband Louis de Salbert. Léa de Bessay, then, arranged intralineal marriages for two of her children: this Henri Isle from her second marriage and Louis de Salbert from her first.
21. ADCM E267: Cession de droits, January 8, 1662, January 14, 1662; ADCM E267: Contrat de mariage, July 23, 1659. The inventory of Léa de Bessay's property at the moment of her remarriage is ADCM E267: Inventaire de lea de Bessay veuve de Zacharie de Salbert, 25 janvier 1639.

22. Jack Goody discusses the importance for family survival of "uxorilocal marriage in a virilocal system of post-marital residence" in "Strategies of Heirship," 9–13.
23. Saint-Saud, *Magistrats*, 83, 169; Saint-Saud, *Nouveaux Essais*, 101–10. The family was maintained noble in the *recherches* of 1697. Sauliere genealogies can also be found in Jougla de Morenas, *Grand Armorial*, 6:175–76 and Callandreau, *Ordre de la Noblesse*, 3:67–68.
24. Foulon, *Belles Demeures de la Charente*, 50; Callandreau, *Ordre de la Noblesse*, 3:67–68; La Morinerie, "Chevalier de Nanteuil," 415–16; Saint-Saud, *Nouveaux Essais*, 104–06.
25. Brantôme, *Vies des grands capitaines françois*, 5:93–94.
26. Delafosse, "Contrats de mariage et dots," 2:47; ADC 4J24: Famille de Sauliere ou Solieres, 1643–1692. Testament de Pierre de Sauliere, April 1, 1593; *Genealogie de m'a mere*; Memoire touchant Nanteuil et Les debtes.
27. This branch would have to go back nearly 400 years—to Aimery II de la Rochefoucauld (ca. 1265–1297) and his wife Dauphine de la Tour d'Auvergne—to find an ancestor in common with the senior line that became the ducal branch in the seventeenth century. Martin, *Histoire et généalogie de la maison de La Rochefoucauld*. Martin's massive genealogical reconstruction, compiled with the help of living family members and largely from family archives, is seriously confused on Casimir and on his posterity, no doubt because, having "fallen into distaff," his line generated no posterity named "La Rochefoucauld" to preserve its memory.
28. ADCM E192 (41): Minute de Salenault, May 30, 1656.
29. Beineix, "Calvin en Saintonge-Angoumois," 115–20. The twenty-five-year-old Calvin went to Poitiers and Angoulême after fleeing from Paris and before taking refuge in Basel.
30. CP A8: Defense by André Robillard against his brother Elie Robillard before the Parlement of Bordeaux, 1534; CP A16: Marriage Contract between Josias de Robillard and Marie de Mazières, 1639; CP A56: Estat et inventaire sommere, Item 91.
31. *Paroisses et communes de France: Charente-Maritime*, 588; Crubaugh, *Balancing the Scales of Justice*, 7–10. Crubaugh uses Torxé to illustrate how "exceedingly diminutive" seigneurial jurisdictions could be in Saintonge.
32. SHD:TV Fonds du Génie MS 187: Claude Masse, Mémoire sur la Carte généralle des côtes de bas Poitou, pays d'Aunis, Saintonge, et Isles adjacentes, Médoc, et partie de celles de la basse guienne (1719), 45; "Etat des paroisses en la généralité de Limoges," 298; Julien-Labruyère, *Saintonge maritime*, 258; Braud, *Torxé*.
33. CP A27: Division of Property by Marie de Mazières, May 21, 1662.
34. CP A30: Division of Inheritance by Josias de Robillard and Casimir Prévost de Touchimbert, April 17, 1669; CP A27: Division of Property by Marie de Mazières, May 21, 1662.
35. ADCM E796: Transaction, March 11, 1686; AMS MS 512.68 (100): Déclaration, December 13, 1685; AMS MS 512.68 (117): Déclaration, June 7, 1688. AMS MS 512.68: Fiefs Paroisses Torxé, Vandré, Champagné contains some thirty or so legal judgments, almost all before 1671 (only two in the 1680s), and half a dozen leases involving Josias' land management at Champagné. Additional documentation is listed in CP A56: Estat et inventaire sommere, Items 92–93. Josias was also actively managing his inherited lands at Voutron during this period. See, for example, the seneschal of Rochefort's ruling on his efforts at debt collection as Seigneur d'Agère. ADCM B1603: Transaction, September 1, 1676.
36. Spangler, "Benefit or Burden?," 66.
37. Collins, "Economic Role of Women," 467–68. On legal constrictions of women's independent action, see Natalie Zemon Davis, "City Women and Religious Change," in her *Society and Culture*, 94; Hanley, "Engendering the State."
38. My interpretation of Susanne Isle's motives here differs from Julie Hardwick's observation that the withdrawal of women from estate management in favor of the son-in-law or son was a sign of weakness, "responding to the disjuncture between widows' legal capacity and pervasive cultural ambivalence about independent women. . . . [In so doing they] confirmed the patriarchial order." Hardwick, "Widowhood and Patriarchy," 140–41.
39. CP A32: Division of Property by Susanne Isle, March 8, 1677.

40. Marie's property was clearly recognized as her own, but she ceded the leading role in its affairs to Josias. Law, custom, the terms of her marriage contract, and personal preference together shaped the spouses' respective parts in administering the seigneury. Marie's experience does not, then, support Rafe Blaufarb's view that because married women's separate property was formally recognized in the law, women lords administering seigneuries in their own right was "commonplace" in Old Regime France. "Once a seigneurie was in the hands of a dame, at least in a Roman-law province, the defense and exercise of its prerogatives were largely unaffected by sex." Blaufarb, "Phenomenon of Female Lordship," 28.
41. AN 1AP: Chartrier de Thouars 2127: 11/6/6,7: Contrat d'échange, June 29, 1494; Texier, *Inventaire archéologique*, 10:53; AN 1AP: Chartrier de Thouars 2127: 11/6/18: Contrat de vente, October 26, 1596 and handwritten note on the reverse; 2127: 11/6/19: Homage fait à Taillebourg par Susanne Isle.
42. ADCM E796: Contrat de ferme du four banal, October 20, 1686.
43. ADCM E797: Contrat de vante de bois, January 20, 1687; CP A55: Josias de Robillard to Marie de La Rochefoucauld, November 2, 1687.
44. CP A47: Division of Inheritance between Marie de La Rochefoucauld and her Sisters, March 8, 1677.
45. ADCM E795: Indenture, December 16, 1683. Neither father nor son could sign his name to the contract.
46. CP A35: Inheritance Agreement between five La Rochefoucauld sisters, May 7, 1680; CP A37: Division of Inheritance between Marie de La Rochefoucauld and her sisters, September 11, 1681; CP A38: Division of Inheritance between Marie de La Rochefoucauld and her sisters, December 3, 1682.
47. The Boutonne above Saint-Jean-d'Angély was bordered by lovely prairies, but below the town "the charm of the banks of the Boutonne disappeared, leaving in sight only marshes without trees, sometimes without grass, and that damage the health of their residents." Aussy, *Chroniques saintongeaises*, 36.
48. Rainguet, *Biographie saintongeaise*, 76–79; Oui, *1763 et 1780*.
49. Marie and Josias had six children by the time they moved to Berneré. Susanne was born February 19, 1668, Uranie August 13, 1669, Elisabeth Sylvie November 19, 1670, François-Casimir December 23, 1671, Josias March 13, 1673, and François-Auguste November 2, 1674. Of these six, three would have died by April 1683, when Marie and Josias made a joint will. Six more children would be born during the family's residence at Berneré: Gédéon October 3, 1677, Marianne May 10, 1679, Henriette-Sylvie November 10, 1680, Susanne-Julie September 16, 1682, René-Casimir April 20, 1684, and Marie Thérèse May 16, 1687. The second through fifth births are recorded in the family's own baptismal register (CP A42), the penultimate only in the Le Douhet Protestant parish register, and the last only in the Saint-Savinien Catholic parish register.
50. CP A56: Estat et inventaire sommere, Items 21, 29, 34, 35, 41; CP A48: Table of Tenants and Rents due at Berneré, undated; Bernage, "Mémoire sur la généralité de Limoges, 1698," 2:174; Claude Masse, quoted in Péret, "De Louis XIV à la Révolution," 302; "Etat des paroisses de la généralité de La Rochelle," 165; ADCM E795: Minute de Bouyer, August 24, 1683; E796: Minute de Bouyer, August 5, 1685; CP A39: Lease of La Borderie by Marie de La Rochefoucauld, May 20, 1683.
51. Rodrigues, *Nobles et bourgeois*, 117; Julien-Labruyère, *Saintonge maritime*, 256–57; Oui, *Marins des trois ports*; Musgrave, "Pottery Production and Proto-Industrialisation." On the evolution of the Charentais brandy trade, see Cullen, *Brandy Trade* and Cullen, *Irish Brandy Houses*. As Cullen shows in both books, the distinction between ordinary brandy and the upstream premium "cognac" was not fully established until the 1720s.
52. Claude Masse, quoted in Teodosijevic, *Saint-Savinien*, 29; SHD:TV Fonds du Génie MS 187: Masse, Mémoire sur la Carte généralle, 100; SHD:MR 1E398: Bégon to Barbezières, June 9, 1693; Bégon to Le Peletier de Souzy, June 9, 1693. In 1685, Saint-Savinien had 538 households (*feux*) and 2,290 inhabitants, according to *Paroisses et communes de France: Charente-Maritime*, 522.
53. Péret, "Vitalité et turbulences," 248. On the salt trade, see Combeau, *Commerce du sel*.

54. Péret, "Vitalité et turbulences," 249; SHD:TV Fonds du Génie MS 187: Masse, Mémoire sur la Carte généralle, 49; Cullen, "Huguenots." A recent study of early-seventeenth-century Dutch trade with France emphasizes the dramatic rise of Nantes after the 1628 defeat of La Rochelle: "The conventional wisdom that La Rochelle functioned as a major wine trade center must be dismissed." Bruyn Kops, *Spirited Exchange*, 25–29, 178–79, 199–203. Brandy for export nonetheless remained a shaping influence on life in the Charentes and a part of the Huguenot story, as the Champagné experience shows.
55. Masse, quoted in Péret, "Vitalité et turbulences," 313; La Rochefoucauld, *Voyages en France*, 2:145–46.
56. "Relation du souslevans des paysans de Saintonge," 2:1105. The *croquants* of the Charentes occupy a chapter in Roland Mousnier's classic work, *Peasant Uprisings*, 53–76. Yves-Marie Bercé critiques the "Relation du souslevans" as a source, which is the only known mention of the events in Saint-Savinien, in his *Histoire des croquants*, 1:380.
57. "Remonstrances faictes par les païsans d'Angoulmois," 118–20.
58. Mousnier, *Peasant Uprisings*, 55.
59. Bégon, "Mémoire," 38; Mours, "Essai sommaire," 316–18. Mours estimated another 15,000 in Angoumois. This number for Saintonge-Aunis-Angoumois was reduced about 5 percent by Benedict, *Huguenot Population*, 10. Benedict estimated the number of Huguenots in the kingdom in 1660–1670 at 796,900, which is a 7 percent reduction from the figure calculated by Mours in *Protestantisme en France*, 86. By either count, about one in ten French Protestants were in the Charentes on the eve of the Revocation. According to both Mours and Benedict, only Basse-Guyenne had more Protestants than the Charentes.
60. The 1670 testament of a pilot in Cozes named Elie Traverrier and his wife Elisabeth Durand, quoted in Dangibeaud, "Cozes," 103.
61. Benedict, "Lesser Nobility and the French Reformation"; Séguin, *Histoire de l'Aunis et de la Saintonge*, 260-61; Pérouas, "Clergé catholique," 262; Pérouas, "Sur la démographie rochelaise"; Chaunu, "Histoire religieuse sérielle," 26–27;
62. Colbert de Croissy, "Rapport au Roy," 22; Chaunu, "Histoire religieuse sérielle," 26–27.
63. La Popelinière, *Histoire de France au xvie siècle* (1582), quoted in *Etat du Poitou*, 94. On the La Trémoïlle in Poitou, see Luria, *Sacred Boundaries*. Henri-Charles de La Trémoïlle, Prince de Tarente, a Protestant until 1670, married Amélie de Hesse-Cassel in 1648; she, as well as her daughter Charlotte-Amélie, would have a continuing role in the Champagné family story. See Part Four.
64. Alès, "Lettre," 157; AN 1AP: Chartrier de Thouars 2127: 10/2/14: Contrat de baillette.
65. ADG B27: Arrêt condamnant au supplice de la claie et au feu Jean Moreau dit Mortaigne, saintongeais, May 6, 1547; B70: Arrêt ordonnant au procureur de Saint-Savinien de faire prendre au corps un serrurier de Saint-Jean-d'Angély, February 27, 1554; B75: Arrêt condamnant Jean Poivert, juge de Saint-Savinien, à diverses réparations et amendes, July 14, 1554.
66. Mours, *Eglises réformées*, 66; BNF MS fr. 15880: Noms des benefices au diocese de Xainctes esquelz ne se faict aulcun exercice de Religion katholicq ancienne, et Romaine, 170v.
67. "Etat contenant le dénombrement des personnes faisant profession de la R.P.R., en 1682," 25–26.This survey makes clear Saint-Savinien's importance in the regional Protestant community, for outside Saint-Savinien and Saint-Jean-d'Angély, only Tonnay-Charente (332 individuals from 127 families), Taillebourg (118 individuals from 29 families), and Tonnay-Boutonne (106 individuals from 36 families) were reported to have as many as 100 *religionnaires*.
68. "Arrêt du parlement de Bordeaux, 6 avril 1569," 406. The sentence was annulled by the Peace of Saint-Germain-en-Laye in 1570.
69. AMS MS 1065: Registre des baptêmes, 520; MS 25.404 MAR: Registre des baptêmes et mariages protestants de la paroisse de Saint-Jean-d'Angély, 1592–1599; Bégon, "Mémoire," 58.
70. AN TT232 (xix:13): Liste des gentilhommes du pays d'aulnis faisant profession de la R.P.R. lesquels ont fait ou font encore faire chez eux l'exercice de leur R.P.R. soit comme ayant haulte Justice ou Maison de fiefs . . . Envoyée par M. de Demuin le x[e.] juillet 1681.

71. CP A42: Private Family Baptismal Record, 1669–1673. Olympe de Cailhault was the wife of Marie de Mazières' brother André.
72. Haag and Haag, *France protestante,* 6:357; D.A., "Histoire de la Réformation à Bordeaux," 44; AN TT263b (ii:26): Memoyre des deputez de Lassemblee de la rochelle, 1612; Fortin de La Hoguette, "Lettres," 43.
73. Saudau, *Saint-Jean-d'Angély,* 253–59; Massiou, *Histoire politique,* 5:317–18; Haag and Haag, *France protestante,* 6:358; AN TT233 (vi:12): Actes du Colloque de St Jean dangely tenu à barbezieux pandant la tenue du sinode, October 7, 1682.
74. Wilkinson, "Wars of Religion"; Saint-Saud, *Nouveaux Essais,* 103–04; ADD B175: Sénéchaussée et présidial de Périgueux, Sentences civiles et criminelles, 1681; AN TT236 (i:24): Memoire des Gentilshommes de la generalité de Bordeaux, qui font faire dans leurs maisons et châteaux, l'exercice de la Religion pretendüe réformée, en qualité de seigneurs hauts-justiciers et pretendans avoir fief de haubert, May 2, 1682; AN TT264 (xxxvi:173): Thenevot to Bernage, August 20, 1699.
75. "Arrêt du parlement de Bordeaux, 6 avril 1569," 401; Beauchet-Filleau et al., *Dictionnaire,* 1:594, 5:147; Texier, *Inventaire archéologique,* 3:27, 16; Saudau, *Miettes et Rogatons,* 106–07; La Bruyère, *Affaire de Saint-Jean-d'Angély,* 17, 22, 169, 181.
76. Mentzer, "Edict of Nantes," 115. On these commissions, see also Garrisson, *Essai* and Hickey, "Enforcing the Edict of Nantes."
77. Colbert de Croissy's firsthand description of the commissioners' work can be found in his "Addition au mémoire concernant l'état du Poitou (1664)," 197–98. An explanation of the decisions reached by these commissioners from 1664 onward can be found in ADCM 4J3322: Claude Chevilliard, "Les Protestants face au pouvoir royal en Saintonge de 1661 à 1685." Mémoire de Maîtrise, Faculté de Nanterre (1971–1972), 16–28.
78. Benoist, *Histoire de l'Edit de Nantes,* 3(1):413–15; [Tessereau], *Histoire des reformés,* 16–17, 264. The *Histoire des reformés* seems to have been assembled from Tessereau's notes for posthumous publication by the refugee pastor Daniel Henri de Laizement. Meschinet de Richemond, "Anciennes églises," 371. Abraham Tessereau came from a prominent Protestant family in La Rochelle and was the author of the great *Histoire chronologique de la grande chancellerie de France* (Paris: P. Le Petit, 1676). A brief biography can be found in Rainguet, *Biographie saintongeaise,* 570. On Tessereau's important role in French Protestantism, see Le Fanu, "Mémoires inédits" and Pittion, "Abraham Tessereau."
79. Haag and Haag, *France protestante,* 6:22. The Haag brothers called Isaac Isle "a man of honor and of conscience, full of moderation and at the same time of zeal." Isaac's military service is detailed in the petition for subsistence he addressed to the States General of Holland. NA/AR, Liasse Requesten, inv. nr. 7540. May 3, 1689.
80. The following examples come from the Protestant parish register of Saint-Savinien. For a discussion of godparentage practice among Protestants, see Cousseau, "Sociabilité, parenté baptismale et protestantisme."
81. Luria, "Rituals of Conversion," 66.
82. ADCM B1977: Audience du comté de Taillebourg. Registre; CP A40: Joint Will of Josias de Robillard and Marie de La Rochefoucauld, April 26, 1683; ADCM E795: Minute de Bouyer, August 24, 1683; CP A29: Marriage contract between Josias de Robillard and Marie de La Rochefoucauld, February 22, 1667.
83. Sottas, "Gouvernement de Brouage," 18–19.
84. ADCM H88: Statistique des établissements religieux de l'Election de Saint-Jean-d'Angély, 1723. Claude Masse said in 1717 that though this had formerly been a very grand monastery with fifty-five monks, it then held only two and they still possessed this half-share of the lord's oven revenue. SHD:TV Fonds du Génie MS 186: Claude Masse, Mémoire des lieux les plus remarquables qui sont dans la province de Saintonge, 238–42.
85. AN 1AP: Chartrier de Thouars 2127: 9/1/9: Requête, June 11, 1675.
86. CP A56: Estat et inventaire sommere, Items 1–5.
87. Rodrigues, *Nobles et bourgeois,* 123; ADCM H47: Prieuré de Saint-Pierre de Torsay. Procès-verbal de visite de l'état de l'église, bâtiments et des lieux, par dom René Rousseau, November 7, 1677; "Etat des paroisses de la généralité de La Rochelle," 166; "Etat des paroisses en la généralité de Limoges," 298.

88. "Arrêt du Parlement de Bordeaux, 6 avril 1569"; Saudau, *Saint-Jean-d'Angély*, 285–87. On Saint-Surin, see Part Four.
89. Robert, "Louis XIV et les protestants," 41–42. Robert lays out the phases of intensification and remission leading up to the Revocation. Yves Krumenacker provides a chronology of repression that demonstrates how it varied with foreign affairs in *Protestants du Poitou*, 174.

Chapter 2

1. Bégon, "Mémoire," 41; Péret, "Vitalité et turbulences," 292; Julien-Labruyère, *Paysans charentais*, 2:257; Krumenacker, *Protestants du Poitou*, 126. Julien-Labruyère estimates (259) that there were about 75,000 Protestants in Saintonge in 1680, that there had been about 125,000 before 1628, and that there would be about 35,000 in 1700. Samuel Mours estimated that 25,000 Protestants of Saintonge-Aunis emigrated, as well as 18,000 from Poitou. *Eglises réformées en France*, 171. The total of departures from France was estimated by Mours at 200,000. "Notes," 231. Estimates continue to vary widely down to the present. Perhaps the most helpful estimates are 200,000 for the entire period 1660–1730 and 140,000–160,000 for 1685–1690, which are given by Jean-Pierre Poussou, "Mobilité et migrations," in Dupâquier, *Histoire de la population française*, 2:130.
2. France had not been a party to the Peace of Augsburg, and the *jus emigrandi* was not adopted in the various peace treaties negotiated inside France by the rival confessions during the sixteenth-century Wars of Religion, though some other aspects of Augsburg served as a model in them. France, however, was a party to the Treaty of Westphalia in 1648, and because the *beneficium emigrandi* had been incorporated into the Westphalia accords, some French Protestants believed they would have this protection if the Edict of Nantes were ever revoked. Labrousse, "Calvinism in France," 310.
3. Calvin, *Institutes*, 73.
4. Massiou, *Histoire politique*, 5:511; Jules Michelet to Eugène Pelletan, June 18, 1859, quoted in Viallaneix, "Relire Michelet," iii, i; Michelet, *Histoire de France*, 15:301.
5. Krumenacker, *Protestants du Poitou*, 121; Marcadé, *Protestants poitevins*, 40; Janzé, *Huguenots*, 241.
6. Philippe Joutard has pointed out that refugee descendants and Protestants in France have remembered and commemorated the same 1685 in fundamentally different ways. "Révocation de l'Edit de Nantes."
7. This focus continues to the present day in French Huguenot studies, as Myriam Yardeni acknowledges: "[it is] France and French Protestantism and not the Refuge that is at the heart of reflection." "France protestante," 27–28.
8. Encrevé, "Image de la Réforme"; Joutard, "Révocation," 310.
9. Lavisse, *Histoire de France illustrée*, 7(2):40, 79.
10. Robert, "Louis XIV et les protestants," 52, 40.
11. Elias, "Expulsion," originally entitled "Die Vertreibung." Elias' essay has scarcely been mentioned by students of his work and has been ignored in Huguenot scholarship. Elias himself would never again so much as touch upon the subject in his writings. The first published English translation appeared only in 1998.
12. Elias, "Notes," 121–23.
13. Nazelle, *Protestantisme en Saintonge*, 12; Joutard, "1685," 22; Maintenon, "Réponse," 401.
14. Butler, *Huguenots in America*, 2. By implication, the few escapees were the fervent remnant of a religion whose heyday was a century behind it. Butler thought this tepid religious allegiance explained how Protestantism could be "so thoroughly uprooted" in France and how the Huguenot refugees in the British colonies could have assimilated so easily and quickly into American society.
15. Léonard, *Protestant français*, 37; Vauban, "Mémoire pour le rappel des huguenots," 15.
16. Quoted in Teodosijevic, *Saint-Savinien*, 38.
17. SHD:TV Fonds du Génie MS 186: Masse, Mémoire des lieux les plus remarquables, 238–42; AMAE, Mémoires et Documents. France 1478: Placet des habitans de st savinien en Xaintonge pour se plaindre contre le Curé de leur paroisse qui mene une vie scandaleuse,

refuse de les confesser, de Baptiser Les Enfans, Et leur repond quil aimeroit beaucoup mesme quils fussent Calvinistes il n'auroit pas tant de peine, fol. 54. This curé, Côme Béchet, was still in place as late as 1737, according to the parish registers.

18. BibSHPF MS E43: "Saint-Savinien Eglise Réformée," 446; BibSHPF MS 869[1]: Papiers Lièvre. Poitou protestant, dr. 4: Registre de l'Eglise de Saint-Savinien-sur-Charente (Charente-Inférieure). In 1886, there would be around 18,000 Protestants in a Charente-Maritime population of 466,416, and 49 temples in the department's 480 communes and 40 cantons. *Annuaire de la Charente-Inférieure pour 1886*, 192, 82, 191–97; "Culte chrétien protestant," 371–72.
19. Marcadé, *Protestants poitevins*, 40.
20. Léonard, *History of Protestantism*, 2:442.
21. Gaxotte, *France de Louis XIV*, 240. Gaxotte calculated this average by simply dividing the total of 1,250,000 Protestants in France among the 630 temples.
22. AN TT271 (xxv:193): Procès Verbal pour constater la distance d'entre le temple de Ceux de La R.P.R du lieu de St Savinien et une Chapelle des Religieux Augustins, November 23, 1681. Demuin had succeeded Colbert de Terron in 1674.
23. *Abbaye des Augustins*; AN 1AP: Chartrier de Thouars 2127: 10/2/14: Contrat de baillette. See also Libaud, *Edifices religieux*, 13–25, 47.
24. AN TT271 (xxv:192): Partage des commissaires pour l'exercice de la R.p.R de s[t] Savinien, February 29, 1664. The eventual *arrêt* ordering demolition of the temple in Saint-Savinien was dated January 12, 1682. This delay in temple closure was typical; action was interrupted by the wartime lull in persecutions during the 1670s.
25. AN TT242 (xxi:1): Advis des sieurs Commissaires pour lExercize de la RPR au Lieu de Coses.
26. Carbonnier-Burkard and Cabanel, eds., *Histoire des protestants*, 58; Haag and Haag, *France protestante*, 6:23; Julien-Labruyère, *Paysans charentais*, 2:252. Between 1661 and the Revocation, 650–700 temples were demolished in France, according to Solange Deyon, "Destruction des temples," 241–42.
27. *Factums pour le syndic du clergé du diocese de Saintes*, no. 25: Saint-Savinien.
28. AN TT271 (xxv:192): Partage des commissaires pour l'exercice de la R.p.R de s[t] Savinien, February 29, 1664 (cover sheet notation); BibSHPF MS 485/6: De Gourgue to Colbert de Croissy, November 16, 1685, fol. 101. Today no one knows just where the temple was located, so thoroughly were all traces of it eradicated. A probable location has recently been identified by Jean Libaud, *Edifices religieux*, 29.
29. Gélin, "Cloches protestantes," 591–607, 652–64; Gélin, "Réformés et les cloches," 144–46.
30. Saudau, *Saint-Jean-d'Angély*, 299, 288; ADCM E Supp. 1366: Registre paroissial de Saint-Jean-d'Angély (église catholique).
31. BibSHPF MS 485/6: De Gourgue to Colbert de Croissy, November 16, 1685, fol. 101.
32. AN TT252 (xii:2): Actes du Sinode provincial des Eglizes refformëes de Xaintonge et aunix et angoulmois, Mauzé, 1677; TT208 (v:6): Saint-Contest, February 12, 1689.
33. AN TT272 (xiii:53–57): Pieces concernant les contestations dentre le Curé de Tonnay-Charente et Ceux de la R.P.R des lieux de Tonnay-Charente et Tonnay-Boutonne, au sujet de l'exercice de la ditte religion; Sanxay, ed., *Sanxay Family*, 45–58, 149. The only surviving Protestant parish register from Tonnay-Boutonne is the one written in Sanxay's hand from 1683–1685 and reprinted as "Registres protestants de Tonnay-Boutonne."
34. AN TT236 (i:24): Memoire des Gentilshommes de la generalité de Bordeaux, May 2, 1682.
35. Culant himself had once held Protestant services in his château, but no longer. AN TT232 (xix:13): Liste des gentilhommes du pays d'aulnis faisant profession de la R.P.R.
36. AMS MS 1065: Registre des baptêmes. The child René-Casimir is not mentioned in any of the Champagné Papers. Losing written track of the family in this way may be attributable to the disarray caused by the shifting of accessible parishes; without a stable home church, the family story became easier to lose.
37. Quoted in André Burguière and François Lebrun, "Priest, Prince, and Family," in Burguière et al., eds., *History of the Family*, 2:105.

38. BibSHPF MS 713, dr. 3, #10: Abraham Tessereau to Elie Bouhéreau, December 8, 1681.
39. AN TT272 (ii:7): Moyens du Syndic du clergé de Saintes Contre Les p.R. de taillebourg.
40. AMS MS 1065: Registre des baptêmes; "Etat contenant le dénombrement des personnes faisant profession de la R.P.R., en 1682," 26.
41. In September 1684, the privilege of *seigneurs hauts-justiciers* to hold such services privately on their fiefs, a concession of the Edict of Nantes, was also suppressed. Arrest du Conseil, du 4 septembre 1684 Concernant l'exercice de la R.P.R. dans les Hautes-Justices, pleins Fiefs de Haubert ou simples Fiefs, reprinted in *Edits, Déclarations et Arrests,* 164–66.
42. CP B4: Josias de Robillard to his children, Paris, July 15, 1685. This is in a notebook and is bound with a second letter, so it must be a copy of the original, if it was ever sent as a literal letter. In the second letter, Josias refers to the first as existing "also elsewhere," so he would seem to have copied it more than once, perhaps in order to give one to each child (as Jean Migault did with the memoir of his family's escape). By the time the children left France in 1687, the three eldest had read the letters, according to CP A55: Josias de Robillard to Marie de La Rochefoucauld, November 2, 1687.
43. CP A56: Estat et inventaire sommere, Item 94.
44. BibSHPF MS 66: Notes extraites par Monsieur Eugène Haag des Registres de l'Etat civil des Protestants qu'il trouva aux Archives du Palais de Justice et aux Archives de l'Hôtel de Ville de Paris, archives qui ont été incendiées depuis, au mois de mai 1871, 254.
45. Protestants customarily avoided using the term Catholic for the rival confession because it meant "universal" and, in their minds, had been usurped by the Rome-based church.
46. ADCM B1486: Présidial de La Rochelle, 1652. Registre; "Emigrés de La Rochelle," 424.
47. Chevalier, *Prêcher sous l'Edit de Nantes,* especially chapter 12.
48. Labrousse, *Bayle,* 296–97; Labrousse, "Calvinism in France"; Benedict, "Two Calvinisms"; Cottret, *Huguenots in England.*
49. Bayle, *Dictionaire historique et critique,* 1:1070.
50. Benedict, "Two Calvinisms," 228; Labrousse, *Bayle,* 296; Labrousse, "Calvinism in France," 291–92.
51. Solé, *Origines intellectuelles de la Révocation,* 11.
52. Popkin, *History of Scepticism.*
53. Protestant theologian Claude Pajon, quoted in Rosa, "'Il était possible," 638. Rosa offers (638–48) an excellent, succinct presentation of this shift and how it gave Catholic disputants "a temporary upper hand in the interconfessional polemic."
54. Quoted in Solé, *Origines intellectuelles de la Révocation,* 30.
55. Chevalier, *Prêcher sous l'Edit de Nantes.*
56. Joutard, "Revocation of the Edict of Nantes," 367–68.
57. Solé, *Origines intellectuelles de la Révocation,* 179.
58. Josias went to the Châtelet in Paris on June 17, 1686 to pay the *procureur* in the Parlement of Paris, Teinturier, who had handled the dispute with the Maréchale de Navailles that took Josias to Paris the preceding summer. CP A56: Estat et inventaire sommere, Items 94–95.
59. Dangeau, *Journal,* 1:218.
60. SHD:TV A^{1}749: Louvois to Boufflers from Chambord, September 8, 1685.
61. *Mercure galant,* December 1685, 203; Orcibal, *Etat présent des recherches,* 25; Pérouas, "Clergé catholique et les protestants," 265. "Durand cy devant ministre" figured on the pensions paid to *nouveaux convertis* in Saint-Jean-d'Angély in 1687, receiving 200 *livres.* AN TT249 (i:39): Estat des pensions des nouveaux convertis qui sont payes a S^{t}. Jean D'angely par les commis de M^{rs}. Les Receveurs generaux des finances, June 13, 1687. Durand was categorized as an apostate, probably unjustly, by later Protestant historians such as Mours in "Pasteurs à la Révocation," 96. Causse corrects the record, showing that Durand, after his ostensible conversion, continued to promote "a familial spirit of evangelical piety" in Saintes, making his own house (as the bishop would describe it) a "little Geneva." Causse, "Audibert Durand," 516, 509.
62. *Mercure galant,* October 1685, 283–96; December 1685, 202–25.
63. BNF MS fr. 7044: Louvois to de Gourgue, September 14, 1685, fol. 155; *Mercure galant,* December 1685, 223–24; AN G^{7}345: De Gourgue from Saint-Jean-d'Angély, September 19, 1685; BNF MS n.a. fr. 21332: Arnoul from Rochefort, September 19, 1685, fol. 119v;

Sourches, *Mémoires*, 1:306–07; BibSHPF MS 485/2: Colbert de Croissy to de Gourgue from Chambord, September 21, 1685, fols. 54–55; SHD:TV A[1]750: Louvois from Fontainebleau, October 7, 1685.

64. SHD:TV A[1]756: Louvois to d'Asfeld from Chambord, September 23, 1685; Pérouas, *Diocèse de La Rochelle*, 320; [Tessereau], *Histoire des reformés de la Rochelle*, 277–82; "Extraits de la Gazette de Haarlem," 262–64; BNF MS n.a. fr. 21332: Arnoul to Louvois from Rochefort, October 21, 1685, fol. 212; Migault, *Journal*, 65.
65. BNF MS n.a. fr. 21331: Arnoul to Seignelay from La Rochelle, July 24, 1685, fol. 352r; Foucault, *Mémoires*, 125; Boisrond, "Mémoires," 10:240–41.
66. BNF MS n.a. fr. 21332: Arnoul from Rochefort, September 15, 1685, fol. 91; SHD:TV A[1]756: Louvois to Boufflers from Chambord, September 19, 1685.
67. Bouffler's address to the assembled Protestant notables of Bergerac, September 1685, as reported in Marsh's Library (Dublin). MS Z 2.2.9: Lettre Escrite de france touchant les violentes persecutions qu'on y fait a ceux de la religion Reformée. Perigort le 5 septembre 1685, in [Abraham Tessereau], Memoires et pieces pour servir A L'histoire generale de La persecution faitte en france Contre Ceux de la Religion Reformée depuis L'année 1656 Jusqu'a la Revocation de l'Edit de Nantes, faitte par celuy donné a Fontainebleau Au moys d'octobre, 1685. 2 vols. 2:item 45, p. 7.
68. [Espagnac], "Relation," 305; BibSHPF MS 485/2: Louvois to de Gourgue from Fontainebleau, October 6, 1685, fol. 71; ULD MS 3613: Autre Relation de la sortie de France de messire Charles de la Motte Fouqué, écrite de sa propre main et trouvée dans ses papiers après son décès.
69. BibSHPF MS 485/4: De Gourgue to Le Pelletier, September 29, 1685, fol. 76; De Gourgue to Colbert, October 6, 1685, fol. 78.
70. BibSHPF MS 485/4: Louvois to de Gourgue, October 17, 1685, fol. 84; See also SHD:TV A[1]751: Louvois to the Duc de Noailles from Fontainebleau, November 5, 1685; BibSHPF MS 485/4. Louvois to the Duc de Noailles, November 8, 1685, with copies to the intendants, fol. 117; BibSHPF MS 485/6. De Gourgue to Colbert de Croissy, January 4, 1686, fol. 106.
71. Fénelon to Seignelay, March 8, 1686, reprinted in Douen, *Intolérance de Fénelon*, 295–96.
72. AMS MS 567.A1: Documents relatifs à la Saintonge: Protestants.
73. The version of abjuration Josias swore resembled the particular wording signed in good conscience by a refugee in Britain, Peter de Cosne: "that he wished to live and die in the Catholic Church where his fathers had lived. It seemed that in this declaration there could be no poison, since the Protestants claimed to be the Catholic Church with yet better title than the Romans." Cosne, "Memoirs," 534.
74. Edit du Roy, Du mois de Janvier 1686 Concernant l'éducation des enfans de ceux de la R.P.R., reprinted in *Edits, Déclarations et Arrests*, 261–63.
75. Ordonnance du Roy, Du 11 Janvier 1686 Concernant les Domestiques dont les P.R. et les Nouveaux Convertis peuvent se servir, reprinted in *Edits, Déclarations et Arrests*, 268–70.
76. Boisrond, "Mémoires," 9:343; 10:240–41, 281; ADCM E796: Ratification, February 2, 1686.
77. "Déclaration donnée et signée par les sieurs de Vigneau, Marchand et des Loges, ministres, à M. l'évêque de Meaux, avant les conférences," reprinted in Douen, *Révocation*, 2:315.
78. BNF MS fr. 7055: Copie dun brouillon dune Lettre ecritte dans le mois davril 1686 a Mr Duvignau, fols. 18–19. Douen, *Révocation* reprints this letter on 2:321 and sets the Catillon case out in detail.
79. Luria, "Rituals of Conversion," 72–76.
80. BibSHPF MS 701: Livre de raison et mémoires de Pierre Lézan, ancien de l'église réformée de Saint Hippolyte du Fort (Gard), 67.
81. Reprinted in "Pourquoi et comment on se soumettait," 543–45.
82. Jurieu, *Lettres pastorales*, August 15, 1688: "When did you begin to judge that you can save yourself in the Roman church? Isn't it when you saw yourself on the verge of losing your property and your repose? . . . Do you not see that cupidity is awakened by the fear of seeing yourself dispossessed of your comforts and conveniences?"

83. *Place des Victoires et ses abords*; Saint-Simon, *Place des Victoires*; Gaehtgens, "Statue de Louis XIV." The captives and the medallions are now displayed in the Cour Puget of the Louvre. Identifications of each captive with a particular country vary, but the emotions conveyed are unambiguous.

Chapter 3

1. [Balthazar], *Histoire*, 298; Pellisson, "Fronde à Cognac," 313–77.
2. Madeleine de Créquy, Duchesse de La Trémoïlle to Demuin, May 23, 1682, reprinted in La Trémoïlle, *Les La Trémoïlle*, 4:222–23; Dez, *Histoire des protestants*, 380. Dragoons were authorized to cost their hosts only limited amounts, according to instructions given by Louvois to Boufflers on July 31: "During the time the troops are in the homes of the said *religionnaires*, you shall not permit them to create other disorders than drawing twenty *sols* per cavalier or dragoon for fodder and utensils, and ten *sols* per foot soldier for the same utensils." Quoted in Noailles, *Histoire de Madame de Maintenon*, 2:415.
3. [Tessereau], *Reformés de la Rochelle*, 286–89. Tessereau had no doubt heard this account directly from Voutron. He mentions that some households had 50, 80, 100, or 150 soldiers billeted on them (281).
4. Colbert de Croissy, "Rapport au Roy," 25.
5. Arrêt du conseil qui dépouille des privilèges de noblesse les descendans des maires de La Rochelle religionnaires. Versailles, March 5, 1685, reprinted in *Recueil général des anciennes lois françaises*, 19:492–93. This annulling of nobility was extended to descendants of the mayors of Angoulême, Saint-Jean-d'Angély, Poitiers and Niort by a further Arrêt du Conseil d'Etat on June 2, 1685. ADV C49: Extrait des Registres du Conseil d'Etat, June 2, 1685.
6. BNF MS n.a. fr. 21331: Arnoul to Seignelay, July 24, 1685, fol. 355r; BNF MS n.a. fr. 21332: Arnoul to Seignelay, December 10, 1685, fol. 393v; Arnoul to Seignelay from Rochefort, September 3, 1685, fol. 57; Arnoul to Seignelay from Rochefort, December 10, 1685, fol.393v; Louvois to Arnoul, forwarding his letter to Foucault from Chambord, September 12, 1685; Louvois to Foucault from Versailles, November 17, 1685, reprinted in Foucault, *Mémoires*, 521.
7. *Catalogue alphabétique des nobles de la généralité de Poitiers*, 318; "Pallet."
8. ADCM E Supp. 1225 (36): Enquête sur les privilèges de la ville de Saint-Jean-d'Angély, faite par Méry de Vicq, 1593. An *arrêt* of the Cour des aides confirmed the nobility of Christophe's sons (including the father of Marie de La Rochefoucauld's Josias) on March 21, 1613.
9. *Catalogue alphabétique des nobles de la généralité de Poitiers*, 290; CP A45: Robillard proofs of nobility as presented for the *recherche de noblesse* in 1666; CP A56: Estat et inventaire sommere, Item 103.
10. Julien-Labruyère, *Paysans charentais*, 2:256.
11. [Tessereau], *Reformés de la Rochelle*, 302–03. Châtelaillon was named governor on May 27, 1686, succeeding Jeurre Milet.
12. Otherwise, she would have had no obligation to perform a *reconnaissance*, as she did upon arriving in England.
13. Marie does not appear in the parish records of Saint-Savinien's Catholic church. Abjurations were sometimes conducted by missionaries outside of churches. The abjuration of Marie Prévost de Touchimbert in January 1686 is recorded on stamped paper, rather than directly on the parish register, and inserted into the register along with other loose sheets. A later curé wrote in the margin of Marie Prévost's stamped paper that several loose sheets listing abjurations were attached thereto by a pin, "all in very poor order." Perhaps Marie de La Rochefoucauld's abjuration was recorded and lost on such a loose sheet.
14. SHD:TV A[1]795. Boufflers to Louvois from Bordeaux, April 27, 1686.
15. Joutard, "1685," 22.
16. Quoted in André Burguière and François Lebrun, "One Hundred and One Families," in Burguière et al., eds., *History of the Family*, 2:65.

17. Spangler, "Benefit or Burden?," 68; Delafosse, "Contrats de mariage et dots," 2:46, 2:49; Dangibeaud, "Cozes," 219.
18. ADCM E796: Déclaration, January 23, 1686.
19. CP A34: Property agreements between Josias de Robillard and Casimir Prévost de Touchimbert, January 24, 1677, January 26, 1677, April 9, 1677.
20. CP A36: Casimir Prévost de Touchimbert, Purchase of Londigny, 1678.
21. CP A49a: Claim of Charles Prévost de Touchimbert (Brassac) against Josias de Robillard, July 20, 1686; CP A49: Parchment order from the Parlement of Bordeaux, May 30, 1686 in favor of Brassac against Josias de Robillard; CP A56: Estat et inventaire sommere, Items 1–4.
22. CP A47: Division between Marie de La Rochefoucauld and her sisters, March 8, 1677; ADCM E795: Obligation, April 7, 1684; ADCM E796: Cession, January 10, 1686.
23. ADCM B736: Sentences, Présidial de Saintes, March 3, 1676. The court awarded Susanne 600 *livres* for four years' maintenance.
24. ADCM B564: Baux judiciaires, Présidial de Saintes, 1686–1688; CP A56: Estat et inventaire sommere, Item 58.
25. CP A35: Inheritance agreement between five La Rochefoucauld sisters, May 7, 1680.
26. ADCM E796: Obligation, July 17, 1686; ADCM E797: Transaction, February 11, 1687, marginal notation dated March 11.
27. E/L9: Vidimus de la Cession faite a Madame de Chambon, August 4, 1677; E/L9b: Marie de La Rochefoucauld, Nos seigneurs de parlement, May 8, 1683; CP A56: Estat et inventaire sommere, Item 56; ADCM B738 (1bis): Sentences, Présidial de Saintes, January 14, 1678; B519: Affirmations de voyage, Présidial de Saintes, 1679–1681; B564: Baux judiciaires, Présidial de Saintes, 1686–1688; B478: Audiences présidiales, Présidial de Saintes, 1680; B564: Baux judiciaires, Présidial de Saintes, 1686–1688; B488: Audiences civiles, Présidial de Saintes, 1692–1693; B519–520: Affirmations de voyage, Présidial de Saintes, 1679–1681, 1692–1693; B530: Enregistrement des procès, Présidial de Saintes, 1679–1693; B562: Baux judiciaires, Présidial de Saintes, 1684.
28. ADCM B488: Audiences civiles, Présidial de Saintes, 1692–1693; ADCM B736: Procédures des procureurs, Bordeaux, April 20, 1676.
29. E/L6: Guy de La Blachière, A nos seigneurs de parlement, January 8, 1683; CP A56: Estat et inventaire sommere, Items 59, 61. The competitive character of debt-pursuit is evident in the ever-shifting alliances in the stages of lawsuits. In the early years, Josias competed against the Saintes merchant Guénon and La Blachière, but when Casimir Prévost de Touchimbert took over the effort after the departure of Josias and Marie, he was often allied with Guénon and La Blachière against other creditors.
30. E/L10: Marie, Elizabeth, Magdellaine Et Suzanne de La Rochefoucaud, A nos seigneurs de Parlemant, February 1, 1683; E/L9: Vidimus de la Cession faite a Madame de Chambon, August 4, 1677; E/L11: Marie et Magdelaine de La rochefoucaud, A Nos seigneurs de parlement, November 23, 1685.
31. CP A56: Estat et inventaire sommere, Item 62; ADCM B564: Baux judiciaires, Présidial de Saintes, 1686–1688; ADCM B750: Sentences, Présidial de Saintes, June 7, 1692.
32. CP A35: Inheritance agreement between five La Rochefoucauld sisters, May 7, 1680; CP A50: Memorandum of sums due on Susanne Isle's division of property, 1689.
33. CP A35: Inheritance agreement between five La Rochefoucauld sisters, May 7, 1680. In the aftermath of a 1675 sedition in their home city, the Parlement of Bordeaux was banished to La Réole, where they operated from May 1678 down to 1690. Boscheron des Portes, *Histoire du Parlement de Bordeaux*, 2:215–17. They had previously been banished to the same location in the aftermath of the Fronde, in which they played a strong anti-crown role.
34. The marriage contract is both E/L1: Contrat de Mariage de Monsieur de soulignonne Aveq Madelaigne de solieres, July 23, 1659 and ADCM E267: Contrat de marriage, July 23, 1659; Colle, *Châteaux, manoirs et forteresses*, 2:307; Amos Barbot, quoted in Brodut, *Tonnay-Charente*, 157; Meschinet de Richemond, "Anciennes églises," 370. Salbert genealogies can be found in Nadaud, *Nobiliaire*, 4:144; Coustures, *Nobiliaire*, 254; Brodut, *Tonnay-Charente*, 634–37.

35. ADCM E267 contains the parchment marriage contract of Jean Isle de Beauchesne and Léa de Bessay dated January 11, 1639.
36. ADCM 3E26/323: Cession de Berneré, January 12, 1710. The 1662 receipt is appended to E/L1: Contrat de Mariage, July 23, 1659.
37. ADCM E267: Contrat de marriage, July 23, 1659; ADCM E267: Inventaire des biens de Léa de Bessay, January 25, 1639; ADCM E267: Inventaire, December 18, 1676; ADCM E267: Cession de droits, January 8, 1662. The division of inheritance between Louis and his sister took place in 1660, a year after his marriage and before payment of Madelene's dowry.
38. ADCM E267: Transaction passée entre Jean Isle, chevalier seigneur de Beauchène d'une part et le seigneur de Celecte, January 14, 1662. Among the children of Bessay's second marriage was the naval officer who would play a role in the Revocation conflict within the Isle kindred (see chapter 5). In 1659, Sara de Salbert married Isaac du Laux, Seigneur de Cellettes. According to Le Brun de la Rochette, *Procez civil et criminel*, 1:315, a stepfather could serve as a tutor to minor children for whom their mother had previously served as guardian.
39. E/L8: *Factum du procez pour dame Marie de la Roche Foucaut, Epouse non commune en biens de Iosias de Robillard Chevalier, Seigneur de Champagné. . .Contre Dame Magdelaine de Solieres veuve en premieres Nopces de Louis Salbert Escuyer sieur de Soulignonne*; E/L5: Madelene de soliere à Madame de Lescure a bernere, undated. "*Ne varietur*" was inscribed on notarized documents and on those submitted as evidence in court cases to indicate that the text must not be changed.
40. E/L8: *Factum du procez pour dame Marie de la Roche Foucaut*; E/L15: *Memoire pour messire Jean-Charles de Lavie, Conseiller au Parlement, au nom et comme Curateur de Dame Marie-Suzanne-Françoise de Gua son Epouse . . . contre dame Suzanne de Lestang*; ADCM 3E 26/323: Cession de Berneré, January 12, 1710; E/L29: Christian de Sèze and Odette de Sèze, *Prospectus*.
41. See chapter 9 for the treatment of Madelene by fellow parishioners in Soulignonne.
42. E/L3: Madelene de soliere à Madame ma tres honoré mere, de paris, May 29, 1672.
43. E/L4: Certificat de mariage, Magdeleine de Saulier et Nicolas Leopol Ignace troisieme De Saxe, May 28, 1672.
44. Biver and Biver, *Abbayes, monastères et couvents de Paris*, 294–302; Colle, *Condition féminine*, 100. For elaboration on Madelene's "marriage," see Carolyn C. Lougee, "The New Princess of Saxony: Paris, Imposture, and Secret Marriage in the Seventeenth Century" (forthcoming, *French History*). This article questions the effect in practice of the "French Marital Law Compact" or "Family-State Compact" posited in Hanley, "Engendering the State," explores the literary and salon culture of seventeenth-century Paris as it may have induced illusions such as Madelene's, and speculates on the treatment Madelene's seducer might have received according to the law.
45. Fierro, *Vie et histoire du XIIe arrondissement*, 17–18, 108–09; Migne, *Encyclopédie théologique*, 20:20–22; Lévesque de Burigny, *Vie du cardinal du Perron*, 368.
46. Le Roy Ladurie, *Saint-Simon and the Court*, 187–91.
47. On the role of Eléonore d'Olbreuse in the Champagné future, see chapter 13.
48. He was Louis Thomas Amédée de Savoie-Carignan, eldest son of Olympe Mancini and Prince Maurice of Savoy.
49. Archives départementales de l'Eure-et-Loire 3E145/1: Parish register La Folie-Herbault, October 12, 1680; D'Aussy, "Dernière comtesse de Soissons," 618; "Appendix XXI: Uranie de la Cropte-Beauvais, Comtesse de Soissons," in Saint-Simon, *Mémoires*, 10:551; Sourches, *Mémoires*, 1:162; Louis XIV to abbé d'Estrades, December 25, 1682, quoted in D'Aussy, "Dernière comtesse de Soissons," 618–19. Uranie de La Cropte was Saint-Surin's ward until 1669 and would inherit his estates because of his emigration. On Saint-Surin, future husband of Susanne de Robillard, and the further involvement of the Comte and Comtesse de Soissons in their lives, see Part Four.
50. Eléonore and the Duke of Brunswick married more than eleven years after the start of their liaison, in 1676, so at the time of Madelene de Solière's "marriage" the Duke had not yet offered to marry Eléonore.

51. E/L30: Petition of Casimir Prévost de Touchimbert to the Parlement of Bordeaux, 1690 or 1691. See chapter 9.
52. E/L7b: Extraits des Registres du Présidial de Saintes, November 14, 1672–December 25, 1672; ADCM B569: Baux judiciaires, Présidial de Saintes, 1692–1693. An order for seizure of the property precisely in 1677 is recorded in ADCM B5161: Présidial de Saintes, Religionnaires, 1653–1715.
53. ADCM B736 (56): Sentences, Présidial de Saintes, 1676; ADCM B745 (43): Sentences, Présidial de Saintes, August 7, 1687.

Chapter 4

1. E/L31: Madelene de Soliere à Madame de Lescure a bernere, [1672].
2. CP A35: Inheritance agreement between five La Rochefoucauld sisters, May 7, 1680.
3. E/L8: *Factum du procez pour dame Marie de la Roche Foucaut.* Many factums, including Marie's, were printed up to distribute to the court and sometimes (especially in the eighteenth century) more widely among the public. Factums often shaped the facts of a case with elements of drama—if not melodrama—in order to move the judges in the client's favor. See Lavoir, "Factums et mémoires d'avocats"; Maza, *Private Lives and Public Affairs.*
4. The three advisors to the guardianship were Benjamin Green de Saint-Marsault, Seigneur de Salignac; Alphée Goulard, Seigneur d'Anville; and François d'Ocoy, Seigneur de Couvrelles.
5. That transaction is ADCM E267 as well as E/L2: Copie de transaction passée entre Messires de bauchesne, de soulignone et de celette, January 8, 1662.
6. E/L5: Madelene de soliere à Madame de Lescure a bernere, undated.
7. CP A56: Estat et inventaire sommere, Item 54.
8. A second dowry or a separate *légitime* plus more than a decade's interest would amount to the entire value of Berneré. So from the outset, there was no way Susanne (or, after her, Marie) could pay Madelene except by handing over Berneré.
9. There were a few nuances to the time limit, but none that played in Madelene's favor. See Ferrière, *Dictionnaire de droit*, "Mineurs," 2:217; "Lettres de rescission," 2:136.
10. E/L7: Acte fait à la Requete de monsieur de La mortmartin, June 5, 1685. Madelene was widowed a second time by 1686.
11. ADCM E794: Procuration, October 14, 1681; E/L8: *Factum du procez pour dame Marie de la Roche Foucaut.*
12. BibSHPF MS E43: *Registre des Abjurations faites dans l'Eglise paroissiale de Saint-Savinien en Xaintonge*, 411–13, 394.
13. CP A56: Estat et inventaire sommere, Item 110a; Hardwick, "Seeking Separations," 175; Audubert, *Régime dotal*, 162; Staves, *Married Women's Separate Property.*
14. Audubert, *Régime dotal*, 47, 163, 113; Portemer, "Statut de la femme en France," 462.
15. CP A40: Joint Will of Josias de Robillard and Marie de La Rochefoucauld, April 26, 1683.
16. Diefendorf, "Women and Property," 179, 187; Wheaton, "Affinity and Descent," 127–28.
17. CP A56: Estat et inventaire sommere, Items 110b, 55; E/L6: Guy de La Blachiere, A nos seigneurs de parlement, January 8, 1683.
18. Hanlon and Carruthers, "Wills, Inheritance and the Moral Order," 153; Wheaton, "Affinity and Descent," 116.
19. The intervals were 12 (marriage to first birth), 18, 15, 13, 15, 20, 35, 19, 18, 22, 19, and 37 months.
20. ADCM E795: Procuration, May 18, 1684.
21. Of the girls baptized in the Protestant temples of La Rochelle, 80 percent were named Marie (27%), Anne, Elisabeth, Susanne, Jeanne, Judith, Esther, Magdelaine, or Marguerite. Faust, "Beleaguered Society," 57. On the fate of baby Thérèse after the departure of her parents and siblings, see chapter 9.
22. AN TT249 (x:38): Estat des biens et Revenus des pretendus reformez et nouveaux convertis fugitifs, Election et ressort de S[t] jean Dangely, 1686–1687; CP A39a: Intendant's order for seizure of Berneré, September 16, 1687; CP A39b: Josias de Robillard, Mesmoire

des advences que Jay faites sur ce que monsieur de la bertramiere porte en comte; CP A39c: Receipt, Rabillard de La Bertramière to Josias de Robillard, March 29, 1688.

23. E/L13: Extrait du Registre du parlement, April 8, 1688; CP A59: Marie de La Rochefoucauld, Ce 10 Ienvier 1690. A further look at Josias' experience between Marie's departure and his own is in chapter 7.
24. E/L8: *Factum du procez pour dame Marie de la Roche Foucaut*; E/L15: *Memoire pour messire Jean-Charles de Lavie.*
25. Quoted in Puaux, "Dessein des pasteurs exilés," 425–26.
26. *Edict du Roy, et Declaration*, 18v; *Edits, Déclarations et Arrests*, 77.
27. Stegmann, *Edits des guerres de religion*, 95–120; Margolf, "Adjudicating Memory"; Margolf, *Religion and Royal Justice.*
28. Boisrond, "Mémoires," 10:189; Weiss, "Poursuites du Présidial de Saintes," 493–94; AN TT242 (xxi:1-10): Pièces Concernant l'Exercice de la R.P.R. au dit lieu de Coses; Dangibeaud, "Cozes," 102.
29. [Tessereau], *Reformés de la Rochelle*, 208; AN TT265 (iii:48): "Au Roy. Requete des habitans de la R.P.R. de Xaintonge, juillet 1684," 261.
30. Dast Le Vacher, *Membres du Parlement de Bordeaux*, 7, 58; AMB MS 796: Registre secret du Parlement de Bordeaux, fols. 663–65; AMB MS 817: Registre secret du Parlement de Bordeaux, fols. 393–97; *Extrait des registres du Parlement*, in Pascal, "Sous la persécution," 407; AN TT265 (iii:48): "Au Roy. Requete des habitans," 259–62.
31. Dubreuilh, "Construction du temple de Sainte-Foy," 362; AN TT236 (i:24): Memoire des Gentilshommes de la generalité de Bordeaux, May 2, 1682; Dast Le Vacher, *Membres du Parlement de Bordeaux*, 29; [Tessereau], *Reformés de la Rochelle*, 208–09.
32. [Tessereau], *Reformés de la Rochelle*, 208–10; AMB MS 796: Registre secret du Parlement de Bordeaux, fol. 706. Duvigier also received a pension of 3,000 *livres* a year from the king for his conversion from April 1680 until at least 1700. He received an extra payment of 3,000 *livres* in September 1684 "as gratification in consideration of his services." AN O[1]605: *Memoire des ordonnances de pensions que le Roy a accordé a aucuns nouveaux convertis a la R.C. ap. et Romaine*, drs 21–34.
33. *Heros de la ligue.* The publication was anonymous, but the overrepresentation of characters from Saintes suggests it was very likely written by a Protestant from Saintonge.
34. ADG contain no record of this case other than the single document relating to the later custody battle, as indicated in chapter 9, notably no indication of the grounds Madelene alleged for her suit before the Parlement. Therefore, her arguments can only be inferred from the attempted refutations in the factum, the court's final decree (ADCM 3E 26/323: Cession de Berneré, January 12, 1710), and the other documents in E/L. The factum is undated, but it must have been produced before Marie de La Rochefoucauld's escape or it could not bear her name as the "defendresse." The latest date mentioned in the text is June 22, 1686. E/L1-50 (fifty-two documents) include the original submissions that Marie de La Rochefoucauld, her partners, and successors made to the Parlement of Bordeaux in defense against Madelene de Solière's suits for Berneré and for custody of Thérèse. It was customary to return such documents to the parties at the time a case was closed. This dossier of documents was passed down in the La Vie family at least as late as the eighteenth century and came into the hands of the present author through the historian Patrick Esclafer de La Rode in Périgord. It will be deposited with the Champagné Papers at Stanford University Libraries. Parallel documents from Madelene de Solière's side, which would have been returned to her, have not been found.
35. Voltaire, "Dialogue entre un plaideur et un avocat," 493–96. The discussion that follows focuses on the provisions of written law adopted and applied by the Parlement of Bordeaux. Some special provisions in the Saintonge *coutume* might be scrutinized further, but, as Cosme Béchet noted in his *Usance de Saintonge*, "on inheritances, wills, and legacies, it is customary to be ruled and governed according to the written law": that is, the sentences and decisions of "the Parlement of Bordeaux, under whose laws we live." (271–72)
36. This sketch of law regimes is based largely upon Le Roy Ladurie, "System of Customary Law," which was adapted from Yver, *Egalité entre héritiers*. Quotations here are taken from Patricia M. Ranum's translation in *Family and Society.*

37. Le Roy Ladurie, "System of Customary Law," 80. The classic discussion of how the egalitarian letter of the law in *coutumes* was manipulated in practice to protect family heritages from partition is Giesey, "Rules of Inheritance."
38. Le Roy Ladurie, "System of Customary Law," 96, 88, 95, 103, 92.
39. Le Roy Ladurie, "System of Customary Law," 78, 96.
40. Staves, "Resentment or Resignation?"
41. Quoted in Audubert, *Régime dotal,* 89; Article 25 of the *Coutume de Normandie,* quoted in Audubert, *Régime dotal,* 89; Audubert, *Régime dotal,* 112, 163, 89–90.
42. Audubert, *Régime dotal,* 109–11, 159, 150, 157, 137, 140–41; Poumarède, "Droit des veuves"; Viollet, *Histoire du droit civil français,* 795, 798, 802; Audubert, *Régime dotal,* 151–52, 158.
43. Viollet, *Histoire du droit civil français,* 796; Tessier, *Traité de la société d'aquêts,* 286.
44. ADCM B738: Sentences. Présidial de Saintes, October 11, 1678; ADC E432: Règlement au sujet du douaire de Marie Gombaud, July 29, 1681; ADCM 3E 26/164: Minute de Gillet, February 3, 1684; 3E 88/60: Minutes de Dalidet, December 2–4, 1690; 3E 26/323: Minute de Senné, November 17, 1710; ADCM 3E 26/384: Transaction, February 5, 1747.
45. The Parlement of Bordeaux recognized no widow's preference over creditors for debts her husband contracted before the marriage. Audubert, *Régime dotal,* 133, 124–25, 96; Poumarède, "Droit des veuves"; Wheaton, "Affinity and Descent"; ADCM E267: Cession de droits, January 8, 1662; ADCM B569: Baux judiciaires, Présidial de Saintes, 1692–1693, April 4, 1693.
46. Audubert, *Régime dotal,* 112, 163.
47. *Recueil général des anciennes lois françaises,* 15:302–03; Déclaration de 1664, quoted in Viollet, *Histoire du droit civil français,* 801; Audubert, *Régime dotal,* 140; Viollet, *Histoire du droit civil français,* 798, 800.
48. Audubert, *Régime dotal,* 65. See also Béchet, *Traité des secondes noces,* 465.
49. Ferrière, *Dictionnaire de droit,* "Enterinement," 1:643; "Rescision," 2:544; "Restitution de fruits," 2:548; "Restitution en entier," 2:547; Brissaud, *History of French Private Law,* 513–18.
50. The following discussion is based largely upon the exposition of the complexities of renunciation offered in Maillet, "Renonciation à succession future des filles dotées."
51. See Staves, "Resentment or Resignation?"
52. So Sarah Hanley, for example, sees the trend toward increasing use of renunciation as prejudicial to women, a means of what she calls "Male Right (entailing female exclusion)." In Hanley's view, Male Right increased in strength simultaneously in private law (family) and public (state rule) across the seventeenth century, and the use of renunciation was a feature of accelerating female exclusion. See Hanley, "From the Law Court," a draft version of "The Family, the State, and the Law." Hanley kindly made the draft available to me in two prepublication versions. This interpretation is questionable in several important respects. The Parisian *coutume* cannot be equated with "French law," nor renunciation with exclusion. Given women's entitlements to inheritance in some legal regimes and access to it in others, the parallel Hanley wants to establish between eligibility for the throne (from which women were excluded even if there were no sons) and inheritance (in which women could be included even if there were sons) seems invalid. And there was no trend, in the South at least, toward exclusion of women from inheritance—quite the opposite, as is evident in the Bordeaux jurisprudence and as has been confirmed by studies elsewhere in the South. See Diefendorf, "Women and Property," 172–74; Darrow, *Revolution in the House;* Collomp, *Maison du père.*
53. Ferrière, *Dictionnaire de droit,* "Mineurs," 2:215–18; "Restitution en entier," 2:547; Audubert, *Régime dotal,* 99; Brissaud, *French Private Law,* 518.
54. An Ordonnance of 1735 finally codified it all. See Maillet, "Renonciation," 250; Gabriel Guéret, quoted in Hanley, "The Family, the State, and the Law," 302; Maillet, "Renonciation," 221, 218, 226.
55. Notaries were to include whatever provisions their clients might want, "provided they be not contrary to good mores or prohibited by laws." Ferrière, *Science parfaite des notaires,* 29–30. See also Lelievre, *Pratique des contrats de mariage,* 14.

56. ADCM 3E 26/249: Minute de Mareschal, December 1, 1691.
57. Maynard, *Notables et singulières questions de droit écrit jugées au Parlement de Toulouse* (1761), quoted in Maillet, "Renonciation," 232.
58. Susanne Isle was already identified as a widow in the marriage contract of her sister Marie, dated October 7, 1636. AN M515: Traitte du Mariage, Remigioux-Isle.
59. Viollet, *Histoire du droit civil français*, 869–70.
60. Seventeenth- and eighteenth-century legal authorities Masse, Dupérier, and Lebrun, quoted in Maillet, "Renonciation," 223–28.
61. Rousseau de la Combe, *Recueil de jurisprudence civile*, quoted in Maillet, "Renonciation," 230; *Recueil par ordre alphabetique des principales questions de Droit*, 279.
62. CP A20: Division of inheritance of Forgette, November 18, 1642; AN M515: Traitte du Mariage, Remigioux-Isle.
63. Hanley, "Family, the State, and the Law," 293; BNF 4°FM 23017-23019: Nemours. Hanley's article is the basis for the following exposition of the Nemours case.
64. [Guéret and Blondeau], *Journal du Palais*, 184–265; Hanley, "From the Law Court," 24; Hanley, "Family, the State, and the Law," 320.
65. Maillet, "Renonciation," 216; Brissaud, *French Private Law*, 518. Perhaps, more simply, the extra payment for Madelene was intended to induce her not to sue. In Layrac, "Relatives could be left a small amount to abandon their lawsuits against previous wills or potential claims they could have against the estate." Hanlon and Carruthers, "Wills, Inheritance, and the Moral Order," 157.
66. E/L1: Contrat de Mariage de Monsieur de soulignonne Aveq Madelaigne de solieres, July 23, 1659.
67. Hardwick, "Widowhood and Patriarchy," 133.

Chapter 5

1. BNF MS n.a. fr. 21331: Arnoul from La Rochelle, June 5, 1685, fol. 228r; Basville to Châteauneuf, January 17, 1698, reprinted in *Mémoires des évêques de France*, 295. Fénelon conveyed to Seignelay a charge similar to Arnoul's: "To all appearances, many obstinate people are still thinking of leaving. . .. It is as much the bad state of their finances as religion that motivates them to go. Some can be seen covering their bankruptcies with the pretext of religion." BNF MS fr. n.a. 507: Lettres autographes de Fénelon, July 1687, fol. 47r.
2. Péret, "Vitalité et turbulences," 253–55; "M. de Saint-Contest, intendant à Limoges au Contrôleur général, du 10 Juin au 22 Juillet 1687," reprinted in *Correspondance des contrôleurs généraux des finances*, 1:106; "Etat des paroisses en la généralité de Limoges," 292.
3. AN TT232 (xix:5): Extrait de l'Estat de liquidation des biens delaissez par ceux de la R.P.R. de la Rochelle et pays d'Aunis, November 12, 1689.
4. ADCM C141: Registre des affaires qui se rattachent aux biens des Religionnaires fugitifs de l'Aunis, 23r; ADCM B1610 (84): Jacques le Goux contre Elisabeth Isle de Loire, 1683; ADCM B736 (200): Transaction, August 12, 1676; E/L38: Requeste dudit sr de la dourville contre ladite dame Isle, 4 novembre 1695. Interestingly, 480 *livres* of Isaac's indebtedness was listed as owing to the intendant Pierre Arnoul.
5. AN TT232 (xix:5): Extrait de l'Estat de liquidation des biens; ADCM C141: Registre des affaires, 40v; ADCM B1610 (22): Sentences. Présidial de La Rochelle. Simon Tayau contre Jozias de Robillard, 29 March 1683; ADCM 3E1795: Reconnoissance, de sr Tayau au sieur de Champagné, March 21, 1688; CP A41: Receipt, Simon Tayau to Josias de Champagné, March 21, 1688.
6. E/L8: *Factum du procez pour Dame Marie de la Roche Foucaut*, 6; Dewald, *Formation of a Provincial Nobility*, 190–91.
7. CP A50: Memorandum of sums due on Susanne Isle's division of property [1689?]; BibSHPF MS 193/1: Journal de Chalmot, 7, 22.
8. Weiss, "Prêtre saintongeais condamné aux galères," 93; AN $G^7$135 (61–64): Burgauld to Pontchartrain from Saintes, April 22, 1696, reprinted in Delavaud, "Révocation," 326;

Bégon to Villermont, quoted in Dangibeaud, "Cozes," 199; Gombauld de Saint-Just to Pontchartrain, May 31, 1694, cited in Delavaud, "Révocation," 320.

9. Quéniart, *Révocation de l'Edit de Nantes,* 35–36; Quoted in Félice, *Histoire des protestants de France,* 448–49; Joutard, "Revocation," 360; Mours and Robert, *Protestantisme en France,* 18–21.
10. The three were brothers-in-law. Benjamin Green had married Susanne d'Ocoy, sister of François and of Marie d'Ocoy, wife of Alphée Goulard. Minute de Maréchal, December 1, 1691, extracted in "Minutes de notaires," 36:258–59; Audiat, "Les d'Auquoy," 132–34.
11. Rodrigues, *Nobles et bourgeois,* 127; Bujeaud, *Chronique protestante,* 223; AN TT232 (xix:13): Liste des gentilhommes du pays d'aulnis faisant profession de la R.P.R.
12. BNF MS n.a. fr. 21332: Arnoul from La Rochelle, September 16, 1685, fol. 98; Arnoul from Rochefort, September 30, 1685, fol.144; BNF MS n.a. fr. 21331: Arnoul to Seignelay from La Rochelle, August 3, 1685, fol. 384v. Fort Lupin was under construction by Vauban on the south bank of the Charente estuary, as part of the outer defenses of the Rochefort naval arsenal.
13. BNF MS n.a. fr. 21332: Arnoul from Rochefort, December 24, 1685, fol. 428; Beauchet-Filleau et al., *Dictionnaire,* 4:388. Châtelaillon held office in La Rochelle continuously from May 1686, the very morrow of his conversion. BMLR MS346: Noms des Gentilshommes de La relligion Du gouvernem[t] de la Rochelle Issus de la Maison de Ville, 52–54.Châtelaillon received continuous pensions of 2,000 *livres* from the king for his conversion from April 1686 through at least 1700. AN O[1]605: Memoire des ordonnances de pensions, drs. 21–34. In April 1689, he received 2,000 *livres* on the grounds that "We have many favorable testimonies about his merit." SHMDR 1E 33: Châteauneuf to Bégon from Versailles, April 6, 1689.
14. BNF MS n.a. fr. 21334: Arnoul to Seignelay from La Rochelle, May 20, 1687, fol. 117v; Arnoul to Seignelay from La Rochelle, May 29, 1687, fol. 120rv; BNF MS n.a. fr. 21333: Arnoul to Seignelay from Rochefort, February 11, 1686; Arnoul to Seignelay from Rochefort, January 21, 1686; Châteauneuf to Laval de Bois-Dauphin, Bishop of La Rochelle, from Marly, April 26, 1690, extracted in Delmas, *Eglise réformée de La Rochelle,* 391–93; Beauchet-Filleau et al., *Dictionnaire,* 4:388.
15. Audiat, "Les d'Auquoy," 132–34; Minute de Richard, extracted in "Minutes de notaires," 36:193. Jeanne d'Ocoy's paternal grandmother was Marie de La Rochefoucauld's great-aunt.
16. AMAE Cp.H 149: Tillieres, April 30, 1686. On the escape attempt by others in the family, see chapter 7.
17. Jeanne d'Ocoy had died by the time of her daughter Gabrielle-Susanne's burial at Agonnay on July 30, 1705.
18. Alphée Goulard's circumstances at the Revocation are unclear.
19. AN TT233 (vi:9): Procez Verbal du sinode de Ceux de la R.P.R. de Xaintonge, Angoumois et Aulnis tenu en la Ville de Barbezieux, October 1682; BNF MS n.a. fr. 21332: To M. Arnoul, October 21, 1685; Arnoul to Seignelay from Rochefort, November 6, 1685, fol. 260. La Rigaudière's petition for return of the land, addressed to Châteauneuf, is in BNF MS n.a. fr. 21442: Collection Arnoul: Affaires diverses, fol. 85. The petition is undated, but its inclusion among Arnoul's papers for 1683–1687 suggests it was dated during that period; AN TT455 (lxxxiv:300): Le s.[r] la rigaudiere nouveau converti de la province de Saintonge, June 20, 1689; (301): Rigaudiere to La Chaise from Paris, June 3, 1689; (302): La Rigaudiere de La Rochefoucauld to the King, 1697.
20. ADCM 3E26/161: Testament, May 19, 1681; ADCM 3E88/60: Minute de Dalidet. Piesse consernent Monsr. Le presiden et madame de magezi et son fis, January 13, 1690.
21. Haag and Haag, *France protestante,* 6:358; Douen, *Révocation,* 2:401–04.
22. Beauchet-Filleau et al., *Dictionnaire,* 5:145; Meyer, "Problème mal posé," 177.
23. BNF MS n.a. fr. 21332: Estat des Gentilshommes du pays daunix qui se sont convertis ou qui restent de la RPR, November 6, 1685, fol. 268v; Louvois to Arnoul from Versailles, August 18, 1685, fol. 7; Arnoul to Seignelay from Rochefort, November 28, 1685, fol. 356v.
24. BNF MS n.a. fr. 21332: Arnoul to Seignelay from Rochefort, December 10, 1685, fol. 393v; BNF MS n.a. fr. 21331: Arnoul to Seignelay from La Rochelle, August 3, 1685,

fol. 384v; BNF MS n.a. fr. 21332: Arnoul from Rochefort, September 3, 1685, fol. 57rv; Arnoul from Rochefort, December 31, 1685, fols. 456v, 428r; Arnoul to Seignelay from Rochefort, December 24, 1685, fol. 428; Lételié, "Fénelon en Saintonge."

25. *Petite histoire locale de la paroisse de Landraye*; BNF MS n.a. fr. 21442: Nicollas Gallais to Arnoul, February 12, 1685, fol. 79; ADCM E52: Papiers de famille Culant, 1475–1784; Rainguet, *Biographie saintongeaise*, 171–73; BNF MS n.a. fr. 21332: Arnoul to Seignelay from Rochefort, December 24, 1685, fol. 428; Arnoul from Rochefort, December 23, 1685, fol. 425v; Arnoul from Rochefort, December 31, 1685, fol. 456v.
26. [Tessereau], *Reformés de la Rochelle*, 265–66. Isaac Isle's own description of his imprisonment and expulsion from France is in his May 3, 1689 pension petition to the States General of Holland. NA/AR, Liasse Requesten, inv. nr. 7540. May 3, 1689. See also Haag and Haag, *France protestante*, 6:22–23; Beauchet-Filleau et al., *Dictionnaire*, 5:146–47; ADCM C141: Registre des affaires qui rattachent aux biens des Religionnaires fugitifs de l'Aunis.
27. Haag and Haag, *France protestante*, 6:22–23; AN TT263[bis] (ix:167): Memoire de M Begon pour la pension de quelques filles a prendre a ce qu'il propose sur les biens des absens, 1689; BNF MS n.a. fr. 21334: Liste de ceux de la Religion qui sont en prison ou dans les couvents du pays daunix pour ne s'estre pas convertis, enclosed in Arnoul to Seignelay, April 20, 1687, fol. 82; Estat des prisonniers de La Religion pretendüe reformée qui sont encore dans les prisons du departement D'Aulnis pour n'avoir pas voulu se convertir, June 17, 1687, fol. 163; AN O[1]32: 1688. 165v.
28. ADCM B736 (200): Transaction, August 12, 1676; ADCM B561: Baux judiciaires, 1682–1684; ADCM B1390 (20): Présidial de La Rochelle, March 28, 1686; B5161: Présidial de Saintes. Fugitifs, June 22, 1686; ADCM B569: Baux judiciaires, December 10, 1692; ADCM B765: Sentences, 1706; E/L38: A Monsieur Le Lieutenant general . . . René Hardy, sieur de La Dourville [against Marguerite Isle, widow Treillebois]; ADCM B501: Audiences. Présidial de Saintes, 1708–1710.
29. BNF MS n.a. fr. 21332: Arnoul to Seignelay from Rochefort, December 10, 1685, fol. 393v; Arnoul from Rochefort, December 31, 1685, fol. 456v; BNF MS n.a. fr. 21334: Arnoul to Seignelay from Marennes, April 26, 1687, fol. 84; Arnoul to Seignelay from Rochefort, June 26, 1687, fol. 184v. This Treillebois was rewarded for his conversion with a naval commission. The arrangement was for Treillebois to render services "on the matter of religion on the coast off La Tremblade": that is, to work the coast against his former coreligionists, as the younger Isaac Isle, his cousin, would do in the same years.
30. Vergé-Franceschi, *Duquesne*, 302.
31. AN TT460 (lxxi:308): Bégon from Rochefort, July 29, 1694; Beauchet-Filleau et al., *Dictionnaire*, 5:146; Lételié, "Fontaine," 436–37; Mauclerc to Chastellars, January 18, 1688, reprinted in Lételié, "Fénelon en Saintonge," 327–29; *Livre des conversions*, 42; *Letters of Denization*, 13, 14, 23; National Archives of Ireland (Dublin) MS M2455: Lord Justices' Letters: Ireland, 1698. Letters from Gallway to Blathwait, January 11, January 29, April 16, May 10, May 27, July 12.
32. *Livre des conversions*, 28, 30; CNRS. Base de données du refuge huguenot, http://www.refuge-huguenot.fr: Notice n° 86549. June 4, 1686–August 28, 1687; ADCM B2205: Juridiction de Mirambeau. Audiences, 1688–1690. Esther Isle abjured at Saint-Savinien on September 28, 1685. AMS. Biographie: Isle, Esther.
33. Gélin, "Cloches protestantes," 653–56; A. M., "Cloche des réformés de Saint-Just," 374–75; Deyon, "Destruction des temples," 253.
34. Belliard, "Baronnie de Champdollent," 260. The parish register entry is reprinted in *RSA* 1 (1879):114. See also AMS. Biographie: Isle.
35. BNF MS n.a. fr. 21334: Liste des nouveaux convertis qui recoivent des pensions du Roy sur les billets du Sieur Arnoul, July 8, 1687, fol. 207; ADCM E267: Inventaire fait au logis noble du Breüil paroisse de villars par dame Lea de Bessay veuve de feu Jean isle ecuyer seigneur de Beauchêne, December 18, 1676; ADCM E267: Transaction, December 11, 1671.
36. AN TT263bis (ii:28): Liste des deputes de lassemblee de La Rochelle, 1612; Beauchet-Filleau et al., *Dictionnaire*, 1:512; ADCM E267: Contrat de mariage, January 11, 1639. Léa

and Jean were still apparently Protestant in November 1664 at the time of the Protestant marriage of their son, a brother of the naval officer: ADCM 3E26/141: Contrat de mariage, November 24, 1664.

37. ADCM E269: Famille Isle, 1673–1691. Brevet de pension, February 2, 1688. The twenty items in this dossier all concern this Isaac Isle's military career. See also ADCM C153 (3): Liste des officiers de marine du département de Rochefort, April 1686, which names Isle as *capitaine de frégate légère*. Unless otherwise indicated, the information in this section comes from the Isle dossiers cited here.
38. The royal edict creating the new, purely military order is reprinted in d'Hozier, *Recueil de tous les membres composant l'Ordre royal et militaire de Saint-Louis*, 1:5–15.
39. ADCM E269: Famille Isle, 1673–1691 includes Pontchartrain's letter from Versailles dated May 12, 1693 notifying Isle of this appointment and the corresponding pension; Quoted in Léonard, "Institution du Mérite Militaire," 299. Some known Protestants did accept the decoration, especially later in the eighteenth century. Presumably they were willing to pay the price of "difficult compromises" (Léonard, 298) or felt that the formality was not important or that they could mouth with impunity words imposed in unjust violence against them. See also Mazas, *Histoire de l'Ordre royal et militaire de Saint-Louis*, 1:286–87.
40. Le Roy Ladurie, "Longue durée et comparatisme."
41. ADCM E270: Famille Isle; Hozier and Hozier de Sérigny, *Armorial général*, 1:313; Vindry, *Demoiselles de Saint-Cyr*, 230; ADCM E268: Bénédiction papale pour Paul Isle et sa famille; Beauchet-Filleau et al., *Dictionnaire*, 5:148–50; ADG C1546: 1691, 4 avril. Rôle des gentilshommes du ressort du siége présidial de Saintes, qui ont comparu à Saintes pour le ban et l'arrière-ban; AN MM816: Noms des Personnes qui demandent d'avoir l'honneur de monter dans les Carosses de Sa Majesté; *Gazette de France*, April 3, 1789.
42. Van Kley, *Religious Origins of the French Revolution*, 26.
43. [Tessereau], *Reformés de la Rochelle*, 303.
44. Bujeaud, *Chronique protestante*, 222–23; ADG MS1546: Rôle des gentilshommes du ressort du siège présidial de Saintes, qui ont comparu à Saintes pour le ban et l'arrière-ban, 4 avril 1691; "Liste des seigneurs de Saint-Xandre," in Tauzin, "Monographie de Saint-Xandre," 43. He was confirmed noble in 1667 by d'Aguesseau and in 1699 by Bégon. His father attended the Protestant national synod held at Alençon in 1637.
45. Boisrond, "Mémoires."
46. Burguière, "Etat monarchique," 329.
47. On this way of looking at the building of Louis XIV's state, see Beik, *Absolutism and Society*; Parker, *Making of French Absolutism*; Mettam, *Power and Faction*; Kettering, *Patrons, Brokers, and Clients*; Collins, *Fiscal Limits of Absolutism*.
48. See Part Four.
49. Quoted in Burguière, "Etat monarchique," 325.
50. Further work is needed on the effects of religious pressure on family solidarity and authority. "Historians have generally ignored this question of religious divisions within the family, and yet there is much we can learn from it about the role of religion and the nature of the family in early modern society." Diefendorf, "Houses Divided," 82.
51. Mentzer, *Blood and Belief*, 45.
52. Mentzer, *Blood and Belief*, 11.
53. Mentzer, *Blood and Belief*, 78–80, 157, 118, 175–76. Mentzer does, however, devote a single paragraph to citing various instances in which brothers sued each other, collateral relatives disputed inheritances and dowries, and so on. Would unraveling them temper the picture of cross-confessional harmony?
54. Mentzer, *Blood and Belief*, 11, 114–16.
55. Quoted in McKee, "Protestants de Sedan," 249–50.
56. Mentzer, *Blood and Belief*, 189, 4.
57. Burguière, "Etat monarchique," 327.
58. Haag and Haag, *France protestante*, 6:358; Beauchet-Filleau et al., *Dictionnaire*, 5:143, 145; Filleau, *Dictionnaire historique*, 2:239.

59. Rivierre, "Notes sur le refuge," 12. Rivierre points out that the Huguenot community in the Charentes "contributed to the Refuge in inverse proportion to the size of each grouping. The isolated succumbed or left in order not to succumb. Where Protestants were more numerous it was less difficult to resist in place and all the less necessary to depart."
60. Quéniart, *Révocation*, 126, 133.
61. Joutard, "1685," 24–25. See also Joutard, "Revocation," 347–49.
62. Burguière, "Etat monarchique," 314.
63. Leslie Tuttle has written, with respect to Colbert's turn to a mercantilist natalist policy in the 1660s, that the crown came to think about "the importance of families within the monarchical order in a new and different way. The social order theoretically assured by patriarchal control of the household was challenged by the realization that the king's interests and those of fathers were not always identical, and that more royal intervention in the sacred union of marriage was necessary to harmonize them." Tuttle, "Gender and Mercantilism," 152. See also her *Conceiving the Old Regime*.
64. Chartier, "Figuration and Habitus," 125. The Champagné case suggests, then, that the push to Huguenot emigration came less from the social forces Norbert Elias fastened upon in his 1936 essay than from the personal interactions that he made the focus of his mature work long after his Huguenot article had been forgotten.

Chapter 6

1. This generalization is supported by both qualitative evidence (escape memoirs) and quantitative. The 1,360 refugees passing through Frankfurt-am-Main in 1686 in Michelle Magdelaine's first set of data included only 104 couples with 184 children, and one cannot assume that even these couples were accompanied by all their children. Joutard, "Revocation," 351. The 5,627 Huguenots arriving in Geneva from 1684 to 1686 were 2,747 men alone, 957 women alone, 345 couples, and 1,233 children. Holtz, "Bourse française."
2. Fontaine, *Mémoires*, 129; Migault, *Journal*, 110–11.
3. "Les Collot d'Escury," 312, 314; AMAE Cp.H 147: Tillieres, August 16, 1686; Jal, *Dictionnaire critique*, 1007–08.
4. AMAE Cp.H 153: Tillieres, March 18, 1687.
5. Philippe Joutard notes how difficult it has been to identify networks facilitating emigration: "too tenuous a phenomenon to appear directly in the documents, but one suspects its existence. . . . We have little information on the preparations for and the conditions of departure." Joutard, "Revocation," 348–49. As their use for the Champagné story demonstrates, spy reports are immensely valuable sources for addressing this gap in historical knowledge.
6. This identification was provided by the spy in Holland, Tillieres: "The woman who helped Madame de Champagné to escape with her children is a first cousin of Monsieur de Champagné. Her husband is still in France, a prisoner." AMAE Cp.H 157: Tillieres, March 16, 1688.
7. ADCM E98: Archives Nicollas de Voutron; ADCM C141: Registre des affaires qui se rattachent aux biens des Religionnaires fugitifs, 28v; Haag and Haag, *France protestante*, 9:534; SHD:MR 1E33: Châteauneuf to Bégon from Versailles, 17 April 1689.
8. AMAE Cp.H 153: Tillieres, June 25, 1687, June 10, 1687, September 23, 1687; 147: Tillieres August 16, 1686; 149: Tillieres, December 30, 1686.
9. ULD MS 3613: Autre Relation de la Sortie de France de Messire Charles de La Motte Fouqué, écrite de sa propre main et trouvée dans ses Papiers après son Décès.
10. AMAE Cp.H 153: Tillieres, June 25, 1687, June 10, 1687, September 23, 1687; 147: Tillieres, August 16, 1686; 149: Tillieres, December 30, 1686. Madame de Puychenin was expelled from France in 1688. Rivierre, "Notes sur le refuge poitevin," 27.
11. AMAE Cp.H 153: Tillieres, April 6, 1687. The spy had this information from Puychenin in Rotterdam himself: "This is what Puychenin told me."
12. NA/PRO E190/1051/8,10,15 and E190/965/1,10. The Exchequer, King's Remembrancer Port Books (E 190 range) record cargos and customs paid on them for each ship (registered by name, tonnage, and master's name as well as home port and port from which arriving) that entered an English port from abroad or from another English port. These

port books reveal the preexisting, lively trading networks between western France and southwestern England that—taking on a new mission—provided transport for escapees. See Grant, "By Sea."

13. CP A59: Marie de La Rochefoucauld, Ce 10 Ienvier 1690.
14. AMAE Cp.H 153: Tillieres, June 25, 1687, July 2, 1687; 152: Tillieres, September 16, 1687.
15. Marie mentions in her memoir that she took advantage of the proximity of Josias' lands to the city: "we had our hay brought there for our horses, wheat for us, and wine." Claude Masse confirmed this bounty in Voutron: "Much hay is gathered around there in the dry salt channels [*estiers*], which gets delivered to La Rochelle." SHD:TV Fonds du Génie MS 185: Masse, Mémoire géographique, 742.
16. ADCM E797: Contrat de vante de bois, January 20, 1687; ADCM E796: Transaction, July 18, 1686; AMAE Cp.H 157: Tillieres, March 16, 1688.
17. Gwynn, "Historical Introduction" to *Minutes of the Consistory*, 1–2.
18. AN Marine $B^3$55: Gastines, commissaire, January 1688, 446–49; Fontaine, *Mémoires*, 127; BNF MS n.a. fr. 21442: Affaires diverses Arnoul, fol. 83v.
19. AMAE Cp.H 147: Tillieres, July 12, 1686; AN TT459 (xxxii:158): Proces verbal de Louis Charette, seneschal de Nantes, January 18–20, 1687; Migault, *Journal*, 107–08.
20. Chauffepié, "Journal," 60; AMAE Cp.H 149: Tillieres, April 30, 1686.
21. Janzé, *Huguenots*, 249; Cosne, "Memoirs," 534; "Biographie de Pierre Changuion," 147, 150; Cabrit, "Histoire de la vie," 534.
22. AN $G^7$133: Bezons to the contrôleur général, March 22, 1687; M. de Harlay, intendant en Bourgogne, au Contrôleur général, December 20, 1685, reprinted in *Correspondance des contrôleurs généraux*, 1:58.
23. AN TT459 (xxxii:154): Estat de l'argent trouvé sur les Religionnaires et nouveaux convertis embarquez sur les vaisseaux Anglois de Samuel lolley et Jean pelton, suivant Le proces verbal du Seneschal de Nantes signé des prisonniers du 17e juin 1687; Sturmer, *Poitevin Protestants in London*, 6; AN TT459 (xxxii:153): Reponces au placet presenté à Sa maiesté par Les sieur Et dame de la Chauvigniere; CP B14: Marriage contract between Susanne de Robillard and Charles de La Motte Fouqué, The Hague, December 12, 1692; CP A59: Marie de La Rochefoucauld, Ce 10 Ienvier 1690.
24. ADCM 3E1795: Reconnoissance du sr Tayau au sieur de Champagné, March 21, 1688. That Josias chose this receipt—from all the documentation of small transactions in his files at Berneré and Champagné—to carry with him in his escape supports the hypothesis that he expected the sum to be pertinent to him in the Refuge. The notarized receipt Tayau gave him is now CP A41. On this transaction with Tayau, see chapter 5.
25. Lettre du Roy, écrite a monsieur le procureur général [en nôtre Cour de Parlement de Paris], du 26 juillet 1686, reprinted in *Edits, déclarations et arrests*, 295.
26. CP B1: Erasmus Dixon Borrowes, Manuscript History of the Champagné Family, 16–17; CP A51: Josias de Robillard, Mesmoire de l'argens que Jay presté ou deposé entre Les mains de mons[r]. de brassac touchaimbert, Et de la maniere que nous avons agy ensemble pour cela. . . . A Voorburg proche la haye en olande çe 3 Oct[bre] 1688.
27. BNF MS fr. 10265: Lettres historiques et anecdotiques, 1682 à 1687, 145 (entry dated Paris, June 22, 1686); CP A49: Parchment order from the Parlement of Bordeaux, May 30, 1686, in favor of Brassac against Josias de Robillard; ADCM B4107: Présidial de la Rochelle. Etats généraux des ventes et baux de biens de fugitifs, 1686–1696, September 2, 1694 (101); BA Archives de la Bastille 12474, fols. 439–41; ADV C52 (12): Estat des filles nouvelles converties qui peuvent payer pension dans les communautéz des nouvelles catholiques dans la parroisse de st hilaire sur lautise, Fontenay, June 28, 1698.
28. CP A51: Josias de Robillard, Mesmoire de l'argens.
29. ADG 7B4: Letter from Bordeaux merchants dated December 17, 1701, to Fénelon, député de Bordeaux au Conseil de Commerce, quoted in Huetz de Lemps, *Géographie du commerce de Bordeaux*, 231; AMAE Cp.H 145: Tillieres, January 17, 1686; 149: Tillieres, July 26, 1686.
30. CP A55: Josias de Robillard to Marie de La Rochefoucauld, November 2, 1687; Delafosse, "Eaux-de-vie," 17; SHD:TV Fonds du Génie MS 187: Masse, Mémoire sur la Carte généralle, 108.

31. Discussion of this transformation is in chapter 13.
32. Cullen, "Merchant Networks," 129; Bosher, "Huguenot Merchants"; Bosher, "Success and Failure"; Bosher, "Political and Religious Origins." For further discussion of refugees' use of preexisting pathways during the Revocation era, see chapter 13.
33. Cullen, *Irish Brandy Houses*; Cullen, *Brandy Trade.*
34. The Champagné case does not illustrate the camouflaging of profit motives with confessional martyrdom—"economic factors as a stimulus for ostensibly 'religious' migration" (Pettegree, "Protestant Migration," 448)—nor Charles Dangibeaud's understanding, gleaned from long immersion in notarial records, that "the rigors of existence"—bad harvests, ever-increasing taxes, depression in crafts and trade, monetary instability, financial disarray—inclined Saintongeais Huguenots to pursue "the mirage of a more tolerable life abroad" ("Cozes," 218). It exemplifies, rather, Andrew Pettegree's sense that "Even the most committed evangelical was necessarily influenced by economic and family circumstances as well as consciencious scruples, in a proportion which it is quite impossible for the historian to disentangle" (Pettegree, "Protestant Migration," 448).
35. *French Protestant Refugees Relieved through the Threadneedle Street Church, London*; BL Coll. Egerton 1705B: Samuel Bernard from Paris to the Princesse de Tarente in Holland, January 5, 1688, fol. 25.
36. AMAE Cp.H 147: Tillieres, August 16, 1686; Cabrit, "Histoire," 540; Chauffepié, "Journal," 63; AN TT459 (xxxii:158): Proces verbal de Louis Charette, seneschal de Nantes, January 18–20, 1687; (151): Au Roy. Henry [sic] de La Chauviniere.
37. Johnston, "Diary of Elie Bouhéreau," 48, 65; Cabrit, "Histoire, " 537, 543. Bouhéreau's contraband exports, including many valuable early French imprints, would be deposited in Marsh's Library in Dublin after he became its first librarian.
38. Cabrit, "Histoire," 539; AMAE Cp.H 147: Tillieres, September 14, 1686; Vigneau and Bomier, Procès-verbal, November 14, 1681, reprinted in Pascal, "Evasion à la Rochelle," 64; Lucas de Demuin to Châteauneuf from Rochefort, November 17, 1681, reprinted in Pascal, "Evasion à la Rochelle," 60.
39. "Biographie de Pierre Changuion," 147–48; AMAE Cp.H 145: Louis XIV to D'Avaux, January 31, 1686; "Les Collot d'Escury," 310–11, 317, 308; AN TT270 (v:23): Procès verbaux concernant la capture d'un bateau qui devait transporter hors de France des Religionnaires, 1687.
40. Davis, "Ghosts, Kin, and Progeny," 97; Furetière, *Dictionaire universel,* article "Exil"; Fontaine, *Mémoires,* 150. On the writing of memoirs as a means of creating identity, see Lougee Chappell, "Paper Memories and Identity Papers."
41. CP A1: Inventory of the Possessions of Marie de La Rochefoucauld, Amsterdam, October 9, 1690.
42. AMAE Cp.H 157: Tillieres, June 16, 1688; CP A56: Estat et inventaire sommere; CP A1: Inventory of the Possessions of Marie de La Rochefoucauld, Amsterdam, October 9, 1690.
43. Le Fanu, "Children of Marie de La Rochefoucauld"; Le Fanu, "Marie de La Rochefoucauld."
44. AMS MS 512.68, 43, 61, 26, 90.
45. For discussion of how these caches of papers were reunited, see the Afterword. For a sketch of the geography and sociology of departures, see Choquette, "Emigration aunisienne" and Sauzeau, "Rochefort et la Nouvelle-France," both in Augeron and Guillemet, eds., *Champlain.*
46. Anonymous, "Journal d'un réfugié sorti du royaume de France par voie de mer, 1685," 62–64.
47. BNF MS n.a. fr. 21331: Arnoul, Mémoire sur le fait de la Religion dans le pays d'Aulnis, January 2, 1685.
48. "Emigrés de la Rochelle," 426–27; Johnston, "Diary of Elie Bouhéreau."
49. Vigneau and Bomier, Procès-verbal, November 14, 1681, reprinted in Pascal, "Evasion à la Rochelle," 60–61, 63.
50. Petition for release to Châteauneuf, quoted in Pascal, "Evasion à la Rochelle," 71.
51. "Emigrés de la Rochelle," 427–28; Anonymous, "Journal d'un réfugié," 62, 65–66.
52. "Emigrés de la Rochelle," 428; Foucault, *Mémoires,* 320.

53. See Beuzart, "Fugitifs protestants."
54. CP A55: Josias de Robillard to Marie de La Rochefoucauld, November 2, 1687.

Chapter 7

1. CP A59: Marie de La Rochefoucauld, Ce 10 Ienvier 1690.
2. CP A55: Josias de Robillard to Marie de La Rochefoucauld, November 2, 1687; Seignelay to Matignon, April 16, 1686, quoted in Jal, *Dictionnaire critique,* 1009; Delavaud, "Révocation," 318.
3. Bujeaud, *Chronique protestante,* 297; Haag and Haag, *France protestante,* 10:440; NA/AR, Liasse Requesten, inv. nr. 7531. October 22, 1687; Haag and Haag, *France protestante,* 10:435, 438; BNF MS n.a. fr. 21334: Estat des prisonniers de la religion p r qui sont encore dans les prisons du dept d'Aulnis pour n'avoir pas voulu se convertir, June 14, 1687.
4. BNF MS n.a. fr. 21333: Arnoul to Seignelay, January 31, 1686; [Tessereau], *Reformés de la Rochelle,* 284–86; BNF MS n.a. fr. 21334: Arnoul to Seignelay, April 20, 1687. Liste de ceux de la Religion qui sont en prison ou dans les couvents du pays daunix pour ne sestre pas convertis.
5. Magnan, quoted in Rivierre and Durand, *Drame de Grand Ry,* 11; Jurieu, *Lettres pastorales,* February 15, 1688.
6. Foucault, *Mémoires,* 219.
7. Jurieu, *Lettres pastorales,* March 15, 1688, April 1, 1688.
8. Migault, *Journal,* 104.
9. "De Paris, 4 novembre 1685. Rose dEscars à son cousin le Marquis de Boisse," reprinted in Alis and Bouillet, *Notice,* 270–72; [Jurieu], *Reflexions,* 42–43; Aubineau, *De la Révocation de l'Edit de Nantes,* xii, 214, 15.
10. Edit du Roy, du mois d'Aout 1669, Portant défenses à tous ses Sujets de se retirer de son Royaume, pour aller s'établir sans sa permission dans les Païs Etrangers, reprinted in *Edits, Déclarations et Arrests,* 26–29; ADCM B5645: Seignelay to Demuin from Rambouillet, October 10, 1681.
11. Demuin to Châteauneuf from Rochefort, November 17, 1681, reprinted in Pascal, "Evasion à la Rochelle," 59.
12. [Tessereau], *Reformés de la Rochelle,* 168–69.
13. Vigneau and Bomier et al., Procès-verbaux, November 14–15, 1681, reprinted in Pascal, "Evasion à la Rochelle," 62–67.
14. Le Fanu, "Mémoires inédits d'Abraham Tessereau," 568.
15. Colbert to Demuin, January 6, 1679, quoted in Jal, *Dictionnaire critique,* 100; AN Marine $B^2$44: Au sr. de Demuin from Versailles, June 7, 1681. Jal opined: "De Muyn était plus catholique que le Roi."
16. Jurieu, *Lettres pastorales,* January 1, 1687.
17. Aubarède to an unnamed missionary from Saint-Martin-de-Ré, October 17, 1687, in *Lettre des nouveaux catholiques,* 24–25.
18. [Tessereau], *Reformés de la Rochelle,* 286–93; Le Fanu, "Mémoires inédits d'Abraham Tessereau," 575; Benoist, *Histoire de l'Édit de Nantes,* 3(3):1020–33, 898–99.
19. Tournier, *Galères de France,* 3:401, 355; "Journal des choses mémorables," 419; Foucault, *Mémoires,* 219; "Louvois à Foucault, À Versailles, le 1er mars 1688," reprinted in Foucault, *Mémoires,* 539.
20. Jurieu, *Lettres pastorales,* March 15, 1688, April 1, 1688.
21. Rivierre and Durand, "Drame de Grand Ry," 5–6.
22. Foucault, *Mémoires,* 213; [Bonnet], *Berthelot,* 52. This is the Orte manuscript at the Bibliothèque wallonne (Leiden).
23. AN TT295 (i:2): Décisions du Conseil relatives aux Pensions, 1700: Angoumois et Limosin, Saintonge; Foucault, *Mémoires,* 172; AN $G^7$133: Bazin de Bezons au Contrôleur-général, March 11, 1687.
24. Jean-Antoine de Mesmes, Comte d'Avaux (1640–1709), scion of the distinguished parlementary family de Mesmes, was ambassador in The Hague from 1679 until 1688. The manuscript dispatches from d'Avaux, some appending the original letters of the spy and

other documentation, are located in two repositories: AMAE Cp.H 140–158 and AN AE B[1] 621–23.

25. AMAE Cp.H 143: Louis XIV to D'Avaux, December 13, 1685; 145: D'Avaux, March 15, 1686, March 28, 1686.
26. AMAE Cp.H 145: Tillieres, January 24, 1686; 148: Tillieres, November 19, 1686.
27. AMAE Cp.H 149: Tillieres, April 3, 1686; 147: Tillieres, August 16, 1686.
28. AMAE Cp.H 145: D'Avaux, March 21, 1686.
29. AMAE Cp.H 149: Tillieres, June 1, 1686, March 2, 1686; 153: Tillieres, May 6, 1687.
30. AMAE Cp.H 155: Tillieres, July 30, 1688; 157: Tillieres, July 27, 1688. For more on this family, in particular this naval officer, see chapter 10.
31. AMAE Cp.H 153: Tillieres, September 9, 1687, June 25, 1687, July 2, 1687.
32. AMAE Cp.H 153: Tillieres, September 9, 1687, December 8, 1687; 152: Tillieres, September 16, 1687 (two letters); AMAE Cp.H 157: Tillieres, February 28, 1688, June 16, 1688.
33. AMAE Cp.H 153: Tillieres, July 2, 1687, June 25, 1687. The manuscript dispatches from D'Avaux were often annotated in the margin at Versailles with the names of persons to whom the information in the dispatch was forwarded. Attention to this marginal detail reveals what action, if any, the ministers took on the information D'Avaux sent them. Some of D'Avaux's dispatches got at least one step beyond Versailles. Pierre Arnoul in Rochefort received verbatim excerpts, for example, from Tillieres' reports about the escape plans of Puychenin and Nieul (BNF n.a. fr. 21442: Collection Arnoul: Affaires diverses, fols. 83–84, 87). Other examples of extracts copied out by the Conseil d'Etat from Tillieres' reports in D'Avaux's dispatches can be found in AN TT430 (111–13): "Extrait des avis donnez au Roy" as well as in AN Marine B[3]57: Correspondance générale. Lettres reçues (1688), 30–38 and B[3]53: Correspondance Ponant (1687), 278–79. A systematic study of crown uses of Tillieres' information might be productively pursued through the correspondence between the ministers and the La Rochelle intendant Pierre Arnoul that is contained in the BNF manuscripts.
34. D'Avaux estimated for Tillieres that he needed eight days advance notice in order to intercept an embarkation in France. AMAE Cp.H 145: D'Avaux, January 24, 1686.
35. AMAE Cp.H 153: Tillieres, July 31, 1687, August 14, 1687, March 18, 1687.
36. AMAE Cp.H 153: Tillieres, October 18, 1687; 149: Tillieres, June 1, 1686, June 27, 1686; 145: Tillieres, March 28, 1686; 157: Tillieres, July 2, 1688; 147: Tillieres, September 16, 1686.
37. Archives des monastères de la Visitation (Paris). "Abregé de la vie et des vertus de feue notre très-chere Soeur Françoise-Henriette Isle de Loire, décédée en ce premier Monastere de la Visitation Sainte-Marie de Paris, le 29. Octobre 1724," in *Circulaires et vies de nos Soeurs de ce 1er Monastère de la Visitation, 1700-1744*, 2: 336.
38. AMAE Cp.H 145: Louis XIV, February 21, 1686; D'Avaux, March 24, 1686, January 10, 1686; 146: D'Avaux, May 9, 1686.
39. AMAE Cp.H 149: D'Avaux, June 5, 1686; 147: D'Avaux, July 16, 1686, July 25, 1686; 147: Louis XIV, August 22, 1686.
40. M. Feydeau de Brou, intendant à Rouen, au Contrôleur-général, June 1, 1687, reprinted in *Correspondance des contrôleurs généraux*, 1:104; Anonymous cahier in the Bibliothèque municipale de Poitiers, reprinted in Lièvre and Weiss, "En Seudre," 81–83; AN G[7]133: Bezons au Contrôleur-général, March 1, 1687, March 11, 1687, March 22, 1687.
41. AN TT459 (xxxii:151–60): Le s.[r] de la Chauvignière, du Poitou, 1687–1688; Brodut, *Tonnay-Charente*, 638; SHD:TV A[1]782: Louvois to Arnoul, April 29, 1687; AMAE Cp.H 153: Tillieres, June 10, 1687.
42. AN Marine B[2]62: A Mr Millet from Fontainebleau, October 30, 1687; AN TT459 (xxxii:151): Au Roy. Henry de La Chauviniere; Foucault, *Mémoires*, 149, 171, 174, 180, 528.
43. "Extraits de la Gazette de Haarlem," March 18 ,1687, 404–05; ADCM C136 (37): Intendance. Religionnaires, 1666–1755; AMAE Cp.H 153: Tillieres, April 15, 1687, July 2, 1687, August 27, 1687, October 18, 1687; Archives des monastères de la Visitation (Paris). "Abregé de la vie et des vertus de feue notre très-chere Soeur Françoise-Henriette Isle de Loire," 2:336–37. Discussion of her case appears in chapter 10.

44. ADCM B5645: Amirauté de La Rochelle. Religionnaires, 1685–1717. Seignelay from Versailles, March 20, 1687.
45. Foucault, *Mémoires*, 172; Anonymous cahier in Lièvre and Weiss, "En Seudre," 82–83; Feydeau de Brou, intendant à Rouen, au Contrôleur général, June 1, 1687, reprinted in *Correspondance des contrôleurs généraux*, 1:104; AN TT459 (xxxii:158): Proces verbal de Louis Charette, sénéchal de Nantes, January 18–20, 1687.
46. Rousset, *Louvois*, 3:438; Orcibal, "Louis XIV," 165.
47. Gregory Monahan's revisionist picture of the suppression of the Camisards in the Protestant stronghold of the Cévennes suggests the low priority the king accorded to the conflict and its objective of Catholic conformity: "He and his ministers simply did not care very much about the rebellion and war in Languedoc. . .. His wider dynastic ambitions trumped even the enforcement of his authority in his own realm." Monahan, *Let God Arise*, 262.
48. AMAE Mémoires et documents. Hollande. 1679–88. 44–45: Négotiations. Précis des négociations du comte d'Avaux à La Haye rédigé par lui-meme. These volumes contain D'Avaux's retrospective on France's political relations with Holland.
49. AMAE Cp.H 150: D'Avaux, January 16, 1687, January 30, 1687; 152: D'Avaux, October 23, 1687; Louis XIV, October 30, 1687.
50. Dangeau, *Journal*, 2:108; Sourches, *Mémoires*, entry dated March 12, 1688, 2:148.
51. [Tessereau], *Reformés de la Rochelle*, 266; "Lettre de M. de Creil," 385; ADCM C141: Liste des religionnaires fugitifs de la Rochelle dont les biens ont été saisis (1685–1688); Chauffepié, "Journal," 264–66; NA/AR, Liasse Requesten, inv. nr. 7536. August 17, 1688; AN O[1]32: A Mad[e]. de Miramion, September 25, 1688; A la Supr[re]. des nouvelles Catholiques, September 24, 1688; BibSHPF MS 485/2: Louvois to de Gourgue, March 10, 1686, fol. 248.
52. BNF MS fr. n.a. 507: Lettres autographes de Fénelon, July 1687, fol. 47v; Bezard, "Intendant Michel Bégon," 155; Lamoignon de Basville, "Réflexions politiques qui doivent porter le roi à contraindre les nouveaux convertis de son royaume de professer la religion catholique," reprinted in the appendix to *Mémoires des évêques de France*, 322–38.
53. The following excerpts from Arnoul's correspondence, and more extended analysis of them, appear in Lougee, "Cross Purposes."
54. AN Marine B[2]61: Seignelay to Arnoul, June 6, 1687.
55. NA/AR, Liasse Requesten, inv. nr. 7536. August 17, 1688.
56. AN G[7]133: Bezons to the Contrôleur-général, March 22, 1687; Dangibeaud, "Cozes," 237.

Chapter 8

1. CP A52: Summary of the decision of the Parlement of Bordeaux, August 20, 1691. See chapter 9 for discussion of the case.
2. Substantial genealogies of the Prévost family can be found in Filleau, *Ancien Poitou*, 2:555–65; Hozier and Hozier de Sérigny, *Armorial général*, 7(2):515–28; Anselme et al., *Histoire généalogique*, 9 (2):933–42; Traversay, *Notice généalogique*; La Chenaye-Desbois and Badier, *Dictionnaire de la noblesse*, 16:386–96.
3. BNF MS fr. 32119: *Preuves de Noblesse des Filles demoiselles Reçuës dans la Maison de S[t]. Louis fondée à S[t]. Cir, par le Roi, au mois de Juin de L'an 1686 Et formée par les soins, et par la conduite de Madame de Maintenon* (Cabinet des titres 294), fols. 33–34; Bourchenin, "Notes sur la géographie calvinienne," 56–57.
4. Filleau, *Ancien Poitou*, 2:560; Hozier, *Armorial général*, 7(2):516–17; Beauchet-Filleau, "Les Prévost de Sansac de Traversay"; Geoffray, *Répertoire*, 128; Du Chatenet, *Amiral Jean-Baptiste de Traversay*.
5. Bujeaud, *Chronique protestante*, Supplément, 21; *Présentation du fonds*, 53; Traversay, *Notice généalogique*, 23; Biais, "Notes et documents," 7–10; Foulon, *Belles Demeures de la Charente*, 7–9. The two sisters were named in the property division but probably took their portions in movables. The Prévost inheritance is clarified in the records of a lawsuit litigated sixty-nine years after the duchess's death. BNF f° Fm.13687 (1): Memoire Pour la Marquise de Pons, 1736.

6. ADV C49: Extrait des Registres du Conseil d'Estat, 8 juin 1682; AN TT266 (xxi:143–54): Pieces concernant les contestations d'Entre le Syndic du clergé du Diocèse de Poitiers et le Seigneur, et les habitans du Lieu de Saveilles de La R.P.R. au Sujet de l'exercice de Lad. Religion, 1682–1683; Haag and Haag, *France protestante*, 8:322; Dez, *Histoire des Protestants*, 1:349; Biais, "Notes et documents," 9–10; Tesseron, *Histoire de l'Angoumois et de la Charente*, 107.
7. Haag and Haag, *France protestante*, 8:323; AN O[1]29: A Mr de la Reynie, June 11, 1685. The parish register of Charenton was destroyed in the 1871 fire at the Hôtel de Ville of Paris, but an earlier extraction from it can be consulted at the BibSHPF.
8. BibSHPF MS 485/2: Louvois to de Gourgue from Paris, October 27, 1685, fol. 102; Louvois to de Gourgue from Paris, October 29, 1685, fol. 105; Colbert de Croissy to de Gourgue from Fontainebleau, October 27, 1685, fol. 103.
9. Benoist, *Histoire de l'Edit de Nantes*, 3(2):483–84; Bibliothèque de Genève Papiers Court 30: Jacques-Jacob de Rossel [Baron d'Aigaliers], Memoires d'un gentilhomme huguenot.
10. Foucault, *Mémoires*, 130, 140–41, 143; Louvois to Foucault, quoted in Foucault, *Mémoires*, 518–19.
11. Archives du Château de Londigny: Petition by François and Casimir Prévost de Touchimbert, brothers, to Louis XIV, October 1685, reprinted in Chevalier, *Verteuil*, 268–70.
12. Louvois to Foucault, October 2, 1685, quoted in Foucault, *Mémoires*, 515–16; SHD:TV A[1]757: Louvois to d'Asfeld, October 27, 1685; Louvois to Foucault, November 7, 1685, quoted in Foucault, *Mémoires*, 519.
13. SHD:TV A[1]757: Le Tellier, November 7 and 9, 1685; Louvois to Besmaus, November 9, 1685; Louvois to de Gourgue, November 11, 1685; BA Archives de la Bastille. MS Register 12474, fols. 439–41; Louvois to Foucault, November 9, 1685, reprinted in Foucault, *Mémoires*, 520; SHD:TV A[1]757: Louvois to de Gourgue from Fontainebleau, November 11, 1685.
14. BA Archives de la Bastille. MS Register 12474, fols. 439–41, 453, 462, 464; *Archives de la Bastille* (Ravaisson-Mollien, ed.), 8:355–58.
15. BA Archives de la Bastille, MS Register 12474, fol. 492; *Archives de la Bastille* (Ravaisson-Mollien, ed.), 8:360; ADCM E796: Transaction, January 10, 1686.
16. *Archives de la Bastille* (Ravaisson-Mollien, ed.), 8:362–65; BA Archives de la Bastille. MS Register 10421, fol. 134; AN O[1]30: A M. de Besmaus, January 14, 1686; Douen, *Révocation*, 3:293; ADCM E796: Transaction, January 10, 1686. By February 2, when she ratified the Soubise contract drawn up in Paris, Marie Prévost de Touchimbert would once again be lodging in the Château de Berneré with the Champagné.
17. Parish register of Londigny, cited in Chevalier, *Verteuil*, 271. Why the sixth daughter, Marie-Anne-Susanne, was absent is unclear. Despite the family's collective abjuration, the two elder daughters, Marie and Angélique, were soon thereafter removed from home: "The King has learned that the two oldest daughters of the sieur de Touchimbert Londigny are so obstinate in their religion that no instruction can make them convert, which is what has given rise to the order I received from His Majesty to inform you that his intention is that you have them put separately in convents in Poitiers until they abjure." SHD:TV A[1]766: Louvois to Foucault, July 7, 1686. At one time or another, then, all six daughters of Casimir Prévost de Touchimbert and Marie de Robillard were sent to convents for reeducation. This Marie and Angélique emigrated to Holland and greeted Marie de La Rochefoucauld on her arrival there.
18. AN O[1]30: Ordre a M. de Besmaus, March 23, 1686; BNF MS fr. 7051: Noms des prisonniers qui sont par ordre du Roy a La Bastille, a Cause de la Religion, December 17, 1686, fol. 252v; ADV 2E183: August 11, 1686, October 21, 1686, March 7, 1687; AMAE Cp.H 149: Tillieres, June 1, 1686; BNF MS fr. 7051: Noms surnoms Et qualitez de Ceux qui sont Nouvellement Convertis et qui sont logez au quartier de la rüe de la harpe et autres en deppendans, 20 decembre 1686, fol. 16.
19. AN O[1]36: A M[r]. de la Bourdonnaye, April 28, 1692; *Archives de la Bastille* (Ravaisson-Mollien, ed.), 8:368.
20. AMAE Cp.H 149: Tillieres, June 1, 1686; 153: Tillieres, June 5, 1687; Stadsarchief Rotterdam: Waals Hervormde Kerk te Rotterdam: Kerkelijke Registers: Lidmaten;

HGA 241.1: Waals Hervormde Kerk te 's-Gravenhage, Kerkelijke Registers: Lidmaten, 1632–1710.

21. AMAE Cp.H 153: Tillieres, June 5, 1687; BNF MS fr. 7051: Noms surnoms et qualitez, fol. 16.
22. Déclaration du Roy, June 17, 1681, reprinted in *Edits, Déclarations et Arrests*, 88.
23. See Lougee, *Paradis des Femmes*, 171–208.
24. Late in 1777, the Minister of War drew up a proposal "that everyone is talking about" to reassign "to the needs of the State" the revenues supporting Saint-Cyr. Bibliothèque municipale de Versailles MSS F629–30: Mémoires de ce qui sest passé de plus remarquable depuis l'Etablissement de la Maison de Saint Cyr. 2 vols., 2:291–92.
25. Saint-Simon, *Mémoires*, 28:232. Saint-Simon went on to link Maintenon herself to the Revocation ("a frightful plot, in which the new spouse was one of the chief conspirators"), but not the school. Saint-Cyr's founding he ascribed, rather, to Maintenon's hopes that it would "smooth the way for a declaration of her marriage . . . while gratifying the poor nobility would cause her to be seen as a protectress in whom all the nobility would feel invested."
26. *Mercure galant*, June 1687, seconde partie, 56–57.
27. Michelet, *Histoire de France*, 16:14; Sée, *Université et Mme de Maintenon*, 41, 93–94.
28. Haag and Haag, *France protestante*. 2d ed., 1:534.
29. AMAE Cp.H 157: Tillieres, July 13, 1688.
30. The marriage was never made public, so its date is uncertain. It probably took place sometime in early to mid-1684, the queen having died in July 1683.
31. She was baptized by the curé of Notre-Dame de Niort on November 28, 1635. ADDS Paroisse de Notre-Dame de Niort, Baptêmes, 1633–1637.
32. Marquise de Villette, "Notice biographique," reprinted in Bonhomme, *Madame de Maintenon et sa famille*, 235; *Notes des Dames de Saint-Cyr*, quoted in Maintenon, *Correspondance générale*, 1:34–35. In Gélin's words, the reworked biography gave Maintenon "for a prelude to her role as converter a role of converted. "Madame de Maintenon convertisseuse," 176.
33. Liselotte to Caroline, Princess of Wales, October 20, 1719, in [Orléans], *Briefe*, 2:248; Liselotte, May 13, 1719, quoted in Read, "Petite-fille d'Agrippa d'Aubigné," 411. Others who assign Maintenon responsibility for the Revocation include Douen, *Révocation*, 1:54 ("Madame de Maintenon recommended the Revocation").
34. Maintenon, "Réponse"; Maintenon to Charles d'Aubigné, quoted in Read, "Petite-fille d'Agrippa d'Aubigné," 406; Labrousse, "Refuge huguenot," 148.
35. Maintenon to Madame de Saint-Géran from Fontainebleau, October 25, 1685 and Maintenon to M. de Villette, April 5, 1681, both reprinted in Maintenon, *Lettres*, 1:363, 594; Maintenon, "Réponse," 402, 408, 405.
36. Maintenon to M. de Villette, April 29, 1675, reprinted in Maintenon, *Lettres*, 1:180; Caylus, *Souvenirs*, 32; Noailles, *Madame de Maintenon*, 2:475; Maintenon to M. l'abbé Gobelin, November 4, 1680 and Maintenon to M. d'Aubigné, 8 December 1680, both reprinted in Maintenon, *Lettres*, 1:348–50. Aymée de Villette-Mursay, Dame de Fontmort collaborated with Maintenon in her conversion efforts. She had no children.
37. Caylus, *Souvenirs*, 33; Maintenon to M. d'Aubigné, December 19, 1680, reprinted in Maintenon, *Lettres*, 1:352; Maintenon to M. d'Aubigné, February 5, 1681, reprinted in Maintenon, *Lettres*, 1:358. Two of the Sainte-Hermine children would have close ties to the Champagné in the Refuge. See Part Four.
38. Maintenon to M. de Villette, September 4, 1687 and Maintenon to M. d'Aubigné, May 19, 1681, both reprinted in Maintenon, *Lettres*, 1:370.
39. BNF MSS fr. 32118–19: *Preuves de Noblesse des Filles demoiselles Reçuës dans la Maison de St. Louis*. The best published list of the pupils of Saint-Cyr is Vindry, *Demoiselles de Saint-Cyr*. Vindry's list is also available on the website of the Archives départementales des Yvelines. Oddly, the Prévost de Touchimbert are the only girls designated as Huguenot in the online list.
40. Douen, *Révocation*, 3:98.

41. *Mercure galant*, February 1686, 208; Haag and Haag, *France protestante*, 4:309; Douen, "Réforme en Picardie," 466–67; AN TT458 (xlix:235): Evêque de Lectoure, June 24, 1742; BibSHPF MS 67: Eugène Haag, Papiers des protestants aux Archives nationales, fol. 115. In the Maravat case, the father may have succeeded in keeping his daughter out of Saint-Cyr, since she does not appear on Vindry's list of the school's pupils.
42. Their two certificates of admission are in ADCM E270: Famille Isle.
43. AN TT89bis (iii:4,7): M.r de Polignac Demande le don des biens des s.r et D.lle Bonniot; ADCM B762: Sentences, Présidial de Saintes, 1703; ADCM B2205: Audiences, Présidial de Saintes, May 17, 1688; Du Pasquier, *Généalogies huguenotes*, 238–39. Madame de Maintenon engineered the transfer of Uranie Isle's properties to the Polignac pupil at Saint-Cyr, who had no kinship claim to them.
44. See chapter 10.
45. AN O[1]33: Ordre du Roy pour tirer du Couvent du port Royal la dlle Touchimberg et la conduire dans la maison de la dame de Miramion, September 14, 1689. Port-Royal was among the convents Maintenon used against Protestants. See AN O[1]30: Seignelay a M. l'archevesque de Paris, April 15, 1686: "Sir, this letter is to advise you that I am sending M. de La Reynie the king's orders to arrest Madame d'Heucourt and take her to the Abbey of Port-Royal. It is Madame de Maintenon who asked this from the King."
46. Biver and Biver, *Abbayes, monastères, couvents de femmes à Paris*, 214–19; Diefendorf, *From Penitence to Charity*, 238. A visitor's description of the education given by the Miramionnes has been reprinted in "Madame de Miramion's School for Girls." The standard biographies of Miramion are Bonneau, *Madame de Beauharnais de Miramion* and the *Vie de Madame de Miramion* by her husband's cousin, abbé de Choisy.
47. Bonneau, *Miramion*, 283.
48. Renaudin, "Dame de Saint-Cyr," 408. Bonneau, *Miramion*, 292–95 reverses the roles of Maintenon and Miramion in this episode.
49. Bonneau, *Miramion*, 282.
50. AN O[1]30: Seignelay to Mère Garnier, May 2, 1686; Seignelay to La Reynie, April 20, 1686; Seignelay to Madame de Miramion, July 21, 1686; Haag and Haag, *France protestante*, 6:357; AN O[1]32: Seignelay to Madame de Miramion, April 24, 1688, September 25, 1688.

Chapter 9

1. ADCM C141: *Estat de Ceux qui ont* [sic] *entrés en pocession des biens des fugitifs en consequence de lEdit du Roy du mois de décembre 1689 dans le ressort de la Rochell pendant l'année 1690*; AN TT249 (x:38): Estat des biens et Revenus des pretendus reformez et nouveaux convertis fugitifs, Election et ressort de St jean Dangely, 1686–1687; Floris and Talon, eds., *Châteaux, Manoirs et Logis*, 463. Casimir continued Josias' efforts to collect the sums owed to Marie de La Rochefoucauld by virtue of her inheritance from her grandmother Susanne Isle, notably the La Valade debt, which he pursued down at least to 1693. ADCM B488: Présidial de Saintes, Audiences civiles, 1692–1693; ADCM B750: Présidial de Saintes, Sentences, 1692.
2. For more on Philippe-Benjamin, see chapter 10.
3. Unless otherwise indicated, the information in this section is taken from the documents related to the battle over inheritance of Susanne Isle's Berneré that were formerly held in the archives of the La Vie family (here referred to as Esclafer/Lougee Manuscripts or E/L).
4. ADCM B1984: Présidial de Saintes, Juridictions seigneuriales, 1690; AN TT452 (xlviii:161): Bishop of Saintes to Père La Chaise, December 16, 1691; BibSHPF MS 156: Information extracted from AN series TT by René Tourlet.
5. Louis de Salbert, Seigneur de Soulignonne, died on June 10, 1669 at the age of thirty-six. Madelene would be widowed again by the death of her second husband Alexandre Roulin, Seigneur de La Mortmartin, by 1686. ADCM B754: Présidial de Saintes, Sentences, 1696.
6. ADCM B754: Présidial de Saintes, Sentences, 1696.
7. ADCM B909: Présidial de Saintes, Sentences criminelles, October 6, 1692, October 9, 1692, July 26, 1693.

8. Colle, *Châteaux, manoirs et forteresses*, 2:307–08. Only one formal gateway and the base of a tower remain of the Château de Soulignonne.
9. Nieul was a New Convert of more recent abjuration than Madelene. As late as 1685, he was still holding Protestant religious exercises at his Château de Nieul, but the Parlement of Bordeaux had suspended them by September of that year. AN TT236 (i:22): Estat des seigneurs de fiefs qui faisoient l'exercice de la religion pretendue reformée dans leurs chateaux et maisons, September 8, 1685. His family's attempted flight from France in 1687 with some of Berneré's neighbors is discussed in chapter 7.
10. Colle, *Châteaux, manoirs et forteresses*, 2:307.
11. Dangibeaud, "Registres paroissiaux de Soulignonnes," 255.
12. ADG Parlement de Bordeaux. Liasse 1021: Arrêt August 20, 1691. An extract is Champagné Papers A52.
13. SHD:TV Fonds du Génie MS 503: Masse, Recueil des Plans de Saintonge, 17. On the Abbaye-aux-Dames, see Feiss, "'Consecrated to Christ'"; Boudet, "Histoire"; Bégon, "Mémoire," 57.
14. She was the granddaughter of Henri de Caumont La Force, marquis de Castelnau, who was a party to the La Rochefaton property division of 1668 that yielded Montalembert to Casimir and Saveilles to François.
15. AMS MS 571D: Documents relatifs à l'Abbaye aux Dames; ADCM H89: Note sur l'Abbaye royale de Notre-Dame de Saintes, envoyée à l'intendant de la généralité de La Rochelle par le monastère, 1723; Audiat, "Abbaye de Notre-Dame de Saintes," 445–48. Daniel de Robillard, Seigneur de Fontbarbeau and father of Gabrielle, was a grandson of Josias' grandfather Christophe. BNF. Cabinet des Titres. Cabinet d'Hozier 292, fol. 7995; Nadaud, *Nobiliaire*, 4:29–30.
16. Childhood and adolescent mortality was 14% in the one sample studied to date. Feiss, "'Consecrated to Christ,'" 270, 281.
17. Audiat, "Les Sainte-Claire," 171, 178, 190.
18. On Jeanne de Lestonnac, see Soury-Lavergne, *Chemin d'éducation*; [Bouzonié], *Histoire*. The Compagnie de Marie Notre-Dame is one of the orders of nuns studied by Rapley, *Social History of the Cloister* and in her *Dévotes*.
19. Bref du pape Paul V, 102–12. The Filles de Notre-Dame remained active in Saintes until the Revolution of 1789, when the convent buildings were converted into a prison.
20. SHD:TV Fonds du Génie MS 503: Masse, Recueil des Plans de Saintonge, 17.
21. Reprinted in "Les Notre-Dame," 114. Because the Filles de Notre-Dame aspired to play the educational role for girls that Jesuits played for boys, they were sometimes nicknamed "Jésuitines." Marcadé, "Filles de Notre-Dame," 218.
22. Quittance donnée par les dames relligieuses de Notre-Dame de Saintes à messire Guilleaume d'Hérisson, chevallier, seigneur de La Grande-Forest et autres lieux, December 31, 1703, reprinted in "Les Notre-Dame," 450–51; ADCM B1984: Juridictions seigneuriales, Présidial de Saintes, 1690; Aussy, "Château de Saintonge," 327; ADCM B569: Présidial de Saintes, Baux judiciaires, 1682–1693; Archives du Séminaire de Saint-Sulpice (Paris) S197: Filles de Notre-Dame. Nécrologie: Saintes, February 29, 1736; AN TT295 (i:2): Décisions du Conseil relatives aux Pensions, 1700: Saintonge; Espanol, ed., *Dictionnaire historique*, 284.
23. AN TT452 (xlviii:161): Bishop of Saintes to Père La Chaise, December 16, 1691; (xlviii:162): Bishop of Saintes to Colbert de Torcy, December 16, 1691. Any appeal to Père La Chaise would likely have elicited involvement from Madame de Maintenon, though this has not been established in this case.
24. ADCM B520: Présidial de Saintes, Affirmations de voyage, 1692–1693; ADCM B521: Présidial de Saintes, Affirmations de voyage, 1693–1695.
25. Marie-Françoise d'Albret, Comtesse de Marsan was the only child of the maréchal César-Phébus d'Albret and Madeleine de Guénégaud. The letter from Louis XIV authorizing Marie d'Albret to found the institution at Pons in 1680 called it an asylum and retreat for Protestant girls "who wish to abjure or have abjured, to be raised and maintained there when they have been abandoned by their parents and ... instructed in the mysteries of

the faith." BMLR MS 658: Lettre de Louis XIV, fol. 134; "Nouvelles Catholiques de Pons" (*Recueil*); "Nouvelles Catholiques de Pons" (*Cahiers*).
26. See chapter 4.
27. AN TT265 (iii:48): "Au Roy. Requete des habitans," 259.
28. A Nosseigneurs du Parlement, May 17, 1684; Grimard to Le Tellier from La Réole, May 18, 1684; and Du Sault from La Réole, May 18, 1684, all reprinted in "Enlèvements d'enfants, séquestrations et violences," 437–45.
29. AN TT265 (iii:48): "Au Roy. Requete des habitans," 260.
30. Rapley, *Social History of the Cloister*, 235; "Enlèvements de jeunes protestantes," 361.
31. Mazoyer, *Enlèvement des enfants*, 8; "Enlèvements de jeunes protestantes," 361; Quoted in Rapley, *Social History of the Cloister*, 250; Chevalier, "Mémoires des noms et qualités," 550–55; ADCM B569: Présidial de Saintes, Baux judiciaires, 1682–1693.
32. The Abbaye-aux-Dames, by contrast, enjoyed annual incomes of 48,000–80,000 *livres* in 1695–1717 from landed and movable endowments stretching back over the centuries since its founding. See *Sites de Saintonge*, 25.
33. ADCM 3E 88/60: Desclaration que fournist dame Claude ozias, Superieure du couvant et monastere des filles Religieuses nostre dame du faubourg de St maurice Les la ville de saintes des biens domaines et heritages que possede led Couvant, 15 Juillet 1690. Mazoyer (*Enlèvement des enfants*, 8) lacks both evidence and example for his charge that "The richer young Huguenots' families are, the more avidly the greedy religious communities seek them out."
34. Bossuet to Tanqueux from Lusanci, November 3, 1687, in Bossuet, *Oeuvres*, 39:654; Françoise d'Aubigné to Madame de Villette, October 12, [1650], reprinted in Maintenon, *Lettres*, 1:95.
35. Chauffepié, "Journal," 257–58.
36. On the two Isle women and the Voutron cousin, see chapter 10.
37. Archives du Séminaire de Saint-Sulpice (Paris) MS S197: Filles de Notre-Dame. Nécrologie, February 29, 1736. This life course from Huguenot to nun appears not to have been common, though it appears numerous times in the families of the Champagné kindred discussed in chapter 10. Among many hundreds of death notices for the Filles de Notre-Dame across France, only four (of whom two commemorate Champagné cousins) identify the late nun as having been born Protestant: Marie-Olympe de Cailhaut at Poitiers (February 18, 1717), Céleste de Voutron at Saintes (February 29, 1736), Renée de Saint-Ours at Sarlat (July 12, 1736), and Jeanne de Beuves at Agde (March 14, 1743).
38. Rapley, *Social History of the Cloister*, 150; Sonnet, *Education des filles*; Rapley, "Women and the Religious Vocation," 623; Marsh's Library (Dublin) MS 30: Diary of Elie Bouhéreau, 1689–1719; "Nouvelles Catholiques de Pons" (*Cahiers*).
39. ADG 1B1048: Arrêt du Parlement de Bordeaux, August 12, 1699.
40. Dubois, "Enlèvements d'enfants protestants," 318. Convents and other closed communities were petrie dishes of fever. Beyond infection, psychological factors have been identified as important contributors to elevated mortality by a statistically precise analysis of the closed convent population at Saint-Cyr. Lougee, "'Its Frequent Visitor.'"
41. ADD E Supplement 5: Baptêmes, mariages et mortuaires de l'église cathédrale Saint-Etienne-Saint-Front de Périgueux, 1684–1792.
42. ADCM 3E26/323: Cession de Berneré, January 12, 1710.
43. E/L15: *Memoire pour messire Jean-Charles de Lavie, Conseiller au Parlement, au nom et comme Curateur de Dame Marie-Suzanne-Françoise de Gua son Epouse . . . contre dame Suzanne de Lestang.*
44. Zacharie de Salbert presumably died sometime shortly after March 1709, when he, as Seigneur de Soulignonne and cavalry lieutenant, agreed, in return for a payment of 2,000 *livres*, to abandon his claims on the estate of his grandmother Léa de Bessay and on the funds his step-grandfather Jean Isle took charge of for his father in 1662. ADCM E270: Famille Isle. Contrat de cession, March 17, 1709. See also Beauchet-Filleau et al., *Dictionnaire*, 5:149.
45. ADCM 3E26/323: Notaire Senné à Saintes. January 23, 1710. "Prise de possession et procès verbal de la terre et seigneurie de Berneré à Saint-Savinien à la demande de

Susanne delestang"; AN 1AP: Chartrier de Thouars 2127 11/6/8bis: Expédition du contrat d'engagement.

46. ADCM B488: Audiences civiles, Présidial de Saintes, 1692–1693; Texier, *Inventaire archéologique,* 11:15; AN 1AP: Chartrier de Thouars 2127 11/6/8ter: Homages rendus; *Mois paroissial de Saint-Savinien,* July 1932; Texier, *Inventaire archéologique,* 10:55.
47. "'Reconnoissances' et abjurations," 91–92; ADCM 3E88/70: Notary Dalidet, August 5, 1701; AN TT265 (iii:50): Estat de ceux de la R.P.R. et nouveaux convertis des Senechaussées de Saintes et Cognac qui ont quitté le Royaume, qui y possedoient des biens fonds, 1687. Two du Gua daughters were interned at the Filles de Notre-Dame de Saintes with Thérèse de Robillard. Louis du Gua was a cousin of Casimir Prévost de Touchimbert and of Marie de La Rochefoucauld de Champagné as well as of his wife Marie Dupuy.
48. See chapter 10.
49. Beauchet-Filleau et al., *Dictionnaire,* 2:769.
50. Chevalier, "Mémoires des noms et qualités," 550–55.
51. E/L15: *Memoire pour messire Jean-Charles de Lavie.* 1732 is the latest date mentioned in the document. The couple had married in July 1727. He was président honoraire de la Première Chambre des Enquêtes in the Parlement of Bordeaux. Minute de Bironneau, August 22, 1756, extracted in "Minutes de notaires," 36:268–69.
52. AN 1AP: Chartrier de Thouars 2127 11/6/8ter: Homages rendus. The Maichin (like the wife's maternal line for four generations) had only daughters; Texier, *Inventaire archéologique,* 10:55–56, 11:16; Colle, *Châteaux, manoirs et forteresses,* 1:89; AMS MS 618: Répertoire des fiefs saintongeais.

Chapter 10

1. Foucault to Seignelay, October 31, 1686, reprinted in Foucault, *Mémoires,* 160.
2. Bibliothèque de Genève. Papiers Court 1: Lettres adressées à Antoine Court: Mr. ministre Viala, November 20, 1740, 13:173–76.
3. AN O[1]38: January 25, 1694; O[1]39: March 7, 1695, April 11, 1695.
4. BNF MS fr. 32107: Preuves de noblesse des pages de la Grande-Ecurie du Roi, 94; Anselme et al., *Histoire généalogique* 9(1):747; Bluche, *Pages de la Grande Ecurie,* 3:n.p; Filleau, *Ancien Poitou,* 2:558; ADV 2E183: Partage des biens de Mrs Prevost, April 26, 1731.
5. ADV C52 (12): Estat des filles nouvelles converties qui peuvent payer pension dans les communautéz des nouvelles catholiques dans la parroisse de st hilaire sur lautise, Fontenay, June 28, 1698; "Maintenues de noblesse," 23:313–14; Lièvre, *Histoire des protestants,* 3:357; http://vaslo.free.fr/Regne/Regne.htm; Bétancourt, *Noms féodaux,* 3:229; ADV 2H5/93: Union chrétienne de Poitiers, 1644–1790: *Registres des professions;* Dez, *Histoire des protestants,* 1:354–55.
6. Will of François Prévost de Touchimbert de Saveilles the younger, February 20, 1711, cited in Chevalier, *Verteuil,* 270; Bégon, "Mémoire," 79; Sepulchre, *Châteaux, villes & villages,* 96, 183; Floris and Talon, eds., *Châteaux, Manoirs et Logis,* 371. The three grooms were the father of the three brothers, brother Charles, and now Isaac son of brother François.
7. In December 1701, the bride was put with her mother, a "very obstinate Huguenot," and two sisters into convents in Bordeaux. Elisabeth made a reliable conversion by the time of her marriage in 1704. AN O[1]45: December 10, 1701; O[1]48: November 12, 1704, July 30, 1704; O[1]46: May 17, 1702, November 1, 1702; Bujeaud, *Chronique protestante,* 297. Isaac fell ill in 1703 and died in 1705. SHD:MR 1E49: Pontchartrain to Bégon, February 14, 1703, March 1, 1703; ADCM B1691: Enquêtes, informations et sentences, 1731.
8. SHD:MR 1E43: Pontchartrain to Bégon, December 29, 1700, December 15, 1700; AN Marine B[2]153: To Bégon, January 12, 1701, January 19, 1701; To François Prévost de Touchimbert, January 19, 1701.
9. Biais, "Notes et documents," 6–7, xxxv–xxxvi.
10. Lettres de chancellerie autorisant Susanne Prévost à accepter sous bénéfice d'inventaire la succession de son père, December 3, 1711, reprinted in Aussy, "Matha," 311; Maintenon to Marie-Susanne Prévost de Sansac, Dame de Saveilles et de Touchimbert, January 31, 1712; Anselme et al., *Histoire généalogique* 9(1):564; *Gazette de France* 93 (November 19,

1773), 424; Aussy, "Matha," 313–14. Maintenon's autograph letter lies loose inside the front cover of ADCM 1J353: *Inventaire des titres du comté de Mastas en Saintonges.* Marie-Susanne is not on Vindry's list of Saint-Cyr pupils, but the letter suggests that she was educated there, and Vindry did sometimes miss girls from families who had sent previous children to the school, for whom only abbreviated paperwork was required.

11. Prévost de Sansac de Traversay, *Actes relevés;* ADCM E121: Liasse Sansac de Traversay.
12. Douen, *Révocation*, 3:116; "Deux prisonniers de la Bastille," 249–52; Waddington, "Ministère sous la croix," 590–95; ADCM C141: *Estat de Ceux qui ont* [sic] *entrés en pocession des biens des fugitifs en consequence de lEdit du Roy du mois de décembre 1689 dans le ressort de la Rochelle pendant l'année 1690*; ADCM B1984: Présidial de Saintes, Juridictions seigneuriales, 1690.
13. Unless indicated otherwise, the following paragraphs are based upon Archives de la Bastille, Carton 10494, fols. 286, 291, 293 and Cartons 5133, 5134; *Archives de la Bastille* (Ravaisson-Mollien, ed.), 9:456–58, 462–63, 471, 475; Funck-Brentano, *Lettres de cachet à Paris*, 107 (item 1476); AN O[1]36: February 24, 1692, March 17, 1692, September 2, 1692; AN O[1]37: January 20, 1693.
14. BMLR MS319: Ernest Jourdan, Mémoires biographiques (de Mazières).
15. According to Jal, *Dictionnaire critique*, 629, the parish register of Saint-Jacques du Haut-Pas (now disappeared) listed the marriage as taking place on February 3, 1693, the groom attended by Jean Gabaret, lieutenant-général des armées navales du Roi, who fifteen months later would stand as godfather for the couple's first-born son.
16. Dangeau, *Journal*, 13 February 1692; Delavaud, "Révocation," 163; Bonnin, *Seigneurs d'Angoulins* (2004) http://angoulinshistoire.blogspot.com/2012/10/les-seigneurs-dangoulins-par-jean.html, 8–9; Jal, *Du Quesne*, 2:529.
17. Chasseboeuf, *Châteaux, manoirs et logis*, 2:465; Floris and Talon, eds., *Châteaux, manoirs et logis*, 375, 447; ADCM B2529: Juridiction de la chatellenie du Passage-Voutron. Registre d'audiences, 1713–1717; AN TT180 (xx:83–85): Le sieur Mazière du Passage Demande permission de vendre, January 1718.
18. ADCM E98: Titres de famille. Nicollas, 1595–1773; 4J662: Acquisition par Marie Chauvet, 1693; Archives du Séminaire de Saint-Sulpice (Paris) S197: Filles de Notre-Dame. Nécrologie: Saintes, February 29, 1736; SHD:MR 1E33: Châteauneuf to Bégon, April 17, 1689; AN TT430 (120): Estat des autres huguenots qu'on a envoyé en hollande par ordre du Roy qui sont partis de bordeaux le 19. du mois de mars dans trois vaisseaux hollandois, 1688.
19. Pierre Vincent Nicolas Voutron signed CP A54: Marriage Contract of Henriette-Sylvie de Robillard de Champagné and Charles Bonnart du Marest d'Antoigny, The Hague, January 5, 1714.
20. ANOM Col. B[21]: Ordre du roi nommant le sieur de La Cave-Voutron enseigne à la Martinique, August 3, 1698, fol. 111; AN Marine C[1]160: Liste générale Alphabétique des Officiers militaires de la Marine, Morts, ou Retirés, 1270–1750, fol. 499.
21. AN Marine B[2]134: Pontchartrain to the bishop of La Rochelle, December 24, 1698; C[1]150: Contrôle général des Officiers de la Marine et des Galères, 1410–1748, fol. 291v; ADCM B1604: Présidial de La Rochelle, Sentences, 1676. A biographical account of Gédéon Nicolas de Voutron and his family appears in the editors' introductory material to Nicolas de Voutron, *Voyages aux Amériques*, 9–56.
22. SHD:MR 1E36: Pontchartrain to Bégon from Versailles, July 7, 1694; 1E40: Pontchartrain to Bégon from Fontainebleau, August 11, 1697; Pontchartrain to Bégon from Versailles, November 6, 1697 and November 13, 1697; "Nouvelles Catholiques de Pons," (*Cahiers*), 797; "Nouvelles Catholiques de Pons," (*Recueil*), 167; "Projet de Mémoire sur les orphelines," 41.
23. AN Marine B[2]126: Pontchartrain to the Bishop of Saintes from Versailles, July 17, 1697; SHD:MR 1E40: Pontchartrain to Bégon from Versailles, July 17, 1697.
24. AN Marine B[2]127: A m. Bégon, October 11, 1697; SHD:MR 1E40: Pontchartrain to Bégon from Fontainebleau, October 11, 1697; Pontchartrain to Bégon from Versailles, November 13, 1697; AN Marine B[2]127: A m. Levesque de xaintes, October 11, 1697.
25. AN Marine B[2]131: A M. l'Evesque de xaintes, March 26, 1698; B[2]134: A Mr Bégon, December 24, 1698.

26. Archives du Séminaire de Saint-Sulpice (Paris). S197: Filles de Notre-Dame. Nécrologie: Saintes, February 29, 1736.
27. Jal, *Du Quesne*, 2:525–26, 559; ADCM 3E379: Quittance, November 20–21, 1688; AN O^{1}32: February 8, 1688; 33: October 23, 1689. On Duquesne-Guiton, see Vergé-Franceschi, *Abraham Duquesne*; Meschinet de Richemond, *Marins rochelais*, 46–50; Venant, "Abraham Marquis Duquesne," 340–56.
28. BNF MS fr. 22802: Bégon to Villermont, March 11, 1692, fol. 17v; Jal, *Du Quesne*, 2:558.
29. AN Marine B^{2}89: A m. du Quesne, March 7, 1693, March 21, 1693.
30. BNF MS fr. 22802: Bégon to Villermont, April 1, 1692, fols. 39r–39v.
31. BNF MS fr. 7045: Bégon, Sur les mariages des nouveaux convertis, Rochefort, May 8, 1695, fols. 42–45. The opposite policy had been enshrined in AN O^{1}24: Edit pour empescher les mariages des Catholiques avec ceux de la R.P.R, November 1680. Three years later, Bégon repeated this call for bishops to relax their marriage rules—"Let the Archbishops be less difficult concerning the marriages of New Converts"—in another memoir addressing the broader question of means for bringing Protestants into the Catholic Church. BNF MS fr. 7045: Mémoire Des differens moyens dont on peut Se Servir pour faire rentrer dans l'Eglise ceux qui sont encore prévenus des Erreurs de Calvin, May 4, 1698, fols. 79–102v.
32. AN Marine B^{2} 92: A m L'Evesque de la Rochelle, October 13, 1693; A m du Quesne, October 13, 1693; AN Marine B^{2}89: A m. l'Esvesque de la Rochelle, March 21, 1693; B^{2}90: A M. L'Eveque de la Rochelle, May 16, 1693; B^{2}91: m. du Quesne, September 29, 1693; A m. l'Evesque de la Rochelle, September 29, 1693.
33. "Projet de Mémoire sur les orphelines," 39; SHD:MR 1E36: Pontchartrain to Bégon, July 14, 1694, July 31, 1694, December 4, 1694; AN Marine B^{2}102: A M. Duquesne, 4 August 1694; B^{2}100: A Monsieur Begon, December 4, 1695; SHD:MR 1E36: Pontchartrain to Bégon, December 4, 1694; AN Marine B^{2}105: Lettre pour faire mettre en liberté la D^{e}. duquesne du couvent de la Providence, January 1, 1695.
34. AN Marine B^{2}131: A M^{r}. du Quesne, March 26, 1698.
35. SHD:MR 1E43: Pontchartrain to Bégon, November 17, 1700, December 1, 1700; AN Marine B^{2}149: A M. Bégon, December 15, 1700; SHD:MR 1E49: Pontchartrain to Bégon, May 30, 1703, June 20, 1703.
36. ANOM Col. B^{36}: A M. de Beauharnois, February 28, 1714, fol. 87v; A M Du Quesne, February 28, 1714, fols. 87–87v; Mémoire pour servir d'instructions à monsieur Duquesne, August 23, 1714, fols. 501v–519v; Lettre du secrétaire d'Etat en complément à ces instructions, August 23, 1714, fols. 519v–524v.
37. ADCM 3E33/13: Procuration, July 21, 1714; Testament, September 17, 1714.
38. ANOM Col. C^{8B} 3 (55):Analyse d'une requête du sieur de Voutron qui demande pour sa soeur, Mme Duquesne, la permission d'aller rejoindre son mari à la Martinique, 1715.
39. ANOM Col. B^{37}: Au sieur de Voutron, July 15, 1715, fols. 129–129v; A M. le Comte de Chamilly, May 25, 1715, fol. 102v; A M le Comte de Chamilly, July 15, 1715, fols. 129v–30.
40. ANOM Col. B^{37}: A M. le Comte de Chamilly, July 15, 1715, fols. 130–31v.
41. ANOM Col. B^{37}: A M. le Comte de Chamilly, August 21, 1715, fols. 152v–153; Au sieur de Voutron, August 21, 1715, fols. 151v–152v; A M. de Beauharnois, August 21, 1715, fols. 153v–154; A monsieur Duquesne au sujet de la venue de sa femme à la Martinique sous certaines conditions, August 21, 1715, fols. 274v–75.
42. Jal, *Du Quesne*, 2:578.
43. *Registre des Vestures*, 10; AN LL1718: *Liste de toutes les Religieuses reçues en ce premier monastere de La visitation ste Marie de Paris depuis son Etablissement*, 19v.
44. Smith, "Mansart Studies," 202–15; Biver and Biver, *Abbayes, monastères, couvents de femmes*, 148–56; Duvignacq-Glessgen, *Ordre de la Visitation*, 237–39, 243. Ironically, the buildings of the convent of the Filles de la Visitation Sainte-Marie have since 1802 housed the Temple Protestant du Marais.
45. Archives des monastères de la Visitation (Paris): Abregé de la vie et des vertus de feue notre très-chere Soeur Françoise-Henriette Isle de Loire, 2:338.
46. "Extrait du contrat de mariage d'Abimélech, marquis de Foucher-Circé," in Menche de Loisne, *Histoire généalogique*, 153, 17; Anselme et al., *Histoire généalogique*, 2:425–28.

47. AN LL1715: Visitation de la rue Saint-Antoine, "Livre de la substance des contrats," fols. 69r, 79v.
48. AN LL1715: "Livre de la substance des contrats," fol. 147rv; AN O[1]35: August 16, 1691; *Registre des vestures*, 10.
49. Archives des monastères de la Visitation (Paris): Abrégé de la vie et des vertus de feue notre très-chere Soeur Françoise-Henriette Isle de Loire, 2:335–42. For a critical look at this type of source, see Rapley, "Women and the Religious Vocation," 616. Rapley concludes that the nuns' death notices circulating among the houses in a religious order "provide a credible body of information." The extent to which "pious fictions" misshape these biographical notices is illuminated by the analysis here of the death notice of Henriette-Lidie Isle de Loire.
50. The narrative suggests a daughter-mother tension and a daughter's longing for absent paternal tenderness that are common in female coming-of-age stories. See the analysis in chapter 12 of the relationship between Susanne de Robillard and her mother Marie de La Rochefoucauld.
51. Drillat, "Visitandines françaises," 190–91; Dompnier, "'Cordiale communication," 277–300.
52. "Abrégé de la vie et des vertus de notre chère soeur Soeur Françoise-Henriette Isle de Loire."
53. Declaration du Roy, du 24 Octobre 1665. Pour obliger les Pères des Enfants de la R.P.R. qui se seront convertis à la Religion Catholique, Apostolique et Romaine, de leur donner pension, reprinted in *Edits, Déclarations et Arrests*, 12–13; Arrêt du Parlement de Paris, June 13, 1663, cited in Labrousse, *Une foi, une loi, un roi?*, 160.
54. Bergin, *Crown, Church, and Episcopate*, 43–44, 144, 247–48, 398; Monahan, *Let God Arise*.
55. Menche de Loisne, *Histoire généalogique*, 67–68; Beauchet-Filleau et al., *Dictionnaire*, 3:518; "Maintenues de noblesse," 342.
56. Audé, "Monsireigne," 293; "Maintenues de noblesse," 214; La Chenaye-Desbois and Badier, *Dictionnaire de la noblesse*, 17:175–80. On Robineau de Chauvinière's escape and capture, nearly contemporaneous with the escape of Marie and her children, see chapter 7.
57. Aillery, *Archives du diocèse de Luçon* reports the marriage (6:395–96). Beauchet-Filleau et al., *Dictionnaire* (5:147) states, on the basis of this report, that she did marry him.
58. A Déclaration du Roy, Concernant la Religion dated May 14, 1724 codified the anti-Protestant legal mandates issued since the Revocation. *Edits, Déclarations et Arrests*, 534–50.
59. AN O[1]37: March 6, 1693, March 3, 1693; O[1]38: March 6, 1694. Pontchartrain notes that he made his request because Maintenon had learned that the daughter was still with the Marquise de Loire.
60. Mesdames de Miossens and de Marsan were both raised in Paris' Marais district in the Hôtel d'Albret, which for Maintenon, according to Saint-Simon, was "the cradle of her fortune" because it was there she met Madame de Montespan, through whom she came to the attention of the king. Saint-Simon, *Mémoires*, 3:221.
61. AN TT236 (i:24): Memoire des Gentilshommes de la generalité de Bordeaux, May 2, 1682; (i:22): Estat des seigneurs de fiefs, September 8, 1685.
62. Quoted in Aumale, *Souvenirs sur madame de Maintenon*, 2:179; Dangeau, *Journal*, 1:288; A. L., "Questions et Réponses," 347. Her husband François Amanieu d'Albret had been killed in a duel in Paris in 1672.
63. AN O[1]38: March 6, 1694, April 5, 1694; O[1]39: August 4, 1695; "Projet de Mémoire sur les orphelines," 37; SHD:MR 1E 36: Pontchartrain to Bégon, July 7, 1694; 1E40: Pontchartrain to Bégon, July 27, 1697; Pontchartrain to Bégon, July 31, 1697; 1E 398: Bégon from La Rochelle, July 20, 1697.
64. Murphy, *Peuple des couvents*, 185; AN O[1]43: October 15, 1699.
65. Rondier, *Historique du monastère de Puyberland*, 28–30, 61–67; Murphy, *Peuple des couvents*, 187–91.
66. ADCM B1622: Présidial de La Rochelle, Sentences, September 3, 1695; Archives d'Etat de Genève. Archives hospitalières. Ka7: Bourse Française. *Délibérations des diacres et livre de memoire, 1692–1699*, fol. 39.

67. CNRS. Base de données du refuge huguenot, http://www.refuge-huguenot.ish-lyon.cnrs.fr: Notice n° 106320, May 26, 1692; Marsh's Library (Dublin) MS 30: Diary of Elie Bouhéreau, 1689–1719: entry April 29/May 9, 1692, entry June 30/July 10, 1692.
68. Centraal Bureau voor Genealogie, Den Haag. Fichier de la Bibliothèque wallonne; ADCM B1622: Présidial de La Rochelle, Sentences, September 3, 1695; SHD:MR 1E50: Pontchartrain to Bégon, December 5, 1703.
69. BNF MS fr. 35706: Cabinet des Titres. Pièces originales 1559, fol. 9: Extrait des Registres des Requestes du Palais du 10 avril 1704. Isaac-Auguste had already received 2,000 *livres* in subsistence allowance, as noted in the award from the Parlement.
70. ADCM B501: Présidial de Saintes, Audiences, November 12, 1708. As late as 1695, she was still identified as Marquise de Loire. ADCM B1392 (22): Présidial ordinaire de La Rochelle, February 8, 1695; ADCM B1622: Présidial de la Rochelle, Sentences, September 3, 1695. See also ADCM B501: Présidial de Saintes, Audiences, November 12, 1708.
71. SHD:TV Fonds du Génie MS 185: Masse, Mémoire géographique, 749. The famous family Le Moyne de Sérigny, which succeeded Isaac-Auguste in possession of Loire, had made its fortune in Canadian commerce and would include a governor of L'Ile Royale as well as the founder of New Orleans. See Library and Archives Canada (Ottawa). Collection de la famille Le Moyne; Rodrigues, *Nobles et bourgeois*, 155; "Le Moyne de Sérigny."

Chapter 11

1. No records survive of the Huguenot congregations in Exeter (one conformist, one nonconformist). Pickard, "Huguenots in Exeter."
2. Bots, "Refuge," 64.
3. HGA MS 241.1: Archief van de Kerkeraad. Livre des Resolutions du Consistoire de l'Eglise francoise de La Haÿe, Commenceant l'an 1618, 259; Bresson, "Eglise wallonne de Rotterdam," 363.
4. Bibliothèque wallonne (Leiden): Fiches op de Waalse Registers, 1500–1828; CP A1: Inventory, October 9, 1690; HGA: Notarielle Protocollen 's-Gravenhage / Periode 1670–1811, 668:343, 739:629–32; NA/AR: Waals Hervormde Kerk te 's-Gravenhage, Kerkelijke Registers: Lidmaten, 1632–1710.
5. Frijhoff, "Uncertain Brotherhood," 128–29; Hans Bots and René Bastiaanse, "Refuge huguenot," in Magdelaine and von Thadden, eds., *Refuge huguenot*, 72–77; Zumthor, *Daily Life*, xix–xx; Van der Linden, *Experiencing Exile*. Frijhoff in his "Uncertain Brotherhood" nicely sketches the ambiguities in Dutch culture that Huguenot refugees stepped into.
6. ULD MS 3613: Récit de la Sortie de France de Madame de Thonnayboutonne en 1687; Cabrol, "Mémoire," 533; [Babault], "Au nom de Dieu!," 11, 14.
7. HGA MS 241.787: Rekeningen van ontvangsten en uitgaven ten behoeve van de refugies, 1689.
8. CP A54: Marriage Contract between Henriette-Sylvie de Robillard de Champagné and Charles Bonnart du Marest d'Antoigny, The Hague, January 5, 1714. Mary Touchimbert was buried on April 8, 1699 at St. Anne Soho in London. Huguenot Library London: Lart Papers T3/12, 83.
9. Mademoiselle des Roches was likely Louis Du Fay's sister Hélène. Marie de La Rochefoucauld in France might well have known *of* these new friends as distant kin of friends and kin of kin. For example, the grandmother of Louis Du Fay was a half-sister of the father of René Culant, Josias' friend and godfather of Josias' baby René-Casimir. They do not, however, appear in Champagné documents from their years in France.
10. Acte d'émancipation . . . de Uranie de La Cropte, fille de François-Paul, chevalier, seigneur de Beauvais, et de feue Charlotte Martel, en présence de Charles de La Mothe Fouqué, chevalier, seigneur de La Grève, son curateur, April 12, 1669, in Aussy, "Inventaire des titres," 199–200.
11. In 1657, Elisabeth (and her as-yet-Protestant daughters) waged a bitter battle over the local church against Françoise de Foix, abbess of the great Abbaye des Dames in Saintes. See ADCM H76: Factum, pour dame Françoise de Foix, abbesse de Saintes, défenderesse contre les demoiselles Martel, demanderesses, 1659–1665.

12. When Anne de Pons married Martel, her half-sister Antoinette de Pons married Henri d'Albret, Comte de Miossens. The D'Albret and Martel families shared the title of Comte de Marennes until the last of the d'Albret-Marennes branch, husband of the future Madame de Marsan, died in a duel in 1678.
13. Caylus, *Souvenirs*, 29; Maintenon to M. le maréchal d'Albret, September 10, 1671, reprinted in Maintenon, *Lettres*, 1:119–21; Maintenon to M. d'Aubigné, April 16, 1677 and May 8, 1677, reprinted in Maintenon, *Lettres*, 1:229–30.
14. Hellot, *Essai historique*; BNF Cabinet des Titres 11546: Martel. The 1726 will of Angélique-Perside Martel is at NA/PRO PROB11/612. It specified legacies of 20 pounds sterling to her godson "Charles Henry Fouquet de Toneboutone" (son of Susanne de Robillard and Saint-Surin), eight pounds sterling to "Mrs des Bonnaird" in The Hague (Henriette-Silvie, daughter of Marie de La Rochefoucauld) and eight pounds sterling to "Mrs de Champagnay" (presumably Marie de La Rochefoucauld).
15. Dumont de Bostaquet, *Mémoires*, 87.
16. Their paternal grandmother Elisabeth Poussard de Vandré was the sister of Eléonore's mother. Louis du Fay became administrator of the Olbreuse estate after the death of the duchess' brother Alexandre.
17. AN TT187A (ii:4–13): Placets, requêtes, mémoires concernant affaires de Religionnaires, XVIIe Siècle; ADCM B755: Présidial de Saintes, Sentences, 1697; B564: Présidial de Saintes, Baux judiciaires, 1686–1688; AN TT265 (iii:50): Estat de ceux de la R.P.R. et nouveaux convertis des Senechaussées de Saintes et Cognac qui ont quitté le Royaume, qui y possedoient des biens fonds, 1687; ADCM B566: Présidial de Saintes. Baux judiciaires, 1689; ADCM 3J48: Etat des protestants et nouveaux convertis de la sénéchaussée de Saintes et Cognac.
18. "De Paris, 4 novembre 1685. Rose dEscars à son cousin le Marquis de Boisse," reprinted in Alis and Bouillet, *Notice*, 270–72.
19. Rome, *Bourgeois protestants*, 395.
20. See Lougee Chappell, "Paper Memories and Identity Papers."
21. AMAE Cp.H 145: D'Avaux, January 3, 1686; Jurieu, *Lettres pastorales*, June 15, 1688.
22. AMAE Cp.H 153: Tillieres, September 9, 1687, December 16, 1687.
23. AMAE Cp.H 157: Tillieres, June 28, 1688, July 2, 1688.
24. AMAE Cp.H 157: Tillieres, June 28, 1688; 153: Tillieres, June 16, 1687; 147: D'Avaux, July 10, 1686; Tillieres, July 12, 1686; 149: Tillieres, May 28, 1686.
25. Frederiks, "Communauté wallonne de Voorburg"; *Livre des Actes des Eglises Wallonnes*, 933; Gagnebin, "Liste des églises wallonnes," 118.
26. AMAE Cp.H 155: D'Avaux, August 20, 1688.
27. AMAE Cp.H 155: D'Avaux, August 26, 1688, August 20, 1688.
28. Bibliothèque de Genève. MS Court 50: Mélanges et Extraits. [Elie Benoist], "Suite De l'Histoire de l'Edit de Nantes," 33–34.
29. [Benoist], "Suite De l'Histoire de l'Edit de Nantes," 34. On Tillieres, see Lougee Chappell, "Through the Eyes of a Spy."
30. CP A59: Marie de La Rochefoucauld, Ce 10 Ienvier, 1690.
31. AMAE Cp.H 156: D'Avaux, October 19 and 28, 1688.
32. [Baux], "Monsieur et très honoré frère," 191–92. The editors attributed this undated letter to 1687, but internal evidence suggests it was written a year later.
33. Dumont de Bostaquet, *Mémoires*, 174, 216, 199; David Onnekink, "'Janisaries, and Spahees and Pretorian Band': Perceptions of Huguenot Soldiers in Williamite England," in Glozier and Onnekink, eds., *War, Religion and Service*, 83. Bostaquet never mentions Josias de Robillard, but his memoir can indirectly illuminate Josias' experience, because even if their paths in the campaigns did not intertwine, they were parallel. He and the Champagné moved in the same circles in Holland; Bostaquet's memoir names the Martel and mentions that when he returned to England with his wife in March 1689, he bid farewell to Madame de Pardaillan, who was Marie de La Rochefoucauld's close friend as well as a cousin of Saint-Surin, and to Madame de Tors, who was Marie's cousin Judic de La Rochefoucauld, Dame du Douhet (209).
34. Dumont de Bostaquet, *Mémoires*, 174; Fontaine, *Mémoires*, 55.

35. Dumont de Bostaquet, *Mémoires*, 191.
36. *True and Exact Relation.*
37. Dumont de Bostaquet, *Mémoires*, 198; Fontaine, *Mémoires*, 156.
38. *True Account Of his Highness.*
39. Dumont de Bostaquet, *Mémoires*, 204. For discussion of Bostaquet's transfer of loyalty to William of Orange through the writing of the early sections of his memoir, see Lougee Chappell, "Paper Memories and Identity Papers."
40. John Childs, "Huguenots and Huguenot Regiments in the British Army, 1660–1702: 'Cometh the moment, cometh the men,'" in Glozier and Onnekink, eds., *War, Religion and Service*, 37, 34. The personnel and history of these French regiments are described at length in Lart, "Huguenot Regiments," 480–99.
41. The four French regiments had a total of 166 regular officers, according to Childs, "Huguenots and Huguenot Regiments," 38. The most comprehensive biographical source for these officers is George Hilton Jones's card index collection of 1,400 French officers in English military service, 1688–1740, which is archived at the Huguenot Library in London. Annotated "Huguenot Regimental Officer Lists" can be found in Glozier, *Huguenot Soldiers of William of Orange*, 149–59.
42. Bodleian Library (Oxford) MS Rawlinson D452: [Pierre Lacoste], Detail de mes etudes, voiages, campagnes et avanteures qui me sont arrivées pendant le cours de 52 annees [1730], 13.
43. *Letter from Chester Of the Twenty Second Instant*; Newsletter dated July 16, 1689, Inventory no. 3570 in *Manuscripts of S.H. Le Fleming*. Dates given here refer to the Julian calendar then in use in England and Ireland.
44. J. F., *Further Account; Letter from Chester Of the 29th of July*; J. F., *Great News.*
45. *Letter from Chester Of the 24th of August; Full and Exact Relation; Exact Account; More Good News; Journal Of what has past in the North of Ireland.*
46. AMAE Cp.H 158: Nouvelles de Rotterdam en Hollande du 19 septembre 1689.
47. Newsletter dated September 15, 1689, Inventory no. 3656 in *Manuscripts of S. H. Le Fleming*; Creighton, *History of Epidemics*, 228, 230.
48. [Story], *True and Impartial History*, 42–43; Walton, *History of the British Standing Army*, 70.
49. Nihell, *Journal Of The Most Remarkable Occurrences*, 4, 7; [Story], *True and Impartial History*, 24; Childs, *Williamite Wars*, 172.
50. Bellingham, *Diary*, 95; Stevens, *Journal*, 96.
51. Dumont de Bostaquet, *Mémoires*, 227–28; Morsier, "Journal" (*Tagebuch*), 2:314–15.
52. Papers of John Cary, quoted in Simms, *War and Politics in Ireland*, 94; Morsier, *Journal* ("Swiss Soldier"), 484.
53. [Story], *True and Impartial History*, 27, 39; [Johnston], "Dear Bargain," 10:362–63.
54. [Story], *True and Impartial History*, 39–41; Dumont de Bostaquet, *Mémoires*, 228. On the Sainte-Hermine, see chapters 8 and 13.
55. "List of the Infantry," 3:119–20.
56. [Johnston], "Dear Bargain," 10:364; Dumont de Bostaquet, *Mémoires*, 228; W[illiam] H[arboard], Letter to the King, 293–94.
57. "List of the Infantry," 3:118.
58. Creighton, *History of Epidemics*, 226. Jacques Dupâquier estimated that 20–25 percent of soldiers died each year on active service (all causes combined); of lives lost in war, 10 percent were killed in action, 30 percent died from wounds or accident, 60 percent from disease. Cited in Corvisier, *France de Louis XIV*, 124.
59. [Story], *True and Impartial History*, 26, 39; Kane, *Campaigns*, 2.

Chapter 12

1. CP A59: Marie de La Rochefoucauld, Ce 10 Ienvier 1690; ULD MS 3613: Récit de La Sortie de France de Madame de Thonnay-boutonne en 1687.
2. The two texts have been published separately: Marie's just twice, Susanne's five times. Corrected versions of both memoirs, translations into English, and discussion of their

publishing history and the extant manuscripts, as well as elaboration on the approach to memoir/autobiography used in this chapter, can be found in Lougee Chappell, "'Pains I Took." After publication of that article, the author located two additional versions of Susanne's account, one in French and one in German, in the La Motte Fouqué family's papers at the Deutsches Literaturarchiv (Marbach), MSS 55.682, 55.683. A version of this chapter previously appeared in *FHS* and is republished here by permission of Duke University Press.

3. Drawing out meanings left latent within texts, to complement their explicit contents, responds to Myriam Yardeni's exhortation that in order to reap full advantage from the the records Huguenots left behind "it is necessary to invent an original method for interrogating each type of document." Yardeni, "Problèmes de fidélité," 258.
4. Domna C. Stanton coins this phrase as a reminder that any autobiography is composed in the midst of life and hence is an artifact of the particular moment at which it is written. "Autogynography."
5. Ariès, "Pourquoi écrit-on des Mémoires," 20; Portelli, "'Time of My Life'," 162.
6. Migault, *Journal*, 111; Fontaine, *Mémoires*, 13, 57, 127, 137.
7. Lejeune, *Pacte autobiographique*; Heilbrun, *Writing a Woman's Life*, 30.
8. Gout, *Pages féminines*, 35–37.
9. Quotations here are from the Rotterdam French Church's register of *reconnaissances*, 1686–1762. Stadsarchief Rotterdam: Waals Hervormde Kerk te Rotterdam, Kerkelijke Registers: Lidmaten. On Dartmouth, see Grant and Gwynn, "Huguenots of Devon." Susanne made her *reconnaissance*, so her memoir states, at Exeter, for which, as for Dartmouth, no parish records survive.
10. NA/AR: Waals Hervormde Kerk te 's-Gravenhage, Kerkelijke Registers: Lidmaten.
11. Further contexts for oral storytelling in the Refuge are discussed in Lougee Chappell, "Writing the Diaspora."
12. The silences in texts signal how the author expects the reader to relate to the text—for example, as an insider or confidant who needs orienting on parts of the story but not on others. On the roles imposed on readers by the rhetoric of texts, see Darnton, "First Steps Toward a History of Reading."
13. The pastor Jean Tirel, for example, denounced the leaving of children behind as a great sin that called for public penitence. BL Harley MS 7024: [Jean Tirel], *Lettres fraternelles d'un prisonnier à ses frères fugitifs et dispersez dans les divers pays* [1686], item 10, fols. 167–217.
14. Adams, *Telling Lies*, ix; Smith, *Poetics of Women's Autobiography*, 18.
15. Marie's narrative is an exception to Natalie Zemon Davis' generalization that memoirs by early modern French women are less self-centered and more relational than men's: "the ones by husbands tell more about themselves than about wives; the ones by wives usually tell at least as much about husbands and children as about themselves." "Ghosts, Kin, and Progeny," 97.
16. Lejeune, *Pacte autobiographique*, 14.
17. For a contrasting case, see Mary Rowlandson's autobiographical narrative of her captivity among Indians in Massachusetts. Rowlandson, a Puritan, not only cited scriptural passages copiously but also structured her narrative as a pilgrim's progress through the wilderness. *Soveraignty and Goodness of God.*
18. Marie's plain language, like Susanne's, could not be farther from the allegorizing biblical prose that Bernard Cottret generalizes as typical of Huguenot refugees' autobiographical writings in "Du Dieu de l'exil." The language of both women is the spare language of the Protestant will and of dialogic Huguenot prayers. See Garrisson, *Homme protestant*, ch. 4 and Stéphan, "Y a-t-il un style protestant?"
19. The argument in Part One multiplies the types of motivations for emigration to include economic and material considerations *alongside* religious commitment, and denies that the former weaken or supersede the latter.
20. Her identity as author is merely tacit, deducible by the reader from the naming in the narrative not of herself but of "M. de Thonnaiboutonne, mon mari."
21. Monod, "Page de la révocation," 486–87; Babucke, "Eigenhändige Aufzeichnungen," 14.

22. Both date in September 1688 the departure that actually occurred around November 1. BL MS 38495: Townshend Papers. Letter-books of Antony Moreau, Polish envoy at The Hague, 1686–1689, fols. 28v–32v is a long letter dated October 12, 1688, that describes preparations for William's upcoming expedition. Furthermore, Josias was still in Voorburg in mid-October, since he wrote a codicil to his will in his own handwriting dated at Voorburg October 13, 1688 (HGA: Notarielle Protocollen 's-Gravenhage, Periode 1670–1811, 676:135–36). According to CP B10: Josias de Robillard to François-Auguste de Robillard, The Hague, January 28, 1722, this was a few days before he left for England.
23. On December 9, 1695, Josias was commissioned a captain in John Tidcomb's Foot. Le Fanu and Manchee, *Dublin and Portarlington Veterans,* 27. This source also indicates that he had been named an ensign in La Melonière's on June 15, 1691, as does NA/PRO 1d.15.3: List of Reformed Officers Serving in Ireland in the Year 1691.
24. The two manuscripts in French, at Darmstadt and Marbach, were executed in a hand that was not Susanne's, which can be seen in the letters she wrote to her brother Josias (CP C). The Deutsches Literaturarchiv Marbach dates its French manuscript (MS 55.682) around 1730. The cover sheet to the handwritten German version in Marbach (MS 55.683) indicates that the translation was done at the behest of Eléonore d'Olbreuse, Duchess of Zell: that is, for the court in Celle while Susanne resided there.
25. Huguenot Library (London): Le Fanu Papers T1/5/2.
26. NA/PRO E190/1051/8,10,15 and E190/965/1,10.
27. Steedman, *Landscape,* 55; [Aulnoy], *Memoirs of the Countess of Dunois,* 3.
28. Psalm 27 is, for example, the first biblical passage Mary Rowlandson cites in her *Soveraignty and Goodness of God.*
29. CP III:B:5 holds the psalter, which has lost its title page; CP A1: Inventory, October 9, 1690; *Sainte Bible.*
30. Perrault, *Histoires.* Susanne's telling did not depend on any of the elements Perrault added, such as the glass slipper.
31. Carolyn Heilbrun, an astute interpreter of women's writings, holds that only in the past few decades have women come to speak frankly of their pain. Perhaps it is true that recent autobiographies by women speak more openly of disappointments and injustices and sorrows than do earlier memoirs. However, a historically informed look at the gendered and genred texts of the past reveals that women have, more often than Heilbrun suggests, found a way to tell their pain and anger without showing them on the surface, where they might be censored by gendered norms of decorum. *Writing A Woman's Life,* 12–13, 60–75.
32. On fairy tales empowering women to speak, see Rowe, "To Spin a Yarn": "To tell a tale for women may be a way of breaking enforced silences" (53).
33. Cohen, "Fond Fathers," 363.
34. For details of the disposition of the family fortune, see chapter 13.
35. AN TT249 (x:38): Estat des biens et Revenus des pretendus reformez et nouveaux convertis fugitifs, Election et ressort de S[t] jean Dangely, 1686–1687; AN TT208 (v:6): Saint Contest, February 12, 1689. Charles fled France in 1685 as Seigneur de La Grève but became heir to the barony of Tonnay-Boutonne on May 27, 1692, when his elder brother Hector died unmarried and childless. ADCM E237: Partage du marais de tonnaiboutonne, September 16, 1657, establishes that Charles (Saint-Surin) was the younger brother of Hector-Louis, baron de Tonnay-Boutonne.
36. Deutsches Literaturarchiv (Marbach) MS 55.678/5: Letter from Tonnay-Boutonne to Charles de La Motte Fouqué; MS 55.678/2: Jernaud in Tonnay-Boutonne to Madame de Tonnay-Boutonne (Susanne de Robillard). Both letters are undated but datable from internal evidence to the mid-1690s.
37. NA/AR, Liasse Requesten, inv. nr. 7583. November 29, 1697; Inv. nr. 7598. December 19, 1700.
38. HGA: Begraven, October 4, 1701. Charles' burial tax was three guilders, a minimal sum but not the least, since the very poorest estates would pay nothing.
39. NA/AR, Liasse Requesten, inv. nr. 7602. October 7, 1701.

40. CP B14 and HGA: Notarielle Protocollen 's-Gravenhage, Periode 1670–1811, 739:629–32: Marriage Contract between Susanne de Robillard and Charles de la Motte Fouqué, The Hague, December 12, 1692.
41. CP A53 and HGA: Notarielle Protocollen 's-Gravenhage, Periode 1670–1811, 749:452–55: Will of Marie de La Rochefoucauld, The Hague, November 22, 1701.
42. Service in a great household was traditionally a means of support for, among others, widows without means. It must have seemed to Susanne a mixed blessing, for "while nobles regarded serving someone higher in rank as honorable, subservience was the everyday reality of such service." Kettering, "Household Service." On Madame von Bülow, see chapter 13. Susanne's sister Marianne served, at least briefly, as companion to Aldenburg's only grandchild Charlotte Sophie, who would marry William, first Count Bentinck. See CP C: Marianne's letters to her brother Josias from Varel dated April 10, 1731, and from Brinkum dated August 1, 1731; Aldenburg, *Autobiography*; Le Blond, *Charlotte Sophie; Une Femme des lumières*.
43. Steedman, *Landscape*, 47.
44. Huguenot Library (London) MS T1/5/2; Tollin, *Magdeburg*, 3:1,B,50.
45. Galland, *Essai*, 229.
46. This analysis is based on the life course approach developed by Tamara K. Hareven in *Transitions* and in *Family Time*.
47. This is Hareven's term for the "goals and aspirations around which an individual or family organizes its life." *Family Time*, 359.
48. Dewald, *Aristocratic Experience*, 73. Though the evidence in *Aristocratic Experience* is often taken from both genders, the chapter on "Family, Education and Selfhood" offers examples exclusively of men's familial conflicts, with the single exception of the sometime employer of Susanne's sister, Charlotte Amélie de La Trémoïlle. Whether responses to familial pressures and conflicts were gendered and whether women's responses might often have paralleled Susanne's rather than those of their brothers would be interesting to discover.
49. The Darmstadt manuscript was inscribed to the princess by the poet Friedrich Heinrich Karl de La Motte Fouqué.
50. Rölleke, "'Utterly Hessian' Fairy Tales," 287–300.
51. La Motte Fouqué, *Lebensbeschreibung*; La Motte Fouqué, *Mémoires*.
52. La Motte Fouqué, *Lebensbeschreibung*, 15, 12, 102.

Chapter 13

1. Alice Clare Carter estimated Huguenot contributions of private capital to the funds underwriting English government debt at 10 percent of the total and the overall contribution of Huguenot financial know-how to the emergence of modern public finance as "incalculable." Carter, *Getting, Spending and Investing*, 91, 77.
2. Lüthy, *Banque protestante*, 1:122.
3. Carter, *Getting, Spending and Investing*, 121.
4. Van Biema, *Huguetan*, 37–38; Carter, *Getting, Spending and Investing*, 89, 80–82.
5. Her annual pension payment of £40 sterling was renewed as late as 1715. "Treasury Warrants, May 1716, 11–20," 236.
6. Majou and Desmé, *Testament*, 6, 8–9.
7. AN TT17 (i:1): Comptes de la Régie: Recepte des biens des fugitifs et Relaps de ladite generallité de la rochelle (1699–1700). This granting of formally forbidden revenues to the Champagné occurred during the "new period of severity" in which the crown attempted to codify procedures for transferring refugees' lands to relatives and strengthen prohibitions on relatives sending revenues to the former owners. Jahan, *Confiscation des biens*, 16–26.
8. Jahan, *Confiscation des biens*, 15; Glozier, *Marshal Schomberg*, 108–09; Ruvigny, "Some Letters," 245.
9. CP A54: Marriage contract of Charles Bonnart, chevalier Seigneur du Marets d'Antogny and Henriette Silvie Robillard de Champagné at The Hague, January 5, 1714. Individuals

from the intermarried clan of Le Coq, Beringhen, Muysson, and Rambouillet signed the marriage contract.

10. To La Reynie, October 28, 1689, and Ordre de faire saisir les biens que M. Lecoq . . . possède en Poitou, October 31, 1689, both quoted in Bujeaud, *Chronique protestante,* 285; "Extraits de la correspondance des ambassadeurs des Provinces-Unies," 384–87.
11. Documentary sources used to track her investments while she lived in Holland, in addition to her own account book and her son Josias' two account books, include multiple notarial documents in HGA as well as BL MS Add. 15,945: Powers of Attorney and Other Documents for the Sale, Transfer, or Receipt of South Sea Stock, 23 (January 5, 1723), 32 (May 23, 1724).
12. Carter, *Getting, Spending and Investing,* 122.
13. Pels himself evidently believed in such annuities, for his family, as well as his bank, invested broadly and deeply in them. BL MS 8223.e.7 (11): *A List of the Several Reversionary Annuities, to which the Million Bank Are Intituled.*
14. Rogers, *First Nine Years,* 165–68; Israel, "England, the Dutch," 84.
15. The connection may also have run through Puychenin, whose wife Marie-Henriette de Chateigner was instrumental in the Champagné escape and who appointed Des Clouseaux executor of his will in 1699. NA/PRO PROB11/451: Will of Samuel Piniott, April 11, 1699.
16. Dickson, *Financial Revolution;* Carter, *Getting, Spending and Investing,* 76–90; Wilson, ed., *Anglo-Dutch Contribution,* 11–32; Gwynn, "Huguenots in Britain," 417; Crouzet, *Britain, France,* 221–66.
17. Carter, *Getting, Spending and Investing,* 92.
18. Carter, *English Public Debt,* 8; Dickson, *Financial Revolution,* 357, 74, 54; Murphy, "Lotteries." Women were disproportionately represented among owners of lottery tickets (around one-third of purchasers).
19. Dickson, *Financial Revolution,* 41–42; Clark, *Betting on Lives.* The English tontine of 1693 was the first long-term loan the English floated, a pioneer, then, in the financial revolution.
20. "Blanks" were lottery tickets that paid only the basic interest, without a chance at prizes.
21. Hunt, *Middling Sort,* 15. According to Gregory King, in England in 1688 the average annual income was £32. The annual income of 12,000 gentry families averaged £280 sterling, that of 8,000 domestic merchants and traders £200, and that of 2,000 maritime merchants and traders £400. King, *Natural and Political Observations,* 31.
22. CP C22: Major Champagné's Small Account Book, 48 r,v.
23. Carter, *Getting, Spending and Investing,* 98.
24. La Primaudaye was a noble family from Anjou and Touraine whose refugees resettled in Celle and Prussia concurrently with Susanne. Lart, "Family of La Primaudaye."
25. CP A59: Marie de La Rochefoucauld, Ce 10 Ienvier 1690.
26. Vickery, *Behind Closed Doors,* 4; Luciani, "Ordering Words."
27. Josias had also specified in the joint will that Marie did not owe the children any accounting of how she used their property during her lifetime. He prescribed division equally to all their children ("as nature has rendered them equally close to us") after "the rights of age and primogeniture previously levied in favor of my eldest son . . . following the usage and *coutumes* of the places where my properties are situated," but gave Marie the power to revise that division "to the prejudice of any of our said children who would act dishonestly or contrary to the respect they owe to my said wife." CP A40: Joint Will of Josias de Robillard and Marie de La Rochefoucauld, April 26, 1683.
28. Connor, *Women, Accounting, and Narrative,* 15, 34.
29. François-Auguste may never have seen his family again. In BL MS 15,945: Power of attorney from François-Auguste, 1723–1724, he was identified as "chevalier de l'ordre de la genérosité, major des gardes du corps, et lieutenant colonel de cavallerie au service de sa majesté le Roy de Pologne, et Electeur de Saxe."
30. According to his will, probated in 1724, Gédéon was a lieutenant in the regiment of Colonel Mainegualt garrisoned in Sluis at the time of his marriage in 1717. NA/PRO PROB11/598: Marriage Contract-Will of Gedion De Champagne or Robillard De Champagne, Lieutenant in the Regiment of the Colonel Mainegualt, written at Sluis August 13, 1717,

read at The Hague June 20, 1724, proved at London July 17, 1724. Josias mentions in his letter to François-Auguste that Gédéon would receive subventions from his mother's assets "until such time as he has a Company or other Employment or source of income that gives him resources for supporting his family a bit better than he can presently." CP B10: Josias de Robillard to François-Auguste de Robillard, The Hague, January 28, 1722.

31. Susanne's memoir added a sort of postscript to Marie's sentence about young Josias' career, explaining another patronage route by which (as she claimed) he got his own regiment in Ireland: "God by his grace took care of us all; my oldest brother also entered English service; some time later he obtained a company there that the Comte de Soissons [marginal note: This count had married a niece of M. de Thonnay-Boutonne, in France] got for him, upon the request M. de Thonnay-Boutonne, my husband, made of him to render service to M. de Champagné, his brother-in-law, which he did graciously, as we know." Soissons had left France in 1694 in semi-disgrace and passed through Holland en route to London, where he would seek new employment. It is therefore plausible that this husband of Saint-Surin's heir and former ward did help forward young Josias's military career.
32. Allégret, "Société des dames françaises."
33. Marianne died at age seventy-five on March 17, 1755. Französisch-reformierte Kirchengemeinde Celle.
34. Of the seven children who left France with their parents, five married and between them bore six children (Susanne four, Josias and Gédéon one each, Henriette-Silvie and François-Auguste none). The firstborns of Susanne and Gédéon died as infants, and two of her three surviving sons died childless. Only General La Motte Fouqué in Prussia and Dean Champagné in Ireland, among Marie's grandchildren, continued the family line, the general with three children, the dean with ten.
35. Flick, "Huguenot Settlements," 82. Flick with this phrase describes the Migault family, whose patriarch Jean lived out his days in Emden while his children settled in England, Holland, Celle, and South Africa.
36. Pollnitz, *Memoirs,* 2:407.
37. On the function of refugee memoirs as plottings of the patronage networks in which the authors and their families "belonged," see Lougee Chappell, "Paper Memories and Identity Papers" and Lougee, "Writing the Diaspora."
38. *Mercure françois* 18 (1632), 418: "On the 18 [of July] the sieur de Sainct-Surin was wounded by a carbine shot in the leg from which he died shortly afterward, much regretted"; *Nouvelles ordinaires de divers endroits,* September 10, 1632.
39. He became a page "at the age of eight" according to several sources, including Tollin, *Magdeburg,* 3:1,B,51. That would be 1706. This information may be no more than approximate, since Tollin says the position had been uncle François-Auguste's at age ten and a half in 1688, whereas François-Auguste took the post in 1688 at age thirteen.
40. Aldenburg, *Autobiography,* 51. This memoir is an important source for the cosmopolitan networks of the great La Trémoïlle family. A generally accurate, if flowery, biography of the La Trémoïlle is Stephens, *La Trémoille Family.*
41. She was Amélie, Princesse de Hesse-Cassel. Her sister Charlotte of Hesse-Cassel was the first wife of the Palatine Elector and the mother of Madame.
42. Aldenburg, *Autobiography,* 50; Beaucaire, *Mésalliance*; Benoist, "Famille d'Olbreuse."
43. It is said that the young J. S. Bach, when a student at Lüneburg's Michaels-Gymnasium in 1700–1702, first heard the music of Lully and Couperin played by this orchestra. "Obituary of The World-Famous Organist, Mr. Johann Sebastian Bach," 217.
44. Duchess of Zell from Lüneburg to M. de La Taillée in Poitou, March 28, 1716, reprinted in Beaucaire, *Mésalliance,* 266.
45. Madeleine-Sylvie was widowed in 1689 and married Oberhauptmann Thomas Christian von Bülow, Grand Bailli of Zell, in 1696. She was *première dame d'atour* of the Duchess of Zell. Her paternal aunt Elisabeth de Sainte-Hermine was Josias de Robillard's maternal aunt, wife of Daniel de Mazières.
46. See chapter 8.
47. Maintenon to M. d'Aubigné, February 5, 1681, reprinted in Maintenon, *Lettres,* 1:358; Duchess of Zell to Alexandre Desmier d'Olbreuse, March 16, 1685, reprinted in Desmier

d'Olbreuse, "Lettres de la duchesse de Zell," 19; Migault, *Journal*, chs. 4–6; Chauffepié, "Journal," 6: 58–59. Migault's extended narrative about the protection his family received in Poitou is in part his tribute to the Duchess of Zell, who was the patron of Migault's son Gabriel in Celle at the time of the writing.

48. AN O[1]30: April 20, 1686, May 2, 1686, July 21, 1686; O[1]32: February 27, 1688; BNF MS fr. 7052: Lettres a Mon dit Sieur De La Reynie par le Commissaire De La Marre, "Aux nouvelles catholiques," October 17, 1686, fol. 25; *Archives de la Bastille* (Ravaisson-Mollien, ed.), 8:381, 399, 400, 405, 407, 453; Archives de la Bastille MSS 10440, 12534; Dumont de Bostaquet, *Mémoires*, 228. A long biographical piece on Philippe de Sainte-Hermine appears in Douen, *Révocation*, 2:409–13. Correspondence concerning his imprisonment, including his request for permission to emigrate, is excerpted in Delavaud, "Marins protestants," 184–85 as well as in Gélin, "Madame de Maintenon convertisseuse," 242–43.
49. Französisch-reformierte Kirchengemeinde Celle (Eglise française de Celle).
50. Groehler and Erfurth, *Alte Dessauer*.
51. The term "cosmopolitan" here refers to ways of thinking and cultural practices among early modern elites who could operate across borders—in sociability, marriage, and military service—because they perceived greater affinity within status across geographical borders than across statuses within a geographical border. The shift to a modern cosmopolitanism based upon universalistic ideologies and cross-border commerce of ideas and goods is insightfully traced in Jacob, *Strangers Nowhere in the World*.
52. On the network of trade and finance that blossomed after the Revocation from preexisting overseas networks of financial relations and commercial activities, see Lüthy, *Banque protestante*; Bosher, "Huguenot Merchants"; Cullen, "Brandy Trade."
53. Robin Gwynn has shown how Huguenot churches in the later seventeenth century served not merely as houses of worship but as social meeting places, marriage markets for lay persons brought into the congregation by family links ("threads of family relationship"), and sites for exchange of information on business and commercial matters. Gwynn, "Huguenots in Britain."
54. Goldgar, *Impolite Learning*; Laursen, ed., *New Essays*.
55. On military recruitment by "ties of affinity and hierarchy" extending across borders and "the long tradition of [Huguenot] service in Dutch pay, with three and four generations sometimes fighting for the United Provinces," see Glozier and Onnekink, eds., *War, Religion and Service*, 9–30, 31–46. Nobles like the Champagné were more numerous among refugees than has sometimes been recognized. Twenty-five percent of Dublin Huguenots (though only 2 percent of the French population) were nobles. Hylton, "Dublin's Huguenot Communities," 229.
56. Brewer, *Sinews of Power*, 45–46; Dangeau, *Journal*, 2:190; Watts, "Notion de patrie." My sense is that the existence of this traditional cosmopolitan network eased the movement of noble Huguenots into exile, serving as a vehicle they could continue to use, but not for long.
57. Hylton, "Dublin's Huguenot Communities."
58. Hanlon, *Confession and Community*, 2. For the British context that shaped such characterizations of Huguenot refugees, see Shaw, *Britannia's Embrace*.
59. A positivist collection of patronage instances on a cosmopolitan scale such as Sharon Kettering assembled to good effect for seventeenth-century French politics could be invaluable. See Kettering, *Patronage*; Kettering, *Patrons, Brokers, and Clients*; Kettering, "Patronage in Early Modern France"; Kettering, "Patronage and Kinship." This might be very like what John Bosher advocated for the financial International in his "Huguenot Merchants": "The serious use of genealogy . . . is a tool that may prove to be as useful in its way for discovering the social movements of early modern times as statistical analysis has already been." (100). An instructive example of a more highly conceptualized mapping of social networks with social science tools is Meadows, "Engineering Exile."
60. HGA Notarielle Protocollen/Periode 1670–1811, 749:452/5 and CP A53: Will of Marie de La Rochefoucauld, The Hague, November 22, 1701.
61. The provision for *préciput* in the *coutumes* applied only to noble possessions in France. So Marie broadens out their meaning here. Of course Josias could not have as part

of his *préciput* the usual "noble residence and principal manor of his predecessors, with their adjoining domains" along with his "fifth of the noble properties" (Béchet, *Usance*, 106).

62. The firstborn son, named Charles Arnaud and baptized on October 29, 1693, died young. The next three sons, all of whom survived to adulthood, were baptized on June 16, 1695 (Henri Charles), February 13, 1698 (Henri Auguste), and June 26, 1701 (Henri Charles Frederic). NA/AR: Waals Hervormde Kerk. 's-Gravenhage. *Livre ou Role des enfans qui ont été batiséz, en L'Eglise Françoise De la Haye.*
63. CP C22: Major Champagné's Small Account Book, 48 r,v; CP B10: Josias de Robillard to François-Auguste de Robillard, The Hague, January 28, 1722.
64. These principles applied in all the *coutumes* of the region: Béchet, *Usance*; Béchet, *Conférence*; Dusault, *Commentaire*; Valin, *Nouveau commentaire*.
65. Diefendorf, "Women and Property," 182.
66. CP B10: Josias de Robillard to François-Auguste de Robillard, The Hague, January 28, 1722.
67. CP B7: Joint agreement on division of Marie de La Rochefoucauld's assets, The Hague, April 24, 1722; CP B10: Josias de Robillard to François-Auguste de Robillard, The Hague, January 28, 1722.
68. Julie died unmarried in the Société de Harlem on October 20, 1719. Leiden Collection. François-Auguste married Sophie de Polentz in 1735, when he was a colonel in the Polish army and commandant of the fortress at Senftenberg, which defended Saxony's northern border. She was the sister of Saxon General Polentz at Warsaw. They had no children. Henriette-Silvie had no children by Du Marest-d'Antoigny and died in 1759. NA/PRO PROB11/678: Will of Sir Charles Bonnard Lord Dumarest of Saint Ann Westminster, Middlesex, written at London February 19, 1731, proved at London August 3, 1736. Gédéon married Adriana Barberina Van Bergen in 1717 and baptised a son, Maximilian Kornelis, at Hulst on June 2, 1723 (Zeeland Rijksarchief, Middelburg. Nederlands Hervormde Kerk, Hulst: Doop Inventaris-Boek) but seems to have had no children at his death in 1724. NA/PRO PROB11/598: Marriage Contract-Will of Gedion De Champagne or Robillard De Champagne.
69. CP C: Dean Champagné to Baron de Saint-Surin, October 12, 1776.
70. She married Henry Bayly (Paget) on July 10, 1767 at St. Anne's Dublin. Huguenot Library (London): Le Fanu Papers T1/5/2.
71. On Anglesey, his siblings, and his descendants, see Anglesey, *One-Leg* and Paget, *Paget Brothers*.
72. The daughter of Lady Jane Paget (daughter of Henry Paget, Earl of Uxbridge and Jane Champagné) and George Stewart, 8th Earl of Galloway, married George Spencer-Churchill, 6th Duke of Marlborough, and was the great-grandmother of Sir Winston Churchill. Lord Paget-Anglesey's great-great-granddaughter Lady Cynthia Hamilton married Albert, 7th Earl Spencer, and was the grandmother of Princess Diana, mother of Prince William.

Conclusion

1. Luc Daireaux noted in 2009: "Most writers have found it very difficult to disengage themselves from a 'militant problematic' inaugurated spectacularly by Elie Benoist in his celebrated *Histoire de l'édit de Nantes*, published in Delft in five volumes between 1693 and 1695, which has been constantly cited or paraphrased for more than three hundred years." "Réflexions," 35. Daireaux borrowed the term "problématique militante" from Labrousse, *Une Foi, Une Loi, Un Roi?*, 26.
2. Stone, *Family and Fortune*, xvii.
3. The logical principle of the black swan—commonly stated as "No number of observations of white swans can allow the inference that all swans are white, but the observation of a single black swan is sufficient to falsify the generalization"—was elaborated by J. S. Mill in his *System of Logic Ratiocinative and Inductive* (1843), in *Collected Works*, 7:314.

4. Jurieu, quoted in Douen, *Premiers pasteurs du desert,* 1:11; Michelet, *Histoire de France,* 15:301.
5. Pérouas, "Clergé catholique," 262; Pérouas, "Sur la démographie rochelaise"; Labrousse, "Calvinism in France," 293; Chaunu, "Histoire religieuse sérielle," 27. Other histories that have elaborated this noble character of Protestantism include Pérouas, *Diocèse de La Rochelle* and Léonard, *History of Protestantism,* 2:359–448.
6. Colbert de Croissy, "Rapport au Roy," 22.
7. Monahan, "Between Two Thieves," 539; Butler, *Huguenots in America,* 21.
8. Marsh's Library (Dublin). MS Z 2.2.9: Lettre Escrite de france, 2:item 45, p. 7; "Une Abjuration collective," 72; Salvaire, *Relation sommaire,* 27; Letter dated February 26, 1687, quoted in Abénon, "Protestants de la Guadeloupe," 41.
9. Merlat, *Traité du pouvoir absolu des souverains;* Bayle, *Nouvelles de la République des lettres,* August 1685, Article VII, in Bayle, *Oeuvres diverses,* 354.
10. Thomas and Znaniecki, *Polish Peasant in Europe and America,* 1:88.
11. Faust, "Beleaguered Society," 16.
12. The pioneering historian of Huguenot finance Herbert Lüthy pointed in this direction decades ago: "The essential work to be done would reconstitute the greatest possible number of family histories—true histories, social and economic histories, not works of piety or jubilee pamphlets—whose materials lie fortuitously in public archives. A global view could only be based on multiple researches in local, family, and social history." *Banque protestante,* 1:35.
13. Spangler, "Benefit or Burden?," 81.
14. Luria, "Rituals of Conversion"; Labrousse, "Refuge huguenot," 152, 158.
15. Cohen, *Hearts Grown Brutal,* xvi.

Afterword

1. A trenchant and thought-provoking objection to submitting autobiographies to verification ("when readers of autobiography become detectives or confessors, when they seek to verify the facts of an autobiography") is found in Gilmore, *Autobiographics,* especially chapter 3, which also appears as "Policing Truth."
2. Le Fanu, "Children of Marie de la Rochefoucauld de Champagné."
3. Chris Tinkler, who drove me daily to and from the Cornmill in Kirkbymoorside, rightly referred to her location, Nunnington, as a "chocolate-box village," relating its charm and beauty to Richard Cadbury's nostalgic paintings on the lids of Cadbury Brothers sweets.
4. The reasons why a modern French reader might be unable to understand Marie's written memoir are evident from the manuscript page illustrating chapter 12 and the associated discussion of her mode of writing and spelling.

BIBLIOGRAPHY

Printed Primary Sources

"Abrégé de la vie et des vertus de notre chère soeur Soeur Françoise-Henriette Isle de Loire, décédée en notre premier Monastère de Paris, l'année 1724, âgée de 54 ans, dont 32 de profession." In *Année sainte des religieuses de la Visitation Sainte-Marie,* 11: 205–11. 12 vols. Annecy: Librairie de la Propagation catholique, 1867–72.

Aldenburg, Charlotte Amélie, Princess of. *Autobiography of Charlotte Amélie, Princess of Aldenburg, née princess de la Trémoïlle, 1652–1732.* Translated and edited by Aubrey Le Blond. New York: McBride, Nast, 1914.

Alès, "Lettre du ministre Alès à monseigneur le duc de La Trimouille à Touars, 10 mars 1604." *AHSA* 1 (1874): 157–58.

"Arrêt du parlement de Bordeaux condamnant à mort 579 protestants, 6 avril 1569." *Archives historiques du département de la Gironde* 13 (1871–72): 399–420.

[Aulnoy, Marie-Catherine Le Jumel de Barneville d']. *Memoirs of the Countess of Dunois.* London: Tho. Cockerill, 1699.

Aumale, [Marie-Jeanne] d'. *Souvenirs sur madame de Maintenon: Les cahiers de mademoiselle d'Aumale.* Edited by G. Hanotaux. 2nd ed. 3 vols. Paris: Calmann-Lévy, 1902–04.

[Babault, Jacob]. "Au nom de Dieu! Papier ou Mémoyre touchant nostre sortye hors de France, arrivée en 1686, et toutes les affaires que nous avons faittes pendant nostre exil vollontaire." Reprinted as *Journal d'un réfugié, 1686–1726.* Edited by Louis Dufour. Geneva: Jules Carey, 1880.

[Balthazar, Jean]. *Histoire de la guerre de Guyenne* (1694). Edited by C. Moreau. Paris: P. Jannet, 1858.

[Baux, G.]. "Monsieur et très honoré frère [1688]." *BSHPF* 43 (1894): 189–98.

Bayle, [Pierre]. *Dictionaire historique et critique.* 2nd ed. 3 vols. Rotterdam: Reinier Leers, 1702.

Bayle, Pierre. *Oeuvres diverses de M^r^. Pierre Bayle.* The Hague: P. Husson, 1727.

Béchet, Cosme. *Conférence de l'usance de Saintes avec la coutume de Sainct Jean d'Angely.* Saintes: Jean Bichon, 1644.

Béchet, Cosme. *Traité des secondes noces.* Saintes: Jean Bichon, 1647.

Béchet, Cosme. *L'Usance de Saintonge entre mer et Charente.* 2nd ed. Saintes: Jean Bichon, 1647.

Bégon, Michel. "Mémoire sur la généralité de La Rochelle (1698)." *AHSA* 2 (1875): 17–174.

Bellingham, Thomas. *Diary of Thomas Bellingham, an Officer under William III.* Edited by Anthony Hewitson. Preston: G. Toulmin & Sons, 1908.

Benoist, Elie. *Histoire de l'Edit de Nantes.* 3 vols. in 5. Delft: Chez Adrien Beman, 1693–95.

Bernage, Louis de. "Mémoire sur la généralité de Limoges, 1698." In *Documents historiques, bas-latins, provençaux et français: Concernant principalement la Marche et le Limousin,* edited by Alfred Leroux et al., 2:149–258. 2 vols. Limoges: Veuve H. Ducourtieux, 1883–85.

Boisrond, René de Saint-Légier de. "Mémoires, 1675–1690." *Recueil de la Commission des arts et monuments historiques de la Charente-Inférieure et Société d'archéologie de Saintes* 9 (1888): 304–24, 338–55, 396–426; 10 (1891): 176–91, 237–43, 280–88, 344–51, 410–38.

[Bonnet, Jacques]. *Berthelot, Le huguenot insaisissable: Récit historique.* Edited by André Pacher and Jean Rivierre. Mougon: Geste Editions, 1995.

Bossuet, Jacques Bénigne. *Oeuvres.* 43 vols. Versailles: J. A. Lebel, 1815–19.

[Bouzonié, Jean]. *Histoire de l'ordre des religieuses filles de Nôtre-Dame.* Poitiers: Chez la Veuve de Jean-Baptiste Braud, 1697.

Brantôme, Pierre de Bourdeille, seigneur de. *Vies des grands capitaines françois.* In *Oeuvres completes.* Edited by Ludovic Lalanne. 11 vols. Paris: Mme Ve Jules Renouard, 1864–82.

"Bref du pape Paul V qui autorise la fondation à Saintes d'un couvent des Notre-Dame et en approuve le règlement, 31 mars 1618." In "Les Notre-Dame." *AHSA* 23 (1894): 102–12.

Cabrit, Jacques. "Histoire de la vie de J. Cabrit écrite par lui-même." *BSHPF* 39 (1890): 533–45, 587–98, 635–45; 40 (1891): 89–96, 213–17, 360–65, 481–87, 584–90, 641–51.

Cabrol, Jean. "Mémoire de l'origine du s[r] Jean Cabrol, natif de Nismes, en Languedoc, et de ce qui lui est arrivé de plus remarquable dans sa famille, jusqu'à l'aage de quatre vint et un an! Au nom de Dieu soit fait. Amen." *BSHPF* 44 (1895): 532–36.

Calvin, Jean. *Institutes of the Christian Religion: 1536 Edition.* Translated by Ford Lewis Battles. Grand Rapids, MI: William B. Eerdmans, 1995.

Catalogue alphabétique des nobles de la généralité de Poitiers maintenus et condamnés roturiers par Colbert, Barentin et Rouillé du Coudray, commissaires du roy, intendants en Poitou. In *Etat du Poitou sous Louis XIV,* 327–485. Fontenay-Le-Comte: Pierre Robuchon, 1865.

Caylus, [Marthe Marguerite de Villette de Mursay,] madame de. *Souvenirs.* Edited by Bernard Noël. Paris: Mercure de France, 1986.

Chauffepié, Anne de. "Journal manuscrit d'Anne de Chauffepié à l'époque des dragonnades et du refuge, 1685–1688." Reprinted in *BSHPF* 6 (1858): 58–68.

Chevalier, M. Supr. "Mémoires des noms et qualités des Protestantes et nouvelles catholiques qui sont dans la ditte Maison de Paris ce dix septième de May 1702." *BSHPF* 43 (1894): 550–55

Choisy, abbé François-Timoléon de. *La Vie de Madame de Miramion.* Paris: Chez Antoine Dezallier, 1706

Colbert de Croissy, Charles. "Addition au mémoire concernant l'état du Poitou (1664)." In *Etat du Poitou sous Louis XIV,* 194–99. Poitiers: Danièle Brissaud, 1976.

Colbert de Croissy, Charles. "Rapport au Roy concernant la province de Poitou (1664)." In *Etat du Poitou sous Louis XIV,* 137–56. Fontenay-Le-Comte: Pierre Robuchon, 1865.

Correspondance des contrôleurs généraux des finances avec les intendants des provinces. Edited by A. M. de Boislisle. 3 vols. Paris: Imprimerie nationale, 1874–97.

Cosne, Peter de. "The MS Memoirs of Peter de Cosne (1658–1748)." *PHSL* 9 (1909–11): 530–44.

Dangeau, Philippe de Courcillon, marquis de. *Journal.* Edited by Eudoxe Soulié et al. 19 vols. Paris: Firmin Didot Frères, 1854–60.

Desmier d'Olbreuse, Eléonore. "Lettres de la duchesse de Zell." *BSHPF* 26 (1877): 15–21.

Desmier d'Olbreuse, Eléonore. "Lettres d'Eléonore Desmier d'Olbreuse, duchesse de Brunswick-Zell." *Archives historiques du Poitou* 4 (1875): 361–89.

Dictionnaire de l'Académie française. 1st ed. 2 vols. Paris: Chez la Veuve de Jean Baptiste Coignard, 1694.

Drelincourt, Charles. *Abrégé des controverses, ou sommaire des erreurs de l'Eglise romaine, avec leur réfutation par des textes exprès de la Bible de Louvain.* 1st ed. Charenton: Jean Anthoine Joallin, 1624.

Dumont de Bostaquet, Isaac. *Mémoires d'Isaac Dumont de Bostaquet, gentilhomme normand sur les temps qui ont précédé et suivi la révocation de l'Edit de Nantes.* Edited by Michel Richard. Paris: Mercure de France, 1968.

Dusault. *Commentaire sur l'usance de Saintes conférée avec la coutume de S. Jean d'Angely.* Bordeaux: Guillaume Boudé-Boé, 1722.

Edict du Roy, et Declaration sur les precedents Edicts de Pacification. Paris: Imprimeurs et Libraires ordinaires du Roy, 1599.

Edits, Déclarations et Arrests concernans la Religion P. Réformée, 1662–1751. Edited by Léon Pilatte. Paris: Librairie Fischbacher, 1885.

"Les Emigrés de La Rochelle: Relation de la fuite de Baudouin de la Bruchardière et de sa famille. 6 décembre 1686." *BSHPF* 18 (1869): 424–28.

[Espagnac, François Sahuguet de Damarzit, Seigneur d']. "Relation de ce qui s'est passé de plus considérable touchant les conversions dans les provinces de Guienne, Béarn, Navarre, Quercy, Limozin, Perigor et Xainct onge, sous le Commendement du marquis de Boufflers en l'année 1685." *RSA* 36 (1916): 217–37, 286–305, 349–57.

"Etat contenant le dénombrement des personnes faisant profession de la R.P.R., en 1682." *BSHPF* 7 (1859): 23–26.

"Etat des paroisses de la généralité de La Rochelle avec l'imposition de l'année 1698, les noms des seigneurs et la qualité du terroir." *AHSA* 2 (1875): 78–174.

"Etat des paroisses en la généralité de Limoges."*AHSA* 28 (1899): 285–326.

Etat du Poitou sous Louis XIV. Fontenay-Le-Comte: Pierre Robuchon, 1865.

An Exact Account of the Duke of Schombergs Happy Voyage from Highlake, to his Safe Arrival at Carick-fergus, 21 August 1689. Edinburgh: 1689.

"Extraits de la correspondance des ambassadeurs des Provinces-Unies à la cour de France de 1680–1725." *BCEW,* 1st ser., 5 (1892): 156–89, 281–348, 372–411

"Extraits de la Gazette de Haarlem sur les persécutions dirigées contre les protestants français de 1679 à 1685." *BSHPF* 29 (1880): 262–69.

Factums pour le syndic du clergé du diocese de Saintes, contre les pretendus reformez de Saintonge, sur le sujet des temples et des exercices publics de leur Religion qu'ils ont établis dans le Diocese de Saintes, par contravention aux Edits (n.p., 1681): #25 "Saint Savinien. Factum Pour le Syndic du Clergé du Diocese de Saintes, demandeur. Contre les Pretendus Reformez de Saint Savinien, défendeurs." (1681).

Ferrière, Claude-Joseph de. *Dictionnaire de droit et de pratique, contenant l'explication des termes de droit, d'ordonnances, de coutumes et de pratique. Avec les jurisdictions de France.* New ed. 2 vols. (Paris: Chez Nyon, 1768).

Ferrière, Claude. *La Science parfaite des notaires, ou le moyen de faire un parfait notaire.* Paris: Chez Charles Osmont, 1682.

Fontaine, Jacques. *Mémoires d'une famille huguenote victime de la révocation de l'édit de Nantes.* Edited by Bernard Cottret. Montpellier: Presses du Languedoc, 1992.

Fortin de la Hoguette, Philippe. "Lettres." *AHSA* 16 (1888): 9–223.

Foucault, Nicolas-Joseph. *Mémoires.* Edited by F. Baudry. Paris: Imprimerie impériale, 1862.

French Protestant Refugees Relieved through the Threadneedle Street Church, London. Edited by A. P. Hands and Irene Scouloudi. London: Huguenot Society of London, 1971.

A Full and Exact Relation Of the Affairs in Ireland, Particularly of the Late K. James's Letter to the French King [August 13, 1689]. London: A. R., 1689.

Furetière, Antoine. *Dictionaire universel, Contenant generalement tous les mots françois tant vieux que modernes, & les Termes de toutes les sciences et des arts.* 3 vols. The Hague: Arnout et Reinier Leers, 1690.

Gazette de France.

[Guéret, Gabriel, and Claude Blondeau]. *Journal du Palais, ou Recueil des principales decisions de tous les Parlemens et Cours Souveraines de France.* Paris: Denys Thierry, 1681.

H[arboard], W[illiam]. Letter to the King, October 16, 1689, from Dundalk. In *Calendar of State Papers, Domestic Series, of the Reign of William and Mary, 13th Feb. 1689–April 1690*, 293–94. London: HMSO, 1895.

Les Heros de la Ligue. Ou La Procession Monacale. conduitte par Louis XIV, pour la conversion des protestans de son royaume. Paris [i.e. Holland]: Chez Père Peters à l'Enseigne de Louis le Grand, 1691.

Hozier, Jean-François-Louis d'. *Recueil de tous les membres composant l'Ordre royal et militaire de Saint-Louis, depuis l'année 1693, époque de sa fondation.* 2 vols. Paris: Bureau général du Bon Français, 1817

Hozier, Louis-Pierre d', and d'Hozier de Sérigny. *Armorial général, ou Registres de la noblesse de France.* 10 vols. Paris: Jacques Collombat, 1738–68.

J. F. *A Further Account of the State of Ireland And the Proceedings Of the Late King James In that Kingdom* [July 31, 1689]. London: J. C., 1689.

J. F. *Great News from the Camp at Chester; Being a true Account of what has occurr'd there since the Arrival of His Grace the Duke of Schomberge at that place* [July 30, 1689]. London: Richard Janeway, 1689.

[Johnston, Nathaniel]. "The Dear Bargain; or, a true Representation of the State of the English Nation under the Dutch. In a Letter to a Friend." [London], 1689.

"Journal des choses mémorables de l'abbaye de Saint-Maixent, 1634–1735." *Archives historiques du Poitou* 18 (1886): 344–452.

"Journal d'un réfugié sorti du royaume de France par voie de mer, 1685." *BSHPF* 31 (1882): 62–66.

A Journal Of what has past in the North of Ireland, Since the Landing of the Duke of Schomberg, to the Surrender of Carrick-Fergus [August 25, 1689]. London: E. Goldin, 1689.

Jurieu, Pierre. *Lettres pastorales adressées aux fideles de France qui gemissent sous la captivité de Babylon.* Edited by Robin Howells. Hildesheim: Georg Olms Verlag, 1988.

[Jurieu, Pierre], *Reflexions sur la cruelle persecution que souffre l'Eglise reformée de France.* 1686.

Kane, Brigadier-General Richard. *Campaigns of King William and Queen Anne: From 1689 to 1712.* London: J. Millan, 1745.

King, Gregory. *Natural and Political Observations And Conclusions upon the State and Condition of England* (1696). In *Two Tracts by Gregory King*, edited by George E. Barnett, 12–56. Baltimore: The Johns Hopkins Press, 1936.

Lamoignon de Basville. "Réflexions politiques qui doivent porter le roi à contraindre les nouveaux convertis de son royaume de professer la religion catholique." In *Mémoires des évêques de France sur la conduite à tenir à l'égard des réformés*, edited by Jean Lemoine, 322–38. Paris: Alphonse Picard et fils, 1902.

La Motte Fouqué, Friedrich Heinrich Karl de. *Lebensbeschreibung des Königl. Preuss. Generals der Infanterie Heinrich August Baron de la Motte Fouqué.* Berlin: Schüppel, 1824.

La Motte Fouqué, Heinrich August de. *Mémoires du baron de La Motte Fouqué, général d'infanterie prussienne.* Edited by G. A. Büttner. 2 vols. Berlin: Chez François de la Garde, 1788.

La Rochefoucauld, François de. *Voyages en France (1781–1783).* Edited by Jean Marchand. 2 vols. Paris: Honoré Champion, 1933–38.

Le Brun de La Rochette, Claude. *Procez civil et criminel, contenants la methodique liaison du Droict et de la Practique Iudiciaire, Civile et Criminelle.* 2 vols. Rouen: Chez Jacques Hollant, 1647.

A Letter from Chester Of the Twenty Second Instant, Giving an Account of some Affairs in Ireland, And of the Arrival and Reception of the General The Duke of Schomberg, And of the Forces there [July 24, 1689]. London: D.K., 1689.

A Letter from Chester Of the 29th of July. Giving an Account of the State of Londonderry and Iniskilling and Of the Defeat the Men of Iniskilling have lately given the Irish. London: John Amery, 1689.

A Letter from Chester Of the 24th of August, Giving a True Account of the Posture of Affairs at Dublin. London: Randal Taylor, 1689.

Letters of Denization and Acts of Naturalization for Aliens in England and Ireland, 1701–1800. Edited by William A. Shaw. Manchester: Huguenot Society of London, 1923.

"Lettre de M. de Creil, Intendant d'Orléans à Mad. la Supérieure des Ursulines de Montargis, Orléans, 9 mars 1688." *BCEW*, 1st ser., 5 (1892): 385–86.

Lettre des nouveaux catholiques de l'Isle d'Arvert en Saintonge a l'auteur des lettres pretendues pastorales. Paris: Chez George & Louis Josse, 1688.

"List of the Infantry Reviewed at Dundalk Camp 18/28 October 1689." In *English Army Lists and Commission Registers, 1661–1714*, edited by Charles Dalton, 3:107–23. 6 vols. London: Eyre & Spottiswoode, 1892–1904.

Livre des Actes des Eglises Wallonnes aux Pays-Bas, 1601–1697. Edited by Guillaume H. M. Posthumus Meyjes and Hans Bots. The Hague: Instituut voor Nederlandse Geschiedenis, 2005.

Livre des conversions et des reconnoissances faites à l'Eglise françoise de la Savoye, 1684–1702. Edited by William Minet and Susan Minet. London: Huguenot Society of London, 1914.

"Madame de Miramion's School for Girls." *The Ranums' Panat Times*. Vol, 1, Dec. 2014. Available online at www.ranumspanat.com/miramion_schools.html.

Maintenon, Françoise d'Aubigné, marquise de. *Correspondance générale de madame de Maintenon*. Edited by Théophile Lavallée. 4 vols. Paris: Charpentier, 1865–66.

Maintenon, Françoise d'Aubigné, marquise de. *Lettres de Madame de Maintenon*. Edited by Hans Bots et al. 7 vols. Paris: Honoré Champion, 2009.

Maintenon, madame de. "Réponse de madame de Maintenon à un Mémoire touchant la manière la plus convenable de travailler à la conversion des Huguenots (1697)." *BSHPF* 39 (1890): 399–408.

"Maintenues de noblesse prononcées par MM. Quentin de Richebourg et Desgalois de Latour, intendants de la généralité de Poitiers (1714–1718)." *Archives historiques du Poitou* 22 (1892): 1–428; 23 (1893): 1–524.

Majou, Samuel, and Marguerite Desmé. *Testament de Samuel Majou et de Marguerite Desmé, 12 janvier 1696*. Edited by Paul Marchegay. Angers: Imprimerie de Cosnier et Lachèse, 1854.

Mémoires des évêques de France sur la conduite à tenir à l'égard des réformés. Edited by Jean Lemoine. Paris: Alphonse Picard et fils, 1902.

Mercure galant.

Mercure françois.

Merlat, Elie. *Traité du pouvoir absolu des souverains, pour servir d'instruction, de consolation et d'apologie aux églises réformées de France qui sont affligées*. Cologne: Chez Jacques Cassander, 1685.

Migault, Jean. *Journal de Jean Migault, ou, Malheurs d'une famille protestante du Poitou (1682–1689)*. Edited by Yves Krumenacker. Paris: Éditions de Paris, 1995.

"Minutes de notaires: Notes de lecture." Edited by Charles Dangibeaud. *RSA* 30 (1910): 82–96, 141–47, 270–93, 339–70; 31 (1911): 51–68, 174–82, 310–14; 32 (1912): 36–59, 286–99; 33 (1913): 89–94, 189–207; 34 (1914): 116–26, 321–28; 35 (1915): 47–67; 36 (1916): 165–97, 249–75, 306–24, 370–80; 37 (1917): 47–57, 112–34, 199–223, 268–79, 338–50, 400–10; 38 (1920): 59–76.

Minutes of the Consistory of the French Church of London, Threadneedle Street, 1679–1692. London: Huguenot Society of Great Britain and Ireland, 1994.

More Good News from Ireland, giving A Faithful Account of the State and Condition of the English Army there, under the Command of his Grace Duke Schomberg, from the Camp at Bangor near Belfast [August 17, 1689]. London: R. Baldwin, 1689.

Morsier, Jean François de. *Journal*. Reprinted as *Tagebuch des Irländischen Feldzugs vom Jahr 1689*, in Johann Friedrich August Kazner, *Leben Friederichs von Schomberg, oder Schoenburg*. 2 vols. Mannheim: Schwan und Götz, 1789.

Morsier, Jean François de. *Journal*. Translated and excerpted in Pádraig Lenihan and Geraldine Sheridan, "A Swiss Soldier in Ireland, 1689–90." *Irish Studies Review* 13 (2005): 479–97.

Newsletter dated July 16, 1689, Inventory no. 3570 in *The Manuscripts of S. H. Le Fleming, Esq., of Rydal Hall*. Great Britain Royal Commission on Historical Manuscripts, 251. London: HMSO, 1890.

Nicolas de Voutron, Gédéon. *Voyages aux Amériques: Journaux de voyage des campagnes de 1696 aux Antilles et de 1706 à Plaisance et en Acadie*. Edited by Frédéric Laux and Christian Huetz de Lemps. Québec: Septention, 2010.

Nihell, James. *A Journal Of The Most Remarkable Occurrences that Happened between His Majesties Army And The Forces Under the Command of Mareschal de Schomberg in Ireland, from the Twelfth of August to the 23th of October, 1689*. Dublin: Alderman James Malone, 1689.

Nouvelles ordinaires de divers endroits. Du dixiesme Septembre, mil six cens trente deux. Paris: Théophraste Renaudot, 1632.

"Obituary of The World-Famous Organist, Mr. Johann Sebastian Bach." In *The Bach Reader*, edited by Hans T. David and Arthur Mendel, 215–24. New York: W. W. Norton & Company, 1945.

[Orléans, Elisabeth Charlotte, duchesse d']. *Briefe der Herzogin Elisabeth Charlotte von Orléans*. Edited by Wilhelm Holland. 6 vols. Stuttgart: Litterarischer Verein, 1867–81.

Perrault, Charles. *Histoires, ou Contes du temps passé, avec des moralitez: Contes de ma mère Loye*. Paris: Claude Barbin, 1697.

Pollnitz, Baron de. *Memoirs of Charles-Lewis, Baron de Pollnitz*. Translated by Stephen Whatley. 2nd ed. 2 vols. London: Daniel Browne, 1739.

"Projet de Mémoire sur les orphelines élevées dans la maison des Dames de la Providence de La Rochelle, depuis le 2 février 1691." *Recueil de la Commission des arts et monuments historiques de la Charente-Inférieure* 12 (1893–94): 33–60.

"'Reconnoissances' et abjurations dans les églises de la Savoie et de Hungerford à Londres (1684–1733)." *BSHPF* 39 (1890): 86–97.

Recueil général des anciennes lois françaises, depuis l'an 420 jusqu'à la Révolution de 1789. Edited by [François-André] Isambert. 29 vols. Paris: Belin-Leprieur, 1821–33.

Recueil par ordre alphabetique des principales questions de Droit, qui se jugent diversement dans les differens Tribunaux du Royaume. Paris: Chez Emery, 1726.

Registre des Vestures et Professions qui se sont faites au premier monastère de la Visitation Sainte-Marie, de Paris, établie rue Saint-Antoine. BSHPF 9 (1860): 10.

"Registres protestants de Tonnay-Boutonne." RSA 22 (1902): 350–54.

"Relation du souslevans des paysans de Saintonge." In *Lettres et mémoires adressés au chancelier Séguier (1633–1649)*, edited by Roland Mousnier, 2: 1103–05. 2 vols. Paris: Presses universitaires de France, 1964.

"Remonstrances faictes par les païsans d'Angoulmois a Messrs de Brassac et de Villemontée, au mois d'aoust 1636." *Bulletins et mémoires de la Société archéologique et historique de la Charente* 12 (1921): 116–22.

Robillard, Susanne de. "Courte notice sur ma fuite de France." *RSA* 10 (1890): 183–89.

Robillard, Susanne de. In Gabriel Monod, "Une Page de la révocation de l'édit de Nantes: Récit autobiographique de la sortie de France de la famille de Robillard, en 1687." *BSHPF* 17 (1868): 486–95.

Robillard, Susanne de, and Charles de la Motte Fouqué. In H. Babucke, "Eigenhändige Aufzeichnungen französischer Flüchtlinge, 1685–1688." *Preussische Jahrbücher* 59 (1887): 13–26.

Robillard, Susanne de. "Récit abrégé de ma sortie de France, pour venir dans les païs étrangers chercher la liberté de ma conscience et l'exercice de notre sainte religion." Reprinted and translated in Carolyn Lougee Chappell, "'The Pains I Took to Save My/His Family': Escape Accounts by a Huguenot Mother and Daughter after the Revocation of the Edict of Nantes." *FHS* 22 (1999): 47–61.

Robillard, Susanne de, and Charles de La Motte Fouqué. "Um des Glaubens willen: Aufzeichnungen der Urgrosseltern des Dichters Friedrich Freiherrn de La Motte Fouqué über ihre Flucht aus Frankreich nach Aufhebung des Ediktes von Nantes." *Der Deutsche Hugenott* 1934: 10–19.

Rowlandson, Mary. *The Soveraignty and Goodness of God, Together, With the Faithfulness of His Promises Displayed; Being a Narrative of the Captivity and Restauration, of Mrs. Mary Rowlandson.* Cambridge, MA: Samuel Green, 1682.

Ruvigny. "Some Letters of the Marquis de Ruvigny." *PHSL* 17 (1943): 224–61.

La Sainte Bible, qui contient le vieux et le nouveau testament. Edition nouvelle, faite sur la version de Genève. Edited by Samuel Des Marets and Henry Des Marets. 4 vols. Amsterdam: Chez Louis & Daniel Elzevier, 1669.

Saint-Simon, Louis de Rouvroy, duc de. *Mémoires.* Edited by A.-M. de Boislisle. 43 vols. Paris: Hachette, 1879–1928.

Salvaire, Elie. *Relation sommaire des désordres commis par les camisards des Cévennes.* Edited by Didier Poton. Montpellier: Presses du Languedoc, 1997.

Sourches, Marquis de. *Mémoires sur le règne de Louis XIV.* 13 vols. Paris: Librairie Hachette, 1882–93.

Stevens, John. *The Journal of John Stevens, Containing a Brief Account of the War in Ireland, 1689–91.* Edited by Robert H. Murray. Oxford: The Clarendon Press, 1912.

[Story, George]. *A True and Impartial History of The Most Material Occurrences in the Kingdom of Ireland during The Two Last Years. With The Present State of Both Armies.* London: Ric. Chiswell, 1691.

Tallemant des Réaux, Gédéon. *Historiettes.* Edited by Antoine Adam. 2 vols. Paris: Librairie Gallimard, 1960–61.

[Tessereau, Abraham]. *Histoire des reformés de la Rochelle et du pais d'Aunis.* Amsterdam: Chez Louis Renard, 1709.

"Treasury Warrants, May 1716, 11–20." In *Calendar of Treasury Books, Volume 30:1716,* edited by William A. Shaw and F.H. Slingsby, 222–40. London: Institute of Historical Research, 1958.

A True Account Of his Highness the Prince of Orange's Coming to St. James's, on Tuesday the 18th. of December 1688. about three of the Clock in the Afternoon. [London],1688.

A True and Exact Relation of the Prince of Orange His Publick Entrance into Exeter. 1688.

Valin, René-Josué. *Nouveau commentaire sur la coutume de La Rochelle et du pays d'Aunis.* 3 vols. La Rochelle, 1756.

Vauban, [Sébastien Le Prestre de]. "Mémoire pour le rappel des huguenots: Addition du 5 avril 1692." In Vauban, *Ecrits divers sur la religion,* edited by Jean-Robert Armogathe, Elisabeth Labrousse, and Jean-François Pernot, 1–32. Saint-Léger-Vauban: Association des amis de la Maison Vauban, 1992.

Voltaire. "Dialogue entre un plaideur et un avocat" (1750). In Voltaire, *Oeuvres complètes,* edited by Louis Moland, 23:493–96. New ed., 52 vols. Paris: Garnier, 1877–1885.

Secondary Sources

Abbaye des Augustins: Saint-Savinien sur Charente. Saint-Savinien: Les Amis de Saint-Savinien, n.d.

Abénon, Lucien. "Les Protestants de la Guadeloupe et la communauté réformée de Capesterre sous l'Ancien Régime." *Bulletin de la Société d'histoire de la Guadeloupe* 32 (1977): 25–62.

"Une Abjuration collective et officielle en Saintonge à la veille de la Révocation, 1685." *BSHPF* 9 (1860): 71–72.

Adams, Timothy Dow. *Telling Lies in Modern American Autobiography.* Chapel Hill: University of North Carolina Press, 1990.

Aillery, Abbé [Eugène]. *Archives du diocèse de Luçon. Chroniques paroissiales.* 13 vols. Luçon: Archives du diocèse de Luçon, 1892–1933.

A. L. "Questions et Réponses." *RSA* 10 (1890): 347.

Alis, Abbé R. L., and Charles Bouillet. *Notice sur le château, les anciens seigneurs et la paroisse de Mauvezin (près Marmande)*. Agen: Michel et Médan, 1887.

Allégret, D. "Société des dames françaises de Harlem." *BSHPF* 27 (1878): 315–22, 518–24, 557–63.

A. M. "La Cloche des réformés de Saint-Just dans l'église de Bourcefranc." *RSA* 5 (1885): 374–75.

Anglesey, G. C. H. V. Paget, Marquess of. *One-Leg: The Life and Letters of Henry William Paget, First Marquess of Anglesey, K.G., 1768–1854*. London: J. Cape, 1961.

Annuaire de la Charente-Inférieure pour 1886. La Rochelle: Imprimerie A. Siret, 1886.

Anselme, Père, et al. *Histoire généalogique et chronologique de la Maison royale de France*. 9 vols. Paris: Librairie de Firmin-Didot, 1879–90.

Archives de la Bastille: D'après des documents inédits. Edited by François Ravaisson-Mollien. 19 vols. Paris: A. Durand et Pedone-Laurel, 1866–1904.

Ariès, Philippe. "Pourquoi écrit-on des Mémoires?" In *Les Valeurs chez les mémorialistes français du XVIIe siècle avant la Fronde*, edited by Noémi Hepp and Jacques Hennequin, 13–20. [Paris]: Klincksieck, 1979.

Aubineau, Léon. *De la Révocation de l'Edit de Nantes*. Paris: Victor Palmé, 1879.

Audé, L. "Etudes historiques et administratives sur la Vendée: Monsireigne." *Annuaire départementale de la Société d'émulation de la Vendée* 3 (1856): 292–301.

Audiat, Louis. "Abbaye de Notre-Dame de Saintes, histoire et documents." *AHSA* 11 (1883): 417–48.

Audiat, Louis. "Les d'Auquoy ou d'Ocoy en Saintonge et à Saint-Brice." *RSA* 20 (1900): 132–34.

Audiat, Louis. "Les Sainte-Claire de Saintes, 1617–1782." *AHSA* 10 (1882): 143–245.

Audubert, Emile. *Le Régime dotal, d'après la coutume et la jurisprudence du Parlement de Bordeaux*. Tulle: Imprimerie du *Corrézien républicain*, 1918.

Augeron, Mickaël, and Dominique Guillemet. *Champlain, ou les portes du nouveau-monde: Cinq siècles d'échanges entre le centre-ouest français et l'Amérique du nord, XVIe–XXe siècles*. La Crèche: Geste Editions, 2004.

Aussy, D. d'. "La Dernière comtesse de Soissons, 1680–1717." *Revue des questions historiques* 32 (1882): 615–23.

Aussy, Denys d'. "Un Château de Saintonge: Crazannes, 1312–1789." *BSA* 2 (1880): 305–40.

Aussy, Denys d'. "Matha, Mornac, Royan et Arvert, 1289–1776." *AHSA* 16 (1888): 224–314.

Aussy, Denys Joly d'. "Inventaire des titres composant les archives du château de Crazannes." *BSA* 2 (1880): 193–207.

Aussy, Hippolyte d'. *Chroniques saintongeaises et aunisiennes*. Saintes: Pathouot, 1857.

Beaucaire, Horric de. *Une Mésalliance dans la maison de Brunswick (1665–1725): Eléonore Desmier d'Olbreuze, duchesse de Zell*. Paris: H. Oudin, 1884.

Beauchet-Filleau, Henri, et al., *Dictionnaire historique et généalogique des familles du Poitou*. 2nd ed. 6 vols. Poitiers: Oudin et al., 1891–1972.

Beauchet-Filleau, Paul. "Les Prévost de Sansac de Traversay." *Bulletin de la Société historique et scientifique des Deux-Sèvres* 5 (1927): 20–24.

Beik, William. *Absolutism and Society in Seventeenth-Century France: State Power and Provincial Aristocracy in Languedoc*. New York: Cambridge University Press, 1985.

Beineix, Joseph. "Calvin en Saintonge-Angoumois." *RSA* 21 (1901): 115–20.

Belliard, V. "Baronnie de Champdollent." *RSA* 44 (1930–32): 137–50, 197–204, 253–64.

Benedict, Philip. *The Huguenot Population of France, 1600–1685: The Demographic Fate and Customs of a Religious Minority*. Philadelphia: American Philosophical Society, 1991.

Benedict, Philip. "The Lesser Nobility and the French Reformation." Unpublished paper, 2015.

Benedict, Philip. "Two Calvinisms." In Philip Benedict, *The Faith and Fortunes of France's Huguenots, 1600–85*, 208–28. Burlington, VT: Ashgate, 2001.

Benjamin, Walter. *The Arcades Project*. Edited by Rolf Tiedemann. Translated by Howard Eiland and Kevin McLaughlin. Cambridge, MA: Harvard University Press, 2002.

Benmayor, Rina, and Andor Skotnes. *Migration and Identity.* New Brunswick, NJ: Transaction Publishers, 2005.

Benoist, André. "La Famille d'Olbreuse et le protestantisme." *Bulletin de la Société historique et scientifique des Deux-Sèvres* 23 (1990): 5–33.

Bercé, Yves-Marie. *Histoire des croquants: études des soulèvements populaires au XVIIe siècle dans le sud-ouest de la France.* 2 vols. Geneva: Librairie Droz, 1974.

Bergin, Joseph. *Crown, Church, and Episcopate under Louis XIV.* New Haven: Yale University Press, 2004.

Bétancourt, Pierre-Louis-Joseph de. *Noms féodaux, ou Noms de ceux qui ont tenu fiefs en France.* 2nd ed. 4 vols. Paris: Schlesinger frères, 1867.

Beuzart, P. "Les Fugitifs protestants devant le parlement de Flandre depuis la Révocation jusqu'à la mort de Louis XIV." *BSHPF* 73 (1924): 173–94, 331–40.

Bezard, Y[vonne]. "L'Intendant Michel Bégon (1638–1710) et la police religieuse." *Revue d'histoire de l'Eglise de France* 18 (1932): 145–62.

Biais, E. "Notes et documents concernant la châtellenie de Saveilles." *Bulletins et mémoires de la Société archéologique et historique de la Charente* 6 (1915): 5–17.

"Biographie de Pierre Changuion." *BSHPF* 14 (1865): 141–58.

Biver, Paul, and Marie-Louise Biver. *Abbayes, monastères, couvents de femmes à Paris des origines à la fin du XVIIIe siècle.* Paris: Presses universitaires de France, 1975.

Biver, Paul, and Marie-Louise Biver. *Abbayes, monastères et couvents de Paris: Des origines à la fin du XVIIIe siècle.* Paris: Editions d'histoire et d'art, 1970.

Blaufarb, Rafe. "The Phenomenon of Female Lordship: The Example of the Comtesse de Sade." In *Women and Work in Eighteenth-Century France,* edited by Daryl Hafter and Nina Kushner, 16–32. Baton Rouge: LSU Press, 2015.

Bluche, François. *Les Honneurs de la Cour.* 2 vols. Paris: Les Cahiers Nobles, 1957.

Bluche, François. *Les Pages de la Grande Ecurie.* 3 vols. Paris: Les Cahiers Nobles, 1966.

Bonhomme, Honoré. *Madame de Maintenon et sa famille: Lettres et documents inédits.* Paris: Didier et cie, 1863.

Bonneau, Alfred. *Madame de Beauharnais de Miramion: Sa vie et ses oeuvres charitables, 1629–1696.* Paris: Librairie Poussielgue Frères, 1868.

Bonnin, Jean-Claude. *Les Seigneurs d'Angoulins* (2004), 8–9. Available online at http://angoulinshistoire.blogspot.com/2012/10/les-seigneurs-dangoulins-par-jean.html.

Boscheron des Portes, C.-B.-F. *Histoire du Parlement de Bordeaux depuis sa création jusqu'à sa suppression (1451–1790).* 2 vols. Bordeaux: Charles Lefebvre, 1877.

Bosher, John F. "Huguenot Merchants and the Protestant International in the Seventeenth Century." *William and Mary Quarterly* 52 (1995): 77–102.

Bosher, John F. "The Political and Religious Origins of La Rochelle's Primacy in Trade with New France, 1627–1685." *French History* 7 (1993): 286–312.

Bosher, John F. "Success and Failure in Trade to New France, 1660–1760." *FHS* 15 (1988): 444–61.

Bots, Hans. "Le Refuge dans les Provinces-Unies." In *La Diaspora des huguenots: Les réfugiés protestants de France et leur dispersion dans le monde (XVIe–XVIIIe siècles),* edited by Eckhart Birnstiel and Chrystel Bernat, 63–74. Paris: Honoré Champion, 2001.

Boudet, [Joseph-Marie]. "Histoire de l'Abbaye de Notre-Dame hors les murs de la ville de Saintes." *AHSA* 12 (1884): 246–312.

Bourchenin, Daniel. "Notes sur la géographie calvinienne." *BSHPF* 77 (1928): 56–57.

Boutin, R. J. *Breuil Magné et Loire dans le passé.* Breuil Magné: La S.E.P., 1981.

Braud, Michel. *Torxé, Une petite commune ordinaire de Saintonge.* Saint-Jean d'Angély: Editions Bordessoules, 2005.

Bresson, L. "L'Eglise wallonne de Rotterdam: Sa vie intérieure, son développement et son influence." *BCEW,* 2nd ser., 4 (1909): 355–98.

Brewer, John. *The Sinews of Power: War, Money and the English State, 1688–1783.* Cambridge: Harvard University Press, 1990.

Brissaud, Jean. *A History of French Private Law.* Translated by Rapelje Howell. Boston: Little, Brown, and Company, 1912.

Brodut, Médéric. *Tonnay-Charente et le canton: Étude historique, géologique, archéologique, généalogique, biographique, religieuse et commerciale.* Rochefort: Ch. Thèze, 1901.

Bruyn Kops, Henriette de. *A Spirited Exchange: The Wine and Brandy Trade between France and the Dutch Republic in its Atlantic Framework, 1600–1650.* Leiden: Brill, 2007.

Buechler, Hans Christian, and Judith Maria Buechler, eds. *Migrants in Europe: The Role of Family, Labor, and Politics.* New York: Greenwood Press, 1987.

Bujeaud, Victor. *Chronique protestante de l'Angoumois: XVIe, XVIIe, XVIIIe siècles.* Paris: Meyrueis, 1860.

Burguière, André. "L'Etat monarchique et la famille (*XVIe–XVIIIe* siècle)." *Annales. Histoire, Sciences Sociales* 56 (2001): 313–35

Burguière, André, et al., eds. *A History of the Family.* 2 vols. Translated by Sarah Hanbury Tenison. Cambridge, MA: Polity Press, 1996.

Butler, Jon. *The Huguenots in America: A Refugee People in New World Society.* Cambridge, MA: Harvard University Press, 1983.

Cabanel, Patrick. *Histoire des protestants en France: (XVIe–XXIe siècle).* Paris: Fayard, 2012.

Cadier-Rey, Gabrielle. "L'Exode des Huguenots." *BSHPF* 133 (1987): 121–24.

Callandreau. *L'Ordre de la Noblesse de l'Angoumois aux Etats provinciaux de 1789.* 3 vols. Cognac: The Author, 1911–14.

Carbonnier-Burkard, Marianne, and Patrick Cabanel, eds. *Une Histoire des protestants en France, XVIe–XXe siècle.* Paris: Desclée de Brouwer, 1998.

Carter, Alice Clare. *The English Public Debt in the Eighteenth Century.* London: The Historical Association, 1968.

Carter, Alice Clare. *Getting, Spending and Investing in Early Modern Times: Essays on Dutch, English and Huguenot Economic History.* Assen: Van Gorcum, 1975.

Causse, Maurice. "Audibert Durand, ministre apostat en Saintonge, 1678–1698." *BSHPF* 128 (1982): 505–16.

Centre national de la recherche scientifique. Base de données du refuge huguenot. Available online at http://refuge-huguenot.ish-lyon.cnrs.fr.

Chartier, Roger. "Figuration and Habitus: Norbert Elias." In Roger Chartier, *On the Edge of the Cliff: History, Language, and Practices,* 105–43. Translated by Lydia G. Cochrane. Baltimore: Johns Hopkins University Press, 1997.

Chasseboeuf, Frédéric. *Châteaux, manoirs et logis: La Charente-Maritime.* 2 vols. Prahecq: Editions Patrimoines et Médias, 2008.

Chaunu, Pierre. "La Décision royale (?): Un système de la Révocation." In *La Révocation de l'Edit de Nantes et le protestantisme français en 1685,* edited by Roger Zuber and Laurent Theis, 13–29. Paris: Société de l'histoire du protestantisme français, 1986.

Chaunu, Pierre. "Une Histoire religieuse sérielle, à propos du diocèse de La Rochelle (1648–1724) et sur quelques exemples normands." *Revue d'histoire moderne et contemporaine* 12 (1965): 5–34.

Chernin, Kim. *In My Mother's House: A Daughter's Story.* New York: HarperCollins, 1994.

Chevalier, Chanoine [Jean-Florentin]. *Verteuil sous la réforme.* Ruffec: Imprimerie F. Dubois, 1934.

Chevalier, Françoise. *Prêcher sous l'Edit de Nantes: La prédication réformée au XVIIe siècle en France.* Geneva: Labor et Fides, 1994.

Childs, John. *The Williamite Wars in Ireland, 1688–1691.* New York: Hambledon Continuum, 2007.

Clark, Geoffrey. *Betting on Lives: The Culture of Life Insurance in England, 1695–1775.* Manchester: Manchester University Press, 1999.

Clédat, Hubert de. "Le Château de La Cave." *BASS* 70 (2012): 5–14.

Cohen, Elizabeth S. "Fond Fathers, Devoted Daughters? Family Sentiment in Seventeenth-Century France." *Histoire sociale: Social History* 19 (1986): 343–63.

Cohen, Roger. *Hearts Grown Brutal: Sagas of Sarajevo.* New York: Random House, 1998.

Colle, Robert. *Châteaux, manoirs et forteresses d'Aunis et de Saintonge.* 3 vols. La Rochelle: Editions Rupella, 1984.

Colle, Robert. *La Condition féminine de la préhistoire à nos jours en Aunis et Saintonge.* La Rochelle: Editions Rupella, 1989.

Collins, James B. "The Economic Role of Women in Seventeenth-Century France." *FHS* 16 (1989): 436–70.

Collins, James B. *Fiscal Limits of Absolutism: Direct Taxation in Early Seventeenth-Century France.* Berkeley: University of California Press, 1988.

Collomp, Alain. *La Maison du père: Famille et village en Haute Provence aux XVIIe et XVIIIe siècles.* Paris: Presses universitaires de France, 1983.

"Les Collot d'Escury réfugiés en hollande et en angleterre, 1685–1834." *BSHPF* 10 (1861): 306–18.

Combeau, Jacques. *Le Commerce du sel dans la seconde moitié du XCII^e^ siècle: Entre Tonnay-Charente et le port de l'Houmeau.* Ruelle: Route des tonneaux et des canons, [2007].

Connor, Rebecca Elisabeth. *Women, Accounting, and Narrative: Keeping Books in Eighteenth-Century England.* New York: Routledge, 2004.

Corvisier, André. *La France de Louis XIV, 1643–1715: Ordre intérieur et place en Europe.* 3d ed. Paris: Sedes, 1990.

Cottret, Bernard. "Du Dieu de l'exil à l'exil de Dieu: Un parcours ambigu." In *Exil, migration et minorités ethniques,* edited by Solange Dayras, 3–14. Paris: Université Paris-Nord, 1990.

Cottret, Bernard. *Huguenots in England: Immigration and Settlement, c. 1550–1700.* Translated by Peregrine and Adriana Stevenson. New York: Cambridge University Press, 1991.

Cousseau, Vincent. "Sociabilité, parenté baptismale et protestantisme: L'exemple de Preuilly (1590–1683)." *BSHPF* 141 (1995): 221–46.

Coustures, Simon des. *Nobiliaire de la généralité de Limoges.* Limoges: H. Ducourtieux, 1901.

Creighton, Charles. *A History of Epidemics in Britain.* 2 vols. Cambridge: University Press, 1891–94.

Crouzet, François. *Britain, France and International Commerce: From Louis XIV to Victoria.* Aldershot: Variorum, 1996.

Crozet, René. *Châteaux de Charente-Maritime.* Paris: Nouvelles Editions Latines, n.d.

Crubaugh, Anthony. *Balancing the Scales of Justice: Local Courts and Rural Society in Southwest France, 1750–1800.* University Park: Pennsylvania State University Press, 2001.

Cullen, L. M. *The Brandy Trade under the Ancien Régime: Regional Specialisation in the Charente.* Cambridge: Cambridge University Press, 1998.

Cullen, L. M. "The Huguenots from the Perspective of the Merchant Networks of Western Europe (1680–1790): The Example of the Brandy Trade." In *The Huguenots and Ireland: Anatomy of an Emigration,* edited by C. E. J. Caldicott, H. Gough, and J.-P. Pittion, 129–50. Dublin: The Glendale Press, 1987.

Cullen, L. M. *The Irish Brandy Houses of Eighteenth-Century France.* Dublin: The Lilliput Press, 2000.

"Culte chrétien protestant." *RSA* 7 (1887): 371–72.

D. A., "Histoire de la Réformation à Bordeaux et dans le ressort du parlement de Guyenne." *RSA* 5 (1885): 41–45.

Daireaux, Luc. *Réduire les Huguenots: Protestants et pouvoirs en Normandie au XVIIe* siècle. Paris: Honoré Champion, 2010.

Daireaux, Luc. "Réflexions sur la politique de 'réduction' du Roi-Soleil, 1643–1685." *Bulletin annuel de l'Institut d'histoire de la Réformation* 31 (2009–2010): 35–51.

Dangibeaud, Charles. "Contribution à l'histoire du protestantisme à Cozes (1675–1699)." *RSA* 41 (1924–25): 59–75, 89–106, 199–237.

Dangibeaud, Charles. "La Mission du Marquis de Boufflers en Béarn, Guyenne, Périgord, Saintonge (1685)." *RSA* 36 (1916): 203–37, 286–305, 349–57.

Dangibeaud, Charles. "Registres paroissiaux de Soulignonnes." *Recueil de la Commission des arts et monuments historiques de la Charente-Inférieure et Société d'Archéologie de Saintes* 10 (1891): 244–57.

Darnton, Robert. "First Steps Toward a History of Reading." In Robert Darnton, *The Kiss of Lamourette: Reflections in Cultural History,* 154–87. New York: W. W. Norton, 1990.

Darrow, Margaret. *Revolution in the House: Family, Class, and Inheritance in Southern France, 1775–1825.* Princeton: Princeton University Press, 1989.

Dast Le Vacher de Boisville, [Jean-Numa]. *Liste générale et alphabétique des membres du Parlement de Bordeaux.* Bordeaux: G. Gounouilhou, 1896.

Davis, Natalie Zemon. "Ghosts, Kin, and Progeny: Some Features of Family Life in Early Modern France." *Daedalus* 106 (1977): 87–114.

Davis, Natalie Zemon. *Society and Culture in Early Modern France.* Stanford: Stanford University Press, 1975.

Delafosse, Marcel. "Contrats de mariage et dots des marchands rochelais au XVIIe siècle." In *Actes du 97e Congrès national des sociétés savantes: Nantes, 1972: Section d'histoire moderne et contemporaine,* 2: 45–51. 2 vols. Paris: Bibliothèque nationale, 1977.

Delafosse, Marcel. "Les Eaux-de-vie de Saintonge et d'Aunis et le fisc au début du XVIIIe siècle." *Revue du Bas-Poitou et des Provinces de l'Ouest* 74 (1963): 16–22.

Delavaud, L[ouis]. "Les Marins protestants sous le règne de Louis XIV." *BSHPF* 31(1882): 181–86.

Delavaud, L[ouis]. "La Révocation de l'Edit de Nantes et ses suites dans la Saintonge et dans l'Aunis (1688–1696)." *BSHPF* 30 (1881): 163–69, 317–29.

Delmas, Louis. *L'Eglise réformée de La Rochelle: Étude historique.* Toulouse: Société des livres religieux, 1870.

"Deux prisonniers de la Bastille: Jean Cardel, de Tours, et Paul Cardel, fils de Jean Cardel, de Rouen. Eclaircissements." *BSHPF* 11(1862): 249–52.

Dewald, Jonathan. *Aristocratic Experience and the Origins of Modern Culture: France, 1570–1715.* Berkeley: University of California Press, 1993.

Dewald, Jonathan. *Formation of a Provincial Nobility: The Magistrates of the Parlement of Rouen, 1499–1610.* Princeton: Princeton University Press, 1980.

Deyon, Solange. "La Destruction des temples." In *La Révocation de l'Edit de Nantes et le protestantisme français en 1685,* edited by Roger Zuber and Laurent Theis, 239–59. Paris: Société de l'histoire du protestantisme français, 1986.

Dez, Pierre. *Histoire des protestants et des Eglises réformées du Poitou.* La Rochelle: Imprimerie de l'Ouest, 1936.

Dickson, P. G. M. *The Financial Revolution in England: A Study in the Development of Public Credit, 1688–1756.* New York: Macmillan, 1967.

Diefendorf, Barbara B. *From Penitence to Charity: Pious Women and the Catholic Reformation in Paris.* New York: Oxford University Press, 2004.

Diefendorf, Barbara B. "Give Us Back Our Children: Patriarchal Authority and Parental Consent to Religious Vocations in Early Counter-Reformation France." *Journal of Modern History* 68 (1996): 265–307.

Diefendorf, Barbara. "Houses Divided: Religious Schism in Sixteenth-Century Parisian Families." In *Urban Life in the Renaissance,* edited by Susan Zimmerman and Ronald F. E. Weissman, 80–99. Newark: University of Delaware Press, 1989.

Diefendorf, Barbara B. "Women and Property in Ancien Régime France: Theory and Practice in Dauphiné and Paris." In *Early Modern Conceptions of Property,* edited by John Brewer and Susan Staves, 170–93. New York: Routledge, 1995.

Dompnier, Bernard. "'La Cordiale communication de nos petites nouvelles': Les lettres circulaires, pratique d'union des monastères." In *Visitation et Visitandines aux XVIIe et XVIIIe siècles,* edited by Bernard Dompnier and Dominique Julia, 277–300. Saint-Etienne: Université de Saint-Etienne, 2001.

Douen, O[rentin]. *L'Intolérance de Fénelon: Études historiques.* Paris: Sandoz & Fischbacher, 1872.

Douen, O[rentin]. *Les Premiers pasteurs du désert (1685–1700).* 2 vols. Paris: Grassart, 1879.

Douen, O[rentin]. "La Réforme en Picardie, 1525–1853." *BSHPF* 8 (1859): 385–609.

Douen, O[rentin]. *La Révocation de l'Edit de Nantes à Paris.* 3 vols. Paris: Librairie Fischbacher, 1894.

Drillat, Geneviève. "Les Visitandines françaises (1667–1767)." In *La Mort des pays de Cocagne: Comportements collectifs de la Renaissance à l'âge classique,* edited by Jean Delumeau, 189–205. Paris: Université de Paris I-Panthéon Sorbonne, 1976.

Dubois, G. "Enlèvements d'enfants protestants et la Communauté des Nouvelles-Catholiques de Rouen." *BSHPF* 85 (1936): 318.

Dubreuilh, Susanne. "Construction du temple de Sainte-Foy (1584–1587)." *BSHPF* 81 (1932): 359–64.

Du Chatenet, Madeleine. *L'Amiral Jean-Baptiste de Traversay: Un français, ministre de la marine des tsars.* Paris: Tallandier, 1996.

Dupâquier, Jacques, et al. *Histoire de la population française.* 4 vols. Paris: Presses universitaires de France, 1988.

Du Pasquier, Thierry. *Généalogies huguenotes.* Paris: Editions Christian, 1985.

Duvignacq-Glessgen, Marie-Ange. *L'Ordre de la Visitation à Paris aux XVIIe et XVIIIe siècles.* Paris: Editions du Cerf, 1994.

Elias, Norbert. "The Expulsion of the Huguenots from France." Translated by Edmund Jephcott. In *The Norbert Elias Reader: A Biographical Selection,* edited by Johan Goudsblom and Stephen Mennell, 18–25. Oxford: Blackwell, 1998.

Elias, Norbert. "Notes on a Lifetime." In Norbert Elias, *Reflections on a Life,* translated by Edmund Jephcott, 81–154. Cambridge, MA: Polity Press, 1994.

Elias, Norbert. "Die Vertreibung der Hugenotten aus Frankreich." *Der Ausweg: Monatschrift für Umschichtung, Wanderung, Siedlung* 1 (1935): 369–76.

Encrevé, André. "Image de la Réforme chez les protestants français de 1830 à 1870." In *Historiographie de la Réforme,* edited by Philippe Joutard, 182–204. Paris: Delachaux et Niestle, 1977.

"Enlèvements d'enfants, séquestrations et violences commis par une fervente catholique: Noble Marie d'Albret, comtesse de Marsan et dame de Pons." *BSHPF* 7 (1859): 435–46.

"Enlèvements de jeunes protestantes en Languedoc, en Poitou et en Guyenne, 1696–1698." *BSHPF* 2 (1854): 358–62.

Espanol, Emmanuel, ed. *Dictionnaire historique du protestantisme en Périgord, Guyenne, Agenais.* Montpeyroux: Editions Barthélémy, 2009.

Faust, Katherine Louise Milton. "A Beleaguered Society: Protestant Families in La Rochelle, 1628–1685." PhD dissertation, Northwestern University, 1980.

Feiss, Hugh. "'Consecrated to Christ, Nuns of this Church Community': The Benedictines of Notre-Dame de Saintes, 1047–1792." *American Benedictine Review* 45 (1994): 269–302.

Félice, G. de. *Histoire des protestants de France.* 8th ed. Toulouse: Société des livres religieux, 1895.

Une Femme des lumières: Ecrits et lettres de la comtesse de Bentinck, 1715–1800. Edited by Anne Soprani and André Magnan. Paris: Editions du CNRS, 1997.

Fierro, Alfred. *Vie et histoire du XIIe arrondissement.* Paris: Editions Hervas, 1988.

Filleau, Henri. *Dictionnaire historique, biographique et généalogique des familles de l'ancien Poitou.* 2 vols. Poitiers: Imprimerie de A. Dupré, 1840–54.

Flick, Andreas. "Huguenot Settlements in Northern Germany: An Unknown Chapter." *Bulletin, Hugenote-Vereniging Van Suid-Afrika* 39 (2002), 82–96.

Floris, Philippe, and Pascal Talon, eds. *Châteaux, manoirs et logis: La Charente-Maritime.* Chauray: Editions Patrimoines et médias, 1993.

Forster, Robert. *The House of Saulx-Tavanes: Versailles and Burgundy, 1700–1830.* Baltimore: Johns Hopkins Press, 1971.

Forster, Robert. "The Provincial Noble: A Reappraisal." *American Historical Review* 68 (1962–63): 681–91.

Foulon, Lydie. *Belles Demeures de la Charente*. Chauray: Editions patrimoines et médias, 1996.

Frederiks, J. G. "La Communauté wallonne de Voorburg." *BCEW*, 1st ser., 5 (1892): 58–75.

Frijhoff, Willem. "Uncertain Brotherhood: The Huguenots in the Dutch Republic." In *Memory and Identity: The Huguenots in France and the Atlantic Diaspora*, edited by Bertrand van Ruymbeke and Randy J. Sparks, 128–71. Columbia: University of South Carolina Press, 2003.

Funck-Brentano, Frantz. *Les Lettres de cachet à Paris: Étude suivie d'une liste des prisonniers de la Bastille (1659–1789)*. Paris: Imprimerie nationale, 1903.

Gaehtgens, Thomas W. "La Statue de Louis XIV et son programme iconographique." In *Place des Victoires: Histoire, architecture, société*, edited by Isabelle Dubois, Alexandre Gady, and Hendrik Ziegler, 9–35. Paris: Editions de la Maison des sciences de l'homme, 2003.

Gagnebin, F. H. "Liste des églises wallonnes des Pays-Bas et des pasteurs qui les ont desservies." *BCEW*, 1st ser., 3(1888): 25–64, 97–120, 209–40, 313–45.

Galland, Jacques Alfred. *Essai sur l'histoire du protestantisme à Caen et en Basse-Normandie de l'édit de Nantes à la Révolution*. Paris: Grassart, 1898.

Garrioch, David. *The Huguenots of Paris and the Coming of Religious Freedom, 1685–1789*. Cambridge: Cambridge University Press, 2014.

Garrioch, David. "The Protestants of Paris and the Old Regime." *French History and Civilization: Papers from the George Rudé Seminar* 2 (2009): 16–24.

Garrisson, Francis, *Essai sur les Commissions d'application de l'Edit de Nantes: Règne de Henri IV*. Montpellier: P. Dehan, 1964.

Garrisson, Janine. *L'Homme protestant*. Brussels: Editions Complexe, 1986.

Gaxotte, Pierre. *La France de Louis XIV*. Paris: Hachette, 1946.

Gélin, Henri. "Les Cloches protestantes." 40 (1891): 591–607, 652–64.

Gélin, Henri. "Madame de Maintenon convertisseuse." *BSHPF* 49 (1900): 169–203, 239–53, 291–96.

Gélin, Henri. "Les Réformés et les cloches pendant les guerres de religion." *Revue poitevine et saintongeaise* 9 (1892): 144–46.

Geoffray, Stéphane. *Répertoire des procès-verbaux des preuves de la noblesse des jeunes gentilshommes admis aux écoles royales militaires, 1751–1792*. Paris: Le Vasseur, 1894.

Giesey, Ralph E. "Rules of Inheritance and Strategies of Mobility in Prerevolutionary France." *American Historical Review* 82 (1977): 271–89.

Gilmore, Leigh. *Autobiographics: A Feminist Theory of Women's Self-Representation*. Ithaca: Cornell University Press, 1994.

Gilmore, Leigh. "Policing Truth: Confession, Gender, and Autobiographical Authority." In *Autobiography and Postmodernism*, edited by Kathleen M. Ashley, Leigh Gilmore, and Gerald Peters, 54–78. Amherst: University of Massachusetts Press, 1994.

Glozier, Matthew. *The Huguenot Soldiers of William of Orange and the "Glorious Revolution" of 1688: The Lions of Judah*. Brighton: Sussex Academic Press, 2002.

Glozier, Matthew. *Marshal Schomberg 1615–1690: 'The Ablest Soldier of His Age'; International Soldiering and the Formation of State Armies in Seventeenth-Century Europe*. Brighton: Sussex Academic Press, 2005.

Glozier, Matthew, and David Onnekink, eds. *War, Religion and Service: Huguenot Soldiering, 1685–1713*. Burlington, VT: Ashgate, 2007.

Goldgar, Anne. *Impolite Learning: Conduct and Community in the Republic of Letters, 1680–1750*. New Haven: Yale University Press, 1995.

Goody, Jack. "Strategies of Heirship." *Comparative Studies in Society and History* 15 (1973): 3–20.

Gout, Raoul. *Pages féminines de la réforme française*. Vol. 2 of *Le Miroir des dames chrétiennes*. Paris: Je Sers, 1937.

Grant, Alison. "By Sea: Huguenot Maritime Links with Seventeenth-Century Devon." *PHSL* 25 (1993): 451–63.

Grant, Alison, and Robin Gwynn. "The Huguenots of Devon." *Reports and Transactions of the Devonshire Association for the Advancement of Science, Literature and the Arts* 117 (1985): 161–94.

Green, Nancy L. "The Politics of Exit: Reversing the Immigration Paradigm." *Journal of Modern History* 77 (2005): 263–89.

Groehler, Olaf, and Helmut Erfurth. *Der Alte Dessauer: Fürst Leopold I. von Anhalt-Dessau.* Berlin: Brandenburgisches Verlagshaus, 1991.

Guitard, Eugène. *Colbert et Seignelay contre la Religion Réformée.* Paris: Auguste Picard, 1912.

Gwynn, Robin. "The Huguenots in Britain, the 'Protestant International' and the Defeat of Louis XIV." In *From Strangers to Citizens: The Integration of Immigrant Communities in Britain, Ireland and Colonial America, 1550–1750,* edited by Randolph Vigne and Charles Littleton, 412–24. London: 2001.

Haag, Eugène, and Emile Haag. *La France protestante ou vies des protestants français qui se sont fait un nom dans l'histoire depuis les premiers temps de la Réformation jusqu'à la reconnaissance du principe de la liberté des cultes par l'assemblée nationale.* 10 vols. Paris: Joël Cherbuliez, 1846–59.

Haag, Eugène, and Emile Haag. *La France Protestante.* 2nd ed. 6 vols. Paris: Librairie Sandoz et Fischbacher, 1877–88.

Hanley, Sarah. "Engendering the State: Family Formation and State Building in Early Modern France." *FHS* 16 (1989): 4–27.

Hanley, Sarah. "The Family, the State, and the Law in Seventeenth- and Eighteenth-Century France: The Political Ideology of Male Right versus an Early Theory of Natural Rights." *Journal of Modern History* 78 (2006): 289–332.

Hanlon, Gregory. *Confession and Community in Seventeenth-Century France: Catholic and Protestant Coexistence in Aquitaine.* Philadelphia: University of Pennsylvania Press, 1993.

Hanlon, Gregory, and Elspeth Carruthers. "Wills, Inheritance and the Moral Order in the Seventeenth-Century Agenais." *Journal of Family History* 15 (1990): 149–61.

Hardwick, Julie. "Seeking Separations: Gender, Marriages, and Household Economies in Early Modern France." *FHS* 21 (1998): 157–80.

Hardwick, Julie. "Widowhood and Patriarchy in Seventeenth-Century France." *Journal of Social History* 26 (1992): 133–48.

Hareven, Tamara K. *Family Time and Industrial Time: The Relationship between the Family and Work in a New England Industrial Community.* New York: Cambridge University Press, 1982.

Hareven, Tamara K. *Transitions: The Family and the Life Course in Historical Perspective.* New York: Academic Press, 1978.

Heilbrun, Carolyn G. *Writing a Woman's Life.* New York: W. W. Norton, 1988.

Hellot, A. *Essai historique sur les Martel de Basqueville et sur Basqueville-en-Caux (1000–1789).* Rouen: Ch. Métérie, 1879.

Hickey, Daniel. "Enforcing the Edict of Nantes: The 1599 Commissions and Local Elites in Dauphiné and Poitou-Aunis." In *The Adventure of Religious Pluralism in Early Modern France,* edited by Keith Cameron et al., 65–83. New York: Peter Lang, 2000.

Holtz, Cécile. "La Bourse française de Genève et le Refuge de 1684 à 1686." In *Genève et la Révocation de l'Edit de Nantes,* edited by O. Reverdin et al., 439–500. Geneva: Droz, 1985.

Huetz de Lemps, Christian. *Géographie du commerce de Bordeaux à la fin du règne de Louis XIV.* Paris: Mouton, 1975.

Hunt, Margaret R. *The Middling Sort: Commerce, Gender, and the Family in England, 1680–1780.* Berkeley: University of California Press, 1996.

Hylton, Raymond Pierre. "Dublin's Huguenot Communities: Trials, Development, and Triumph, 1662–1701." *PHSL* 24 (1985): 221–31.

Israel, Jonathan. "England, the Dutch, and the Struggle for Mastery of World Trade in the Age of the Glorious Revolution (1682–1702)." In *The World of William and Mary: Anglo-Dutch Perspectives On the Revolution of 1688–89*, edited by Dale Hoak and Mordechai Feingold, 75–86. Stanford, CA: Stanford University Press, 1996.

Jacob, Margaret C. *Strangers Nowhere in the World: The Rise of Cosmopolitanism in Early Modern Europe*. Philadelphia: University of Pennsylvania Press, 2006.

Jahan, Emmanuel. *La Confiscation des biens des religionnaires fugitifs de la révocation de l'édit de Nantes à la Révolution*. Paris: Pichon and Durand-Auzias, 1959.

Jal, A[ugustin]. *Abraham Du Quesne et la marine de son temps*. 2 vols. Paris: Henri Plon, 1873.

Jal, A[ugustin]. *Dictionnaire critique de biographie et d'histoire*. 2nd ed. Paris: Henri Plon, 1872.

Janzé, Charles Alfred de. *Les Huguenots: Cent ans de persécution, 1685–1789*. Paris: Grassart, 1886.

Johnston, Elsie. "The Diary of Elie Bouhéreau." PHSL 15 (1933–37): 46–68.

Jougla de Morenas, Henri. *Grand Armorial de France: catalogue général des armoiries des familles nobles de France*. Paris: Editions héraldiques, 1934–52.

Jouhaud, Christian. "Camisards! We Were Camisards!" *History and Memory* 21 (2009): 5–24.

Joutard, Philippe. "1685, une fin et une nouvelle chance pour le protestantisme français." In *Le Refuge Huguenot*, edited by Michelle Magdelaine and Rudolf von Thadden, 13–30. Paris: Armand Colin, 1985.

Joutard, Philippe. "La Révocation de l'Edit de Nantes, événement mémorable?" In *La Révocation de l'Edit de Nantes et le protestantisme français en 1685*, edited by Roger Zuber and Laurent Theis, 299–311. Paris: Société de l'histoire du protestantisme français, 1986.

Joutard, Philippe. "The Revocation of the Edict of Nantes: End or Renewal of French Calvinism?" In *International Calvinism, 1541–1715*, edited by Menna Prestwich, 339–68. Oxford: Clarendon Press, 1985.

Julien-Labruyère, François. *Paysans charentais: Histoire des campagnes d'Aunis, Saintonge, et bas Angoumois*. 2 vols. La Rochelle: Rupella, 1982.

Julien-Labruyère, François. *A la recherche de la Saintonge maritime*. Versailles: Chez l'Auteur, 1974.

Kettering, Sharon. "The Household Service of Early Modern French Noblewomen." *FHS* 20 (1997): 55–85.

Kettering, Sharon. "Patronage and Kinship in Early Modern France." *FHS* 16 (1989): 408–35.

Kettering, Sharon. "Patronage in Early Modern France." *FHS* 17 (1992): 839–62.

Kettering, Sharon. *Patronage in Sixteenth- and Seventeenth-Century France*. Aldershot: Ashgate, 2002.

Kettering, Sharon. *Patrons, Brokers, and Clients in Seventeenth-century France*. New York: Oxford University Press, 1986.

Krumenacker, Yves. *Les Protestants du Poitou au XVIIIe siècle, 1681–1789*. Paris: Honoré Champion, 1998.

Labrousse, Elisabeth. "Calvinism in France, 1598–1685." In *International Calvinism, 1541–1715*, edited by Menna Prestwich, 285–314. Oxford: Clarendon Press, 1985.

Labrousse, Elisabeth. *Une foi, une loi, un roi?: La Révocation de l'Edit de Nantes*. Geneva: Labor et Fides, 1985.

Labrousse, Elisabeth. *Pierre Bayle: Hétérodoxie et rigorisme*. Paris: Editions Albin Michel, 1996.

Labrousse, Elisabeth. "Le Refuge Huguenot." *Le Genre humain* 19 (1989): 147–71.

La Bruyère, René. *L'Affaire de Saint-Jean-d'Angély, ou le mystère de la mort du prince de Condé*. Paris: Le Croît vif, 1995.

La Chenaye-Desbois, [François-Alexandre Aubert] de, and Badier. *Dictionnaire de la noblesse*. 3rd ed. 19 vols. Paris: Schlesinger frères, 1863–1876.

La Morinerie. "Le Chevalier de Nanteuil (1763)." *RSA* 20 (1900): 415–16.

Lart, C. E. "The Family of La Primaudaye." *PHSL* 15 (1934–35): 338–41.

Lart, Charles E. "The Huguenot Regiments." *PHSL* 9 (1909–11): 476–516.

La Trémoïlle, Louis de. *Les La Trémoïlle pendant cinq siècles.* 5 vols. Nantes: Emile Grimaud, 1890–96.

Laursen, John Christian, ed. *New Essays on the Political Thought of the Huguenots of the Refuge.* New York: E. J. Brill, 1995.

Lavisse, Ernest. *Histoire de France illustrée depuis les origines jusqu'à la Révolution.* 9 vols. New York: AMS Press, 1969 [1900–11].

Lavoir, Lise. "Factums et mémoires d'avocats aux XVIIe et XVIIIe siècles: Un regard sur une société (environ 1620–1760)." *Histoire, économie et société* 7 (1988): 221–42.

Le Blond, Aubrey. *Charlotte Sophie, Countess Bentinck: Her Life and Times, 1715–1800.* 2 vols. London: Hutchinson, 1912.

Le Fanu, Thomas Philip. "The Children of Marie de la Rochefoucauld de Champagné." *PHSL* 13 (1923–29): 560–78.

Le Fanu, Thomas Philip. "Marie de la Rochefoucauld de Champagné and Her Escape from France in 1687." *PHSL* 13 (1923–29): 454–73.

Le Fanu, Thomas Philip. "Mémoires inédits d'Abraham Tessereau." *PHSL* 15 (1937): 566–85.

Le Fanu, T. P., and W. H. Manchee. *Dublin and Portarlington Veterans: King William III's Huguenot Army.* London: Huguenot Society of London, 1946.

Lejeune, Philippe. *Le Pacte autobiographique.* Paris: Editions du Seuil, 1975.

Lelievre, Jacques. *Pratique des contrats de mariage chez les notaires au Châtelet de Paris de 1769 à 1804.* Paris: Editions Cujas, 1959.

"Le Moyne de Sérigny et de Loire, Joseph." In *Dictionnaire biographique du Canada,* 2: 424–26. 15 vols. Toronto: Les Presses de l'Université Laval, 1966–2005.

Léonard, Emile G. *A History of Protestantism.* Translated by R. M. Bethell. 2 vols. London: Thomas Nelson, 1967.

Léonard, Emile. "L'Institution du Mérite Militaire." *BSHPF* 82 (1933): 297–320, 455–81.

Léonard, Emile G. *Le Protestant français.* Paris: Presses universitaires de France, 1953.

Le Roy Ladurie, Emmanuel. "Longue durée et comparatisme: Révocation de l'Edit de Nantes et glorieuse révolution d'Angleterre." *Revue de la Bibliothèque nationale* 29 (1988): 3–18.

Le Roy Ladurie, Emmanuel. *Saint-Simon and the Court of Louis XIV.* Translated by Arthur Goldhammer. Chicago: University of Chicago Press, 2001.

Le Roy Ladurie, Emmanuel. "A System of Customary Law: Family Structures and Inheritance Customs in Sixteenth-Century France." *Annales: Economies, Sociétés, Civilisations* 27 (1972): 825–46. Reprinted in *Family and Society,* edited by Robert Forster and Orest Ranum, 75–103. Baltimore: Johns Hopkins University Press, 1976 and in *Family and Inheritance: Rural Society in Western Europe, 1200–1800,* edited by Jack Goody, Joan Thirsk, and E. P. Thompson, 37–70. Cambridge: Cambridge University Press, 1976.

Lételié, André. "Fénelon en Saintonge et la Révocaton de l'Edit de Nantes, 1685–88." *AHSA* 13 (1885): 209–34.

Lételié, André. "Histoire d'un réfugié. Jacques Fontaine." *BSA* 8 (1888): 422–38.

Lévesque de Burigny, Jean. *Vie du cardinal du Perron.* Paris: Chez de Bure, 1768.

Libaud, Jean. *Edifices religieux de Saint-Savinien: Leur histoire, leurs secrets.* Saint-Savinien: Recherche historique en pays savinois, 2010.

Lièvre, Auguste. *Histoire des protestants et des églises réformées du Poitou.* 3 vols. Paris: Grassart, 1856–60.

Lièvre, A., and N. Weiss. "En Seudre: Pilotes huguenots, émigration en masse, arrestations, etc.; Récits et procès-verbaux contemporains, 1681–1687." *BSHPF* 43 (1894): 79–88.

Lougee, Carolyn C. "Cross Purposes: The Intendant of La Rochelle and Protestant Policy at the Revocation." In *Tocqueville and Beyond: Essays on the Old Regime,* edited by Robert M. Schwartz and Robert A. Schneider, 155–71. Newark: University of Delaware Press, 2003.

Lougee, Carolyn C. "'Its Frequent Visitor': Death at Boarding School in Early-Modern Europe." In *Women's Education in Early Modern Europe: A History, 1500–1800,* edited by Barbara Whitehead, 193–224. New York, Garland, 1999.

Lougee, Carolyn C. "The New Princess of Saxony: Paris, Imposture, and Secret Marriage in the Seventeenth Century." *French History* (forthcoming).

Lougee, Carolyn C. *Le Paradis des Femmes: Women, Salons, and Social Stratification In Seventeenth-Century France.* Princeton: Princeton University Press, 1976.

Lougee Chappell, Carolyn. "'The Pains I Took to Save My/His Family': Escape Accounts by a Huguenot Mother and Daughter after the Revocation of the Edict of Nantes." *FHS* 22 (1999): 1–64.

Lougee Chappell, Carolyn. "Paper Memories and Identity Papers: Why Huguenot Refugees Wrote Memoirs." In *Narrating the Self In Early Modern Europe,* edited by Bruno Tribout and Ruth Whelan, 121–38. Oxford: Peter Lang, 2007.

Lougee Chappell, Carolyn. "Through the Eyes of a Spy: Venom and Value in an Enemy's Report on the Huguenot Emigration." In *The Huguenots: France, Exile and Diaspora,* edited by Jane McKee and Randolph Vigne, 77–88. Brighton: Sussex Academic Press, 2013.

Lougee Chappell, Carolyn. "Writing the Diaspora: Escape Memoirs and the Construction of Huguenot Memory." In *L'Identité huguenote: Faire mémoire et écrire l'histoire* (XVIe–XXIe siècle), edited by Philip Benedict, Hugues Daussy, and Pierre-Olivier Léchot, 261–77. Geneva: Librairie Droz, 2014.

Luciani, Isabelle. "Ordering Words, Ordering the Self: Keeping a *Livre de Raison* In Early Modern Provence, Sixteenth through Eighteenth Centuries." *FHS* 38 (2015): 529–48.

Luria, Keith P. "Rituals of Conversion: Catholics and Protestants In Seventeenth-Century Poitou." In *Culture and Identity In Early Modern Europe, 1500–1800,* edited by Barbara B. Diefendorf and Carla Hesse, 65–81. Ann Arbor: University of Michigan Press, 1993.

Luria, Keith P. *Sacred Boundaries: Religious Coexistence and Conflict In Early Modern France.* Washington, DC: Catholic University of America Press, 2005.

Lüthy, Herbert. *La Banque protestante en France, de la Révocation de l'Edit de Nantes à la Révolution.* 2 vols. Paris: S.E.V.P.E.N., 1959, 1961.

Magdelaine, Michelle, and Rudolf von Thadden, eds. *Le Refuge Huguenot.* Paris: Armand Colin, 1985.

Maillet, J. "La Renonciation à succession future des filles dotées dans la doctrine et la jurisprudence méridionales des XVIme–XVIIIme siècles." In *Etudes d'histoire du droit dédiées à M. Auguste Dumas: Annales de la Faculté de droit d'Aix,* 215–51. Aix-en-Provence: Imprimerie d'éditions provençales, 1950.

Marcadé, Jacques. "Les Filles de Notre-Dame à Poitiers (XVIIe–XVIIIe siècles)." *Bulletin de la Société des antiquaires de l'Ouest et des Musées de Poitiers* 16 (1981): 217–35.

Marcadé, Jacques. *Protestants poitevins de la Révocation à la Révolution.* La Crèche: Geste Editions, 1998.

Margolf, Diane. "Adjudicating Memory: Law and Religious Difference In Early Seventeenth-Century France." *Sixteenth-Century Journal* 27 (1996): 399–418.

Margolf, Diane C. *Religion and Royal Justice In Early Modern France: The Paris Chambre de l'Edit, 1598–1665.* Kirksville, MO: Truman State University Press, 2004

Martin, Georges. *Histoire et généalogie de la maison de La Rochefoucauld.* La Ricamarie: Chez l'Auteur, 1975.

Massiou, D. *Histoire politique, civile et religieuse de la Saintonge et de l'Aunis depuis les premiers temps historiques jusqu'à nos jours.* 2nd ed. 6 vols. Saintes: A. Charrier, 1846.

Maza, Sara C. *Private Lives and Public Affairs: The Causes Célèbres of Prerevolutionary France.* Berkeley: University of California Press, 1993.

Mazas, Alexandre. *Histoire de l'Ordre royal et militaire de Saint-Louis depuis son institution en 1693 jusqu'en 1830.* 2nd ed. 3 vols. Paris: Firmin Didot, 1860–61.

Mazoyer, Louis. *L'Enlèvement des enfants: une page douloureuse dans l'histoire des persécutions aux XVIIe et XVIIIe siècles contre la R.P.R.* Mialet: Musée du Désert, 1991.

McKee, Denis. "Les Protestants de Sedan et la Révocation de l'Edit de Nantes: opposition, fuites et résistance." *BSHPF* 127 (1981): 219–54.

Meadows, R. Darrell. "Engineering Exile: Social Networks and the French Atlantic Community, 1789–1809." *FHS* 23 (2000): 67–102.

Menche de Loisne, Auguste Charles Henri. *Histoire généalogique de la maison de Foucher.* Abbeville: Imprimerie Fourdrinier, 1898.

Mendelsohn, Daniel. *The Lost: A Search for Six of Six Million.* New York: HarperCollins, 2006.

Mentzer, Raymond A. *Blood and Belief: Family Survival and Confessional Identity among the Provincial Huguenot Nobility.* West Lafayette, IN: Purdue University Press, 1994.

Mentzer, Raymond. "The Edict of Nantes and Its Institutions." In *Society and Culture In the Huguenot World, 1559–1685*, edited by Raymond A. Mentzer and Andrew Spicer, 98–116. Cambridge: Cambridge University Press, 2002.

Mentzer, Raymond A., and Bertrand Van Ruymbeke, eds., *A Companion to the Huguenots.* Leiden and Boston: Brill, 2015.

Meschinet de Richemond, Louis. "Anciennes églises et lieux de culte des réformés à La Rochelle." *BSHPF* 44 (1895): 364–83.

Meschinet de Richemond, L. *Les Marins rochelais: Notes biographiques.* 2nd ed. Niort: G. Clouzot, 1906.

Mettam, Roger. *Power and Faction In Louis XIV's France.* New York: Basil Blackwell, 1988.

Meyer, Jean. "Un Problème mal posé: La noblesse pauvre; l'exemple breton au XVIIe siècle." *Revue d'histoire moderne et contemporaine* 18 (1971): 161–88.

Michelet, Jules. *Histoire de France.* 19 vols. Paris: C. Marpon et E. Flammarion, 1879–84.

Migne, J. P. *Encyclopédie théologique.* 168 vols. Paris: Chez l'éditeur, 1845–1873.

Mill, John Stuart. *The Collected Works of John Stuart Mill.* Edited by J. M. Robson. 33 vols. London: Routledge and Kegan Paul, 1963–1991.

Monahan, W. Gregory. "Between Two Thieves: The Protestant Nobility and the War of the Camisards." *FHS* 30 (2007): 537–58.

Monahan, W. Gregory. *Let God Arise: The War and Rebellion of the Camisards.* New York: Oxford University Press, 2014.

Mours, Samuel. *Les Eglises réformées en France: Tableaux et cartes.* Paris: Librairie Protestante, 1958.

Mours, Samuel. "Essai sommaire de géographie du protestantisme réformé français au XVIIe siècle." *BSHPF* 111 (1965): 303–21.

Mours, Samuel. "Notes sur les galériens protestants (1683–1775)." *BSHPF* 116 (1970): 178–231.

Mours, Samuel. "Les Pasteurs à la Révocation de l'Edit de Nantes." *BSHPF* 114 (1968): 67–105, 292–316, 521–24.

Mours, Samuel. *Le Protestantisme en France au 17e siècle, 1598–1685.* Paris: Librairie protestante, 1967.

Mours, Samuel, and Daniel Robert. *Le Protestantisme en France du XVIIIe siècle à nos jours.* Paris: Librairie protestante, 1972.

Mousnier, Roland. *Peasant Uprisings In Seventeenth-Century France, Russia, and China.* Translated by Brian Pearce. New York: Harper Torchbooks, 1970.

Moya, Jose C. *Cousins and Strangers: Spanish Immigrants In Buenos Aires, 1850–1930.* Berkeley: University of California Press, 1998.

Murphy, Anne L. "Lotteries In the 1690s: Investment or Gamble?" *Financial History Review* 12 (2005): 227–46.

Murphy, Gwénaël. *Le Peuple des couvents: Religieuses et laïques du diocèse de Poitiers sous l'ancien régime.* La Crèche: Geste éditions, 2007.

Musgrave, Elizabeth. "Pottery Production and Proto-Industrialisation: Continuity and Change In the Rural Ceramics Industries of the Saintonge Region, France, 1250 to 1800." *Rural History* 9 (1998): 1–18.

Nadaud, Joseph. *Nobiliaire du diocèse et de la généralité de Limoges.* 4 vols. Limoges: H. Ducourtieux, 1863–1882.

Nazelle, L.-J. *Le Protestantisme en Saintonge sous le régime de la Révocation, 1685–1789.* Alençon: Imprimerie Veuve Félix Guy, 1907.

Noailles, Paul, duc de. *Histoire de Madame de Maintenon et des principaux événements du règne de Louis XIV.* 4 vols. Paris: Comptoir des imprimeurs-unis, 1849–58.

"Les Notre-Dame." *AHSA* 23 (1894): 102–24.

"Les Nouvelles Catholiques de Pons." *Cahiers du Centre de généalogie protestante* 12 (1985): 619–29; 14 (1986): 754–72; 15 (1986): 787–97.

"Nouvelles Catholiques de Pons." *Recueil de la Commission des arts et monuments historiques de la Charente-Inférieure* 11 (1891): 112–69.

Orcibal, Jean. *Etat présent des recherches sur la répartition géographique des 'nouveaux catholiques' à la fin du XVIIe siècle.* Paris: Librairie philosophique J. Vrain, 1948.

Orcibal, J[ean]. "Louis XIV and the Edict of Nantes." In *Louis XIV and Absolutism*, edited by Ragnhild Hatton, 154–76. Columbus: Ohio State University Press, 1976.

Oui, R. *1763 et 1780: Importants séjours d'étrangers à Saint-Savinien, ou Conséquences de la salubrité de l'air à St. Savinien.* Saint-Savinien: F.R.G.S., n.d.

Oui, René. *Les Marins des trois ports: Saint-Savinien, Port-d'Envaux, Taillebourg, au XVIIIe siècle.* Saint-Savinien-sur-Charente: Les Amis de Saint-Savinien et Sa Région, n.d.

Paget, Sir Arthur. *The Paget Brothers, 1790–1840.* Edited by Lord Hylton. London: John Murray, 1918.

"Pallet." *Annuaire de la noblesse de France* 30 (1874): 221–27.

Parker, David. *The Making of French Absolutism.* New York: St. Martin's Press, 1983.

Paroisses et communes de France: Dictionnaire d'histoire administrative et démographique; Charente-Maritime. Paris: Editions du CNRS, 1985.

Pascal, César. "Une Evasion à la Rochelle en 1681." *BSHPF* 39 (1890): 57–78.

Pascal, César. "Sous la persécution en Saintonge au XVIIe siècle." *BSHPF* 50 (1901): 393–444.

Pellisson, Jules. "La Fronde à Cognac, 1650–1657." *AHSA* 12 (1884): 313–77.

Péret, Jacques. "De Louis XIV à la Révolution, des provinces sages aux évolutions contrastées." In *Histoire du Poitou et des pays charentais: Deux-Sèvres, Vienne, Charente, Charente-Maritime*, edited by Jean Combes, 283–323. Clermont-Ferrand: Editions Gérard Tisserand, 2001.

Péret, Jacques. "Vitalité et turbulences (1515–1660)." In *Histoire du Poitou et des pays charentais: Deux-Sèvres, Vienne, Charente, Charente-Maritime*, edited by Jean Combes, 241–82. Clermont-Ferrand: Editions Gérard Tisserand, 2001.

Pérouas, Louis. "Le Clergé catholique et les protestants au pays rochelais, 1630–1730." *Istina* 1963: 261–78.

Pérouas, Louis. "Sur la Démographie rochelaise." *Annales: Economies, Sociétés, Civilisations* 16 (1961): 1131–40.

Pérouas, Louis. *Le Diocèse de La Rochelle de 1648 à 1724: Sociologie et pastorale.* Paris: S.E.V.P.E.N., 1964.

Petite histoire locale de la paroisse de Landraye en Aunis, de son origine à nos jours. Surgères: Editions F. Bayle, 1937.

Pettegree, Andrew. "Protestant Migration during the Early Modern Period." In *Le Migrazioni In Europa Secc. XIII–XVIII*, edited by Simonetta Cavaciocchi, 441–58. Florence: Le Monnier, 1994.

Pickard, Ransom. "The Huguenots in Exeter." *Report and Transactions of the Devonshire Association for the Advancement of Science, Literature and Art* 68 (1936): 261–97.

Pittion, Jean-Paul. "Abraham Tessereau: An Address Given in Saint Patrick's Cathedral, Dublin, 2 October 2011." Available online at http://huguenotsinireland.com/wp-content/uploads/2014/04/Abraham-Tessereau-pdf-Oct-2011.pdf.

La Place des Victoires et ses abords. Paris: Mairie du 1er arrondissement, 1983.

Popkin, Richard H. *The History of Scepticism from Savonarola to Bayle.* New York: Oxford University Press, 2003.

Portelli, Alessandro. "'The Time of My Life': Functions of Time in Oral History." *International Journal of Oral History* 2 (1981): 162–80.

Portemer, Jean. "Le Statut de la femme en France depuis la réformation des coutumes jusqu'à la rédaction du Code civil." *La Femme: Recueils de la Société Jean Bodin* 12 (1962): 447–97.

Poumarède, Jacques. "Le Droit des veuves sous l'ancien régime (XVIIe–XVIIIe siècles) ou comment gagner son douaire." In *Femmes et Pouvoirs sous l'ancien régime,* edited by Danielle Haase-Dubosc and Eliane Viennot, 64–76. Paris: Editions Rivages, 1991.

"Pourquoi et comment on se soumettait à Montauban en 1685." *BSHPF* 51 (1902): 543–45.

Présentation du fonds ancien des Archives de l'hôpital et Hôtel-Dieu Notre Dame des Anges de Ruffec (XVIIe siècle–1830). Edited by Jean-François Comte. Ruffec: Office de Tourisme, 1983.

Prévost de Sansac de Traversay, [Jules-Marie]. *Actes relevés dans les registres de la paroisse de Plibou (Deux-Sèvres) sur le territoire de laquelle était situé le château de Traversay.* Blois: Imprimerie C. Migault, 1907.

Puaux, Frank. "Un dessein des pasteurs exilés en hollande après la Révocation de l'Edit de Nantes." *BSHPF* 61 (1912): 425–34.

Quéniart, Jean. *La Révocation de l'Edit de Nantes: Protestants et catholiques en France de 1598 à 1685.* Paris: Desclée de Brouwer, 1985.

Rainguet, Pierre-Damien. *Biographie saintongeaise.* Saintes: Chez M. Niox, 1851.

Rapley, Elizabeth. *The Dévotes: Women and Church in Seventeenth-Century France.* Montreal: McGill-Queen's University Press, 1990.

Rapley, Elizabeth. *A Social History of the Cloister: Daily Life in the Teaching Monasteries of the Old Regime.* Montreal: McGill-Queen's University Press, 2001.

Rapley, Elizabeth. "Women and the Religious Vocation in Seventeenth-Century France." *FHS* 18 (1994): 613–31.

Read, Charles. "La Petite-fille d'Agrippa d'Aubigné devant la légende et l'histoire, étude contradictoire et documentaire." *BSHPF* 36 (1887): 393–412, 449–68, 625–37; 37 (1888): 13–24, 70–79.

Renaudin, Paul. "Une Dame de Saint-Cyr: Madame de la Maisonfort." *Revue des deux mondes* 28 (1915): 390–428.

Rivierre, Jean. "Notes sur le refuge poitevin en hollande." *BCEW,* 5th ser., 4 (1950): 5–37.

Rivierre, Jean. *La Vie des protestants du Poitou après la Révocation (1685–1700).* 2 vols. Ivry-sur-Seine: Phénix Editions, 2002.

Rivierre, Jean, and Roger Durand, *Le Drame de Grand Ry.* La Couarde: Editions du Malpertuis, 1995.

Robert, Daniel. "Louis XIV et les protestants." *XVIIe siècle* 76–77 (1967): 39–52.

Rodrigues, Georges. *Nobles et bourgeois en Aunis et Saintonge.* Royan: G. Rodrigues, 1989.

Roelker, Nancy Lyman. "The Appeal of Calvinism to French Noblewomen in the Sixteenth Century." *Journal of Interdisciplinary History* 2 (1971–72): 391–418.

Roelker, Nancy Lyman. "The Role of Noblewomen in the French Reformation." *Archiv für Reformationsgeschichte* 63 (1972): 168–95.

Rölleke, Heinz. "The 'Utterly Hessian' Fairy Tales by 'Old Marie': The End of a Myth." In *Fairy Tales and Society: Illusion, Allusion, and Paradigm,* edited by Ruth B. Bottigheimer, 287–300. Philadelphia: University of Pennsylvania Press, 1986.

Rogers, James E. Thorold. *The First Nine Years of the Bank of England.* Oxford: Clarendon Press, 1887.

Rome, Catherine. *Les Bourgeois protestants de Montauban au XVIIe siècle: Une élite urbaine face à une monarchie autoritaire.* Paris: Honoré Champion, 2002.

Rondier, R. F. *Historique du monastère de Puyberland.* Niort: L. Clouzot, 1868.

Rosa, Susan. "'Il était possible aussi que cette conversion fût sincère': Turenne's Conversion in Context." *FHS* 18 (1994): 632–66.

Rousset, Camille. *Histoire de Louvois et de son administration politique et militaire.* 4 vols. Paris: Librairie académique Didier, 1886–91.

Rowe, Karen E. "To Spin a Yarn: The Female Voice in Folklore and Fairy Tale." In *Fairy Tales and Society: Illusion, Allusion, and Paradigm,* edited by Ruth B. Bottigheimer, 53–74. Philadelphia: University of Pennsylvania Press, 1986.

Saint-Affrique, Olga de. "L'Aunis au 17e siècle." In *Histoire des protestants charentais (Aunis, Saintonge, Angoumois)*, edited by Francine Ducluzeau, 126. Paris: Le Croît vif, 2001.

Saint-Saud, Comte [Aymard] de. *Magistrats des sénéchaussées, présidiaux et élections, Périgord.* Bergerac: Imprimerie générale du sud-ouest, 1931.

Saint-Saud, Comte [Aymard] de. *Nouveaux Essais généalogiques périgourdins.* Paris: Librairie Gaston Saffroy, 1942.

Saint-Simon, F. de. *La Place des Victoires.* Paris: Editions Vendôme, 1984.

Sanxay, Theodore F., ed. *The Sanxay Family, and Descendants of Reverend Jacques Sanxay, Huguenot Refugee to England in 1685.* New York, 1907.

Saudau, Louis-Claude. *Miettes et Rogatons de l'histoire locale.* Saint-Jean-d'Angély: Imprimerie A. Rogé, 1912.

Saudau, Louis-Claude. *Saint-Jean-d'Angély d'après les archives de l'échevinage et les sources directes de son histoire.* Saint-Jean-d'Angély: Imprimerie A. Roge, 1903.

Sauzet, Robert. *Les Cévennes catholiques: Histoire d'une fidélité (XVIe–XXe siècle).* Paris: Perrin, 2002.

Sée, Camille. *L'Université et Mme de Maintenon.* Paris: Librairie Léopold Cerf, 1894.

Séguin, Marc. *Histoire de l'Aunis et de la Saintonge: Le début des temps modernes, 1480–1610.* La Crèche: Geste Editions, 2005.

Sepulchre, Bruno. *Châteaux en ruines ou disparus en Angoumois.* Barbezieux: Imprimerie Calmels, 1973.

Sepulchre, Bruno. *Châteaux, villes & villages de l'Angoumois, Aunis, Saintonge & Poitou au XVIIe siècle par Claude Chastillon, Ingénieur du roi (1560–1616).* N.p.: B. Sepulchre, 1992.

Shaw, Caroline. *Britannia's Embrace: Modern Humanitarianism and the Imperial Origins of Refugee Relief.* New York: Oxford University Press, 2015.

Simms, J. G. *War and Politics in Ireland, 1649–1730.* London: Hambledon Press, 1986.

Sites de Saintonge: L'Abbaye-aux-Dames de Saintes. Saintes: Atelier du patrimoine Saintonge, 1990.

Smith, James E., and Jim Oeppen. "Estimating Numbers of Kin in Historical England Using Demographic Microsimulation." In *Old and New Methods in Historical Demography*, edited by David S. Reher and Roger Schofield, 280–317. New York: Oxford University Press, 1993.

Smith, Peter. "Mansart Studies III: The Church of the Visitation in the Rue S. Antoine." *Burlington Magazine* 106 (1964): 202–15.

Smith, Sidonie. *A Poetics of Women's Autobiography: Marginality and the Fictions of Self-Representation.* Bloomington, 1987.

Solé, Jacques. "La Diplomatie de Louis XIV et les protestants français réfugiés aux Provinces-Unies, 1678–1688." *BSHPF* 115 (1969): 625–60.

Solé, Jacques. *Les origines intellectuelles de la Révocation de l'Edit de Nantes.* Saint-Etienne: Publications de l'Université de Saint-Etienne, 1997.

Sonnet, Martine. *L'Education des filles au temps des Lumières.* Paris: Editions du Cerf, 1987.

Sottas, Jules. "Le Gouvernement de Brouage et La Rochelle sous Mazarin, 1653–1661." *RSA* 42 (1926): 5–81.

Soury-Lavergne, Françoise. *Chemin d'éducation sur les traces de Jeanne de Lestonnac.* Chambray-lès-Tours, 1984.

Spangler, Jonathan. "Benefit or Burden? The Balancing Act of Widows in French Princely Houses." *Proceedings of the Western Society for French History* 31 (2003): 65–83.

Stanton, Domna C. "Autogynography: The Case of Marie de Gournay's *Apologie pour celle qui escrit.*" In *Autobiography in French Literature*, 18–31. Columbia: University of South Carolina, 1985.

Staves, Susan. *Married Women's Separate Property in England, 1660–1833.* Cambridge, MA: Harvard University Press, 1990.

Staves, Susan. "Resentment or Resignation? Dividing the Spoils among Daughters and Younger Sons." In *Early Modern Conceptions of Property*, edited by John Brewer and Susan Staves, 194–218. New York: Routledge, 1995.

Steedman, Carolyn Kay. *Landscape for a Good Woman: A Story of Two Lives*. New Brunswick, NJ: Rutgers University Press, 1987.

Stegmann, André. *Edits des guerres de religion*. Paris: J. Vrin, 1979.

Stéphan, Raoul. "Y a-t-il un style protestant?" In Raoul Stéphan. *Histoire du protestantisme français*, 343–65. Paris: Arthème Fayard, 1961.

Stephens, Winifred. *The La Trémoille Family*. Boston and New York: Houghton Mifflin, 1914.

Stone, Lawrence. *Family and Fortune: Studies in Aristocratic Finance in the Sixteenth and Seventeenth Centuries*. Oxford: Clarendon Press, 1973

Sturmer, Herbert H. *Some Poitevin Protestants in London: Notes about the Families of Ogier from Sigournais and Creuzé of Châtellerault and Niort*. London: The Author, 1896.

Tauzin, E. "Monographie de Saint-Xandre." *Recueil de la Commission des arts et monuments historiques de la Charente-Inférieure et Société d'archéologie de Saintes* 13 (1895–96): 11–58.

Teodosijevic, Michel. *Saint-Savinien: Terre de libre passage*. Saint-Savinien: Bordessoules, 1999.

Tesseron, Gaston. *Histoire de l'Angoumois et de la Charente: La Charente sous Louis XIV; le grand siècle de la monarchie*. Angoulême: Editions Coquemard, 1958.

Tessier, Honoré. *Traité de la société d'aquêts suivant les principes de l'ancienne jurisprudence du Parlement de Bordeaux*. 2nd ed. Bordeaux: H. Duthu, 1881.

Texier, Jean. *Inventaire archéologique de l'arrondissement de Saint-Jean-d'Angély*. 11 vols. Saint-Jean-d'Angély: Imprimerie Brisson, 1963–82).

Thomas, William Isaac, and Florian Znaniecki. *The Polish Peasant in Europe and America: Monograph of an Immigrant Group*. 5 vols. Boston: Gorham Press, 1918–1920.

Tollin, Henri. *Geschichte der französischen Colonie von Magdeburg*. 3 vols. Magdeburg: Verlag der Faber'schen Buchdruckerei, 1886–94.

Tollin, Henri. "Geschichte der hugenottischen Gemeinde von Celle." *Geschichtsblätter des Deutschen Hugenotten-Vereins* 2 (1893), Heft 7–8.

Tournier, Gaston. *Les Galères de France et les galériens protestants des XVIIe et XVIIIe siècles*. 3 vols. Montpellier: Presses du Languedoc, 1984.

Traversay, François de. *Notice généalogique sur la famille Prévost: Angoumois et Poitou*. Bordeaux: Imprimerie nouvelle F. Pech, 1925.

Tuttle, Leslie. *Conceiving the Old Regime: Pronatalism and the Politics of Reproduction in Early Modern France*. New York, Oxford University Press, 2010.

Tuttle, Leslie. "Gender and Mercantilism: The Example of Natalist Policy." *Proceedings of the Western Society for French History* 30 (2002): 145–54.

Van Biema, Eduard. *Les Huguetan de Mercier et de Vrijhoeven*. The Hague: M. Nijhoff, 1918.

Van der Linden, David. *Experiencing Exile: Huguenot Refugees in the Dutch Republic, 1680–1700*. Burlington, VT: Ashgate, 2015.

Van Kley, Dale. *The Religious Origins of the French Revolution: From Calvin to the Civil Constitution, 1560–1791*. New Haven: Yale University Press, 1996.

Venant, Henry. "Abraham Marquis Duquesne, lieutenant général des armées navales et la seigneurie de Bellébat (Commune de Champdolent)." *RSA* 35 (1915): 340–56.

Vergé-Franceschi, Michel. *Abraham Duquesne: Huguenot et marin du roi-soleil*. Paris: Editions France-Empire, 1992.

Viallaneix, Paul. "Relire Michelet," avant-propos to J[ules] Michelet, *De la Révocation de l'Edit de Nantes à la guerre des Cévennes, 1685–1704*. Montpellier: Presses du Languedoc, 1985.

Vickery, Amanda. *Behind Closed Doors: At Home in Georgian England*. New Haven: Yale University Press, 2009.

Vindry, Fleury. *Les Demoiselles de Saint-Cyr (1686–1793)*. Paris: Librairie Honoré Champion, 1908.

Viollet, Paul. *Histoire du droit civil français*. 2nd ed. Paris: L. Larose and Forcel, 1893.

Waddington, Francis. "Le Ministère sous la croix, en France." *BSHPF* 3 (1855): 590–95.

Walton, Clifford. *History of the British Standing Army, A.D. 1660 to 1700*. London: Harrison and Sons, 1894.

Watts, Derek A. "La Notion de patrie chez les mémorialistes d'avant la Fronde: le problème de la trahison." In *Les Valeurs chez les mémorialistes français du XVIIe siècle avant la Fronde*, edited by Noémi Hepp and Jacques Hennequin, 195–209. [Paris]: Klincksieck, 1979.

Weiss, N. "Poursuites du Présidial de Saintes: enfants saisis, apothicaires et orfèvres, baptêmes, etc. (1684)." *BSHPF* 42 (1893): 493–96.

Weiss, N. "Un Prêtre saintongeais condamné aux galères pour avoir été tolérant, août 1731." *BSHPF* 46 (1897): 93–95.

Wheaton, Robert. "Affinity and Descent in Seventeeenth-Century Bordeaux." In *Family and Sexuality in French History*, edited by Robert Wheaton and Tamara Hareven, 111–34. Philadelphia: University of Pennsylvania Press, 1980.

Whelan, Ruth. "Persecution and Toleration: The Changing Identities of Ireland's Huguenot refugees." *PHSL* 27 (1998): 20–35.

Wilkinson, Maurice. "The Wars of Religion in the Périgord." *English Historical Review* 21 (1906): 650–72.

Wilson, Charles, ed. *The Anglo-Dutch Contribution to the Civilization of Early Modern Society*. Oxford: Oxford University Press, 1976.

Wrigley, E. A. "Fertility Strategy for the Individual and the Group." In *Historical Studies of Changing Fertility*, edited by Charles Tilly, 135–54. Princeton: Princeton University Press, 1978.

Yardeni, Myriam. "La France protestante et le Refuge huguenot." In *La Diaspora des huguenots: Les réfugiés protestants de France et leur dispersion dans le monde (XVIe–XVIIIe siècles)*, edited by Eckhart Birnstiel, 27–42. Paris: Honoré Champion, 2001.

Yardeni, Myriam. "Problèmes de fidélité chez les protestants français à l'époque de la révocation." In *Hommage à Roland Mousnier: Clientèles et fidélités en Europe à l'époque moderne*, edited by Yves Durand, 297–314. Paris: Presses universitaires de France, 1981.

Yver, Jean. *Egalité entre héritiers et exclusion des enfants dotés: Essai de géographie coutumière*. Paris: Editions Sirey, 1966.

INDEX